Table of Contents

Ultimate Guide to Medical Schools

Second Edition

Josh Fischman and the staff of U.S.News & World Report

Foreword by Bernadine Healy, M.D.

Anne McGrath, Editor

Robert Morse, Director of Data Research

Brian Kelly, Series Editor

SOURCEBOOKS, INC.®
NAPERVILLE, ILLINOIS

Published by Sourcebooks, Inc.
P.O. Box 4410
Naperville, Illinois 60567-4410
(630) 961-3900 FAX: (630) 961-2168
www.sourcebooks.com

ISBN 13: 978-1-4022-0705-1
ISBN 10: 1-4022-0705-0
Second Edition
Printed and bound in the United States of America
CH 10 9 8 7 6 5 4 3 2 1

Foreword

On Being a Doctor

by Bernadine Healy, M.D.

Medicine is a way of life. It is a way of knowing and thinking, of seeing the world, and of feeling about people. No one
is born a doctor, and the long road to becoming one requires
unrelenting study, discipline, and the cultivation of unique
talents and skills. But whatever the domain of medical pursuit and however removed from the bedside one's work may
ultimately be, its ethos and raison d'être stems from that
one enduring relationship: physician and patient.

In our time, this most personal of human services has
burgeoned into a $1.5 trillion enterprise employing one in
ten Americans. It is a growth propelled by the endless fron-
tier of medical discovery, translating into better ways to care
for people. In that sense, a medical career is the intellectual

journey of a lifetime. In a field where the sands shift so quickly and one technology is swept away by another, medical school is not about teaching you all the facts you'll ever need to know. Rather, it is the place in which students are slowly converted from lay people into doctors.

This conversion takes time, with and beyond the books, journals, and professorial pronouncements. Ultimately, one becomes a doctor from an immersion in the unpredictable, varied, and complex ways in which patients fall ill, and the momentous efforts of people and technology to make them well. It comes from learning the secrets of the body, the passages of life from birth to death, the tortured times and the peaceful times of human souls, and the uplifting (and carefully harnessed) power of the physician to make a difference every step along the way. For the best of students, by the time they walk across the stage and accept their medical diploma, doctorhood has seeped into the marrow of their bones, the depth of their hearts. Whatever their chosen line of work, they will always see the world through the lens of a doctor.

That lens is broad. Medicine embraces a continuum of knowledge and practice from the micro to macro level—from the medical scientist in the laboratory, to the doctor at the bedside, to the public health specialist tracking down the latest epidemic anywhere in the world. And along that broad spectrum, one can carve out a professional life of research, teaching, practice or administration, or some combination of all four. There is a place for generalists and specialists, writers and policy wonks, computer jocks and business gurus—all part of a medical community doing something that is in its ultimate purpose about helping another human being.

That the profession helps human beings in a profound and measurable way is in fact why young people dream of being a doctor, and it is the single most common reason medical school applicants give for pursing a medical career. Indeed, it is that perspective that ultimately overrides some of the negative sides of a career in medicine, which in today's world can discourage even the strongest-hearted premed. For medicine as we know it today brings its own set of hassles: managed care, increasing government regulations, and malpractice premiums (and massive malpractice awards), on top of discouraging medical school debt averaging nearly $100,000 at a time when physician's incomes are relatively stagnant.

Although there are two applicants for every medical school slot, and the quality of prospective students is thought to be as good as ever, there is widespread belief among medical school educators that because of these strains, fewer students are interested in applying to medical school now than a decade ago, a phenomenon masked by the dramatic increase in female applicants. But the reality is that no profession—and nothing worth pursuing in life—is free from its own set of hassles. The reward-to-hassle ratio is what counts. It is something each prospective doctor must sort out for himself or herself.

And the rewards of today's medicine are many. The expanding knowledge base is truly compelling and ever changing to the betterment of patient and doctor. There is virtually no illness we cannot make better, if not cure, and with improved drugs and technology and emerging knowledge of human genomes, we see more tailored treatment of individual patients with better results. As for the doctor's personal life, the hours today are more reasonable and controllable than in the past. The solo doc is becoming a rare breed; large group practices and clinics enable medical practitioners to escape the direct brunt of administrative hassles while at the same time gaining camaraderie and an enriched practice environment. Medicine is a tough and fulfilling career, immutably purpose driven, value laden, intellectually stimulating, and emotionally gratifying. But it is a profession that demands the right stuff of those who serve.

Certain deeply held personal qualities are essential; without them, from my perspective as a former medical school dean, students quite simply need not apply. Think hard about them, for they are the essence of the art and the science of being a doctor.

Compassion and generosity. Kindness goes beyond "bedside manner." It is reflected in generosity of time and self, and sensitivity to the unique circumstance of any given situation. Making an extra stop by the room of a lonely patient; giving a worried family member your home phone number; being calm and measured with an ornery, angry, or noncompliant patient. Sickness can bring out the best in people but also the worst, and a physician can lighten a patient's load by being a source of hope, caring, and cheerleading—along with providing technical expertise.

Hard work and grit. It takes a lot of stamina to be part of a world that is always on call in some fashion. The stress might come from a rather mundane struggle with an insurance company for an extra day in the hospital or a needed MRI, or from perseverance against an engulfing bureaucracy. But stress most especially comes from the challenge of caring for the very sick. This demands the courage to make tough medical decisions, and in the face of risk and uncertainty, to proceed with

a risky operation, or embark on a drastic course of medical therapy. It takes grit to confront one's inevitable failures and learn from them—without becoming timid because of them. In their hearts, doctors must live with the confidence that at the end of the day, they did the best they could, and tirelessly so.

Scholarship and good sense. With medical practice reborn almost every day in new knowledge and emerging technology, new approaches are an essential part of medicine, disseminated in hospital corridors, medical rounds, mortality and morbidity conferences, journal clubs, and national medical gatherings. The wise and learned physicians are those who can sift through the flood of new knowledge and the latest evidence to make it apply to any given patient. That's why we teach medicine at the bedside and through individual case studies of real people. And that's why we respect reasoned judgment that often comes out with different advice. Should that 30-year-old woman with a newly discovered benign heart tumor have prompt heart surgery, as is the practice? Of course—but she is six months pregnant and with surgery, risks losing the baby, so dare we wait? The PSA is intermittently elevated in a 55-year-old man. Do you watch, or biopsy? Yes, a lumpectomy is the conventional wisdom for this precancerous change detected by mammogram, but this patient wants a mastectomy as an alternative because she has a breast cancer gene running through her family. Do we go along? The hyperactive child is driving his family to distraction with behaviors that another family could manage better. Do you medicate?

Medical wisdom is about knowing when conventional practice guidelines apply, particularly in the context of the unlimited variables that confound any given patient's illness or circumstance.

The best decisions come from the marriage of scholarship and good sense.

Integrity and trust. Despite the variability of human illness, one of the great insights of medicine is that with regard to reaction to their disease, all patients are fundamentally the same. Though they may show it differently, they share the same fears and vulnerabilities; and have the same needs for comfort, support, and trust. The physician is the focus of that trust, and that is a heavy responsibility. Never give advice that you yourself would not take—or you would not recommend to a loved one. Imagine you are the patient, particularly when the going gets tough. Matters of privacy, conflicts of interest, participation of patients in research trials—these are all issues of trust. Underpinning this essential quality of being a doctor is a quiet reverence for what it means to be a doctor and what it feels like to care—in the deepest sense—for a patient in your charge. The late Dr. George Crile, Jr., a pioneering Cleveland surgeon and son of one of the founders of the Cleveland Clinic, wrote a short passage in his book on cancer back in 1955 that captures the quiet reverence of a profession that has the ability to restore health or even life, and always to relieve human suffering. His words mean as much now as they did then:

No physician, sleepless and worried about a patient, can return to the hospital in the midnight hours without feeling the importance of his faith. The dim corridor is silent; the doors are closed. At the end of the corridor in the glow of the desk lamp, the nurse watches over those who sleep or lie lonely and wait behind closed doors. No physician entering the hospital in these quiet hours can help feeling that the medical institution of which he is a part is in essence religious, that it is built on trust. No physician can fail to be proud that he is part of his patient's faith.

The student who understands that faith is the one who is ready to embark on life as doctor.

Dr. Healy graduated from Harvard Medical School and spent much of her career caring for patients and teaching and researching at the Johns Hopkins School of Medicine and the Cleveland Clinic Foundation. She served as the dean of the College of Medicine and Public Health at Ohio State University, president of the American Red Cross, and was the first woman to be the director of the National Institutes of Health. Currently she writes health and medical columns for U.S.News & World Report, where she speaks to some twenty million "patients."

Introduction

There are certainly easier careers than medicine. You'll struggle through difficult science courses, indenture yourself for a *long* decade of school and training, and lose countless hours of sleep. The reward? You may end up owing $100,000, being mired in paperwork that robs you of time for patients (or for a life outside of work), and holding a job that leaves you a ripe target for malpractice lawsuits.

And it spite of it all, medicine could be the best choice you ever make. You could be the person who turns pain and suffering into relief and hope. You might solve the mystery of an illness that has stumped generations of doctors. Your colleagues will be extraordinary people. You will see babies safely born, and you will save people's lives.

"I think I have the best job on Earth," said Ronald Drusin, a doctor and associate dean at Columbia University's College of Physicians and Surgeons. "Half of my time, I deal with students and help make sure they get the best education. And half the time I'm in practice as a cardiologist, working at our heart transplant center. So I get to see miracles everyday."

"I can't put into words how wonderful this job is," said Cynthia Romero, a family practice doctor in Virginia Beach, Virginia. "I spend my time seeing my patients as people, not just handing out medications. I get to know them, see them again and again and help them to live a healthy lifestyle. And I can see that it makes a big difference in my community."

It sounds ideal—and idyllic. But before you rush into medical school, stop and think about whether the vision of the profession you carry in your head matches today's reality. Medicine has always demanded a lot of physicians, even in the pre-HMO days of small practices and house calls. For many years, however, it has been changing in ways that doctors simply don't like. Lawrence Klein, an internist who enjoys his private practice in Washington, D.C., feels frustrated that increasing bureaucracy and financial pressures steal time from his patients. After all, seeing patients and giving them good care is what drew him to medicine in the first place. Would he go to medical school today? "Yes, but I'd think about it a bit more."

He'd consider, for example, the skyrocketing malpractice insurance premiums now hitting doctors—price hikes that insurers blame on outrageous jury awards in malpractice cases. "It's a dangerous situation for everyone," said Donald Palmisano, former president of the American Medical Association. "The costs are forcing doctors to close practices." Indeed, physicians in Pennsylvania, West Virginia, Connecticut, and many other states have held protest marches to plead for relief.

Klein would also factor in the pressure that hospitals, practice groups, and HMOs exert on doctors to bring in more revenue by seeing more patients and seeing them faster. And he would certainly think about one unfortunate consequence of rising health care costs: Employers, looking for the best deals, are switching health plans frequently—every two years, in many cases—and that means that patients have to switch doctors, too. As a result of these switches and the hurried patient visits, many physicians find it impossible to build the long-term relationships they feel are so essential to effective patient care. Indeed, fewer med school graduates are even going into primary care, opting instead for specialties such as radiology where they believe they will be insulated from these forces.

Because of the time, vast sums of money, and effort involved, it's important to take a hard look at yourself—your motives, your goals, your personality—before embarking on this course. One undergrad at the University of Virginia, after slogging through organic chemistry and other premed courses, getting top marks, and prepping for and acing the all-important Medical College Admissions Test (MCAT), began collecting school applications. Then, she remembers, she was sitting in the school library one night and looking across the table at a bunch of med students hunched over their books. "That's all they ever do: work," she said to her best friend. "That's not a life. It's a huge sacrifice. And I don't think I can do that." She didn't.

At least she realized her mismatch early.

"Sometimes we have alums who stop med school after two or three years," said Carol Baffi-Dugan, director of health profession advising at Tufts University. "It's not often, but when it happens, it's the saddest thing. They've got debt coming out of their ears. And they've devoted an incredible amount of time and energy learning skills that are not really transferable."

So how can you give yourself a reality test before medical school tests you? The Association of American Medical Colleges poses several general questions, such as: Do I care deeply about other people, their problems, and their pain? Do I enjoy helping people with my skills and knowledge? Do I enjoy learning and gaining new understanding? Do I often dig deeper into a subject than my teacher requires? Surely, your response in all cases ought to be a well-considered and resounding "yes" if you're about to start writing tuition checks. But a "yes" could just as easily foreshadow a brilliant career in social work.

So as you go about measuring your reservoir of empathy and intellectual drive, check your motives, too. "People want to go into medicine for all sorts of reasons," said a student at Columbia's College of Physicians and Surgeons. "Sometimes it's money or prestige. And that's just stupid. Look, you'll always make a comfortable living as a doctor. But there's got to be something more for you to be happy." Larry Sullivan, the prehealth professions advisor at Avila University in Kansas City, Kansas, often sees students who "have 'inherited' the idea of being a doctor. It comes from pressure from their family, or their peers." This, said Baffi-Dugan, is "one of the biggest pitfalls: the idea that 'it's going to make my parents happy.'" Still others want to practice because they've always watched *ER* on television and think that medicine is

dramatic and exciting. They don't consider how little independence doctors often have in real life and how difficult a workplace the health care system can be.

It's also worth considering whether or not you have some specific strengths that seem to stand out in the profession. Admissions directors and advisors agree that good doctors come in a whole range of personality types. "Is every good doctor an extrovert? No," said Baffi-Dugan. But beyond an honest desire to help sick people, good doctors do share some important characteristics, chief among them self-discipline, an ability to think clearly and make decisions in a crisis, and conscientiousness.

A mix of great attention to detail and a desire to strive for high-quality work proves extremely valuable in medical school, too. In an unpublished study of 610 Belgian medical students over six years of their education, across the board, conscientiousness predicted the strongest performance in medical school. This finding mirrors an earlier study of 176 English med students, in which teacher references, student personality statements, and personality scores were all compared to see what factor best predicted med school performance, and the winner was conscientiousness.

Why does care and thoroughness mean so much? "You have to have remarkable perseverance to get through medical school," said psychologist Cheryl Weinstein of Harvard Medical School, who studies learning and learning disabilities. "If you are reasonably intelligent and can learn facts, you can get through the MCAT. If you have high intelligence and love science you are likely to get the references. But once you have to start spending the long hours, once you have to sustain attention and be able to plan and attend, if you don't have [perseverance] you will be found out." Ask yourself: Are you someone who meticulously proofreads a paper before handing it in, not relying on the caprices of computerized spelling and grammar programs to do your work? Did you work extra hours as a hospital volunteer because there was work that needed to be done? And when former professors or former employers write your recommendations, will they note that assignments and projects were never late?

> *"You have to have remarkable perseverance to get through medical school."*

Perhaps the most practical way to research the depth of your commitment is to actually watch what real doctors do. Marilyn Becker, director of admissions for the University of Minnesota Medical School, said that her picks usually have some serious experience in a medical setting before med school, often in a community clinic, a doctor's office, or a hospital. Applicants are strongly encouraged to get this sort of exposure, perhaps part-time while they're in college or over the summers. Sullivan said that Avila University makes such work a part of a course called Introduction to Health Care Careers. More typically, students arrange it on their own. In college, Virginia Beach doctor Cynthia Romero set herself up with what she calls "mini rotations" by asking different doctors if she could shadow them for a week or more. (And she did this even though she already had more than a passing familiarity with the profession: Her mother is a physician.)

Romero liked what she saw, but for others, work experience can be a jolting reality check. "People volunteered in hospitals and realized they didn't have the patience to see patients," Romero

recalled. "Or they couldn't handle the pressure, or they couldn't stand seeing sick children. Some got really upset at the sight of blood." That's a fairly safe sign that you should bail out.

Those who stay the course but aren't truly enthusiastic are easy to identify when you meet them, said Charles Bardes, admissions director at Weill Medical College at Cornell University. "That's why you can't get into medical school without an interview," he notes. What are the signs of true commitment to an activity mentioned in an application? "Did they do this work in a perfunctory way, say for just one hour per week? Were they involved in the leadership of this activity, or did they just show up?" he said. "We try and get a feel for all this when we interview the students." Nor is Becker impressed by someone who emphasizes his or her family's illustrious medical past as qualification—two doctor-uncles, a grandfather on the faculty of a renowned med school—rather than a personal passion for the profession.

One student at Columbia remembers that he felt it was really important to take time off after college to put to rest any doubts about his career direction. He worked as a chef for a while, and then as a high school teacher. Not only did he gain confidence in his decision to go to med school, but "now I have some sense of professionalism," he said. "Being a doctor is a position of responsibility. You need a solid sense of yourself. School won't teach you that."

Assuming that all this soul searching reveals you're meant to be in medicine, this book is your step-by-step guide to getting there. The first chapter offers snapshots of what you'll experience as a first-year med student, followed by a discussion in Chapter 2 of how to choose a medical school that meets your particular needs. Chapter 3 profiles the life and academics at five very different types of medical schools. In Chapter 4, you'll learn how to fine-tune your application so that your first-choice school chooses you. Chapter 5 is a primer on that all-important topic: financing your education. And Chapter 6 explores second chances, telling you what to do if you don't get accepted the first time.

Beginning on page 77, you'll find a series of exclusive lists that allow you to compare medical schools on all kinds of key attributes: which are the hardest and easiest to get into, for example, and which ones leave graduates with the most and least debt. Finally, in the directory at the back of the book, you'll find detailed information on the country's medical schools, including schools offering the D.O. degree in osteopathy. This alternative medical degree involves a slightly different course of training, which is described in Chapter 2.

As you go through the extensive—some would say excruciating—application process, bear in mind that the interview, recommendation letters, and work experiences act as a final filter. They separate good students who *like* the idea of being a doctor from those who really would *be* a good doctor. Assuming that you possess all of the right qualifications, your best chance of making it through this sieve is to do what Harvard's Weinstein, and several ancient philosophers, suggest: "Know thyself." Perhaps friends, parents, mentors, school counselors, or trusted doctors will be able to ask you all the right questions to help you make this important decision. Regardless, there is only one person who can give the right answer. You.

Chapter One

A Med Student's First Year

Let's say you make it through your premed coursework, do well on the MCATs, and actually get into medical school. What happens next? Rachel Sobel was a young medical writer when she decided that the world she'd been covering as a journalist was something she wanted to experience firsthand. She'd majored in the history of science at Harvard and finished her premed coursework shortly after college. In 2002 she enrolled at the University of California, San Francisco School of Medicine (UCSF). "The process of becoming a physician is exhilarating," she said. "You will learn more about yourself and the world around you than you ever have." When she started school, Sobel also chronicled her experiences as a new med student. Here's her report from the front lines.

Fall, Year One

Meet Mr. Danovic

Sirens were blaring when the paramedics wheeled in John Danovic. The twenty-nine-year-old motorcyclist, who had just been laid off from his trucking job, had been drinking. He got hit by a car and thrown from his bike. Blood oozed from wounds in his scalp and chest, and a broken bone was jutting out of one arm.

The scene could have come straight out of any ER, but the case of John Danovic unfolded before my eyes in a lecture hall, not a hospital. The "blood" was actually a viscous burgundy concoction, and the team of doctors and nurses attending to the actor playing Mr. Danovic were my professors.

Welcome to my first lecture at medical school.

Med school isn't famous for its drama, nor is it known for its openness to change. Yet as the Mr. Danovic lecture reveals, change is afoot. Indeed, there is something of a revolution underway, transforming the first years of medical education. Many schools are dramatically revamping their curricula to prepare future physicians for an increasingly fragmented health care system in which any body of biomedical knowledge is bound to be quickly outdated.

Medical education has been virtually unchanged since the early twentieth century, when educators first standardized training. The "2+2" curriculum devoted the first two years to basic science lectures and the last two years to hospital training. Most med schools still use that general framework, but at UCSF and several other places, the first two years would be unrecognizable to a physician who graduated even five years ago.

Forget lectures from 8 a.m. until 5 p.m. Professors here have trimmed away esoteric hard science, keeping only what's essential to patient care. The reasoning is that you don't have to be a biochemist to be a skillful internist. In place of all that lab time, new disciplines are now considered essential to medical training, such as psychology, ethics, and even anthropology. For example, a patient assaulted by a gang (a real victim, unlike Mr. Danovic) talked to us about the psychological dimensions of healing.

David Irby, vice dean of education at UCSF, told me that the school's overhaul was driven in part by studies saying that newly minted M.D.s were unprepared to navigate today's health care system. There was also a widespread sense that medical school, rather than being an inspiring experience, had become a deadening one. Why did education have to be a boring exercise in memorization?

Mr. Danovic's case teaches that it can be otherwise. From him we learned the proper way to insert a chest tube (over the rib so you don't hit the nerves or vessels) and to recognize the signs of shock. Making the material more clinically relevant is not only more compelling but also more practical: According to Irby, study after study suggests that human memory is better wired for narrative than for rote learning.

Another major change taking place in medical training is an increased emphasis on cooperation, which grew out of the frequent observation that new doctors had great difficulty working in teams. You can imagine twenty- and thirty-somethings scoffing at the nursery school notion of cooperative learning, but in fact it's instilled so subtly that it's the way we're learning to think about how medicine works. Grades are pass/fail, which discourages competition. Half our classes take place in small groups, where the only way to learn is from one another. Picture a class where everyone doffs their shirts (women wear sports bras) and students draw on each other with Mr. Sketch markers to learn the complex intertwining of nerves, arteries, and veins of the arm. Being half-naked with classmates in "surface anatomy" isn't exactly a breeding ground for cutthroat rivalry.

Speaking of anatomy, I know my Uncle Peter will ask me over winter break how it went. Before I left for California, he regaled me with tales from his own medical school days—and reminded me to get there early for anatomy to get the best cadaver. I'm bracing for the next "In my day..." speech. But at UCSF, we learn from already dissected cadavers, and there is no competition to get the best one. Instead of spending hours trying to dig out, say, the renal artery, the idea is to save time and learn first from an intact specimen. To be sure, students still do a lot of memorizing. (For the eight wrist bones, remember: Some Lovers Try Positions That They Can't Handle: scaphoid, lunate, triquetrum, pisiform....You get the idea.) And budding surgeons can take a dissection elective, on, say, the abdomen or the pelvis.

No one knows if this new approach will prove better than the old one. Other schools that have made similar switches admit to growing pains. The ultimate measure is whether this generation of M.D.s will be better doctors in the modern health care system. On that, we'll have to wait to hear from the real Mr. Danovic.

Winter, Year One

The Art of Listening

One of my first epiphanies at med school came not from a gray-haired professor nor from *Gray's Anatomy* but from a fellow classmate. During our orientation in the fall, Jane (not her real name) told our entering class at UCSF about her heart surgery just a few weeks earlier.

Jane was a teenager when she first noticed an odd fluttering sensation inside her chest. The doctor did a quick exam and chalked it up to palpitations from too much caffeine. Later, while in college, Jane was getting ready for bed when her heart began racing and her room suddenly started spinning. Different symptoms, different doctor, but the same cursory approach: In this case, the diagnosis was anxiety.

Not until a recent checkup—six years after her initial complaint—did a keen physician find what was really wrong. He took a meticulous history and then listened to her heart with a stethoscope. Medicine's fancy term for this is auscultation: basically, listening to the body's various sounds. According to Jane, this physician "wasn't just going through the motions." He placed the stethoscope on her chest, closed his eyes, and listened for a long time. It paid off. The doc discovered a dangerous murmur, and further tests showed a two-inch hole in the wall between two chambers of her heart. Left untreated, such a defect could have caused heart and lung failure.

I was reminded of Jane's ordeal when I heard that the U.S. Medical Licensing Examination Committee had approved a new requirement for all medical students: a clinical-skills exam. The new test measures two things: communication skills and the ability to gather information through the physical exam. Students will interview and examine a series of "patients" (all actors) and complete a write-up for each one.

Many students were miffed that we would have to shell out an extra $1,000 or more to get licensed—not pocket change, considering that our average debt will close in on $100,000 by graduation. What's more, most schools already offer their own clinical-skills exams. Still, the new test sets important priorities. After all, isn't this what we came to school for, to learn the art of bedside diagnosis?

Kanu Chatterjee, a UCSF cardiologist who is legendary at performing physical examinations, has seen these vital skills atrophy in the profession over time. The repercussions, he says, include not only missed diagnoses but also the erosion of the patient–doctor relationship. Chatterjee trained in the 1950s when a physician's main diagnostic tool was a stethoscope. Now younger doctors rely more on sophisticated technology. He doesn't blame them; there is limited teaching time and technology is powerful. Still, he says, the physical exam "is the only tool to really get to know your patient."

A physical exam includes everything from inspecting a patient's appearance to palpating the abdomen to finding various pulses. As straightforward as that sounds, it is not easy. Last quarter, one of my professors played a recording of aberrant heart sounds during a lecture. I could not identify most of them. He played them again. Was that the abnormal "gallop"? I desperately clung to some fleeting rumble. Or was I just deluding myself into hearing something—anything?

My classmates and I got into medical school based in large part on our aptitude for science. But the art of physical diagnosis calls upon an entirely new sensibility: a heightened ability to listen, and look, and feel. Textbooks and flashcards can't teach these skills. They require practice, more practice, and an entirely new awareness of our own bodies to nourish the senses we have long neglected at the library.

An equally essential part of the bedside exam, obvious as it may seem, is good communication.

In fact, educators who pushed for the new licensing exam say part of the rationale is to weed out poor communicators and encourage schools to emphasize this competency in training. They cite a growing body of literature suggesting that the rising rate of malpractice complaints is linked to poor interpersonal skills.

This quarter, Jane and I took an in-house clinical-skills test. When our grader, a doctor from a nearby hospital, told a colleague she was going to be an evaluator, the colleague quipped: "They still teach that stuff?" Jane looked at me and said: "I can think of a few reasons why."

Spring, Year One

My future life?

The red-headed lady doesn't want her toddler to know she smokes. The man sitting next to her suffered two heart attacks this year and says it's time to quit. Another man, who has asthma, wants cleaner lungs. And in the corner, a transgendered woman undergoing hormone therapy vows to cut back on her two-pack-a-day habit because the combination puts her at increased risk for blood clots.

The motives for quitting might have been familiar, but clearly this was no ordinary smoking cessation meeting. It took place near the end of my first year as a medical student at a shelter in the squalid Tenderloin district of San Francisco, and its participants were a group of determined homeless people. Yes, they had unfathomable troubles to deal with, such as finding work and somewhere permanent to sleep, but they also had an unbending desire to take care of their own health.

The participants inspired not only each other but also the medical students who led the meetings each week. Medical school coursework is rigorous, yet many of us still squeeze in time to volunteer during the classroom years. At UCSF, for example, students set up pediatric health fairs in underserved areas, teach science to high schoolers, and coordinate bone marrow drives, among other things. It is here that we continue to cultivate what brought many of us into medicine in the first place: a desire to serve others through improving health care.

After the first two medical school years, where classroom learning dominates, in the final two years students are immersed in clinical experience and get to funnel all of their idealism, passion, and brain cells into taking care of patients. Enthusiastic friends who are in those years tell me, "you finally get to do what you came here for." Yet, at the same time, students are charged with figuring out their next step—their choice of specialty—and it is quite a complex decision. A new sense of pragmatism emerges.

During my first year, when I was on the wards for a few days during our winter "clinical interlude," I simply wasn't used to the new rhetoric about career choice. A third-year student told me in casual conversation that he wanted to specialize in radiology because of the "great lifestyle." I was shocked at first because I at least expected him to mention something intrinsically attractive about the field, such as its visual elegance or the satisfaction of nailing down diagnoses through images.

But then I began to hear more about this "ROAD to happiness"—radiology, ophthalmology, anesthesia, dermatology. The hours are good and the pay is at the top of the profession. These specialties are so popular that others are getting short shrift. For example, in 2002, less than half of all family practice residencies were filled by recent U.S. graduates.

Indeed, a recent study reported that lifestyle factors, such as adequate time for hobbies and family and control of weekly work hours, are a major reason for recent shifts in specialty career choices. The proportion of students who ranked anesthesiology as their first career choice, for example, went up more than fivefold in the last six years. At the same time, family practice applications have dropped 40 percent and the popularity of general surgery has also significantly declined.

There are many possible reasons why. One explanation is that more and more women are going into medicine and they are choosing more family-friendly fields. Another is that some students quickly become jaded in the modern medical climate. And who could blame them? Their role models are weary. A fourth-year student at an East Coast medical school told me that the attending physicians on his primary care rotation spent the whole time trying to convince him not to go into their field. The sacrifices such specialties call for, the student said, just aren't as appealing during these days of managed care pressures, high malpractice costs, and lower reimbursement rates.

Medical schools are concerned. Harvard's associate dean for student affairs, Nancy Oriol, believes that much of the growing acclaim of "lifestyle specialties" is simply urban legend passed around by students who haven't actually experienced these careers. She advises her students to pick their specialty based on their gut love of the field and then carve out the lifestyle they want once they begin practicing. "If you start off saying 'what are the lifestyle specialties?' then you may miss the ones you really love," she says. In almost every field, Oriol contends, a doctor can find a position that fits his or her choice of hours. There are surgeons who work part time, she says,

How med school works

Though schools vary widely in the courses they teach, most of this variation is grafted on top of a basic curriculum: two years of medical science followed by two years of clinical practice. This is followed by an apprenticeship period, or residency, that lasts from three to seven years. Here's a general outline:

Years One and Two: Coursework covers these topics: anatomy and embryology, physiology, biochemistry, histology, neuroscience, medical genetics, pharmacology, microbiology, pathology, and immunology. These first two years may also include courses on sexuality, nutrition, health care delivery, ethics, and other subjects.

Years Three and Four: You start clinical rotations in hospitals, usually beginning with surgery, family medicine, pediatrics, neuroscience, and obstetrics and gynecology. As you gain experience in patient care, these are followed by more rotations with advanced responsibility. You can also take elective courses in areas such as end-of-life care, psychiatry, or public and community health. Year four is also when students apply for residencies at various hospitals around the country in particular medical specialties. You graduate at the end of four years, and you can put an M.D. or D.O. after your name.

Year Five Postgraduate: You begin the first year of your residency, sometimes called an internship, taking primary responsibility for patient care while being supervised yourself by experienced doctors. Depending on the program—surgery, for instance, is very time-consuming—residencies can last as long as seven years.

Beyond Year Five: There's a lot of hard work involved in residency programs. After completing them successfully and passing national medical exams and state licensing tests, you are a full-fledged physician.

and there are academicians in radiology and dermatology who work all the time.

I recently spoke with a friend who is graduating from the University of Pennsylvania medical school. He is going into pediatrics, as did about one-sixth of the Penn class that graduated a year before him. Pediatrics is, on average, the lowest-paying field. "The majority of people," he observes, "still end up doing what their heart has told them to do from the beginning."

Now that I've finished my first year and have some perspective on it, I count my blessings: how privileged I am to be studying medicine and starting to work in the field. I know that in my training there will be elation and frustration, excitement and exhaustion—as there has been for many of my predecessors. Still, in the whirlwind events of a day during my training, I hope to always find meaning in the simple wonders of medicine—like the wonder I witnessed in the Tenderloin, as that group of homeless people threw away their lighters and cigarettes to begin a tough journey toward healthier living.

Chapter Two

Which Is the Right School for You?

There are essentially two ways to choose a medical school. There's the cynical approach: "You don't really have much choice," said one student. That is, you'll apply to the very few schools that might take you, and if you're lucky "get into one or maybe two. And there you go." This view gets some support from many medical school admissions officers, although they phrase it a little more diplomatically: All schools offer a similarly fine education because of medicine's rigid accreditation requirements. (Still, their own schools are better than most, these officers hasten to add.) So what does it matter where you go, in the end?

Then there's the smarter approach. It won't make getting in any easier, but it greatly improves your odds of thriving if you make it. "Schools really aren't created equal," said Lucy Wall, assistant dean for admissions at the University of Wisconsin Medical School. "There are differences in teaching methods and curriculum, some schools are more research oriented, public schools can be very different environments than private schools....There are lots of things to consider." A school's location can make a huge difference in the kind of experience you have, both academically and in terms of your quality of life. An institution's

---

"Schools really aren't created equal....There are lots of things to consider."

---

reputation—whether it's viewed as a topflight research school or the place to go to become a primary care physician—can influence your chances of getting the residency slot you want after graduation. And since the learning environment is greatly affected by the other students and the campus culture, the most important consideration may be "that gut feeling you get about a school, how comfortable you feel there," said Lauren Oshman, a former president of the American Medical Student Association and a graduate of Baylor College of Medicine in Houston.

Take Fernanda Musa's experience as a first-year student at Columbia University's College of Physicians and Surgeons in New York City. Musa wanted to attend a big-city institution doing cutting-edge research ("our teachers are some of the top names in their fields") where she would see the greatest variety of patients and conditions. Columbia was the perfect fit, she said. "The school culture is so happy. We're a really close, supportive group. We study together, and we also go out to concerts and bars. Most first-year students live together in Bard Hall, and that's where we get this great sense of community." Jessica Vorpahl, when she came to the University of Wisconsin a few years ago as a student interested in family practice, felt equally thrilled about her Midwestern, primary-care oriented, smaller-town school: "There's absolutely no better place. I'm totally convinced."

The hard numbers—your overall grade point average, your all-important science GPA, and your score on the Medical College Admissions Test—will narrow the field considerably by telling you which schools are within your reach. (See Chapter 4 for tips on figuring out the extent of your reach, then check out the directory at the back of this book for a sense of the numbers needed for entry at each school.) But your proper place in the field will depend on more, much more, than collections of statistics. Examining how the school teaches students (Does it rely on huge lectures? Will you get clinical experience early on or not until the latter half of your med school career?), what its curricular strengths are, what specialties graduates go on to practice, and how current students feel about the school will give you the best chance of finding, like Vorpahl, "no better place."

Consider the school culture

At the University of Iowa's Carver College of Medicine, students from all four years are grouped into small "learning communities" and interact both in class and out. First-year students relish the contact with upperclassmen, who are founts of invaluable advice about choosing courses and figuring out ways to fit all your hospital rotations into a tight schedule.

At more traditionally organized schools, such as the University of Chicago Pritzker School of Medicine, older students can disappear from sight once they start their clinical rotations. "Insanely competitive" is the phrase one student from the University of Alabama School of Medicine used to describe class-mates. While the med school at Johns Hopkins University also has a reputation for intense competi-tion, many students there protest that this is a myth—though they concede that, as a group, they tend to drive themselves hard and aren't exactly famous for kicking back and relaxing. At Yale, on the other hand, a policy of optional exams and no grades (students get evaluations from faculty) seems to create a less-pressured atmosphere, aided by the school schedule, which mandates a few weekday afternoons off.

Clearly, getting a feel for the ambience of a school requires some on-the-ground reporting. When you visit campus for your interview—which every med school requires—you'll be taken on a guided tour set up by the admissions office and designed to impress. Figure out how to break away and do some independent poking around. One way to gather information is to visit a school early in the application process—before you're called in. Medical school admission offices aren't set up for drop-in visits the way college admissions offices are, so you may not get a lot of help from them. But you can contact alumni from your college at a particular med school, and they should be able to find you people to talk with and places to stay. Once you're on campus, don't be shy about but-tonholing a few students and asking them some pointed questions:

What is student life like outside the classroom? Columbia students might tell you about the school's P & S Club, a student-run group central to most medical students' social lives that one day is running a wine tasting and another is producing *West Side Story* with students in the starring roles. One student at Iowa reports that in Iowa City, "the world stops for college athletics. This place is overwhelmed by Hawkeye fever, and it's a lot of fun. Everyone goes to football and basketball games. At hospitals, you even see doctors with Hawkeye lapel pins next to their name badges." Hopkins students, in contrast, say they have to work to find extracurricular activities in Baltimore; the fun is there, but you need to dig for it. At Northwestern University's Feinberg School of Medicine, as at Columbia, a social life is easy to come by. First-year students at Northwestern live together in Lake Shore Center, which leads to impromptu gatherings, study sup-port, and therapeutic venting sessions.

How intense is the competition? Often a lot less so than you might think. Sure, there are people at Hopkins who are intensely competitive, said one student, "but it hasn't affected me." Study groups and note-sharing are more the norm. A student at Case Western Reserve University School of Medicine said, "I had heard students at Case were kind of snobby and I was concerned that might lead to competition, but that's definitely not the case!" At Alabama, too, the "insanity" is more exception than rule. "The students are very helpful if you ask," said an Alabama student. "I think there are really only a few people who don't like to help others, and nobody likes them anyway."

Many new med students may *fear* competition because they remember, all too clearly, how fiercely they fought to get into medical school in the first place. But the reality is that once admitted, students feel a kinship with each other—that they're in this often-grueling, often-exhilarating experience together, said Jack Snarr, former associate dean for student programs at Northwestern. They want to do well so as to get into a good residency program, but aren't willing to do it by hurting others. "I know what I want to score on an exam, because I know what I'm capable of. But I don't want to get that score by withholding information from another student," said a student at Wright State University School of Medicine in Dayton, Ohio.

How accessible are the professors? Try to get input from a number of people because opinions may differ a lot within schools: Students who hang back may find they have very little contact with faculty, while more assertive students have no complaints. A lecture format, which predominates during the first years of school at the University of Chicago, for example, will probably make it more difficult to get to know faculty, especially if the school and the lectures are large. In the faculty-led small discussion and problem-solving groups that pepper the first years at Cornell University's Weill Medical College in New York City, by contrast, even the shyest students are soon known by name. At the University of Minnesota School of Medicine at Duluth, where entering class sizes hover around 50 rather than the more typical 100 to 150, faculty and administration "really feel more like family," said one student. "People have open-door policies, and you can just walk in and discuss something if you have a problem or are confused by something."

Yet even at schools like Chicago, professors have office hours. Find out whether they keep them, and whether those who go up and knock on the door are welcome or treated as nuisances. Keep in mind that even though medical schools list particular faculty members as "course directors" in their catalogs, at some schools you may see that professor only at the first lecture and then spend the rest of the semester dealing with assistants.

How welcoming is the school and the student body to people of different backgrounds? You can often tell a lot by just walking around with your eyes open. How diverse does the population seem to be? How much a part of things are the minority students? "We do OK on women here," said Philip Farrell, dean at Wisconsin. "But we don't do so well on minorities."

Nor do a good many other medical schools, but finding and encouraging would-be minority doctors is a goal that some are now getting serious about. Wisconsin has initiated "pipeline" programs to try and remedy the shortage, running summer science and math workshops for disadvantaged and minority high school students. Some med schools, such as Columbia and the University of California–San Francisco, have tried to build special support networks for minority students to reduce feelings of isolation and deal with any academic troubles. At UCSF, for example, the Medical Scholars Program was started because some underrepresented minority students found a few of the science courses to be tough going. Students who want help can meet twice a week in small workshops to discuss coursework, problem-solving skills, and better ways of organizing their study time. The workshops also serve as social hubs, where students meet one another and forge friendships.

If you can't manage to get to a school in person, some virtual exploration might be in order. Student perspectives can be found on the website of the Student Doctor Network (www.studentdoctor. net), a volunteer not-for-profit group that collects questionnaires about medical schools from premed students who have visited them. "Really laid back, friendly and enjoyable. Interviews were conversational. I had to explain my nontraditional stuff, which I expected (I'm 25). Really got me excited about the school," wrote one visitor to the University of Michigan–Ann Arbor. Another visitor to the same school, however, had this to say: "I got the real picture from some of the students. They told me most people are sons of doctors, or their parents are wealthy benefactors of the school. Lots of Ivy Leaguers too over there, not much room for people without money."

Obviously, opinions can differ, and you're sure to get conflicting information. But complaints can clue you in to areas that bear further investigation. The SDN site also features chat rooms where you can quiz students at schools of interest. You can also trade impressions with premeds and med students at another online community, www.medschoolchat.com.

Weigh the location

Beyond student culture, one of the most important features of a school to consider is its address. Location affects the kinds of patients you'll see, the range of diseases you'll be trained in, and the emphasis the school puts on different medical specialties—not to mention whether or not your significant other will have to give up his or her job and follow you out of state.

"An urban setting exposes you to a wide variety of patients, simply because that's the population. And that's going to make you a more well-rounded clinician." said Charles Bardes, admissions director at Cornell, which sits on the east side of Manhattan. It's important, he said, for applicants comparing schools to get a sense of the patient populations when they're visiting campus. "Walk up and down the hospital halls, and talk to students." If the school has a spectrum of hospitals, he said, there will in all likelihood be a spectrum of patients. A student at Cornell, for instance, might spend time in a hospital where a number of patients are elderly and have brittle bones, then move on to a hospital in a poor neighborhood and

> *"An urban setting exposes you to a wide variety of patients, simply because that's the population."*

see pregnant teenagers and children affected by lead poisoning. And because the school is affiliated with the world-renowned Memorial Sloan-Kettering Cancer Center, the student might well see more rare cancers than the average medical student—and the latest in treatment.

But don't take this to mean that all noncity schools will offer you an all-white or otherwise one-dimensional experience. Even though Wisconsin is located in the small city of Madison, for example, it sends students to training sites across the state. They can spend weeks seeing patients in small towns like Chippewa Falls, where many people have adequate health insurance and are easily available for follow-up care. But they can also go to Milwaukee, which has a large Latino population, and where patient care might involve surmounting language barriers that don't exist in Chippewa Falls. That said, schools like Minnesota–Duluth and Iowa, in rural states, do tend to focus more on family practice medicine because that specialty is much in demand in these areas.

The "other" medical degree

Connor Shannon was the son of a doctor and he knew, very early, that he wanted to be an M.D., too. So after graduating from the University of Colorado, he trained as an emergency medical technician, spent a couple of years working, and applied to 25 medical schools. Because his science background was relatively weak, which in turn "made me not do so well on the MCATs," he was rejected by 23 schools and waitlisted by the remaining two.

In the months that followed, Shannon got to know several doctors with the "other" medical degree—a doctor of osteopathy or D.O.—and began to suspect he might be chasing the wrong kind of training. "I liked [the D.O.s'] bedside manner better," he said. Shannon went to—and loved—the Chicago College of Osteopathic Medicine at Midwestern University.

Many medical school advisors recommend applying to a combination of D.O. and M.D. schools right from the start. "Both produce well-trained doctors," said Carol Baffi-Dugan,

program director for health professions advising at Tufts University. Curricula at both cover the same basic scientific principles of medicine, and osteopaths are licensed in all 50 states in surgery, internal medicine, and every other medical discipline.

Where the two schools of medicine differ is in philosophy. Doctors of osteopathy "treat people, not just symptoms," says Karen Nichols, dean of the Chicago College of Osteopathic Medicine. "The course list looks exactly the same, but the M.D.'s focus is on discreet organs. The osteopathic focus is that all of those pieces are interrelated. You can't affect one with out affecting another." That means more than paying simple lip-service to the idea of the "whole" patient: It means examining his or her environment, family, and general situation in life, too. Michael Kuchera, a D.O., described the emphasis as being on health rather than disease. Not surprisingly, more than 65 percent of the 52,000 licensed osteopaths in the United States are primary care

physicians—in family practice or pediatrics, for example. The American Association of Colleges of Osteopathic Medicine provides a description of osteopathic training, as well as short profiles of 20 schools, on its website (www.aacom.org). The D.O. programs and their contact information are listed in the Directory section of this book.

Beyond their other medical studies, osteopathic students get 200 hours of training in "osteopathic manipulative medicine," a hands-on technique for diagnosis and healing. Limited motion in the lower ribs, for instance, can cause pain in the stomach that seems a lot like irritable bowel syndrome. Identifying the muscle strain in the ribs through manipulation, and then treating it, can relieve the stomach distress. An osteopath learns to apply specific amounts of pressure on a body part, attempting to relax it or stimulate it. While such an approach might have raised eyebrows in the profession a decade or two ago, these days no one—except perhaps the crustiest old M.D.s—dismisses it as New Age nonsense. Manipulative medicine is based on the not-terribly-heretical idea that structures in the body influence function, and that a problem in the structure of one body part can cause problems in the function of other parts.

Don't think of applying to D.O. schools as a fallback plan. Some of them accept a greater percentage of applicants than do M.D. schools, but many are just as selective. And all D.O. schools are searching for a particular kind of person. "Students have to understand the osteopathic schools are not looking for people who couldn't get into M.D. schools," said Nichols. "I want them to understand the osteopathic philosophy, to have spent time with a D.O. so they can get a strong letter of recommendation." And as for Connor Shannon, he decided that his rejections were a good thing because they allowed him to land where he was always meant to be.

Indeed, public institutions supported by state money generally emphasize medical training targeted to state and local needs. While it's possible to be trained in ophthalmology or oncology at the University of Washington in Seattle, for example, there's a definite push to turn out primary care docs who will stay in the Northwestern corner of the country and practice. Wisconsin offers many more opportunities to learn about rural health care than does Columbia. At SUNY Downstate Medical Center College of Medicine in Brooklyn, students get exposure to a high-risk obstetrics program because there are so many high-risk pregnancies in that community.

Another way state schools fulfill state objectives is by educating their own residents, and doing so relatively cheaply. "The first issue I usually ask students to think about when thinking about schools is where they live," said John Friede, the health professions advisor at Villanova University in Philadelphia.

"Staying in-state can often mean real savings, and getting out of school with less debt." Pennsylvania residents who choose Pennsylvania State University College of Medicine pay about $30,000 per year in tuition, for instance. The school charges students from out of state an extra $10,000 per year. If Pennsylvania residents go to Duluth to study medicine, they pay $35,000 for the first year, while the Minnesota locals pay $28,000. The next year, Minnesota residents' tuition drop to $19,000, while out-of-staters stay above $33,000. Likewise, leaving state for a private institution could mean tuition bills of $30,000–40,000 a year. (See Chapter 5 for other strategies for financing your education.)

You'll probably find that staying close to home gives you a better chance of getting in, too. Recently, for example, the University of California–San Diego School of Medicine had about 3,000 in-state applicants and admitted 120; of about 1,100 applicants from out-of-state, it took just 2. Wisconsin's med school is committed to taking 80 to 90 percent of its students from the Badger State. Finally, of course, a school's location can mean a great deal for your personal life. One of the reasons Columbia worked so well for one student is that her family members, who lived in Brazil, found it easy to fly up and visit her on the East Coast; a California school would have called for a longer, more expensive trip.

"Staying in-state can often mean real savings, and getting out of school with less debt."

Put prestige in perspective

You might be tempted to pay any amount of money to get your M.D. from a great medical school—a really, really great school. Someplace you've always heard about, like Harvard, or Stanford, or Cornell, or Johns Hopkins, whose name alone says "first-rate education."

Not so fast, cautions Bardes. As admissions director at Cornell, he can certainly brag about a top-notch faculty and state-of-the-art facilities. He just can't say that Cornell's strengths add up to a quality of education that's significantly better than most others. "The quality range in medical schools is much narrower than in other types of schools," he said. Andrew Frantz, associate dean of admissions at Columbia, which usually scores near the top in the annual *U.S.News & World Report* ranking of med schools, agreed: "For maybe 90 percent of the schools, the quality seems very tight, and very high." Or as Delores Brown, associate dean for admissions at Northwestern's med school, put it: "For medical training, there is no bad school."

Why would medicine produce such a tight bunch? There are a few reasons. Bardes points out that because the public has a life-and-death interest in highly skilled physicians, the accreditation process for medical schools is unusually elaborate and demanding. That process, overseen by both the Association of American Medical Colleges and the American Medical Association, examines everything from the technology at student clinical sites to the teaching qualifications of the faculty to the curriculum content, ensuring that it covers not just the scientific basis of medicine but also behavioral and socioeconomic aspects. The resulting accreditation reports for any given school are as bulky as a Los Angeles telephone directory. "They ask a lot of questions and want very specific answers," said Wisconsin's Farrell, hefting his school's report off his desk. "There are about 120 certification standards in here. With us, they liked our faculty development program and our mentoring program for students. But they thought we had too many lectures and not enough self-directed study."

Another equalizer? The national standardized tests students must take during their four years in school. Passing the initial U.S. Medical Licensing Examination, which tests knowledge of basic medical science, is required for promotion from the second to the third year, and students have to pass further stages of the test during their final two years in order to graduate. Obviously, failure doesn't just hurt the student: A pattern of failures reflects badly on the school and may jeopardize its accreditation.

Schools that do enjoy an aura of prestige tend to be the ones with the big research programs, said Thomas Langhorne, the prehealth professions advisor at Binghamton University in New York. "These are schools with lots of Nobel Prize winners, or researchers that make discoveries about diseases, or get big grants, and so they get a lot of press," he said. "You read the names 'Harvard' and 'Stanford' a lot. But these are things that, to me, don't have a lot to do with your training to be a physician."

It's not that a strong and active research program is irrelevant; in fact, the research might well enhance your academic experience. If you find yourself drawn to the study of glaucoma or the genetics of antibiotic resistance, for example, it should be relatively easy at a school pulling in lots of grants in these areas to get funding for a short research project, often working alongside a faculty member. The research may also inform course content—indeed, the experts may be teaching the classes. At a smaller school with less research money—say, a state school focused on primary care—you'll have fewer opportunities to "follow your nose" and go in unexpected directions. And anyone who tells you that having Harvard or Cornell on a résumé won't open a few extra doors simply isn't being honest.

In certain cases, however, a great research reputation might actually be a career handicap, said Phyllis Guze, former president of the Association of Program Directors in Internal Medicine—the people who run residency programs and thus hire med school graduates for their first job. "You can come from a school with a stellar academic reputation, and depending on the residency you're applying for, that's not going to help you," she said. If she were looking at applicants for an inner-city hospital residency without a big research component, a Stanford résumé wouldn't be the top one on her pile. "It's a school noted for great scholarship and academic physicians," she said, "so why would the student be interested in this kind of hospital? Program directors really think about things like this."

Rather than focusing on reputation, advisors and med school faculty suggest taking a hard look at the concrete—and the metal and the electronics. Good facilities are a harbinger of a good educational experience. Wisconsin's new health sciences building, for

"The quality range in medical schools is much narrower than in other types of schools."

instance, has Ethernet jacks at every classroom desk, so if a lecturer is using a PowerPoint presentation, students can download it right onto their laptops. The University of Pittsburgh School of Medicine is going totally wireless, so students can do the same thing even when sprawled out in a hallway.

Pittsburgh also has installed high-resolution cameras and monitors that cover every inch of its anatomy lab. Typically, when new students are dissecting a cadaver and people at one table find something interesting, like the heart, "a buzz goes through the room and 150 students line up to look," said John Mahoney, the school's assistant dean for medical education. "That takes forever and number 150 probably can't see anything. But with our cameras, an image immediately shows up over every dissecting table, so all students have to do is look up for a great view." Features like these indicate that the school is investing in education, and not neglecting students to pay hospital debts.

One aspect of a school's reputation that should matter to you a lot is how well-regarded it is among residency directors who aim to hire the most skilled doctors they can find. Examining the school's record on residency matches will give you a good idea. In general, academic hospitals—those closely affiliated with a university—tend to be more sought after because they are better teaching environments than stand-alone hospitals. And how many of the students get into their top choices? At most schools, 90 percent of graduates get into their first-, second,- or

---

"You read the names 'Harvard' and 'Stanford' a lot. But these are things that, to me, don't have a lot to do with your training to be a physician."

---

third-choice program. If the school reports a lower number, that should be a warning.

There are other signs of trouble, and they have to do with money. If a school is strapped, count on it: You'll be affected. In the late 1990s, for instance, MCP-Hahnemann University School of Medicine in Philadelphia was in dire straits because its hospitals were hemorrhaging money. Morale among faculty was low and researchers had trouble getting the school to pay their bills on time. Since then, Hahnemann has merged with another Philly school to form the Drexel University College of Medicine. There's new management, new money flowing in, new technology, new ownership arrangements for the hospitals, and much more happiness on campus. So check the local newspapers for stories about financial worries. You might even call a broker. If a school or medical center has floated bond issues, agencies like Moody's rate those bonds based on the financial soundness of the institution issuing them.

What and how you'll learn

A school's curriculum and the style faculty use to teach it are crucial elements of your decision, even though the topics covered during the first and second years are pretty much the same wherever you go. Anatomy and embryology, physiology, biochemistry, histology, neuroscience, genetics, pharmacology, microbiology, pathology, and immunology—all are basic science areas that every budding doctor needs to cover.

What varies is the way in which they are taught; many schools present the facts in tried-and-true large lectures, while others emphasize small-group discussions that center around solving problems. Some schools use a mix of the two styles. At Harvard and Pittsburgh, two institutions that rely heavily on "problem-based learning," or PBL, a group of first-year students studying anatomy or immunology or microbiology will meet for, say, 90 minutes to discuss a hypothetical patient with specific symptoms—Mr. X has come to his family doctor complaining of fever and chills—and brainstorm ways to figure out what's wrong. If the course is microbiology, someone might suggest an infection. Then the question becomes: What kind of infection? Everyone goes off to research possible conditions and appropriate diagnostic tests, and the group meets again and again during the week, eventually arriving at a solution: Mr. X has a staph infection. The idea is that by teaching themselves how to solve problems, students are better equipped for the real world. "When they present to you one specific disease and you talk about it in PBL, it really sticks with you," noted a Pittsburgh student.

A microbiology lecture on staph, in contrast, might present a list of germs, symptoms they can cause, and antibiotics that might kill them.

Not everyone is a believer in PBL. One Columbia student pointed out that while it gives students the needed information, it can also take a lot of extra time. "It's great when everyone in the group comes in with a different knowledge base and can exchange information. But the first year of med school is *not* like that. People actually know very little. So you end up spending an awful lot of time running around to the library, looking up basic things. It's not efficient at all." The Columbia faculty agrees with him for the most part and has emphasized lectures, adopting PBL techniques in just a few courses. One University of Chicago med student added that she got more with less fuss out of the science lectures that dominate at her school: "You need to have the basic sciences down first in order to do something good later. It might not seem interesting but we can't help patients without it."

Another variation is the way schools serve up the required topics. For example, many are moving away from courses that cover discrete subjects such as microbiology or pharmacology as overviews of the entire body, moving instead toward interdisciplinary "organ-based" courses that examine all aspects of, say, the kidneys. Students learn about kidney anatomy, microbiology, immunology, and the drugs that affect this organ. Next, they might move on to the heart and circulatory system, then go on to the nervous system, and so on throughout the body. "I think it helps you put things together and see how the body actually works," said a Duluth student. Her school, along with Brown, Yale, the University of Texas Medical Branch at Galveston, and many others, have switched to this way of teaching.

The amount of time spent helping patients—or at the very least seeing patients—is an increasingly important variable, too. For a large part of the last century, the basic science courses during the

"You need to have the basic sciences down first in order to do something good later."

first years of med school kept students in large lecture halls or with their noses buried in textbooks. Then, in the third year, they'd enter the hospital for clinical training and encounter their first real patients. Often they were ill-prepared. "Our faculty was getting worried that students weren't making the connections between science and patient care that they could be making," said Donald Innes, associate dean for curriculum at the University of Virginia's medical school. That concern was shared nationwide, said Robert Eaglen of the Liaison Committee on Medical Education, the curriculum guidance arm of the Association of American Medical Colleges. Medical schools across the country began revamping their first-year curriculum so that student–patient encounters would occur early on.

It's a welcome change for many students. "I want the science backed up by experience," said one student at the University of New Mexico, explaining that the promise of early and plentiful experience with patients drew him to that school. As a supplement to time in class, New Mexico places first-year students in local clinics where they work with supervising physicians in actual practice. "Having a real face behind these medical problems is really helpful," said the student. Moreover, students learn early how to interact with patients—a skill you can't get from a textbook, said Scott Obenshain, New Mexico's former associate dean for undergraduate medical education. The

---

"Our faculty was getting worried that students weren't making the connections between science and patient care that they could be making."

---

contact is helpful to patients, too—which is why New Mexico originally started making it happen. "We're in a rural area and we have a great call for physicians who have general skills, rather than specialists," said Obenshain. Case Western pairs students in their first month of school with expectant mothers at local clinics. The students work as patient advocates until these mothers give birth.

Some schools simulate patient interaction instead. Virginia, for instance, uses "standardized patients" in first-year lecture classes. These are not real patients, but people who have been trained to complain of symptoms that are signs of a particular illness. Students learn to take medical histories from working with them and progress to giving them physical exams.

Most schools also now require that first-year students "shadow" practicing physicians on their rounds, perhaps once a week or once a month. But beware: Not all shadowing experiences are equally useful. "Applicants really should ask if shadowing is an active or passive experience," said Cornell's

Bardes, who believes that just sitting around watching the doctor work doesn't do much good. A more active role, which Cornell asks of its students, is to function as a patient advocate or a kind of social worker in a medical clinic, talking to the patient and making sure any concerns are addressed by the medical team. "Not only does that get the student involved with the patient," Bardes said, "it also involves the student with the doctors and nurses directly, and helps the student understand that care is a team effort."

New topics are also shouldering their way into the mix. At Pritzker in Chicago, first-years take a course called Introduction to Clinical Medicine, which gets away from science and into interpersonal relationships and ethics; at Iowa, this course is called Foundations of Clinical Practice. UCSF offers an introduction to pain treatment. And Emory, in Atlanta, teaches Complementary Medical Practices as an elective, in which students visit acupuncture studios and Chinese herbalists. Other schools have added complementary medicine to the curriculum, too, as doctors begin to realize how many of their patients take herbs and supplements.

Finally, although medical students often joke that "C equals M.D." (meaning that you can count on being a doctor as long as you don't flunk out), it's worth considering the way schools on your list handle grades. The traditional "ABC" system may be the most comfortable one for you if you like getting fairly specific feedback about how firm a grasp you have of the material. Some students at Yale, in fact, say that school's relaxed no-grade approach can cause people to slip far behind unless they are highly motivated and disciplined.

On the other hand, many students find that simple pass/fail grades relieve some of the pressure that comes with a letter system. One student at Case Western noted that grading policies helped him choose between Case in Cleveland and Ohio State in Columbus. Ohio State was a lot cheaper and "in a town that felt more like home." Yet he decided on Case largely because the first two years of the program are graded pass/fail. To him, that meant the likelihood that Case "might be more humane than the rest," and that there would be more cooperation with other students. Indeed, he reports that his time in school was filled with fun as well as work, and much of the credit goes to his fellow students. "So I'll take my Case Western degree and smile."

Chapter Three

Inside Five Top Schools

There's more than one way to become a doctor—146 ways, in fact, if you count all of the accredited medical schools in the country. (Turn to the Directory for details.) The five top schools profiled in this chapter each typify a different approach to the teaching of medicine. All place highly in the annual *U.S.News & World Report* rankings. Two are public schools, one in a small Midwestern city (the University of Wisconsin in Madison) and the other in a dense, urban West Coast setting (the University of Washington in Seattle). Both of these schools try to meet local needs by turning out world-class primary care doctors, but they do so in very different ways.

The remaining three are private institutions. Duke University, in the Southeast, has an accelerated program of science courses for first-year students, setting them up to do complex research. At Yale University in the Northeast, students don't take exams unless they want to, yet are required to write a thesis. Then there is Johns Hopkins University in the mid-Atlantic, a research power-house whose students serve urban Baltimore when they are not busy in the school's labs.

Of course, each school boasts features that defy the limits of any stereotype: Washington, for instance, creates family doctors while also pulling in more research money than most other schools in the nation. That's why any school you're interested in merits a closer look. To give you a head start, here are profiles, including student and faculty viewpoints, of each member of this medical Fab Five.

University of Wisconsin Medical School

- Madison, Wisconsin
- Public
- Enrollment 2005–2006 academic year: 619
- Overall rank in the 2007 *U.S. News* medical school rankings (research): 28
- Overall rank in the 2007 *U.S. News* medical school rankings (primary care): 6
- Average MCAT score: 10.4
- Average undergraduate GPA: 3.70

Stroll over to Wisconsin's anatomy department and you'll be able to talk to—or take a class from—James Thomson, the scientist who first isolated human stem cells from an embryo, a giant break-through that has raised hopes for dramatic new medical therapies and embroiled the country in an ethical debate over use of these cells. Nearly 600 of Wisconsin's other 1,100 faculty members are involved in leading medical science programs in aging, neuroscience, cancer, and other key areas. The university as a whole pulled in $770 million in research money in a recent year, making it one of the top public schools doing this kind of work. So what draws most students to Madison? Surprisingly, *not* the lure of the lab. "I came because we train some of the best primary care physicians around," said one student. It's a senti-ment fellow students echo again and again.

Philip Farrell, dean of the medical school, said there's no contradiction here, given Wisconsin's status as both a fine academic institution and a state university. "We have a superb clinical care program; that's absolutely true. It's a core part of our mission. Yet we're also part of this enormous research university." The med school has almost as many Ph.D. students as it does M.D. students; joint M.D./Ph.D. degrees in the Medical Scientist Training Program are also popular. Pioneering research programs on the connection between cancer and nutrition, and on cardiac electrophysi-ology, have spawned courses for medical students. "But yeah," Farrell said, "we produce fine, caring doctors."

This, then, is the "Wisconsin idea": While the university is tucked away on a narrow isthmus of land, almost cut off by two surrounding beautiful lakes, Mendota and Monona, the medical school itself is a statewide institution. Students do research in Madison at the highly regarded cancer center, for example, but also go to Milwaukee and work with the urban poor, or head out to small towns like Eagle River or Ashland, where they learn about rural health care issues and everyone around knows their names. Feeling a strong responsibility to make sure Wisconsin has the necessary supply of doctors, the university's Board of Regents presses Farrell to reserve 80 to 90 percent of the spots in each entering class for in-state students, many of whom will stay in the area once they get their M.D.

To fan interest in treating patients, the school pairs first- and second-year students with family practice doctors, internists, or pediatricians for a half-day each month. Students themselves run a program called MEDIC (Medical Information Center), which puts them to work advising patients at clinics in the Madison area. For at least six weeks during the third year, the school boots everyone out for rotations in small-town clinics and hospitals throughout the state. "It's not that they absolutely want to push us in that direction, but they definitely want to expose us to that," said one student interested in family practice. (The school does look beyond the Dairy State borders: It runs a summer medical clinic in Ecuador, for example.) And the exposure definitely gets results: Since 1999, about 20 percent of each graduating class has gone into family medicine residencies. Internal medicine has drawn an additional 12 to 20 percent, and the third most popular specialty has been pediatrics. In contrast, about five or six percent choose surgery, and a fraction of a percent go into neurology.

Whatever specialty students explore, they do it in close contact with their professors. Particularly at the small-town sites, there's often just one student rotating through at a time, which translates into a lot of attention from teacher-physicians. That's true on campus, too. Faculty members have a reputation for being very approachable and often come in during the evenings to tutor students. "There's a lot of interaction with professors," one student said. "When I went to get recommendations for residency programs, there was no shortage of people I could talk to. I was on a first-name basis with a lot of them." Indeed, teaching skill, not just the number of publications or amount of grant funding brought in, is weighed more heavily

"When I went to get recommendations for residency programs, there was no shortage of people I could talk to."

in promotion decisions than at most schools, and junior faculty are assigned a senior faculty mentor to help them along.

The warm, intimate feeling extends to fellow students. "I got into here, and Dartmouth, and Yale," said one third-year student. "This place seemed different. People at Madison take time out of their schedules to stop and discuss the school with you, in the classrooms and in the hallways, because they like it so much. I remember I visited one other school where I didn't see a student all day, and I know they weren't all on vacation." Students call the culture supportive, not competitive; there are even side bets in each class on how many members will end up marrying one another. And while everyone studies hard, people here "also know how to have a good time," said another student. Yet another one noted that she liked the fact that much of her class was older and brought mature, diverse perspectives to discussions about subjects such as medical ethics.

Not everything about the school gets rave reviews. There are too many basic science lectures, according to some students and faculty. Unlike schools that try to pepper the first year with small-group learning experiences, Wisconsin has retained the large-lecture format. "I'd say that small-group learning is our biggest weakness right now," said Susan Skochelak, the senior associate dean for academic affairs. Her concern is echoed by students. "There were six or seven hours of lectures per day during the first year," said one. "They don't take attendance, so you don't have to be there. But I felt that much structured time was excessive, at least for me." There are also complaints that the school buildings are old and overcrowded and that there's no student parking.

Class sizes and facilities were drastically improved in the fall of 2004, when the school's new Health Sciences Learning Center is set to opened, giving Wisconsin one of the most modern medical school buildings in the country. Numerous classrooms and labs allow for smaller course sections and discussion groups. The school's formerly separate libraries are now consolidated here and equipped with more computer terminals as well as wireless access. The entire building, in fact, is a wireless heaven, with numerous "hot spots" where students can download course materials and medical data out of the ether. The building also houses Wisconsin's nursing and physician assistant programs, allowing for a lot of cross-pollination of ideas and staff.

Parking spaces are still going to be a problem, however. If that's a big issue for you, Madison is not going to make you happy. But everything else—the patient contact, the access to leading research if you want it, the new building, the famously rich university-made ice cream sold at the student center—makes for some of the best-trained (and happiest) future doctors around.

Duke University School of Medicine

- **Durham, North Carolina**
- **Private**
- **Enrollment 2005–2006 academic year: 406**
- **Overall rank in the 2007 *U.S. News* medical school rankings (research): 6**
- **Overall rank in the 2007 *U.S. News* medical school rankings (primary care): 6**
- **Average MCAT score: 11.9**
- **Average undergraduate GPA: 3.80**

Most medical students spend their third year of school racing around hospitals, going from cardiology units to pediatric wards to try out various clinical specialties. But by Brian Griffith's third year at Duke, he had already been there and done that. Instead, Griffith was holed up in his own little corner of a bustling microbiology lab, surrounded by rows and rows of petri dishes filled with a fungus that can cause meningitis in people with weak immune systems. Griffith was designing tests to identify genes that help the fungus become virulent.

Meanwhile, across town at a Duke clinic, Griffith's classmate Jennifer Kim was interviewing and examining 100 patients enrolled in a new study on the reliability of various blood pressure monitors. "Blood pressure is used so often for diagnosis and patient status info," said Kim, whose goal was to bring better, more reliable devices into hospitals and clinics. "I think this sort of research is key to the practice of medicine."

This notion—that research is the cornerstone of health care—dominates the Duke experience. To this end, the school packs all basic science classes into the first 11 months, running August through July, instead of spreading them across the first two years as most schools do. The science acceleration gets students into the hospital sooner—during year two instead of year three, so their third year is devoted full-time to research.

Clearly, Duke is not aiming to swell the ranks of family practice docs. Instead, the program is geared toward producing physician-scientists who can easily move between the lab bench and the bedside. "Our current body of knowledge will have nothing to do with the practice of medicine in ten years," said R. Sanders Williams, dean of the school. "We aim to provide graduates with both the tools and the ethos of lifetime scholarship." He noted that a full 40 percent of students go on to pursue dual degrees such as an M.D./Ph.D. or an M.D. combined with a new master's degree in translational medicine, which focuses on turning basic research into clinically useful models.

The pressure can be great here, especially early on, so Duke students must hit the ground running. That early push to cover everything from physiology and neurobiology to pathology in the first year means spending all day, every day in a lecture hall and then a lab. It's difficult, say students, but doable. "We're learning the essentials, not a lot of fluff, because you don't need it," said one second-year student, adding that she felt extremely well-prepared for her clinical rotations. In fact, most students are eager to hit the wards. "I came to med school to practice medicine, to put a white coat on and get out into the hospital—not to sit in a classroom for two years," explained a student in the fourth year of a combined M.D./Ph.D. program in medical sociology and health policy.

Then it's on to the third year for research.

The school pushes this hard, said Edward Halperin, vice dean of the med school, in part because of a belief that would-be doctors need to be able to interpret constantly advancing research. "Just because a study is in the *Journal of the American Medical Association* doesn't mean it's true," he said. "You have to learn how to critically read scientific literature—*how* do you read

---

"We aim to provide graduates with both the tools and the ethos of lifetime scholarship."

---

what's published and decide when things change research to therapy? And there's no better way to assess the value of research than to do it yourself." The individualized research process requires a lot of initiative and self-motivation—much like the rest of the Duke experience—but gives students exceptional benefits. It provides an opportunity to work closely with a faculty mentor, for one thing, perhaps one of the big names you see on the covers of your textbooks. It can also be an important résumé boost when you start shopping for a residency, particularly if you've published a scientific paper or two, as both Griffith and Kim planned to do.

There are a few complaints about the pace. Some students say that the chock-full first year ignores important areas such as embryology; others say that it's particularly difficult to cover gross anatomy—and dissect a human body—in only nine weeks. (Other schools spend twice as much time teaching these skills.) Currently, Duke is in the midst of revamping its curriculum to better address changes in the field. The traditional first-year lecture courses will be regrouped into three blocks—Molecules and Cells, Normal Body, and Body and Disease—with a focus on individual organ systems rather than broad topics, and more emphasis on interaction and case-based learning. In the second year, there will be five weeklong "mini courses" that cover diagnostic exercises and exposure to areas of health care like

> "There's no better way to assess the value of research than to do it yourself."

physical rehabilitation and social work. In addition, the research year will expand from eight to ten months and require a written thesis.

Already, though, both research and clinical opportunities abound throughout the relatively young and rich Duke University Medical Center, a $1.3 billion system closely affiliated with the medical school, encompassing myriad health care providers from the Duke Hospital and Clinics to the Duke Community Hospice. That range provides chances for students to gain exposure to many different areas of medicine. This is perhaps another reason why the vast majority of students here end up focusing on competitive specialties and subspecialties like dermatology, pediatrics, plastic surgery, orthopedics, and radiology, as opposed to primary care or family medicine. A good number go on to obtain coveted residencies in these areas at top institutions, including nearly a quarter at Duke itself. After they graduate, some 20 percent of Duke students go on to hold academic positions; the remaining 80 percent pursue a wide variety of career paths,

from running biotech companies to working in government health organizations. And, yes, a few do serve as physicians in small towns.

Although Duke is filled with one hyperqualified overachiever after another, students say the culture here is overwhelmingly collegial. Many tell tales of sharing notes and study charts with their whole class during the first year, perhaps because students aren't grubbing for A's. The grading system here is pass, fail, and honors; some complain that the latter designation can be arbitrary, but most say they're happy with the results. It helps that faculty are said to be very accessible. In the first year, students are assigned to an advisory dean and meet with that person and a handful of peers for lunch once a week; these gatherings let students discuss current events and schoolwide issues, or simply blow off steam. In the second year, larger groups of 25 congregate to talk about being in the hospital and share important milestones, like delivering a baby for the first time.

This collegiality was crucial, students say, when the unthinkable happened a few years back. In a case that made major headlines, a Duke surgeon infamously botched an organ transplant on a young illegal immigrant named Jesica Santillan, who eventually died. "I think we were all shocked, to say the least," recalled one student. "But we talked about it a lot [in advising groups and classes] and I think we learned from it. It made me more aware of how vigilant you have to be at all times, even with the most routine things." In the aftermath, some students say they feel more empowered to speak up to physicians if they notice a mistake or an inconsistency.

In addition to its many academic advantages, Duke, surprisingly, can also provide a relatively inexpensive medical education. The low cost of living in Durham, combined with a famously generous financial aid office, results in a much lower average debt burden: the mean for Duke grads is $74, 790, compared to the national average of slightly more than $100,000. That, say students, relieves a lot of anxiety about the future. The med school offers 11 full-tuition scholarships per class; and recently, 65 out of 100 third-year students received research scholarships from sources such as the Howard Hughes Medical Institute. And despite the hard work, students say, there's plenty of time to hang out with friends and enjoy Durham Bulls minor league baseball and the university's nationally ranked basketball teams. (The comprehensive, student-produced *Duke Med School Made Ridiculously Simple* is a favorite resource for information about how you'll spend your free time, in addition to academics.)

Duke is, in short, a school of tremendous challenges but also tremendous opportunities. Said the school's dean: "Being here is about dreaming big, following your dream, and not being afraid." The fearless thrive and go on to push back the current boundaries of medicine.

Yale University School of Medicine

- ■ New Haven, Connecticut
- ■ Private
- ■ Enrollment 2005–2006 academic year: 441
- ■ Overall rank in the 2007 *U.S. News* medical school rankings (research): 9
- ■ Overall rank in the 2007 *U.S. News* medical school rankings (primary care): N/A
- ■ Average MCAT score: 11.6
- ■ Average undergraduate GPA: 3.75

When Yale students invite friends from other med schools for some weekend fun, such as skiing or a trip to the ballpark, the response is usually something along the lines of "Are you kidding?" That's because most med students spend their weekends cramming for exams. But not at Yale. Most exams here are optional, anonymous, online self-evaluations. What's more, students get two free afternoons each week. So perhaps it's not surprising that they jokingly refer to laid-back Yale as the "Utopia School of Medicine."

Officially, though, the school's approach is called "The Yale System." It aims to give med students wide latitude in constructing their own educational experiences, akin to Ph.D. programs in, say, genetics or history. And if this is utopia, it requires plenty of self-discipline. "Students must assume more than usual responsibility for their education," reads the school's literature. "Memorization of facts should be far less important than a well-rounded education in fundamental principles, training in methods of investigation, and the acquisition of the scientific habit of mind."

For the academic overachievers who populate Yale's ranks, The System can take some getting used to. It tries to transform students who have previously succeeded by being extremely competitive into team players. "Yale is full of people who are Type A personalities but are trying to be Type B," said one second-year student. The reason? Success in modern medicine depends more than ever before on collaboration. There's so much knowledge to absorb and then put into practice that doctors and researchers have to team up. "At

---

"Yale is full of people who are Type A personalities but are trying to be Type B."

Yale, it's all about getting through this stuff together," said a student. "It's not like, 'I won't give you the answer because you'll get a better orthopedics residency.'" Said another second-year student: "Students here study for the right reasons. You take self-evaluations to see if you understand the material, not to see who got a 94 percent and who got a 97 percent." The school's size—each class is roughly 100 students—also breeds an intimate, cooperative atmosphere. For second-year students who cycle through a long series of total-immersion modules—a few weeks on the cardiovascular system followed by a few weeks of psychiatry, and so on—classes outside the lectures are invariably tiny. In labs and workshops, class size stays below 20.

But the system has its pitfalls, students say. Basic science lectures for first and second years are often poorly attended, probably due in part to lecturers not taking attendance. And because self-evaluations are optional, some students never get around to taking them, which could mean playing catch-up before taking national licensing exams.

"If one is too liberal in slacking," said a first-year student, "the system will give you enough rope to hang yourself." Still, most students learn to keep up with the curriculum; Yale's pass rate on the national exams is similar to other top-ranked med schools.

What Yale does require is a thesis, an unusual demand among medical schools. This project, usually begun during the first or second year and completed during the fourth and final year of school, may be lab research or an investigation of clinical, epidemiological, or sociological subjects. Recent papers have examined the stigma attached to AIDS in Africa and the causes of type II diabetes in lab mice. Students doing this work can tap into Yale's resources as a leading research institution (it received $300.7 million in National Institutes of Health grants in 2005), funding thesis-related research through grants and getting access to top faculty for thesis advisors. Meeting with his advisor for the first time, one third-year student remembered, "we had a fifteen-minute appointment and [the advisor] stayed for two hours. His eyes shone as he talked—I didn't think you could get that excited about basic science." Most students secure research funding for the summer between their first and second year, often for overseas projects and thesis-related work. Roughly half of each class takes an extra year to graduate, often to devote a full year to the thesis; in these cases, Yale waives fifth-year tuition.

Because of this program, Yale is known for breeding academic physicians. Even students who aren't drawn to Yale for the thesis often wind up getting hooked on research. Many publish their papers in medical journals. "Our purpose here is to turn out individuals who are going to be the leading physician-scientists in the country," said Dennis Spencer, a professor of neurosurgery and, until very recently, the school's acting dean. "We don't turn out many people who are going to do primary care." Indeed, Yale New Haven Hospital, the school's main teaching hospital, doesn't count family medicine among the residencies it offers, though a large number of Yale students do take residencies in pediatrics.

Despite the heady academic atmosphere, students are not locked in an ivory research tower. The M.D. program puts students in touch with patients early on. From the first year, all students meet weekly to practice taking medical histories from fellow students, then from actual patients—sometimes within the first few weeks of med school. This is a big help when students hit the hospital wards full-time in their third year. One third-year student said he didn't appreciate the weekly meetings until he had to tell a former drug user that he'd need regular kidney dialysis for the rest of his life—a test of interpersonal, rather than medical, skills. "By the time third-year rolls around," he said, "you spend time caring for the patient instead of figuring out how to gather information from them." Even during their time in the hospitals, students are encouraged to take control of their learning. "The structure on the wards is flat as opposed to hierarchical," one student said. "There's no objection to saying, 'I don't think that's right' to an attending [physician]. Just because they've had all this training doesn't mean they can't be challenged."

During that third year, which can be quite intense, Yale still prides itself on maintaining free afternoons. Most students don't use these to sleep in or goof off, however. Many spend the time doing volunteer work, like educating local school children on AIDS/HIV prevention or creating basic medical records for New Haven's homeless population. An annual auction, organized by students, raises tens of thousands of dollars for the homeless. With plenty of low-income residents,

> "We don't turn out many people who are going to do primary care."

New Haven is flush with volunteer opportunities. "You can't be isolated here," said Spencer. "You have to engage in the community." The medical school is also a short walk from Yale's main campus, which allows students to interact with other university departments.

Most of their engagement, however, is at the med school itself, where the administration seems unusually responsive to student input. When a pair of students recently developed a formula that allowed third-year students to schedule their clinical clerkships more easily, administrators agreed to adopt it. And when international students lobbied to extend financial aid to foreign students last year, the school obliged. After all, if a school urges students to take their education into their own hands, it has to face the consequences.

Johns Hopkins University School of Medicine

- Baltimore, Maryland
- Private
- Enrollment 2005–2006 academic year: 464
- Overall rank in the 2007 *U.S. News* medical school rankings (research): 2
- Overall rank in the 2007 *U.S. News* medical school rankings (primary care): 41
- Average MCAT score: 11.5
- Average undergraduate GPA: 3.84

Johns Hopkins researchers invented the implantable pacemaker, discovered restriction enzymes that let geneticists manipulate DNA, and developed CPR. The medical school received $475.3 million in National Institutes of Health funding in 2005. Hopkins surgeons routinely make newspaper headlines by, say, separating conjoined twins in intricate operations. So what is it like at the bottom of the Hopkins pecking order, as a lowly medical student? Like being taught by the best in the world, said a fourth-year student. "Even the greatest researchers there completely feel that part of their job is to train students."

And they should feel teaching is important—modern medical education was born at Hopkins. When the school opened in 1893, most medical institutions offered only lectures—future doctors never laid eyes on a live patient. But Quaker merchant Johns Hopkins stipulated that the medical school carrying his name had to be connected to a hospital with the size and means to train medical students. As a result, Hopkins students learned through hands-on experience. Eventually, this model spread throughout American medical education. Since its founding, the school has been home to over a century of influential medical educators, such as William Osler and William Halsted, inventors of the modern medical residency.

"I think that the tradition here is important," said Frank Herlong, former associate dean of student affairs. "And I think we have to be careful that it doesn't become oppressive." He gave the example of the resident who, several years ago, announced that she just wanted to be a regular old doctor, not an academic. A faculty member called her into his office to ask "Where have we failed?" Today, however, Herlong said that Hopkins students are "pluripotent"—like the human embryo's primordial stem cells, they could develop into anything, not just academic physicians. "The person who has been a leader in some small community by influencing the health care for the underserved, that person may not be famous or in the newspaper, but I hope that we would continue to embrace that," he noted. Still, more than half of Hopkins graduates spend some part of their career in academic medicine, whether as full professors or as part-timers at local medical schools. Only about 10 percent of graduates focus exclusively on primary care.

Medical education at Hopkins, overall, follows the traditional pattern: science lectures until April of the second year, then just over two years of learning by watching and doing in the hospital. But several years ago, the school reassessed first-year courses, which leapt from biochemistry to genetics to immunology with no attempt to explore the relationships between these topics. Now the curriculum starts with the molecule, builds up to cells, then to organs, and finishes with organ functions in a healthy person. Although lectures dominate in the beginning, most of the teaching in later years happens one-on-one, with a research mentor or on the wards, said pediatrician David Nichols, vice dean for education. "Teaching how to develop a bedside manner—that's really a one-on-one kind of experience," he said. "You can't teach it in a lecture and you can't read about it in a book."

Even before bedside manners are taught, however, Hopkins students begin feeling the research tug: More than 80 percent do some kind of research as an elective, most often in the summer after their first year. One fourth-year student said she came to school with a strong interest in international health. She'd been an anthropology major in college, and said there was no way anyone was getting her to sit at a lab bench for months at a stretch. "Then all of a sudden here I was working in a lab and, you know, I took a year off to do it." Her research, on how HIV lives in the body even during antiviral treatment, taught her how the lab relates to patient care—in her case, to the international HIV prevention work that she eventually wants to do.

Besides its name for fostering cutting-edge research, Hopkins also has a reputation for generating cutthroat competition. Hopkins takes only 120 of its 4,000 or so applicants every year, so its students are among the best in the country academically. But reputation isn't necessarily reality, one student said. "My experience has been that there are always a handful of people who are very, very intensely competitive and that's kind of their thing." Many students say they usually study in groups, helping each other get through the difficult science courses. And during those first few years of school, students spend a great deal of time together, in and out of class.

Professors seem to be supportive as well. After the first exam of her first year, one student recalled

getting "the worst grade I've ever seen in my life." She went to see the professor and "just started bawling like an idiot." But her prof calmed her down, reassuring her that everyone goes through tough times in medical school, and she wasn't destined to fail. After talking about the situation, the student realized she had to overhaul her study habits to focus on learning, not grades. When she had to

"Even the greatest researchers there completely feel that part of their job is to train students."

explain the material to other students in study groups, she finally knew that she had it down pat.

Hopkins' urban home, Baltimore, may be known as "Charm City," but those charms are usually not immediately evident to med students. "Baltimore is a great place once you get to know it, but at first it seems maybe not the most friendly place that I've ever been," said one student. The hospital and school are wedged into a dense urban campus in rough East Baltimore, although the neighborhood has been improving in recent years. Security officers check IDs by every entrance, and the students consider the hospital campus to be safe. Eventually, they learn to navigate Baltimore's many neighborhoods, such as nightclub-packed Fell's Point and tree-lined, pet-friendly Butchers Hill, and many fall in love with the city. Washington, D.C., is less than an hour away, and students can get to New York City in a few hours. One med student noted that he spent his spare time exploring Maryland's state parks—in addition to the horse racing scene, which includes the Preakness, Baltimore's leg of the Triple Crown.

The city plays a role in students' education, too. Part of the hospital's mission is to take care of the poor. While students see many unusual cases referred from other hospitals (because Hopkins has so many top specialists), they also tackle the day-to-day health problems of their closest neighbors. Many students work on community health projects: Some teach sex education workshops in Baltimore middle schools, work on a program to introduce local high school kids to health careers, or mentor pregnant teenagers.

While students are working to change the area around the school, the school is working hard to change itself. Committees of faculty and students are discussing an overhaul of the curriculum to take effect in 2006 or 2007. As more and more conditions are treated without a hospital stay, medical students rarely see a patient with pneumonia. Doctors are spending less time with patients, which means new doctors have less time to learn clinical skills, such as listening to the way lung and heart sounds change as people get better or worse. In the next few years, the school will start using more high-tech simulations to train students, such as special mannequins that can be programmed to make different heart sounds and mimic these changes. Another major debate about the curriculum is how new research on genetics will change medical practice— for example, whether doctors should drop the old idea of a sick body as a machine that needs fixing and focus instead on each patient's genes, environment, and personal history.

In the meantime, the school is still turning out new doctors with an impressive entry on their résumés. "To be honest, the name helps a lot," a student said, but added that it was more than just a name; it was a superior education. "They set me up to do whatever I wanted to do after medical school."

University of Washington School of Medicine

- Seattle, Washington
- Public
- Enrollment 2005–2006 academic year: 810
- Overall rank in the 2007 *U.S. News* medical school rankings (research): 7
- Overall rank in the 2007 *U.S. News* medical school rankings (primary care): 1
- Average MCAT score: 10.4
- Average undergraduate GPA: 3.65

It's puzzling: Why would more than half the graduates of a huge school with an expansive academic research program like the University of Washington School of Medicine go into primary care? And why would so many graduates leave this urban Seattle campus to practice medicine in rural areas, many outside the state?

The answer, it seems, is WWAMI. That's the acronym for five Northwestern states— Washington, Wyoming, Alaska, Montana, and Idaho—that together make up more than a quarter of the land mass in the United States, yet have only one medical school among them. People in these states need good primary care in fields such as family medicine and pediatrics. So for thirty years, all five states have united behind that one school, UW, pooling far-flung resources, doctors, and science faculty at local colleges to bring WWAMI residents to Seattle—and get them back to WWAMI states once they've graduated.

The route many of them take is, for med students, a little unusual. One, Courtney Paterson, grew up in Bozeman, Montana, where she also went to college. After getting into UW's medical program, she spent her first year not in Seattle, but at Montana State University, where there is no med school. There she took the basic medical science courses—physiology, microbiology, and so on—with visiting faculty and the school's own science staff. Paterson then went to work for a summer at a clinic in tiny Ronan, Montana (population 1,800) which had six primary care docs and not much else. She followed the doctors around, watching how they did their work, and also did research on local rates of sexually transmitted diseases. She finally set foot on UW's campus at the beginning of her second year—the first time she'd been there since her admissions interview. "It was a little weird to have to mix with all these people who've already been here for a year when I didn't even know where the main office was yet," she said, "But I knew I wasn't alone."

Far from it. Nearly half of the 178 students in Paterson's med school class spent their first year like her, doing basic science at one of four Northwestern schools outside Seattle. More than a hundred UW students spend their first-year summers working side-by-side with local docs in underserved, rural areas. And ultimately more than 50 percent of UW graduates end up practicing medicine in a WWAMI state.

This commitment to rural primary care came about, said Paul Ramsey, the school's dean, because 37 percent of the population in the region lives in rural areas. "Over two billion people in the world have no access to a physician," he said, "Does the world really need more big city specialists?" Not from UW, which has sent graduates everywhere from Kodiak Island, Alaska, to Thermopolis, Wyoming.

Primary care "is just part of the culture" that suffuses UW and its affiliated hospitals, said Kristi Nix. Recently a pediatrics resident at a UW children's hospital in Seattle, Nix worked with both students and faculty from the med school. She said that you get a feel, watching the professors, for what it is to be a "good doctor." Nix didn't go to UW for medical school herself, and at other

"I was in a clinic taking a personal history the first week of my first year."

schools, she said, the good doctors all "have labs and see patients half-time and do research eighty hours a week. Out here, most of the docs are living lives as physicians, they're actually taking care of people—and they don't have that aggressive, 'you've got to publish' type of feeling."

Instead, faculty push clinical skills on their students early and often. In both first and second years, students take the required course Introduction to Clinical Medicine, where they are tutored in interviewing skills, usually in small groups of six or seven. "I was in a clinic taking a personal history the first week of my first year," said one student.

In their third and fourth years, when a lot of other med students are touring specialty areas in big teaching hospitals, UW students are encouraged to do their rotations outside Seattle, in more than one hundred WWAMI towns from Pocatello to Coeur d'Alene to Mountain Home. "It's just an unbeatable experience out there," said Joe Woodward, a student who did his family medicine rotation in a five-doctor clinic in eastern

Washington. The doctors there had known their patients for years. In some cases, they were delivering the babies of people they'd delivered. "I saw things I'd never see in an urban hospital with a hundred interns running around," he said.

When students do rotations as far away as Alaska, the isolation puts a premium on developing diverse medical skills. "Out there you have no

---

"Sometimes specialists just take care of a problem, you know? In primary care, your job really is to take care of people."

---

idea what could walk in the door at any moment," said Woodward. "If you can't handle it, the patient gets choppered a hundred miles to someone who can," and the helicopter ride can, for critically injured patients, take too long.

This emphasis on primary care does have its downside. It "can be a good thing as an introduction to medicine, but it's a double-edged sword," said one student torn between hospital-based primary care and infectious diseases. She worried that UW students who don't know what they want to specialize in can easily fall into something like family medicine for lack of extensive exposure to anything else. "It's entirely possible to find yourself at the end of your third year, and you haven't rotated in any other fields." Other students say UW does offer plenty of options outside primary care for those who truly want them. "If you're proactive, it's easy to find [an advisor] in something else," said one, who

specialized in internal medicine yet made space in her schedule for classes in anesthesiology.

Many of those options come from UW's enormous research presence. In 2005, the school scored nearly $540 million in grants from the National Institutes of Health, one of the highest totals in the nation. Over 1,600 full-time faculty wend their ways through the fir trees on the shores of Lake Washington each day to the school's Pentagon-sized labyrinth of laboratories. Calling Washington home are 25 members of the Institute of Medicine, and students can also work with dozens of award-winning cancer vaccine researchers at the Fred Hutchinson Cancer Research Center a few miles from campus. Scott Sears, a recent grad now working as a general internist in Billings, Montana, earned three separate grants at UW to work with the school's collection of human and primate eyeballs, one of the largest in the country, studying ophthalmology and developmental proteins in retinas.

Still, for Paterson and so many of her classmates, the UW road will lead to WWAMI's primary needs. "When I was 16, I wanted to be a brain surgeon," she said. "When I was 18, it was obstetrics/gynecology. I was never interested in family practice until that summer" in Ronan. And after graduation, Paterson planned to head back to Montana. "Sometimes specialists just take care of a problem, you know? In primary care, your job really is to take care of people."

Chapter Four

Getting In

There are lots of good reasons for wanting to be a doctor. Maybe you think you have a healing touch, or you want to serve the community, or there's something about solving the puzzle of an illness that satisfies your mind and your soul. And there are probably some bad reasons, like doing it for the money, or because your family will be disappointed if you don't make medicine a career. But no matter what the motives, everyone has to jump over the same hurdle: medical school admissions.

It's not an easy leap. More than 34,000 people try to get in every year, yet just 16,000 succeed. And that's only the overall picture. Individual schools can be much more picky. The University of Chicago Pritzker School of Medicine recently received over 5,700 applications for its incoming class of about 100 students. Georgetown University School of Medicine had over 7,000 applicants for about 170 spaces. You do the math.

If you want in, you'd better be *able* to do the math. This is a brainy crowd. Admissions committees are swamped with applications from students whose undergraduate grade point averages hover at 3.4 and who average a score of 27 out of 45 on the Medical College Admission Test (MCAT). Those who attend the most competitive schools consistently score well over 30. "The competition is very intense," said

---

"The competition is very intense. There are a whole bunch of applicants who, in terms of numbers, are all equally qualified."

Greg Goldmakher, a medical school advisor with AdmissionsConsultants, Inc. in Vienna, Virginia. "There are a whole bunch of applicants who, in terms of numbers, are all equally qualified."

To stand out—and get in—applicants must find ways to distinguish themselves from the rest of the premed pack. In this chapter, you'll learn how. *U.S. News* asked admissions directors at the nation's top medical schools to describe what they look for in candidates who get the green light. All of them said good grades and MCATs are a great start. But science smarts are not enough. Admissions committees are looking for unique, highly motivated people who excel in and out of the classroom. "It's a very special segment of the human race," said Andrew Frantz, associate dean of admissions at Columbia University's College of Physicians and Surgeons in New York. "They have to be intelligent, sensitive to others, compassionate, committed to finding joy in their work and they should want to be of service to others." Here are tips to best let you show those traits, along with ways to get the best test scores and grades that you can.

Making the grades

It all starts in the classroom. Science is the backbone of medicine, and no matter how caring or compassionate you may be, medical schools want to know that you can handle the academic material. You will need to complete certain science courses before you can apply to medical school and you should start taking them freshman year, if possible. By the time you apply to medical school, you should have completed one year each (including labs) of chemistry, biology, physics, and organic chemistry. In addition, medical schools often want to see a year of English and a year of math, including a semester of calculus. The American Medical Student Association (AMSA) tells premeds to head for their school's preprofessional health advisor, usually found in the career counseling office, and together plot a course for completing all of the classes.

Tip: Pace yourself. A heavy load of rigorous courses can drag down your performance in each class, so don't take more than two prerequisites a semester.

If you decide to jump on the premed track a bit later—say, well into your sophomore year—you may need to take summer classes to make up for lost time. Find a summer school that is comparable to the one you attend during the school year; admissions committees do take note of the difference. "We are troubled by someone taking one or two semesters of something like organic chemistry at a community college over the summer," said Robert Witzburg, associate dean and director of admissions at Boston University School of Medicine. But if the course is taken at a school like

The "nontraditional" student

There was a time when almost every applicant to medical school came directly from college. No longer. An ever-increasing number are taking time after they graduate to pursue other interests or get some work experience. Called "nontraditional applicants," even though their path is becoming a tradition in itself, these people are often viewed favorably, even prized, by admissions committees. Boston University's medical school admissions office says the school's nontraditional students, many of whom have put off their physician training to work in jobs serving communities without many resources, demonstrate "flexible intelligence" and an ability to interact well with patients. Henry Ralston, who was the associate dean of admissions at the University of California–San Francisco agreed—that's why he encouraged premeds to take a year off and get some experience outside of the school setting. "I prefer older students," he said.

But not all schools feel this way, cautioned Trina Denton, a nontraditional applicant who served as director of premedical affairs at AMSA, the medical student advocacy group. Some medical schools may worry that applicants who have taken time away from studying will find it hard to get back into the habit. Applicants can ask the schools they are interested in if taking time off could harm their chances of getting in—or better yet, ask for the numbers of nontraditional students in the entering class.

Some nontraditional applicants decide after finishing college that they want to apply to medical school, but have not taken the prerequisite science courses. Such applicants should consider a premed, postbaccalaureate program. You get the basic courses plus the chance to take some advanced electives. At Georgetown University, the postbaccalaureate program "gives students the courses they need so they will qualify as premed despite the fact that they may have majored in poetry," said Douglas Eagles, a former program director. Programs take one to two years and offer students some valuable structure and help when they get ready to take the MCAT and prepare their school applications. Some people find this much easier than going it all alone. And because postbaccalaureate programs can include some of the same courses a first-year med student would take, they let the admissions office see that you can really do the work—because you have.

The Association of American Medical Colleges offers a searchable database to find these programs nationwide. Go to www.aamc.org and search "postbaccalaureate programs." (For a list of several well-regarded programs, see 352.) An alternative is to take the classes on a full- or part-time basis at a local university under a nondegree-seeking status, and med schools will usually accept them. Some are more restrictive, however, so check with the schools before signing up.

the one you're already studying at, he said, "no one here is going to be bothered by that."

If you plan on using Advanced Placement courses taken during high school to fulfill these requirements, be wary. Many med schools won't accept them, and whether they do or not can depend on your other science courses. Remember, schools want to see that you can

---

"The ideal candidate has strong performance in science, but also has taken humanities."

---

handle the material. So college students who major in science and also received AP credit can demonstrate they know the basics by performing well in their upper-level science courses. Med schools are more likely to let their AP work count for a college course. But applicants who do not take more advanced college science classes may not be able to use their AP scores. If you already have an idea about the med schools you want to apply to, check with those admissions offices about their AP credit policies.

This focus on science doesn't mean you have to major in biology or physics. In fact, admissions committees look for students who have challenged themselves academically and taken a broad range of classes throughout their undergraduate years. "The ideal candidate has strong performance in science, but also has taken humanities," said Albert Kirby, associate dean for admissions at Case Western Reserve University School of Medicine in Cleveland, Ohio. "We love students who are nonscience majors," said William Eley, executive associate

dean for education and former director of admissions at Emory University School of Medicine in Atlanta, Georgia. "We are looking for that breadth because it indicates involvement in the human side of medicine."

Indeed, majoring in something nonscientific might actually help you. In a crowd of biology and physics students, that history degree stands out.

According to the Association of American Medical Colleges (AAMC), 52 percent of humanities and social science majors who applied were accepted to medical school in 2001. That's actually a little better than the 48 percent of successful applicants who majored in biology.

Tip: Take some humanities courses. Applicants who focus solely on science can be viewed as weaker candidates than those who have performed well across many fields.

Testing, testing

In addition to science classes, undergraduates must take the MCAT, an eight-hour standardized test given by the AAMC. Typically, applicants take the test in April of their junior year, although the MCAT is also given in August. You must preregister at www.aamc.org/mcat. Registration usually begins on February 1 for the April test and on June 1 for the August test. Aim for the April date because then you have August as a fallback if your scores aren't as high as you want. Try to register early because space can be limited at certain testing sites and slots are filled in the order in which they are received. The fee can be paid by credit card or by an electronic money transfer.

Unlike other standardized tests that attempt to predict a student's ability (such as the SAT), the MCAT is content-driven, testing your mastery of the basic science material covered in premed courses. The test consists of four sections: physical sciences, which includes physics and chemistry; biological sciences, which includes biology and organic chemistry; verbal reasoning; and the writing sample. You can score up to 15 points in each of the two science sections and in verbal reasoning, for a possible total score of 45. (Most med school applicants, successful and unsuccessful, score in the high 20s and low 30s.) The writing sample is graded according to an eleven-letter system that goes alphabetically from "J" (lowest) to "T" (highest).

Obviously, it's best to have completed all of the science prerequisites before you take the test. Even so, to adequately prepare, you should plan to devote between 200 and 300 hours to studying. Many applicants, perhaps as many as three-quarters, choose to take a preparatory class to help them structure their studying and to ensure that they cover all of the material. Princeton Review and Kaplan, Inc., offer widely available courses. You get multiple classroom sessions, prep materials, and practice tests. The courses are expensive, running well over $1,000, but if you are not satisfied with your score, the companies will refund your fee or let you take the course again. (That's not going to help you, however, if you're not satisfied with your score and not satisfied with the course itself.) There are many local prep companies, too. But prep courses certainly aren't a must; if you feel you can be both disciplined and organized in your studying, you can purchase practice tests from the AAMC and a study guide from a bookstore, and prepare on your own.

Tip: Consider prepping. Prep classes can particularly help because they provide proctored practice tests to get you used to the grueling task of sitting and answering questions for eight hours straight.

Taken together, your GPA and MCAT score form the basis of the initial cut medical schools make in their applicant pool. Why? Studies have shown that performance on the MCAT and in undergraduate courses is a reliable predictor of how well an applicant will do during the first two years of medical school.

It takes about two months to get your scores back. If your April MCAT score falls well below what you expected, consider taking the test again in August. Medical schools vary on whether they will use your highest or your most recent score, with some averaging the two. Call admissions offices to find out how they handle the second set. But be warned: Waiting for the August score to come in could slow down the admission committee's review of your application, and when schools offer admissions on a rolling basis, that may reduce your chances of getting a spot.

Apply yourself

Once you have completed the MCAT in April, it is time to start thinking about assembling your application. This is one-stop shopping: Most medical schools use the American Medical College Application Service (AMCAS), a division of the AAMC, to process all the paperwork. You submit one completed application online, and that includes an application form, a personal statement, transcripts from all the undergraduate schools you have attended, and other paperwork, as well as a list of schools you want to apply to. For a fee, AMCAS assembles your application file, verifies it, and forwards it to the schools you have designated. The service also sends along your MCAT scores if you

What schools want...and what they don't

Some of our most difficult applicants are the majors from technical schools who took AP English in high school and never took another humanities course. They generally don't do well in the application process.
—*Robert Witzburg, associate dean of admissions, Boston University School of Medicine*

Don't ask *me* why you should pick our school. It's a turn-off.
—*Andrew Frantz, associate dean of admissions, Columbia University College of Physicians and Surgeons in New York*

We value individuals who will bring different strengths to the class. If everyone in the class had the same background, it would be dull.
—*Albert Kirby, associate dean for admissions, Case Western Reserve University School of Medicine in Cleveland*

Write about something you really experienced, not a two-week trip to a developing country where you saw poverty and were moved by it.
—*Henry Ralston, former associate dean of admissions, UCSF School of Medicine in San Francisco*

We are looking for people who can do lots of things well. I like to see someone who is engaged in events and issues, someone who is not just interested in medicine.
—*Gaye Sheffler, director of admissions, University of Pennsylvania School of Medicine in Philadelphia*

I do not view the goal of the essays as either to entertain me, persuade me that the applicant would be 'fun to teach,' or regale me with stories of wondrous achievements and world travel. I expect applicants to take the writing of the essays seriously.
—*Edward Halperin, vice dean, Duke University School of Medicine*

tell them to do so. (If you plan on retaking the test, you have the option to withhold your scores.)

The application, along with timelines, resources, and worksheets, is available at www.aamc.org/amcas. You should be able to get the application about mid-March, and the service begins accepting completed applications on June 1. It stops accepting applications two weeks before whatever deadline is set by the medical schools you are applying to, and that's generally from October to mid-December. It is your responsibility to meet these deadlines.

Tip: Double check. Some schools do not use the AMCAS application and rely on some other form instead. Contact the schools you are interested in to see if you need other application materials.

After AMCAS, there's still more application paperwork to deal with. Once the service has sent a copy of your application to each of your chosen medical schools, the schools themselves may send you a "secondary application." Some schools send secondary applications to all applicants, others send them only to those who make the initial cut after a review of GPAs and MCATs. The secondary application usually asks for additional personal essays, letters of recommendation, and an application fee. AMSA recommends that applicants fill out and return secondary applications no later than two weeks after they are received to avoid paperwork pileup.

Because the competition is so steep, plan to send out about 10 to 15 applications, maximizing your chances of success. Include three or four "reach" schools—where you just might have good enough credentials to get in—two backup schools, and five to ten schools that you have a reasonable chance of getting into. What's a reach and what's a backup? Look at the mean GPA and MCAT scores for the incoming class of each medical school, which you can find in the directory section of this book. If your numbers are higher, you can think of the school as a backup. If they are lower, consider the school a reach—and the greater the gap, the longer the reach. Close matches are just that: By the numbers, you're a good fit. (See Chapter 2 for details about other important factors—things to consider before you worry about your chances for successful admission—in choosing schools.) Of course, the rest of your application has to be strong: Good numbers are ultimately no substitute for a poor essay or lackluster recommendations.

Getting personal

The next phase of application review, if you have the grades and MCAT scores to make it past a school's cut-off points, is when the school tries to

get to know you as more than a set of numbers. Admissions committees are keenly interested in learning who you are, based on what you have done and how you express yourself. Here is where your written statements, recommendation letters, and interview come into play.

Keep in mind that medical schools receive thousands of applications from people who appear

"It is very important in medicine to be able to extend yourself emotionally."

to be pretty much the same as one another. They have good grades, good MCATs, experience working in a research lab for a summer or two, have worked in a hospital shadowing a physician, and have volunteered with a community organization delivering food to homeless people. These are strong candidates, said Goldmakher—but they are not distinctive. If you want to get into an ultra-selective school, you will need to be all this and more. That could mean demonstrating a longer commitment to one of these extracurricular activities or to the pursuit of something that is entirely unrelated to medicine, but is challenging nonetheless. The depth of your involvement in a project will indicate to medical schools how important that activity was to you.

Schools really are not looking for any one type of person or set of experiences. They want individuals with traits such as leadership, compassion, commitment, enthusiasm, and competence. For example, athletics can be an excellent way to show that you can work with a team—an important trait in many fields of medicine—as well as demonstrate that you have leadership skills and the ability to make quick decisions. Athletics also demonstrates physical stamina, which can be important in certain fields, such as surgery. Admissions committees will consider all of these traits, so include hobbies and talents that you are passionate about in your application even if you think they are not relevant to your interest in becoming a doctor. These outside interests reveal a lot to admissions committees about who you are and what you are capable of. Andrew Frantz from Columbia University said he is drawn to applicants with an interest in theater because acting "forces you to put yourself in another person's shoes. It is very important in medicine to be able to extend yourself emotionally."

Of course, actors and lacrosse goalies still must know something about taking care of people, in sickness and in health. "Applicants need to show that they can deal with illness," said Henry Ralston, former associate dean of admissions at the University of California–San Francisco School of Medicine. Volunteering at a hospital or nursing home, shadowing a physician, or even having personal exposure to serious illness, such as a terminally ill family member, are all avenues to gain such experience.

But even here you can find ways to set yourself apart from the typical medical school applicant and further bolster your application. Gaye Sheffler, director of admissions at the University of Pennsylvania School of Medicine, recalled one student who, along with his wife, developed a program for Hispanic residents in his community who were having difficulty accessing health care. That showed inner strength, she said, and an ability to take a project to its end, in addition to hands-on experience in the medical field.

Recommendation letter 101

Letters of recommendation should speak to these experiences or personality traits, and they should be written by people who know you well. It is better to have a letter from someone who can provide details about how you work and what kind of a person you are than one from some well-known professor who only taught you in a 250-student lecture and cannot say very much about you as an individual. If you have been engaged in a variety of activities outside of the classroom, it should not be hard to find people who can write about you in detail. Athletic coaches, employers, and volunteer work supervisors are all good sources of letters.

Tip: Choose wisely. Avoid asking for letters from people like your minister or congressman unless they can speak directly to your ability to lead, teach others, put forth the extra effort, or learn new skills.

Medical schools will want to see letters of recommendation from your college professors. Students who attend large universities may have a harder time establishing a close relationship with their teachers, especially in basic science classes with 100 or more students. The folks at AMSA suggest a way around this problem: Approach professors of larger classes near the beginning of the term to let them know that you will be applying to medical school and may ask them for a letter of recommendation at the end of the semester. Throughout the semester, attend the professor's office hours to ask questions about the material. After the class has ended and your grade has been determined, then make the request for the letter. Bring a copy of your résumé and perhaps your personal statement and be ready to sit down to discuss your interests and desire to become a

Countdown to med school

WHEN	WHAT YOU SHOULD DO
College freshman year and sophomore year	Get some medical experience
	Contact your premed advisor about planning coursework
	Do some community work
	Check out the nonmedical world—don't be one-dimensional
Junior year	
Sept. through Dec.	Take an MCAT prep course if you can afford it
Jan./Feb.	Register for the April MCAT
	Take a prep course if you still need it
March	Last chance to register for April MCAT
April	MCAT test date
May	Start writing your personal statement
June	Turn in AMCAS application; register for August MCAT if you're taking the test again
August	MCAT test date
Senior year	
Sept./Oct./Nov.	Fill out secondary applications and send them in
	Go on interviews
Oct.	Early decision applicants receive admission letters
Jan.	Another chance to register for an MCAT, if you plan to start med school more than a year from now
April	MCAT test date
	Regular admission applicants receive admission letters
May/June	Graduate and start packing for med school

doctor. Make sure you ask the professor if she or he can write a *strong* letter of recommendation on your behalf. If the answer is no, look elsewhere. If it is yes, send a thank-you note two weeks after you ask for the letter, both to be polite and as a gentle reminder to finish the letter in time to meet your application deadlines. (And don't forget to send along a stamped, addressed envelope.)

Your undergraduate school may have a pre-professional committee, generally made up of faculty members from different academic departments and a preprofessional advisor. They will ask you for your academic record, personal statement, letters of recommendation, employment and volunteer experience, and extracurricular activities. You may be called in for an interview as well. Using this information, the committee will write a single letter of recommendation, which you then send to all of the medical schools you are applying to.

Making a statement

The personal statement is your chance to show that you can express a point of view clearly while also explaining a little bit about yourself. It's also probably the hardest part of the application process, prompting a lot of staring at a blank computer screen, multiple drafts, and much anxiety. Here are strategies to make things easier.

Pick a topic that reveals something about you that admissions committee members would not otherwise have known. It should come from your life experiences, such as an event or person that has made a deep impression on you. And it should reflect you and your life in an honest, thoughtful way. "Tell me something I don't know, not just 'I love science and I want to help people,'" said Emory's Eley. "There are moments in life that teach. Tell us about them. It could be about being sick, or a special grandparent, or climbing a mountain."

Structure the personal statement either around a theme or as a chronology, advised Goldmakher. A thematic essay about being sick, for example, might focus on shepherding a friend or family member through illness. Admissions committees want to see that you can write and express yourself well, but they also want to get to know something about your insights and attributes. A chronological essay might focus more on

a series of events or activities and how you grew or changed as a result. One example might be an essay about a year spent abroad.

Tip: Gimmicks are not impressive. Although you want your essay to stand out, avoid tricks that fall flat, such as poems, plays, or mock press releases.

Face to faces

If your written application sparks enough interest, the admissions committee will invite you to visit the school for an interview. At some schools, this will be a one-on-one with a faculty member, but at others you may sit down with a group of senior medical students and professors. Whatever the configuration, interviews have some things in common. Someone is probably going to ask you to elaborate on some experience you wrote about, or will ask you to talk about your interests in medicine or your background. Some typical questions: Why do you want to be a doctor? What makes you think you'll make a good one? What experiences in your life led to this decision? What weaknesses do you struggle against in yourself? The committee is looking for signs that you are mature, confident without being arrogant, and able to communicate well.

You can write passionately about many things in your application, but in an interview, applicants often reveal how truly meaningful an experience was. "If they are doing all of these things because they think it's what they are supposed to do, it will be a boring interview," said Eley. "If they have followed their heart, their eyes will light up, and that's what we look for."

To prepare for the interview, brush up on current events, especially those related to medicine as well as some issues like medical ethics. Goldmakher said that admissions committees generally aren't looking for one particular answer when they ask you these less personal kinds of questions. They are interested in how you think and whether you can see different points of view. He advises his clients to take a deep breath, come up with a few points they want to make, and try to express them clearly. Don't rehearse your answers too much: Admissions directors say canned answers are a good way for an applicant to get, well, canned.

Be sure to know something about the school before you arrive for the interview. It is a big turn-off to admissions committees if they ask you why you are interested in their program and it becomes clear you don't know very much about the school. Take advantage of the chance to ask about something specific to the school—and not something easily answered in the brochure. It shows you have genuine interest. After the interview, remember to send a thank-you note to the people who interviewed you as well as anyone else who helped you throughout the interview day. This is a good way to get them to remember you.

"If they have followed their heart, their eyes will light up, and that's what we look for."

After all this, what's left? You get to sit back and wait for your acceptance letters.

Chapter Five

Finding the Money

Make no mistake: It costs an arm and a leg to become a doctor. The tab at private medical schools—for tuition, living expenses, and books—easily tops $200,000 over four years. At the George Washington University School of Medicine, for instance, the four-year budget is almost $250,000—and that's before allowing for the inevitable tuition increases. Costs are equally high for out-of-state students at public institutions. A nonresident at the University of North Carolina–Chapel Hill School of Medicine will pay nearly $235,000. Even in-state students at public medical schools can expect to spend $150,000 or more to earn an M.D. degree.

Most medical students borrow heavily to cover the bills. Total debts in excess of $100,000 are typical for new doctors, and that's not counting whatever they may have borrowed as an undergraduate. Not surprisingly, many young docs continue to feel strapped for cash even after their incomes begin to soar.

How can you limit the damage? While financial aid in the form of grants and scholarships is not as plentiful as it is for undergraduates, most schools do make modest need-based or merit-based awards to some medical students. A handful of outside scholarships are available, too—especially for members of minority groups. Uncle Sam's largesse, in the form of tax credits for the cost of higher education, can also free up some extra cash. And students who are willing to serve in the military or commit to practicing medicine in underserved communities can go to medical school practically for free—or at least have a portion of their debts forgiven.

Even if you do have to borrow a bundle, you can take some comfort in the fact that education debt is as cheap as it ever has been because interest rates are relatively low. And through your tax deductions, the federal government will chip in on the interest you do pay. Here's what you need to know to pay for your degree.

Need-based grants might help a little—very little

As you'll probably remember from your undergraduate days, anyone applying for financial aid funds handed out by the federal government has to fill out the Free Application for Federal Student Aid, also known as the FAFSA. That's where you'll start, but the truth is that most medical schools have only a modest amount of money available for need-based grants. They assume that most students will borrow to finance their degrees and will easily be able to repay their debts once they are

doctors. At the University of Missouri School of Medicine, for example, only about 50 percent of students receive need-based awards—and they average a measly $2,780 yearly, a drop in the bucket compared to tuition.

Even schools with more money available generally won't meet your full need with grants: There simply aren't enough funds available at the graduate level to fulfill the requirements of students no longer dependent on their parents. At Johns Hopkins University School of Medicine in Baltimore, for instance, the average need-based grant is $22,513; tuition runs about $33,000 for first-year students, who need an estimated $54,645 to cover everything. (The school offers over 200 endowed scholarships to help meet students' financial need.)

You may find that your eligibility for need-based aid varies dramatically from school to school. That's because medical schools, like undergraduate colleges and universities, use different formulas to calculate how big a discrepancy there is between what med school will cost and what your income and assets are. Under the formula used to hand out federal aid, for example, all graduate students are considered *independent:* supporting themselves, regardless of their age or whether they have financial help from their parents. Bottom line: Full-time students at schools using the federal formula will have significant need.

But most medical schools use their own institutional formulas, which classify many students as *dependent.* You'll provide schools with information about your parents' income and assets on additional needs-analysis forms (GAPS–FAS, CSS, and Need Access are the common ones), and the financial aid office will consider those resources to be available to pay the bills. At Johns Hopkins, parent resources are weighed on a case-by-case basis. "If someone is the son or daughter of elderly parents, we won't expect much," said Paul T. White, assistant dean for admissions and financial aid. "But there are also children well over 30 whose parents are still supporting them. We consider that," White said.

Parents' income and assets also are used in determining who is eligible for federal Scholarships for Disadvantaged Students. These are need-based awards, specifically for medical students who come from disadvantaged backgrounds, based on family income or ethnicity. The size of the award varies from school to school.

Regardless of which forms are required, be sure to get them in as soon as possible after January. Some aid is awarded on a first-come, first-served basis.

Apply with an eye on the merit money

Harvard Medical School does not award any merit scholarships. At the University of Michigan Medical School, by contrast, about one-third of each entering class receives a renewable scholarship ranging from $1,000 to $30,000 a year. At Vanderbilt School of Medicine in Tennessee, about 16 percent of students receive full-tuition scholarships, some based solely on academic merit and extracurricular record (such as the Canby-Robinson Scholarship), others based on a combination of merit and need. The school also awards money to applicants who will diversify the student body; recipients have included not only students of color, but also students of Jewish background (not so common in the Southeast), students from Appalachian Tennessee, and one recipient who grew up in Montana and was a cowboy, according to J. Harold Helderman, assistant dean for admissions.

Schools that do have merit money to dole out usually base their awards on the admission application. High MCAT scores and undergraduate grades are a big factor, but, like Vanderbilt, many schools are also looking to attract people with varied strengths and backgrounds. Many of the awards are endowed scholarships handed out based on the donor's wishes. One award might be reserved for residents of a certain state or county, for example, another for students studying cardiology or pediatrics.

Search for outside scholarships

Scholarships from foundations, associations, and civic organizations are not as plentiful in medicine as they are for other graduate students, and many are reserved for minority students, residents of specific states or counties, or students concentrating in specific areas of medicine. Regardless, it's well worth checking an online search engine for possibilities. (Good search engines include www.fastweb.com and www.collegenet.com. Also try the excellent listing of grants on Michigan State University's website at www.lib.msu.edu/harris23/grants/3gradinf.htm.) Check with any civic, religious, or community groups you or your family members belong to, as well. And be sure to ask your med school's financial aid officer for other leads. Shelley Corrigan at the University of Vermont College of Medicine has been able to lead students to a variety of special scholarships—including ones for people with epilepsy and diabetes.

How varied are the opportunities? Here's a sampling of scholarships:

• The Jack Kent Cooke Foundation Graduate Scholarship program (www.jackkentcooke foundation.org) makes approximately 35 awards a year to college seniors or recent grads who are pursuing graduate study. The scholarship pays for full tuition, fees, room, board, and books (up to $50,000 a year) for up to six years of graduate study. Candidates must be nominated by their undergraduate institution.

• The Medical Scientist Training Program (www.nigms.nih.gov/Training/Mechanisms/NRS A/InstPredoc/PredocOverview-MSTP.htm) is for students pursuing a combined M.D./Ph.D. degree at one of 41 participating medical schools, including Harvard, Stanford, Tufts, and the University of Michigan. Students accepted into the program, which is funded by the National Institutes of Health, earn full tuition plus a stipend; $21,000 to $26,000 per year is typical.

• The Nicholas Pisacano Family Practice Scholarship is awarded by the American Board of Family Practice (www.fpleaders.org/leaderfrm. html). Five awards of $7,000 per year, up to $28,000, are made to third-year med school students planning to specialize in family medicine.

• National Medical Fellowships (www.nmf-online.org) are awards of up to $10,000 for med students who have financial need and who are African American, mainland Puerto Rican, Mexican American, American Indian, or native Alaskan or Hawaiian. The group also offers numerous other merit-based fellowships and scholarships for minorities.

Get set to borrow

The average medical student borrows roughly $120,000; a third borrow more than $150,000,

and 9 percent borrow more than $200,000, according to the Association of American Medical Colleges. Ultralow interest rates will help ease the sting. And if you shop around for a lender, you may save a bit more in upfront fees.

Federal loans. Government-guaranteed Stafford loans are a staple for most medical students; a typical full-time student borrows the annual maximum of $8,500 in a "subsidized" Stafford loan plus at least a portion of the additional $30,000 allowed each year in "unsubsidized" loans, for a total of up to $38,500 per year. The federal government pays the interest on a subsidized loan while you're in school and for six months after you graduate or drop below half-time status. Interest accrues on the unsubsidized loan while you're a student, so the grand total mounts, but with both types of loan you can delay making payments until after graduation—or even until after your residency. In total, you can borrow up to $189,125 in Stafford loans to finance your education, including whatever you've already taken on as an undergraduate.

To qualify for a subsidized loan, you have to show on your FAFSA form that you have "need" (a gap between what you've got and the cost of school), which is fairly easy to do with medical school costs being so high. If your school participates in the Federal Direct Student Loan Program, you'll borrow directly from the federal government. Otherwise you can choose your own funding source using a list of preferred lenders provided by your school. While all lenders offer the same interest rate on Stafford loans, some waive the up-front origination and guarantee fees (which can run up to 4 percent of the loan amount), some reduce the interest rate in repayment if you sign up for automatic payments or make a certain number of payments on time, and some do both. Rates on these variable-rate loans change every summer, but will not exceed a cap of 8.25 percent.

Students with high financial need—the FAFSA shows that they're expected to contribute very little or nothing to their medical school education—will also qualify for a Perkins loan of up to $40,000 per year. The interest rate is a fixed 5 percent. In addition, there are no up-front origination fees. The Perkins is a subsidized loan, so no interest accrues until nine months after you graduate or drop below half-time status—or until after your residency if you qualify for a deferment (page 52).

The federal government also makes certain loans available specifically to medical students. Federal Loans for Disadvantaged Students are available to needy students from disadvantaged backgrounds, based on family income or ethnicity. The interest rate is a fixed 5 percent, with no loan fees, and interest is subsidized. Primary Care Loans, which have the same rate and no fees, go to students who agree to enter family medicine, internal medicine, pediatrics, or preventive medicine—and to practice primary care until the loan is fully repaid. There's a big catch, though: The interest rate jumps to 18 percent if you change your mind and practice in another specialty.

Private loans. If the federal loan limits leave you short, private lenders stand ready to lend you up to the full cost of your education, less any financial aid. (Some medical schools also have their own loan programs.) Interest rates tend to be only slightly higher than the rates on Stafford loans, but origination fees can be significantly higher—up to 6 percent of the loan amount—and interest begins accruing right away. Some lenders who market specifically to medical students will even lend you up to $13,000 to cover the costs of traveling to your residency interviews.

Some popular programs include MEDLOANS Alternative Loan Program, from Sallie Mae and the Association of American Medical Colleges (www.aamc.org/students/medloans), Medical Access Loan, from Access Group, Inc. (www.accessgroup.org), CitiAssist Health Profession Loans, from Citibank (www.studentloan.com), and MedAchiever, from KeyBank (www.keybank.com/educate).

To qualify for a private loan, you need a clean credit history—or a cosigner. It's a good idea to check your credit reports for errors before you apply.

Home-equity loans. For students who own a home, a home-equity line of credit is another attractive choice. Rates are low, fees are minimal, and the interest on up to $100,000 in debt is tax deductible if you itemize. If you expect to graduate into a high-paying job, home-equity debt may be a better choice than other debt because you won't qualify to deduct the interest on government or private student loans. Interest on student loans will be fully tax deductible only if your income falls below $50,000 if you're a single taxpayer and below $100,000 if you file jointly. Remember, though, that a home-equity line of credit is secured by your home. Will you be able to make the payments when you're a struggling resident?

Find help paying the money back

At 2006 rates, the payment on $100,000 in Stafford loan debt is roughly $1,000 a month over the standard ten-year repayment term. Those payments usually aren't manageable on a typical resident's pay of $40,000 or so a year. But there are ways to ease the burden.

Deferment and forbearance. Most medical residents with high levels of debt will qualify for an economic hardship deferment on their Stafford loans, which allows them to push off making payments for up to three years. Interest continues to accrue on unsubsidized loans (at the "in-school" rate, which is somewhat lower than the "repayment" rate that kicks in when payments are due) but does not accrue on subsidized loans. After three years, residents can continue to have their payments suspended for the remainder of their residency by requesting "forbearance," during which interest accrues on all loans at the repayment rate. You file an application for deferment or forbearance with your lender.

Flexible repayment options. The standard 10-year repayment term for Stafford loans—which for most new doctors begins after residency ends—can be stretched in various ways to reduce your monthly payments. With an extended repayment plan, for instance, you can lengthen the loan term to up to 30 years. Another option, a graduated repayment schedule that extends over 12 to 30 years, starts you off with lower payments than the standard plan would call for and then ratchets them up annually as your paycheck presumably grows. Income-contingent or income-sensitive repayment plans adjust your payment each year based on your income. In the end, you'll pay more interest over the longer payback periods, but you can always boost your payments as your income rises to pay down the loan more quickly than you're asked to.

Loan consolidation. You may also be able to reduce the interest you pay on Stafford loans by consolidating them when interest rates are low. That locks in current interest rates instead of allowing them to fluctuate annually. You may even be able to consolidate your undergraduate and early medical school loans to take advantage of low rates while you're still in school. For more details on student loan consolidation, see loanconsolidation.ed.gov at the Department of Education's web site, or www.federalconsolidation.org, a website sponsored by Access Group, Inc., a private nonprofit lender.

Student loan interest deduction. You can deduct up to $2,500 a year in student loan interest if you earn less than $50,000 as a single taxpayer or less than $100,000 if you are married and filing jointly. (You can deduct a lesser amount with income up to $65,000 filing singly or $130,000 filing jointly.)

Note to parents: You get to take this deduction on your own return if you're legally obligated to pay back the debt and you claim the student as a dependent on your tax return.

Loan repayment programs. Doctors who agree to practice certain kinds of medicine where there are shortages or who work in underserved areas of the country can qualify to have significant portions of their debt forgiven. Through the National Health Service Corps, for instance, doctors practicing primary care medicine in underserved areas can have up to $50,000 of their debt repaid by the federal government during a two-year minimum service commitment. An additional $35,000 a year in debt repayment is available to doctors who sign up for a third or fourth year of service.

Many states have similar debt repayment programs for doctors who live or are licensed in the state and who practice primary care medicine in-state. Doctors in Massachusetts, for instance, can earn $20,000 a year in debt payments if they work a minimum of two years in a Massachusetts community health center. A listing of state programs is available at the website of the Association of American Medical Colleges, at www.aamc.org/students/financing/repayment.

The National Institutes of Health offers a debt repayment program for employees engaged in various kinds of research, including AIDS research, pediatric research, and clinical research, whose debt load is at least 20 percent of their annual salary. M.D. researchers can have up to $35,000 per year of debt repaid during a two-year service period.

Get a job

One reason M.D. students tally up so much debt is that most cannot work part-time while earning their degree, even during summers. "There is no time to work," said Conway Jones, coordinator of financial aid at the University of Missouri–Columbia School of Medicine. For that reason, most financial aid officers do not include a federal work-study job in financial aid packages for med students. But for students who feel they can handle it, work-study is available and can reduce the need to borrow. An award of $1,500 to $2,000 might typically cover 10 to 15 hours of work a week in the university hospital or in a lab.

In most programs, there is a summer break between the first and second years of med school, after which the academic year runs 11 or 12 months. During the first-year summer break, some students earn extra money assisting faculty with a research project or participating in a summer preceptorship in which they shadow a doctor in exchange for a stipend. At the University of California–San Francisco, for instance, students can earn $3,000 for a four- to six-week full-time summer preceptorship.

Take advantage of Uncle Sam

If your household income is modest, the federal government offers help in the form of a tax credit or tax deduction for educational expenses.

Medical students who qualify will want to take advantage of the Lifetime Learning tax credit, worth $2,000 a year (20 percent of the first $10,000 you spend in tuition and fees each year). You qualify for the full credit if you file a single tax return and your income is $43,000 or less, and for a partial credit if you make up to $53,000. If you're married and filing jointly, the full credit is available when income is less than $87,000, and a partial credit is available up to $107,000. (A tax credit reduces your tax bill dollar for dollar.)

Most full-time medical students won't exceed those thresholds. (In fact, those with little or no income won't benefit at all from the credits because they won't owe any taxes to begin with.) But if you do cross the line—perhaps because you are married and your spouse earns a good income—you may still qualify for a tax deduction for your educational expenses. In 2004 and 2005, students can take a deduction for up to $4,000 in tuition and fees if their incomes don't exceed $65,000 filing singly or $130,000 filing jointly. That's worth up to $1,000 to a taxpayer in the 25 percent tax bracket. Note: You can't take both the credit and the deduction.

Medical students who are willing to pay for their education with a service commitment to the military or to the National Health Service Corps can start their medical careers with little or no debt. An Armed Forces Health Professions Scholarship, for instance, pays for tuition, fees, books, and supplies, plus a living-expense stipend of about $1,200 a month. After your residency, you repay the armed forces with a year of service for each year of support you received. You can get in touch with an Army, Army Reserve, Navy, or Air Force recruiter for more information. (Anyone who is gay or lesbian will want to keep in mind the

If there's time, plan ahead

If you're looking ahead to medical school in the next couple of years and can set aside some savings, take advantage of the tax benefits of a state-sponsored 529 plan. While most investors use these plans to save for a child's undergraduate expenses, the plans generally allow you to open an account and name yourself as the beneficiary.

The primary benefit is that the earnings on your savings will be tax-free, and your state may throw in a deduction for your contributions. All 529 plans include investments that are appropriate for adults who will need to tap the money soon, such as bonds and money-market accounts.

While many of the broker-sold 529s impose up-front sales fees that would minimize or offset any tax benefits over just a year or two, many of the direct-sold plans, such as those offered by TIAA-CREF and Vanguard, do not. Several are paying a guaranteed 3 percent or so right now. Not a bad parking place for a couple of years, especially when Uncle Sam isn't claiming any of the gains.

military's policy on homosexuality; one website that provides an overview is gaylife.about.com/cs/politicsactivism.)

Students on a National Health Service Corps scholarship also get a free ride that covers tuition, fees, books, and supplies, plus a stipend. The tradeoff: These students agree that, for each year of support, they'll practice a year of primary care medicine in an underserved area, which may be a rural community or even a prison. What if you renege? You'll owe the government the loan amount plus interest, and $7,500 for each month of service that you miss. This is not a commitment to make lightly.

Chapter Six

What If You Don't Get In?

Dreams have a predictable way of taking unpredictable turns. For many, the dream of med school started in childhood with a mini doctor's bag molded in black plastic, and continued through grueling college organic chemistry classes and cram sessions for the MCAT. But for all too many, what comes next is a mailbox full of rejection letters—and an uncertain future. These rude awakenings are unavoidable: Many medical schools accept fewer than 1 in 10 or 15 of those who apply.

So what happens next?

Your first priority should be to put things in perspective. "A lot of high quality kids can't make the cut," said William Harvey, who recently retired after spending years advising aspiring medical students at Earlham College in

Richmond, Indiana. While this sometimes can be the result of unrealistic aspirations, he notes, it may be for reasons as impersonal as that you hail from the same state as a huge number of other applicants that year.

And take heart: You do have options. You can rethink your goals altogether. You can retake your MCATs and get more science courses—perhaps a master's degree—and reapply. Or you can do what thousands of successful doctors have done: study abroad.

Trying again

You might as well start by reassessing your goals. Are you so sure that you belong in medicine that you're really prepared to go through all this again? "The hardest thing about medical school is not getting in, it's getting through," warned Karen Nichols, dean of Midwestern University Chicago College of Osteopathic Medicine. If an honest second look tells you that "you aren't motivated by all the right reasons, you must not come." Added Nancy Nielsen, senior associate dean at the University at Buffalo School of Medicine and Biomedical Sciences: "Ask [yourself] how badly you want to be a doctor, and if the answer is 'more than anything,' consider reapplying."

That's assuming you've got the grades, of course. You may have spent your last four summers working at an inner-city clinic and every scrap of free time reading journal articles about cancer research, but if your college grades are mediocre, "you can apply till the cows come home, but you're not going to get in" to a U.S. school, said Nielsen. Even if you do have a respectable grade point average, statistics from the Association of American Medical Colleges show that repeat applicants are less likely than first-timers to be accepted, so you may have to target less-competitive schools this go around.

Ask admissions officers at the schools that sent rejection letters to explain your shortcomings. Often, they're happy to offer insights. The University of Minnesota Medical School–Twin Cities, in fact, sends out rejections with an explicit offer: "I am very willing to speak with applicants by phone or in a personal interview and give them very, very specific information about what they can do to improve their applications," said the director of admissions, Marilyn Becker. Good scores may have been overshadowed by weak essays, flat letters of recommendation, or an unimpressive science background. The tell-all postrejection interview "takes the mystery out of it and gives concrete ideas" about what to do next, Becker said.

If the admissions staff isn't helpful—and even if they are—pose the same question to your undergraduate advisor, said Nichols. "Ask them to be ruthless—and have thick skin." Then apply their answers to the next application. While you're tapping undergrad resources, you might also ask someone in your college admissions office to give you a mock interview. The right answer, expressed in the wrong way, can tank an acceptance. Nichols once had an applicant say, "'I would really like to go to your school because I really don't want to work that hard,'" she recalled. "What he meant was, 'Your school really understands the importance of a balanced approach.'" The end result of his poor phrasing: He didn't get in.

It's probably a given that you'll revisit your MCAT scores; taking the test again and raising your numbers will certainly be a big help. So find a study group. Take a prep class. Hire a tutor. And take as many practice tests as you can. Admissions deans further recommend looking critically at your science background and doing whatever you need to do to bolster it. Indeed, one of the best ways to upgrade your application is to get a master's degree in one of the sciences.

It pays to get work or service experience, too; exposure to the health care field will enhance an application, admissions deans say. If grades and MCAT scores are equal, "the person who has a history of volunteering has an edge," Nielsen said. Volunteering for a medical facility that interests you, such as a clinic, a pediatric cancer ward, or a nursing home, underscores your commitment to medicine and desire to learn and can also offer evidence that you've got other valued attributes. Leadership, for example, "is one quality that is highly weighted," said Gregory Vercellotti, former senior associate dean for education at the University of Minnesota. So are level-headedness and heart. The admissions committee is on the lookout for "students who have a sense of well-being and balance and can demonstrate compassion," he said.

When your new, improved application is ready to go, don't worry too much that your rejection will taint it. "Given the number of applications and number of students who have to try more than once, there's nothing really adverse about a second application," said Vercellotti. Indeed, it's worth remembering that some people are accepted on the third or occasionally the fourth try.

Looking abroad

During Peter Burke's first two years of college, he was "a student athlete, with more emphasis on 'athlete,'" he said. Though he "got serious" by junior year and worked for a few years as a lab technician after graduation, his early history hurt him when he decided on medical school. "I was always having to explain my first two years in college," he said—and American medical schools were not forgiving. So he joined more than 8,000 Americans currently taking an alternate "offshore" route and went to The American University of the Caribbean School of Medicine, located in St. Maarten.

Many aspiring doctors look at the offshore schools as a poor substitute for U.S. institutions, but the reality is that more than 25 percent of doctors practicing in the United States today got their education outside of the country, according to the American Association of International Medical Graduates. Some 43,000, or 6 percent, of these doctors are United States citizens. "There are a number of international schools that are worth looking at," said former Earlham advisor Harvey. (For a list of foreign schools that educate significant numbers of American students, see page 361.)

Look carefully, though, because the quality of overseas programs varies enormously. Some of the most highly regarded schools in Europe are just as selective as U.S. medical schools and are not known for training Americans who failed to make the cut stateside. Besides AUC, foreign schools that do take large numbers of U.S. citizens—and that have track records for turning out solid doctors—include St. George's University School of Medicine in Grenada, Tel Aviv University Sackler School of Medicine in Israel, and Ross University School of Medicine in Dominica (which is now owned by DeVry University).

How do you determine which schools are worth your time and money? Separating the winners from the losers is a chore made both easier and harder by the Internet, which will probably be your first route to campus. Building an impressive website is much easier than building a high-quality faculty or campus; on the other hand, the Web can be a source of expert advice and an insider's point of view. The American Association of International Medical Graduates (www.aaimg.com) issues reports on schools in different areas of the world, providing pros and cons along with "words of wisdom." The organization evaluates schools using such criteria as

---

"There are a number of international schools that are worth looking at."

---

recruiting practices; basic science curriculum; student concerns like affordable housing and health care; clinical training programs; faculty qualifications; and history of problems with regulatory agencies, licensing boards, student loans, and student records. AAIMG notes whether each school is deficient or meets or exceeds the AAIMG standards. You'll also find a list of schools that don't meet the group's standards.

Approach your search with a similarly critical eye, advised Harvey. The overseas medical schools that cater to Americans follow a curriculum essentially the same as that of U.S. schools— two years of basic sciences followed by two years of clinical rotations in hospitals—in preparation for the same set of licensing exams all U.S. doctors-to-be must pass. But you may find considerable variation in the quality of the faculty (Where did they train? What kind of research are they engaged in? Will you be taught by full-time professors or part-time local practitioners?) and how accessible they are. While a dedicated, permanent staff is ideal, some students note that

they have had excellent courses taught by gifted U.S. professors enjoying the adventure of a year in an exotic locale.

The faculty/student ratio will provide a clue as to how likely you are to get professors' attention; in the U.S., ratios range from 13.6 faculty members per student at Mayo Medical School to 1 professor for every 31 students at the New York College of Osteopathic Medicine. Anyone considering a European or other medical school that doesn't teach in English will want to find out whether there's an English-language program and if foreign students have the same access to faculty as native students do.

To assess how well schools prep students for the U.S. Medical Licensing Examination (USMLE), compare their students' pass rates on "Step 1," the portion of the exam taken after second year, and "Step 2," generally taken during the last clinical year of medical school or around graduation. Pass rates vary. For example, Tel Aviv's Sackler School's recent pass rate for Step 1 was 98 percent; St. George's in Grenada had a 90 percent pass rate. Lesser schools have lower rates—sometimes much lower. As is true for American medical schools, too, you'll want to find out what type of clinical experience you can expect, and how early. Ask what kind of support services students have available: stress management? counseling? help with study skills?

A number of offshore schools have come and gone in the last several years, particularly in Mexico, Central America, and the Caribbean. So focus from the start on schools with a history. Indeed, before you invest in a place, make sure the place has invested in itself. Be wary of a school operating in rented space—some marginal schools have been known to hold classes in hotels or even private homes—because, as the AAIMG website cautions, "the school that rents a few classrooms has little incentive to remain open during hard times."

Make a visit before you commit so you can gauge quality and viability by sitting in on classes, quizzing students, and checking out the library and labs. While a listing in the "World Directory of Medical Schools," published by the World Health Organization, doesn't guarantee that a school is worthy, being included is considered a good sign. Another tip: The U.S. Department of Education Federal School Code Search (www.fafsa.ed.gov/fotwo607/fslookup.htm) lets you plug in a foreign institution's code number and find out if it can receive and distribute American financial aid.

Find out, too, who the school considers a worthy candidate. At Ross University School of Medicine in Dominica, the class admitted in January 2004 had an average undergraduate GPA of 3.18. And whereas "most U.S. schools are looking at [MCAT scores of] 27 and above, our average was 21," said Andrew Serenyi, director of marketing for the school. At American University of the Caribbean, the incoming classes often include "people who are nurses, paramedics and EMTs; career transfers; people who are young, didn't study well in college and didn't get the grades that they needed; and people who are waitlisted," said Susan Atchley, professor of immunology and director of community services. "They judge you based on what you are doing now instead of on what you did as an 18-year-old," said Burke, who was 28 when he arrived at AUC in September 2000. "But then you have to prove yourself. My class started with 180 [students] and is now about 90. If you're not meeting the criteria you'll get weeded out of the system."

Many students attending offshore schools return to the United States after the second year to do their clinical rotations in U.S. hospitals; before applying to any overseas school, ask if the school is affiliated with clinical sites in the United States. Students often find residencies in the States, too, through the same match system as do their stateside peers (students pick schools and schools pick students and the computer matches them up). The website of the Educational Commission for Foreign Medical Graduates (www.ecfmg.org) walks students through the required steps to a U.S. residency.

The chances of making a match are good for students from reputable international programs who have strong USMLE scores. While some 15,000 students graduate from U.S. medical schools each year, there are about 21,500 postgraduate residency positions available. Among the eligible U.S. citizens attending St. George's University Medical School who applied in a typical recent year, 99 percent landed U.S. residency positions. Students from Ross University School of Medicine have been offered residencies at such noted hospitals as Yale–New Haven Hospital, Loma Linda University Medical Center in California, Georgetown University Medical Center, and UCLA Medical Center. As you shop for a school, ask those that interest you to provide a contact list of graduates who are now practicing in the U.S., as well as a history of residency placements.

"The great equalizer is standardized tests," said Burke, who said he scored in the 95th percentile on Step 1 and in the 99th on Step 2. Before he finished his fourth year in a cardiology rotation at Providence Hospital in Southfield, Michigan, he was matched to a residency in internal medicine with the hospital. From there, he planned to move on to a cardiology fellowship.

Finding your Plan B

What do you do if, in the end, your dream is dashed? "You need to think about Plan B: a different career choice," said Harvey.

But Plan B may well be a modification of Plan A: a career in public health or another health-related field, or the pursuit of a Ph.D. in the biological sciences, for example. Carol Baffi-Dugan, who advises undergrads going into health professions at Tufts University in Massachusetts, said the first thing she asks students who have been rejected by a medical school is why they were attracted to medicine in the first place. "Sometimes a student is motivated by an incredible love of science. It may be that that student would be intellectually stimulated and more successful doing a Ph.D.," she said. "But if they say the classic, 'I want to help people and use science,'

then I start to talk about the clinical health professions and the area of public health. Other health professions are playing an increasingly important role in health care delivery." She has also pointed to physician assistants, who can specialize in cardiology or surgery, or nurse practitioners, who can specialize in pediatrics. (For an introduction to a number of health care options, see Chapter 7.)

Baffi-Dugan said she hopes that the students she advises have at least been thinking about other possibilities all along. At a recent freshman orientation she told the incoming class, "Look at all areas [in medicine], even if you do decide that a M.D. degree is what you want. You will understand that medical care is a team effort [and] you'll be better prepared." You will also be more likely to make a thoughtful and heartfelt choice. No one wants "the dentist who wanted to be a doctor," Baffi-Dugan said.

Chapter Seven

Other Choices, Other Paths

So you like medicine and you like making people feel better, yet you don't want to be a doctor? Good. Though it may surprise many physicians, there are plenty of good health careers that *don't* take you through medical school. Physical therapy, physician assistant, and nursing are among some of the booming fields in the allied health professions. People working in them say the intellectual challenges, emotional rewards, and relationships with patients are often more satisfying than in the doctor's world. "I can see a patient for ten consecutive weeks, make corrections in their treatment, and see steady progress," said one physical therapist. "How many doctors can do that?"

Here we profile eight such professions, highlighting the pluses and minuses of each, the training needed, and tips on how to get into a program or school. We also list the top three schools in each field (or more in the case of a third-place tie) according to the latest *U.S News & World Report* rankings, which are based on opinion surveys of faculty and administrators at accredited schools. (Note: There are no rankings for dentistry programs.)

Physician Assistant

Health care has changed enormously over the last 20 years, and as a result, the role physician assistants play in medicine has been transformed. Treating acute illnesses is now less important than preventing them. Widespread use of routine screening and an arsenal of new drugs has made managing chronic illness a top priority. Today, there is a premium on controlling costs, and four of five Americans are enrolled in managed care plans. Health care is delivered not only by physicians but by a team of medical providers, and physician assistants have become some of the team's most sought-after players.

Physician assistants (PAs) are licensed to practice medicine under the supervision of physicians. They are nationally certified after graduating from an accredited program, usually about two years in length, and passing a certifying exam. More than half of the nation's 50,000 PAs specialize in primary care—family medicine, internal medicine, pediatrics, or obstetrics and gynecology. Over a third specialize either in surgery or emergency medicine. They see patients, take histories, evaluate tests, make diagnoses, prescribe drugs, give advice, suture cuts, perform simple surgeries such as biopsies, and more.

"I love the potpourri of family practice," said Julie Theriault, who has been a physician assistant at the Sutter Medical Group in Elk Grove, California. "I do see some complicated things, and one of the key factors in the job of a PA is knowing when to get the doctor involved. I just had a diabetic patient who was on three medications and yet her blood sugar level was still out of whack. So I called the doctor." Theriault was able to describe the patient's test results and other factors, allowing the physician to make a diagnosis and advise treatment—even though he was located in another office miles away. The ability of one highly paid doctor to supervise a number of PAs who can manage patient care on-site not only cuts costs, it also allows rural and medically vulnerable communities access to care when they may have had none before. A study of primary care providers in two Western states showed that more physician assistants were practicing in rural areas than any other type of provider, and in vulnerable minority and poor communities, physician assistants, along with family physicians and internists, provide the majority of medical services available.

Pluses. PAs end up in much the same place as primary care physicians but spend about half the time in school and probably one-fifth of the money to get there. Salaries are high, and many practices and hospitals work out flexible schedules to allow PAs to have lives outside of work. Women find the PA career—with its high skill levels, good salaries, and flexible hours—particularly rewarding: They make up nearly 60 percent of the profession.

Minuses. Some doctors worry that the huge growth in nonphysician clinicians may lead to competition—rather than cooperation—between doctors and PAs. Physician assistants estimate that they can treat 50 to 75 percent of the complaints that send patients to doctors. The ability of physician assistants to treat so many conditions, coupled with a two- to four-fold increase in the number of PAs and other nonphysician clinicians, has left doctors wondering if there may be less need for M.D.s in the future. Still, Joseph Kaplowe, physician assistant coordinator at New Britain Hospital in New Britain, Connecticut, said that's unlikely. "With so many people in the population getting into their 50s and 60s, and that being the age at which people need more health and hospital care, there will be a need for more docs *and* more PAs."

> *"With so many people in the population getting into their 50s and 60s...there will be a need for more docs and PAs."*

Training. Many of the first PAs were Navy medical corpsmen who had received training and experience in Vietnam, but returned home to find there were no similar positions in the civilian health care system. At the same time, the nation faced a shortage of primary care physicians, particularly in rural and inner-city communities, so PA positions were created for these veterans.

Today most PAs are trained not on the battlefield but in programs that offer a master's degree. The coursework is divided into two parts spread over two years. The preclinical curriculum during the first year includes medical science courses—topics such as pharmacology, signs and symptoms of diseases, and primary care aspects of every medical specialty. The second year consists of clinical clerkships where PA students work with physicians treating patients and managing their cases. Many programs now require a thesis or "capstone" project on a medical topic of interest such as obesity or childhood depression. Newly minted PAs must pass a national certification exam, and then must acquire 100 hours of continuing medical education every two years and be recertified every six years.

Tips on getting started. Nationally, there are about two applicants for every opening in PA programs, and at some schools the competition is stiffer. Applicants to PA programs must complete at least two years of college-level courses in basic and behavioral sciences as prerequisites. There are 133 PA programs at various schools across the country, and for about 80 of them applications can be submitted online through a central system, at www.caspaonline.org. At this site, you can click on the schools, look at what their programs offer, and get details on requirements, prerequisites, and more. You can apply to more than one program and add to your list if your application is turned down at your first few choices.

Most PA students already hold undergraduate degrees in a wide variety of fields and have worked in health care for four years before beginning training. Kaplowe said, "the most competitive applicant for PA school is 28 or older and this is a second career for them. They have a liberal arts degree and they understand the way the world works. They'll be able to communicate better to patients, staffs, and to write clearly. The person who has a strong work ethic, who understands they will be part of a team, who understands the boundaries that they work in— he or she will be a successful PA applicant."

Top schools. master's programs, ranked in 2003: 1) Duke University, North Carolina, 2) University of Iowa, 3) (tie) Emory University, Georgia; George Washington University, Washington, D.C.

To find out more. The American Academy of Physician Assistants (703-836-2272; www.aapa.org) has extensive resources about schools, training, and careers on its site.

> *"The person who has a strong work ethic, who understands they will be part of a team, will be a successful PA applicant."*

Nursing

In Victorian England, nursing was routinely considered "menial employment needing neither study nor intelligence." But then came Florence Nightingale, whose lifesaving work during the Crimean War in the mid-1800s transformed the practice into a respected and highly skilled profession. Today, nurses are witnessing an explosion in demand for their services, from geriatric care in nursing homes to cutting-edge work in high-tech medical facilities. There is now a veritable "candy store" of opportunities in the field, said Patricia Rowell, senior policy fellow at the American Nurses Association. Ruth Corcoran, CEO of the National League for Nursing, concurred: "The job security is amazing, the salaries are very fair, and it's an opportunity to make a difference every day in work that is appreciated and needed."

This is still an intimate career, requiring empathy and close relationships with patients who may be sick or dying. In general, nurses collect and analyze data on patients' physical and psychological situations, help diagnose ailments, provide continuous care and monitoring, and offer critical support to physicians. But there's more than one kind of nurse, and they are classified by their skill levels.

First come licensed vocational or practical nurses. They are typically high school graduates with a year of nursing training from a vocational school or junior college. They work under the direction of higher-level nurses and focus on the physical care of the patient, such as monitoring vital signs, making beds, and caring for some wounds.

Above LPNs are registered nurses, and they make up the majority of the field. They are state-licensed and have earned either an associate degree in nursing from a community college or a bachelor's of science in nursing from a four-year school. Unlike LPNs, they handle medications, complex treatments, patient assessments, and plans for care. RNs can remain generalist nurses and serve in operating rooms, pediatric and maternity wards, rehabilitation centers, or psychiatric units, to name just a few places.

There are more options for students who earn postgraduate degrees, such as a master's in nursing. These are gateways to a variety of specialized paths. Nurse practitioners, for instance, see patients in primary care settings and help set up treatment plans. Clinical nursing specialists provide expert care in fields like oncology. Nurse anesthetists take care of a patient's anesthesia needs during surgery or childbirth. There's also academia: Some highly motivated baccalaureate students go directly into Ph.D. programs that prepare them for teaching and research positions.

Pluses. Many hospitals allow nurses to negotiate their work schedules, which is a boon for working parents. "If you have a child who is in school all day, you may want to work days so you can be home at night," Rowell said. If you want regular hours, you can find them in public health clinics or doctors' offices. Nursing is also a highly mobile profession, with opportunities growing overseas as well. The current nursing shortage means plenty of jobs, and salaries that keep going up.

Minuses. Nurses in some hospitals are asked to work different hours every week, or even every day. As an acute care nurse, Rowell worked three separate shifts: Days were 7 a.m. to 3:30 p.m., for five or ten days straight, followed by a couple of days off, and then a stretch of night and evening shifts. "You can't really plan anything more than a month ahead of time," she said.

Training. LPNs start with that one-year vocational training program. The first step in the RN path is usually the associate or bachelor's degree. There are 569 such bachelor's degree programs in the United States, which take four years to complete, and 885 associate degree programs, which take from two to three years. Most bachelor's degree programs require students to first apply for general undergrad admissions. After completing the school's required courses, students may then apply to the nursing program. The University of Washington's school of nursing in Seattle is a good example. It requires students to take ninety credits—usually during freshman and sophomore year—in English composition, problem-solving, statistics, art, sociology, and the sciences before they can begin the nursing program. Applicants also must maintain at least a 2.0 GPA and provide a résumé outlining health care experience (volunteer and paid), a recommendation from a health care provider, and various essays. Once admitted, nursing students take various courses ranging from anatomy to pharmacotherapeutics to ethics. There also are several required clinical practicums. Clinical nurse specialists and other advanced nursing degree candidates take more advanced courses and must do a thesis or research project.

Once students have completed their undergraduate program, there's yet another hurdle: a state license. That means passing a nationally standardized test from the National Council Licensure Examination (NCLEX). Depending on your state nursing board, additional certification may be required for clinical nurse specialists and nurse anesthetists. You can find links to those boards through the National Council of State Boards of Nursing site at www.ncsbn.org.

The cost of a nursing degree varies enormously depending on the program and the school. Community colleges are the least expensive, costing $3,000 to $5,000 per year. At the other end of the spectrum, a private, four-year college can cost more than $20,000 per year.

Tips on getting started. Preparing for a nursing program is no cakewalk. High school students should take the most rigorous college prep courses, especially in biology, chemistry, and math. They must also show excellent writing skills because documentation is a big part of nursing. Clear communication is essential because nurses assess patients and relay information to other health care providers. Each undergraduate nursing program has its own set of admission prerequisites, but there are some basic requirements: the SAT or ACT exam and high school courses in math, biology, chemistry, English, and a foreign language. The American Nurses Association also recommends courses in computer science and the behavioral and social sciences. Rowell said volunteer work in a nursing setting is key for students "to see if it's what they really want to do. We see students drop out because they had an idealized notion of what a nurse was. Try it out a bit."

Top schools. Master's, ranked in 2003: 1) University of Washington; 2) University of California–San Francisco; 3) (tie) University of Michigan–Ann Arbor; University of Pennsylvania.

To find out more. The National Student Nurses Association (718-210-0705; www.nsna.org/career) has information about the variety of nursing careers. So does the American Nurses Association (800-274-4ANA; www.ana.org). The American Association of Colleges of Nursing (202-463-6930; www.aacn.nche. edu) has details on schools and programs.

Dentistry

Dentists roll up their sleeves, put on their surgical gloves, and get down to work in patients' mouths. They pull out painful wisdom teeth, fill cavities, and fit prosthetics where teeth used to be; some operate on cleft palates or even do cosmetic surgery. Research has linked oral health to general health, so dentists see their work as helping to keep their patients hale and hearty overall. Dentists work with their hands more than most physicians do, said Laura Neumann, of the American Dental Association, and that's a stimulating part of the job. "They work in a small space. It requires very fine motor skills," she said. Those skills are applied not only to the mouth's function, but also to its appearance. "We like to say it's an art and a science," said Neumann. "The art that goes into restoring or improving aesthetics can be both challenging and fun, and people always feel good when you've done something like that for them."

Over 80 percent of dentists are general practitioners, and most are in private practice. The rest specialize: Orthodontists correct poorly aligned teeth, for instance, while oral surgeons operate in and around the mouth. Other specialties include prosthodontics (restoring or replacing teeth) and periodontics (treating diseases of gums and other structures around the teeth).

Pluses. Dentistry can drastically improve a patient's life without placing the life-and-death stress of medicine on its practitioners. "Sometimes medical problems can be a little bit depressing," said Neumann. But in dentistry, "you tend to deal with less life-threatening situations." Plus dentists get to treat diseases directly, not just by writing prescriptions, and there's a great deal of satisfaction in that approach. Dentists earn a healthy income, and demands from work don't take over their lives. "Especially if you have your own practice or you're an associate, you can control your hours," Neumann said. That makes it an attractive career for women, she noted. She had three children—one before dental school, one during, and one just after. "I started practicing right away. I'm not going to say it was a piece of cake, but it was doable."

Minuses. In addition to learning how to pull teeth, anyone interested in private practice should be willing to learn how to manage a payroll and a small business. There's also the inescapable fact that people don't like coming to see you. But with improving technology, things have gotten much more pleasant for the patient—although they never seem to get used to the sound of the drill.

Training. Dental schools offer a D.D.S (doctor of dental surgery) or the equivalent D.M.D. (doctor of dental medicine); both degrees are universally accepted. Like medical school, dental school lasts four years. In the first two years, students take classes in basic sciences—such as anatomy, microbiology, and physiology—concentrated on the head and neck. They try out techniques on synthetic models or extracted teeth. Since most dentists end up in private practice, courses on management are also part of the dental training. Students learn how to lead a dental team—which usually includes a hygienist and a dental assistant—and follow employment and tax laws.

Students may begin to see real, live patients in their second year, or sooner in some cases. That clinical experience accelerates in the third and fourth years, when they treat patients under the supervision of faculty dentists. A few schools have students rotate through community-based clinics or hospitals, but the majority of clinical work is in dental schools' own clinics.

Before they can practice, dentists have to pass a national written exam and a clinical licensing exam that may vary from state to state. In every state but Delaware, you can start practicing as soon as you get your degree, but about 40 percent of graduates go on to a residency for further training. Some residencies are in dental schools, others in hospitals. The length of residency depends on the specialty. Most general practice residencies are one year, while orthodontics and periodontics take three years and oral surgery takes four years. Some oral surgeons get an M.D. as part of their residency, which takes an additional two years. Having an M.D. can make it easier to get hospital privileges. There are a variety of other programs, such as one- to two-year residencies in public health. A public health dentist might work for a city, running dental education and screening programs.

Tips on getting started. Dentistry isn't a fallback for students who don't have high enough numbers to get into medical school. Recent entering classes of Harvard's medical and dental schools had the same average GPA: 3.8. In addition to great grades, schools also usually require students to have had courses in English, biology, chemistry, and physics—these are part of an established predental curriculum, and

---

"Sometimes medical problems can be a little bit depressing," but in dentistry, "you tend to deal with less life-threatening situations."

---

your school's health advisor can fill you in on other details. Remember, too, that aligning teeth and making sure they look good is also an art—admissions offices take that seriously. Students should consider taking studio art classes to help with their spatial skills. And get some experience: schools want applicants to prove they care about dentistry, and part of that proof is spending time with professionals, doing "chairside observation," and shadowing dentists.

Applicants should also decide whether they are most interested in a practice or in doing research: Some dental schools focus on clinical skills, others on scientific research. Schools do try to simplify the application process by using a central service: AADSAS, the Associated American Dental Schools Application Service (www.adea.org), will send your application to all the schools you select. As part of your application, you have to take the computerized DAT, or Dental Admissions Test. The test covers biology and chemistry, perceptual ability (matching shapes and judging distances), reading comprehension, and math. Registration is online at the American Dental Association's website (www.ada.org; look for their Education and Testing section), and you can schedule the test for almost any time at one of a few hundred testing centers across the country. You can spend $1,000 on a DAT prep class, it's not necessary if you buy practice tests and study on your own. Some schools also require a manual dexterity test, like carving a piece of chalk or soap to specifications.

To find out more. The American Dental Association has information on careers in dentistry and on the DAT test (312-440-2500; www.ada.org). The American Dental Education Association (1-800-353-2237; www.adea.org) publishes the *Official Guide to Dental Schools* ($35), which describes the programs at U.S. and Canadian schools and explains the application process.

Psychology

Psychologists have moved far beyond the "talking cure" during the century since Sigmund Freud set up his couch in Vienna. Therapists still talk, of course, and still try to cure. But the field has broadened significantly. Through a wide variety of psychotherapies—some short-term, some long, some directed at modifying behavior, some focused on the thinking behind that behavior—psychologists may work with clients to identify and change unhealthy or irrational attitudes that make people dissatisfied with their lives and, in some cases, utterly miserable. They may also test applicants' fitness for jobs using paper-and-pencil questionnaires, perform IQ tests, and do other kinds of assessments. Some teach and do academic research in different topics, such as a culture's effect on the way people feel. School psychologists work with students' behavior problems and may help teachers learn to manage

classrooms. Psychologists may also bring their understanding of the mind to bear on physical illnesses, cooperating with physicians to help patients with stress-related ulcers or others who don't stick with their medications.

One thing all psychologists have in common is that they view distress as a complex problem, not one simply rooted in body chemistry or solved solely by antidepressants. "If you see the solutions to mental illness lying in biology, then I'd probably go to medical school," said George Stricker, a clinical psychologist recently retired from Adelphi University in Garden City, New York. (Unlike psychiatrists, psychologists can't prescribe drugs—except in New Mexico, where they recently won that right.)

Pluses. When clinical psychologist Tom Olkowski worked in a suburban Colorado school system, he evaluated children and helped them, their families, and teachers understand how the kids could learn better. "When you see a kid who's been struggling doing better in school, that's something tangible," he said. Variety is another advantage: Olkowski's psychology Ph.D. gave him the background in research and theory to work in many fields. In his 30-year career, he worked not only in schools, but also in a mental health center; written a book on the stress of moving with children; and made two videos for a real estate company on the same topic.

Minuses. Psychology can be stressful, especially when you deal with clients who may turn suicidal or violent. Olkowski cautioned that doctoral training doesn't prepare you for running a private practice, when you have to know about things like marketing and cash flow. Insurance restrictions on the number of therapy sessions with a client can add to the hassle factor. And training is expensive:

Clinical psychologists often emerge from school $30,000 to $60,000 in debt.

Training. In most states, you need a doctorate in order to practice independently, without a doctorate-level psychologist supervising you. To get that doctorate, Ph.D.s used to be the only option for psychologists. But today, the Psy.D. (doctor of psychology) degree has become popular (although there are still more Ph.D. programs than Psy.D. programs). A Ph.D. has more emphasis on original research and requires an extensive dissertation. Students usually spend five years taking classes, doing research, and learning clinical skills, plus at least another year completing the dissertation. Psy.D. programs concentrate more on clinical practice and therapeutic methods. Students still learn how to do research and how to use the findings, but have to write a shorter paper to graduate. The clinical emphasis makes the Psy.D. attractive, but the Ph.D. makes it easier to get an academic job.

All doctoral students also learn the foundations of the discipline, including skills such as assessing patients using a variety of tests and how to practice ethically. Many students study statistics and research design. They also learn the cognitive, social, and biological bases of behavior, which may include classes in neurological and physiological psychology. Many states only license psychologists with doctorates from programs accredited by the American Psychological Association (most programs are APA-accredited). Graduates who want to be licensed as psychologists also have to take a national written exam and, in some states, a separate test that may cover the state's ethical codes and mental health laws. Many states also require that psychologists practice under supervision for a while before they can get an independent license.

Are you doctorate-phobic? Consider a master's in psychology. Master's programs are short—two or three years—and thus relatively cheap. The degree allows you to do marriage and family counseling, mental health counseling, and social work. Master's programs are accredited by the Masters in Psychology Accreditation Council.

Tips on getting started. You don't have to be a psych major in college to get into graduate school, although it may be tougher to work the classes you'll need into your art history major. Most programs require undergrad courses in statistics and experimental psychology. Stricker also recommends getting some experience with emotionally troubled people to be sure you want to work with them professionally. He suggests volunteering with a peer counseling service, for example. If you plan on going to a Ph.D. program, research experience can be very helpful; try finding a professor who will let you volunteer in his or her lab. About half of the U.S. doctoral programs in psychology require applicants to take the Graduate Record Examinations. Some programs also require the psychology subject GRE, which has multiple-choice questions about experimental and natural sciences, social sciences, and general psychology, including the history of the discipline and research design. Scores on these tests are important, but schools place even more emphasis on the applicant's statement of goals, recommendations from professors, and research experience.

Doctoral students who responded to a 1999 survey funded by the Pew Charitable Trusts said one extremely important factor in picking a school was choosing an advisor you can work with. A Ph.D. student and her advisor may work together closely or meet a few times a year, depending on the school and the person, so it's important to choose someone whose style fits your own. It's also a good idea to ask about funding when you're looking at schools to find out how students there are financially supported. Ph.D. students can be carried on an advisor's research grant. But because Psy.D.s are usually offered by smaller schools that don't have a lot of research money, most Psy.D. students have to come up with loans, which means more postgrad debt.

Top schools. Doctorate programs in clinical psychology, ranked in 2004: 1) University of California–Los Angeles; 2) (tie) University of California–Berkeley; University of Wisconsin–Madison.

To find out more. The American Psychological Association (800-374-2721; www.apa.org) has information on psychology careers and education. The APAs *Graduate Study in Psychology* (www.apa.org/books; $24.95 in print, $19.95 for three months' access to the online version) lists psychology programs in the United States and Canada, and is updated yearly. The Pew-funded survey on Ph.D. student experiences (www.phd-survey.org) has a valuable section devoted to psychology.

Physical Therapy

The human body is pretty good at self-repair, knitting torn muscles and fractured bones together after an injury. But sometimes it can't handle the workload alone. Physical therapists help the healing process by flexing stiffened muscles, stretching limbs, and teaching balance to people who have been off their feet for a while. "It's the study of movement and its application, but it's more than that," said Sue Schafer, associate director of the School of Physical Therapy at Texas Woman's University in Dallas, Texas. It's understanding individual needs, she said, and matching them to individual capabilities. When assessing a patient—

from a hulking football player to a stroke survivor to a tiny infant—the therapist determines what structures are damaged, and what a patient needs to do to recover—given his or her particular physical limits—and then oversees the appropriate rehabilitation therapy. Techniques include exercise, massage, ultrasound, and heat therapy.

Sports medicine is one of the better known PT subfields, but therapists don't just rehab athletes. Today, for example, they are often called on to work with breast cancer patients, advising them on how to remain active while undergoing chemotherapy and radiation treatments, and also working to reduce postsurgery side effects such as painful swelling of the arms. Although they often work in tandem with occupational therapists, physical therapists focus on increasing mobility and strength and decreasing pain, while occupational therapists tackle the ability to perform specific tasks.

Pluses. Hanging out with professional sports teams and mixing with world-famous ballerinas isn't too shabby, but in reality, very few physical therapists have celeb-studded jobs. The rest relish the opportunity to work extensively one-on-one with patients and see the fruits of their labor in every step that patients make. PT's also have the flexibility to work in either a hospital or private practice, and the range of patients—from kids with cerebral palsy to senior citizens recovering from hip replacement surgery—keeps them on their toes.

Minuses. The work takes a toll on therapists' own bodies. The job can require heavy lifting—moving around large patients or large equipment—and standing or crouching for long periods of time. "It's a physical profession and eventually we have personal limitations," Schafer said. "I don't do well getting on the ground any more and that's what you have to do when you work with children." Other therapists say that the greatest frustration is patients who are not willing to do the work needed for recovery. Physical therapy often demands that patients be not only cooperative, but determined.

Training. Either a master's or doctorate is required to practice. (The Commission on Accreditation in Physical Therapy stopped recognizing baccalaureate professional degrees a few years ago, and by 2020, the American Physical Therapy Association hopes to make the profession an all-doctorate field.) Master's programs usually take two years and teach students basic sciences such as chemistry and biology as well as the psychosocial aspects of disease, intervention and treatment options, and current PT research directions. In addition to classroom work, students receive an average of fifteen weeks of field training at hospitals, rehab centers, schools, or outpatient clinics.

Doctorates, which take about three years, supplement this training with expanded work in areas like pharmacology, radiology, health care management, and pathology. They also insist on more field training—as long as a year. Graduates must pass a national exam as well as fulfill any individual state requirements, which may include additional training to maintain licensure.

Tips for getting started. To get into a PT program, applicants need some prerequisite undergrad courses, which include psychology, biology, physics, chemistry, statistics, and the humanities. A high GPA in these courses is important, as is performance on the GRE. But program directors warn that numbers alone won't get you in. Applicants need to show a knack for working with people. Work as a physical therapy assistant (an accredited aide who has completed a two-year program) or volunteer experience at a nursing home or hospital can also make an application shine.

Top schools. Master's and doctorate programs, ranked in 2004: 1) University of Southern California; 2) Washington University in St. Louis; 3) University of Pittsburgh.

To find out more. The American Physical Therapy Association (703-684-2782; www.apta. org) lists accredited programs and residency and fellowship information and offers financial aid advice.

Occupational Therapy

Most people view occupations as that thing they do from 9 to 5. Occupational therapists don't. While OT's most often help patients with temporary or permanent disabilities function smoothly in the workplace, they handle every aspect of the business of life, from inventing ways for handicapped parents to make lunches for their kids to teaching premature babies the proper movements for nursing. Retired folks don't stare into computer monitors or punch time cards every day, but they can call on occupational therapists to help them relearn how to dress and bathe themselves after a hip replacement or stroke.

As in physical therapy, the long-term goal of occupational therapy is to increase independence. But while physical therapists focus on overall strength and movement, OT's tackle obstacles to particular activities. When consulting with a patient, a therapist must break down an activity into each of its components, whether they are physical, environmental, mental, or behavioral. "Bowling isn't just picking up a ball and rolling it," explained Janet Falk-Kessler, director of Columbia University's occupational therapy programs. "It involves everything from posture, bilateral motor coordination, aspects of vision, sound, and strength. It also has social components, like how one behaves in a bowling alley."

It's a field that requires a lot of creative problem-solving. When some of Falk-Kessler's students were working with the homebound elderly, they discovered that the Meals on Wheels packaging was too difficult to open. So the therapists created a tool specifically designed to cut the boxes.

Pluses. Not bound to hospitals, occupational therapists can ply their trade in a range of industries. Some work with architects—helping design accessible homes and buildings—while others, who are interested in mental health, can work with children and teenagers who have anxiety disorders or substance abuse problems, improving their ability to stay on task and interact better with peers and adults.

Minuses. Sometimes patients have difficulty understanding the purpose of therapy. "We're not here to take away the pain. You have to feed your dog and we have to figure out how to do that," explained one therapist. Dealing with insurance companies that offer patients only limited therapy coverage can also be frustrating.

Training. Undergraduate degrees for OT are on their way out: As of January 2007, the Accreditation Council for Occupational Therapy Education will only recognize those programs that confer a master's or doctorate. Anyone now enrolling in an undergrad program is going to need summer coursework to finish by the deadline. The new emphasis is on the master's degree, which requires two years of classroom study, including courses in anatomy, sociology, psychology, and biology. This is followed by six to nine months of fieldwork under the guidance of a licensed therapist. Some combined baccalaureate/master's programs can shorten the amount of schooling by

a year. A national certification exam is required to practice.

Tips for getting started. Proof of a commitment to community service looks stellar on any kind of application, but for almost all occupational therapy programs, it is required. To impress admissions officers, work beyond the minimum number of hours and try to volunteer in hospitals that will allow you to shadow members of the occupational therapy unit. Experience in varied settings, like homeless shelters or schools, helps demonstrate your dedication as well. There are some required undergrad courses, including biology, physiology, and psychology. Programs also examine GPAs and scores on the Graduate Record Exam.

Top schools. Master's and doctorate programs, ranked in 2004: 1) University of Southern California; 2) Boston University, Sargent College of Health & Rehabilitation Sciences; 3) Washington University in St. Louis.

To find out more. The American Occupational Therapy Association (301-652-2682; www.aota.org) has resources on education and snagging a job in the field. The American Occupational Therapy Foundation (301-652-6611, ext. 2250; www.aotf.org) has information on financial aid.

Social Work

When life gets tough, social workers get moving. People at high risk for AIDS, or low-income parents who are caught between the demands of work and the need to find decent child care, have traditionally been able to get counseling and practical help from social workers employed by public welfare agencies and hospitals. Today private companies, including HMOs and for-profit health service organizations, have added social workers to their payroll to advise patients and their families. While specialties aren't strictly defined in the field, most social workers build an area of expertise or gain certification in the areas of family care, public health, or mental health.

Pluses. No surprises here—the positive impact you have is a big reason for doing this job. Many social workers also praise the diversity of the work, which can range from grief counseling to supervising a homeless outreach program. Some social work positions also allow for flexible working hours; private firms, in particular, often hire counselors on a part-time basis.

Minuses. The emotional rewards typically are higher than the monetary ones, and the long, intense hours often lead to burnout.

Training. Education requirements for social workers vary in each state; the Association of Social Work Boards lists all of them. A master's degree as well as a passing score on a licensing exam are needed for most positions, especially clinical or management ones. However, some entry-level positions, such as child welfare case workers or counseling jobs in the private sector, only call for an undergraduate degree in social work. That degree, offered at many universities, involves the study of social welfare policies and methods. As part of the major, most schools require seminars on dealing with individuals and families, and an internship where students are placed in a public or private social service organization to get hands-on experience dealing with patients.

The master's degree is similar but more intense. In over 150 programs accredited by the Council on Social Work Education, students take two years of classes in social welfare policy and practice, human behavior, and research methods. Other courses may include applied psychology, sociology, and ethics. Budding social workers also need to take a nine-hundred-hour practicum. At the University of Illinois–Urbana-Champaign, for instance, graduate students work Monday

"Patients get what their policy covers, not necessarily what they need."

through Thursday at anywhere from a school to a nursing home depending on their area of interest; the work typically includes client interviews and case evaluations. On Fridays, students attend a seminar at the school to discuss and learn from their experiences.

An increasing number of graduate schools are offering minors and dual-degree programs for students who want to demonstrate an expertise in a certain area—and get a step ahead in the job market. Columbia University is starting a dual-degree program in social work and international affairs that will help graduates land positions with international organizations like the United Nations. "We know that there isn't a single social problem that requires one profession to intervene," said Jeanette Takamura, dean of the university's School of Social Work. "So why should we offer one single degree?" The program at Columbia takes three years to finish, and students graduate with two master's degrees. The school also offers dual social work degrees in other areas such as urban planning and Jewish studies.

If you want to become a clinical social worker who provides mental health therapy, you need to receive still more training. Clinical social workers who work as psychotherapists, doing in-depth counseling, can receive reimbursement for their services from HMOs. Besides a master's degree, psychotherapists need two years of supervised work experience and a passing score on a clinical licensing test.

Tips on getting started. "You need to have passion if you want to be a social worker. And that

To find out more. The National Association of Social Workers (202-408-8600; www.social workers.org) has general information and career advice The Council on Social Work Education (703-683-8080; www.cswe.org) has complete listings of accredited school programs. The Association of Social Work Boards (800-225-6880; www. aswb.org) administers the licensing exams and maintains information on each state's test and license requirements.

"Social workers work with some of the most seriously troubled individuals in American culture."

---

passion can't be taught," one social work professor said. The best way to demonstrate this kind of dedication is to show it on your résumé. If you haven't been working in a related field such as teaching or nursing, volunteer experience is very important for an applicant—even as little as spending one evening each week playing cards at a nearby nursing home or one Saturday a month helping mentally-ill children. While universities do not require an undergraduate degree in social work, most schools do give preference to students who have performed well in social sciences courses like psychology and sociology. Many graduate schools of social work do not require applicants to take the Graduate Record Exam but they do want to see a high undergraduate GPA.

Top schools. Master's programs, ranked in 2004: 1) University of Michigan–Ann Arbor; 2) Washington University in St. Louis; 3) (tie) Columbia University, New York; University of California–Berkeley; University of Chicago; University of Washington.

Speech-Language Pathology

Humans need to communicate. It's an essential characteristic of the species. But sometimes it doesn't come easy. That's where speech-language pathologists (SLP) come in. They work in hospitals, clinics, schools, corporate offices, or private practice, diagnosing speaking and communication problems and developing treatment plans. For example, children who have trouble articulating certain words and sounds can learn to talk fluently with proper training. For stroke victims who suffer aphasia—trouble speaking, comprehending, or writing language—early treatment by an SLP can help preserve and improve language skills by using verbal or visual drills and conversational role-playing.

Pluses. Good salaries and opportunities to work in a variety of settings with all kinds of patients keep SLPs happy. Those that tire of working in a hospital, for instance, can easily find another job in a school helping students with speech problems. New SLPs say they are amazed and gratified when they see a struggling student finally turn a corner.

Minuses. "It's not like giving somebody a pill," said Diane Paul-Brown of the American Speech-

Language-Hearing Association. Some patients with severe disabilities may never reach normal levels, and their progress can be slow and frustrating. There are also hassles in getting compensation from schools and insurers.

Training. In almost every state, practicing speech-language pathologists must have a master's degree in the field, pass a national licensing exam, and complete a nine-month supervised fellowship. Programs are accredited by a council of the American Speech-Language-Hearing Association, and a typical master's curriculum involves four semesters and a summer of full-time study. Classes focus on specific disorders. For example, at the University of Maryland–College Park, besides a diagnostic methods course and an audiology course, all students must study aphasia, voice disorders, stuttering, child language disorders, and phonological disorders. They can also take electives such as augmentative communications (using technology to enhance innate ability). Once graduate students have a grasp of their field and its tools, they begin clinical rotations where they learn how to evaluate and diagnose actual patients and design customized courses of treatment. Some programs also require a thesis.

Tips on getting started. Aspiring undergrads can major in speech pathology or communication sciences and disorders, which gives them many of the prerequisite courses for grad school. (Some grad programs only accept applicants with these majors.) The prerequisites include anatomy and physiology of speech, anatomy and physiology of hearing, speech science, hearing science, speech and language development, phonetics, psychology of language, and acoustics.

You're not barred from becoming an SLP if you didn't major in it, however. Some students without

"You need to have passion if you to want to be a social worker. And that passion can't be taught."

this background do postbaccalaureate work before applying to grad programs, while others apply anyway, and are accepted with the provision that they first take a year of make-up classes. In general, schools are looking for high GPAs and GRE scores. Students with better chances of admission usually have volunteered or worked in nursing homes and preschools.

Top schools. Master's programs, ranked in 2004: 1) (tie) University of Iowa; University of Wisconsin–Madison; 3) (tie) Northwestern University, Illinois; Purdue University–West Lafayette, Indiana; University of Washington.

To find out more. The American Speech-Language-Hearing Association (800-498-2071; www.asha.org) has extensive student materials with a guide to accredited programs by state.

The U.S. News Insider's Index

How Do the Schools Stack Up?

Which are the hardest and easiest medical schools to get into?

While the number of applications to medical schools has dropped in recent years, it is still extremely hard to get in. Many of the most competitive only accept 1 in 20 of those who apply—or even fewer. Schools are ranked here from most to least selective based on a formula that combines average MCAT scores and undergraduate GPA for the Fall 2005 entering class as well as the school's acceptance rates. Average GPAs and MCATs will give you a sense of the competition.

Most to least selective

School	Overall acceptance rate	Acceptance rate (men)	Acceptance rate (women)	Acceptance rate (minorities)	Average undergraduate GPA	Average composite MCAT score (scale: 1-15)	Average MCAT score, verbal reasoning (scale: 1-15)	Average MCAT score, physical sciences (scale: 1-15)	Average MCAT score, biological (scale: 1-15)	Average MCAT score, writing (scale: J-T)
Washington University in St. Louis	9.9%	9.0%	10.9%	10.7%	3.85	12.3	11.6	12.7	12.8	Q
Duke University (NC)	4.4%	4.3%	4.6%	10.1%	3.80	11.9	10.6	11.9	11.8	N
Columbia Univ. Col. of Physicians and Surgeons (NY)	5.3%	N/A	N/A	N/A	3.79	11.8	11.2	12.2	12.1	Q
Johns Hopkins University (MD)	5.9%	5.7%	6.2%	6.5%	3.84	11.5	10.9	11.6	11.9	Q
Harvard University (MA)	5.2%	4.2%	6.4%	3.3%	3.76	11.7	11.0	12.0	12.0	R
University of Pennsylvania	4.8%	4.5%	5.1%	4.8%	3.79	11.6	11.0	11.8	11.8	Q
Yale University (CT)	5.9%	5.1%	6.9%	5.6%	3.75	11.6	11.1	11.9	11.9	R
Cornell University (Weill) (NY)	4.3%	3.3%	5.5%	4.8%	3.73	11.5	10.8	11.9	11.9	P
University of California–San Francisco	4.9%	4.0%	5.7%	6.1%	3.79	11.3	10.6	11.5	11.7	P
Baylor College of Medicine (TX)	6.7%	6.7%	6.6%	7.8%	3.77	11.3	10.8	11.6	11.6	P
University of Michigan–Ann Arbor	7.8%	8.4%	7.1%	N/A	3.72	11.4	10.8	11.7	11.8	Q
Vanderbilt University (TN)	6.7%	5.6%	8.0%	7.2%	3.73	11.3	10.6	11.5	11.7	Q
Mayo Medical School (MN)	2.3%	1.9%	2.7%	N/A	3.82	10.8	10.3	10.7	11.3	Q
Northwestern University (Feinberg) (IL)	5.8%	5.5%	6.0%	6.7%	3.72	11.3	10.7	11.6	11.5	Q
Stanford University (CA)	2.9%	2.9%	2.9%	3.2%	3.71	11.2	10.5	11.3	11.8	Q
University of Texas Southwestern Medical Center–Dallas	13.3%	13.7%	12.8%	13.7%	3.78	11.0	10.3	11.3	11.4	P
New York University	5.8%	5.7%	5.9%	5.2%	3.73	11.0	10.4	11.1	11.3	Q
University of California–San Diego	6.0%	6.0%	6.0%	7.0%	3.73	11.0	10.2	11.3	11.5	Q
University of Colorado–Denver and Health Sciences Center	9.7%	9.2%	10.4%	6.4%	3.74	11.0	11.0	11.0	11.0	Q
University of Chicago (Pritzker)	7.2%	6.9%	7.6%	9.0%	3.74	10.9	10.5	11.0	11.3	Q
Mount Sinai School of Medicine (NY)	5.0%	5.0%	5.0%	4.4%	3.67	11.0	10.6	11.0	11.4	Q
University of Pittsburgh	8.7%	8.2%	9.3%	6.7%	3.62	11.3	10.6	11.6	11.6	P
Brown University (RI)	4.3%	3.7%	4.7%	4.2%	3.62	11.1	10.4	11.5	11.5	R
Emory University (GA)	8.2%	7.9%	8.5%	7.1%	3.64	11.1	10.7	11.2	11.4	P
Ohio State University	9.6%	10.1%	8.9%	7.7%	3.72	10.8	10.3	10.9	11.2	P
University of California–Los Angeles (Geffen)	4.5%	4.1%	4.9%	7.3%	3.71	10.8	9.7	10.8	11.1	Q
University of Virginia	8.7%	7.8%	9.7%	8.8%	3.74	10.7	10.4	10.9	11.0	P
Dartmouth Medical School (NH)	7.2%	7.0%	7.4%	7.8%	3.70	10.7	10.4	10.7	10.9	N/A
Case Western Reserve University (OH)	8.6%	8.2%	9.0%	8.5%	3.62	11.0	10.5	11.2	11.3	P
University of Rochester (NY)	7.5%	6.5%	8.6%	6.3%	3.68	10.7	10.5	10.8	11.0	P
University of Southern California (Keck)	7.0%	6.2%	7.9%	6.0%	3.60	11.0	10.5	11.2	11.4	Q
Boston University	4.7%	4.0%	5.4%	N/A	3.65	10.7	10.1	10.9	11.0	Q
St. Louis University	8.7%	10.1%	6.8%	6.6%	3.70	10.5	10.1	10.4	10.8	P
University of California–Irvine	7.3%	6.5%	8.1%	7.0%	3.65	10.6	9.8	10.9	11.1	Q
University of North Carolina–Chapel Hill	7.1%	6.7%	7.5%	5.8%	3.65	10.6	10.3	10.5	10.9	N
Tufts University (MA)	7.0%	6.9%	7.0%	5.4%	3.61	10.7	10.2	10.9	11.1	Q
University of Wisconsin–Madison	10.6%	9.1%	12.4%	6.0%	3.70	10.4	10.1	10.4	10.7	P
Stony Brook University (NY)	10.5%	10.3%	10.6%	9.2%	3.60	10.7	10.0	11.0	11.0	P

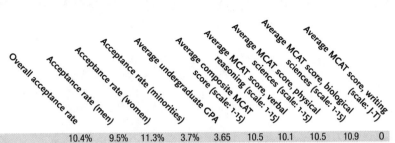

	Overall acceptance rate	Acceptance rate (men)	Acceptance rate (women)	Acceptance rate (minorities)	Average undergraduate GPA	Average composite MCAT score (scale: 1-15)	Average MCAT score, verbal reasoning (scale: 1-15)	Average MCAT score, physical sciences (scale: 1-15)	Average MCAT score, biological sciences (scale: 1-15)	Average MCAT score, writing (scale: J-T)
University of Florida	10.4%	9.5%	11.3%	3.7%	3.65	10.5	10.1	10.5	10.9	O
Yeshiva University (Einstein) (NY)	8.8%	7.7%	9.8%	7.5%	3.65	10.5	9.9	10.7	11.0	Q
Oregon Health and Science University	6.2%	5.1%	7.4%	4.4%	3.67	10.3	10.3	10.0	10.6	P
University of Iowa (Carver)	11.9%	11.3%	12.8%	9.2%	3.71	10.2	9.9	10.2	10.6	P
University of Washington	7.2%	6.9%	7.6%	5.2%	3.65	10.4	10.2	10.1	10.7	Q
University of Alabama–Birmingham	12.3%	13.2%	11.3%	7.9%	3.72	10.1	9.8	10.1	10.4	N/A
University of Maryland	8.4%	7.4%	9.2%	7.5%	3.66	10.3	10.3	10.0	10.4	P
University of Massachusetts–Worcester	22.8%	21.0%	24.2%	N/A	3.64	10.6	10.3	10.7	10.7	Q
University of Minnesota Medical School	10.3%	9.8%	10.9%	8.1%	3.68	10.2	9.9	10.2	10.5	Q
Creighton University (NE)	6.2%	N/A	N/A	N/A	3.72	9.9	9.9	9.8	10.2	P
Medical College of Wisconsin	8.4%	8.2%	8.7%	N/A	3.72	9.9	9.7	9.9	10.2	P
University of California–Davis	4.9%	4.5%	5.4%	4.9%	3.61	10.3	10.0	10.0	11.0	Q
University of Connecticut	7.2%	N/A	N/A	N/A	3.66	10.1	9.7	9.9	10.6	Q
University of Missouri–Columbia	16.2%	14.3%	18.5%	10.7%	3.75	9.9	10.0	9.6	10.2	P
Georgetown University (DC)	5.2%	4.7%	5.7%	N/A	3.61	10.2	10.1	10.2	10.3	N/A
Jefferson Medical College (PA)	6.7%	6.5%	7.0%	5.1%	3.57	10.4	10.3	10.2	10.6	Q
Rush University (IL)	6.2%	6.0%	6.4%	5.1%	3.65	10.1	9.8	10.3	10.3	P
University of Miami (Miller) (FL)	8.6%	8.6%	8.7%	9.2%	3.71	9.8	9.6	9.7	10.0	P
University of Nebraska College of Medicine	15.3%	15.6%	15.1%	8.2%	3.75	9.7	9.6	9.5	10.0	N/A
Wake Forest University (NC)	4.7%	4.7%	4.6%	N/A	3.63	10.1	10.1	10.1	10.1	P
Indiana University–Indianapolis	14.8%	15.3%	14.3%	N/A	3.68	9.9	9.7	9.8	10.3	P
Medical College of Georgia	14.8%	16.5%	13.3%	8.9%	3.66	10.0	9.9	9.9	10.3	N/A
Tulane University (LA)	4.8%	N/A	N/A	N/A	3.50	10.5	N/A	N/A	N/A	N/A
UMDNJ-Robert Wood Johnson Medical School	12.3%	11.8%	12.6%	10.9%	3.62	10.1	9.4	10.2	10.6	P
Loyola University Chicago (Stritch)	6.6%	6.5%	6.6%	6.3%	3.62	9.9	9.5	9.9	10.2	P
University of Cincinnati	11.5%	11.4%	11.7%	N/A	3.59	10.1	9.7	10.1	10.5	O
University of South Florida	11.1%	10.9%	11.3%	11.0%	3.68	9.7	9.4	9.7	9.9	N/A
Medical University of Ohio	11.4%	14.1%	8.7%	N/A	3.59	10.0	10.0	9.9	10.2	N/A
Temple University (PA)	7.8%	8.1%	7.7%	7.6%	3.59	10.0	9.5	10.0	10.4	P
University of Arizona	28.4%	25.8%	31.3%	N/A	3.67	9.9	9.8	9.8	10.2	P
Northeastern Ohio Universities College of Medicine	14.9%	16.0%	14.0%	18.5%	3.79	9.2	9.2	9.2	9.3	O
Texas A&M University System Health Science Center	11.6%	12.0%	11.3%	10.8%	3.73	9.3	8.8	9.3	9.5	Q
University of Oklahoma	19.6%	20.1%	18.9%	16.3%	3.68	9.6	9.7	9.5	9.7	O
University of Texas Medical Branch–Galveston	8.4%	8.3%	8.5%	9.4%	3.72	9.3	9.0	9.0	10.0	P
University of Texas Health Science Center–Houston	7.9%	8.1%	7.6%	4.9%	3.66	9.5	9.3	9.3	10.0	P
Drexel University (PA)	13.3%	12.9%	13.5%	13.1%	3.44	10.3	10.0	10.0	11.0	Q
University of Kansas Medical Center	14.7%	14.3%	15.3%	11.7%	3.66	9.5	9.6	9.2	9.8	P
New York Medical College	10.5%	9.2%	11.8%	8.2%	3.50	10.0	9.5	10.2	10.5	Q
University of Utah	12.8%	11.0%	17.1%	5.7%	3.64	9.5	9.3	9.2	10.1	O
Eastern Virginia Medical School	7.5%	N/A	N/A	N/A	3.45	10.1	10.3	9.7	10.4	N/A
SUNY–Syracuse	12.3%	11.9%	12.7%	11.0%	3.54	9.8	9.6	9.9	10.1	P
University at Buffalo–SUNY	12.9%	11.6%	14.3%	N/A	3.57	9.7	9.3	9.9	10.1	P
University of Illinois–Chicago	13.2%	12.4%	14.0%	12.2%	3.49	10.0	N/A	N/A	N/A	N/A
University of Kentucky	19.1%	18.8%	19.4%	N/A	3.58	9.7	9.8	9.7	9.9	P
University of South Dakota	9.2%	7.3%	11.8%	1.6%	3.66	9.3	9.4	8.9	9.7	O
UMDNJ-New Jersey Medical School	10.2%	10.3%	10.2%	N/A	3.51	9.8	9.6	9.8	10.1	O
University of New Mexico	9.3%	8.9%	9.6%	9.0%	3.59	9.5	9.5	9.1	9.8	N/A
West Virginia University	13.0%	18.7%	5.0%	27.8%	3.65	9.3	9.0	9.2	9.6	O
East Tennessee State University (Quillen)	12.0%	10.8%	13.5%	5.1%	3.63	9.3	9.8	8.8	9.2	O
Medical University of South Carolina	17.7%	17.9%	17.4%	11.5%	3.59	9.5	9.7	9.1	9.6	O
Uniformed Services Univ. of the Health Sciences (MD)	15.2%	16.5%	13.0%	8.5%	3.52	9.7	9.4	9.8	9.9	O

Which are the hardest and easiest medical schools to get into?

	Overall acceptance rate	Acceptance rate (men)	Acceptance rate (women)	Acceptance rate (minorities)	Average undergraduate GPA	Average composite MCAT score (scale: 1-15)	Average MCAT score, verbal reasoning (scale: 1-15)	Average MCAT score, physical sciences (scale: 1-15)	Average MCAT score, biological sciences (scale: 1-15)	Average MCAT score, writing (scale: J-T)
George Washington University (DC)	4.6%	N/A	N/A	N/A	3.56	9.3	9.1	9.2	9.8	P
Texas Tech University Health Sciences Center	6.5%	7.1%	5.9%	7.0%	3.56	9.3	9.0	9.2	9.9	O
Michigan State University	6.6%	5.8%	7.6%	6.3%	3.52	9.4	9.2	9.1	9.9	P
University of North Dakota	33.6%	33.8%	33.3%	N/A	3.70	9.1	8.9	8.9	9.7	O
University of Vermont	5.9%	5.7%	6.0%	3.6%	3.50	9.5	9.8	9.1	9.6	Q
University of Arkansas for Medical Sciences	24.9%	22.5%	27.9%	18.0%	3.62	9.2	9.4	8.8	9.4	O
University of Tennessee Health Science Center	23.6%	24.6%	22.3%	21.3%	3.58	9.3	9.0	9.0	10.0	O
Virginia Commonwealth University	7.5%	7.2%	7.9%	10.0%	3.50	9.4	9.0	9.4	9.8	O
University of South Carolina	10.0%	9.4%	10.6%	5.5%	3.55	9.2	9.6	8.5	9.4	O
Rosalind Franklin University of Medicine and Science (IL)	7.5%	9.9%	5.1%	3.6%	3.45	9.5	9.0	10.0	10.0	O
Wright State University (OH)	8.3%	N/A	N/A	N/A	3.58	9.0	9.1	8.6	9.3	O
U. of N. TX Health Sci. Center (TX Col. of Osteopathic Med.)	10.4%	9.7%	11.2%	8.1%	3.52	9.2	9.0	8.9	9.6	P
Florida State University	10.9%	9.0%	12.7%	12.6%	3.59	8.7	8.2	8.5	8.9	N
East Carolina University (Brody) (NC)	14.9%	N/A	N/A	N/A	3.50	9.0	9.1	8.8	9.0	P
Mercer University (GA)	12.9%	13.8%	12.2%	8.1%	3.52	8.9	9.0	8.5	9.2	M
Morehouse School of Medicine (GA)	5.1%	N/A	N/A	N/A	N/A	N/A	N/A	N/A	N/A	N/A
Des Moines University Osteopathic Medical Center (IA)	18.7%	18.4%	19.0%	10.6%	3.56	8.6	8.5	8.3	9.0	O
UMDNJ–School of Osteopathic Medicine	7.9%	6.8%	8.9%	3.9%	3.48	8.8	8.5	8.7	9.2	Q
Oklahoma State University Center for Health Sciences	27.5%	26.6%	28.5%	22.3%	3.59	8.5	9.0	8.0	9.0	O
Southern Illinois University–Springfield	19.0%	16.8%	21.3%	N/A	3.50	8.8	8.9	8.5	9.0	O
Touro University College of Osteopathic Medicine (CA)	13.3%	N/A	N/A	N/A	3.45	8.8	8.6	8.9	9.0	O
College of Osteopathic Medicine of the Pacific (CA)	23.1%	21.6%	24.7%	21.3%	3.45	8.9	8.5	8.9	9.6	O
New York College of Osteopathic Medicine	16.4%	15.4%	17.2%	16.4%	3.50	8.6	8.2	8.5	9.0	O
Chicago College of Osteopathic Medicine	23.2%	21.6%	24.7%	18.5%	3.50	8.6	8.5	8.3	9.0	N/A
Michigan State University College of Osteopathic Medicine	17.2%	17.9%	16.6%	10.5%	3.49	8.5	8.5	8.2	8.8	O
A.T. Still University of Health Sciences (Kirksville) (MO)	14.7%	13.3%	16.5%	10.1%	3.47	8.4	8.3	8.2	8.8	O
Ohio University	6.7%	5.7%	7.7%	5.5%	3.54	8.0	8.0	7.6	8.3	O
Nova Southeastern Univ. Col. of Osteopathic Med. (FL)	14.4%	13.7%	15.1%	N/A	3.41	8.3	8.4	8.0	8.6	M
Univ. of New England Col. of Osteopathic Medicine (ME)	9.0%	7.7%	10.4%	2.2%	3.37	8.4	8.5	7.8	8.6	R
Howard University (DC)	5.9%	5.9%	5.9%	7.8%	3.35	8.0	7.6	7.8	8.5	O
Philadelphia College of Osteopathic Medicine	10.8%	10.4%	11.3%	2.2%	3.23	8.3	8.4	8.1	8.6	O
Lake Erie College of Osteopathic Medicine (PA)	12.2%	14.7%	9.6%	8.1%	3.32	7.9	7.9	7.6	8.2	O
West Virginia School of Osteopathic Medicine	19.0%	19.8%	18.1%	8.6%	3.43	7.5	7.8	7.1	7.4	M
Pikeville College School of Osteopathic Medicine (KY)	26.9%	28.7%	24.7%	19.6%	3.30	7.3	7.3	6.9	7.5	N/A
Edward Via Virginia College of Osteopathic Medicine	15.3%	15.2%	15.5%	12.2%	3.45	7.5	7.8	7.1	7.7	P

Who's the priciest? Who's the cheapest?

The total cost of an M.D. degree can easily top $200,000 at the most expensive private schools once you factor in living expenses. Private medical schools are ranked here by tuition and fees for the 2003–2004 academic year, with the most expensive at the top. Public institutions follow, sorted by in-state tuition so you can easily see what you might save by sticking close to home.

Private Schools

	Tuition and fees	Room and board
Tufts University (MA)	$43,579	$7,820
Columbia University College of Physicians and Surgeons (NY)	$41,873	$15,471
George Washington University (DC)	$41,553	$18,647
St. Louis University	$41,092	$15,518
University of Southern California (Keck)	$40,454	$12,950
New York Medical College	$40,276	$17,326
Northwestern University (Feinberg) (IL)	$40,001	$14,625
Boston University	$39,960	$11,381
Yeshiva University (Einstein) (NY)	$39,800	$14,300
Washington University in St. Louis	$39,720	$8,824
Georgetown University (DC)	$39,699	$14,835
Albany Medical College (NY)	$39,637	N/A
Duke University (NC)	$39,537	$13,872
University of Pennsylvania	$39,467	$16,050
Case Western Reserve University (OH)	$39,384	$16,172
Rush University (IL)	$39,024	$8,560
Harvard University (MA)	$38,776	$14,515
Stanford University (CA)	$38,431	$19,053
Creighton University (NE)	$38,325	$12,500
Jefferson Medical College (PA)	$38,316	$15,609
New York University	$38,175	$12,000
Drexel University (PA)	$37,890	$9,500
Yale University (CT)	$37,655	$10,150
Brown University (RI)	$37,453	$14,667
University of Rochester (NY)	$37,379	$15,000
Rosalind Franklin University of Medicine and Science (IL)	$36,900	$16,000
Dartmouth Medical School (NH)	$36,850	$8,750
Loyola University Chicago (Stritch)	$36,771	$16,099
Emory University (GA)	$36,534	$14,640
Vanderbilt University (TN)	$36,001	$8,640
Johns Hopkins University (MD)	$35,965	$9,080
University of New England College of Osteopathic Medicine (ME)	$35,270	$11,000
College of Osteopathic Medicine of the Pacific (Western University) (CA)	$35,260	$10,430
New York College of Osteopathic Medicine	$34,984	$20,275
University of Chicago (Pritzker)	$34,701	$10,071
Philadelphia College of Osteopathic Medicine	$34,272	N/A
Wake Forest University (NC)	$34,006	$15,040
A.T. Still University of Health Sciences (Kirksville) (MO)	$33,945	$10,010
Cornell University (Weill) (NY)	$33,345	$9,947

Who's the priciest? Who's the cheapest?

Private Schools, cont'd.

	Tuition and fees	Room and board
Touro University College of Osteopathic Medicine (CA)	$33,200	$14,798
Chicago College of Osteopathic Medicine	$32,250	$9,735
Mercer University (GA)	$30,220	$13,190
Des Moines University Osteopathic Medical Center (IA)	$30,210	$14,690
University of Miami (Miller) (FL)	$29,848	$22,917
Morehouse School of Medicine (GA)	$28,557	$11,760
Medical College of Wisconsin	$28,098	$7,500
Pikeville College School of Osteopathic Medicine (KY)	$28,000	$0
Howard University (DC)	$26,566	$11,855
Lake Erie College of Osteopathic Medicine (PA)	$25,220	$10,500
Nova Southeastern University College of Osteopathic Medicine (FL)	$24,740	$10,431
Eastern Virginia Medical School	$24,048	N/A
Mayo Medical School (MN)	$14,250	$11,990
Baylor College of Medicine (TX)	$10,583	$18,172

Public Schools

	In-state tuition and fees	Out-of-state tuition and fees	Room and board
East Carolina University (Brody) (NC)	$7,676	$32,633	$9,856
Texas A&M University System Health Science Center	$9,012	$24,212	$10,884
University of Texas Medical Branch–Galveston	$9,378	$22,478	N/A
University of Texas Southwestern Medical Center–Dallas	$10,632	$23,732	$15,277
University of North Carolina–Chapel Hill	$10,740	$34,406	$24,384
Texas Tech University Health Sciences Center	$10,807	$23,907	$10,210
U. of North Texas Health Sci. Center (Texas Col. of Osteopathic Medicine)	$10,974	$26,724	$10,857
University of Texas Health Science Center–Houston	$11,505	$24,605	$12,410
Medical College of Georgia	$12,436	$34,660	$14,211
University of Massachusetts–Worcester	$14,037	N/A	$12,563
University of Arizona	$14,462	N/A	$9,070
University of New Mexico	$14,642	$38,781	$8,312
University of Washington	$14,859	$34,697	$12,603
University of Arkansas for Medical Sciences	$14,861	$28,949	$0
University of Alabama–Birmingham	$15,478	$38,210	$10,780
West Virginia University	$16,454	$37,452	$8,226
University of South Dakota	$16,731	$35,197	$19,375
Oklahoma State University Center for Health Sciences	$16,938	$32,158	$7,300
University of Oklahoma	$17,021	$39,109	N/A
Florida State University	$17,570	$52,121	N/A
University of Utah	$17,646	$32,805	$8,604
West Virginia School of Osteopathic Medicine	$17,850	$45,878	N/A
University of Tennessee Health Science Center	$18,065	$34,949	$13,251
University of South Florida	$18,431	$50,515	$9,420
East Tennessee State University (Quillen)	$18,559	$36,691	$12,900
University of Kentucky	$19,238	$38,212	$10,175
University of Kansas Medical Center	$19,337	$35,092	$22,464
University of South Carolina	$19,570	$56,496	$10,930
Stony Brook University (NY)	$19,736	$34,436	$21,350
SUNY–Syracuse	$19,840	$34,540	N/A

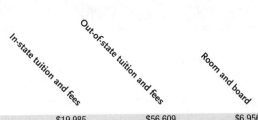

	In-state tuition and fees	Out-of-state tuition and fees	Room and board
Southern Illinois University–Springfield	$19,985	$56,609	$6,956
University of Florida	$20,036	$47,073	$8,685
University at Buffalo–SUNY	$20,099	$34,799	$9,301
University of North Dakota	$20,125	$51,699	$8,704
University of Maryland	$20,262	$36,129	$18,315
University of Iowa (Carver)	$21,076	$40,282	$9,000
University of Colorado–Denver and Health Sciences Center	$21,218	$72,791	$11,250
University of Nebraska College of Medicine	$21,475	$49,105	$13,500
University of California–Los Angeles (Geffen)	$21,506	$33,751	$14,385
Indiana University–Indianapolis	$21,613	$41,298	$13,290
Medical University of South Carolina	$21,702	$57,754	N/A
University of Wisconsin–Madison	$21,818	$32,942	$13,860
University of Missouri–Columbia	$21,895	$42,620	$8,433
University of California–San Diego	$22,008	$34,253	$11,657
Medical University of Ohio	$22,072	$50,332	N/A
University of California–San Francisco	$22,328	$34,573	$18,570
University of Michigan–Ann Arbor	$22,435	$34,787	$20,880
University of Connecticut	$22,540	$42,780	N/A
University of California–Davis	$22,820	$35,065	$11,229
University of California–Irvine	$22,820	$35,065	$10,520
Ohio University	$22,845	$32,277	$10,071
Wayne State University (MI)	$23,314	$46,766	$18,733
University of Cincinnati	$23,580	$41,004	$15,191
Michigan State University	$23,700	$51,600	$12,024
Michigan State University College of Osteopathic Medicine	$23,700	$51,600	$12,024
Ohio State University	$23,872	$28,717	$7,080
UMDNJ–School of Osteopathic Medicine	$23,977	$36,059	$10,000
Wright State University (OH)	$24,082	$32,806	$10,560
Virginia Commonwealth University	$24,137	$38,166	$9,372
UMDNJ-New Jersey Medical School	$24,332	$36,414	$11,140
UMDNJ-Robert Wood Johnson Medical School	$24,392	$36,474	$10,026
Northeastern Ohio Universities College of Medicine	$24,599	$47,906	$10,000
University of Vermont	$25,477	$43,487	$9,767
University of Illinois–Chicago	$26,230	$54,284	$12,967
University of Virginia	$28,700	$38,524	$16,549
Oregon Health and Science University	$28,760	$38,760	$15,000
Edward Via Virginia College of Osteopathic Medicine	$29,500	$29,500	$23,000
University of Minnesota Medical School	$30,875	$37,769	$11,220
University of Pittsburgh	$32,868	$37,608	$15,000
Temple University (PA)	$34,305	$41,885	$13,776
Mount Sinai School of Medicine (NY)	$37,050	$37,050	$13,800

Which schools award the most and the least financial aid?

Compared to what you're going to need, you may be surprised at how little you get: Medical schools assume that their students will borrow to pay the bills because they'll make enough after graduation to manage the loan payments. However, a lucky few with top scores and undergraduate grades may find a merit award on the table. Schools are ranked here by percentage of students receiving aid.

Private Schools

	% receiving aid of any kind	% receiving loans	% receiving grants/scholarships	% receiving work-study benefits
Mayo Medical School (MN)	100%	57%	100%	N/A
Pikeville College School of Osteopathic Medicine (KY)	98%	98%	66%	N/A
Des Moines University Osteopathic Medical Center (IA)	95%	91%	23%	N/A
Medical College of Wisconsin	95%	87%	62%	0%
Morehouse School of Medicine (GA)	95%	88%	58%	0%
Nova Southeastern University College of Osteopathic Medicine (FL)	95%	95%	20%	3%
A.T. Still University of Health Sciences (Kirksville) (MO)	94%	94%	18%	18%
Loyola University Chicago (Stritch)	94%	87%	67%	0%
Mercer University (GA)	94%	91%	76%	0%
New York College of Osteopathic Medicine	94%	87%	27%	0%
Touro University College of Osteopathic Medicine (CA)	94%	93%	11%	10%
Philadelphia College of Osteopathic Medicine	93%	90%	45%	15%
University of New England College of Osteopathic Medicine (ME)	93%	92%	29%	0%
Howard University (DC)	92%	87%	49%	0%
Lake Erie College of Osteopathic Medicine (PA)	92%	92%	25%	0%
New York Medical College	92%	90%	14%	3%
University of Chicago (Pritzker)	92%	79%	85%	2%
University of Rochester (NY)	92%	84%	46%	22%
Washington University in St. Louis	92%	52%	76%	0%
Creighton University (NE)	90%	86%	24%	0%
University of Southern California (Keck)	90%	90%	35%	0%
College of Osteopathic Medicine of the Pacific (Western University) (CA)	89%	87%	12%	0%
University of Miami (Miller) (FL)	88%	88%	27%	0%
Rush University (IL)	87%	85%	60%	4%
Duke University (NC)	87%	68%	73%	0%
Vanderbilt University (TN)	86%	71%	58%	N/A
Georgetown University (DC)	86%	80%	40%	1%
Wake Forest University (NC)	86%	82%	76%	0%
Albany Medical College (NY)	86%	85%	37%	37%
Drexel University (PA)	85%	84%	12%	21%
Jefferson Medical College (PA)	85%	80%	49%	8%
University of Pennsylvania	84%	73%	61%	1%
Dartmouth Medical School (NH)	83%	75%	44%	N/A
Columbia University College of Physicians and Surgeons (NY)	82%	71%	54%	10%
Yale University (CT)	82%	69%	55%	0%
Case Western Reserve University (OH)	81%	79%	59%	0%
Rosalind Franklin University of Medicine and Science (IL)	81%	81%	39%	5%
Cornell University (Weill) (NY)	80%	66%	59%	16%
Emory University (GA)	80%	72%	50%	0%

	% receiving aid of any kind	% receiving loans	% receiving grants/scholarships	% receiving work-study benefits
George Washington University (DC)	80%	80%	24%	0%
Yeshiva University (Einstein) (NY)	80%	80%	45%	0%
Boston University	79%	74%	34%	0%
Brown University (RI)	79%	74%	50%	0%
Johns Hopkins University (MD)	78%	68%	64%	20%
New York University	77%	70%	65%	15%
Tufts University (MA)	77%	73%	19%	1%
Baylor College of Medicine (TX)	77%	68%	47%	13%
Northwestern University (Feinberg) (IL)	76%	71%	58%	0%
Harvard University (MA)	71%	70%	43%	3%
Stanford University (CA)	65%	57%	52%	8%

Public Schools

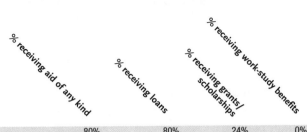

	% receiving aid of any kind	% receiving loans	% receiving grants/scholarships	% receiving work-study benefits
University of Nebraska College of Medicine	100%	93%	64%	0%
University of California–Los Angeles (Geffen)	99%	93%	99%	0%
Oklahoma State University Center for Health Sciences	98%	94%	44%	25%
University of Texas Health Science Center–Houston	98%	98%	49%	0%
University of North Dakota	98%	95%	55%	0%
West Virginia School of Osteopathic Medicine	97%	94%	12%	11%
University of Iowa (Carver)	96%	90%	60%	1%
University of South Dakota	96%	93%	74%	2%
University of Kansas Medical Center	95%	85%	71%	0%
Oregon Health and Science University	95%	90%	80%	2%
University of California–Davis	95%	90%	93%	0%
University of Connecticut	95%	90%	45%	0%
University of Kentucky	95%	85%	64%	8%
University of Missouri–Columbia	95%	95%	44%	0%
Michigan State University College of Osteopathic Medicine	94%	92%	88%	0%
University of Arkansas for Medical Sciences	94%	89%	44%	0%
Michigan State University	93%	87%	80%	0%
Southern Illinois University–Springfield	93%	91%	40%	0%
University of Arizona	93%	88%	88%	4%
University of Minnesota Medical School	93%	81%	73%	1%
Virginia Commonwealth University	93%	86%	38%	0%
University of Colorado–Denver and Health Sciences Center	92%	89%	56%	4%
University of Texas Southwestern Medical Center–Dallas	92%	84%	66%	6%
East Tennessee State University (Quillen)	92%	91%	35%	0%
University of Washington	92%	85%	60%	0%
Ohio University	92%	90%	31%	2%
University of South Carolina	91%	86%	39%	0%
University of California–San Francisco	91%	85%	88%	1%

Which schools award the most and the least financial aid?

Public Schools, cont'd.

	% receiving aid of any kind	% receiving loans	% receiving grants/ scholarships	% receiving work-study benefits
Mount Sinai School of Medicine (NY)	91%	85%	45%	9%
University of Florida	91%	86%	77%	0%
University of Utah	91%	89%	50%	0%
East Carolina University (Brody) (NC)	90%	90%	36%	0%
Indiana University–Indianapolis	90%	89%	41%	0%
U. of North Texas Health Sci. Center (Texas Col. of Osteopathic Medicine)	90%	90%	41%	1%
University of Vermont	90%	88%	64%	0%
Medical University of Ohio	90%	87%	24%	17%
University of Oklahoma	90%	86%	42%	0%
Temple University (PA)	89%	88%	45%	6%
UMDNJ–School of Osteopathic Medicine	89%	87%	45%	7%
University of New Mexico	89%	86%	81%	0%
University of Tennessee Health Science Center	89%	84%	42%	1%
University of Massachusetts–Worcester	89%	89%	26%	0%
SUNY–Syracuse	89%	83%	44%	7%
University at Buffalo–SUNY	88%	84%	70%	0%
University of Maryland	88%	84%	64%	2%
West Virginia University	88%	82%	41%	0%
University of Virginia	87%	84%	65%	0%
Wayne State University (MI)	87%	86%	41%	3%
Stony Brook University (NY)	87%	84%	35%	9%
University of California–Irvine	87%	80%	83%	0%
University of Cincinnati	87%	85%	40%	2%
Ohio State University	87%	80%	58%	0%
Texas A&M University System Health Science Center	86%	83%	86%	0%
University of Pittsburgh	86%	75%	59%	0%
UMDNJ-New Jersey Medical School	85%	82%	35%	6%
University of Alabama–Birmingham	85%	81%	22%	N/A
University of Wisconsin–Madison	85%	85%	25%	0%
University of California–San Diego	84%	82%	63%	2%
University of North Carolina–Chapel Hill	84%	80%	80%	0%
University of Texas Medical Branch–Galveston	84%	80%	60%	8%
University of South Florida	83%	79%	42%	0%
Medical College of Georgia	83%	78%	40%	2%
University of Michigan–Ann Arbor	83%	76%	56%	0%
Medical University of South Carolina	82%	80%	18%	3%
Northeastern Ohio Universities College of Medicine	82%	81%	26%	0%
UMDNJ-Robert Wood Johnson Medical School	82%	79%	43%	6%
Texas Tech University Health Sciences Center	78%	69%	51%	0%
Uniformed Services University of the Health Sciences (Hebert) (MD)	0%	0%	0%	0%

Which are the largest and smallest medical schools?

As you compare schools, you'll want to pay attention to the total enrollment, the size of the first-year class, and the faculty-to-student ratio. All will have an impact on the schools' personalities, the availability of professors outside of class, and the extent to which you engage with your classmates.

	Total enrollment	% in-state enrollment	Size of first-year class	Faculty-to-student ratio
University of Illinois–Chicago	1,403	78%	333	0.6
Lake Erie College of Osteopathic Medicine (PA)	1,206	34%	389	0.1
New York College of Osteopathic Medicine	1,176	64%	310	N/A
Indiana University–Indianapolis	1,162	90%	280	1.1
Wayne State University (MI)	1,063	92%	N/A	N/A
Philadelphia College of Osteopathic Medicine	1,041	57%	266	0.1
Drexel University (PA)	1,016	30%	231	0.5
University of Minnesota Medical School	937	77%	220	1.7
Jefferson Medical College (PA)	935	44%	254	2.6
University of Texas Southwestern Medical Center–Dallas	904	86%	229	1.6
University of Texas Health Science Center–Houston	848	97%	210	0.9
Ohio State University	839	88%	210	2.3
University of Texas Medical Branch–Galveston	830	94%	210	1.3
Des Moines University Osteopathic Medical Center (IA)	819	24%	215	N/A
Nova Southeastern University College of Osteopathic Medicine (FL)	819	52%	236	0.1
Medical College of Wisconsin	811	47%	204	1.3
University of Washington	810	88%	180	2.4
New York Medical College	765	35%	186	1.6
Rosalind Franklin University of Medicine and Science (IL)	756	23%	185	0.9
Harvard University (MA)	739	N/A	165	10.2
Virginia Commonwealth University	737	59%	184	1.0
University of North Carolina–Chapel Hill	732	84%	160	1.7
Yeshiva University (Einstein) (NY)	732	45%	180	3.5
Temple University (PA)	725	62%	176	0.6
College of Osteopathic Medicine of the Pacific (Western University) (CA)	724	69%	212	N/A
Georgetown University (DC)	718	1%	190	2.5
Medical College of Georgia	711	100%	180	0.7
University of Kansas Medical Center	709	85%	175	0.7
New York University	703	48%	160	2.2
Tufts University (MA)	703	36%	168	1.9
UMDNJ-New Jersey Medical School	700	100%	170	1.1
George Washington University (DC)	699	2%	177	0.9
Chicago College of Osteopathic Medicine	690	46%	174	N/A
University of California–Los Angeles (Geffen)	690	98%	122	3.0
University of Michigan–Ann Arbor	688	46%	177	2.8
University of Alabama–Birmingham	683	93%	160	1.6
Baylor College of Medicine (TX)	678	86%	168	2.6
Northwestern University (Feinberg) (IL)	678	28%	171	2.6
A.T. Still University of Health Sciences (Kirksville) (MO)	671	16%	172	0.1

Which are the largest and smallest medical schools?

	Total enrollment	% in-state enrollment	Size of first-year class	Faculty-to-student ratio
Uniformed Services University of the Health Sciences (Hebert) (MD)	665	6%	169	0.4
University of Southern California (Keck)	665	79%	171	1.8
UMDNJ-Robert Wood Johnson Medical School	642	100%	157	1.3
University of Miami (Miller) (FL)	641	80%	182	1.8
Columbia University College of Physicians and Surgeons (NY)	634	38%	149	2.8
Boston University	632	19%	155	1.9
University of Cincinnati	629	94%	160	2.2
Tulane University (LA)	627	N/A	N/A	0.9
Case Western Reserve University (OH)	624	54%	167	2.9
University of Wisconsin–Madison	619	88%	163	1.7
University of Pennsylvania	617	41%	147	3.3
Michigan State University College of Osteopathic Medicine	616	91%	205	0.3
SUNY–Syracuse	615	95%	153	0.6
St. Louis University	614	43%	164	0.9
Medical University of Ohio	611	91%	147	0.4
University of Maryland	604	84%	150	1.9
Medical University of South Carolina	601	92%	138	1.6
University of California–San Francisco	600	95%	141	2.7
University of Tennessee Health Science Center	600	97%	150	1.2
Washington University in St. Louis	593	7%	123	2.5
University of Pittsburgh	584	29%	148	3.0
University of Oklahoma	582	96%	152	1.3
University of Arkansas for Medical Sciences	581	98%	150	1.7
University of Virginia	563	70%	141	1.6
University of Iowa (Carver)	562	71%	142	1.5
University at Buffalo–SUNY	561	100%	136	0.8
University of Colorado–Denver and Health Sciences Center	561	92%	143	2.7
Loyola University Chicago (Stritch)	552	46%	140	1.2
Albany Medical College (NY)	538	47%	N/A	N/A
Texas Tech University Health Sciences Center	538	94%	140	0.9
Touro University College of Osteopathic Medicine (CA)	526	N/A	135	0.1
U. of North Texas Health Sci. Center (Texas Col. of Osteopathic Medicine)	520	95%	135	0.6
Rush University (IL)	511	83%	128	0.9
University of California–San Diego	503	97%	122	1.6
University of New England College of Osteopathic Medicine (ME)	500	19%	121	0.2
University of Florida	491	97%	131	2.2
Oregon Health and Science University	489	52%	112	3.0
Creighton University (NE)	485	13%	125	0.6
Stanford University (CA)	476	43%	86	1.5
University of Nebraska College of Medicine	476	87%	122	1.2
Edward Via Virginia College of Osteopathic Medicine	470	36%	160	0.1
Mount Sinai School of Medicine (NY)	470	45%	120	2.5
Johns Hopkins University (MD)	464	23%	121	4.7
Emory University (GA)	462	33%	114	3.8
Northeastern Ohio Universities College of Medicine	461	94%	120	0.6
University of Arizona	461	99%	110	1.8
University of South Florida	458	99%	120	1.1
Michigan State University	454	78%	106	0.7
Howard University (DC)	448	6%	116	0.5
Stony Brook University (NY)	447	98%	101	1.1
Yale University (CT)	441	12%	100	2.3

	Total enrollment	% in-state enrollment	Size of first-year class	Faculty-to-student ratio
Eastern Virginia Medical School	436	65%	110	0.7
Vanderbilt University (TN)	436	30%	105	3.7
Wake Forest University (NC)	431	36%	108	2.0
Ohio University	430	97%	108	0.2
West Virginia University	424	75%	98	1.4
University of Chicago (Pritzker)	416	35%	104	1.9
University of Massachusetts–Worcester	412	99%	102	2.3
Cornell University (Weill) (NY)	410	50%	101	4.9
University of Vermont	410	32%	102	1.2
University of Rochester (NY)	408	41%	100	3.2
Duke University (NC)	406	17%	101	4.2
University of California–Davis	404	100%	91	1.4
University of Kentucky	400	92%	103	1.6
University of Utah	398	76%	102	2.4
West Virginia School of Osteopathic Medicine	397	55%	104	0.1
University of California–Irvine	388	100%	103	1.2
Wright State University (OH)	386	96%	100	0.9
UMDNJ–School of Osteopathic Medicine	382	99%	100	0.4
University of Missouri–Columbia	368	98%	96	1.2
Oklahoma State University Center for Health Sciences	352	89%	88	0.2
Brown University (RI)	345	16%	73	2.0
University of New Mexico	325	98%	75	2.0
University of South Carolina	319	94%	80	0.7
University of Connecticut	313	58%	79	1.4
Texas A&M University System Health Science Center	299	92%	81	2.4
Dartmouth Medical School (NH)	296	8%	82	2.7
Southern Illinois University–Springfield	291	100%	72	1.0
East Carolina University (Brody) (NC)	286	100%	72	1.4
Pikeville College School of Osteopathic Medicine (KY)	284	45%	80	0.1
Mercer University (GA)	242	100%	60	N/A
East Tennessee State University (Quillen)	238	94%	60	1.1
University of North Dakota	236	85%	61	0.7
Florida State University	220	100%	80	0.4
University of South Dakota	206	96%	50	1.2
Morehouse School of Medicine (GA)	196	51%	52	1.1
Mayo Medical School (MN)	166	23%	43	13.6

Which get the most research money? Which get the least?

How much research does the school support? One prime indicator is the amount of grant money the medical school and its affiliated hospitals are awarded by the National Institutes of Health, the federal research department devoted to medicine. Institutions with an asterisk have received grants to the medical school only.

	Amount of NIH grants in 2005, in millions	Number of NIH grants in 2005	Number of principal investigators associated with NIH-funded grants	Number of full-time faculty associated with NIH research grants
Harvard University (MA)	$1,171.0	2,818	1,964	3,932
University of Washington	$538.8	1,082	704	1,073
University of Pennsylvania	$500.8	1,088	747	1,063
Johns Hopkins University (MD)	$475.4	1,032	684	1,501
Baylor College of Medicine (TX)	$454.2	1,073	714	1,894
University of California–Los Angeles (Geffen)	$426.8	1,178	712	1,944
University of California–San Francisco	$422.9	941	633	845
Washington University in St. Louis	$358.9	759	489	878
Duke University*	$330.8	713	441	524
University of Pittsburgh	$330.0	846	522	637
University of Michigan–Ann Arbor	$315.2	771	532	1,499
Yale University (CT)	$300.7	839	598	1,083
Columbia University College of Physicians and Surgeons (NY)	$300.3	723	722	781
Cornell University (Weill) (NY)	$286.2	810	380	518
University of California–San Diego	$273.7	578	318	461
Vanderbilt University (TN)	$249.3	690	366	772
Stanford University*	$244.5	609	324	365
Case Western Reserve University (OH)	$240.2	618	435	652
Ohio State University	$227.1	759	461	844
University of Colorado–Denver and Health Sciences Center	$223.1	683	365	N/A
University of North Carolina–Chapel Hill	$212.3	565	327	420
Northwestern University (Feinberg) (IL)	$205.9	663	366	455
Yeshiva University (Einstein) (NY)	$203.8	438	289	464
Mayo Medical School (MN)	$201.8	436	277	651
University of Alabama–Birmingham*	$193.4	N/A	N/A	N/A
University of Chicago (Pritzker)	$197.8	596	311	445
Boston University	$196.4	584	341	698
University of Cincinnati	$190.2	710	394	N/A
Oregon Health and Science University	$188.5	628	414	635
University of Texas Southwestern Medical Center–Dallas	$187.9	581	331	880
Emory University (GA)	$187.1	544	327	765
University of Wisconsin–Madison	$182.8	545	311	436
Mount Sinai School of Medicine*	$174.1	494	291	600
University of Maryland*	$159.8	441	239	504
University of Southern California (Keck)	$159.0	288	201	N/A
Georgetown University (DC)	$158.8	455	257	392
University of Minnesota Medical School	$148.4	458	278	278
University of Virginia*	$146.2	430	230	662
University of Iowa (Carver)	$145.9	355	233	233
University of Rochester (NY)	$140.6	370	283	402
New York University	$138.8	373	255	733
Wake Forest University*	$128.2	273	200	246
University of Massachusetts–Worcester*	$121.0	416	209	225
Dartmouth Medical School (NH)	$109.4	386	217	230
Brown University (RI)	$103.8	298	205	252
Indiana University–Indianapolis*	$101.1	295	206	380

	Amount of NIH grants in 2005, in millions	Number of NIH grants in 2005	Number of principal investigators associated with NIH-funded grants	Number of full-time faculty associated with NIH research grants
University of Utah	$101.7	255	175	N/A
University of Texas Medical Branch–Galveston	$100.8	253	253	242
Jefferson Medical College (PA)	$95.4	330	168	282
Medical College of Wisconsin*	$87.3	233	177	N/A
Tufts University (MA)	$85.9	264	117	209
Medical University of South Carolina	$85.2	280	190	315
University of Illinois–Chicago	$84.4	384	188	468
University of Florida	$82.7	363	218	249
University of Miami (Miller) (FL)	$82.5	233	149	428
University of California–Irvine	$82.2	371	147	385
Stony Brook University (NY)	$75.3	329	177	212
Tulane University (LA)	$73.3	N/A	N/A	N/A
University of California–Davis	$72.8	272	158	316
University of Connecticut*	$70.0	N/A	150	N/A
University at Buffalo–SUNY	$68.0	227	140	188
University of Arizona*	$66.6	173	118	393
Virginia Commonwealth University*	$65.1	215	119	345
University of South Florida	$63.8	121	81	N/A
University of Kentucky*	$63.3	199	127	N/A
University of Vermont*	$62.6	148	98	200
UMDNJ-New Jersey Medical School	$54.6	114	84	172
University of Arkansas for Medical Sciences	$52.7	162	110	133
University of Texas Health Science Center–Houston	$52.4	157	105	N/A
UMDNJ-Robert Wood Johnson Medical School	$52.3	217	128	256
University of Kansas Medical Center*	$44.6	110	79	64
Medical College of Georgia	$42.8	171	115	146
St. Louis University	$40.4	132	83	136
University of New Mexico	$40.1	101	71	N/A
George Washington University (DC)	$38.1	101	65	284
Rush University (IL)	$37.8	69	55	142
University of Oklahoma	$37.0	92	67	132
Morehouse School of Medicine (GA)	$36.7	42	37	124
University of Nebraska College of Medicine	$33.0	93	67	136
Uniformed Services University of the Health Sciences (Hebert)*	$28.6	63	57	57
Rosalind Franklin University of Medicine and Science (IL)	$26.7	40	27	27
Temple University (PA)	$26.0	93	58	77
Drexel University*	$23.1	69	68	73
Loyola University Chicago (Stritch)	$22.1	87	74	103
New York Medical College	$21.7	63	42	N/A
SUNY–Syracuse	$18.9	87	58	58
Michigan State University*	$17.5	64	39	N/A
Medical University of Ohio	$16.5	77	43	93
Howard University (DC)	$15.6	38	38	26
West Virginia University	$15.5	49	40	90
University of Missouri–Columbia	$15.3	52	37	46
U. of North Texas Health Sci. Center (Texas Col. of Osteopathic Medicine)	$12.9	50	30	64
University of South Dakota	$11.8	17	14	34
Creighton University (NE)	$11.5	65	35	54
Texas A&M University System Health Science Center	$11.5	51	42	42
Wright State University*	$11.2	34	23	35
University of North Dakota*	$8.8	18	12	26
University of South Carolina	$7.6	44	41	59
Michigan State University College of Osteopathic Medicine	$7.5	31	28	52
Eastern Virginia Medical School	$6.8	41	26	30
Florida State University	$4.9	9	6	6

Which get the most research money? Which get the least?

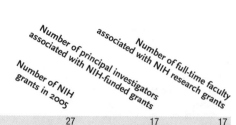

	Amount of NIH grants in 2005, in millions	Number of NIH grants in 2005	Number of principal investigators associated with NIH-funded grants	Number of full-time faculty associated with NIH research grants
Southern Illinois University–Springfield*	$4.8	27	17	17
UMDNJ–School of Osteopathic Medicine	$4.6	17	15	18
Texas Tech University Health Sciences Center	$4.4	17	12	14
East Carolina University (Brody) (NC)	$3.4	19	18	32
East Tennessee State University (Quillen)*	$3.3	18	17	28
Northeastern Ohio Universities College of Medicine	$2.4	10	7	7
Nova Southeastern University College of Osteopathic Medicine (FL)	$1.7	5	1	3
Edward Via Virginia College of Osteopathic Medicine	$.9	11	7	2
Oklahoma State University Center for Health Sciences	$.5	5	5	5
Philadelphia College of Osteopathic Medicine	$.4	4	4	4
University of New England College of Osteopathic Medicine*	$.3	2	2	3
A.T. Still University of Health Sciences (Kirksville) (MO)	$.2	1	3	4
College of Osteopathic Medicine of the Pacific (Western University) (CA)	$.1	1	1	1
Des Moines University Osteopathic Medical Center*	$.0	0	2	

Whose graduates have the most debt? The least?

How much should you expect to borrow? On average, medical school grads who need to take out loans start their residencies with debt of $100,000—and that's not counting any college loans. This table shows the average amount of debt incurred by borrowers in the Class of 2005, from highest to lowest.

	Average medical school debt		Average medical school debt
Touro University College of Osteopathic Medicine (CA)	$182,000	University of Minnesota Medical School	$119,868
Rosalind Franklin University of Medicine and Science (IL)	$174,932	University of Cincinnati	$119,355
Philadelphia College of Osteopathic Medicine	$172,491	Medical College of Wisconsin	$119,340
Nova Southeastern Univ. Col. of Osteopathic Medicine (FL)	$165,110	University of Maryland	$118,700
Univ. of New England College of Osteopathic Medicine (ME)	$164,516	University of Oklahoma	$118,000
New York Medical College	$163,000	Texas Tech University Health Sciences Center	$117,482
Drexel University (PA)	$160,488	Morehouse School of Medicine (GA)	$116,518
Tufts University (MA)	$158,336	Virginia Commonwealth University	$115,314
New York College of Osteopathic Medicine	$158,000	Emory University (GA)	$114,078
College of Osteopathic Medicine of the Pacific (CA)	$154,572	SUNY–Syracuse	$113,231
West Virginia School of Osteopathic Medicine	$148,147	Wayne State University (MI)	$113,000
Des Moines University Osteopathic Medical Center (IA)	$146,689	University of Michigan–Ann Arbor	$110,738
University of Southern California (Keck)	$146,300	Indiana University–Indianapolis	$110,723
University of Chicago (Pritzker)	$144,900	Southern Illinois University–Springfield	$109,255
A.T. Still University of Health Sciences (Kirksville) (MO)	$144,801	Ohio State University	$109,139
Creighton University (NE)	$144,229	East Tennessee State University (Quillen)	$109,000
Michigan State University College of Osteopathic Medicine	$141,850	Medical University of South Carolina	$108,952
Boston University	$141,681	University of Missouri–Columbia	$108,805
Mercer University (GA)	$141,006	University of North Dakota	$108,710
Jefferson Medical College (PA)	$140,916	University of Colorado–Denver and Health Sciences Center	$105,755
Temple University (PA)	$140,266	University of South Dakota	$104,497
Lake Erie College of Osteopathic Medicine (PA)	$140,000	UMDNJ–School of Osteopathic Medicine	$104,005
University of Miami (Miller) (FL)	$139,100	UMDNJ–Robert Wood Johnson Medical School	$103,897
Albany Medical College (NY)	$138,897	Vanderbilt University (TN)	$103,200
Rush University (IL)	$136,663	University of Tennessee Health Science Center	$103,193
George Washington University (DC)	$136,500	UMDNJ–New Jersey Medical School	$103,118
Michigan State University	$136,461	Harvard University (MA)	$102,625
Oklahoma State University Center for Health Sciences	$136,000	University of Pennsylvania	$101,318
Loyola University Chicago (Stritch)	$134,929	Columbia University College of Physicians and Surgeons (NY)	$100,970
Georgetown University (DC)	$134,482	University of Nebraska College of Medicine	$100,875
University at Buffalo–SUNY	$134,121	University of South Florida	$100,823
Northwestern University (Feinberg) (IL)	$132,346	University of Iowa (Carver)	$99,812
University of Vermont	$131,945	University of Arkansas for Medical Sciences	$98,582
University of Wisconsin–Madison	$130,000	University of Texas Medical Branch–Galveston	$98,517
University of Rochester (NY)	$129,342	Northeastern Ohio Universities College of Medicine	$98,494
Pikeville College School of Osteopathic Medicine (KY)	$128,000	University of Texas Health Science Center–Houston	$98,345
Wake Forest University (NC)	$126,634	University of Illinois–Chicago	$97,556
Medical University of Ohio	$125,473	University of Kentucky	$97,171
Ohio University	$124,795	University of Alabama–Birmingham	$96,786
Oregon Health and Science University	$124,486	New York University	$95,935
University of Pittsburgh	$123,256	Johns Hopkins University (MD)	$95,919
Case Western Reserve University (OH)	$123,100	West Virginia University	$95,308
Howard University (DC)	$120,829	Yeshiva University (Einstein) (NY)	$95,000
Stony Brook University (NY)	$120,300	Yale University (CT)	$94,568

Whose graduates have the most debt? The least?

	Average medical school debt
U. of N. Texas Health Sci. Center (TX Col. of Osteopathic Med)	$93,207
Texas A&M University System Health Science Center	$93,152
University of New Mexico	$92,687
Washington University in St. Louis	$92,501
University of Massachusetts–Worcester	$92,069
Mount Sinai School of Medicine (NY)	$91,460
Brown University (RI)	$91,174
Cornell University (Weill) (NY)	$91,048
University of Kansas Medical Center	$89,949
Dartmouth Medical School (NH)	$86,500
University of South Carolina	$86,311
University of California–Los Angeles (Geffen)	$86,122
University of Washington	$85,953
University of Arizona	$85,706
University of Connecticut	$79,000
University of Virginia	$78,790

	Average medical school debt
University of California–San Francisco	$76,573
University of Florida	$75,975
University of Texas Southwestern Medical Center–Dallas	$75,400
Duke University (NC)	$74,790
University of North Carolina–Chapel Hill	$74,605
University of California–Davis	$69,345
University of California–Irvine	$69,000
Baylor College of Medicine (TX)	$67,679
University of California–San Diego	$66,642
Mayo Medical School (MN)	$65,772
University of Utah	$65,386
Medical College of Georgia	$63,907
East Carolina University (Brody) (NC)	$63,793
Stanford University (CA)	$61,566
Uniformed Services University of the Health Sciences (MD)	$0

Which schools have the most minority students? The fewest?

If you're looking for a medical school culture that is welcoming to students from a wealth of backgrounds, one way to judge is by the percentage of minority students already there.

	% minority	American Indian	Asian-American	Black	Hispanic	White	International	Men	Women
Howard University (DC)	96%	0.0%	8.7%	74.8%	2.0%	3.8%	10.7%	46%	54%
Morehouse School of Medicine (GA)	86%	0.0%	14.8%	69.4%	2.0%	13.3%	0.5%	36%	64%
University of California–Los Angeles (Geffen)	64%	0.4%	38.0%	8.8%	15.9%	32.8%	1.0%	47%	53%
UMDNJ-New Jersey Medical School	58%	0.1%	30.3%	13.4%	14.3%	40.4%	0.0%	51%	49%
University of California–Davis	55%	1.7%	40.1%	3.5%	9.7%	44.8%	0.2%	46%	54%
Baylor College of Medicine (TX)	54%	1.6%	33.9%	8.7%	9.9%	45.4%	0.4%	52%	48%
UMDNJ-Robert Wood Johnson Medical School	54%	0.2%	34.3%	12.9%	5.3%	46.4%	0.0%	47%	53%
Stanford University (CA)	53%	1.5%	31.3%	5.0%	15.1%	42.9%	4.2%	51%	49%
University of Illinois–Chicago	53%	N/A	N/A	N/A	N/A	N/A	N/A	52%	48%
UMDNJ–School of Osteopathic Medicine	53%	0.3%	23.8%	21.7%	6.5%	47.4%	0.3%	43%	57%
Stony Brook University (NY)	51%	0.9%	37.1%	9.2%	4.0%	48.3%	0.4%	47%	53%
Northwestern University (Feinberg) (IL)	51%	1.2%	39.5%	5.0%	5.5%	42.3%	3.7%	51%	49%
Rosalind Franklin University of Medicine and Science (IL)	50%	0.3%	43.8%	4.8%	1.5%	47.1%	2.2%	55%	45%
University at Buffalo–SUNY	50%	0.4%	25.7%	5.9%	1.6%	66.5%	0.0%	45%	55%
University of California–San Diego	49%	1.0%	38.6%	2.0%	7.8%	37.4%	0.0%	51%	49%
Boston University	49%	0.5%	32.9%	8.2%	7.6%	46.8%	2.8%	47%	53%
University of California–San Francisco	49%	1.3%	32.5%	4.3%	11.8%	48.8%	0.2%	44%	57%
Harvard University (MA)	48%	1.6%	26.4%	12.3%	8.1%	45.9%	4.3%	50%	50%
Brown University (RI)	48%	0.3%	26.4%	12.5%	6.1%	51.0%	3.8%	42%	58%
University of Michigan–Ann Arbor	47%	1.2%	29.9%	10.3%	5.4%	51.5%	0.0%	55%	45%
Johns Hopkins University (MD)	46%	0.4%	32.1%	9.7%	4.1%	52.6%	1.1%	50%	50%
College of Osteopathic Medicine of the Pacific (Western University) (CA)	46%	0.6%	39.8%	1.2%	4.6%	46.4%	1.5%	50%	50%
University of Southern California (Keck)	45%	0.2%	32.6%	3.5%	9.2%	49.3%	1.5%	51%	49%
New York College of Osteopathic Medicine	45%	0.2%	26.4%	9.2%	7.1%	55.6%	0.1%	46%	54%
Cornell University (Weill) (NY)	44%	0.7%	24.4%	12.0%	6.6%	55.1%	0.7%	50%	50%
Drexel University (PA)	44%	0.8%	35.8%	4.1%	3.6%	50.5%	0.2%	50%	50%
New York Medical College	44%	0.1%	39.2%	3.0%	1.6%	53.3%	0.4%	50%	50%
Rush University (IL)	44%	1.2%	35.8%	3.1%	1.6%	56.6%	0.0%	45%	55%
Mount Sinai School of Medicine (NY)	44%	1.1%	22.3%	6.0%	14.3%	53.4%	1.5%	47%	53%
University of Texas Southwestern Medical Center–Dallas	43%	0.3%	26.3%	5.9%	10.6%	51.5%	0.8%	56%	44%
University of California–Irvine	43%	0.3%	31.7%	1.5%	9.5%	53.6%	0.0%	52%	48%
University of Miami (Miller) (FL)	43%	0.6%	22.0%	6.2%	14.0%	56.5%	0.3%	51%	49%
University of Texas Medical Branch–Galveston	43%	0.5%	17.5%	9.5%	15.4%	51.3%	0.7%	50%	50%
Tufts University (MA)	43%	0.3%	31.7%	5.0%	5.8%	54.3%	0.7%	54%	46%
Florida State University	43%	0.9%	13.6%	12.7%	14.5%	57.3%	0.0%	43%	57%
Duke University (NC)	42%	1.7%	20.0%	14.0%	3.0%	50.7%	7.4%	52%	48%
University of New Mexico	40%	4.0%	7.4%	0.6%	28.0%	59.7%	0.0%	43%	57%
Northeastern Ohio Universities College of Medicine	40%	0.7%	34.1%	3.9%	1.1%	59.7%	0.0%	50%	50%
Texas Tech University Health Sciences Center	40%	0.4%	25.1%	3.0%	11.2%	57.8%	0.4%	57%	43%
George Washington University (DC)	39%	0.7%	22.5%	8.2%	2.6%	59.1%	1.0%	48%	52%
University of Pittsburgh	39%	0.0%	26.7%	9.6%	2.6%	61.1%	0.0%	53%	47%
Temple University (PA)	38%	0.1%	22.8%	8.8%	6.1%	61.7%	0.0%	54%	46%
Texas A&M University System Health Science Center	38%	0.7%	21.7%	4.7%	10.7%	57.9%	1.7%	49%	51%
Columbia University College of Physicians and Surgeons (NY)	37%	0.6%	19.7%	8.5%	6.5%	58.0%	3.5%	53%	47%
University of South Florida	37%	2.0%	18.1%	7.0%	9.6%	63.1%	0.0%	47%	53%
U. of North Texas Health Sci. Center (Texas Col. of Osteopathic Medicine)	37%	0.8%	26.3%	1.9%	7.7%	62.5%	0.6%	47%	53%
University of Pennsylvania	36%	0.6%	18.8%	9.1%	7.3%	63.7%	0.5%	50%	50%

Which schools have the most minority students? The fewest?

	% minority	American Indian	Asian	Black	Hispanic	White	International	Men	Women
Michigan State University	36%	0.9%	15.4%	10.4%	9.0%	63.4%	0.9%	43%	57%
New York University	36%	0.1%	25.2%	5.4%	5.0%	54.1%	1.0%	50%	50%
Albany Medical College (NY)	36%	0.6%	29.2%	3.9%	2.0%	61.3%	3.0%	46%	54%
Yale University (CT)	36%	0.9%	21.1%	7.3%	6.3%	54.9%	6.8%	45%	55%
University of Maryland	36%	0.0%	21.2%	12.7%	1.7%	59.8%	1.2%	40%	60%
Case Western Reserve University (OH)	35%	0.2%	22.8%	10.9%	1.6%	58.8%	2.9%	54%	46%
University of Chicago (Pritzker)	34%	0.2%	20.4%	8.2%	5.0%	62.5%	3.4%	49%	51%
University of Florida	34%	0.6%	18.5%	6.3%	8.4%	65.0%	0.0%	47%	53%
Washington University in St. Louis	34%	0.7%	26.1%	4.7%	2.2%	58.7%	4.4%	53%	47%
University of Connecticut	34%	0.6%	12.5%	14.1%	3.8%	65.2%	2.6%	37%	63%
East Carolina University (Brody) (NC)	33%	3.5%	6.6%	15.4%	2.8%	70.3%	0.0%	51%	49%
Ohio State University	32%	1.1%	21.7%	6.2%	2.5%	66.9%	1.0%	63%	37%
Mayo Medical School (MN)	32%	1.8%	15.1%	10.2%	4.8%	68.1%	0.0%	49%	51%
Nova Southeastern University College of Osteopathic Medicine (FL)	32%	0.7%	13.8%	3.8%	13.3%	62.0%	N/A	50%	50%
University of Rochester (NY)	31%	0.0%	20.6%	7.6%	2.9%	66.7%	0.0%	45%	55%
Wake Forest University (NC)	30%	1.2%	14.2%	11.4%	3.7%	64.5%	5.1%	56%	44%
Wayne State University (MI)	30%	0.2%	16.1%	12.9%	0.8%	65.9%	2.1%	52%	48%
Vanderbilt University (TN)	30%	0.2%	17.9%	7.6%	1.6%	67.4%	4.1%	53%	47%
University of North Carolina–Chapel Hill	29%	N/A	N/A	N/A	N/A	N/A	N/A	48%	52%
Yeshiva University (Einstein) (NY)	29%	0.3%	24.2%	7.4%	3.7%	56.4%	1.6%	47%	53%
Emory University (GA)	29%	0.6%	16.0%	10.0%	1.5%	66.5%	1.9%	52%	48%
University of Arizona	29%	2.8%	14.1%	1.5%	10.2%	71.4%	0.0%	50%	50%
SUNY–Syracuse	29%	0.7%	22.0%	5.5%	0.5%	68.1%	3.3%	52%	48%
University of Virginia	28%	N/A	N/A	N/A	N/A	N/A	N/A	49%	51%
University of Cincinnati	28%	0.0%	18.6%	8.4%	0.3%	72.7%	N/A	56%	44%
Virginia Commonwealth University	28%	0.3%	28.0%	6.6%	0.1%	58.2%	0.0%	52%	48%
Medical College of Georgia	28%	0.3%	17.2%	8.6%	1.1%	72.4%	0.0%	56%	44%
University of Texas Health Science Center–Houston	27%	0.2%	11.6%	2.9%	12.7%	69.9%	0.2%	52%	48%
St. Louis University	26%	0.2%	19.9%	3.7%	1.8%	60.1%	1.8%	56%	44%
Southern Illinois University–Springfield	25%	1.4%	10.3%	10.7%	3.1%	74.6%	0.0%	48%	52%
Georgetown University (DC)	25%	0.1%	17.4%	6.1%	1.7%	71.4%	1.7%	48%	52%
Jefferson Medical College (PA)	25%	0.4%	20.4%	1.8%	3.1%	72.0%	2.2%	51%	49%
Ohio University	24%	0.7%	8.6%	10.7%	4.4%	75.6%	0.0%	45%	55%
Chicago College of Osteopathic Medicine	24%	N/A	N/A	N/A	N/A	N/A	N/A	47%	53%
University of Washington	24%	1.6%	15.2%	2.2%	5.1%	73.6%	0.0%	48%	52%
University of Oklahoma	24%	7.2%	14.6%	1.4%	0.7%	73.9%	0.0%	61%	39%
University of Tennessee Health Science Center	23%	0.5%	12.0%	9.3%	1.3%	75.0%	0.0%	62%	38%
Lake Erie College of Osteopathic Medicine (PA)	22%	0.3%	15.8%	2.3%	3.9%	77.5%	0.1%	54%	46%
Oklahoma State University Center for Health Sciences	22%	11.6%	4.8%	4.3%	1.4%	76.4%	0.0%	53%	47%
University of Alabama–Birmingham	22%	1.2%	12.9%	6.7%	0.9%	77.9%	N/A	59%	41%
Wright State University (OH)	22%	0.5%	13.2%	8.8%	2.6%	74.4%	0.0%	45%	55%
Indiana University–Indianapolis	22%	0.8%	10.6%	6.2%	3.0%	77.4%	1.4%	54%	46%
Medical College of Wisconsin	22%	1.4%	14.4%	2.8%	3.2%	75.2%	1.0%	56%	44%
Medical University of South Carolina	21%	0.5%	7.7%	9.3%	2.7%	77.4%	1.2%	53%	47%
Medical University of Ohio	21%	1.0%	16.9%	1.5%	2.0%	76.1%	0.8%	61%	39%
Loyola University Chicago (Stritch)	21%	0.9%	14.6%	2.9%	2.4%	78.5%	0.0%	50%	50%
Dartmouth Medical School (NH)	21%	0.7%	13.2%	3.4%	3.4%	73.0%	4.7%	51%	49%
University of Kansas Medical Center	21%	1.3%	10.6%	5.9%	2.8%	69.1%	0.0%	55%	45%
Edward Via Virginia College of Osteopathic Medicine	20%	0.4%	10.4%	7.0%	3.5%	74.8%	0.4%	51%	49%
University of Massachusetts–Worcester	20%	1.0%	14.6%	3.2%	1.7%	79.4%	0.0%	45%	55%
University of Minnesota Medical School	20%	2.8%	11.8%	1.9%	2.2%	79.3%	1.9%	50%	50%

	% minority	American Indian	Asian	Black	Hispanic	White	International	Men	Women
Philadelphia College of Osteopathic Medicine	20%	0.2%	11.0%	5.9%	3.0%	76.4%	0.8%	47%	53%
Uniformed Services University of the Health Sciences (Hebert) (MD)	20%	1.1%	15.0%	3.0%	0.3%	74.7%	0.0%	69%	31%
University of Wisconsin–Madison	20%	0.5%	7.9%	4.0%	4.2%	82.6%	0.0%	47%	53%
Eastern Virginia Medical School	19%	N/A	N/A	N/A	N/A	N/A	N/A	47%	53%
University of Colorado–Denver and Health Sciences Center	19%	0.9%	8.2%	2.9%	7.1%	80.9%	0.0%	52%	48%
University of Iowa (Carver)	19%	0.7%	6.8%	3.6%	7.8%	76.2%	0.0%	53%	47%
Creighton University (NE)	18%	2.1%	6.8%	3.5%	5.2%	82.5%	N/A	53%	47%
University of Vermont	17%	0.2%	15.1%	0.5%	0.7%	78.5%	0.7%	38%	62%
University of South Carolina	17%	0.3%	10.7%	6.0%	0.0%	82.8%	0.0%	52%	48%
University of Missouri–Columbia	16%	0.0%	7.3%	5.7%	1.4%	85.6%	0.0%	52%	48%
Michigan State University College of Osteopathic Medicine	16%	0.6%	12.3%	2.1%	1.1%	83.8%	0.0%	48%	52%
East Tennessee State University (Quillen)	16%	2.5%	6.7%	6.3%	0.4%	84.0%	0.0%	50%	50%
University of Kentucky	15%	0.0%	8.3%	4.8%	0.5%	83.3%	2.3%	57%	43%
University of Utah	15%	0.5%	6.5%	1.8%	1.8%	84.2%	4.0%	62%	38%
A.T. Still University of Health Sciences (Kirksville) (MO)	14%	0.6%	12.7%	0.6%	1.8%	79.9%	1.6%	60%	40%
Mercer University (GA)	14%	0.4%	9.9%	3.3%	0.4%	86.0%	0.0%	52%	48%
University of Arkansas for Medical Sciences	12%	1.4%	7.9%	5.9%	0.2%	84.7%	0.0%	58%	42%
Oregon Health and Science University	12%	1.6%	13.3%	1.4%	2.0%	81.6%	0.0%	44%	56%
University of North Dakota	11%	8.9%	1.7%	N/A	0.8%	88.6%	N/A	48%	52%
West Virginia School of Osteopathic Medicine	11%	0.5%	8.3%	0.5%	1.3%	88.7%	0.0%	53%	47%
West Virginia University	11%	0.0%	9.7%	0.7%	1.9%	87.7%	0.0%	61%	39%
Des Moines University Osteopathic Medical Center (IA)	11%	0.5%	6.8%	1.1%	2.1%	84.9%	1.3%	52%	48%
University of New England College of Osteopathic Medicine (ME)	10%	0.2%	7.8%	1.0%	1.0%	89.2%	0.8%	48%	52%
Pikeville College School of Osteopathic Medicine (KY)	10%	0.4%	5.6%	2.1%	2.5%	85.9%	0.0%	57%	43%
University of Nebraska College of Medicine	8%	0.6%	3.8%	2.1%	1.1%	91.8%	0.0%	59%	41%
University of South Dakota	5%	3.4%	1.9%	0.0%	0.0%	94.7%	0.0%	52%	48%

Which schools turn out the most primary care residents? The fewest?

If you are interested in family practice, general pediatrics, or general internal medicine, you probably want to consider schools that send most of their graduates on to primary care residency programs.

	Average % 2003-2005 graduates entering primary care residencies
West Virginia School of Osteopathic Medicine	87.3%
Michigan State University College of Osteopathic Medicine	85.8%
Pikeville College School of Osteopathic Medicine (KY)	78.0%
U. of N. Texas Health Sci. Center (TX Col. of Osteopathic Med.)	77.7%
Nova Southeastern Univ. College of Osteopathic Medicine (FL)	77.0%
Univ. of New England College of Osteopathic Medicine (ME)	67.2%
Oklahoma State University Center for Health Sciences	67.0%
East Carolina University (Brody) (NC)	62.0%
Lake Erie College of Osteopathic Medicine (PA)	61.0%
University of Nebraska College of Medicine	61.0%
Ohio University	58.0%
University of Massachusetts–Worcester	57.0%
University of Vermont	55.0%
Yeshiva University (Einstein) (NY)	55.0%
Drexel University (PA)	52.0%
Touro University College of Osteopathic Medicine (CA)	52.0%
University of Arkansas for Medical Sciences	52.0%
University of Missouri–Columbia	52.0%
East Tennessee State University (Quillen)	50.6%
University of Connecticut	50.3%
George Washington University (DC)	50.2%
SUNY–Syracuse	50.2%
Michigan State University	50.1%
Temple University (PA)	50.0%
Eastern Virginia Medical School	49.0%
Wake Forest University (NC)	49.0%
Loyola University Chicago (Stritch)	48.6%
University of North Carolina–Chapel Hill	48.0%
University of Minnesota Medical School	47.4%
University of Illinois–Chicago	47.3%
University of California–Davis	47.1%
University of Chicago (Pritzker)	47.0%
University of Maryland	47.0%
University of Oklahoma	46.8%
St. Louis University	46.6%
University of Wisconsin–Madison	46.6%
Des Moines University Osteopathic Medical Center (IA)	46.5%
Brown University (RI)	46.3%
University of Washington	46.0%
University of South Carolina	45.9%
A.T. Still University of Health Sciences (Kirksville) (MO)	45.7%
Baylor College of Medicine (TX)	45.6%
New York Medical College	45.4%
University of Kansas Medical Center	45.2%

	Average % 2003-2005 graduates entering primary care residencies
New York College of Osteopathic Medicine	45.0%
Rush University (IL)	45.0%
University of Florida	45.0%
University of Kentucky	45.0%
Wright State University (OH)	45.0%
University of Texas Medical Branch–Galveston	44.3%
Stony Brook University (NY)	44.1%
Medical College of Wisconsin	44.0%
Medical University of Ohio	44.0%
University of Texas Southwestern Medical Center–Dallas	44.0%
Case Western Reserve University (OH)	43.3%
Dartmouth Medical School (NH)	43.1%
Duke University (NC)	43.1%
University at Buffalo–SUNY	43.1%
University of Iowa (Carver)	43.1%
Ohio State University	43.0%
University of California–Irvine	43.0%
University of New Mexico	43.0%
University of Southern California (Keck)	43.0%
University of Colorado–Denver and Health Sciences Center	42.7%
Southern Illinois University–Springfield	42.5%
Medical College of Georgia	42.3%
Texas A&M University System Health Science Center	42.1%
Emory University (GA)	42.0%
Tufts University (MA)	42.0%
Virginia Commonwealth University	42.0%
University of California–San Diego	41.4%
Indiana University–Indianapolis	41.3%
University of South Florida	41.1%
Harvard University (MA)	41.0%
Oregon Health and Science University	41.0%
West Virginia University	41.0%
Jefferson Medical College (PA)	40.7%
Northwestern University (Feinberg) (IL)	40.5%
Cornell University (Weill) (NY)	40.4%
Medical University of South Carolina	40.0%
University of California–Los Angeles (Geffen)	39.7%
Georgetown University (DC)	39.1%
Creighton University (NE)	39.0%
University of Arizona	39.0%
University of Miami (Miller) (FL)	39.0%
UMDNJ-Robert Wood Johnson Medical School	38.9%
New York University	38.8%
Mount Sinai School of Medicine (NY)	38.2%

	Average % 2003-2005 graduates entering primary care residencies
University of Alabama–Birmingham	38.0%
Tulane University (LA)	37.9%
Florida State University	37.0%
Johns Hopkins University (MD)	37.0%
Philadelphia College of Osteopathic Medicine	37.0%
UMDNJ-New Jersey Medical School	37.0%
University of Pennsylvania	37.0%
University of Virginia	37.0%
University of Utah	36.3%
Texas Tech University Health Sciences Center	36.0%
University of Cincinnati	36.0%
University of Texas Health Science Center–Houston	35.3%
Howard University (DC)	35.0%
Uniformed Services University of the Health Sciences (MD)	35.0%
University of Pittsburgh	34.9%

	Average % 2003-2005 graduates entering primary care residencies
Boston University	34.7%
University of California–San Francisco	34.5%
Northeastern Ohio Universities College of Medicine	33.0%
Columbia University College of Physicians and Surgeons (NY)	32.7%
University of South Dakota	32.3%
Stanford University (CA)	32.1%
University of Rochester (NY)	32.1%
Mayo Medical School (MN)	32.0%
Vanderbilt University (TN)	31.0%
Yale University (CT)	30.2%
University of Tennessee Health Science Center	30.0%
Washington University in St. Louis	30.0%
University of Michigan–Ann Arbor	29.9%
University of North Dakota	28.0%

Which schools' grads are most likely to stay in state? The least likely?

If you want to stay close to where you study after you graduate, you may want to consider schools whose new doctors choose residencies in-state. Some states also offer incentives to graduates who stay and practice in underserved areas. Doctors in Massachusetts, for instance, can receive as much as $20,000 a year in debt payments if they work at least two years in a Massachusetts community health center.

School	Average % 2004-2005 graduates accepting in-state residencies
Michigan State University College of Osteopathic Medicine	90%
University of Southern California (Keck)	79%
Ohio University	77%
University of California–Irvine	75%
University of California–Los Angeles (Geffen)	75%
Mount Sinai School of Medicine (NY)	75%
University of California–San Diego	70%
Stony Brook University (NY)	69%
University of California–Davis	69%
New York College of Osteopathic Medicine	67%
University at Buffalo–SUNY	67%
University of California–San Francisco	64%
University of Texas Medical Branch–Galveston	63%
Stanford University (CA)	61%
Yeshiva University (Einstein) (NY)	60%
University of Texas Health Science Center–Houston	58%
U. of N. Texas Health Sci. Center (TX Col. of Osteopathic Med.)	58%
Oklahoma State University Center for Health Sciences	58%
University of Arkansas for Medical Sciences	57%
Rush University (IL)	56%
Texas A&M University System Health Science Center	54%
SUNY–Syracuse	53%
New York University	52%
University of Minnesota Medical School	52%
Philadelphia College of Osteopathic Medicine	52%
Texas Tech University Health Sciences Center	52%
Cornell University (Weill) (NY)	51%
Harvard University (MA)	51%
University of Massachusetts–Worcester	51%
Columbia University College of Physicians and Surgeons (NY)	50%
Baylor College of Medicine (TX)	50%
Northeastern Ohio Universities College of Medicine	50%
University of Texas Southwestern Medical Center–Dallas	50%
Indiana University–Indianapolis	49%
Ohio State University	49%
Florida State University	48%
University of Cincinnati	48%
University of Colorado–Denver and Health Sciences Center	47%
University of Illinois–Chicago	47%
Michigan State University	47%
University of South Florida	46%

School	Average % 2004-2005 graduates accepting in-state residencies
Temple University (PA)	46%
University of Alabama–Birmingham	46%
University of Arizona	45%
West Virginia University	45%
University of Missouri–Columbia	44%
University of South Carolina	44%
Jefferson Medical College (PA)	44%
Drexel University (PA)	43%
Loyola University Chicago (Stritch)	43%
Medical College of Georgia	43%
University of Chicago (Pritzker)	43%
University of Miami (Miller) (FL)	43%
University of Kansas Medical Center	43%
New York Medical College	43%
University of Kentucky	42%
East Carolina University (Brody) (NC)	41%
Johns Hopkins University (MD)	41%
University of Washington	41%
Virginia Commonwealth University	41%
University of Florida	41%
Touro University College of Osteopathic Medicine (CA)	40%
Wright State University (OH)	40%
University of Nebraska College of Medicine	39%
University of Tennessee Health Science Center	38%
University of Oklahoma	37%
East Tennessee State University (Quillen)	37%
Nova Southeastern University Col. of Osteopathic Medicine (FL)	37%
Mayo Medical School (MN)	36%
Medical University of Ohio	36%
University of New Mexico	36%
Washington University in St. Louis	36%
Case Western Reserve University (OH)	35%
Emory University (GA)	35%
Medical University of South Carolina	35%
Southern Illinois University–Springfield	35%
Northwestern University (Feinberg) (IL)	35%
Medical College of Wisconsin	34%
West Virginia School of Osteopathic Medicine	34%
University of Rochester (NY)	33%
University of Michigan–Ann Arbor	33%
University of Pittsburgh	33%

	Average % 2004-2005 graduates accepting in-state residencies
University of Wisconsin–Madison	32%
Eastern Virginia Medical School	31%
Lake Erie College of Osteopathic Medicine (PA)	31%
Oregon Health and Science University	31%
UMDNJ-New Jersey Medical School	31%
University of North Carolina–Chapel Hill	31%
University of Pennsylvania	31%
Boston University	30%
University of Iowa (Carver)	30%
Tufts University (MA)	30%
University of Connecticut	30%
University of Maryland	29%
UMDNJ-Robert Wood Johnson Medical School	26%
University of Virginia	26%
Wake Forest University (NC)	26%
University of Utah	26%
Vanderbilt University (TN)	25%

	Average % 2004-2005 graduates accepting in-state residencies
Yale University (CT)	25%
University of South Dakota	24%
Howard University (DC)	24%
St. Louis University	23%
Pikeville College School of Osteopathic Medicine (KY)	23%
University of Vermont	23%
Creighton University (NE)	22%
Georgetown University (DC)	22%
Duke University (NC)	20%
George Washington University (DC)	20%
University of North Dakota	19%
Des Moines University Osteopathic Medical Center (IA)	18%
University of New England College of Osteopathic Medicine (ME)	18%
Brown University (RI)	17%
A.T. Still University of Health Sciences (Kirksville) (MO)	15%
Dartmouth Medical School (NH)	8%

The U.S.News & World Report

Ultimate Medical School Directory

How to use the directory

In the following pages, you'll find in-depth profiles of medical schools fully accredited by the Liaison Committee on Medical Education, plus schools that offer the Doctor of Osteopathy degree accredited by the American Osteopathic Association. The schools are listed alphabetically in two sections: those conferring the M.D. degree, followed by schools of osteopathy.

The data were collected by *U.S. News* from the schools during late 2005 and early 2006. If a medical school did not supply the data requested, or if the data point does not apply to the school, you'll see an N/A, for "not available." Schools that did not return the *U.S. News* questionnaire are listed at the end of the directory.

You may also want to consult the online version of the directory at www.usnews.com, which allows you to do a customized search of our database.

Essential Stats

In addition to the medical school's address and the year the school was founded, you'll find the following key facts and figures here:

Tuition: for the 2005-2006 academic year.

Enrollment: full-time students during the 2005-2006 academic year.

Specialty ranking: the school's 2007 *U.S. News* ranking in various specialty areas, where applicable (the possible areas are women's health, geriatrics, internal medicine, AIDS, drug/alcohol abuse, rural medicine, pediatrics, and family medicine).

GPA and MCAT: The undergraduate grade point averages and Medical College Admission

Test (MCAT) scores shown are for the fall 2005 entering class. The MCAT score is the average of the scores on the verbal, physical sciences, and biological sciences portions of the test.

Acceptance rate: percentage of applicants accepted for the fall 2005 entering class.

***U.S. News* ranking:** A school's overall rank indicates where it sits among its peers in the 2007 ranking of medical schools published by *U.S. News* (at www.usnews.com) and in its annual guide *America's Best Graduate Schools*. Schools are ranked separately in research and primary care, and the schools in the top 60 are ranked numerically. Schools below the top 60 are listed as "unranked."

Admissions

Application website: Many medical schools allow you to complete and submit an application online.

Applicants and acceptees: The acceptance rates for the fall 2005 entering class are broken down by in-state, out-of-state, minority, and international students. The admissions statistics—numbers of applicants and of people interviewed and accepted—are also for the fall 2005 entering class.

Profile of admitted students: Besides the GPA and MCAT scores of fall 2005 entrants, we list the proportion majoring in biological sciences, physical sciences, non-sciences, other health professions, and other disciplines. The percentage who took time off between college and medical school is also shown.

Admission dates and details: We note whether the university uses the American Medical College Application Service (AMCAS), and whether it asks for a second, school-specific application form. Besides key deadlines for applicants to the 2007-2008 first-year class, you'll find information on whether the school has an Early Decision Plan (EDP), whether a personal interview is required for admission, whether admission can be deferred, and what undergraduate coursework is required.

Admissions policy: The text describing admissions policies was written by the schools. *U.S. News* edited the information for style but did not verify it.

Financial Aid

Tuition and other expenses: for the 2005-2006 academic year. For public schools, we list both in-state and out-of-state tuition.

Financial aid profile: The data on financial aid awards and the percentage of students receiving grants, loans, and scholarships are for the 2005-2006 academic year. The average debt burden of borrowers who graduated in 2004 does not include their undergraduate debt.

Student Body Stats

What will your classmates be like? This section supplies the breakdown of male and female students, the in-state enrollments, and the ethnic makeup of the student body during the 2005-2006 academic year (which may not add up to 100 percent due to rounding).

Academic Programs

Besides information on areas of specialization, you can look here for a sense of how early in your training you'll have contact with patients.

Joint degrees awarded: Some medical students pursue a second degree in another university department to marry their interests or gain an edge in the job market. One common joint degree, the M.D./M.B.A., combines medicine and business. Another, for those interested in research, is the M.D./Ph.D. degree. Other degree combos include the M.D. /J.D. (law) and the M.D./M.P.H. (public health).

Research profile: An indicator of how big a role research plays at the medical school is the amount of grant money the faculty brings in. We list the total amount of National Institutes of Health (NIH) grants awarded to the medical school and affiliated hospitals in fiscal 2005.

Curriculum

The text describing the curriculum was provided by the schools. *U.S. News* edited the text for style but did not verify the information.

Faculty Profile

Here, you'll find the number of full-time and part-time teaching faculty during fall 2005, as well as information on whether they teach in the basic sciences or in clinical programs. The full-time faculty/student ratio gives some indication of how accessible your professors are likely to be.

Support Services

How does the school help students deal with the pressure of medical school?

Residency Profile

This section provides data on the residency placements of graduates—the most popular residency and specialty programs chosen by the 2004 and 2005 graduates, plus the proportion of graduates who enter into primary care specialties (family practice, general pediatrics, or general internal medicine). The latter figures are three-year average percentages from 2003-2005 and the proportion of 2004-2005 graduates who accepted in-state residencies.

Albany Medical College

- 47 New Scotland Avenue, Albany, NY 12208
- Private
- Year Founded: 1839
- Tuition, 2005-2006: $39,637
- Enrollment 2005-2006 academic year: 538
- Website: http://www.amc.edu
- Specialty ranking: N/A

3.50 AVERAGE GPA, ENTERING CLASS FALL 2005

9.8 AVERAGE MCAT, ENTERING CLASS FALL 2005

N/A ACCEPTANCE RATE, ENTERING CLASS FALL 2005

Unranked 2007 U.S. NEWS MEDICAL SCHOOL RANKING (RESEARCH)

Unranked 2007 U.S. NEWS MEDICAL SCHOOL RANKING (PRIMARY CARE)

ADMISSIONS

Admissions phone number: **(518) 262-5521**
Admissions email address: **admissions@mail.amc.edu**
Application website: **N/A**
Acceptance rate: **N/A**
In-state acceptance rate: **N/A**
Out-of-state acceptance rate: **N/A**
Minority acceptance rate: **N/A**
International acceptance rate: **N/A**

Profile of admitted students

Average undergraduate grade point average: **3.50**
MCAT averages (scale: 1-15; writing test: J-T):
Composite score: **9.8**
Verbal reasoning score: **9.5**, Physical sciences score: **9.8**, Biological sciences score: **10.1**, Writing score: **N/A**
Proportion with undergraduate majors in: Biological sciences: **N/A**, Physical sciences: **N/A**, Non-sciences: **N/A**, Other health professions: **N/A**, Mixed disciplines and other: **N/A**
Percentage of students not coming directly from college after graduation: **N/A**

Dates and details

The American Medical College Application Service (AMCAS) application is accepted.
School asks for a school-specific application as part of the admissions process.
Oldest MCAT considered for Fall 2007 entry: **2003**
Earliest application date for the 2007-2008 first-year class: **June 1, 2006**
Latest application date: **November 15, 2006**

Acceptance dates for regular application for the class entering in fall 2007:
Earliest: **N/A**
Latest: **N/A**
The school N/A consider requests for deferred entrance.
Starting month for the class entering in 2007–2008: **N/A**
The school N/A have an Early Decision Plan (EDP).
A personal interview is required for admission.

Undergraduate coursework required

Medical school requires undergraduate work in these subjects: biology, organic chemistry, inorganic (general) chemistry, physics.

COSTS AND FINANCIAL AID

Financial aid phone number: **(518) 262-5435**
Tuition, 2005-2006 academic year: **$39,637**
Room and board: **N/A**
Percentage of students receiving financial aid in 2005-06: **86%**
Percentage of students receiving: Loans: **85%**, Grants/scholarships: **37%**, Work-study aid: **37%**
Average medical school debt for the Class of 2004: **$138,897**

STUDENT BODY

Fall 2005 full-time enrollment: **538**
Men: **46%**, Women: **54%**, In-state: **47%**, Minorities: **36%**, American Indian: **0.6%**, Asian-American: **29.2%**, African-American: **3.9%**, Hispanic-American: **2.0%**, White: **61.3%**, International: **3.0%**, Unknown: **0.0%**

Baylor College of Medicine

- One Baylor Plaza, Houston, TX 77030
- Private
- **Year Founded:** 1900
- **Tuition, 2005-2006:** $10,583
- **Enrollment 2005-2006 academic year:** 678
- **Website:** http://www.bcm.edu
- **Specialty ranking:** AIDS: 17, drug/alcohol abuse: 19, family medicine: 16, geriatrics: 20, internal medicine: 24, pediatrics: 5, women's health: 21

3.77 AVERAGE GPA, ENTERING CLASS FALL 2005

11.3 AVERAGE MCAT, ENTERING CLASS FALL 2005

6.7% ACCEPTANCE RATE, ENTERING CLASS FALL 2005

10 2007 U.S. NEWS MEDICAL SCHOOL RANKING (RESEARCH)

11 2007 U.S. NEWS MEDICAL SCHOOL RANKING (PRIMARY CARE)

ADMISSIONS

Admissions phone number: **(713) 798-4842**
Admissions email address: **admissions@bcm.tmc.edu**
Application website:
 http://public.bcm.edu/admissions/suppapp.htm
Acceptance rate: **6.7%**
In-state acceptance rate: **13.4%**
Out-of-state acceptance rate: **3.4%**
Minority acceptance rate: **7.8%**
International acceptance rate: **4.6%**

Fall 2005 applications and acceptees

	Applied	Interviewed	Accepted	Enrolled
Total:	4,285	664	285	168
In-state:	1,376	399	185	129
Out-of-state:	2,909	265	100	39

Profile of admitted students

Average undergraduate grade point average: **3.77**
MCAT averages (scale: 1-15; writing test: J-T):
 Composite score: **11.3**
 Verbal reasoning score: **10.8**, Physical sciences score: **11.6**, Biological sciences score: **11.6**, Writing score: **P**
Proportion with undergraduate majors in: Biological sciences: **43%**, Physical sciences: **28%**, Non-sciences: **17%**, Other health professions: **0%**, Mixed disciplines and other: **12%**
Percentage of students not coming directly from college after graduation: **8%**

Dates and details

The American Medical College Application Service (AMCAS) application is accepted.
School asks for a school-specific application as part of the admissions process.
Oldest MCAT considered for Fall 2007 entry: **2002**
Earliest application date for the 2007-2008 first-year class: **June 1, 2006**
Latest application date: **November 1, 2006**
Acceptance dates for regular application for the class entering in fall 2007:

Earliest: **October 15, 2006**
Latest: **June 1, 2007**
The school considers requests for deferred entrance.
Starting month for the class entering in 2007–2008: **July**
The school has an Early Decision Plan (EDP).
A personal interview is required for admission.

Undergraduate coursework required

Medical school requires undergraduate work in these subjects: biology, English, organic chemistry, inorganic (general) chemistry.

ADMISSIONS POLICY
(TEXT PROVIDED BY SCHOOL):

Baylor College of Medicine participates in the American Medical College Application Service. An application is available at the AMCAS website starting in May. Baylor also has a supplemental application.

Among the students enrolled in the class of 2005, 76 percent were Texas residents, 45 percent were women and 24 percent were underrepresented minority students. All entering students had completed work for the baccalaureate degree and five percent had obtained graduate degrees.

The student's record in premedical work offers the Admissions Committee a reasonable basis on which to estimate potential success with the medical school curriculum. The majority of applicants accepted have overall grade-point averages of 3.5 or higher (where 4.0 = A). An overall college GPA of less than B indicates a student might not be able to handle the work of medical school. In evaluating the academic records of applicants, attention is paid to course selection, academic challenge imposed by the student's curriculum, and the extent to which extracurricular activities and employment might have limited the student's opportunity for high academic achievement. Baylor does not require applicants to major in a scientific field.

All applicants offered places in the first-year class are interviewed personally at Baylor. The Admissions Committee invites for interviews those applicants it perceives to be competitive for admission.

Although high intellectual ability and a record of academic achievement are essential for success in the study of medicine, the Admissions Committee also looks for strong motivation for a career in medicine, human compassion, an abiding interest in the problems of people, leadership skills, the ability to communicate ideas effectively, and a high level of personal integrity. Additional criteria include socioeconomic background, being the first person in the immediate family to graduate from college, multilingual proficiency, responsibilities while attending secondary and/or undergraduate schools, community involvement, and geographic diversity.

COSTS AND FINANCIAL AID

Financial aid phone number: **(713) 798-4603**
Tuition, 2005-2006 academic year: **$10,583**
Room and board: **$18,172**
Percentage of students receiving financial aid in 2005-06: **77%**
Percentage of students receiving: Loans: **68%**, Grants/scholarships: **47%**, Work-study aid: **13%**
Average medical school debt for the Class of 2004: **$67,679**

STUDENT BODY

Fall 2005 full-time enrollment: **678**
Men: **52%**, Women: **48%**, In-state: **86%**, Minorities: **54%**, American Indian: **1.6%**, Asian-American: **33.9%**, African-American: **8.7%**, Hispanic-American: **9.9%**, White: **45.4%**, International: **0.4%**, Unknown: **0.0%**

ACADEMIC PROGRAMS

The school's curriculum very frequently gives first-year students substantial contact with patients.
There are opportunities for first- or second-year students to work in community health clinics.
Program offerings: AIDS, drug/alcohol abuse, family medicine, geriatrics, internal medicine, pediatrics, rural medicine, women's health
Joint degrees awarded: M.D./Ph.D., M.D./MBA, M.D./MPH, M.D./JD
Total National Institutes of Health (NIH) grants awarded to the medical school and affiliated hospitals: **$454.2 million**

CURRICULUM

(TEXT PROVIDED BY SCHOOL):
Baylor College of Medicine's curriculum is designed so that students acquire a solid foundation in the scientific concepts underlying medicine, a working knowledge of the core clinical sciences for resident training in any medical specialty, and the skills and attitudes required to be a competent and compassionate physician and lifelong learner. There is a high degree of coordination and integration between the basic and clinical sciences across a curriculum uniquely divided into 1.5 years of preclinical coursework and 2.5 years of highly individualized clinical experiences.

The preclinical curriculum consists of organ-systems-based modules. Baylor's unique approach sequences these modules so that students progressively cycle through the organ systems twice, with normal being emphasized in the first cycle and abnormal in the second. All didactic coursework occurs in the morning, protecting the afternoon for organized, small-group problem solving, skills practice and clinical applications, and independent study. Students benefit from early clinical training exposure, which includes biweekly afternoon preceptors in the offices of nearby community physicians.

The clinical curriculum consists of individually tailored sequences of core clerkships (medicine, pediatrics, obstetrics/gynecology, surgery, psychiatry, family and community medicine, and neurology), selectives (selection of required rotations primarily in the surgical subspecialties), and electives (from over 200 offerings). During the clinical curriculum, Baylor students work with residents, faculty, and community physicians in seven affiliated teaching hospitals and outpatient or ambulatory clinics.

Throughout the entire clinical curriculum, students are freed from rotation duties for one half day per week to participate in other required activities, including the Clinical Application of Biomedical Science course in the second year, the Longitudinal Ambulatory Care Experience course in the third year, and Mechanisms and Management of Disease in the fourth year.

Current and planned dual-degree programs are offered in collaboration with Rice University, the University of Houston, and the University of Texas at Houston.

FACULTY PROFILE (FALL 2005)

Total teaching faculty: **1,774 (full-time)**, **337 (part-time)**
Of full-time faculty, those teaching in basic sciences: **16%**; in clinical programs: **84%**
Of part-time faculty, those teaching in basic sciences: **5%**; in clinical programs: **95%**
Full-time faculty/student ratio: **2.6**

SUPPORT SERVICES

The school offers students these services for dealing with stress: expanded-hour gym access, peer counseling, professional counseling, support groups.

RESIDENCY PROFILE

Most popular residency and specialty programs chosen by the 2004 and 2005 M.D. graduating classes: anesthesiology, internal medicine, ophthalmology, orthopaedic surgery, otolaryngology, pediatrics, radiology–diagnostic, urology.

WHERE GRADS GO

45.6%
Proportion of 2003-2005 graduates who entered primary care specialties

50.2%
Proportion of 2004-2005 graduates who accepted in-state residencies

Boston University

- 715 Albany Street, L-103, Boston, MA 02118
- Private
- Year Founded: 1848
- Tuition, 2005-2006: $39,960
- Enrollment 2005-2006 academic year: 632
- Website: http://www.bumc.bu.edu
- Specialty ranking: drug/alcohol abuse: 13, geriatrics: 17, internal medicine: 25

3.65 AVERAGE GPA, ENTERING CLASS FALL 2005

10.7 AVERAGE MCAT, ENTERING CLASS FALL 2005

4.7% ACCEPTANCE RATE, ENTERING CLASS FALL 2005

28 2007 U.S. NEWS MEDICAL SCHOOL RANKING (RESEARCH)

Unranked 2007 U.S. NEWS MEDICAL SCHOOL RANKING (PRIMARY CARE)

ADMISSIONS

Admissions phone number: **(617) 638-4630**
Admissions email address: **medadms@bu.edu**
Application website:
https://www.bumc.bu.edu/busm/myapplication/shared/signin.aspx
Acceptance rate: **4.7%**
In-state acceptance rate: **12.6%**
Out-of-state acceptance rate: **4.2%**
Minority acceptance rate: **N/A**
International acceptance rate: **2.7%**

Fall 2005 applications and acceptees

	Applied	Interviewed	Accepted	Enrolled
Total:	9,589	1,038	454	155
In-state:	653	148	82	23
Out-of-state:	8,936	890	372	132

Profile of admitted students

Average undergraduate grade point average: **3.65**
MCAT averages (scale: 1-15; writing test: J-T):
  Composite score: **10.7**
  Verbal reasoning score: **10.1**, Physical sciences score: **10.9**, Biological sciences score: **11.0**, Writing score: **Q**
Proportion with undergraduate majors in: Biological sciences: **56%**, Physical sciences: **22%**, Non-sciences: **10%**, Other health professions: **N/A**, Mixed disciplines and other: **13%**
Percentage of students not coming directly from college after graduation: **55%**

Dates and details

The American Medical College Application Service (AMCAS) application is accepted.
School asks for a school-specific application as part of the admissions process.
Oldest MCAT considered for Fall 2007 entry: **2004**
Earliest application date for the 2007-2008 first-year class: **June 1, 2006**
Latest application date: **November 1, 2006**

Acceptance dates for regular application for the class entering in fall 2007:
  Earliest: **January 1, 2007**
  Latest: **September 9, 2007**
The school doesn't consider requests for deferred entrance.
Starting month for the class entering in 2007–2008:
  August
The school has an Early Decision Plan (EDP).
A personal interview is required for admission.

Undergraduate coursework required

Medical school requires undergraduate work in these subjects: biology, English, organic chemistry, inorganic (general) chemistry, physics, humanities, demonstration of writing skills.

ADMISSIONS POLICY
(TEXT PROVIDED BY SCHOOL):

We draw upon a large and highly qualified applicant pool, with more than 90 applicants for every seat in the entering class. Our students represent the full range of geographic, cultural, ethnic, and educational diversity of our pluralistic society, and we believe that this diversity contributes to the strength of the experience for all of us.

COSTS AND FINANCIAL AID

Financial aid phone number: **(617) 638-5130**
Tuition, 2005-2006 academic year: **$39,960**
Room and board: **$11,381**
Percentage of students receiving financial aid in 2005-06: **79%**
Percentage of students receiving: Loans: **74%**, Grants/scholarships: **34%**, Work-study aid: **0%**
Average medical school debt for the Class of 2004: **$141,681**

STUDENT BODY

Fall 2005 full-time enrollment: **632**
Men: **47%**, Women: **53%**, In-state: **19%**, Minorities: **49%**, American Indian: **0.5%**, Asian-American: **32.9%**,

African-American: **8.2%**, Hispanic-American: **7.6%**, White: **46.8%**, International: **2.8%**, Unknown: **1.1%**

ACADEMIC PROGRAMS

The school's curriculum very frequently gives first-year students substantial contact with patients.

There are opportunities for first- or second-year students to work in community health clinics.

Program offerings: AIDS, drug/alcohol abuse, family medicine, geriatrics, internal medicine, pediatrics, rural medicine, women's health

Joint degrees awarded: M.D./Ph.D., M.D./MBA, M.D./MPH

Total National Institutes of Health (NIH) grants awarded to the medical school and affiliated hospitals: **$196.4 million**

CURRICULUM
(TEXT PROVIDED BY SCHOOL):

The basic science curriculum is taught in an innovative format, integrating traditional lecture-style classes with small-group problem seminars and laboratory exercises. There is an emphasis on self-directed learning and teamwork. Patient contact is introduced in the first week of the first-year curriculum, and the formal clinical training in the third and fourth years offers broad-based preparation for postgraduate training in the full range of disciplines that make up modern medicine.

FACULTY PROFILE (FALL 2005)

Total teaching faculty: **1,183 (full-time)**, **1,213 (part-time)**

Of full-time faculty, those teaching in basic sciences: **14%**; in clinical programs: **86%**

Of part-time faculty, those teaching in basic sciences: **1%**; in clinical programs: **99%**

Full-time faculty/student ratio: **1.9**

SUPPORT SERVICES

The school offers students these services for dealing with stress: expanded-hour gym access, peer counseling, professional counseling, support groups.

RESIDENCY PROFILE

Most popular residency and specialty programs chosen by the 2004 and 2005 M.D. graduating classes: emergency medicine, family practice, internal medicine, obstetrics and gynecology, ophthalmology, orthopaedic surgery, pathology–anatomic and clinical, pediatrics, radiology–diagnostic, surgery–general.

WHERE GRADS GO

34.7%

Proportion of 2003-2005 graduates who entered primary care specialties

30.3%

Proportion of 2004-2005 graduates who accepted in-state residencies

Brown University

- 97 Waterman Street, Box G-A212, Providence, RI 02912-9706
- Private
- **Year Founded:** 1764
- **Tuition, 2005-2006:** $37,453
- **Enrollment 2005-2006 academic year:** 345
- **Website:** http://bms.brown.edu
- **Specialty ranking:** drug/alcohol abuse: 13, women's health: 16

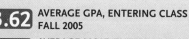

3.62	AVERAGE GPA, ENTERING CLASS FALL 2005
11.1	AVERAGE MCAT, ENTERING CLASS FALL 2005
4.3%	ACCEPTANCE RATE, ENTERING CLASS FALL 2005
38	2007 U.S. NEWS MEDICAL SCHOOL RANKING (RESEARCH)
16	2007 U.S. NEWS MEDICAL SCHOOL RANKING (PRIMARY CARE)

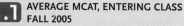

ADMISSIONS

Admissions phone number: **(401) 863-2149**
Admissions email address:
medschool_admissions@brown.edu
Application website:
http://bms.brown.edu/admissions/applications
Acceptance rate: **4.3%**
In-state acceptance rate: **14.3%**
Out-of-state acceptance rate: **4.1%**
Minority acceptance rate: **4.2%**
International acceptance rate: **2.8%**

Fall 2005 applications and acceptees

	Applied	Interviewed	Accepted	Enrolled
Total:	4,324	294	184	73
In-state:	77	15	11	9
Out-of-state:	4,247	279	173	64

Profile of admitted students

Average undergraduate grade point average: **3.62**
MCAT averages (scale: 1-15; writing test: J-T):
    Composite score: **11.1**
    Verbal reasoning score: **10.4**, Physical sciences score: **11.5**, Biological sciences score: **11.5**, Writing score: **R**
Proportion with undergraduate majors in: Biological sciences: **37%**, Physical sciences: **12%**, Non-sciences: **37%**, Other health professions: **1%**, Mixed disciplines and other: **13%**
Percentage of students not coming directly from college after graduation: **34%**

Dates and details

The American Medical College Application Service (AMCAS) application is accepted.
School asks for a school-specific application as part of the admissions process.
Oldest MCAT considered for Fall 2007 entry: **2002**
Earliest application date for the 2007-2008 first-year class: **July 1, 2006**
Latest application date: **December 31, 2006**

Acceptance dates for regular application for the class entering in fall 2007:
    Earliest: **January 15, 2007**
    Latest: **September 1, 2007**
The school considers requests for deferred entrance.
Starting month for the class entering in 2007–2008:
    September
The school doesn't have an Early Decision Plan (EDP).
A personal interview is required for admission.

Undergraduate coursework required

Medical school requires undergraduate work in these subjects: biology, organic chemistry, inorganic (general) chemistry, physics, behavioral science, calculus, social sciences.

ADMISSIONS POLICY
(TEXT PROVIDED BY SCHOOL):

All applicants are selected on the basis of academic achievement, faculty evaluations, evidence of maturity, motivation, leadership, integrity, and compassion. Applicants to the M.D./Ph.D. program also are evaluated on the basis of their research accomplishments and potential.

To be eligible for consideration, candidates generally must present a minimum cumulative grade-point average of 3.0 (on a 4.0 scale) in courses taken as a matriculated student at an undergraduate college or graduate school. In addition, applicants must have completed the requirements for a baccalaureate degree prior to matriculation into the medical school. The mean undergraduate GPA for Brown Medical School students is approximately 3.6.

COSTS AND FINANCIAL AID

Financial aid phone number: **(401) 863-1142**
Tuition, 2005-2006 academic year: **$37,453**
Room and board: **$14,667**
Percentage of students receiving financial aid in 2005-06: **79%**
Percentage of students receiving: Loans: **74%**, Grants/scholarships: **50%**, Work-study aid: **0%**
Average medical school debt for the Class of 2004: **$91,174**

STUDENT BODY

Fall 2005 full-time enrollment: **345**

Men: **42%**, Women: **58%**, In-state: **16%**, Minorities: **48%**, American Indian: **0.3%**, Asian-American: **26.4%**, African-American: **12.5%**, Hispanic-American: **6.1%**, White: **51.0%**, International: **3.8%**, Unknown: **0.0%**

ACADEMIC PROGRAMS

The school's curriculum very frequently gives first-year students substantial contact with patients.

There are opportunities for first- or second-year students to work in community health clinics.

Program offerings: AIDS, drug/alcohol abuse, family medicine, geriatrics, internal medicine, pediatrics, rural medicine, women's health

Joint degrees awarded: M.D./Ph.D., M.D./MPH, M.D./MS

Total National Institutes of Health (NIH) grants awarded to the medical school and affiliated hospitals: **$103.8 million**

CURRICULUM

(TEXT PROVIDED BY SCHOOL):

The medical program at Brown University has three major goals for its graduates: that they be broadly and liberally educated men and women, that they view medicine as a socially responsible human service profession, and that they be prepared for the lifelong intellectual and scholarly challenge that is the practice of medicine.

Our graduates must be well educated in the medical sciences and capable of approaching problems from a variety of perspectives. We view the boundaries of medicine as wide, encompassing all of the factors that lead to human disease, including those of a social, cultural, and economic nature.

Brown is the only medical school in Rhode Island, and the school's affiliated institutions encompass more than half of the hospital beds in the state. Half of the state's physicians are members of the Brown faculty. These factors contribute to our responsibility to serve the community. We encourage and support student leadership and participation in response to the needs of those we serve.

The medical school curriculum is undergoing renewal and redesign; principles that guided us in the past will apply to this process. Brown Medical School was the first in the nation to implement a competency-based curriculum, and our new curriculum will continue in this tradition. We will maintain the high level of flexibility that allows students to pursue scholarly goals both within and beyond the traditional areas of medical education. Our new curriculum will also retain the combination of lecture-based courses and organ-system, problem-based learning that currently occupies the first two years. In Fall 2005 we introduced a course, Doctoring, that places students in the community medical setting at the start of their education. This course teaches the essential skills required for the practice of medicine, history taking and physical diagnosis, and incorporates professional development, biomedical ethics, medical civics, and the application of the sciences to the practice of medicine. As our new curriculum is developed, we will further incorporate these essential areas into all four years of the medical education experience, thereby preparing students as best we know how for the challenges of a career in medicine.

FACULTY PROFILE (FALL 2005)

Total teaching faculty: **703 (full-time), 0 (part-time)**

Of full-time faculty, those teaching in basic sciences: **26%**; in clinical programs: **74%**

Of part-time faculty, those teaching in basic sciences: **N/A**; in clinical programs: **N/A**

Full-time faculty/student ratio: **2.0**

SUPPORT SERVICES

The school offers students these services for dealing with stress: expanded-hour gym access, peer counseling, professional counseling, religious support, support groups.

RESIDENCY PROFILE

Most popular residency and specialty programs chosen by the 2004 and 2005 M.D. graduating classes: family practice, internal medicine, internal medicine–pediatrics, pediatrics, psychiatry, radiology–diagnostic, surgery–general, internal medicine/pediatrics.

WHERE GRADS GO

46.3%

Proportion of 2003-2005 graduates who entered primary care specialties

16.9%

Proportion of 2004-2005 graduates who accepted in-state residencies

Case Western Reserve University

- 10900 Euclid Avenue, Cleveland, OH 44106
- Private
- Year Founded: 1843
- Tuition, 2005-2006: $39,384
- Enrollment 2005-2006 academic year: 624
- Website: http://casemed.case.edu/
- Specialty ranking: AIDS: 16, family medicine: 11, pediatrics: 12

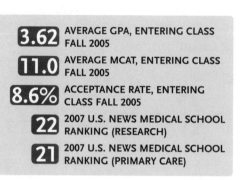

3.62 AVERAGE GPA, ENTERING CLASS FALL 2005

11.0 AVERAGE MCAT, ENTERING CLASS FALL 2005

8.6% ACCEPTANCE RATE, ENTERING CLASS FALL 2005

22 2007 U.S. NEWS MEDICAL SCHOOL RANKING (RESEARCH)

21 2007 U.S. NEWS MEDICAL SCHOOL RANKING (PRIMARY CARE)

ADMISSIONS

Admissions phone number: **(216) 368-3450**
Admissions email address: **axh65@case.edu**
Application website: **N/A**
Acceptance rate: **8.6%**
In-state acceptance rate: **10.9%**
Out-of-state acceptance rate: **8.2%**
Minority acceptance rate: **8.5%**
International acceptance rate: **10.2%**

Fall 2005 applications and acceptees

	Applied	Interviewed	Accepted	Enrolled
Total:	4,975	1,027	427	167
In-state:	734	216	80	44
Out-of-state:	4,241	811	347	123

Profile of admitted students

Average undergraduate grade point average: **3.62**
MCAT averages (scale: 1-15; writing test: J-T):
  Composite score: **11.0**
  Verbal reasoning score: **10.5**, Physical sciences score: **11.2**, Biological sciences score: **11.3**, Writing score: **P**
Proportion with undergraduate majors in: Biological sciences: **24%**, Physical sciences: **35%**, Non-sciences: **15%**, Other health professions: **2%**, Mixed disciplines and other: **24%**
Percentage of students not coming directly from college after graduation: **N/A**

Dates and details

The American Medical College Application Service (AMCAS) application is accepted.
School asks for a school-specific application as part of the admissions process.
Oldest MCAT considered for Fall 2007 entry: **2003**
Earliest application date for the 2007-2008 first-year class: **July 1, 2006**
Latest application date: **November 1, 2006**
Acceptance dates for regular application for the class entering in fall 2007:
  Earliest: **October 15, 2006**

Latest: **N/A**
The school considers requests for deferred entrance.
Starting month for the class entering in 2007–2008: **July**
The school doesn't have an Early Decision Plan (EDP).
A personal interview is required for admission.

Undergraduate coursework required

Medical school requires undergraduate work in these subjects: biology/zoology, English, organic chemistry, inorganic (general) chemistry, physics.

ADMISSIONS POLICY
(TEXT PROVIDED BY SCHOOL):

The Admissions Committee selects students without regard to age, national origin, race, religion, sex, or sexual orientation. With respect to disability, technical standards for admissions are available upon request. The School of Medicine deliberately seeks a diverse student body. Over 20 states of residence and 70 to 80 undergraduate colleges are represented in a typical entering class.

While the committee does not rely on grades and Medical College Admission Test scores alone in the selection process, all students have demonstrated exceptional academic strength. Completed secondary applications are reviewed with great attention given to the candidate's written statements and letters of recommendation in the decision to invite an applicant for an interview.

Although it has accepted transfer students from LCME-accredited schools in cases of extreme hardship, recent changes in the curriculum will not allow such transfers in the future, effective for the academic year 2006-2007.

COSTS AND FINANCIAL AID

Financial aid phone number: **(216) 368-3666**
Tuition, 2005-2006 academic year: **$39,384**
Room and board: **$16,172**
Percentage of students receiving financial aid in 2005-06: **81%**
Percentage of students receiving: Loans: **79%**, Grants/scholarships: **59%**, Work-study aid: **0%**

Average medical school debt for the Class of 2004: **$123,100**

STUDENT BODY
Fall 2005 full-time enrollment: **624**
Men: **54%**, Women: **46%**, In-state: **54%**, Minorities: **35%**, American Indian: **0.2%**, Asian-American: **22.8%**, African-American: **10.9%**, Hispanic-American: **1.6%**, White: **58.8%**, International: **2.9%**, Unknown: **2.9%**

ACADEMIC PROGRAMS
The school's curriculum frequently gives first-year students substantial contact with patients.
There are opportunities for first- or second-year students to work in community health clinics.
Program offerings: AIDS, drug/alcohol abuse, family medicine, geriatrics, internal medicine, pediatrics, rural medicine, women's health
Joint degrees awarded: M.D./Ph.D., M.D./MBA, M.D./MPH, M.D./JD, M.D./MS, M.D./M.A.
Total National Institutes of Health (NIH) grants awarded to the medical school and affiliated hospitals: **$240.2 million**

CURRICULUM
(TEXT PROVIDED BY SCHOOL):
Case offers three paths to the M.D. degree: the 4-year University Program (University Campus, about 130 students per year), the 5-year Cleveland Clinic Lerner College of Medicine program (College Program, Cleveland Clinic, 32 students per year), and the NIH-funded Medical Scientist Training Program (MSTP) (about 12 students per year, University Program) where students simultaneously pursue an M.D. and a Ph.D in a basic science field. In the University Program, the organ-system based pre-clerkship courses are lecture based, supplemented by case-based small group discussions. Every medical student is required to complete a research thesis, and coursework has been condensed to create a 16-week block of time dedicated to a mentored research project that serves as the basis for their theses.

Through the newly established Rotating Apprenticeships in Medical Practice Program, patient care in the first two years initially centers on a series of preceptorships relating to birth, childhood, adult care, geriatrics, acute care, mental health and end of life care. Students then undertake a weekly longitudinal preceptorship in the clinical setting of their choice with a single preceptor. Students can choose an area of concentration or select from a broad range of clinical and non-clinical electives. The University Program also offers

M.D./MS, M.D./MBA, and M.D./JD degrees. MSTP students complete the first two years of the University Program along with most of their Ph.D coursework, then spend 3-4 years researching and preparing a Ph.D thesis before returning to the M.D. clerkship curriculum. The College Program is designed to prepare physician investigators by combining an extensive integrated curriculum in basic and clinical research skills with a required research thesis. Organ system courses center on weekly problem-based learning cases and interactive seminars and labs. Students care for patients in the office of a primary care preceptor one-half day per week during the first two years. Clinical clerkships for both programs (years 3-4) are offered at the Cleveland Clinic, VA Medical Center, St. Vincent Charity Hospital, MetroHealth Medical Center, and University Hospitals of Cleveland. Required clerkships include family medicine, medicine, neurosciences, obstetrics/gynecology, pediatrics, psychiatry, and surgery. Student advising plays a key role in ensuring success in each program.

FACULTY PROFILE (FALL 2005)
Total teaching faculty: **1,780 (full-time)**, **1,975 (part-time)**
Of full-time faculty, those teaching in basic sciences: **23%**; in clinical programs: **77%**
Of part-time faculty, those teaching in basic sciences: **8%**; in clinical programs: **92%**
Full-time faculty/student ratio: **2.9**

SUPPORT SERVICES
The school offers students these services for dealing with stress: expanded-hour gym access, peer counseling, professional counseling, religious support, support groups.

RESIDENCY PROFILE
Most popular residency and specialty programs chosen by the 2004 and 2005 M.D. graduating classes: emergency medicine, family practice, internal medicine, ophthalmology, orthopaedic surgery, pediatrics, psychiatry, radiology–diagnostic, surgery–general, internal medicine/pediatrics.

WHERE GRADS GO

43.3%
Proportion of 2003-2005 graduates who entered primary care specialties

35.4%
Proportion of 2004-2005 graduates who accepted in-state residencies

Columbia University

COLLEGE OF PHYSICIANS AND SURGEONS

- 630 W. 168th Street, New York, NY 10032
- Private
- Year Founded: 1767
- Tuition, 2005-2006: $41,873
- Enrollment 2005-2006 academic year: 634
- Website: http://www.cumc.columbia.edu/dept/ps
- Specialty ranking: AIDS: 9, drug/alcohol abuse: 6, internal medicine: 11, pediatrics: 12, women's health: 14

3.79 AVERAGE GPA, ENTERING CLASS FALL 2005

11.8 AVERAGE MCAT, ENTERING CLASS FALL 2005

5.3% ACCEPTANCE RATE, ENTERING CLASS FALL 2005

11 2007 U.S. NEWS MEDICAL SCHOOL RANKING (RESEARCH)

Unranked 2007 U.S. NEWS MEDICAL SCHOOL RANKING (PRIMARY CARE)

ADMISSIONS
Admissions phone number: **(212) 305-3595**
Admissions email address: **psadmissions@columbia.edu**
Application website:
   http://www.cumc.columbia.edu/dept/ps
Acceptance rate: **5.3%**

Fall 2005 applications and acceptees

	Applied	Interviewed	Accepted	Enrolled
Total:	5,768	1,247	307	149
In-state:	N/A	152	51	32
Out-of-state:	N/A	1,095	256	117

Profile of admitted students
Average undergraduate grade point average: **3.79**
MCAT averages (scale: 1-15; writing test: J-T):
   Composite score: **11.8**
   Verbal reasoning score: **11.2**, Physical sciences score: **12.2**, Biological sciences score: **12.1**, Writing score: **Q**
Proportion with undergraduate majors in: Biological sciences: **34%**, Physical sciences: **32%**, Non-sciences: **28%**, Other health professions: **0%**, Mixed disciplines and other: **7%**
Percentage of students not coming directly from college after graduation: **37%**

Dates and details
The American Medical College Application Service (AMCAS) application is accepted.
School asks for a school-specific application as part of the admissions process.
Oldest MCAT considered for Fall 2007 entry: **2003**
Earliest application date for the 2007-2008 first-year class: **June 1, 2006**
Latest application date: **October 15, 2006**
Acceptance dates for regular application for the class entering in fall 2007:
   Earliest: **March 1, 2007**
   Latest: **August 16, 2007**
The school considers requests for deferred entrance.

Starting month for the class entering in 2007–2008:
   August
The school doesn't have an Early Decision Plan (EDP).
A personal interview is required for admission.

Undergraduate coursework required
Medical school requires undergraduate work in these subjects: biology, English, organic chemistry, physics, general chemistry.

ADMISSIONS POLICY
(TEXT PROVIDED BY SCHOOL):
Admission is offered to applicants showing the greatest evidence of excellence and leadership potential in both the science and the art of medicine. Beyond academic ability, the art of medicine also demands personal qualities of integrity, the ability to relate easily to other people, and concern for their welfare. These qualities are evaluated by several means: the tenor of letters of recommendation, the extent of the applicant's participation in extracurricular and summer activities, the breadth of his or her interests and undergraduate education (the choice of field of concentration is not an important consideration), and the personal interview.

Each year, some applicants are accepted who display extraordinary promise for either the science or the art of medicine, although they may not fully meet all criteria described above.

The Admissions Committee seeks diversity of background, geographical and otherwise, among its applicants; no preference is given to state of residence. Admission is possible for all qualified applicants regardless of sex, race, age, religion, sexual orientation, national origin, or handicap. Members of underrepresented minority groups are encouraged to apply, and Columbia has been successful in this regard: 16.4% of enrollment comes from underrepresented minority groups, and another 19.7% are Asian/Pacific Islander.

COSTS AND FINANCIAL AID
Financial aid phone number: **(212) 305-4100**
Tuition, 2005-2006 academic year: **$41,873**

Room and board: **$15,471**
Percentage of students receiving financial aid in 2005-06:
82%
Percentage of students receiving: Loans: **71%**,
Grants/scholarships: **54%**, Work-study aid: **10%**
Average medical school debt for the Class of 2004:
$100,970

STUDENT BODY

Fall 2005 full-time enrollment: **634**
Men: **53%**, Women: **47%**, In-state: **38%**, Minorities: **37%**,
American Indian: **0.6%**, Asian-American: **19.7%**,
African-American: **8.5%**, Hispanic-American: **6.5%**,
White: **58.0%**, International: **3.5%**, Unknown: **3.2%**

ACADEMIC PROGRAMS

The school's curriculum frequently gives first-year students
substantial contact with patients.
There are opportunities for first- or second-year students to
work in community health clinics.
Program offerings: AIDS, drug/alcohol abuse, family
medicine, geriatrics, internal medicine, pediatrics, rural
medicine, women's health
Joint degrees awarded: M.D./Ph.D., M.D./MBA,
M.D./MPH
Total National Institutes of Health (NIH) grants awarded to
the medical school and affiliated hospitals: **$300.3
million**

CURRICULUM

(TEXT PROVIDED BY SCHOOL):
Columbia University College of Physicians & Surgeons
(P&S) provides the fundamental scientific basis for the
study of medicine while also coordinating basic science and
clinical subjects throughout four years to make these connections clear from the start of medical school.

P&S students begin clinical work early in the first year to
acquire the skills and attitudes they will need to see patients
as individuals and as members of families and communities,
and to see themselves as members of a healthcare team.

The cornerstone of the first-year curriculum is a course
called Science Basic to the Practice of Medicine. The course
weaves together biochemistry, cell biology, genetics, and
physiology to explain how the body works.

The second year is transitional, synthesizing the science
of pathophysiology and pharmacology with history-taking
and physical diagnosis. Second-year students learn to take a
comprehensive medical history and to conduct a thorough
physical examination under faculty supervision at affiliated
hospitals.

The strength and depth of the P&S curriculum are most
evident in the third year, when students complete clerkships
in a wide range of clinical disciplines. Clerkship sites
include inner-city, suburban, Indian Health Service, and
rural settings.

In the fourth year, besides seven months of electives, students take "back to the classroom" courses to re-emphasize
the foundation of medical knowledge and critical data
appraisal in day-to-day patient care management.

To become a successful physician, a medical student
must develop the skills and orientation to pursue lifelong
learning. Small-group teaching in the basic sciences is a
hallmark of the curriculum. P&S has reduced the number
of required lectures and increased the time students spend
working in small groups on case-based, problem-oriented
projects. P&S also prepares its graduates to understand and
participate in the ongoing organizational changes in
American healthcare.

P&S encourages greater emphasis on humanism in the
practice of medicine. To affirm commitment to the highest
ethical principles, students entering P&S don a white coat
and take the Hippocratic oath. This ceremony, launched at
P&S in 1993, has since been adopted by medical schools
across the nation. To encourage and empower third-year
students entering the clinical stage of their medical training, P&S is one of a handful of medical schools to also
introduce the Student Clinician's Ceremony.

FACULTY PROFILE (FALL 2005)

Total teaching faculty: **1,778 (full-time), 2,540 (part-time)**
Of full-time faculty, those teaching in basic sciences: **11%**;
in clinical programs: **89%**
Of part-time faculty, those teaching in basic sciences: **5%**;
in clinical programs: **95%**
Full-time faculty/student ratio: **2.8**

SUPPORT SERVICES

The school offers students these services for dealing with
stress: expanded-hour gym access, peer counseling, professional counseling, religious support, support groups.

RESIDENCY PROFILE

Most popular residency and specialty programs chosen by
the 2004 and 2005 M.D. graduating classes: emergency
medicine, internal medicine, neurology, obstetrics and
gynecology, orthopaedic surgery, pathology–anatomic and
clinical, medical microbiology, pediatrics, psychiatry, radiology–diagnostic.

WHERE GRADS GO

32.7%
*Proportion of 2003-2005 graduates who entered primary
care specialties*

50.3%
*Proportion of 2004-2005 graduates who accepted in-state
residencies*

Cornell University

WEILL

- 1300 York Avenue at 69th Street, New York, NY 10021
- Private
- Year Founded: 1898
- Tuition, 2005-2006: $33,345
- Enrollment 2005-2006 academic year: 410
- Website: http://www.med.cornell.edu
- Specialty ranking: AIDS: 21, drug/alcohol abuse: 19, internal medicine: 21

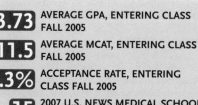

3.73 AVERAGE GPA, ENTERING CLASS FALL 2005

11.5 AVERAGE MCAT, ENTERING CLASS FALL 2005

4.3% ACCEPTANCE RATE, ENTERING CLASS FALL 2005

15 2007 U.S. NEWS MEDICAL SCHOOL RANKING (RESEARCH)

49 2007 U.S. NEWS MEDICAL SCHOOL RANKING (PRIMARY CARE)

ADMISSIONS

Admissions phone number: **(212) 746-1067**
Admissions email address: **cumc-admissions@med.cornell.edu**
Application website:
http://www.med.cornell.edu/education/admissions
Acceptance rate: **4.3%**
In-state acceptance rate: **4.9%**
Out-of-state acceptance rate: **4.2%**
Minority acceptance rate: **4.8%**
International acceptance rate: **1.4%**

Fall 2005 applications and acceptees

	Applied	Interviewed	Accepted	Enrolled
Total:	5,177	759	225	101
In-state:	1,203	162	59	36
Out-of-state:	3,974	597	166	65

Profile of admitted students

Average undergraduate grade point average: **3.73**
MCAT averages (scale: 1-15; writing test: J-T):
Composite score: **11.5**
Verbal reasoning score: **10.8**, Physical sciences score: **11.9**, Biological sciences score: **11.9**, Writing score: **P**
Proportion with undergraduate majors in: Biological sciences: **40%**, Physical sciences: **21%**, Non-sciences: **19%**, Other health professions: **N/A**, Mixed disciplines and other: **20%**
Percentage of students not coming directly from college after graduation: **65%**

Dates and details

The American Medical College Application Service (AMCAS) application is accepted.
School asks for a school-specific application as part of the admissions process.
Oldest MCAT considered for Fall 2007 entry: **2004**
Earliest application date for the 2007-2008 first-year class: **June 1, 2006**
Latest application date: **October 15, 2006**

Acceptance dates for regular application for the class entering in fall 2007:
Earliest: **March 1, 2007**
Latest: **N/A**
The school considers requests for deferred entrance.
Starting month for the class entering in 2007–2008: **August**
The school has an Early Decision Plan (EDP).
A personal interview is required for admission.

Undergraduate coursework required

Medical school requires undergraduate work in these subjects: biology/zoology, English, organic chemistry, inorganic (general) chemistry, physics.

ADMISSIONS POLICY
(TEXT PROVIDED BY SCHOOL):

Weill-Cornell seeks applicants who uphold the highest standards. WMC is among the most selective medical schools in the nation. Each year the Committee on Admissions selects 101 students from more than 5,000 applicants. The committee seeks students who are best prepared for future leadership roles in medicine. Applicants should have a broad liberal arts education with demonstrated accomplishment in the humanities and social sciences, as well as a thorough preparation in the basic sciences.

The committee equally considers students with backgrounds in the basic sciences, social sciences, and liberal arts. We encourage applicants to pursue premedical curricula that allow them to sample a broad range of academic disciplines and explore one or more areas in depth.

Letters of recommendation play an important role in the committee's assessment of an application. We prefer letters from persons who know the applicant well to letters from persons who may be well known but do not know the applicant well personally.

The committee regards the Medical College Admission Test as a standardized tool that allows for one form of comparison among applicants. There are no cutoffs for MCAT scores.

Meaningful participation in extracurricular activities is of extreme interest. Such participation should demonstrate commitment and involvement.

Applicants should explore medicine in some form before entering medical school. The committee also values applicants' research experiences.

The practice of medicine requires the highest level of personal integrity. The committee seeks applicants who show emotional maturity, personal depth, commitment to others' well-being, and ethical and moral integrity.

About 700 applicants are selected for interview. The committee makes acceptance decisions by consensus. While a small number of students are accepted in December, most are accepted in early March.

COSTS AND FINANCIAL AID

Financial aid phone number: **(212) 746-1066**
Tuition, 2005-2006 academic year: **$33,345**
Room and board: **$9,947**
Percentage of students receiving financial aid in 2005-06: **80%**
Percentage of students receiving: Loans: **66%**, Grants/scholarships: **59%**, Work-study aid: **16%**
Average medical school debt for the Class of 2004: **$91,048**

STUDENT BODY

Fall 2005 full-time enrollment: **410**
Men: **50%**, Women: **50%**, In-state: **50%**, Minorities: **44%**, American Indian: **0.7%**, Asian-American: **24.4%**, African-American: **12.0%**, Hispanic-American: **6.6%**, White: **55.1%**, International: **0.7%**, Unknown: **0.5%**

ACADEMIC PROGRAMS

The school's curriculum very frequently gives first-year students substantial contact with patients.
There are opportunities for first- or second-year students to work in community health clinics.
Program offerings: AIDS, drug/alcohol abuse, family medicine, geriatrics, internal medicine, pediatrics, women's health
Joint degrees awarded: M.D./Ph.D., M.D./MBA.
Total National Institutes of Health (NIH) grants awarded to the medical school and affiliated hospitals: **$286.2 million**

CURRICULUM

(TEXT PROVIDED BY SCHOOL):
Key features of the curriculum: integration of the teaching of the basic and clinical sciences; problem-based learning in the basic sciences; reorganization of the core basic science curriculum into highly integrated block courses; teaching the basic and clinical sciences across the four years of medical school; acquisition of clinical skills in the first two years; a three-year, integrated sequence in public health, behavioral sciences, psychosocial medicine, ethics, and clinical skills; a primary-care clerkship; and increased flexibility in the scheduling of clerkships and clinical electives.
The first-year curriculum includes:

Molecules, Genes and Cells: an integration of biochemistry, cell biology, molecular biology, cellular physiology and biophysics, the genetic basis of diseases, and the fundamentals of pharmacology.

Human Structure and Function: dedicated to the study of gross anatomy, histology, embryology, physiology of organ systems, and clinical imaging of the normal human body.

Host Defenses: introducing the student to the basic concepts of abnormal human biology and devoted to the study of general pathology, immunology, and the principles of microbiology and pharmacology.

Medicine, Patients, and Society I: approaches the patient-physician relationship from conceptual and practical perspectives.

The second-year curriculum includes:

Brain and Mind: content ranges from basic neuroscience and gross anatomy of the head and neck to neurological diagnosis and psychopathology.

Basis of Disease: organized into nine modules covering the major organ systems.

Medicine, Patients, and Society II: building upon the principles introduced in Medicine, Patients, and Society I, including an introduction to physical examination.

Introductory Clerkship: designed to provide an orientation to experiences common to all clerkships over three weeks.

Anesthesia, Ventilation, and Circulation: introducing the fundamental principles of anesthesiology over one week.

FACULTY PROFILE (FALL 2005)

Total teaching faculty: **2,025 (full-time)**, **1,907 (part-time)**
Of full-time faculty, those teaching in basic sciences: **12%**; in clinical programs: **88%**
Of part-time faculty, those teaching in basic sciences: **2%**; in clinical programs: **98%**
Full-time faculty/student ratio: **4.9**

SUPPORT SERVICES

The school offers students these services for dealing with stress: professional counseling, religious support, support groups.

RESIDENCY PROFILE

Most popular residency and specialty programs chosen by the 2004 and 2005 M.D. graduating classes: anesthesiology, dermatology, emergency medicine, internal medicine, ophthalmology, pediatrics, psychiatry, radiology–diagnostic, surgery–general.

WHERE GRADS GO

40.4%
Proportion of 2003-2005 graduates who entered primary care specialties

51.3%
Proportion of 2004-2005 graduates who accepted in-state residencies

Creighton University

- 2500 California Plaza, Omaha, NE 68178
- Private
- Year Founded: 1878
- Tuition, 2005-2006: $38,325
- Enrollment 2005-2006 academic year: 485
- Website: http://medicine.creighton.edu
- Specialty ranking: N/A

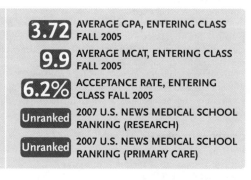

3.72 AVERAGE GPA, ENTERING CLASS FALL 2005

9.9 AVERAGE MCAT, ENTERING CLASS FALL 2005

6.2% ACCEPTANCE RATE, ENTERING CLASS FALL 2005

Unranked 2007 U.S. NEWS MEDICAL SCHOOL RANKING (RESEARCH)

Unranked 2007 U.S. NEWS MEDICAL SCHOOL RANKING (PRIMARY CARE)

ADMISSIONS

Admissions phone number: **(402) 280-2799**
Admissions email address: **medschadm@creighton.edu**
Application website:
  http://medicine.creighton.edu/medschool/admissions/
Acceptance rate: **6.2%**

Fall 2005 applications and acceptees

	Applied	Interviewed	Accepted	Enrolled
Total:	**4,962**	**578**	**310**	**125**
In-state:	N/A	N/A	N/A	**17**
Out-of-state:	N/A	N/A	N/A	**108**

Profile of admitted students

Average undergraduate grade point average: **3.72**
MCAT averages (scale: 1-15; writing test: J-T):
  Composite score: **9.9**
  Verbal reasoning score: **9.9**, Physical sciences score: **9.8**,
  Biological sciences score: **10.2**, Writing score: **P**
Proportion with undergraduate majors in: Biological
  sciences: **58%**, Physical sciences: **26%**, Non-sciences:
  6%, Other health professions: **5%**, Mixed disciplines and
  other: **6%**
Percentage of students not coming directly from college
  after graduation: **N/A**

Dates and details

The American Medical College Application Service
  (AMCAS) application is accepted.
School asks for a school-specific application as part of the
  admissions process.
Oldest MCAT considered for Fall 2007 entry: **2004**
Earliest application date for the 2007-2008 first-year class:
  January 6, 2006
Latest application date: **January 12, 2006**
Acceptance dates for regular application for the class
  entering in fall 2007:
  Earliest: **January 6, 2006**
  Latest: **January 2, 2007**
The school considers requests for deferred entrance.

Starting month for the class entering in 2007–2008:
  August
The school has an Early Decision Plan (EDP).
A personal interview is required for admission.

Undergraduate coursework required

Medical school requires undergraduate work in these subjects: biology, English, organic chemistry, inorganic (general) chemistry, physics.

ADMISSIONS POLICY
(TEXT PROVIDED BY SCHOOL):

The MCAT and three years (at least 90 semester hours) of
accredited college work are mandatory. Preference is given,
however, to holders of the baccalaureate degree. Applicants
may take the MCAT in the fall of the year preceding their
entry into medical school. All requirements must be completed by June prior to entry. Coursework must include 8
hours general biology with lab; 8 hours inorganic or general
chemistry with lab; 8-10 hours of organic chemistry with
lab; 8 hours of general physics with lab; and 6 hours of
English. Although no additional coursework is required,
advanced study in human biology, especially biochemistry
and/or genetics, is strongly encouraged. Applicants may
pursue a baccalaureate degree with any major in science or
liberal arts (except military science) appropriate to their
interests. Nonscience majors should elect to take advanced
science study to the extent possible. Up to 27 semester
hours of credit are accepted under CLEP and/or advanced
placement programs. A record that includes significant
service to humanity and medical experience is deemed
important. The preprofessional committee evaluations and
letters of recommendation are equally important. There are
no restrictions placed on applicants because of race, religion, sex, national or ethnic origin, age, disability, or status
as a disabled veteran. Advantage is given to applicants who
have undertaken their preprofessional education at
Creighton University. Because the cumulative and science
GPAs of the 120 candidates selected for the 2004 entering
class were 3.68 and 3.63, respectively, it is suggested that no
candidate apply whose GPA in either situation is below 3.2.

The AMCAS application is the principal source of information on the candidates. Additional (secondary) information is requested of all the applicants upon receipt of the AMCAS form. Transfers from LCME medical schools are admitted on a space-available basis. In addition to federally insured student loan programs and funds available from major foundation grants, a limited number of scholarships and fellowships are available for upperclassmen and for a few well-qualified entering students. Scholarship aid is awarded on the basis of overall qualifications and personal financial need. Approximately 95 percent of all the students receive some form of financial aid during a part or all of their four years of study. Students are discouraged from accepting outside employment because of the lack of available time during a heavy academic schedule, but spouses of students usually have no difficulty in finding employment in the Omaha metropolitan area.

COSTS AND FINANCIAL AID

Financial aid phone number: **(402) 280-2666**
Tuition, 2005-2006 academic year: **$38,325**
Room and board: **$12,500**
Percentage of students receiving financial aid in 2005-06: **90%**
Percentage of students receiving: Loans: **86%**, Grants/scholarships: **24%**, Work-study aid: **0%**
Average medical school debt for the Class of 2004: **$144,229**

STUDENT BODY

Fall 2005 full-time enrollment: **485**
Men: **53%**, Women: **47%**, In-state: **13%**, Minorities: **18%**, American Indian: **2.1%**, Asian-American: **6.8%**, African-American: **3.5%**, Hispanic-American: **5.2%**, White: **82.5%**, International: **N/A**, Unknown: **N/A**

ACADEMIC PROGRAMS

The school's curriculum frequently gives first-year students substantial contact with patients.
There are opportunities for first- or second-year students to work in community health clinics.
Program offerings: drug/alcohol abuse, family medicine, internal medicine, pediatrics, rural medicine, women's health
Joint degrees awarded: M.D./Ph.D.
Total National Institutes of Health (NIH) grants awarded to the medical school and affiliated hospitals: **$11.5 million**

CURRICULUM

(TEXT PROVIDED BY SCHOOL):
Students participate in an integrated curriculum that incorporates basic and clinical science in all four years.

The educational program has been divided into four components. Component 1, Biomedical Fundamentals, serves as the foundation of the educational program, followed by more complex basic science information presented in a clinically relevant context in Component 2. This component consists of a series of organ-based and disease-based courses. Component 3 consists of required core clerkships emphasizing basic medical principles and acquisition of core clinical skills in a variety of inpatient and ambulatory settings. Component 4 provides additional responsibilities for patient care, including an eight-week block of critical care medicine, a four-week surgery elective, a four-week primary care subinternship, and 24 weeks of elective study.

Clinical experience is a prominent part of the curriculum in all components, beginning with the physical-diagnosis instruction in the first year. Students interact with standardized patients in the first year and are assigned to longitudinal clinics during the second year. The curriculum also integrates ethical and societal issues into all four components. Instructional methodology utilizes case-based, small-group sessions and computer-assisted instruction in all components. A close faculty-student relationship provides for mentoring and advising of students in choosing courses that will broaden their backgrounds for careers in medicine, as well as satisfying their special interests.

Competency-based evaluation is used in all components, and the students are graded on a pass/fail/honors system. Students compete against standards and not against one another.

FACULTY PROFILE (FALL 2005)

Total teaching faculty: **286 (full-time)**, **21 (part-time)**
Of full-time faculty, those teaching in basic sciences: **24%**; in clinical programs: **76%**
Of part-time faculty, those teaching in basic sciences: **29%**; in clinical programs: **71%**
Full-time faculty/student ratio: **0.6**

SUPPORT SERVICES

The school offers students these services for dealing with stress: expanded-hour gym access, peer counseling, professional counseling, religious support, support groups.

RESIDENCY PROFILE

Most popular residency and specialty programs chosen by the 2004 and 2005 M.D. graduating classes: anesthesiology, family practice, internal medicine, obstetrics and gynecology, orthopaedic surgery, pediatrics, psychiatry, radiology–diagnostic, surgery–general.

WHERE GRADS GO

39%
Proportion of 2003-2005 graduates who entered primary care specialties

22%
Proportion of 2004-2005 graduates who accepted in-state residencies

Dartmouth Medical School

- 3 Rope Ferry Road, Hanover, NH 03755-1404
- Private
- **Year Founded:** 1797
- **Tuition, 2005-2006:** $36,850
- **Enrollment 2005-2006 academic year:** 296
- **Website:** http://www.dartmouth.edu/dms
- **Specialty ranking:** family medicine: 22, rural medicine: 10

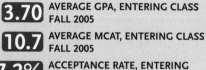

3.70	AVERAGE GPA, ENTERING CLASS FALL 2005
10.7	AVERAGE MCAT, ENTERING CLASS FALL 2005
7.2%	ACCEPTANCE RATE, ENTERING CLASS FALL 2005
32	2007 U.S. NEWS MEDICAL SCHOOL RANKING (RESEARCH)
21	2007 U.S. NEWS MEDICAL SCHOOL RANKING (PRIMARY CARE)

ADMISSIONS

Admissions phone number: **(603) 650-1505**
Admissions email address:
 dms.admissions@dartmouth.edu
Application website:
 **http://www.dartmouth.edu/dms/admissions/instrs_to_a
 pplicants.shtml**
Acceptance rate: **7.2%**
In-state acceptance rate: **22.0%**
Out-of-state acceptance rate: **7.0%**
Minority acceptance rate: **7.8%**
International acceptance rate: **N/A**

Fall 2005 applications and acceptees

	Applied	Interviewed	Accepted	Enrolled
Total:	3,599	669	259	82
In-state:	50	29	11	8
Out-of-state:	3,549	640	248	74

Profile of admitted students

Average undergraduate grade point average: **3.70**
MCAT averages (scale: 1-15; writing test: J-T):
 Composite score: **10.7**
 Verbal reasoning score: **10.4**, Physical sciences score:
 10.7, Biological sciences score: **10.9**, Writing score: **N/A**
Proportion with undergraduate majors in: Biological
 sciences: **61%**, Physical sciences: **7%**, Non-sciences:
 23%, Other health professions: **0%**, Mixed disciplines
 and other: **9%**
Percentage of students not coming directly from college
 after graduation: **N/A**

Dates and details

The American Medical College Application Service
 (AMCAS) application is accepted.
School asks for a school-specific application as part of the
 admissions process.
Oldest MCAT considered for Fall 2007 entry: **2004**
Earliest application date for the 2007-2008 first-year class:
 June 1, 2006
Latest application date: **November 1, 2006**

Acceptance dates for regular application for the class
 entering in fall 2007:
 Earliest: **October 15, 2006**
 Latest: **N/A**
The school considers requests for deferred entrance.
Starting month for the class entering in 2007-2008:
 August
The school doesn't have an Early Decision Plan (EDP).
A personal interview is required for admission.

Undergraduate coursework required

Medical school requires undergraduate work in these subjects: biology, organic chemistry, inorganic (general) chemistry, physics, calculus.

ADMISSIONS POLICY
(TEXT PROVIDED BY SCHOOL):

DMS seeks students with academic excellence and social
diversity. Although the vast majority of students, typically
over 90%, come from out of state, Dartmouth maintains a
commitment to residents of New Hampshire and a similar
commitment to Maine residents who apply through the
FAME/ACCESS program.

 Admissions requirements include one year of general
chemistry, organic chemistry, biology, and physics, and a
half-year of calculus. Also required is the equivalent of at
least three years' college work at an American or Canadian
college or university.

 The most recent entering class has average undergraduate GPAs of 3.7 and average combined MCATs of 32.
However, the committee does not use cutoffs and considers
candidates who present special qualities. Dartmouth values
and supports diversity in all of its programs and we always
encourage applications from minority students.

COSTS AND FINANCIAL AID

Financial aid phone number: **(603) 650-1919**
Tuition, 2005-2006 academic year: **$36,850**
Room and board: **$8,750**
Percentage of students receiving financial aid in 2005-06:
 83%

Percentage of students receiving: Loans: **75%**, Grants/scholarships: **44%**, Work-study aid: **N/A**
Average medical school debt for the Class of 2004: **$86,500**

STUDENT BODY

Fall 2005 full-time enrollment: **296**
Men: **51%**, Women: **49%**, In-state: **8%**, Minorities: **21%**, American Indian: **0.7%**, Asian-American: **13.2%**, African-American: **3.4%**, Hispanic-American: **3.4%**, White: **73.0%**, International: **4.7%**, Unknown: **1.7%**

ACADEMIC PROGRAMS

The school's curriculum frequently gives first-year students substantial contact with patients.
There are opportunities for first- or second-year students to work in community health clinics.
Program offerings: AIDS, drug/alcohol abuse, family medicine, geriatrics, internal medicine, pediatrics, rural medicine, women's health
Joint degrees awarded: M.D./Ph.D., M.D./MBA, M.D./MPH, M.D./MS
Total National Institutes of Health (NIH) grants awarded to the medical school and affiliated hospitals: **$109.4 million**

CURRICULUM

(TEXT PROVIDED BY SCHOOL):
Dartmouth Medical School's response to the rapid changes in medicine is to train dynamic learners. Our curriculum mixes lectures, small-group sessions, problem-based learning, computer-assisted instruction, preceptorships, interdisciplinary coursework, and independent study. Our class size is about 65 M.D. students, with joint degree programs of M.D./MBA, M.D./MPH, and M.D./Ph.D also offered.

Year I of the M.D. curriculum introduces students to the basic and fundamental biomedical sciences and to the normal structure and function of the human organism. In week I, students are paired with community physicians and/or core faculty preceptors to develop clinical skills.

Year II exposes students to an integrated, organ-system-based, multidisciplinary examination of pathophysiology, pharmacology, genetics, pathology, and medicine.

Students continue to study in the clinical environment with their preceptors.

Year III students strengthen and apply clinical skills in the principal branches and disciplines of medicine, working in both hospital and ambulatory settings. Coupled with 2 on-site teaching hospitals, students choose training sites in locations from Bethel, AK, the Florida Keys, Orange County, CA, and Augusta, ME.

Year IV includes 4 capstone courses, clinical clerkships, a subinternship in the discipline of the student's choice, and significant elective opportunities. The Capstone courses are "Health Society and the Physician", "Clinical Pharmacology and Therapeutics"; "Advanced Medical Sciences"; and "Advanced Cardiac Life Support."

FACULTY PROFILE (FALL 2005)

Total teaching faculty: **803 (full-time)**, **1,050 (part-time)**
Of full-time faculty, those teaching in basic sciences: **10%**; in clinical programs: **90%**
Of part-time faculty, those teaching in basic sciences: **4%**; in clinical programs: **96%**
Full-time faculty/student ratio: **2.7**

SUPPORT SERVICES

The school offers students these services for dealing with stress: peer counseling, professional counseling, support groups.

RESIDENCY PROFILE

Most popular residency and specialty programs chosen by the 2004 and 2005 M.D. graduating classes: anesthesiology, emergency medicine, family practice, internal medicine, obstetrics and gynecology, orthopaedic surgery, pediatrics, psychiatry, radiology–diagnostic, surgery–general.

WHERE GRADS GO

43.1%
Proportion of 2003-2005 graduates who entered primary care specialties

8%
Proportion of 2004-2005 graduates who accepted in-state residencies

Drexel University

■ 2900 Queen Lane, Philadelphia, PA 19129
■ Private
■ Year Founded: 1848
■ Tuition, 2005-2006: $37,890
■ Enrollment 2005-2006 academic year: 1,016
■ Website: http://www.drexelmed.edu
■ Specialty ranking: women's health: 16

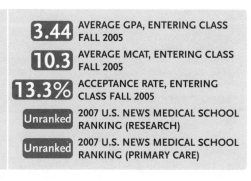

3.44 AVERAGE GPA, ENTERING CLASS FALL 2005

10.3 AVERAGE MCAT, ENTERING CLASS FALL 2005

13.3% ACCEPTANCE RATE, ENTERING CLASS FALL 2005

Unranked 2007 U.S. NEWS MEDICAL SCHOOL RANKING (RESEARCH)

Unranked 2007 U.S. NEWS MEDICAL SCHOOL RANKING (PRIMARY CARE)

ADMISSIONS
Admissions phone number: **(215) 991-8202**
Admissions email address: **Medadmis@drexel.edu**
Application website:
  http://www.aamc.org/students/start.htm
Acceptance rate: **13.3%**
In-state acceptance rate: **23.5%**
Out-of-state acceptance rate: **12.0%**
Minority acceptance rate: **13.1%**
International acceptance rate: **N/A**

Fall 2005 applications and acceptees

	Applied	Interviewed	Accepted	Enrolled
Total:	6,475	1,523	858	231
In-state:	680	263	160	64
Out-of-state:	5,795	1,260	698	167

Profile of admitted students
Average undergraduate grade point average: **3.44**
MCAT averages (scale: 1-15; writing test: J-T):
  Composite score: **10.3**
  Verbal reasoning score: **10.0**, Physical sciences score:
  10.0, Biological sciences score: **11.0**, Writing score: **Q**

Dates and details
The American Medical College Application Service
  (AMCAS) application is accepted.
School asks for a school-specific application as part of the
  admissions process.
Oldest MCAT considered for Fall 2007 entry: **2004**
Earliest application date for the 2007-2008 first-year class:
  June 1, 2006
Latest application date: **December 1, 2006**
Acceptance dates for regular application for the class
  entering in fall 2007:
  Earliest: **October 15, 2006**
  Latest: **N/A**
The school considers requests for deferred entrance.
Starting month for the class entering in 2007–2008:
  August
The school has an Early Decision Plan (EDP).

A personal interview is required for admission.

Undergraduate coursework required
Medical school requires undergraduate work in these subjects: biology, English, organic chemistry, inorganic (general) chemistry, physics.

ADMISSIONS POLICY
(TEXT PROVIDED BY SCHOOL):
In accordance with this institution's commitment, women,
students interested in careers as generalist physicians, those
who come from Pennsylvania, and those from populations
that are underrepresented in medicine are particularly
encouraged to apply. Applicants must be U.S. citizens or
permanent residents.

Applications are complete when the medical school
receives a verified AMCAS application, a secondary application with the $75 fee, and premedical letters of recommen-
dation. An admissions committee member will then review
the application in its entirety: GPA, MCAT scores, advisor
recommendations, the essay, and extracurricular activities
are all taken into consideration when choosing who to interview.

Typically, about 10 percent of the applicants are invited
for interviews. Interviews are conducted by both an experienced faculty member and a current medical student.

When these evaluations are returned to the office of
admissions, the entire applicant file is given to one of the 18
medical school applicant admissions committee members
for a blind review. The blind reviewer is someone on the
committee who has not personally met or interviewed the
applicant. The role of the blind reviewer is to give a subjective review of the applicant file including the essay and letters of recommendation.

Once this process is complete, a total overall score from
1-5 is given to each applicant based on all of the evaluations.
An agenda is then generated for the medical school admissions committee in rank order from 5 (highest) to 1 (lowest).
Each applicant file is presented to the admissions committee, and one of the members can make a recommendation
to accept, pur on a waitlist, or reject the applicant. Another

member of the committee must second the motion in order for our committee to vote. Once it is seconded, the committee votes and majority rules. The admissions committee meets every Thursday and decision letters are mailed to the applicants on Monday. This is process takes approximately 6 weeks from interview to receipt of a decision.

Applicants who are accepted to the medical college are sent an official acceptance packet and are required to submit a response with a $100 deposit fee to confirm his/her seat into the medical school. The time frame is 21 days to respond. The applicant has up until May 15 of the application year to withdrawal his/her acceptance.

COSTS AND FINANCIAL AID
Financial aid phone number: **(215) 991-8210**
Tuition, 2005-2006 academic year: **$37,890**
Room and board: **$9,500**
Percentage of students receiving financial aid in 2005-06: **85%**
Percentage of students receiving: Loans: **84%**, Grants/scholarships: **12%**, Work-study aid: **21%**
Average medical school debt for the Class of 2004: **$160,488**

STUDENT BODY
Fall 2005 full-time enrollment: **1,016**
Men: **50%**, Women: **50%**, In-state: **30%**, Minorities: **44%**, American Indian: **0.8%**, Asian-American: **35.8%**, African-American: **4.1%**, Hispanic-American: **3.6%**, White: **50.5%**, International: **0.2%**, Unknown: **4.9%**

ACADEMIC PROGRAMS
The school's curriculum occasionally gives first-year students substantial contact with patients.
There are opportunities for first- or second-year students to work in community health clinics.
Program offerings: AIDS, drug/alcohol abuse, family medicine, geriatrics, internal medicine, pediatrics, women's health
Joint degrees awarded: M.D./Ph.D., M.D./MBA, M.D./MPH
Total National Institutes of Health (NIH) grants awarded to the medical school and affiliated hospitals: **N/A**

CURRICULUM
(TEXT PROVIDED BY SCHOOL):
With its dedication to academic and clinical excellence, Drexel University College of Medicine has earned national recognition as an institution that provides innovation in medical education. Medical students are trained to consider each patient's case and needs in a comprehensive, integrated manner. The medical college is dedicated to preparing "physician healers"—doctors who practice the art, science, and skill of medicine.

Students choose between two innovative academic curricula for their first two years of study, both of which prepare students to pursue a career as either a generalist or specialist. Both stress problem solving, lifelong learning skills, and the coordinated teaching of basic science with clinical medi-

cine. Both tracks give early exposure to clinical skills training by using standardized patients.

The Interdisciplinary Foundations of Medicine curriculum integrates basic science courses and presents them through clinical symptom-based modules. Each first-year module features material from the perspective of several basic and behavioral science disciplines. By the end of the first year, the basic and behavioral science courses have presented their entire core content. In the second year, students study basic and clinical sciences using an organ-system approach.

Students who choose the Program for Integrated Learning will learn primarily in small groups. There are seven 10-week blocks over the first two years. Each block contains 10 case studies, detailing real patient issues, that serve as the stimulus and context for students to search out the information they need to understand, diagnose, and treat clinical problems. Laboratories and lectures complement the case studies.

The third year is devoted to required clinical clerkship rotations in medicine, family medicine, obstetrics and gynecology, pediatrics, psychiatry, and surgery. Students spend 30 percent of their clinical time in expanded ambulatory care experiences.

The fourth-year curriculum is structured in the form of "pathways," courses that give students a well-rounded educational experience with some focus on potential careers. The pathway system is structured so that students take both required courses and electives.

FACULTY PROFILE (FALL 2005)
Total teaching faculty: **510 (full-time)**, **59 (part-time)**
Of full-time faculty, those teaching in basic sciences: **20%**; in clinical programs: **80%**
Of part-time faculty, those teaching in basic sciences: **8%**; in clinical programs: **92%**
Full-time faculty/student ratio: **0.5**

SUPPORT SERVICES
The school offers students these services for dealing with stress: expanded-hour gym access, peer counseling, professional counseling, religious support, support groups.

RESIDENCY PROFILE
Most popular residency and specialty programs chosen by the 2004 and 2005 M.D. graduating classes: anesthesiology, emergency medicine, family practice, internal medicine, orthopaedic surgery, pediatrics, psychiatry, radiology–diagnostic, surgery–general.

WHERE GRADS GO

52%
Proportion of 2003-2005 graduates who entered primary care specialties

43%
Proportion of 2004-2005 graduates who accepted in-state residencies

Duke University

- **DUMC, Durham, NC 27710**
- **Private**
- **Year Founded:** 1930
- **Tuition, 2005-2006:** $39,537
- **Enrollment 2005-2006 academic year:** 406
- **Website:** http://dukemed.duke.edu
- **Specialty ranking:** AIDS: 7, family medicine: 8, geriatrics: 4, internal medicine: 4, pediatrics: 15, women's health: 10

3.80 AVERAGE GPA, ENTERING CLASS FALL 2005

11.9 AVERAGE MCAT, ENTERING CLASS FALL 2005

4.4% ACCEPTANCE RATE, ENTERING CLASS FALL 2005

6 2007 U.S. NEWS MEDICAL SCHOOL RANKING (RESEARCH)

6 2007 U.S. NEWS MEDICAL SCHOOL RANKING (PRIMARY CARE)

ADMISSIONS

Admissions phone number: **(919) 877-2985**
Admissions email address: **armst002@.mc.duke.edu**
Application website:
   http://dukemed.duke.edu/AdmissionsFinancialAid/index.cfm
Acceptance rate: **4.4%**
In-state acceptance rate: **5.7%**
Out-of-state acceptance rate: **4.3%**
Minority acceptance rate: **10.1%**
International acceptance rate: **3.0%**

Fall 2005 applications and acceptees

	Applied	Interviewed	Accepted	Enrolled
Total:	5,042	1,024	222	101
In-state:	367	223	21	17
Out-of-state:	4,675	801	201	84

Profile of admitted students

Average undergraduate grade point average: **3.80**
MCAT averages (scale: 1-15; writing test: J-T):
   Composite score: **11.9**
   Verbal reasoning score: **10.6**, Physical sciences score: **11.9**, Biological sciences score: **11.8**, Writing score: **N**
Proportion with undergraduate majors in: Biological sciences: **48%**, Physical sciences: **31%**, Non-sciences: **17%**, Other health professions: **0%**, Mixed disciplines and other: **5%**
Percentage of students not coming directly from college after graduation: **15%**

Dates and details

The American Medical College Application Service (AMCAS) application is accepted.
School asks for a school-specific application as part of the admissions process.
Oldest MCAT considered for Fall 2007 entry: **2003**
Earliest application date for the 2007-2008 first-year class: **January 6, 2006**
Latest application date: **March 11, 2006**

Acceptance dates for regular application for the class entering in fall 2007:
   Earliest: **January 3, 2007**
   Latest: **July 7, 2007**
The school considers requests for deferred entrance. Starting month for the class entering in 2007–2008:
   August
The school doesn't have an Early Decision Plan (EDP).
A personal interview is required for admission.

Undergraduate coursework required

Medical school requires undergraduate work in these subjects: biology, English, organic chemistry, inorganic (general) chemistry, physics, mathematics, calculus.

ADMISSIONS POLICY
(TEXT PROVIDED BY SCHOOL):

Duke University School of Medicine's approach to the identification, recruitment, and matriculation of students for the study of medicine is guided by our desire to select those candidates who will benefit maximally from the educational and experiential resources and unique curricula at Duke Med.

The missions of the school, to train scholars and leaders for medicine across a broad spectrum of career opportunities, are embodied in specific parameters that describe those qualities necessary for the study of medicine in the new millennium. This means that in addition to prediction of academic success using bottom-line grade-point average, Medical College Admission Test scores, academic honors, and detailed review of the breadth, depth, and level of academic rigor in undergraduate and graduate transcripts, the Admissions Committee evaluates the impact that the following factors have contributed toward the kind of humanism necessary for the needs of our increasingly diverse society:

   1) Sustained participation in and leadership of campus and community service activities.
   2) The need to work to financially support education.
   3) Where applicable, the demands imposed by varsity athletics.

4) Family educational achievement, resources, and socioeconomic background and the obstacles that these may introduce to accelerate or impede the achievement of an applicant's educational goals.

5) Significant exposure to medicine through volunteer experiences in clinical settings.

6) Exposure to research through experiences in research laboratories.

Through the American Medical College Application Service and Duke supplemental application and required interview process, we are able to gain insight into the impact that students' academic and experiential activities have had on the development of compassion, altruism, leadership, professionalism, oral/written communication skills, humanism, intellectual curiosity, critical thinking, and problem-solving skills, all of which are compelling attributes for those to whom the healthcare of the country will be entrusted. Duke University School of Medicine seeks applicants from diverse communities, including but not limited to geographically, culturally, socially, economically, intellectually, and racially diverse populations.

COSTS AND FINANCIAL AID

Financial aid phone number: **(919) 684-6649**
Tuition, 2005-2006 academic year: **$39,537**
Room and board: **$13,872**
Percentage of students receiving financial aid in 2005-06: **87%**
Percentage of students receiving: Loans: **68%**, Grants/scholarships: **73%**, Work-study aid: **0%**
Average medical school debt for the Class of 2004: **$74,790**

STUDENT BODY

Fall 2005 full-time enrollment: **406**
Men: **52%**, Women: **48%**, In-state: **17%**, Minorities: **42%**, American Indian: **1.7%**, Asian-American: **20.0%**, African-American: **14.0%**, Hispanic-American: **3.0%**, White: **50.7%**, International: **7.4%**, Unknown: **3.2%**

ACADEMIC PROGRAMS

The school's curriculum frequently gives first-year students substantial contact with patients.
There are opportunities for first- or second-year students to work in community health clinics.
Program offerings: AIDS, drug/alcohol abuse, family medicine, geriatrics, internal medicine, pediatrics, rural medicine, women's health
Joint degrees awarded: M.D./Ph.D., M.D./MBA, M.D./MPH, M.D./JD, M.D./MS

Total National Institutes of Health (NIH) grants awarded to the medical school and affiliated hospitals: **N/A**

CURRICULUM
(TEXT PROVIDED BY SCHOOL):
The Duke medical school curriculum emphasizes the development of independent thinkers committed to the generation, conservation, and dissemination of knowledge regarding the causes, prevention, and treatment of human disease.

The Duke curriculum is unique in that all required basic science coursework is taken in the first year. In the second year, students do the core required clinical rotations. The third year is a year of scholarship in which about two thirds of the class pursue laboratory or clinical research. Approximately one third of the students pursue combined degree programs (M.D./Ph.D., M.D./MPH, M.D./MS in clinical research, M.D./JD, M.D./MBA). During the fourth year, students return to clinical rotations or clinical electives.

FACULTY PROFILE (FALL 2005)

Total teaching faculty: **1,695 (full-time), 18 (part-time)**
Of full-time faculty, those teaching in basic sciences: **8%**; in clinical programs: **92%**
Of part-time faculty, those teaching in basic sciences: **6%**; in clinical programs: **94%**
Full-time faculty/student ratio: **4.2**

SUPPORT SERVICES

The school offers students these services for dealing with stress: expanded-hour gym access, peer counseling, professional counseling, religious support, support groups.

RESIDENCY PROFILE

Most popular residency and specialty programs chosen by the 2004 and 2005 M.D. graduating classes: anesthesiology, dermatology, emergency medicine, internal medicine, ophthalmology, orthopaedic surgery, pediatrics, radiology–diagnostic, surgery–general.

WHERE GRADS GO

43.1%
Proportion of 2003-2005 graduates who entered primary care specialties

19.7%
Proportion of 2004-2005 graduates who accepted in-state residencies

East Carolina University

BRODY

- 600 Moye Boulevard, Greenville, NC 27834
- Public
- Year Founded: 1975
- Tuition, 2005-2006: In-state: $7,676; Out-of-state: $32,633
- Enrollment 2005-2006 academic year: 286
- Website: http://www.ecu.edu/bsomadmissions
- Specialty ranking: family medicine: 9, rural medicine: 7

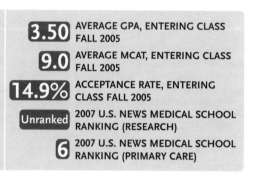

3.50 AVERAGE GPA, ENTERING CLASS FALL 2005

9.0 AVERAGE MCAT, ENTERING CLASS FALL 2005

14.9% ACCEPTANCE RATE, ENTERING CLASS FALL 2005

Unranked 2007 U.S. NEWS MEDICAL SCHOOL RANKING (RESEARCH)

6 2007 U.S. NEWS MEDICAL SCHOOL RANKING (PRIMARY CARE)

ADMISSIONS

Admissions phone number: **(252) 744-2202**
Admissions email address: **somadmissions@mail.ecu.edu**
Application website: **N/A**
Acceptance rate: **14.9%**
In-state acceptance rate: **14.9%**

Fall 2005 applications and acceptees

	Applied	Interviewed	Accepted	Enrolled
Total:	745	400	111	72
In-state:	745	400	111	72
Out-of-state:	0	0	0	0

Profile of admitted students

Average undergraduate grade point average: **3.50**
MCAT averages (scale: 1-15; writing test: J-T):
  Composite score: **9.0**
  Verbal reasoning score: **9.1**, Physical sciences score: **8.8**, Biological sciences score: **9.0**, Writing score: **P**
Proportion with undergraduate majors in: Biological sciences: **53%**, Physical sciences: **24%**, Non-sciences: **12%**, Other health professions: **10%**, Mixed disciplines and other: **1%**
Percentage of students not coming directly from college after graduation: **62%**

Dates and details

The American Medical College Application Service (AMCAS) application is accepted.
School asks for a school-specific application as part of the admissions process.
Oldest MCAT considered for Fall 2007 entry: **3**
Earliest application date for the 2007-2008 first-year class: **June 1, 2006**
Latest application date: **November 15, 2006**
Acceptance dates for regular application for the class entering in fall 2007:
  Earliest: **October 15, 2006**
  Latest: **N/A**
The school doesn't consider requests for deferred entrance.

Starting month for the class entering in 2007-2008:
  August
The school has an Early Decision Plan (EDP).
A personal interview is required for admission.

Undergraduate coursework required

Medical school requires undergraduate work in these subjects: biology/zoology, English, organic chemistry, inorganic (general) chemistry, physics.

ADMISSIONS POLICY

(TEXT PROVIDED BY SCHOOL):

Factors considered by Admissions Committee members as they review applicants to the Brody School of Medicine encompass the intellectual, personal, and social development of each individual. In order to assess these areas, the committee uses a variety of data, including grades and other indicators of academic achievement; performance on the Medical College Admission Test and any other available standardized tests; the personal, professional, and employment experiences of the applicant; evaluations from faculty members who have taught the applicant; letters of reference from employers, acquaintances, and other individuals; interviews conducted by members of the Admissions Committee; and any other pertinent information.

Since there are no rigid cutoffs or formulas used in the selection of medical students, each applicant is viewed as an individual. All available information is considered in order to best determine that applicant's character and qualifications for the study of medicine.

The Brody School of Medicine acknowledges its responsibility as a state-supported school to select students and train physicians who will meet the needs of all residents of North Carolina. In meeting this responsibility, the Brody School of Medicine seeks competent students of diverse personalities and backgrounds. In particular, special effort is made to include in each entering class students from a variety of geographical, economic, and ethnic groups. It follows that all applicants are evaluated by the Admissions Committee without regard to race, religion, sex, color, national origin, age, or disability.

Since the Brody School of Medicine is a state-supported medical school, very strong preference is given to qualified residents of North Carolina who apply for admission. No out-of-state students have been admitted in nearly 20 years.

COSTS AND FINANCIAL AID
Financial aid phone number: **(252) 744-2278**
Tuition, 2005-2006 academic year: **In-state: $7,676; Out-of-state: $32,633**
Room and board: **$9,856**
Percentage of students receiving financial aid in 2005-06: **90%**
Percentage of students receiving: Loans: **90%**, Grants/scholarships: **36%**, Work-study aid: **0%**
Average medical school debt for the Class of 2004: **$63,793**

STUDENT BODY
Fall 2005 full-time enrollment: 286
Men: 51%, Women: 49%, In-state: 100%, Minorities: 33%, American Indian: 3.5%, Asian-American: 6.6%, African-American: 15.4%, Hispanic-American: 2.8%, White: 70.3%, International: 0.0%, Unknown: 1.4%

ACADEMIC PROGRAMS
The school's curriculum very frequently gives first-year students substantial contact with patients.
There are opportunities for first- or second-year students to work in community health clinics.
Program offerings: drug/alcohol abuse, family medicine, geriatrics, internal medicine, pediatrics, rural medicine, women's health
Joint degrees awarded: M.D./Ph.D., M.D./MBA, M.D./MPH.
Total National Institutes of Health (NIH) grants awarded to the medical school and affiliated hospitals: **$3.4 million**

CURRICULUM
(TEXT PROVIDED BY SCHOOL):
The medical school curriculum has been carefully developed and is regularly monitored and adjusted to reflect the changes occurring in contemporary medical education and practice. The curriculum provides a logical integration of basic science and clinical science knowledge over the four-year span.
Early experience in the patient care setting is achieved through individual preceptorships at physician offices

throughout the state and through contact with both standardized and clinic patients in the Doctoring and Clinical Skills course in the first two years. Innovative teaching methods such as small-group discussions, computer-assisted instruction, use of standardized patients and medical simulations are employed during the entire four years, as a complement to the traditional venues of the lecture hall and the laboratory.

The third- and fourth-year clinical experiences are gained at a major regional teaching hospital center, outpatient clinics, and physician office settings as students progress through the six major clinical areas. The fourth year includes opportunities to explore medical topics, specialties, and individually designed selectives. Research projects are encouraged and supported through the medical student research program in the first and second years.

FACULTY PROFILE (FALL 2005)
Total teaching faculty: **400 (full-time)**, **47 (part-time)**
Of full-time faculty, those teaching in basic sciences: **19%**; in clinical programs: **81%**
Of part-time faculty, those teaching in basic sciences: **19%**; in clinical programs: **81%**
Full-time faculty/student ratio: **1.4**

SUPPORT SERVICES
The school offers students these services for dealing with stress: expanded-hour gym access, peer counseling, professional counseling, religious support, support groups.

RESIDENCY PROFILE
Most popular residency and specialty programs chosen by the 2004 and 2005 M.D. graduating classes: emergency medicine, family practice, internal medicine, obstetrics and gynecology, orthopaedic surgery, pediatrics, physical medicine and rehabilitation, surgery–general, internal medicine/pediatrics, internal medicine/psychiatry.

WHERE GRADS GO

62%
Proportion of 2003-2005 graduates who entered primary care specialties

41%
Proportion of 2004-2005 graduates who accepted in-state residencies

Eastern Virginia Medical School

- 721 Fairfax Avenue, PO Box 1980, Norfolk, VA 23501-1980
- Private
- Year Founded: 1973
- Tuition, 2005-2006: $24,048
- Enrollment 2005-2006 academic year: 436
- Website: http://www.evms.edu
- Specialty ranking: N/A

3.45	AVERAGE GPA, ENTERING CLASS FALL 2005
10.1	AVERAGE MCAT, ENTERING CLASS FALL 2005
7.5%	ACCEPTANCE RATE, ENTERING CLASS FALL 2005
Unranked	2007 U.S. NEWS MEDICAL SCHOOL RANKING (RESEARCH)
52	2007 U.S. NEWS MEDICAL SCHOOL RANKING (PRIMARY CARE)

ADMISSIONS

Admissions phone number: **(757) 446-5812**
Admissions email address: **nanezkf@evms.edu**
Application website: **http://www.evms.edu/admissions**
Acceptance rate: **7.5%**

Fall 2005 applications and acceptees

	Applied	Interviewed	Accepted	Enrolled
Total:	3,424	N/A	256	110
In-state:	720	N/A	N/A	73
Out-of-state:	2,704	N/A	N/A	37

Profile of admitted students

Average undergraduate grade point average: **3.45**
MCAT averages (scale: 1-15; writing test: J-T):
Composite score: **10.1**
Verbal reasoning score: **10.3**, Physical sciences score: **9.7**, Biological sciences score: **10.4**, Writing score: **N/A**
Proportion with undergraduate majors in: Biological sciences: **40%**, Physical sciences: **18%**, Non-sciences: **9%**, Other health professions: **18%**, Mixed disciplines and other: **14%**
Percentage of students not coming directly from college after graduation: **N/A**

Dates and details

The American Medical College Application Service (AMCAS) application is accepted.
School asks for a school-specific application as part of the admissions process.
Oldest MCAT considered for Fall 2007 entry: **2004**
Earliest application date for the 2007-2008 first-year class: **June 1, 2006**
Latest application date: **November 15, 2006**
Acceptance dates for regular application for the class entering in fall 2007:
Earliest: **October 15, 2006**
Latest: **N/A**
The school considers requests for deferred entrance.
Starting month for the class entering in 2007–2008: **August**

The school has an Early Decision Plan (EDP).
A personal interview is required for admission.

Undergraduate coursework required

Medical school requires undergraduate work in these subjects: biology, organic chemistry, inorganic (general) chemistry, physics.

ADMISSIONS POLICY

(TEXT PROVIDED BY SCHOOL):

As a medical school dedicated since its inception to the healthcare needs of eastern Virginia, EVMS shows preference to applicants from the Commonwealth of Virginia, especially legal residents of Hampton Roads. For an applicant to be considered as an in-state Virginia resident, he or she must have been legally domiciled in the Commonwealth of Virginia for at least one year prior to matriculation.

Out-of-state students who have strong academic credentials and the personal traits valued by EVMS are also encouraged to apply. Applicants from rural or other underserved regions and those who have been disadvantaged or underrepresented for economic, racial, or social reasons, and who possess the motivation and aptitude required for the study of medicine, are also strongly encouraged to apply.

The body of knowledge a physician must assimilate is vast and complex. For this reason, EVMS requires academic excellence of those students admitted to the medical school. The Committee on Admissions gauges an applicant's academic ability by his or her performance in undergraduate courses and scores on the Medical College Admission Test. The MCAT and a minimum of 100 semester hours at an accredited American or Canadian university are required.

Coursework must include one year each of biology, general chemistry, organic chemistry, and physics, all with lab work. Applicants are expected to have grades of C or better in all required courses. Credits earned through Advanced Placement programs or the College Level Examination Program are acceptable. Applicants may enhance their chances of acceptance by taking graduate coursework in natural science. In recent years, students matriculating at EVMS have had a mean grade-point average of 3.44 and a mean MCAT of 30.

COSTS AND FINANCIAL AID

Financial aid phone number: **(757) 446-5814**
Tuition, 2005-2006 academic year: **$24,048**
Work-study aid: **0%**

STUDENT BODY

Fall 2005 full-time enrollment: **436**
Men: **47%**, Women: **53%**, In-state: **65%**, Minorities: **19%**

ACADEMIC PROGRAMS

The school's curriculum very frequently gives first-year students substantial contact with patients.
There are opportunities for first- or second-year students to work in community health clinics.
Program offerings: AIDS, drug/alcohol abuse, family medicine, geriatrics, internal medicine, pediatrics, rural medicine
Joint degrees awarded: M.D./MPH
Total National Institutes of Health (NIH) grants awarded to the medical school and affiliated hospitals: **$6.8 million**

CURRICULUM

(TEXT PROVIDED BY SCHOOL):
The mission of the M.D. program is to educate medical students who will be noted for their excellence in practice, human values, collegiality, and scientific curiosity and rigor.

The curriculum is designed to educate compassionate, skillful physician-scientists, with an emphasis on preparation of physicians for residency training in the primary care disciplines. Excellence in patient care requires a firm foundation in the medical sciences and clinical skills, combined with an empathetic attitude and the ability to apply the scientific method to the solution of medical problems.

To meet the challenges created by the rapid development of new technologies and new understanding in medical science, the physician of the future will need not only accurate, current information but also the ability to obtain, evaluate, and assimilate information about the rapid advances in medicine. Essential to this ability is a habit of critical scientific inquiry. With the increasing complexity of medicine, deductive reasoning and problem solving become increasingly important.

With these concepts in mind, the EVMS curriculum is designed to: provide a firm foundation in medical sciences and clinical skills; address medical problems using the best available medical evidence; cultivate habits of independent learning and scholarship; help students recognize the broad social and economic responsibilities of members of the medical profession; encourage the development of self-awareness and communication skills; and emphasize human values in the practice of medicine.

The instructional approach at EVMS emphasizes an integrated program of basic and clinical sciences from the first week of medical school throughout all four years of study. Students participate as active learners in a carefully sequenced program designed to achieve competency in all areas required for the general professional education of the physician. Small study groups help students develop their interpersonal skills, professional attitudes, and problem-solving abilities. The four-year curriculum includes both interdisciplinary and discipline-based instruction. Progress toward achieving the expected professional competence is assessed periodically through the Professional Skills Center in all four years and through standardized testing.

FACULTY PROFILE (FALL 2005)

Total teaching faculty: **313 (full-time)**, **60 (part-time)**
Of full-time faculty, those teaching in basic sciences: **14%**; in clinical programs: **86%**
Of part-time faculty, those teaching in basic sciences: **2%**; in clinical programs: **98%**
Full-time faculty/student ratio: **0.7**

SUPPORT SERVICES

The school offers students these services for dealing with stress: peer counseling, professional counseling, religious support.

RESIDENCY PROFILE

Most popular residency and specialty programs chosen by the 2004 and 2005 M.D. graduating classes: anesthesiology, emergency medicine, family practice, internal medicine, obstetrics and gynecology, ophthalmology, pediatrics, psychiatry, radiology–diagnostic, surgery–general.

WHERE GRADS GO

49%
Proportion of 2003-2005 graduates who entered primary care specialties

31%
Proportion of 2004-2005 graduates who accepted in-state residencies

East Tennessee State University

J.H. QUILLEN

- PO Box 70694, Johnson City, TN 37614
- Public
- Year Founded: 1974
- Tuition, 2005-2006: In-state: $18,559; Out-of-state: $36,691
- Enrollment 2005-2006 academic year: 238
- Website: http://com.etsu.edu
- Specialty ranking: family medicine: 22, rural medicine: 3

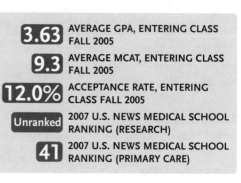

3.63 AVERAGE GPA, ENTERING CLASS FALL 2005

9.3 AVERAGE MCAT, ENTERING CLASS FALL 2005

12.0% ACCEPTANCE RATE, ENTERING CLASS FALL 2005

Unranked 2007 U.S. NEWS MEDICAL SCHOOL RANKING (RESEARCH)

41 2007 U.S. NEWS MEDICAL SCHOOL RANKING (PRIMARY CARE)

ADMISSIONS

Admissions phone number: **(423) 439-2033**
Admissions email address: **sacom@etsu.edu**
Application website: **http://www.aamc.org**
Acceptance rate: **12.0%**
In-state acceptance rate: **25.8%**
Out-of-state acceptance rate: **2.8%**
Minority acceptance rate: **5.1%**
International acceptance rate: **N/A**

Fall 2005 applications and acceptees

	Applied	Interviewed	Accepted	Enrolled
Total:	1,187	197	142	60
In-state:	472	163	122	53
Out-of-state:	715	34	20	7

Profile of admitted students

Average undergraduate grade point average: **3.63**
MCAT averages (scale: 1-15; writing test: J-T):
   Composite score: **9.3**
   Verbal reasoning score: **9.8**, Physical sciences score: **8.8**,
   Biological sciences score: **9.2**, Writing score: **O**
Proportion with undergraduate majors in: Biological
   sciences: **36%**, Physical sciences: **30%**, Non-sciences:
   17%, Other health professions: **2%**, Mixed disciplines
   and other: **15%**
Percentage of students not coming directly from college
   after graduation: **20%**

Dates and details

The American Medical College Application Service
   (AMCAS) application is accepted.
School asks for a school-specific application as part of the
   admissions process.
Oldest MCAT considered for Fall 2007 entry: **2004**
Earliest application date for the 2007-2008 first-year class:
   June 1, 2006
Latest application date: **November 15, 2006**
Acceptance dates for regular application for the class
   entering in fall 2007:
   Earliest: **October 15, 2006**

Latest: **August 1, 2007**
The school considers requests for deferred entrance.
Starting month for the class entering in 2007–2008:
   August
The school has an Early Decision Plan (EDP).
A personal interview is required for admission.

Undergraduate coursework required

Medical school requires undergraduate work in these subjects: biology/zoology, English, organic chemistry, inorganic
(general) chemistry, physics.

ADMISSIONS POLICY

(TEXT PROVIDED BY SCHOOL):
Quillen's multilevel review process employs consideration
of the qualities important in making a successful physician
and meeting the stated goals and values of both Quillen and
ETSU. This whole-person concept evaluates applicants on
the basis of objective and subjective criteria: demonstrated
academic achievement, Medical College Admission Test
scores, letters of recommendation, pertinent extracurricular
work and research experience, evidence of nonscholastic
accomplishment, motivation for the study and practice of
medicine, and interest in a primary-care practice in a rural
or underserved area.

Because Quillen College of Medicine is a state-supported
institution, preference for admission is given to Tennessee
residents. Out-of-state applicants from the contiguous
Appalachian region interested in primary-care medicine
may receive a higher admissions priority than other nonresident applicants. There are no quotas or set-asides; all applicants are considered in the same competitive pool using the
same policies, procedures, and Admissions Committee
members.

Through its 25-year history, Quillen's admissions process
has proved to consistently produce a diverse student body
with high graduation rates, with more than half of the graduates entering a field of primary care, often in underserved
rural regions.

COSTS AND FINANCIAL AID

Financial aid phone number: (423) 439-2035
Tuition, 2005-2006 academic year: **In-state: $18,559;** Out-of-state: $36,691
Room and board: **$12,900**
Percentage of students receiving financial aid in 2005-06: **92%**
Percentage of students receiving: Loans: **91%**, Grants/scholarships: **35%**, Work-study aid: **0%**
Average medical school debt for the Class of 2004: **$109,000**

STUDENT BODY

Fall 2005 full-time enrollment: **238**
Men: **50%**, Women: **50%**, In-state: **94%**, Minorities: **16%**, American Indian: **2.5%**, Asian-American: **6.7%**, African-American: **6.3%**, Hispanic-American: **0.4%**, White: **84.0%**, International: **0.0%**, Unknown: **0.0%**

ACADEMIC PROGRAMS

The school's curriculum frequently gives first-year students substantial contact with patients.
There are opportunities for first- or second-year students to work in community health clinics.
Program offerings: AIDS, drug/alcohol abuse, family medicine, geriatrics, internal medicine, pediatrics, rural medicine, women's health
Joint degrees awarded: N/A
Total National Institutes of Health (NIH) grants awarded to the medical school and affiliated hospitals: **N/A**

CURRICULUM

(TEXT PROVIDED BY SCHOOL):
The James H. Quillen College of Medicine (JHQCOM) has both a generalist track and a rural primary care track (RPCT). Up to 25 percent of the entering class may elect to be in the RPCT. The core curriculum is common to both tracks, but the RPCT students are in an experiential and interdisciplinary learning environment in rural communities from the first month; 20 percent of their first two years, one-third of their junior clerkship experiences and one-half of their required four months of senior selective experiences are in rural primary care settings.

The first-year core curriculum provides the biomedical science basis for human anatomy and function. The case-oriented learning, workshops, the human patient simulator, preceptorship program and standardized-patient clinical skills program provide clinical relevance and reinforce the basic science learning. Communication skills, psychological development, psychosocial issues and the behavioral basis for psychiatric disease are introduced in the first year.

The second year builds on the first year with an introduction to the altered states produced by microorganisms and disease. A year-long course that uses student presentations in a grand round format integrates closely with other course topics to reinforce learning, focus on pathophysiology, and provide introduction to clinical thinking and problem solving.

Third year consists of six eight-week clerkships: Family Medicine, Internal Medicine, Pediatrics, Obstetrics/Gynecology, Psychiatry and Surgery. Junior students have supervised responsibility and are required to become part of the health care team. Each clerkship has clearly defined objectives, a core lecture series, and defined opportunities for formative feedback.

The fourth year consists of four months of required "Selective" experiences, four months of electives, and a one month "Keystone" experience. Elective experiences allow students to address individual needs and two of the four electives may be taken in other medical schools. The "Keystone" month combines clinical workshops, simulator experience, and a lecture series to prepare students for starting residency training. Topics in the lecture series include practice management, financial management, medical-legal issues, ethics, and a "favorite professor" lecture series.

FACULTY PROFILE (FALL 2005)

Total teaching faculty: **250 (full-time)**, **38 (part-time)**
Of full-time faculty, those teaching in basic sciences: **24%**; in clinical programs: **76%**
Of part-time faculty, those teaching in basic sciences: **3%**; in clinical programs: **97%**
Full-time faculty/student ratio: **1.1**

SUPPORT SERVICES

The school offers students these services for dealing with stress: expanded-hour gym access, peer counseling, professional counseling, religious support.

RESIDENCY PROFILE

Most popular residency and specialty programs chosen by the 2004 and 2005 M.D. graduating classes: emergency medicine, family practice, internal medicine, obstetrics and gynecology, orthopaedic surgery, otolaryngology, pathology–anatomic and clinical, pediatrics, psychiatry, surgery–general.

WHERE GRADS GO

50.6%
Proportion of 2003-2005 graduates who entered primary care specialties

37.3%
Proportion of 2004-2005 graduates who accepted in-state residencies

Emory University

- 1440 Clifton Road NE, Atlanta, GA 30322-1053
- Private
- Year Founded: 1854
- Tuition, 2005-2006: $36,534
- Enrollment 2005-2006 academic year: 462
- Website: http://www.med.emory.edu
- Specialty ranking: AIDS: 17, drug/alcohol abuse: 19, internal medicine: 18

3.64 AVERAGE GPA, ENTERING CLASS FALL 2005

11.1 AVERAGE MCAT, ENTERING CLASS FALL 2005

8.2% ACCEPTANCE RATE, ENTERING CLASS FALL 2005

26 2007 U.S. NEWS MEDICAL SCHOOL RANKING (RESEARCH)

41 2007 U.S. NEWS MEDICAL SCHOOL RANKING (PRIMARY CARE)

ADMISSIONS

Admissions phone number: **(404) 727-5660**
Admissions email address: **medadmiss@emory.edu**
Application website: **N/A**
Acceptance rate: **8.2%**
In-state acceptance rate: **15.0%**
Out-of-state acceptance rate: **7.4%**
Minority acceptance rate: **7.1%**
International acceptance rate: **3.2%**

Fall 2005 applications and acceptees

	Applied	Interviewed	Accepted	Enrolled
Total:	3,759	752	308	114
In-state:	400	139	60	35
Out-of-state:	3,359	613	248	79

Profile of admitted students

Average undergraduate grade point average: **3.64**
MCAT averages (scale: 1-15; writing test: J-T):
  Composite score: **11.1**
  Verbal reasoning score: **10.7**, Physical sciences score: **11.2**, Biological sciences score: **11.4**, Writing score: **P**
Proportion with undergraduate majors in: Biological sciences: **40%**, Physical sciences: **18%**, Non-sciences: **21%**, Other health professions: **0%**, Mixed disciplines and other: **20%**
Percentage of students not coming directly from college after graduation: **26%**

Dates and details

The American Medical College Application Service (AMCAS) application is accepted.
School asks for a school-specific application as part of the admissions process.
Oldest MCAT considered for Fall 2007 entry: **2003**
Earliest application date for the 2007-2008 first-year class: **June 1, 2006**
Latest application date: **October 15, 2006**
Acceptance dates for regular application for the class entering in fall 2007:
  Earliest: **November 1, 2006**

Latest: **July 17, 2007**
The school considers requests for deferred entrance.
Starting month for the class entering in 2007-2008: **July**
The school doesn't have an Early Decision Plan (EDP).
A personal interview is required for admission.

Undergraduate coursework required

Medical school requires undergraduate work in these subjects: biology, English, organic chemistry, inorganic (general) chemistry, physics, humanities, behavioral science, demonstration of writing skills, social sciences.

ADMISSIONS POLICY
(TEXT PROVIDED BY SCHOOL):

When you apply to Emory, we will look at you as an individual. To be a competitive applicant, we recommend that you present a file that features a strong academic record; recommendations from those who can attest to both your work in the classroom as well as your personal character, compassion, integrity, and motivation for a career in medicine; exposure to patients in a clinical setting; and evidence of your interests in areas outside of medicine.

There are eight recommended steps that need to be completed in the application process and that can be easily downloaded at the Emory Web site. It is to your advantage to apply though the American Medical College Application Service and complete your application as early as possible, as Emory receives thousands of applications for our entering class of 112 students. Your file will not be screened for an interview until the Office of Medical Education and Student Affairs receives your AMCAS application, Medical College Admission Test scores, recommendations, and supplemental application with fee payment. If you have specific questions about how to improve your application, please contact your premed adviser or visit our website.

COSTS AND FINANCIAL AID

Financial aid phone number: **(800) 727-6039**
Tuition, 2005-2006 academic year: **$36,534**
Room and board: **$14,640**

Percentage of students receiving financial aid in 2005-06:
80%
Percentage of students receiving: Loans: 72%,
Grants/scholarships: 50%, Work-study aid: 0%
Average medical school debt for the Class of 2004:
$114,078

STUDENT BODY

Fall 2005 full-time enrollment: 462
Men: 52%, Women: 48%, In-state: 33%, Minorities: 29%,
American Indian: 0.6%, Asian-American: 16.0%,
African-American: 10.0%, Hispanic-American: 1.5%,
White: 66.5%, International: 1.9%, Unknown: 3.5%

ACADEMIC PROGRAMS

The school's curriculum occasionally gives first-year
students substantial contact with patients.
There are opportunities for first- or second-year students to
work in community health clinics.
Program offerings: AIDS, drug/alcohol abuse, family
medicine, geriatrics, internal medicine, pediatrics,
women's health
Joint degrees awarded: M.D./Ph.D., M.D./MPH
Total National Institutes of Health (NIH) grants awarded to
the medical school and affiliated hospitals: $187.1
million

CURRICULUM

(TEXT PROVIDED BY SCHOOL):
Come to Emory, and you'll partake in a medical curriculum
that is continually extending its program into areas beyond
the bounds of traditional medical education for the benefit
of the student and society. It is a combination of lectures,
laboratory work, research opportunities, conferences,
demonstrations, examinations, clinical instruction, and
small- group discussions, including problem-based learning
and interaction with patient actors in a clinical skills/stan-
dardized patient program.
    The first two years of basic science coursework are con-
ducted on the Emory campus with enhanced patient contact
and experience that includes problem-based learning and
clinical instruction. Emory students are well prepared to

begin caring for patients when they transition into the more
clinical two years of the program. Dual-degree programs
offer in-depth opportunities to pursue research and public-
health projects.
    The vast number of outpatient and inpatient visits within
the Emory Healthcare environment and throughout the
state of Georgia offers students a rewarding experience
within a broad range of facilities. Couple this with more
than 1,600 dedicated faculty, and the medical curriculum
makes Emory a rich environment for learning clinical medicine and providing important research opportunities.

FACULTY PROFILE (FALL 2005)

Total teaching faculty: 1,772 **(full-time)**, 180 **(part-time)**
Of full-time faculty, those teaching in basic sciences: 10%;
in clinical programs: 90%
Of part-time faculty, those teaching in basic sciences: 3%;
in clinical programs: 97%
Full-time faculty/student ratio: 3.8

SUPPORT SERVICES

The school offers students these services for dealing with
stress: expanded-hour gym access, peer counseling, professional counseling, religious support, support groups.

RESIDENCY PROFILE

Most popular residency and specialty programs chosen by
the 2004 and 2005 M.D. graduating classes: anesthesiology,
dermatology, emergency medicine, internal medicine,
orthopaedic surgery, otolaryngology, pediatrics, psychiatry,
radiology–diagnostic, surgery–general.

WHERE GRADS GO

42%
*Proportion of 2003-2005 graduates who entered primary
care specialties*

35%
*Proportion of 2004-2005 graduates who accepted in-state
residencies*

Florida State University

- 1115 W. Call Street, Tallahassee, FL 32306-4300
- Public
- Year Founded: 2000
- Tuition, 2005-2006: In-state: $17,570; Out-of-state: $52,121
- Enrollment 2005-2006 academic year: 220
- Website: http://www.med.fsu.edu/
- Specialty ranking: N/A

3.59 AVERAGE GPA, ENTERING CLASS FALL 2005

8.7 AVERAGE MCAT, ENTERING CLASS FALL 2005

10.9% ACCEPTANCE RATE, ENTERING CLASS FALL 2005

Unranked 2007 U.S. NEWS MEDICAL SCHOOL RANKING (RESEARCH)

Unranked 2007 U.S. NEWS MEDICAL SCHOOL RANKING (PRIMARY CARE)

ADMISSIONS

Admissions phone number: **(850) 644-7904**
Admissions email address: **medadmissions@med.fsu.edu**
Application website: **N/A**
Acceptance rate: **10.9%**
In-state acceptance rate: **12.5%**
Out-of-state acceptance rate: **0.0%**
Minority acceptance rate: **12.6%**
International acceptance rate: **N/A**

Fall 2005 applications and acceptees

	Applied	Interviewed	Accepted	Enrolled
Total:	1,209	196	132	80
In-state:	1,055	196	132	80
Out-of-state:	154	0	0	0

Profile of admitted students

Average undergraduate grade point average: **3.59**
MCAT averages (scale: 1-15; writing test: J-T):
  Composite score: **8.7**
  Verbal reasoning score: **8.2**, Physical sciences score: **8.5**, Biological sciences score: **8.9**, Writing score: **N**
Proportion with undergraduate majors in: Biological sciences: **51%**, Physical sciences: **10%**, Non-sciences: **10%**, Other health professions: **10%**, Mixed disciplines and other: **19%**
Percentage of students not coming directly from college after graduation: **29%**

Dates and details

The American Medical College Application Service (AMCAS) application is accepted.
School asks for a school-specific application as part of the admissions process.
Oldest MCAT considered for Fall 2007 entry: **2002**
Earliest application date for the 2007-2008 first-year class: **May 5, 2006**
Latest application date: **December 1, 2006**
Acceptance dates for regular application for the class entering in fall 2007:
  Earliest: **October 15, 2006**

Latest: **June 1, 2007**
The school considers requests for deferred entrance.
Starting month for the class entering in 2007-2008: **May**
The school has an Early Decision Plan (EDP).
A personal interview is required for admission.

Undergraduate coursework required

Medical school requires undergraduate work in these subjects: biology, English, organic chemistry, inorganic (general) chemistry, physics, biochemistry, mathematics.

ADMISSIONS POLICY
(TEXT PROVIDED BY SCHOOL):

The FSU College of Medicine is searching for students who have demonstrated through their lifestyle a commitment of service to others.

The College encourages applications from traditional students, nontraditional students, and students from rural, inner city or other medically underserved areas of Florida.

FSU College of Medicine is an Early Start Program—classes begin May 30, 2006. Students apply through the AMCAS. Some are invited to submit a secondary application. FSU COM accepts approximately 50 students each year.

An applicant should be a legal resident of Florida.

An applicant should have completed the required prerequisite courses: English, biology, chemistry, organic chemistry, physics, biochemistry.

An applicant should meet academic standards predictive of success in medical school—academic grade point average and MCAT (Medical College Aptitude Test) score. An applicant's MCAT score should be dated no more than three years prior to the beginning of the year of the application cycle.

A bachelor's degree is required by the time of matriculation to medical school. If an applicant is currently enrolled in a degree program, the program must be completed and final transcripts provided to the College of Medicine Admissions Office prior to the beginning of classes in May.

Non-U.S. citizens must possess a permanent resident visa.

COSTS AND FINANCIAL AID

Financial aid phone number: N/A

Tuition, 2005-2006 academic year: **In-state: $17,570**; **Out-of-state: $52,121**

Room and board: N/A

Percentage of students receiving financial aid in 2005-06: N/A

Percentage of students receiving: Loans: N/A, Grants/scholarships: 59%, Work-study aid: 0%

Average medical school debt for the Class of 2004: N/A

STUDENT BODY

Fall 2005 full-time enrollment: 220

Men: 43%, Women: 57%, In-state: 100%, Minorities: 43%, American Indian: 0.9%, Asian-American: 13.6%, African-American: 12.7%, Hispanic-American: 14.5%, White: 57.3%, International: 0.0%, Unknown: 0.9%

ACADEMIC PROGRAMS

The school's curriculum very frequently gives first-year students substantial contact with patients.

There are opportunities for first- or second-year students to work in community health clinics.

Program offerings: family medicine, geriatrics, internal medicine, pediatrics, rural medicine

Joint degrees awarded: N/A

Total National Institutes of Health (NIH) grants awarded to the medical school and affiliated hospitals: **$4.9 million**

CURRICULUM

(TEXT PROVIDED BY SCHOOL):

The Florida State University College of Medicine focuses on educating outstanding physicians who are well prepared to meet the health care needs of diverse communities.

Students benefit from a well-structured continuum of education in the biomedical, behavioral and clinical sciences. Subjects such as anatomy and pathology are presented in a clinically relevant context using medical cases, as well as the latest educational technologies. Problem-based and small-group learning experiences help students develop their clinical acumen and learn to work as a team.

Community-based clinical education spans the four-year curriculum. During the first two years, clinical education takes place in physician practices in the Tallahassee area, as well as in the medical school's Clinical Learning Center. In the third and fourth years, students complete their required clinical rotations at one of the medical school's four regional campuses, located in Orlando, Pensacola, Sarasota and Tallahassee. In these urban centers and the surrounding rural areas, the clinical training program extends into hospitals, skilled nursing facilities, managed care organizations, private clinics and other outpatient settings.

FACULTY PROFILE (FALL 2005)

Total teaching faculty: **93 (full-time)**, **696 (part-time)**

Of full-time faculty, those teaching in basic sciences: 45%; in clinical programs: 55%

Of part-time faculty, those teaching in basic sciences: 5%; in clinical programs: 95%

Full-time faculty/student ratio: 0.4

SUPPORT SERVICES

The school offers students professional counseling for dealing with stress.

RESIDENCY PROFILE

Most popular residency and specialty programs chosen by the 2004 and 2005 M.D. graduating classes: emergency medicine, family practice, internal medicine, orthopaedic surgery, pediatrics, surgery–general.

WHERE GRADS GO

37%

Proportion of 2003-2005 graduates who entered primary care specialties

48%

Proportion of 2004-2005 graduates who accepted in-state residencies

Georgetown University

- 3900 Reservoir Road NW, Med-Dent Building, Washington, DC 20007
- Private
- Year Founded: 1851
- Tuition, 2005-2006: $39,699
- Enrollment 2005-2006 academic year: 718
- Website: http://som.georgetown.edu/index.html
- Specialty ranking: N/A

3.61 AVERAGE GPA, ENTERING CLASS FALL 2005

10.2 AVERAGE MCAT, ENTERING CLASS FALL 2005

5.2% ACCEPTANCE RATE, ENTERING CLASS FALL 2005

46 2007 U.S. NEWS MEDICAL SCHOOL RANKING (RESEARCH)

Unranked 2007 U.S. NEWS MEDICAL SCHOOL RANKING (PRIMARY CARE)

ADMISSIONS

Admissions phone number: **(202) 687-1154**
Admissions email address:
   medicaladmissions@georgetown.edu
Application website:
   http://som.georgetown.edu/admissions/index.html
Acceptance rate: **5.2%**
In-state acceptance rate: **16.7%**
Out-of-state acceptance rate: **5.1%**
Minority acceptance rate: **N/A**
International acceptance rate: **N/A**

Fall 2005 applications and acceptees

	Applied	Interviewed	Accepted	Enrolled
Total:	7,944	1,312	413	190
In-state:	36	14	6	3
Out-of-state:	7,908	1,298	407	187

Profile of admitted students

Average undergraduate grade point average: **3.61**
MCAT averages (scale: 1-15; writing test: J-T):
   Composite score: **10.2**
   Verbal reasoning score: **10.1**, Physical sciences score: **10.2**, Biological sciences score: **10.3**, Writing score: **N/A**
Proportion with undergraduate majors in: Biological sciences: **52%**, Physical sciences: **14%**, Non-sciences: **28%**, Other health professions: **4%**, Mixed disciplines and other: **3%**
Percentage of students not coming directly from college after graduation: **66%**

Dates and details

The American Medical College Application Service (AMCAS) application is accepted.
School asks for a school-specific application as part of the admissions process.
Oldest MCAT considered for Fall 2007 entry: **2004**
Earliest application date for the 2007-2008 first-year class: **June 1, 2006**
Latest application date: **November 1, 2006**

Acceptance dates for regular application for the class entering in fall 2007:
   Earliest: **October 15, 2006**
   Latest: **August 7, 2007**
The school considers requests for deferred entrance.
Starting month for the class entering in 2007–2008:
   August
The school doesn't have an Early Decision Plan (EDP).
A personal interview is required for admission.

Undergraduate coursework required

Medical school requires undergraduate work in these subjects: biology, English, organic chemistry, inorganic (general) chemistry, physics, mathematics.

ADMISSIONS POLICY
(TEXT PROVIDED BY SCHOOL):

A secondary application packet is mailed to each applicant who applies to the School of Medicine through the American Medical College Application Service. The packet provides applicants with information on the application requirements, process and procedures, and selection factors of the Committee on Admissions.

Georgetown University School of Medicine requires the Medical College Admission Test and a minimum of three years of college (90 semester hours, including the standard basic science core courses) and a personal essay unique to Georgetown University School of Medicine for consideration of admission. Upon completion of the secondary application process, the applicant's file is personally read during an administrative review. While a solid preparation in the sciences is essential, a broad background in the humanities and computer science is also important. An applicant must not only present a strong academic profile but also demonstrate well-developed noncognitive qualities. The Committee on Admissions selects students on the basis of academic achievement, character, maturity, and motivation. In rendering its decisions, the committee evaluates the applicant's entire academic record, performance on the MCAT, college premedical advisory committee evaluations, letters of recommendation, essays, healthcare-related experiences, and personal interview. The interview evaluates the applicant's motivation, maturity, compassion, commitment to serving others, problem-solving abilities, sense of humor, and reasons for and interest in applying to Georgetown.

The Committee on Admissions meets biweekly to make final decisions on interviewed applicants. Members base their votes on all aspects of the application without a weight or score being assigned to any individual aspect. The School of Medicine does not discriminate on the basis of race, sex, creed, sexual orientation, age, handicap, or national or ethnic origin. Neither citizenry nor residency plays any role in the selection process.

COSTS AND FINANCIAL AID

Financial aid phone number: **(202) 687-1693**
Tuition, 2005-2006 academic year: **$39,699**
Room and board: **$14,835**
Percentage of students receiving financial aid in 2005-06: **86%**
Percentage of students receiving: Loans: **80%**, Grants/scholarships: **40%**, Work-study aid: **1%**
Average medical school debt for the Class of 2004: **$134,482**

STUDENT BODY

Fall 2005 full-time enrollment: **718**
Men: **48%**, Women: **52%**, In-state: **1%**, Minorities: **25%**, American Indian: **0.1%**, Asian-American: **17.4%**, African-American: **6.1%**, Hispanic-American: **1.7%**, White: **71.4%**, International: **1.7%**, Unknown: **1.5%**

ACADEMIC PROGRAMS

The school's curriculum frequently gives first-year students substantial contact with patients.
There are opportunities for first- or second-year students to work in community health clinics.
Program offerings: AIDS, drug/alcohol abuse, family medicine, geriatrics, internal medicine, pediatrics, rural medicine, women's health
Joint degrees awarded: M.D./Ph.D., M.D./MBA, M.D./MS, M.D./M.A.
Total National Institutes of Health (NIH) grants awarded to the medical school and affiliated hospitals: **$158.8 million**

CURRICULUM

(TEXT PROVIDED BY SCHOOL):
The first two years at Georgetown provide students with an early introduction to the patient, as well as to the spiritual and ethical dimensions of medicine. In the first and second years, departmental courses provide the student with the scientific knowledge basic to the practice of medicine, including the anatomic and chemical characteristics of the normal body and the changes that are produced by diseases, drugs, and other agents. First-year courses are particularly concerned with how bodily organs interact. Finally, students are introduced to the care of patients; the fundamental principles and theories of clinical ethics; the broader demo-

graphic and political dimensions of the American health-care system; and the role of spirituality in the experience of health and illness as well as in the physician-patient relationship.

A focus of the second year is the study of disease processes, especially those caused by microbes: the body's own immunological defenses against microbes and other pathological agents, and the principles governing the action of pharmacological agents, their major uses, and their consequences. In addition, students continue their introduction to clinical practice through ambulatory care experiences and through a course in physical diagnosis. They also continue their study of clinical ethics. Finally, students take an interdepartmental course called Clinical Problem Solving, which provides a bridge to the clinical emphasis of the third and fourth years.

The third year contains 48 weeks divided into four 12-week blocks. The student serves clinical clerkships in medicine, surgery, pediatrics, obstetrics/gynecology, neurology, psychiatry, and family medicine.

The fourth year contains 44 weeks of instructional time and provides the student with substantial but supervised responsibility in the clinical management of patients. Patient experience is gained during six weeks on the medical and surgical services as an acting intern, 12 weeks on a primary/ambulatory rotation that includes emergency medicine, and a selection of two other four-week rotations.

FACULTY PROFILE (FALL 2005)

Total teaching faculty: **1,760 (full-time)**, **258 (part-time)**
Of full-time faculty, those teaching in basic sciences: **13%**; in clinical programs: **87%**
Of part-time faculty, those teaching in basic sciences: **17%**; in clinical programs: **83%**
Full-time faculty/student ratio: **2.5**

SUPPORT SERVICES

The school offers students these services for dealing with stress: expanded-hour gym access, professional counseling, religious support, support groups.

RESIDENCY PROFILE

Most popular residency and specialty programs chosen by the 2004 and 2005 M.D. graduating classes: anesthesiology, emergency medicine, family practice, internal medicine, internal medicine–pediatrics, obstetrics and gynecology, orthopaedic surgery, pediatrics, surgery–general.

WHERE GRADS GO

39.1%
Proportion of 2003-2005 graduates who entered primary care specialties

22%
Proportion of 2004-2005 graduates who accepted in-state residencies

George Washington University

■ 2300 Eye Street NW, Room 713W, Washington, DC 20037
■ Private
■ Year Founded: 1821
■ Tuition, 2005-2006: $41,553
■ Enrollment 2005-2006 academic year: 699
■ Website: http://www.gwumc.edu/
■ Specialty ranking: N/A

3.56	AVERAGE GPA, ENTERING CLASS FALL 2005
9.3	AVERAGE MCAT, ENTERING CLASS FALL 2005
4.6%	ACCEPTANCE RATE, ENTERING CLASS FALL 2005
Unranked	2007 U.S. NEWS MEDICAL SCHOOL RANKING (RESEARCH)
Unranked	2007 U.S. NEWS MEDICAL SCHOOL RANKING (PRIMARY CARE)

ADMISSIONS

Admissions phone number: **(202) 994-3506**
Admissions email address: **medadmit@gwu.edu**
Application website: **http://www.gwumc.edu/edu/admis/**
Acceptance rate: **4.6%**
In-state acceptance rate: **N/A**
Out-of-state acceptance rate: **N/A**
Minority acceptance rate: **N/A**
International acceptance rate: **N/A**

Fall 2005 applications and acceptees

	Applied	Interviewed	Accepted	Enrolled
Total:	**7,778**	**1,083**	**358**	**177**
In-state:	**N/A**	**N/A**	**N/A**	**3**
Out-of-state:	**N/A**	**N/A**	**N/A**	**174**

Profile of admitted students

Average undergraduate grade point average: **3.56**
MCAT averages (scale: 1-15; writing test: J-T):
  Composite score: **9.3**
  Verbal reasoning score: **9.1**, Physical sciences score: **9.2**,
  Biological sciences score: **9.8**, Writing score: **P**
Proportion with undergraduate majors in: Biological
  sciences: **37%**, Physical sciences: **11%**, Non-sciences:
  28%, Other health professions: **23%**, Mixed disciplines
  and other: **1%**
Percentage of students not coming directly from college
  after graduation: **38%**

Dates and details

The American Medical College Application Service
  (AMCAS) application is accepted.
School asks for a school-specific application as part of the
  admissions process.
Oldest MCAT considered for Fall 2007 entry: **2004**
Earliest application date for the 2007-2008 first-year class:
  July 1, 2006
Latest application date: **December 1, 2006**
Acceptance dates for regular application for the class
  entering in fall 2007:
  Earliest: **August 26, 2006**

Latest: **June 29, 2007**
The school considers requests for deferred entrance.
Starting month for the class entering in 2007–2008:
  August
The school has an Early Decision Plan (EDP).
A personal interview is required for admission.

Undergraduate coursework required

Medical school requires undergraduate work in these subjects: biology, biology/zoology, English, organic chemistry,
inorganic (general) chemistry, physics, demonstration of
writing skills.

ADMISSIONS POLICY
(TEXT PROVIDED BY SCHOOL):

As the 11th-oldest medical school in the country, George
Washington University has a rich history of being at the
forefront of medical technology. The School of Medicine
and Health Sciences is enriched by the diversity of its more
than 600 medical students. Four of every 10 students hold
undergraduate degrees in the liberal arts. In the fall 2005
entering class, 31 states were represented plus the District of
Columbia, with the top five states being California,
Maryland, New York, Virginia, and New Jersey. The entering
class ranged in age from 20 to 47 years old, with an average
age of 24. Females made up 56 percent of the entering
class.

The initial overall evaluation is based on data contained
in the American Medical College Application Service and
supplemental applications. This evaluation screens applicants on the basis of academic performance; Medical
College Admission Test scores; extracurricular, health-
related, research, and work experiences; and evidence of
nonscholastic accomplishments. Evidence of strong performance in recent, relevant coursework is to an applicant's
advantage. Some additional consideration is given to applicants from the District of Columbia and its metropolitan
area as well as to applicants from GWU's undergraduate
schools.

The next phase of the selection procedure depends on
careful examination of personal comments and letters of

recommendation. The most promising applicants are then invited for a personal interview either at the school or with a regional interviewer. The last phase includes the review by the Committee on Admissions of the entire dossier. This phase is designed to select academically prepared students with motivation and personal characteristics the committee considers important in future physicians. There is no discrimination in the selection process because of race, gender, religion, age, marital status, sexual orientation, disability, or national or regional origin.

COSTS AND FINANCIAL AID

Financial aid phone number: **(202) 994-2960**
Tuition, 2005-2006 academic year: **$41,553**
Room and board: **$18,647**
Percentage of students receiving financial aid in 2005-06: **80%**
Percentage of students receiving: Loans: **80%**, Grants/scholarships: **24%**, Work-study aid: **0%**
Average medical school debt for the Class of 2004: **$136,500**

STUDENT BODY

Fall 2005 full-time enrollment: **699**
Men: **48%**, Women: **52%**, In-state: **2%**, Minorities: **39%**, American Indian: **0.7%**, Asian-American: **22.5%**, African-American: **8.2%**, Hispanic-American: **2.6%**, White: **59.1%**, International: **1.0%**, Unknown: **6.0%**

ACADEMIC PROGRAMS

The school's curriculum very frequently gives first-year students substantial contact with patients.
There are opportunities for first- or second-year students to work in community health clinics.
Program offerings: AIDS, drug/alcohol abuse, family medicine, geriatrics, internal medicine, pediatrics, women's health
Joint degrees awarded: M.D./Ph.D., M.D./MPH
Total National Institutes of Health (NIH) grants awarded to the medical school and affiliated hospitals: **$38.1 million**

CURRICULUM

(TEXT PROVIDED BY SCHOOL):
The George Washington University School of Medicine and Health Sciences provides a diverse spectrum of learning opportunities. These include lectures, laboratories, small groups, problem-based-learning tutorials, and traditional clinical clerkships and electives. Most courses utilize computer-assisted instructional materials and are delivered with Web-based course management software tools. Assessment techniques include National Board of Medical Examiners subject examinations, multiple choice and essay examinations, practical examinations, and structured faculty observations. We incorporate extensive assessment of clinical skills utilizing standardized patients. Training in and evaluation of interviewing skills, technical skills, communication skills, physical diagnosis skills, and clinical decision making are completed in our state-of-the-art Clinical

Learning/Simulation Center throughout the four-year curriculum. Students must pass steps 1 and 2 of the U.S. Medical Licensing Examination in order to graduate.

The first two years include traditional disciplinary courses in the basic and clinical sciences. Year 1 is divided on a "structure-function" continuum; the second year is structured on an organ-based interdisciplinary model. A comprehensive note service is provided. This includes lecture transcripts, audiotapes, and digital streaming audio.

The Practice of Medicine (POM) course runs throughout the four years. During the first two years, it includes small-group instruction in the doctor-patient relationship (interviewing, physical diagnosis), the Clinical Apprenticeship Program (office-based practice experience one half day every other week), and problem-based-learning tutorials. In years 3 and 4, POM incorporates ongoing instruction in the doctor-patient relationship with issues in professionalism, ethics, epidemiology/medical decision making, and cultural competency. There is a required research project that spans the two years.

The third year includes six core clinical clerkships in surgery, internal medicine, primary care, psychiatry, obstetrics and gynecology, and pediatrics. Several short elective opportunities are offered.

Year 4 includes required neuroscience, emergency medicine, anesthesiology, and "acting internship" (medicine or pediatrics) clerkships with up to six months of elective time.

FACULTY PROFILE (FALL 2005)

Total teaching faculty: **626 (full-time), 1,648 (part-time)**
Of full-time faculty, those teaching in basic sciences: **12%**; in clinical programs: **88%**
Of part-time faculty, those teaching in basic sciences: **5%**; in clinical programs: **95%**
Full-time faculty/student ratio: **0.9**

SUPPORT SERVICES

The school offers students professional counseling for dealing with stress.

RESIDENCY PROFILE

Most popular residency and specialty programs chosen by the 2004 and 2005 M.D. graduating classes: anesthesiology, emergency medicine, family practice, internal medicine, obstetrics and gynecology, pediatrics, psychiatry, radiology–diagnostic, surgery–general, transitional year.

WHERE GRADS GO

50.2%
Proportion of 2003-2005 graduates who entered primary care specialties

19.6%
Proportion of 2004-2005 graduates who accepted in-state residencies

Harvard University

- 25 Shattuck Street, Boston, MA 02115-6092
- Private
- **Year Founded:** 1782
- **Tuition, 2005-2006:** $38,776
- **Enrollment 2005-2006 academic year:** 739
- **Website:** http://hms.harvard.edu
- **Specialty ranking:** AIDS: 3, drug/alcohol abuse: 3, geriatrics: 4, internal medicine: 2, pediatrics: 1, women's health: 1

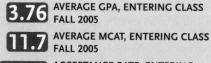

3.76 AVERAGE GPA, ENTERING CLASS FALL 2005

11.7 AVERAGE MCAT, ENTERING CLASS FALL 2005

5.2% ACCEPTANCE RATE, ENTERING CLASS FALL 2005

1 2007 U.S. NEWS MEDICAL SCHOOL RANKING (RESEARCH)

25 2007 U.S. NEWS MEDICAL SCHOOL RANKING (PRIMARY CARE)

ADMISSIONS

Admissions phone number: **(617) 432-1550**
Admissions email address:
admissions_office@hms.harvard.edu
Application website:
http://www.hms.harvard.edu/education.html
Acceptance rate: **5.2%**
In-state acceptance rate: **N/A**
Out-of-state acceptance rate: **N/A**
Minority acceptance rate: **3.3%**
International acceptance rate: **5.3%**

Fall 2005 applications and acceptees

	Applied	Interviewed	Accepted	Enrolled
Total:	4,598	1,041	239	165
In-state:	N/A	N/A	N/A	N/A
Out-of-state:	N/A	N/A	N/A	N/A

Profile of admitted students

Average undergraduate grade point average: 3.76
MCAT averages (scale: 1-15; writing test: J-T):
Composite score: 11.7
Verbal reasoning score: 11.0, Physical sciences score: 12.0, Biological sciences score: 12.0, Writing score: **R**
Proportion with undergraduate majors in: Non-sciences: 17%, Mixed disciplines and other: 11%
Percentage of students not coming directly from college after graduation: **N/A**

Dates and details

The American Medical College Application Service (AMCAS) application is accepted.
School asks for a school-specific application as part of the admissions process.
Oldest MCAT considered for Fall 2007 entry: **2003**
Earliest application date for the 2007-2008 first-year class: **July 1, 2006**
Latest application date: **October 15, 2006**
Acceptance dates for regular application for the class entering in fall 2007:
Earliest: **March 6, 2006**

Latest: **March 15, 2007**
The school considers requests for deferred entrance.
Starting month for the class entering in 2007–2008: **August**
The school doesn't have an Early Decision Plan (EDP).
A personal interview is required for admission.

Undergraduate coursework required

Medical school requires undergraduate work in these subjects: biology, English, organic chemistry, inorganic (general) chemistry, physics, molecular and cell biology, mathematics, demonstration of writing skills, calculus.

ADMISSIONS POLICY
(TEXT PROVIDED BY SCHOOL):

The Faculty of Medicine accepts applications from current students in good standing and graduates of accredited colleges. Applicants must present evidence that their credentials are of such quality as to predict success in the study and practice of medicine. Academic excellence is expected. Students are encouraged to take advanced courses, if qualified, as the Committee on Admissions takes the level of courses into account when considering academic performance.

Selection is based on a total and comparative appraisal of the candidates' suitability for medicine. Applicants are expected to have demonstrated aptitude in the biological and physical sciences during their undergraduate years, but narrow specialization in science to the exclusion of the humanities and social sciences is undesirable. A study at the Harvard Medical School has shown that students are successful in their medical studies regardless of undergraduate concentration, providing that they have had adequate science preparation. Students are urged to strive for a balanced and liberal education over specialization. No preference is given to applicants who have majored in science over those who have majored in humanities.

In addition to academic records, information considered by the Committee on Admissions includes the essay written by the student, MCAT scores, extracurricular activities, summer occupations, and life experiences. Any experience in the health fields, including research or community work, is also noted as well as the comments contained in letters of evaluation. We look for evidence of integrity, maturity, concern for others, leadership potential, and an aptitude for working with people.

Interviews are scheduled selectively, and all invitations for interview are issued by early January. The Committee on Admissions welcomes applications from qualified students representing groups that historically have had few members in the field of medicine.

COSTS AND FINANCIAL AID
Financial aid phone number: **(617) 432-1575**
Tuition, 2005-2006 academic year: **$38,776**
Room and board: **$14,515**
Percentage of students receiving financial aid in 2005-06: **71%**
Percentage of students receiving: Loans: **70%**, Grants/scholarships: **43%**, Work-study aid: **3%**
Average medical school debt for the Class of 2004: **$102,625**

STUDENT BODY
Fall 2005 full-time enrollment: **739**
Men: **50%**, Women: **50%**, In-state: **N/A**, Minorities: **48%**, American Indian: **1.6%**, Asian-American: **26.4%**, African-American: **12.3%**, Hispanic-American: **8.1%**, White: **45.9%**, International: **4.3%**, Unknown: **1.4%**

ACADEMIC PROGRAMS
The school's curriculum frequently gives first-year students substantial contact with patients.
There are opportunities for first- or second-year students to work in community health clinics.
Program offerings: AIDS, drug/alcohol abuse, family medicine, geriatrics, internal medicine, pediatrics, rural medicine, women's health
Joint degrees awarded: M.D./Ph.D., M.D./MBA, M.D./MPH.
Total National Institutes of Health (NIH) grants awarded to the medical school and affiliated hospitals: **$1,171 million**

CURRICULUM
(TEXT PROVIDED BY SCHOOL):
The Harvard Medical School offers two distinct curricula that are designed to accommodate the variety of interests, educational backgrounds, and career goals that characterize the student body; it also provides a general medical education for all kinds of physicians and serves as the foundation for later career specialization.

The New Pathway is a restructuring of the traditional medical school curriculum that gives students a core of biomedical and clinical knowledge and also provides the skills, tools, and attitudes that will enable them to become lifelong learners, to use new information, and to provide better patient care. Basic science and clinical content are interwoven throughout the four years. In the first- and second-year interdisciplinary block courses, a problem-based approach emphasizing small-group tutorials and self-directed learning is complemented by laboratories, conferences, and lectures. Clinical skills and the patient-doctor relationship are addressed in a three-year longitudinal sequence; instruction in taking patient histories begins in the first weeks of school. The third and fourth years emphasize experiences in direct patient care through clinical clerkships conducted in hospitals and institutions.

The Health Sciences and Technology (HST) curriculum is oriented toward students with an interest in a biomedical research career or a strong interest and background in quantitative or molecular science. It is appropriate for students who are planning interdisciplinary research careers in academic medicine. The approach is quantitative and rigorous, emphasizing modern biology, biotechnology, engineering, and physical sciences. Courses in the first two years are taught at HMS and MIT. The curriculum affords students the opportunity to take advantage of elective courses offered at Harvard's Graduate School of Arts and Sciences and MIT's Graduate School of Science and Engineering. HST students join students of New Pathway for clinical clerkships in the third and fourth years. An M.D. thesis is required for graduation.

Harvard Medical School is in the midst of a medical education reform initiative that focuses on: enhanced integration of basic sciences and clinical medicine and integration within and among courses and clerkships; increased opportunities for student-faculty interactions and partnerships; a new model of clinical education that emphasizes longitudinal personal and professional development during an integrated core-clerkship year; and a faculty-mentored in-depth scholarly experience as a requirement for graduation. The new curriculum will be launched for the class entering in the fall of 2006.

FACULTY PROFILE (FALL 2005)
Total teaching faculty: **7,519 (full-time)**, **2,613 (part-time)**
Of full-time faculty, those teaching in basic sciences: **8%**; in clinical programs: **92%**
Of part-time faculty, those teaching in basic sciences: **1%**; in clinical programs: **99%**
Full-time faculty/student ratio: **10.2**

SUPPORT SERVICES
The school offers students these services for dealing with stress: professional counseling, religious support, support groups.

RESIDENCY PROFILE
Most popular residency and specialty programs chosen by the 2004 and 2005 M.D. graduating classes: dermatology, emergency medicine, internal medicine, ophthalmology, orthopaedic surgery, pediatrics, psychiatry, radiology–diagnostic, surgery–general.

WHERE GRADS GO

41%
Proportion of 2003-2005 graduates who entered primary care specialties

51%
Proportion of 2004-2005 graduates who accepted in-state residencies

Howard University

- **520 W. Street NW, Washington, DC 20059**
- **Private**
- **Year Founded:** 1868
- **Tuition, 2005-2006:** $26,566
- **Enrollment 2005-2006 academic year:** 448
- **Website:** http://www.med.howard.edu
- **Specialty ranking:** N/A

3.35 AVERAGE GPA, ENTERING CLASS FALL 2005

8.0 AVERAGE MCAT, ENTERING CLASS FALL 2005

5.9% ACCEPTANCE RATE, ENTERING CLASS FALL 2005

Unranked 2007 U.S. NEWS MEDICAL SCHOOL RANKING (RESEARCH)

Unranked 2007 U.S. NEWS MEDICAL SCHOOL RANKING (PRIMARY CARE)

ADMISSIONS
Admissions phone number: **(202) 806-6279**
Admissions email address: **jwalk@howard.edu**
Application website: **N/A**
Acceptance rate: **5.9%**
In-state acceptance rate: **11.0%**
Out-of-state acceptance rate: **5.8%**
Minority acceptance rate: **7.8%**
International acceptance rate: **1.9%**

Fall 2005 applications and acceptees
	Applied	Interviewed	Accepted	Enrolled
Total:	4,131	369	243	116
In-state:	100	27	11	8
Out-of-state:	4,031	342	232	108

Profile of admitted students
Average undergraduate grade point average: **3.35**
MCAT averages (scale: 1-15; writing test: J-T):
 Composite score: **8.0**
 Verbal reasoning score: **7.6**, Physical sciences score: **7.8**,
 Biological sciences score: **8.5**, Writing score: **O**
Proportion with undergraduate majors in: Biological
 sciences: **66%**, Physical sciences: **16%**, Non-sciences:
 10%, Other health professions: **4%**, Mixed disciplines
 and other: **5%**
Percentage of students not coming directly from college
 after graduation: **N/A**

Dates and details
The American Medical College Application Service
 (AMCAS) application is accepted.
School asks for a school-specific application as part of the
 admissions process.
Oldest MCAT considered for Fall 2007 entry: **2004**
Earliest application date for the 2007-2008 first-year class:
 June 1, 2006
Latest application date: **December 15, 2006**
Acceptance dates for regular application for the class
 entering in fall 2007:
 Earliest: **October 16, 2006**

Latest: **July 12, 2007**
The school considers requests for deferred entrance.
Starting month for the class entering in 2007–2008: **July**
The school doesn't have an Early Decision Plan (EDP).
A personal interview is required for admission.

Undergraduate coursework required
Medical school requires undergraduate work in these subjects: biology, English, organic chemistry, inorganic (general) chemistry, physics, mathematics.

ADMISSIONS POLICY
(TEXT PROVIDED BY SCHOOL):
The application deadline is December 15. All applicants are invited to complete a secondary application. The application fee cannot be waived. There are no GPA or MCAT cutoffs, although a total MCAT of 21 or better is considered most competitive, as is a BCPM (biology/chemistry/physics/math) GPA of 2.8 or better. In prescreening for an interview, leadership experience, research experience, and a demonstrated commitment to serve in medically underserved communities are also considered. Howard students, including those in the BS/MD combined program, are favored over those from other schools, other factors being equal. There are no other geographic or institutional preferences or relationships. Undergraduate institutions are not ranked, and there are no correction factors applied to applicant criteria. However, general knowledge of, and experience with, particular undergraduate institutions is taken into consideration.

The most recent MCAT is used in evaluation, but all scores are reviewed with a focus on improvement. The Admissions Committee may consider the highest scores earned in individual sections. Minimally, eight semester hours each of biology, general chemistry, physics and organic chemistry are required, along with six semester hours of college math and English. Science course requirements must include a laboratory. Students with AP/CLEP credit in required courses need to take additional upper-level courses in that discipline at a college or university. It is essential to have health care experiences with patient contact as a demonstration of motivation for a career in medicine. A composite, confidential pre-health professions committee letter is preferred, but two letters of recommendation from science faculty who have taught the applicant will suffice. The committee and/or faculty letters of recommendation are not considered in screening for an interview, but are used in the Admissions Committee's evaluation of the interviewed candidate. Acceptances are offered throughout the application year. A $100 good-faith deposit, refundable until May 15, and a nonrefundable $300 enrollment fee are required to hold the slot in the incoming class. There is a wait-list, which is also filled on a rolling basis and not rank-ordered. Each year, several alternate list applicants are offered admission, most after May 15.

COSTS AND FINANCIAL AID

Financial aid phone number: **(202) 806-6388**
Tuition, 2005-2006 academic year: **$26,566**
Room and board: **$11,855**
Percentage of students receiving financial aid in 2005-06: **92%**
Percentage of students receiving: Loans: **87%**, Grants/scholarships: **49%**, Work-study aid: **0%**
Average medical school debt for the Class of 2004: **$120,829**

STUDENT BODY

Fall 2005 full-time enrollment: **448**
Men: **46%**, Women: **54%**, In-state: **6%**, Minorities: **96%**, American Indian: **0.0%**, Asian-American: **8.7%**, African-American: **74.8%**, Hispanic-American: **2.0%**, White: **3.8%**, International: **10.7%**, Unknown: **0.0%**

ACADEMIC PROGRAMS

The school's curriculum occasionally gives first-year students substantial contact with patients.
There are opportunities for first- or second-year students to work in community health clinics.
Program offerings: AIDS, drug/alcohol abuse, family medicine, geriatrics, internal medicine, pediatrics, women's health
Joint degrees awarded: M.D./Ph.D.
Total National Institutes of Health (NIH) grants awarded to the medical school and affiliated hospitals: **$15.6 million**

CURRICULUM

(TEXT PROVIDED BY SCHOOL):
During the first semester of the first year, instructional units in the Molecules and Cells block include macromolecules and metabolism, molecular and cell biology, tissue histology, nutrition, basic microbiology, genetics and immunology. During the second semester, the Structure and Function blocks covers all organ systems. There is a Medicine and Society block in both semesters.

The second year curriculum has two blocks covering the Organ Systems, one block covering Physical Diagnosis, and two blocks of Medicine and Society. During the first semester, instructional units in the Organ Systems block include general principles; the hematopoetic, lymphoreticular, and cardiovascular systems; the respiratory system; and the renal and urinary systems. During the second semester, the

Organ Systems block includes the gastrointestinal, central nervous, endocrine, reproductive, and musculoskeletal systems; skin and related connective tissue; and special topics. One block each of Physical Diagnosis and Medicine and Society are also taught.

The third and fourth years consist of instruction in a continuum of clerkships (internal medicine, surgery, pediatrics, psychiatry, neurology and rehabilitation, obstetrics and gynecology, and family medicine). All junior medical students are required to take a course in Introduction to Health Care Ethics and Jurisprudence. There are two required clerkships during the fourth year: internal medicine and general surgery.

Beginning in the second semester of the first year, each medical student may enroll in one elective per semester through the second year. Electives are not required during the first two years. A maximum of six elective periods (minimum of five) are available in the fourth year.

Academic support is offered to all students. Throughout the academic year, the Office of Medical Education identifies students in academic difficulty and provides them with tutoring and counseling. Re-examinations and summer instruction are offered to eligible students needing additional time to master course work.

For promotion and graduation, satisfactory student performance is mandatory in all units/blocks/courses, clerkships, and electives. Students are required to pass the United States Medical Licensing Examination (USMLE) Step 1 for promotion to the third year and Step 2 (both Clinical Knowledge and Clinical Skills) for graduation.

FACULTY PROFILE (FALL 2005)

Total teaching faculty: **240 (full-time)**, **168 (part-time)**
Of full-time faculty, those teaching in basic sciences: **27%**; in clinical programs: **73%**
Of part-time faculty, those teaching in basic sciences: **10%**; in clinical programs: **90%**
Full-time faculty/student ratio: **0.5**

SUPPORT SERVICES

The school offers students these services for dealing with stress: professional counseling, support groups.

RESIDENCY PROFILE

Most popular residency and specialty programs chosen by the 2004 and 2005 M.D. graduating classes: anesthesiology, family practice, internal medicine, obstetrics and gynecology, orthopaedic surgery, pathology–anatomic and clinical, pediatrics, surgery–general, transitional year, internal medicine/pediatrics.

WHERE GRADS GO

35%			

Proportion of 2003-2005 graduates who entered primary care specialties

24.1%			

Proportion of 2004-2005 graduates who accepted in-state residencies

Indiana University–Indianapolis

- 1120 South Drive, Indianapolis, IN 46202
- Public
- Year Founded: 1903
- Tuition, 2005-2006: In-state: $21,613; Out-of-state: $41,298
- Enrollment 2005-2006 academic year: 1,162
- Website: http://www.medicine.iu.edu
- Specialty ranking: rural medicine: 23

3.68 AVERAGE GPA, ENTERING CLASS FALL 2005

9.9 AVERAGE MCAT, ENTERING CLASS FALL 2005

14.8% ACCEPTANCE RATE, ENTERING CLASS FALL 2005

45 2007 U.S. NEWS MEDICAL SCHOOL RANKING (RESEARCH)

33 2007 U.S. NEWS MEDICAL SCHOOL RANKING (PRIMARY CARE)

ADMISSIONS

Admissions phone number: **(317) 274-3772**
Admissions email address: **inmedadm@iupui.edu**
Application website: **http://www.aamc.org/students/amcas**
Acceptance rate: **14.8%**
In-state acceptance rate: **47.1%**
Out-of-state acceptance rate: **4.8%**
Minority acceptance rate: **N/A**
International acceptance rate: **20.9%**

Fall 2005 applications and acceptees

	Applied	Interviewed	Accepted	Enrolled
Total:	2,760	953	409	280
In-state:	656	623	309	242
Out-of-state:	2,104	330	100	38

Profile of admitted students

Average undergraduate grade point average: **3.68**
MCAT averages (scale: 1-15; writing test: J-T):
  Composite score: **9.9**
  Verbal reasoning score: **9.7**, Physical sciences score: **9.8**,
  Biological sciences score: **10.3**, Writing score: **P**
Proportion with undergraduate majors in: Biological
  sciences: **42%**, Physical sciences: **21%**, Non-sciences:
  8%, Other health professions: **1%**, Mixed disciplines and
  other: **28%**
Percentage of students not coming directly from college
  after graduation: **38%**

Dates and details

The American Medical College Application Service
  (AMCAS) application is accepted.
School does not ask for a school-specific application as part
  of the admissions process.
Oldest MCAT considered for Fall 2007 entry: **2002**
Earliest application date for the 2007-2008 first-year class:
  May 1, 2006
Latest application date: **December 15, 2006**
Acceptance dates for regular application for the class
  entering in fall 2007:
  Earliest: **October 15, 2006**

Latest: **August 15, 2007**
The school considers requests for deferred entrance.
Starting month for the class entering in 2007–2008:
  August
The school has an Early Decision Plan (EDP).
A personal interview is required for admission.

Undergraduate coursework required

Medical school requires undergraduate work in these subjects: biology, organic chemistry, inorganic (general) chemistry, physics.

ADMISSIONS POLICY

(TEXT PROVIDED BY SCHOOL):

Learners wishing to join our medical student community
must have: (a) submitted an application online through the
American Medical College Application Service, (b) adequate
preparatory work including a minimum number of
required science courses (at least one year each of general
chemistry, organic chemistry, physics, and biological science); (c) taken a significant number of courses in the
humanities and social and behavioral sciences; (d) competency in written and spoken English; (e) completed the
MCAT; and (f) pledged to uphold our school's honor code.
  Invitations to join our community are based on scholarship, character, references, academic performance, and personal interview. IUSM gives preference to Indiana residents
and non-residents with significant ties to the state of
Indiana; however, each year we also invite non-residents to
join our community. We uphold and honor equal opportunity guidelines.

COSTS AND FINANCIAL AID

Financial aid phone number: **(317) 274-1967**
Tuition, 2005-2006 academic year: **In-state: $21,613; Out-
of-state: $41,298**
Room and board: **$13,290**
Percentage of students receiving financial aid in 2005-06:
  90%
Percentage of students receiving: Loans: **89%**,
  Grants/scholarships: **41%**, Work-study aid: **0%**

Average medical school debt for the Class of 2004: **$110,723**

STUDENT BODY
Fall 2005 full-time enrollment: **1,162**
Men: **54%**, Women: **46%**, In-state: **90%**, Minorities: **22%**, American Indian: **0.8%**, Asian-American: **10.6%**, African-American: **6.2%**, Hispanic-American: **3.0%**, White: **77.4%**, International: **1.4%**, Unknown: **0.7%**

ACADEMIC PROGRAMS
The school's curriculum frequently gives first-year students substantial contact with patients.

There are opportunities for first- or second-year students to work in community health clinics.

Program offerings: AIDS, drug/alcohol abuse, family medicine, geriatrics, internal medicine, pediatrics, rural medicine, women's health

Joint degrees awarded: M.D./Ph.D., M.D./MBA, M.D./MPH, M.D./MS, M.D./M.A.

Total National Institutes of Health (NIH) grants awarded to the medical school and affiliated hospitals: **N/A**

CURRICULUM
(TEXT PROVIDED BY SCHOOL):
With an undergraduate student body of 1,120 and an average class size of 280, Indiana University School of Medicine (IUSM) is the nation's second largest medical school. The only medical school in the state, IUSM is committed to producing knowledgeable, skilled and caring physicians.

Recognizing that the art of medicine requires more than excellent medical knowledge and procedural skill, IUSM was one of the first schools in the nation to adopt an innovative competency based curriculum. Nine competencies have been sequentially integrated into each year of the curriculum: (1) Effective Communication; (2) Basic Clinical Skills; (3) Using Science to Guide Diagnosis, Management, Therapeutics and Prevention; (4) Lifelong Learning; (5) Self-Awareness, Self-Care and Personal Growth; (6) The Social and Community Context of Health Care; (7) Moral Reasoning and Ethical Judgment; (8) Problem Solving; and (9) Professionalism and Role Recognition. Additional information can be found at http://meded.iusm.iu.edu/.

IUSM recognizes that the formation of a physician's professional identity is not accomplished only through the formal curriculum. Therefore, we are in the third year of the Relationship-Centered Care program to transform our social environment, or informal curriculum, by fostering relationship and attentiveness to human interactions. Additional information can be found at http://meded.iusm.iu.edu/Resources/RCCIInfo.htm.

FACULTY PROFILE (FALL 2005)
Total teaching faculty: **1,289 (full-time)**, **79 (part-time)**
Of full-time faculty, those teaching in basic sciences: **14%**; in clinical programs: **86%**
Of part-time faculty, those teaching in basic sciences: **8%**; in clinical programs: **92%**
Full-time faculty/student ratio: **1.1**

SUPPORT SERVICES
The school offers students these services for dealing with stress: expanded-hour gym access, peer counseling, professional counseling, religious support, support groups.

RESIDENCY PROFILE
Most popular residency and specialty programs chosen by the 2004 and 2005 M.D. graduating classes: anesthesiology, emergency medicine, family practice, internal medicine, neurology, obstetrics and gynecology, orthopaedic surgery, pediatrics, radiology–diagnostic, surgery–general.

WHERE GRADS GO
41.3%
Proportion of 2003-2005 graduates who entered primary care specialties

48.6%
Proportion of 2004-2005 graduates who accepted in-state residencies

Jefferson Medical College

- 1025 Walnut Street, Room 100, Philadelphia, PA 19107-5083
- Private
- Year Founded: 1824
- Tuition, 2005-2006: $38,316
- Enrollment 2005-2006 academic year: 935
- Website: http://www.tju.edu
- Specialty ranking: family medicine: 18, rural medicine: 25

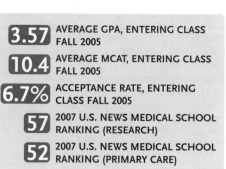

3.57 AVERAGE GPA, ENTERING CLASS FALL 2005

10.4 AVERAGE MCAT, ENTERING CLASS FALL 2005

6.7% ACCEPTANCE RATE, ENTERING CLASS FALL 2005

57 2007 U.S. NEWS MEDICAL SCHOOL RANKING (RESEARCH)

52 2007 U.S. NEWS MEDICAL SCHOOL RANKING (PRIMARY CARE)

ADMISSIONS

Admissions phone number: **(215) 955-6983**
Admissions email address: **jmc.admissions@jefferson.edu**
Application website: **http://www.jefferson.edu**
Acceptance rate: **6.7%**
In-state acceptance rate: **19.0%**
Out-of-state acceptance rate: **5.0%**
Minority acceptance rate: **5.1%**
International acceptance rate: **N/A**

Fall 2005 applications and acceptees

	Applied	Interviewed	Accepted	Enrolled
Total:	7,702	771	517	254
In-state:	963	265	183	107
Out-of-state:	6,739	506	334	147

Profile of admitted students

Average undergraduate grade point average: **3.57**
MCAT averages (scale: 1-15; writing test: J-T):
Composite score: **10.4**
Verbal reasoning score: **10.3**, Physical sciences score: **10.2**, Biological sciences score: **10.6**, Writing score: **Q**
Proportion with undergraduate majors in: Biological sciences: **46%**, Physical sciences: **17%**, Non-sciences: **25%**, Other health professions: **2%**, Mixed disciplines and other: **10%**
Percentage of students not coming directly from college after graduation: **37%**

Dates and details

The American Medical College Application Service (AMCAS) application is accepted.
School asks for a school-specific application as part of the admissions process.
Oldest MCAT considered for Fall 2007 entry: **2002**
Earliest application date for the 2007-2008 first-year class: **June 1, 2006**
Latest application date: **November 15, 2006**
Acceptance dates for regular application for the class entering in fall 2007:
Earliest: **October 15, 2006**

Latest: **August 4, 2007**
The school considers requests for deferred entrance.
Starting month for the class entering in 2007–2008:
August
The school has an Early Decision Plan (EDP).
A personal interview is required for admission.

Undergraduate coursework required

Medical school requires undergraduate work in these subjects: biology, organic chemistry, inorganic (general) chemistry, physics.

ADMISSIONS POLICY

(TEXT PROVIDED BY SCHOOL):
The medical profession is a career for those prepared for a lifetime of service to the ill regardless of diagnosis. It has as its objective the development of professional men and women prepared to adhere to the highest standards of conduct and behavior asked of few others in our society.

A strong preparation in the sciences basic to medical school studies is advised. Courses taken should be supplemented by laboratory experiences. Studies in the humanities and the social and behavioral sciences and the development of effective writing skills are strongly suggested.

The Medical College Admission Test and a baccalaureate degree from an accredited college or university in the United States or Canada are required.

The selection of students is made after careful consideration of many factors: college attended, academic record, letters of recommendation, MCAT scores, performance in nonacademic areas, and assessment by the Committee on Admissions, following a personal interview, of motivation, maturity, compassion, dedication, integrity, and commitment. Almost every applicant selected for interview has demonstrated a commitment to community service through volunteer work.

Jefferson Medical College is committed to providing equal opportunities without regard to race, color, national and ethnic origin, religion, sex, age, disability, sexual orientation, or veteran status. Preference is given to Pennsylvania residents. Special consideration may also be given to off-spring of faculty and alumni, to applicants whose background is underrepresented in medicine, and to applicants in JMC's cooperative programs with a number of colleges and universities in Pennsylvania. Each year, as the official medical school of Delaware, JMC provides for up to 20 places for Delaware residents in Jefferson's first-year class. The Physician Shortage Area Program admits students from rural areas and small towns who are committed to practicing family medicine in these areas.

COSTS AND FINANCIAL AID

Financial aid phone number: (215) 955-2867
Tuition, 2005-2006 academic year: $38,316
Room and board: $15,609
Percentage of students receiving financial aid in 2005-06:
  85%
Percentage of students receiving: Loans: 80%,
  Grants/scholarships: 49%, Work-study aid: 8%
Average medical school debt for the Class of 2004:
  $140,916

STUDENT BODY

Fall 2005 full-time enrollment: 935
Men: 51%, Women: 49%, In-state: 44%, Minorities: 25%,
  American Indian: 0.4%, Asian-American: 20.4%,
  African-American: 1.8%, Hispanic-American: 3.1%,
  White: 72.0%, International: 2.2%, Unknown: 0.0%

ACADEMIC PROGRAMS

The school's curriculum frequently gives first-year students
  substantial contact with patients.
There are opportunities for first- or second-year students to
  work in community health clinics.
Program offerings: AIDS, drug/alcohol abuse, family
  medicine, geriatrics, internal medicine, pediatrics, rural
  medicine, women's health
Joint degrees awarded: M.D./Ph.D., M.D./MBA,
  M.D./MPH, M.D./M.H.A.
Total National Institutes of Health (NIH) grants awarded to
  the medical school and affiliated hospitals: $95.4 million

CURRICULUM

(TEXT PROVIDED BY SCHOOL):
Jefferson Medical College seeks to provide its students with learning opportunities that will enable them to acquire fundamental knowledge and skills in the basic and clinical sciences as well as develop professional behaviors.

JMC is committed to helping its students understand the tentative nature of scientific conclusions and to encouraging students to assume responsibility for their own education. Recognizing that our students have multiple backgrounds and goals, and will pursue varied careers, educational opportunities at Jefferson incorporate sufficient flexibility to address this diversity.

Two years of preclinical instruction are provided in areas of basic science, followed by two years of clinical instruction. However, there is considerable integration across the four years. For example, the preclinical curriculum includes patient contact in the first year, and the clinical curriculum includes basic science reinforcement in the last year.

During the first year, Jefferson students focus on the function of the human organism in its physical and psychosocial context. Coursework provides first-year students with a strong basic science grounding. Clinical coursework focuses on the doctor-patient relationship, medical interviewing and history taking, the human developmental trajectory, behavioral science principles, and core clinical skills and reasoning.

In addition to increasing emphasis on clinical skills, the curriculum shifts in the second year to the study of pathophysiology and disease. After an introductory block of general pathology and general pharmacology, the subjects of immunology, microbiology, and systems-based pharmacology, pathology, and clinical medicine are presented as an interdisciplinary curriculum. The curriculum includes small-group sessions.

The clinical curriculum consists of 84 weeks, including six-week core rotations in family practice, obstetrics and gynecology, pediatrics, psychiatry, and general surgery, as well as 12 weeks of internal medicine in the third year. The fourth year includes 16 weeks of elective time and required rotations in the surgical subspecialties, neurology/rehabilitation medicine, outpatient and inpatient subinternships, and courses in advanced basic science and emergency medicine/advanced clinical skills.

FACULTY PROFILE (FALL 2005)

Total teaching faculty: 2,408 (full-time), 566 (part-time)
Of full-time faculty, those teaching in basic sciences: 10%;
  in clinical programs: 90%
Of part-time faculty, those teaching in basic sciences: 1%;
  in clinical programs: 99%
Full-time faculty/student ratio: 2.6

SUPPORT SERVICES

The school offers students these services for dealing with stress: expanded-hour gym access, peer counseling, professional counseling, religious support, support groups.

RESIDENCY PROFILE

Most popular residency and specialty programs chosen by the 2004 and 2005 M.D. graduating classes: anesthesiology, emergency medicine, family practice, internal medicine, obstetrics and gynecology, ophthalmology, orthopaedic surgery, pediatrics, psychiatry, surgery–general.

WHERE GRADS GO

40.7%
Proportion of 2003-2005 graduates who entered primary care specialties

43.5%
Proportion of 2004-2005 graduates who accepted in-state residencies

Johns Hopkins University

- 733 N. Broadway, Baltimore, MD 21205
- Private
- **Year Founded:** 1893
- **Tuition, 2005-2006:** $35,965
- **Enrollment 2005-2006 academic year:** 464
- **Website:** http://www.hopkinsmedicine.org
- **Specialty ranking:** AIDS: 2, drug/alcohol abuse: 1, geriatrics: 2, internal medicine: 1, pediatrics: 3, women's health: 3

3.84 AVERAGE GPA, ENTERING CLASS FALL 2005

11.5 AVERAGE MCAT, ENTERING CLASS FALL 2005

5.9% ACCEPTANCE RATE, ENTERING CLASS FALL 2005

2 2007 U.S. NEWS MEDICAL SCHOOL RANKING (RESEARCH)

41 2007 U.S. NEWS MEDICAL SCHOOL RANKING (PRIMARY CARE)

ADMISSIONS

Admissions phone number: **(410) 955-3182**
Admissions email address: **somadmiss@jhmi.edu**
Application website:
  http://www.hopkinsmedicine.org/admissions
Acceptance rate: **5.9%**
In-state acceptance rate: **7.7%**
Out-of-state acceptance rate: **5.8%**
Minority acceptance rate: **6.5%**
International acceptance rate: **5.2%**

Fall 2005 applications and acceptees

	Applied	Interviewed	Accepted	Enrolled
Total:	4,289	643	255	121
In-state:	299	52	23	12
Out-of-state:	3,990	591	232	109

Profile of admitted students

Average undergraduate grade point average: **3.84**
MCAT averages (scale: 1-15; writing test: J-T):
  Composite score: **11.5**
  Verbal reasoning score: **10.9**, Physical sciences score: **11.6**, Biological sciences score: **11.9**, Writing score: **Q**
Proportion with undergraduate majors in: Biological sciences: **29%**, Physical sciences: **31%**, Non-sciences: **24%**, Other health professions: **0%**, Mixed disciplines and other: **16%**
Percentage of students not coming directly from college after graduation: **36%**

Dates and details

The American Medical College Application Service (AMCAS) application is accepted.
School asks for a school-specific application as part of the admissions process.
Oldest MCAT considered for Fall 2007 entry: **2003**
Earliest application date for the 2007-2008 first-year class:
  June 1, 2006
Latest application date: **October 15, 2006**
Acceptance dates for regular application for the class entering in fall 2007:

Earliest: **October 1, 2006**
Latest: **April 15, 2007**
The school considers requests for deferred entrance.
Starting month for the class entering in 2007–2008:
  August
The school has an Early Decision Plan (EDP).
A personal interview is required for admission.

Undergraduate coursework required

Medical school requires undergraduate work in these subjects: biology, organic chemistry, inorganic (general) chemistry, physics, humanities, behavioral science, calculus.

ADMISSIONS POLICY
(TEXT PROVIDED BY SCHOOL):

All applicants must be or have previously been in attendance at a fully accredited institution in the country where the academic work was completed. Prospective applicants who have exclusively studied outside the United States, in most cases, must have their academic coursework supplemented by a year or more of coursework in an accredited U.S. university.

The applicant must arrange for an official transcript to be sent to Johns Hopkins from each college or university attended outside the United States. The committee requires that all of the coursework submitted in fulfillment of admission requirements must be evaluated on the basis of a traditional grading system. Grades of Pass or Credit will be considered acceptable for only a limited number of courses.

Applicants for admission must fulfill the following seven prerequisites:

Mathematics: one year of calculus or statistics. One semester of calculus and one semester of statistics is also acceptable. Advanced Placement credit for calculus, acceptable to the student's undergraduate college, may be used in fulfillment of the Hopkins math requirement.

General chemistry: one year with lab. Applicants with acceptable Advanced Placement credit for general chemistry must take one additional semester of advanced college chemistry with lab.

Organic chemistry: one year with lab. A semester of biochemistry with lab may be substituted for the second semester of organic chemistry.

Biology: one year with lab. Advanced Placement credit may not be used to satisfy the biology requirement.

Physics: one year of general physics with lab. Advanced Placement credit for physics, acceptable to the student's undergraduate college, may be used in fulfillment of the Hopkins physics requirement.

Humanities, and/or social and behavioral sciences: Applicants are required to complete at least 24 semester hours in these disciplines. The TOEFL exam for foreign applicants is not needed to apply to the School of Medicine. However, the applicant must be proficient in spoken and written English. Advanced Placement credits may not be used to satisfy the Humanities and/or Social and Behavioral Sciences requirement.

Each applicant must have received their bachelor's (B.A. or B.S.) degree prior to matriculation.

COSTS AND FINANCIAL AID

Financial aid phone number: **(410) 955-1324**
Tuition, 2005-2006 academic year: **$35,965**
Room and board: **$9,080**
Percentage of students receiving financial aid in 2005-06: **78%**
Percentage of students receiving: Loans: **68%**,
  Grants/scholarships: **64%**, Work-study aid: **20%**
Average medical school debt for the Class of 2004:
  $95,919

STUDENT BODY

Fall 2005 full-time enrollment: **464**
Men: **50%**, Women: **50%**, In-state: **23%**, Minorities: **46%**,
  American Indian: **0.4%**, Asian-American: **32.1%**,
  African-American: **9.7%**, Hispanic-American: **4.1%**,
  White: **52.6%**, International: **1.1%**, Unknown: **0.0%**

ACADEMIC PROGRAMS

The school's curriculum frequently gives first-year students substantial contact with patients.
There are opportunities for first- or second-year students to work in community health clinics.
Program offerings: AIDS, drug/alcohol abuse, family medicine, geriatrics, internal medicine, pediatrics, rural medicine, women's health
Joint degrees awarded: M.D./Ph.D.
Total National Institutes of Health (NIH) grants awarded to the medical school and affiliated hospitals: **$475.4 million**

CURRICULUM

(TEXT PROVIDED BY SCHOOL):
The regular M.D. curriculum comprises four academic years. The academic requirements of this program can be combined with graduate study leading to a master's or Ph.D. degree. The course of instruction is based on a core of required basic sciences and clinical courses, supplemented with ample elective time for special advanced study.

The first year primarily centers on normal human structure and function. Required courses include Molecules and Cells, Anatomy (including developmental biology), Neuroscience and Introduction to Behavioral Science, and Clinical Epidemiology and Organ Systems. The year also begins a four-year course, The Physician and Society, involving ethics, history of medicine, cultural arts, the physician-patient relationship, and the role of physicians in prevention and research. In the Introduction to Medicine course, students spend time working with a community-based, private-practice physician.

Second-year students study the causes and effects of diseases in Pathology and Human Pathophysiology. They also learn about the action of drugs in Pharmacology. Students are introduced to the elements of history taking, physical examination, and clinical medicine.

Beginning in the final quarter of the second year, each student follows an educational program adapted to his or her particular interests and needs. Clinical clerkships are devoted to the study of health and disease. The student is introduced to practical clinical problems through instruction conducted largely in small groups; correlative study involving two or more clinical fields is common. Elective courses available in every department range from direct participation in current biomedical research to advanced clinical work. Students may elect, within certain limits, the order in which they pursue the required instruction.

The total number of students in each class of the regular four-year program is limited to 120.

FACULTY PROFILE (FALL 2005)

Total teaching faculty: **2,198 (full-time)**, **1,190 (part-time)**
Of full-time faculty, those teaching in basic sciences: **10%**;
  in clinical programs: **90%**
Of part-time faculty, those teaching in basic sciences: **3%**;
  in clinical programs: **97%**
Full-time faculty/student ratio: **4.7**

SUPPORT SERVICES

The school offers students these services for dealing with stress: expanded-hour gym access, peer counseling, professional counseling, support groups.

RESIDENCY PROFILE

Most popular residency and specialty programs chosen by the 2004 and 2005 M.D. graduating classes: anesthesiology, dermatology, emergency medicine, internal medicine, neurological surgery, ophthalmology, orthopaedic surgery, pediatrics, radiology–diagnostic, surgery–general.

WHERE GRADS GO

37%
Proportion of 2003-2005 graduates who entered primary care specialties

41%
Proportion of 2004-2005 graduates who accepted in-state residencies

Loyola University Chicago

STRITCH

- 2160 S. First Avenue, Building 120, Maywood, IL 60153
- Private
- Year Founded: 1909
- Tuition, 2005-2006: $36,771
- Enrollment 2005-2006 academic year: 552
- Website: http://www.meddean.lumc.edu
- Specialty ranking: N/A

3.62 AVERAGE GPA, ENTERING CLASS FALL 2005

9.9 AVERAGE MCAT, ENTERING CLASS FALL 2005

6.6% ACCEPTANCE RATE, ENTERING CLASS FALL 2005

Unranked 2007 U.S. NEWS MEDICAL SCHOOL RANKING (RESEARCH)

Unranked 2007 U.S. NEWS MEDICAL SCHOOL RANKING (PRIMARY CARE)

ADMISSIONS

Admissions phone number: **(708) 216-3229**
Admissions email address: **N/A**
Application website: **N/A**
Acceptance rate: **6.6%**
In-state acceptance rate: **12.2%**
Out-of-state acceptance rate: **5.3%**
Minority acceptance rate: **6.3%**
International acceptance rate: **N/A**

Fall 2005 applications and acceptees

	Applied	Interviewed	Accepted	Enrolled
Total:	4,413	531	290	140
In-state:	839	183	102	65
Out-of-state:	3,574	348	188	75

Profile of admitted students

Average undergraduate grade point average: **3.62**
MCAT averages (scale: 1-15; writing test: J-T):
   Composite score: **9.9**
   Verbal reasoning score: **9.5**, Physical sciences score: **9.9**,
   Biological sciences score: **10.2**, Writing score: **P**
Proportion with undergraduate majors in: Biological
sciences: **36%**, Physical sciences: **14%**, Non-sciences:
21%, Other health professions: **1%**, Mixed disciplines
and other: **29%**
Percentage of students not coming directly from college
after graduation: **51%**

Dates and details

The American Medical College Application Service
   (AMCAS) application is accepted.
School asks for a school-specific application as part of the
   admissions process.
Oldest MCAT considered for Fall 2007 entry: **2003**
Earliest application date for the 2007-2008 first-year class:
   June 1, 2006
Latest application date: **November 15, 2006**
Acceptance dates for regular application for the class
   entering in fall 2007:
   Earliest: **October 15, 2006**

Latest: **N/A**
The school considers requests for deferred entrance.
Starting month for the class entering in 2007-2008: **July**
The school doesn't have an Early Decision Plan (EDP).
A personal interview is required for admission.

Undergraduate coursework required

Medical school requires undergraduate work in these subjects: biology/zoology, organic chemistry, inorganic (general) chemistry, physics.

ADMISSIONS POLICY
(TEXT PROVIDED BY SCHOOL):

Premedical students interested in applying for admission to
Loyola's Stritch School of Medicine must apply through the
American Medical College Application Service no later than
November 15 of the year preceding desired entrance into
medical school. After screening, some applicants are invited
to complete a Stritch supplemental application that includes
short-answer and essay questions that allow students to
comment on their personal experiences and insights.
Completed applicant files also include letters of recommendation and a $70 application fee, unless it is waived.

Applicants who present academic credentials that indicate they are capable of succeeding in the rigors of a medical education will be evaluated for evidence of the personal
qualifications they can bring to the medical profession.
Essential characteristics include an interest in lifelong learning, integrity, compassion, and the ability to assume responsibility. Of particular concern will be an applicant's
exploration of the field of medicine, the nature of the motivation to enter this career, and the degree of involvement in
extracurricular activities.

Each year approximately 600 applicants are invited to
interview with members of the Committee on Admissions
at Loyola's medical center campus. Generally, applicants are
notified of their status within one month of the interview
date. Once the class has been filled, most interviewed candidates are placed on an alternate list and considered for
acceptance as positions in the class become available.

Applicants must earn a bachelor's degree prior to matriculation into the medical school. Any course of study is acceptable. Coursework in molecular biology and genetics is strongly recommended, and an introduction to statistics is helpful.

Applicants must submit scores from the Medical College Admission Test. The MCAT should be taken in the spring of the year in which application is made to Loyola and should be repeated if one's scores are not near the national averages.

COSTS AND FINANCIAL AID

Financial aid phone number: (708) 216-3227
Tuition, 2005-2006 academic year: $36,771
Room and board: $16,099
Percentage of students receiving financial aid in 2005-06: 94%
Percentage of students receiving: Loans: 87%, Grants/scholarships: 67%, Work-study aid: 0%
Average medical school debt for the Class of 2004: $134,929

STUDENT BODY

Fall 2005 full-time enrollment: 552
Men: 50%, Women: 50%, In-state: 46%, Minorities: 21%, American Indian: 0.9%, Asian-American: 14.6%, African-American: 2.9%, Hispanic-American: 2.4%, White: 78.5%, International: 0.0%, Unknown: 0.7%

ACADEMIC PROGRAMS

The school's curriculum very frequently gives first-year students substantial contact with patients.
There are opportunities for first- or second-year students to work in community health clinics.
Program offerings: AIDS, drug/alcohol abuse, family medicine, geriatrics, internal medicine, pediatrics, women's health
Joint degrees awarded: N/A
Total National Institutes of Health (NIH) grants awarded to the medical school and affiliated hospitals: $22.1 million

CURRICULUM

(TEXT PROVIDED BY SCHOOL):
Stritch School of Medicine is a Catholic and Jesuit institution where individuals from a variety of backgrounds and traditions come together and learn the demanding art and science of medicine. Stritch emphasizes personal growth, excellence in academics and character, strong personal work ethic, openness to the spiritual dimensions of life, and a clear intent of developing women and men who will serve others. We encourage individual achievement and have high standards to bring out the best in all our students, but we also prize teamwork, good communication, and development of an atmosphere where students are good friends, help one another, and work cooperatively. We foster a strong

ethical framework that emphasizes respect for human life and dignity and considers medicine a profession dedicated to the service of others. We welcome students with strong backgrounds in academics, service work, and a variety of life experiences who are open to personal reflection, willing to learn about dimensions of caring that go beyond the physical, and show respect for those of differing cultures, backgrounds, faiths, and experiences.

Years 1 and 2 provide a combination of instruction in the basic sciences and in developing skills in communicating with patients, taking a history, and performing a physical examination. All courses feature a combination of lecture and small-group experiences. Some have required laboratory sessions. Practical experience is provided by the Patient Centered Medicine course.

During the third and fourth years, students participate in required and elective clerkships. Third-year required clerkships include internal medicine, surgery, family medicine, obstetrics/gynecology, pediatrics, and psychiatry. Clerkships combine inpatient experience with extensive time in the ambulatory setting, using one of the private office settings available to students and taking advantage of the Loyola University Hospital, the adjoining Hines Veterans Affairs Hospital, and community hospitals.

FACULTY PROFILE (FALL 2005)

Total teaching faculty: 640 (full-time), 696 (part-time)
Of full-time faculty, those teaching in basic sciences: 9%; in clinical programs: 91%
Of part-time faculty, those teaching in basic sciences: 3%; in clinical programs: 97%
Full-time faculty/student ratio: 1.2

SUPPORT SERVICES

The school offers students these services for dealing with stress: expanded-hour gym access, peer counseling, professional counseling, religious support, support groups.

RESIDENCY PROFILE

Most popular residency and specialty programs chosen by the 2004 and 2005 M.D. graduating classes: anesthesiology, emergency medicine, family practice, internal medicine, internal medicine–pediatrics, neurology, obstetrics and gynecology, orthopaedic surgery, pediatrics, surgery–general.

WHERE GRADS GO

48.6%
Proportion of 2003-2005 graduates who entered primary care specialties

43%
Proportion of 2004-2005 graduates who accepted in-state residencies

Mayo Medical School

- 200 First Street SW, Rochester, MN 55905
- Private
- Year Founded: 1972
- Tuition, 2005-2006: $14,250
- Enrollment 2005-2006 academic year: 166
- Website: http://www.mayo.edu/mms/
- Specialty ranking: internal medicine: 14

3.82 AVERAGE GPA, ENTERING CLASS FALL 2005

10.8 AVERAGE MCAT, ENTERING CLASS FALL 2005

2.3% ACCEPTANCE RATE, ENTERING CLASS FALL 2005

22 2007 U.S. NEWS MEDICAL SCHOOL RANKING (RESEARCH)

57 2007 U.S. NEWS MEDICAL SCHOOL RANKING (PRIMARY CARE)

ADMISSIONS

Admissions phone number: (507) 284-3671
Admissions email address:
  medschooladmissions@mayo.edu
Application website:
  http://www.aamc.org/stuapps/start.htm
Acceptance rate: 2.3%
In-state acceptance rate: 4.5%
Out-of-state acceptance rate: 2.0%
Minority acceptance rate: N/A
International acceptance rate: N/A

Fall 2005 applications and acceptees

	Applied	Interviewed	Accepted	Enrolled
Total:	2,883	295	65	43
In-state:	310	45	14	11
Out-of-state:	2,573	250	51	32

Profile of admitted students

Average undergraduate grade point average: 3.82
MCAT averages (scale: 1-15; writing test: J-T):
  Composite score: 10.8
  Verbal reasoning score: 10.3, Physical sciences score:
  10.7, Biological sciences score: 11.3, Writing score: Q
Proportion with undergraduate majors in: Biological
  sciences: 30%, Physical sciences: 33%, Non-sciences:
  26%, Other health professions: 0%, Mixed disciplines
  and other: 11%
Percentage of students not coming directly from college
  after graduation: 43%

Dates and details

The American Medical College Application Service
  (AMCAS) application is accepted.
School does not ask for a school-specific application as part
  of the admissions process.
Oldest MCAT considered for Fall 2007 entry: 2004
Earliest application date for the 2007-2008 first-year class:
  June 1, 2006
Latest application date: November 1, 2006

Acceptance dates for regular application for the class
  entering in fall 2007:
  Earliest: October 15, 2006
  Latest: July 23, 2007
The school considers requests for deferred entrance.
Starting month for the class entering in 2007-2008: July
The school doesn't have an Early Decision Plan (EDP).
A personal interview is required for admission.

Undergraduate coursework required

Medical school requires undergraduate work in these subjects: biology, biology/zoology, organic chemistry, inorganic
(general) chemistry, physics, biochemistry.

ADMISSIONS POLICY
(TEXT PROVIDED BY SCHOOL):

Mayo Medical School enrolls students with superior academic credentials, leadership characteristics, and a sincere
desire to commit their lives to service. Recognizing the
strength of diversity, we encourage individuals with diverse
backgrounds to apply. Equal opportunity and access are
embraced throughout the admissions process.

Once an applicant has completed the standardized telephone and on-campus interviews, his or her application is
presented to the Admissions Committee for discussion and
deliberation. The Admissions Committee meets weekly
from October through March. A periodic review of all
ranked candidates will occur every four to six weeks, at
which time several appointment offers are made.

Those applicants not receiving appointments during this
review will receive notification of their "hold status." During
each subsequent periodic review, however, all previously
reviewed applicants remain eligible to receive appointment
offers. This periodic and rolling admissions process allows
for all applicants to remain active for admissions consideration, irrespective of their interview dates.

U.S. citizenship or permanent resident status is required
for admission. All M.D. program applicants must obtain a
baccalaureate degree from an accredited institution of
higher education in the United States or Canada prior to

matriculation. No major field is preferred. Mayo Medical School does not routinely accept transfer students.

The following courses are required: one year of biology and/or zoology; one year of inorganic chemistry (with lab); one year of organic chemistry (with lab); one year of physics (with lab); and one course in biochemistry.

Applicants must complete the Medical College Admission Test. Only MCAT scores reported within three years of the application year are considered in admission decisions.

Students must apply through the American Medical College Application Service from June 1 through November 1.

COSTS AND FINANCIAL AID
Financial aid phone number: **(507) 284-4839**
Tuition, 2005-2006 academic year: **$14,250**
Room and board: **$11,990**
Percentage of students receiving financial aid in 2005-06: **100%**
Percentage of students receiving: Loans: **57%**, Grants/scholarships: **100%**, Work-study aid: **N/A**
Average medical school debt for the Class of 2004: **$65,772**

STUDENT BODY
Fall 2005 full-time enrollment: **166**
Men: **49%**, Women: **51%**, In-state: **23%**, Minorities: **32%**, American Indian: **1.8%**, Asian-American: **15.1%**, African-American: **10.2%**, Hispanic-American: **4.8%**, White: **68.1%**, International: **0.0%**, Unknown: **0.0%**

ACADEMIC PROGRAMS
The school's curriculum occasionally gives first-year students substantial contact with patients.
There are opportunities for first- or second-year students to work in community health clinics.
Program offerings: AIDS, drug/alcohol abuse, family medicine, geriatrics, internal medicine, pediatrics, rural medicine, women's health
Joint degrees awarded: M.D./Ph.D., M.D./MBA, M.D./MPH, M.D./JD.
Total National Institutes of Health (NIH) grants awarded to the medical school and affiliated hospitals: **$201.8 million**

CURRICULUM
(TEXT PROVIDED BY SCHOOL):
Mayo's innovative, patient-based curriculum is characterized by two prominent features: extensive patient interaction starting in the first year and integration of the basic sciences into all segments of the curriculum.

Mayo Medical School annually enrolls 42 students in three related medical degree programs: M.D. program, enrolling 34 students per year; M.D./Ph.D. program, enrolling six students per year; and M.D./O.M.S. program, enrolling two students per year.

Patient contact begins early in the first year and increases commensurate with student progress. The integration of basic and clinical sciences occurs in a manner that strengthens basic science concepts, stresses the patient orientation appropriate for an undergraduate medical school, and uses a variety of active, problem-oriented, faculty-guided, and self-learning techniques to aid student comprehension.

Curriculum integration is promoted by the organization of course material into broad functional units that span several curricular years. The curricular units are: The Organ; The Patient, Physician, and Society; The Scientific Foundations of Medical Practice; Clinical Experiences; and The Research Semester.

This curricular organization promotes content integration of the basic and clinical sciences and between basic and clinical science.

FACULTY PROFILE (FALL 2005)
Total teaching faculty: **2,254 (full-time)**, **N/A (part-time)**
Of full-time faculty, those teaching in basic sciences: **10%**; in clinical programs: **90%**
Of part-time faculty, those teaching in basic sciences: **N/A**; in clinical programs: **N/A**
Full-time faculty/student ratio: **13.6**

SUPPORT SERVICES
The school offers students these services for dealing with stress: expanded-hour gym access, peer counseling, professional counseling, religious support, support groups.

RESIDENCY PROFILE
Most popular residency and specialty programs chosen by the 2004 and 2005 M.D. graduating classes: anesthesiology, emergency medicine, internal medicine, pediatrics, radiology–diagnostic, transitional year.

WHERE GRADS GO
32%
Proportion of 2003-2005 graduates who entered primary care specialties

36%
Proportion of 2004-2005 graduates who accepted in-state residencies

Medical College of Georgia

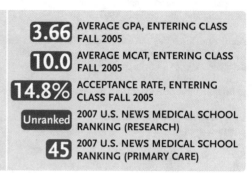

- 1120 15th Street, Augusta, GA 30912-4750
- Public
- Year Founded: 1828
- Tuition, 2005-2006: In-state: $12,436; Out-of-state: $34,660
- Enrollment 2005-2006 academic year: 711
- Website: http://www.mcg.edu/som/index.html
- Specialty ranking: rural medicine: 23

3.66 AVERAGE GPA, ENTERING CLASS FALL 2005

10.0 AVERAGE MCAT, ENTERING CLASS FALL 2005

14.8% ACCEPTANCE RATE, ENTERING CLASS FALL 2005

Unranked 2007 U.S. NEWS MEDICAL SCHOOL RANKING (RESEARCH)

45 2007 U.S. NEWS MEDICAL SCHOOL RANKING (PRIMARY CARE)

ADMISSIONS

Admissions phone number: **(706) 721-3186**
Admissions email address: **stdadmin@mail.mcg.edu**
Application website: **N/A**
Acceptance rate: **14.8%**
In-state acceptance rate: **26.2%**
Out-of-state acceptance rate: **0.4%**
Minority acceptance rate: **8.9%**
International acceptance rate: **N/A**

Fall 2005 applications and acceptees

	Applied	Interviewed	Accepted	Enrolled
Total:	1,742	447	258	180
In-state:	973	437	255	178
Out-of-state:	769	10	3	2

Profile of admitted students

Average undergraduate grade point average: **3.66**
MCAT averages (scale: 1-15; writing test: J-T):
  Composite score: **10.0**
  Verbal reasoning score: **9.9**, Physical sciences score: **9.9**,
  Biological sciences score: **10.3**, Writing score: **N/A**
Proportion with undergraduate majors in: Biological
sciences: **67%**, Physical sciences: **17%**, Non-sciences:
14%, Other health professions: **0%**, Mixed disciplines
and other: **2%**
Percentage of students not coming directly from college
after graduation: **39%**

Dates and details

The American Medical College Application Service
(AMCAS) application is accepted.
School asks for a school-specific application as part of the
admissions process.
Oldest MCAT considered for Fall 2007 entry: **2004**
Earliest application date for the 2007-2008 first-year class:
June 1, 2006
Latest application date: **November 1, 2006**
Acceptance dates for regular application for the class
entering in fall 2007:
  Earliest: **October 15, 2006**

Latest: **N/A**
The school considers requests for deferred entrance.
Starting month for the class entering in 2007–2008:
  August
The school has an Early Decision Plan (EDP).
A personal interview is required for admission.

Undergraduate coursework required

Medical school requires undergraduate work in these subjects: biology, biology/zoology, English, organic chemistry,
inorganic (general) chemistry, physics, molecular and cell
biology.

ADMISSIONS POLICY
(TEXT PROVIDED BY SCHOOL):

The admissions committee strives to identify and accept
applicants who will help meet the health care needs of a
widely dispersed and highly diverse population in Georgia.
We seek applicants with the academic ability, personal
attributes and interests consistent with our institution's
mission and which produce quality physicians. The admissions committee expects applicants to have experiences
shadowing physicians and volunteering in a clinical setting.
Information used for assessing an individual's academic
accomplishments, personal attributes and interests includes
but is not limited to the applicant's: responsibilities prior to
application to medical school; involvement in extracurricular and community activities; ethnic, socioeconomic and
cultural background; region of residence with respect to its
health professional needs; commitment to practice in
underserved area of Georgia; letters of recommendation by
the premedical advisor and 2 personal references; motivation and potential for serving as a physician, personal interviews; performance on MCAT; college grades including
undergraduate, graduate and post-baccalaureate. Preference
is given to residents of Georgia. No more than 5 percent of
the entering class each year can be non-residents of the
state of Georgia.

COSTS AND FINANCIAL AID

Financial aid phone number: **(706) 721-4901**

Tuition, 2005-2006 academic year: **In-state: $12,436; Out-of-state: $34,660**
Room and board: **$14,211**
Percentage of students receiving financial aid in 2005-06: **83%**
Percentage of students receiving: Loans: **78%**, Grants/scholarships: **40%**, Work-study aid: **2%**
Average medical school debt for the Class of 2004: **$63,907**

STUDENT BODY
Fall 2005 full-time enrollment: **711**
Men: **56%**, Women: **44%**, In-state: **100%**, Minorities: **28%**, American Indian: **0.3%**, Asian-American: **17.2%**, African-American: **8.6%**, Hispanic-American: **1.1%**, White: **72.4%**, International: **0.0%**, Unknown: **0.4%**

ACADEMIC PROGRAMS
The school's curriculum frequently gives first-year students substantial contact with patients.
There are opportunities for first- or second-year students to work in community health clinics.
Program offerings: AIDS, drug/alcohol abuse, family medicine, geriatrics, internal medicine, pediatrics, rural medicine, women's health
Joint degrees awarded: M.D./Ph.D.
Total National Institutes of Health (NIH) grants awarded to the medical school and affiliated hospitals: **$42.8 million**

CURRICULUM
(TEXT PROVIDED BY SCHOOL):
During the two preclinical years, students acquire the building blocks of basic science that underlie medical practice and the skills required for clinical decision making and patient interaction. The modular content of the curriculum is taught in lectures, labs with integrated clinical conferences, and small-group activities.
In the first semester of Year 1, the Cellular and Systems Structures module introduces students to gross anatomy, histology, and development. In the second semester, biochemistry, genetics, and physiology are taught in the Cellular and Systems Processes module while the Brain and Behavior module gives students an understanding of the interplay between psychiatry and neuroscience. The yearlong Essentials of Clinical Medicine emphasizes familial cultural, and population aspects of healthcare; communication skills and information retrieval and analysis; health promotion/disease prevention; ethics; history taking with children and adults; and a community project. The ECM is a two-year sequence that emphasizes skills needed for success in the third year. In Year 2, ECM addresses interviewing and physical exam, common medical problems, and interdisciplinary topics such as ethics, nutrition, and the impact of behavior on health, while highlighting principles of patient care for each stage of life. Cellular and Systems

Disease States is a yearlong module running in parallel that exposes students to medical microbiology, pathology, and pharmacology. Passing the U.S. Medical Licensing Examination Step 1 is a requirement for promotion to Year 3.
Year 3 consists of required core clerkships in internal medicine (eight weeks), surgery (eight weeks), family medicine (six weeks), pediatrics (six weeks), psychiatry (six weeks), obstetrics/gynecology (six weeks), and neurology (four weeks). Core clerkships take place at the Medical College of Georgia Hospitals and Clinics, the Children's Medical Center, and other sites throughout Georgia. Students may rotate to affiliated community hospitals for part of the core curriculum.
During Year 4, students must complete four-week rotations in emergency medicine and critical care, and an acting internship in medicine, family medicine, pediatrics, surgery, and obstetrics/gynecology. The remainder of Year 4 is for elective study, which can include both clinical and research courses. Evaluation during the clinical years is based on assessment of knowledge, clinical skills, and professional behavior. Passing the USMLE Step 2 is a requirement for graduation.

FACULTY PROFILE (FALL 2005)
Total teaching faculty: **466 (full-time)**, **118 (part-time)**
Of full-time faculty, those teaching in basic sciences: **29%**; in clinical programs: **71%**
Of part-time faculty, those teaching in basic sciences: **9%**; in clinical programs: **91%**
Full-time faculty/student ratio: **0.7**

SUPPORT SERVICES
The school offers students these services for dealing with stress: expanded-hour gym access, peer counseling, professional counseling, religious support, support groups.

RESIDENCY PROFILE
Most popular residency and specialty programs chosen by the 2004 and 2005 M.D. graduating classes: anesthesiology, emergency medicine, family practice, internal medicine, neurology, obstetrics and gynecology, orthopaedic surgery, pediatrics, radiology–diagnostic, surgery–general.

WHERE GRADS GO
42.3%
Proportion of 2003-2005 graduates who entered primary care specialties

43%
Proportion of 2004-2005 graduates who accepted in-state residencies

Medical College of Wisconsin

- 8701 Watertown Plank Road, Milwaukee, WI 53226
- Private
- Year Founded: 1893
- Tuition, 2005-2006: $28,098
- Enrollment 2005-2006 academic year: 811
- Website: http://www.mcw.edu/acad/admission
- Specialty ranking: N/A

3.72 AVERAGE GPA, ENTERING CLASS FALL 2005

9.9 AVERAGE MCAT, ENTERING CLASS FALL 2005

8.4% ACCEPTANCE RATE, ENTERING CLASS FALL 2005

54 2007 U.S. NEWS MEDICAL SCHOOL RANKING (RESEARCH)

41 2007 U.S. NEWS MEDICAL SCHOOL RANKING (PRIMARY CARE)

ADMISSIONS

Admissions phone number: **(414) 456-8246**
Admissions email address: **medschool@mcw.edu**
Application website: **N/A**
Acceptance rate: **8.4%**
In-state acceptance rate: **29.0%**
Out-of-state acceptance rate: **6.2%**
Minority acceptance rate: **N/A**
International acceptance rate: **1.8%**

Fall 2005 applications and acceptees

	Applied	Interviewed	Accepted	Enrolled
Total:	5,645	701	475	204
In-state:	552	208	160	96
Out-of-state:	5,093	493	315	108

Profile of admitted students

Average undergraduate grade point average: **3.72**
MCAT averages (scale: 1-15; writing test: J-T):
  Composite score: **9.9**
  Verbal reasoning score: **9.7**, Physical sciences score: **9.9**,
  Biological sciences score: **10.2**, Writing score: **P**
Proportion with undergraduate majors in: Biological
  sciences: **49%**, Physical sciences: **14%**, Non-sciences:
  12%, Other health professions: **0%**, Mixed disciplines
  and other: **24%**
Percentage of students not coming directly from college
  after graduation: **45%**

Dates and details

The American Medical College Application Service
  (AMCAS) application is accepted.
School asks for a school-specific application as part of the
  admissions process.
Oldest MCAT considered for Fall 2007 entry: **2004**
Earliest application date for the 2007-2008 first-year class:
  June 1, 2006
Latest application date: **November 1, 2006**
Acceptance dates for regular application for the class
  entering in fall 2007:
  Earliest: **October 15, 2006**

Latest: **N/A**
The school considers requests for deferred entrance.
Starting month for the class entering in 2007–2008:
  August
The school has an Early Decision Plan (EDP).
A personal interview is required for admission.

Undergraduate coursework required

Medical school requires undergraduate work in these subjects: biology, English, organic chemistry, inorganic (general) chemistry, physics, mathematics.

ADMISSIONS POLICY

(TEXT PROVIDED BY SCHOOL):
The Admissions Committee bases its decisions on a
thoughtful appraisal of each candidate's suitability for the
profession of medicine. Decisions are based upon scholastic
record, Medical College Admission Test scores, recommendations, involvement in college and community activities,
the personal interview, and also by the less tangible qualities
of personality, character, and maturity.

COSTS AND FINANCIAL AID

Financial aid phone number: **(414) 456-8208**
Tuition, 2005-2006 academic year: **$28,098**
Room and board: **$7,500**
Percentage of students receiving financial aid in 2005-06:
  95%
Percentage of students receiving: Loans: **87%**,
  Grants/scholarships: **62%**, Work-study aid: **0%**
Average medical school debt for the Class of 2004:
  $119,340

STUDENT BODY

Fall 2005 full-time enrollment: **811**
Men: **56%**, Women: **44%**, In-state: **47%**, Minorities: **22%**,
  American Indian: **1.4%**, Asian-American: **14.4%**,
  African-American: **2.8%**, Hispanic-American: **3.2%**,
  White: **75.2%**, International: **1.0%**, Unknown: **2.0%**

ACADEMIC PROGRAMS

The school's curriculum occasionally gives first-year students substantial contact with patients.

There are opportunities for first- or second-year students to work in community health clinics.

Program offerings: family medicine, geriatrics, internal medicine, pediatrics, rural medicine, women's health

Joint degrees awarded: M.D./Ph.D.

Total National Institutes of Health (NIH) grants awarded to the medical school and affiliated hospitals: **N/A**

CURRICULUM

(TEXT PROVIDED BY SCHOOL):

The M.D. curriculum at the Medical College of Wisconsin consists of carefully sequenced learning experiences that enable students to acquire the knowledge and skills that are necessary for the effective practice of medicine.

The learning activities of the first two years are a mix of traditional curriculum formats (lectures, labs, dissection, and discussion groups) and newer educational methods—computer-aided instruction, problem-based learning, and independent study options. There are mentor experiences and a medical interviewing course utilizing standardized patients.

During the third and fourth years of study, education shifts from the lecture hall and laboratory to the bedside. Required clerkships in a variety of patient care settings enable third-year students to draw from their working knowledge of the basic medical sciences as they begin to participate in the care of patients. They develop the skills necessary to diagnose and treat those patients, including the use of Objective Structured Clinical Examinations (OSCE's).

Fourth-year students continue their training in required and elective experiences. By choosing electives that meet their individual educational needs, students gain experiences that enhance their autonomy and prepare them to enter the specialty of their choice.

FACULTY PROFILE (FALL 2005)

Total teaching faculty: **1,092 (full-time)**, **58 (part-time)**

Of full-time faculty, those teaching in basic sciences: **10%**; in clinical programs: **90%**

Of part-time faculty, those teaching in basic sciences: **29%**; in clinical programs: **71%**

Full-time faculty/student ratio: **1.3**

SUPPORT SERVICES

The school offers students these services for dealing with stress: expanded-hour gym access, professional counseling, religious support, support groups.

RESIDENCY PROFILE

Most popular residency and specialty programs chosen by the 2004 and 2005 M.D. graduating classes: anesthesiology, emergency medicine, family practice, internal medicine, pediatrics, radiology–diagnostic, surgery–general, transitional year.

WHERE GRADS GO

44%

Proportion of 2003-2005 graduates who entered primary care specialties

34%

Proportion of 2004-2005 graduates who accepted in-state residencies

Medical University of Ohio

- 3000 Arlington Avenue, Toledo, OH 43614
- Public
- Year Founded: 1969
- Tuition, 2005-2006: In-state: $22,072; Out-of-state: $50,332
- Enrollment 2005-2006 academic year: 611
- Website: http://www.meduohio.edu
- Specialty ranking: N/A

3.59 AVERAGE GPA, ENTERING CLASS FALL 2005

10.0 AVERAGE MCAT, ENTERING CLASS FALL 2005

11.4% ACCEPTANCE RATE, ENTERING CLASS FALL 2005

Unranked 2007 U.S. NEWS MEDICAL SCHOOL RANKING (RESEARCH)

Unranked 2007 U.S. NEWS MEDICAL SCHOOL RANKING (PRIMARY CARE)

ADMISSIONS
Admissions phone number: **(419) 383-4229**
Admissions email address: **admissions@meduohio.edu**
Application website: **N/A**
Acceptance rate: **11.4%**
In-state acceptance rate: **21.8%**
Out-of-state acceptance rate: **6.3%**
Minority acceptance rate: **N/A**
International acceptance rate: **N/A**

Fall 2005 applications and acceptees

	Applied	Interviewed	Accepted	Enrolled
Total:	2,787	447	318	147
In-state:	918	269	200	97
Out-of-state:	1,869	178	118	50

Profile of admitted students
Average undergraduate grade point average: **3.59**
MCAT averages (scale: 1-15; writing test: J-T):
  Composite score: **10.0**
  Verbal reasoning score: **10.0**, Physical sciences score: **9.9**, Biological sciences score: **10.2**, Writing score: **N/A**
Proportion with undergraduate majors in: Biological sciences: **59%**, Physical sciences: **17%**, Non-sciences: **11%**, Other health professions: **4%**, Mixed disciplines and other: **9%**
Percentage of students not coming directly from college after graduation: **17%**

Dates and details
The American Medical College Application Service (AMCAS) application is accepted.
School asks for a school-specific application as part of the admissions process.
Oldest MCAT considered for Fall 2007 entry: **2003**
Earliest application date for the 2007-2008 first-year class: **June 15, 2006**
Latest application date: **November 1, 2006**
Acceptance dates for regular application for the class entering in fall 2007:
  Earliest: **October 15, 2006**

  Latest: **N/A**
The school considers requests for deferred entrance.
Starting month for the class entering in 2007–2008:
  August
The school has an Early Decision Plan (EDP).
A personal interview is required for admission.

Undergraduate coursework required
Medical school requires undergraduate work in these subjects: biology, English, organic chemistry, inorganic (general) chemistry, physics, mathematics.

ADMISSIONS POLICY
(TEXT PROVIDED BY SCHOOL):
The MCAT is required unless the student is accepted through the MEDStart program. A baccalaureate degree is required. A comprehensive command and understanding of the English language are essential. Beyond these requirements, concentration in humanities, sciences, or other areas is viewed with equal favor. Close attention will be paid to the general scope of the applicant's academic background and to whether or not there is an adequate understanding of the physical, biological, chemical, and social sciences and some reasonable sensitivity to the humanities. In selecting applicants, the Medical University of Ohio looks more for evidence of general competence and capability than for specific areas of study. Students are admitted on the basis of individual qualifications, regardless of sex, religion, race, age, or disability.

COSTS AND FINANCIAL AID
Financial aid phone number: **(419) 383-4232**
Tuition, 2005-2006 academic year: **In-state: $22,072; Out-of-state: $50,332**
Room and board: **N/A**
Percentage of students receiving financial aid in 2005-06: **90%**
Percentage of students receiving: Loans: **87%**, Grants/scholarships: **24%**, Work-study aid: **17%**
Average medical school debt for the Class of 2004: **$125,473**

STUDENT BODY

Fall 2005 full-time enrollment: **611**

Men: **61%**, Women: **39%**, In-state: **91%**, Minorities: **21%**,
American Indian: **1.0%**, Asian-American: **16.9%**,
African-American: **1.5%**, Hispanic-American: **2.0%**,
White: **76.1%**, International: **0.8%**, Unknown: **1.8%**

ACADEMIC PROGRAMS

The school's curriculum occasionally gives first-year
students substantial contact with patients.

There are opportunities for first- or second-year students to
work in community health clinics.

Program offerings: AIDS, drug/alcohol abuse, family
medicine, geriatrics, internal medicine, pediatrics, rural
medicine, women's health

Joint degrees awarded: M.D./Ph.D., M.D./MPH, M.D./MS

Total National Institutes of Health (NIH) grants awarded to
the medical school and affiliated hospitals: **$16.5 million**

CURRICULUM

(TEXT PROVIDED BY SCHOOL):

The curriculum of the Medical College of Ohio is composed
of an integrated basic science/clinical science four-year
approach to medical education, with emphasis on clinically
oriented objectives and problem-based learning.

The first year is devoted to integrated blocks of cellular
and molecular biology, growth and development, human
structure and neuroscience, and behavioral science. Each of
these sections will have a corresponding integrated clinical,
applied component. Also included will be Fundamentals of
Clinical Practice, which runs concurrently throughout the
first two years.

The second year is composed of Immunity and Infection,
an integrated systems course involving pathology, pharmacology, and physiology. During the first two years, approximately 45 percent of the student's time will be spent in a
nonlecture format, with emphasis placed on small-group
interaction. Students are required to pass Step 1 of the U.S.

Medical Licensing Examination before beginning their third
year and Step 2 prior to graduation.

The last two years of the curriculum are devoted to
mandatory clerkships in internal medicine, surgery, pediatrics, obstetrics and gynecology, neurology, psychiatry, family practice, and electives. All students are required to rotate
through a clinical Area Health Education Center, account-
ing for 10 percent of their total clerkship time.

FACULTY PROFILE (FALL 2005)

Total teaching faculty: **255 (full-time)**, **40 (part-time)**

Of full-time faculty, those teaching in basic sciences: **28%**;
in clinical programs: **72%**

Of part-time faculty, those teaching in basic sciences: **5%**;
in clinical programs: **95%**

Full-time faculty/student ratio: **0.4**

SUPPORT SERVICES

The school offers students these services for dealing with
stress: expanded-hour gym access, peer counseling, professional counseling, support groups.

RESIDENCY PROFILE

Most popular residency and specialty programs chosen by
the 2004 and 2005 M.D. graduating classes: emergency
medicine, family practice, internal medicine, obstetrics and
gynecology, pediatrics, psychiatry, radiology–diagnostic,
urology.

WHERE GRADS GO

44%

*Proportion of 2003-2005 graduates who entered primary
care specialties*

36%

*Proportion of 2004-2005 graduates who accepted in-state
residencies*

Medical University of South Carolina

- 171 Ashley Avenue, Charleston, SC 29425
- Public
- Year Founded: 1824
- Tuition, 2005-2006: In-state: $21,702; Out-of-state: $57,754
- Enrollment 2005-2006 academic year: 601
- Website: http://www2.musc.edu
- Specialty ranking: drug/alcohol abuse: 9

3.59 AVERAGE GPA, ENTERING CLASS FALL 2005

9.5 AVERAGE MCAT, ENTERING CLASS FALL 2005

17.7% ACCEPTANCE RATE, ENTERING CLASS FALL 2005

Unranked 2007 U.S. NEWS MEDICAL SCHOOL RANKING (RESEARCH)

57 2007 U.S. NEWS MEDICAL SCHOOL RANKING (PRIMARY CARE)

ADMISSIONS

Admissions phone number: **(843) 792-2055**
Admissions email address: **taylorwl@musc.edu**
Application website: **http://www.musc.edu/es/apply/**
Acceptance rate: **17.7%**
In-state acceptance rate: **41.4%**
Out-of-state acceptance rate: **3.0%**
Minority acceptance rate: **11.5%**
International acceptance rate: **0.0%**

Fall 2005 applications and acceptees

	Applied	Interviewed	Accepted	Enrolled
Total:	1,064	357	188	138
In-state:	406	309	168	134
Out-of-state:	658	48	20	4

Profile of admitted students

Average undergraduate grade point average: **3.59**
MCAT averages (scale: 1-15; writing test: J-T):
 Composite score: **9.5**
 Verbal reasoning score: **9.7**, Physical sciences score: **9.1**,
 Biological sciences score: **9.6**, Writing score: **O**
Percentage of students not coming directly from college
 after graduation: **8%**

Dates and details

The American Medical College Application Service
 (AMCAS) application is accepted.
School asks for a school-specific application as part of the
 admissions process.
Oldest MCAT considered for Fall 2007 entry: **2002**
Earliest application date for the 2007-2008 first-year class:
 June 1, 2006
Latest application date: **December 1, 2006**
Acceptance dates for regular application for the class
 entering in fall 2007:
 Earliest: **October 1, 2006**
 Latest: **March 16, 2007**
The school considers requests for deferred entrance.
Starting month for the class entering in 2007-2008:
 August

The school has an Early Decision Plan (EDP).
A personal interview is required for admission.

ADMISSIONS POLICY
(TEXT PROVIDED BY SCHOOL):

The College of Medicine is a participant in the American
Medical College Application Service (AMCAS). The applica-
tion-filing period is from June 1 to December 1 prior to the
year in which the applicant wishes to enter. AMCAS will
forward verified applications to the medical school after July
1 for screening by the Admissions Committee. All applicants who apply through AMCAS are requested to complete
a supplemental application for MUSC. Before a final admission decision is made, three personal interviews—one with
an Admissions Committee member, one with a MUSC faculty member, and one with a South Carolina private physician—are required. Only students who meet the academic
cutoff established by the Admissions Committee are invited
for interviews. Offers of acceptance are made on a rolling
basis; final decisions on all applications are made by mid-
March.

Medical College Admission Test (MCAT) scores and a
minimum of three years of college work (90 semester
hours) are required for admission. Preference is given to
applicants who have earned a baccalaureate degree.
Students who choose to major in a science should select a
broad range of studies outside the sciences as well. Because
the MCAT requires knowledge of the natural sciences, students are expected to study college courses in introductory
biology, introductory physics, general chemistry, and
organic chemistry.

Selection is based on a total evaluation of the applicant.
Intellectual capability for successful performance in medical
school is evaluated by reviewing an applicant's cumulative
undergraduate grade-point average and MCAT scores.
Those passing the academic cutoff are invited for interviews. Non cognitive skills desirable in future physicians are
evaluated during the interviews. These traits include emotional stability, integrity, reasoning skills, enthusiasm, and
genuine concern for others. Accomplishments, as determined by the letters of recommendation, leadership experi-

ences, volunteerism/charitable works, and shadowing/clinical exposure, are also rated during the interviews.

South Carolina residency is a primary admission consideration. Foreign students without a permanent residence visa are not eligible for consideration.

COSTS AND FINANCIAL AID

Financial aid phone number: **(843) 792-2536**
Tuition, 2005-2006 academic year: **In-state: $21,702; Out-of-state: $57,754**
Room and board: N/A
Percentage of students receiving financial aid in 2005-06: 82%
Percentage of students receiving: Loans: 80%, Grants/scholarships: 18%, Work-study aid: 3%
Average medical school debt for the Class of 2004: $108,952

STUDENT BODY

Fall 2005 full-time enrollment: **601**
Men: 53%, Women: 47%, In-state: 92%, Minorities: 21%, American Indian: 0.5%, Asian-American: 7.7%, African-American: 9.3%, Hispanic-American: 2.7%, White: 77.4%, International: 1.2%, Unknown: 1.3%

ACADEMIC PROGRAMS

The school's curriculum frequently gives first-year students substantial contact with patients.
There are opportunities for first- or second-year students to work in community health clinics.
Program offerings: AIDS, family medicine, geriatrics, internal medicine, pediatrics, rural medicine
Joint degrees awarded: M.D./Ph.D., M.D./MBA, M.D./MPH, M.D./M.H.A.
Total National Institutes of Health (NIH) grants awarded to the medical school and affiliated hospitals: **$85.2 million**

CURRICULUM

(TEXT PROVIDED BY SCHOOL):
The goal of the College of Medicine is to produce caring and competent physicians who are capable of succeeding in their postgraduate career. The four-year program, which leads to an M.D. degree, is divided into two years of preclinical instruction, which consists of education in the basic sciences and an introduction to clinical medicine, followed by two years of clinical science education.

During the first two years, the curriculum addresses four major objectives: provision of basic science concepts; acquisition of problem-solving strategies; development of skills that permit the performance of an adequate history and physical examination; and an introduction to the role of the physician in society. Throughout, emphasis is placed on small-group instruction. The curriculum provides opportunities for independent, self-directed learning. As a result, students are exposed earlier to certain clinical skills.

The junior year consists of seven core clerkships: eight weeks each of internal medicine, obstetrics/gynecology, pediatrics, and surgery, as well as four weeks each of family medicine, psychiatry, and neurology. In addition, all students take a block of 40 hours of clinical nutrition. During the clerkships, emphasis is placed on the development of clinical, interpersonal, and professional competence.

During the senior year, students take a minimum of seven four-week rotations. The student is required to take a clinical externship in general medicine, pediatrics, or surgery. The remaining four blocks are elective and can be taken at approved sites throughout the state or country. The clinical offerings of the Area Health Education Centers throughout the state play an integral part in the college's clinical curriculum.

FACULTY PROFILE (FALL 2005)

Total teaching faculty: **945 (full-time)**, **127 (part-time)**
Of full-time faculty, those teaching in basic sciences: 21%; in clinical programs: 79%
Of part-time faculty, those teaching in basic sciences: 9%; in clinical programs: 91%
Full-time faculty/student ratio: 1.6

SUPPORT SERVICES

The school offers students these services for dealing with stress: expanded-hour gym access, peer counseling, professional counseling, religious support, support groups.

RESIDENCY PROFILE

Most popular residency and specialty programs chosen by the 2004 and 2005 M.D. graduating classes: anesthesiology, emergency medicine, family practice, internal medicine, obstetrics and gynecology, orthopaedic surgery, pediatrics, psychiatry, radiology–diagnostic, surgery–general.

WHERE GRADS GO

40%
Proportion of 2003-2005 graduates who entered primary care specialties

35%
Proportion of 2004-2005 graduates who accepted in-state residencies

Mercer University

- 1550 College Street, Macon, GA 31207
- Private
- Year Founded: 1982
- Tuition, 2005-2006: $30,220
- Enrollment 2005-2006 academic year: 242
- Website: http://medicine.mercer.edu
- Specialty ranking: family medicine: 22, rural medicine: 30

3.52	AVERAGE GPA, ENTERING CLASS FALL 2005
8.9	AVERAGE MCAT, ENTERING CLASS FALL 2005
12.9%	ACCEPTANCE RATE, ENTERING CLASS FALL 2005
Unranked	2007 U.S. NEWS MEDICAL SCHOOL RANKING (RESEARCH)
Unranked	2007 U.S. NEWS MEDICAL SCHOOL RANKING (PRIMARY CARE)

ADMISSIONS

Admissions phone number: **(478) 301-2542**
Admissions email address: **faust_ek@mercer.edu**
Application website: **N/A**
Acceptance rate: **12.9%**
In-state acceptance rate: **12.9%**
Out-of-state acceptance rate: **N/A**
Minority acceptance rate: **8.1%**
International acceptance rate: **N/A**

Fall 2005 applications and acceptees

	Applied	Interviewed	Accepted	Enrolled
Total:	689	237	89	60
In-state:	689	237	89	60
Out-of-state:	0	0	0	0

Profile of admitted students

Average undergraduate grade point average: **3.52**
MCAT averages (scale: 1-15; writing test: J-T):
  Composite score: **8.9**
  Verbal reasoning score: **9.0**, Physical sciences score: **8.5**,
  Biological sciences score: **9.2**, Writing score: **M**
Proportion with undergraduate majors in: Biological
  sciences: **48%**, Physical sciences: **20%**, Non-sciences:
  6%, Other health professions: **6%**, Mixed disciplines
  and other: **20%**
Percentage of students not coming directly from college
  after graduation: **10%**

Dates and details

The American Medical College Application Service
  (AMCAS) application is accepted.
School asks for a school-specific application as part of the
  admissions process.
Oldest MCAT considered for Fall 2007 entry: **2004**
Earliest application date for the 2007-2008 first-year class:
  June 1, 2006
Latest application date: **November 1, 2006**
The school considers requests for deferred entrance.
Starting month for the class entering in 2007–2008:
  August

The school has an Early Decision Plan (EDP).
A personal interview is required for admission.

Undergraduate coursework required

Medical school requires undergraduate work in these subjects: biology, organic chemistry, inorganic (general) chemistry, physics.

ADMISSIONS POLICY

(TEXT PROVIDED BY SCHOOL):

To help Mercer fulfill its mission to Georgia, the School of
Medicine accepts only Georgia residents into the doctor of
medicine program. Admissions decisions made by a faculty
committee are based on an applicant's potential for achievement in medical school and compliance with Mercer's mission. No particular major is required, but all accepted
applicants must have successfully completed three years of
course work leading to a baccalaureate degree and one-year
laboratory courses in biology, general or inorganic chemistry, organic chemistry or organic-biochemistry, and
physics. Mercer encourages applications from all qualified
persons, regardless of age, sex, race, religion or national or
ethnic origin. Applications can be accessed online through
the American Medical College Application Service
(AMCAS). Mercer's deadline is November 1, and the Mercer
Medical School Code Number is GA-832. The Early
Decision Program is also available, for which the deadline is
August 1.

COSTS AND FINANCIAL AID

Financial aid phone number: **(478) 301-2853**
Tuition, 2005-2006 academic year: **$30,220**
Room and board: **$13,190**
Percentage of students receiving financial aid in 2005-06:
  94%
Percentage of students receiving: Loans: **91%**,
  Grants/scholarships: **76%**, Work-study aid: **0%**
Average medical school debt for the Class of 2004:
  $141,006

STUDENT BODY

Fall 2005 full-time enrollment: **242**
Men: **52%**, Women: **48%**, In-state: **100%**, Minorities: **14%**,
 American Indian: **0.4%**, Asian-American: **9.9%**,
 African-American: **3.3%**, Hispanic-American: **0.4%**,
 White: **86.0%**, International: **0.0%**, Unknown: **0.0%**

ACADEMIC PROGRAMS

The school's curriculum occasionally gives first-year
 students substantial contact with patients.
There are opportunities for first- or second-year students to
 work in community health clinics.
Program offerings: family medicine, geriatrics, internal
 medicine, pediatrics, rural medicine, women's health
Total National Institutes of Health (NIH) grants awarded to
 the medical school and affiliated hospitals: **N/A**

CURRICULUM

(TEXT PROVIDED BY SCHOOL):

Mercer University School of Medicine was one of the first
medical schools in the country to replace the traditional
classroom lecture curriculum with small-group tutorials.

In this supportive learning environment, medical students utilize a problem-based or case study method, which
requires participants to study and learn the basic sciences
requisite to medical practice and know how to organize and
apply the information to medical situations.

This problem-based curriculum results in a high level of
student interaction. This active learning approach enables
Mercer medical students to develop the tools and skills to be
life-long learners, something critical for providing quality
health care. With its small 60-member class size, a close
student/faculty relationship exists, offering individualized
attention and a supportive atmosphere.

Because patient care involves more than textbook learning, Mercer students are placed in clinical settings within
the first few weeks of medical school. Interviewing techniques and physical examination skills, learned through
encounters with simulated patients on campus, are

strengthened through these clinical experiences, which continue throughout the first two years of medical school.

To provide this clinical component and to help students
understand their role in the community and in the medical
profession, Mercer has developed an extensive network of
physicians who precept, or teach, Mercer students. Students
are matched to a particular community, which they visit
throughout medical school to learn about personal care, disease prevention and health promotion. In addition to the
hands-on experiences students receive, they also have the
opportunity to give back to the profession by conducting
needs assessments to determine the health status of the
communities they serve.

Following their second year, students participate in core
clinical clerkships in Macon or Savannah, which are offered
at the school's primary teaching hospitals: Medical Center
of Central Georgia in Macon or Memorial Health University
Medical Center in Savannah. Additional rotations are
offered at affiliate medical centers and hospitals in Rome,
Albany, Atlanta and Columbus. All third-year students experience clerkships in family medicine, internal medicine,
obstetrics and gynecology, pediatrics, emergency medicine,
psychiatry and surgery.

Senior year includes clerkships in acute/critical care, substance abuse and community-based primary care medicine,
as well as electives in areas that complement and
strengthen the student's knowledge of their chosen area of
medical practice.

SUPPORT SERVICES

The school offers students these services for dealing with
stress: expanded-hour gym access, professional counseling.

RESIDENCY PROFILE

Most popular residency and specialty programs chosen by
the 2004 and 2005 M.D. graduating classes: family practice, internal medicine, obstetrics and gynecology, pediatrics, surgery–general.

Michigan State University

- A110 E. Fee Hall, East Lansing, MI 48824
- Public
- Year Founded: 1964
- Tuition, 2005-2006: In-state: $23,700; Out-of-state: $51,600
- Enrollment 2005-2006 academic year: 454
- Website: http://humanmedicine.msu.edu
- Specialty ranking: family medicine: 18, rural medicine: 16

3.52 AVERAGE GPA, ENTERING CLASS FALL 2005

9.4 AVERAGE MCAT, ENTERING CLASS FALL 2005

6.6% ACCEPTANCE RATE, ENTERING CLASS FALL 2005

Unranked 2007 U.S. NEWS MEDICAL SCHOOL RANKING (RESEARCH)

14 2007 U.S. NEWS MEDICAL SCHOOL RANKING (PRIMARY CARE)

ADMISSIONS

Admissions phone number: **(517) 353-9620**
Admissions email address: **MDadmissions@msu.edu**
Application website: **N/A**
Acceptance rate: **6.6%**
In-state acceptance rate: **14.5%**
Out-of-state acceptance rate: **2.8%**
Minority acceptance rate: **6.3%**
International acceptance rate: **4.1%**

Fall 2005 applications and acceptees

	Applied	Interviewed	Accepted	Enrolled
Total:	3,165	369	210	106
In-state:	1,042	263	151	83
Out-of-state:	2,123	106	59	23

Profile of admitted students

Average undergraduate grade point average: **3.52**
MCAT averages (scale: 1-15; writing test: J-T):
  Composite score: **9.4**
  Verbal reasoning score: **9.2**, Physical sciences score: **9.1**,
  Biological sciences score: **9.9**, Writing score: **P**
Proportion with undergraduate majors in: Biological
  sciences: **67%**, Physical sciences: **8%**, Non-sciences:
  19%, Other health professions: **4%**, Mixed disciplines
  and other: **2%**
Percentage of students not coming directly from college
  after graduation: **20%**

Dates and details

The American Medical College Application Service
  (AMCAS) application is accepted.
School asks for a school-specific application as part of the
  admissions process.
Oldest MCAT considered for Fall 2007 entry: **2003**
Earliest application date for the 2007-2008 first-year class:
  June 1, 2006
Latest application date: **November 15, 2006**
Acceptance dates for regular application for the class
  entering in fall 2007:
  Earliest: **October 15, 2006**

Latest: **N/A**
The school considers requests for deferred entrance.
Starting month for the class entering in 2007–2008:
  August
The school has an Early Decision Plan (EDP).
A personal interview is required for admission.

Undergraduate coursework required

Medical school requires undergraduate work in these subjects: biology, English, organic chemistry, inorganic (general) chemistry, physics, humanities, mathematics, social sciences.

ADMISSIONS POLICY
(TEXT PROVIDED BY SCHOOL):

The College seeks to admit an academically proficient class that reflects both the rural and urban characteristics of Michigan and includes a wide spectrum of personalities, backgrounds, and talents. Students who may be disadvantaged due to economic circumstances, lack of educational opportunities, and/or family circumstances, yet have the desire and aptitude to become physicians, are encouraged to apply. Approximately 80 percent of the entering class are Michigan residents.

The Committee on Admissions reviews approximately 3,500 applications each year and subsequently awards 800 Secondary Applications. About 400 applicants are invited to attend Interview Day at the East Lansing campus. Applicants interview with faculty members and current medical students. Selection is based on many factors: academic profile, including review of GPA and MCAT scores; fit with the school's mission; relevant community service; clinical experience; interviewer assessments of motivation, ability to communicate, problem-solving ability, maturity, and suitability for the MSU program; state of residence, and potential to contribute to the overall quality of the entering class.

COSTS AND FINANCIAL AID

Financial aid phone number: **(517) 353-5188**

Tuition, 2005-2006 academic year: **In-state: $23,700; Out-of-state: $51,600**

Room and board: **$12,024**

Percentage of students receiving financial aid in 2005-06: **93%**

Percentage of students receiving: Loans: **87%**, Grants/scholarships: **80%**, Work-study aid: **0%**

Average medical school debt for the Class of 2004: **$136,461**

STUDENT BODY

Fall 2005 full-time enrollment: **454**

Men: **43%**, Women: **57%**, In-state: **78%**, Minorities: **36%**, American Indian: **0.9%**, Asian-American: **15.4%**, African-American: **10.4%**, Hispanic-American: **9.0%**, White: **63.4%**, International: **0.9%**, Unknown: **N/A**

ACADEMIC PROGRAMS

The school's curriculum frequently gives first-year students substantial contact with patients.

There are opportunities for first- or second-year students to work in community health clinics.

Program offerings: AIDS, drug/alcohol abuse, family medicine, geriatrics, internal medicine, pediatrics, rural medicine, women's health

Joint degrees awarded: M.D./MS, M.D./M.A., M.D./M.H.A.

Total National Institutes of Health (NIH) grants awarded to the medical school and affiliated hospitals: **N/A**

CURRICULUM

(TEXT PROVIDED BY SCHOOL):

The MSU/CHM curriculum integrates basic biological, behavioral, and social sciences using a developmental approach to learning, early teaching of clinical skills, attention to professional development, and a community-integrated approach to clinical training using the Block System.

Block 1, a three-semester experience, presents fundamental basic science concepts and principles in a structured, discipline-based format. Clinical skills training, mentor groups, a longitudinal patient care experience (LPCE), supplementary learning experiences, and a clinical correlations course integrate basic science information.

Block 2, which comprises two semesters, presents advanced basic science concepts organized into an integrated, problem-based format that utilizes small-group instruction and problem solving to learn basic science concepts in clinical scenarios. Clinical skills training, LPCE, and mentor groups continue, and topical seminars addressing contemporary issues in society and medicine are added.

Block 3 consists of 56 weeks of required clerkships and 20 weeks of elective clerkships which provide students with hospital and ambulatory care experience in one of the six community campus settings. Family practice/primary care is a required clerkship. The Rural Physician Program and the Leadership in Medicine for the Underserved Program address special interests.

FACULTY PROFILE (FALL 2005)

Total teaching faculty: **308 (full-time)**, **37 (part-time)**

Of full-time faculty, those teaching in basic sciences: **58%**; in clinical programs: **42%**

Of part-time faculty, those teaching in basic sciences: **46%**; in clinical programs: **54%**

Full-time faculty/student ratio: **0.7**

SUPPORT SERVICES

The school offers students these services for dealing with stress: expanded-hour gym access, professional counseling, support groups.

RESIDENCY PROFILE

Most popular residency and specialty programs chosen by the 2004 and 2005 M.D. graduating classes: emergency medicine, family practice, internal medicine, obstetrics and gynecology, pediatrics, radiology–diagnostic, surgery–general.

WHERE GRADS GO

50.1%

Proportion of 2003-2005 graduates who entered primary care specialties

46.6%

Proportion of 2004-2005 graduates who accepted in-state residencies

Morehouse School of Medicine

- 720 Westview Drive SW, Atlanta, GA 30310
- Private
- Year Founded: 1975
- Tuition, 2005-2006: $28,557
- Enrollment 2005-2006 academic year: 196
- Website: http://www.msm.edu
- Specialty ranking: N/A

N/A	AVERAGE GPA, ENTERING CLASS FALL 2005
N/A	AVERAGE MCAT, ENTERING CLASS FALL 2005
5.1%	ACCEPTANCE RATE, ENTERING CLASS FALL 2005
Unranked	2007 U.S. NEWS MEDICAL SCHOOL RANKING (RESEARCH)
Unranked	2007 U.S. NEWS MEDICAL SCHOOL RANKING (PRIMARY CARE)

ADMISSIONS

Admissions phone number: **(404) 752-1650**
Admissions email address: **mdadmissions@msm.edu**
Application website: **N/A**
Acceptance rate: **5.1%**
In-state acceptance rate: **11.5%**
Out-of-state acceptance rate: **3.8%**
Minority acceptance rate: **N/A**
International acceptance rate: **N/A**

Fall 2005 applications and acceptees

	Applied	Interviewed	Accepted	Enrolled
Total:	2,144	247	110	52
In-state:	373	85	43	30
Out-of-state:	1,771	162	67	22

Profile of admitted students

Average undergraduate grade point average: **N/A**
MCAT averages (scale: 1-15; writing test: J-T):
Composite score: **N/A**
Verbal reasoning score: **N/A**, Physical sciences score:
N/A, Biological sciences score: **N/A**, Writing score: **N/A**
Proportion with undergraduate majors in: Biological sciences: **65%**, Physical sciences: **8%**, Non-sciences: **21%**, Other health professions: **4%**, Mixed disciplines and other: **2%**
Percentage of students not coming directly from college after graduation: **30%**

Dates and details

The American Medical College Application Service (AMCAS) application is accepted.
School asks for a school-specific application as part of the admissions process.
Oldest MCAT considered for Fall 2007 entry: **2004**
Earliest application date for the 2007-2008 first-year class: **June 1, 2006**
Latest application date: **December 1, 2006**
Acceptance dates for regular application for the class entering in fall 2007:
Earliest: **June 1, 2006**

Latest: **December 1, 2006**
The school considers requests for deferred entrance.
Starting month for the class entering in 2007–2008: **July**
The school has an Early Decision Plan (EDP).
A personal interview is required for admission.

Undergraduate coursework required

Medical school requires undergraduate work in these subjects: biology, English, organic chemistry, physics, mathematics, general chemistry.

ADMISSIONS POLICY
(TEXT PROVIDED BY SCHOOL):

The selection of students by the committee is made after careful consideration of many factors. Among them are intelligence, preparedness, motivation and aptitude. In the evaluation, account is taken of the candidate's score on the Medical College Admission Test (MCAT), evidence of academic achievement, the extent of academic improvement, balance and depth of academic program, difficulty of courses taken and other indications of maturation of learning ability. The Committee is also interested in the activities of the applicant outside of the classroom including the nature of extracurricular activities that indicate concurrence with the school's mission and evidence of pursuing interests in talents in depth. Finally, the Committee looks for evidence of which, in the Committee's opinion, indicate that the applicant shows promise of contributing to the advancement of the art, science, and practice of medicine after obtaining the M.D. Degree. The Committee's consideration of these factors are based on all components of the applicant's file including letters of recommendation, the academic record, the supplemental application, and the interview if the latter is granted. Qualified residents of the State of Georgia will be given high priority. Students who have been dismissed from medical school will not be considered for admission. International applicants must have a permanent visa.

COSTS AND FINANCIAL AID

Financial aid phone number: **(404) 752-1655**

Tuition, 2005-2006 academic year: **$28,557**
Room and board: **$11,760**
Percentage of students receiving financial aid in 2005-06:
   95%
Percentage of students receiving: Loans: **88%**,
   Grants/scholarships: **58%**, Work-study aid: **0%**
Average medical school debt for the Class of 2004:
   $116,518

STUDENT BODY

Fall 2005 full-time enrollment: **196**
Men: **36%**, Women: **64%**, In-state: **51%**, Minorities: **86%**,
   American Indian: **0.0%**, Asian-American: **14.8%**,
   African-American: **69.4%**, Hispanic-American: **2.0%**,
   White: **13.3%**, International: **0.5%**, Unknown: **0.0%**

ACADEMIC PROGRAMS

The school's curriculum frequently gives first-year students
   substantial contact with patients.
There are opportunities for first- or second-year students to
   work in community health clinics.
Program offerings: AIDS, drug/alcohol abuse, family
   medicine, internal medicine, pediatrics, rural medicine,
   women's health
Joint degrees awarded: M.D./MPH
Total National Institutes of Health (NIH) grants awarded to
   the medical school and affiliated hospitals: **$36.7 million**

CURRICULUM

(TEXT PROVIDED BY SCHOOL):
The educational program offered by Morehouse School of
Medicine which leads to the Doctor of Medicine (M.D.)
degree focuses both on scientific medicine and on meeting
the primary healthcare needs of patients who are underserved. Most of the first and second year classes are offered
in the Hugh Gloster Basic Medical Sciences Building on the
main campus. Clinical experience begins in the first year
with clinical preceptorships in private offices. Learning in
community service is also an element of the first year curriculum. Clinical instruction is given in hospitals and clinics affiliated with MSM, which include: Grady Memorial
Hospital, Southwest Hospital Medical Center, West Fulton
Mental Health Center, Ridgeview Institute, Southside
Healthcare, Inc., and others. In addition, clinical preceptorships in health clinics and physicians' offices are part of the
educational program. The first year begins with a five-week

summer component designed to assist students in finding
the most efficient way to approach the curriculum. On the
basis of their performance, students may elect to, or be
required to, participate in the five-year program. This decel-
erated curriculum allows three years to complete the first
two years of the basic sciences curriculum. This five-year
program is a recognized and legitimate course of study. The
entire first year curriculum extends over ten and one/half
months. The second year of the curriculum begins in early
August and concludes with the United States Medical
Licensing Examination, Step I (USMLE, Step I). The ten-
month curriculum includes course work in clinical medicine taught in affiliated hospitals and clinics. The academic
schedule for the third year begins in early August and ends
in late July. During this twelve-month period, students must
complete all of the following clerkships: Surgery, Family
Medicine, Maternal Child Health, Psychiatry, Radiology,
Internal Medicine, Pediatrics, and Obstetrics & Gynecology.
The academic schedule for the fourth year begins in early
August and ends in late April. During this nine-month
period, students must complete the remaining two clinical
rotations, i.e., Rural Primary Care and Ambulatory
Medicine, in addition to a minimum of five clinical electives. The electives program, which must be approved for
each student in order to ensure a balanced program, may
include electives at other LCME accredited medical schools.

FACULTY PROFILE (FALL 2005)

Total teaching faculty: **216 (full-time)**, **43 (part-time)**
Of full-time faculty, those teaching in basic sciences: **26%**;
   in clinical programs: **74%**
Of part-time faculty, those teaching in basic sciences: **14%**;
   in clinical programs: **86%**
Full-time faculty/student ratio: **1.1**

SUPPORT SERVICES

The school offers students these services for dealing with
stress: expanded-hour gym access, peer counseling, professional counseling, religious support, support groups.

RESIDENCY PROFILE

Most popular residency and specialty programs chosen by the
2004 and 2005 M.D. graduating classes: dermatology, emergency medicine, family practice, internal medicine, obstetrics
and gynecology, pediatrics, pediatrics–adolescent medicine,
psychiatry, radiology–diagnostic, surgery–general.

Mount Sinai School of Medicine

- One Gustave L. Levy Place, PO Box 1475, New York, NY 10029
- Public
- Year Founded: 1963
- Tuition, 2005-2006: In-state: $37,050; Out-of-state: $37,050
- Enrollment 2005-2006 academic year: 470
- Website: http://www.mssm.edu/
- Specialty ranking: AIDS: 14, geriatrics: 2, internal medicine: 28

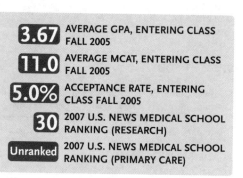

3.67	AVERAGE GPA, ENTERING CLASS FALL 2005
11.0	AVERAGE MCAT, ENTERING CLASS FALL 2005
5.0%	ACCEPTANCE RATE, ENTERING CLASS FALL 2005
30	2007 U.S. NEWS MEDICAL SCHOOL RANKING (RESEARCH)
Unranked	2007 U.S. NEWS MEDICAL SCHOOL RANKING (PRIMARY CARE)

ADMISSIONS

Admissions phone number: **(212) 241-6696**
Admissions email address: **admissions@mssm.edu**
Application website:
  http://fusion.mssm.edu/admissions/submit
Acceptance rate: **5.0%**
In-state acceptance rate: **7.3%**
Out-of-state acceptance rate: **4.3%**
Minority acceptance rate: **4.4%**
International acceptance rate: **2.9%**

Fall 2005 applications and acceptees

	Applied	Interviewed	Accepted	Enrolled
Total:	6,591	737	329	120
In-state:	1,532	253	112	47
Out-of-state:	5,059	484	217	73

Profile of admitted students

Average undergraduate grade point average: **3.67**
MCAT averages (scale: 1-15; writing test: J-T):
  Composite score: **11.0**
  Verbal reasoning score: **10.6**, Physical sciences score: **11.0**, Biological sciences score: **11.4**, Writing score: **Q**
Proportion with undergraduate majors in: Biological sciences: **32%**, Physical sciences: **11%**, Non-sciences: **43%**, Other health professions: **0%**, Mixed disciplines and other: **14%**
Percentage of students not coming directly from college after graduation: **30%**

Dates and details

The American Medical College Application Service (AMCAS) application is accepted.
School asks for a school-specific application as part of the admissions process.
Oldest MCAT considered for Fall 2007 entry: **2004**
Earliest application date for the 2007-2008 first-year class: **June 1, 2006**
Latest application date: **November 28, 2006**
Acceptance dates for regular application for the class entering in fall 2007:

Earliest: **November 1, 2006**
Latest: **N/A**
The school considers requests for deferred entrance.
Starting month for the class entering in 2007–2008: **August**
The school has an Early Decision Plan (EDP).
A personal interview is required for admission.

Undergraduate coursework required

Medical school requires undergraduate work in these subjects: biology, English, organic chemistry, inorganic (general) chemistry, physics, mathematics.

ADMISSIONS POLICY
(TEXT PROVIDED BY SCHOOL):

Mount Sinai seeks to attract individuals of diverse backgrounds who have the ability and potential to become physician-scholars dedicated to excellence in their chosen career paths. Applicants for admission are considered based on their total qualifications. We assess intellectual capability, academic achievement, motivation for a career in medicine, community service, leadership abilities, enthusiasm for shaping one's own learning experience, and personal maturity. We give no preference to in-state applicants. We are seeking students who are dedicated to becoming the next generation of leaders in a constantly changing profession. We pride ourselves in a class that has broad representation of geography, undergraduate colleges, fields of study, race, gender, and previous accomplishments.

COSTS AND FINANCIAL AID

Financial aid phone number: **(212) 241-5245**
Tuition, 2005-2006 academic year: **In-state: $37,050; Out-of-state: $37,050**
Room and board: **$13,800**
Percentage of students receiving financial aid in 2005-06: **91%**
Percentage of students receiving: Loans: **85%**, Grants/scholarships: **45%**, Work-study aid: **9%**
Average medical school debt for the Class of 2004: **$91,460**

STUDENT BODY

Fall 2005 full-time enrollment: **470**
Men: **47%**, Women: **53%**, In-state: **45%**, Minorities: **44%**,
American Indian: **1.1%**, Asian-American: **22.3%**, African-American: **6.0%**, Hispanic-American: **14.3%**, White: **53.4%**, International: **1.5%**, Unknown: **1.5%**

ACADEMIC PROGRAMS

The school's curriculum frequently gives first-year students substantial contact with patients.
There are opportunities for first- or second-year students to work in community health clinics.
Program offerings: AIDS, drug/alcohol abuse, family medicine, geriatrics, internal medicine, pediatrics, women's health
Joint degrees awarded: M.D./Ph.D., M.D./MBA, M.D./MPH.
Total National Institutes of Health (NIH) grants awarded to the medical school and affiliated hospitals: **N/A**

CURRICULUM

(TEXT PROVIDED BY SCHOOL):

Mount Sinai School of Medicine's innovative curriculum promotes exposure to patients during the first two years and integrates clinical medicine with the basic sciences. The teaching faculty is interdisciplinary and there is vertical integration of themes (e.g. ethics, evidence-based medicine, palliative care) organized in a matrix entitled Courses Without Walls. Art and Science of Medicine is a two year course which integrates aspects of doctoring, including history taking, physical examination, bioethics, and health policy. Lectures are used in the first two years for information best taught in that format. Other large group formats have been replaced with interactive small group and laboratory sessions which are co-taught by clinical preceptors. The elective component of the curriculum in years one and two encourages students to participate in community-based experiences and research.

We have implemented an Introduction to Clinical Skills week before the clerkships begin, and an Intersession week during the spring of the third year. During Intersession students participate in integrated problem-based learning exercises and incorporate the fundamentals of clinical practice through didactic and small group experiences. Our educational program includes a network of affiliates that serves diverse communites of patients. Students have ample elective time in years three and four to sample clinical disciplines, participate in research, or complete other advanced

degrees (e.g. MPH, MBA). Critical Care and Anatomic Radiology have been included in the fourth year to provide advanced clinical experience and integrate Physiology and Anatomy. A sub-Internship in Medicine or Pediatrics and an Emergency Medicine experience are required. Many innovative resources are available to students: a web-based curriculum for all courses and clerkships, a web-based assessment tool for all educational offerings, and Human Simulator and Standardized Patient centers for skills training and assessment. Abundant faculty resources allow for individualized educational and research experiences, as well as intensive career counseling. Our unique Comprehensive Skills Assessment programs (COMPASS) take place at the end of year two and at the end of year three, and prepare our students for the clerkships and Clinical Skills National Board examination. Our curriculum promotes self-directed learning, information retrieval skills, problem solving and reasoning, and scientific inquiry.

FACULTY PROFILE (FALL 2005)

Total teaching faculty: **1,188 (full-time)**, **192 (part-time)**
Of full-time faculty, those teaching in basic sciences: **33%**; in clinical programs: **67%**
Of part-time faculty, those teaching in basic sciences: **23%**; in clinical programs: **77%**
Full-time faculty/student ratio: **2.5**

SUPPORT SERVICES

The school offers students these services for dealing with stress: expanded-hour gym access, peer counseling, professional counseling, religious support, support groups.

RESIDENCY PROFILE

Most popular residency and specialty programs chosen by the 2004 and 2005 M.D. graduating classes: anesthesiology, emergency medicine, internal medicine, neurology, obstetrics and gynecology, ophthalmology, pediatrics, psychiatry, radiology–diagnostic, surgery–general.

WHERE GRADS GO

38.2%
Proportion of 2003-2005 graduates who entered primary care specialties

74.5%
Proportion of 2004-2005 graduates who accepted in-state residencies

New York Medical College

- Administration Building, Valhalla, NY 10595
- Private
- **Year Founded:** 1860
- **Tuition, 2005-2006:** $40,276
- **Enrollment 2005-2006 academic year:** 765
- **Website:** http://www.nymc.edu
- **Specialty ranking:** N/A

3.50 AVERAGE GPA, ENTERING CLASS FALL 2005

10.0 AVERAGE MCAT, ENTERING CLASS FALL 2005

10.5% ACCEPTANCE RATE, ENTERING CLASS FALL 2005

Unranked 2007 U.S. NEWS MEDICAL SCHOOL RANKING (RESEARCH)

Unranked 2007 U.S. NEWS MEDICAL SCHOOL RANKING (PRIMARY CARE)

ADMISSIONS

Admissions phone number: **(914) 594-4507**
Admissions email address: **mdadmit@nymc.edu**
Application website:
   http://www.nymc.edu/admit/medical/info/proced.htm
Acceptance rate: **10.5%**
In-state acceptance rate: **16.6%**
Out-of-state acceptance rate: **9.0%**
Minority acceptance rate: **8.2%**
International acceptance rate: **4.4%**

Fall 2005 applications and acceptees

	Applied	Interviewed	Accepted	Enrolled
Total:	7,073	1,394	743	186
In-state:	1,415	378	235	57
Out-of-state:	5,658	1,016	508	129

Profile of admitted students

Average undergraduate grade point average: **3.50**
MCAT averages (scale: 1-15; writing test: J-T):
   Composite score: **10.0**
   Verbal reasoning score: **9.5**, Physical sciences score:
   10.2, Biological sciences score: **10.5**, Writing score: **Q**
Proportion with undergraduate majors in: Biological
   sciences: **50%**, Physical sciences: **18%**, Non-sciences:
   16%, Other health professions: **1%**, Mixed disciplines
   and other: **15%**
Percentage of students not coming directly from college
   after graduation: **65%**

Dates and details

The American Medical College Application Service
   (AMCAS) application is accepted.
School asks for a school-specific application as part of the
   admissions process.
Oldest MCAT considered for Fall 2007 entry: **2003**
Earliest application date for the 2007-2008 first-year class:
   July 1, 2006
Latest application date: **December 15, 2006**
Acceptance dates for regular application for the class
   entering in fall 2007:

Earliest: **December 4, 2006**
Latest: **July 31, 2007**
The school considers requests for deferred entrance.
Starting month for the class entering in 2007–2008:
   August
The school has an Early Decision Plan (EDP).
A personal interview is required for admission.

Undergraduate coursework required

Medical school requires undergraduate work in these subjects: biology, English, organic chemistry, inorganic (general) chemistry, physics.

ADMISSIONS POLICY
(TEXT PROVIDED BY SCHOOL):

The Admissions Committee selects students after considering factors of intellect, character and personality that point
toward their ability to become informed and caring physicians. This basic platform must include a history of academic excellence. Although the majority of students have
had undergraduate majors in the sciences, it is not at all a
factor in selection. We welcome applicants with a broad
education in the humanities. In addition to purely academic
factors, we look for students who show clear evidence
through their activities of strong motivation toward medicine and a sense of dedication to the service of others.
Personal qualities of character and personality are evaluated
from letters of recommendation, from the personal statement and from the interview. New York Medical College
does not deny admission to any applicant on the basis of
any legally prohibited discrimination involving, but not limited to, such factors as race, color, creed, religion, national
or ethnic origin, age, sex, sexual orientation or disability.

COSTS AND FINANCIAL AID

Financial aid phone number: **(914) 594-4491**
Tuition, 2005-2006 academic year: **$40,276**
Room and board: **$17,326**
Percentage of students receiving financial aid in 2005-06:
   92%

Percentage of students receiving: Loans: 90%,
Grants/scholarships: 14%, Work-study aid: 3%
Average medical school debt for the Class of 2004:
$163,000

STUDENT BODY

Fall 2005 full-time enrollment: **765**
Men: **50%**, Women: **50%**, In-state: **35%**, Minorities: **44%**,
American Indian: **0.1%**, Asian-American: **39.2%**,
African-American: **3.0%**, Hispanic-American: **1.6%**,
White: **53.3%**, International: **0.4%**, Unknown: **2.4%**

ACADEMIC PROGRAMS

The school's curriculum frequently gives first-year students
substantial contact with patients.
There are opportunities for first- or second-year students to
work in community health clinics.
Program offerings: AIDS, drug/alcohol abuse, family
medicine, geriatrics, internal medicine, pediatrics, rural
medicine, women's health
Joint degrees awarded: M.D./Ph.D., M.D./MPH
Total National Institutes of Health (NIH) grants awarded to
the medical school and affiliated hospitals: **$21.7 million**

CURRICULUM

(TEXT PROVIDED BY SCHOOL):
New York Medical College's goal is to provide a general professional education that prepares students for all career
options in medicine. There is emphasis on critical thinking,
evidence-based decision making and cultural sensitivity
throughout the entire curriculum. Particular strengths
include an integrated four-year curriculum in Biomedical
Ethics; a rigorous subinternship in Medicine or Pediatrics;
and a required fourth-year rotation in Geriatric Medicine or
Chronic Care Pediatrics. A non-credit elective in Medical
Spanish is offered during the preclinical years. International
medical electives are available during the fourth year. An
optional Summer Research Fellowship Program is offered
between the first and second years. The College sponsors a
wide array of community-oriented service programs. In
addition to traditional lectures and laboratory exercises, the
basic science courses utilize small group learning, clinical
correlation sessions, case-based discussions, problem-based
learning and computer-assisted instruction. Particular
emphasis in the second year is on self-directed learning.
Throughout the first two years, all students have a longitudinal clinical experience with assigned physician preceptors.
Third-year clerkships are offered in a variety of hospitals
located throughout the New York metropolitan area. The
Family Medicine clerkship is entirely community-based.

There is a palliative care component of the Medicine clerkship. All students gain experience in medical informatics
and in the application of PDAs to the clinical setting. In the
fourth-year subinternship, students are expected to function
at the level of a beginning resident. The College utilizes an
array of evaluation tools to assess student performance.
These include in-house written exams; laboratory practical
exams, including autopsy; participation in interactive small
group tutorials and problem solving exercises; case presentations, discussions and write-ups; cardiology simulator sessions; observed clinical interviews and physical
examinations; formal Observed Supervised Clinical
Evaluations; evidence-based medicine projects; and standardized checklist rating forms with narrative comments
for clinical clerkships. Most basic science courses and all
third-year clerkships require a passing score on the relevant
National Board Subject Examination (shelf exam). USMLE
Step 1 is required for promotion into fourth year. USMLE
Step 2 CK (clinical knowledge) is required for graduation.
Students are also required to take USMLE Step 2 CS.

FACULTY PROFILE (FALL 2005)

Total teaching faculty: **1,246 (full-time)**, **109 (part-time)**
Of full-time faculty, those teaching in basic sciences: **10%**;
in clinical programs: **90%**
Of part-time faculty, those teaching in basic sciences: **3%**;
in clinical programs: **97%**
Full-time faculty/student ratio: **1.6**

SUPPORT SERVICES

The school offers students these services for dealing with
stress: expanded-hour gym access, professional counseling,
religious support, support groups.

RESIDENCY PROFILE

Most popular residency and specialty programs chosen by
the 2004 and 2005 M.D. graduating classes: anesthesiology,
emergency medicine, family practice, internal medicine,
obstetrics and gynecology, orthopaedic surgery, pediatrics,
psychiatry, radiology–diagnostic, surgery–general.

WHERE GRADS GO

45.4%
*Proportion of 2003-2005 graduates who entered primary
care specialties*

42.5%
*Proportion of 2004-2005 graduates who accepted in-state
residencies*

New York University

- 550 First Avenue, New York, NY 10016
- Private
- **Year Founded:** 1841
- **Tuition, 2005-2006:** $38,175
- **Enrollment 2005-2006 academic year:** 703
- **Website:** http://www.med.nyu.edu/medicaldegree
- **Specialty ranking:** AIDS: 13, drug/alcohol abuse: 11

3.73 AVERAGE GPA, ENTERING CLASS FALL 2005

11.0 AVERAGE MCAT, ENTERING CLASS FALL 2005

5.8% ACCEPTANCE RATE, ENTERING CLASS FALL 2005

32 2007 U.S. NEWS MEDICAL SCHOOL RANKING (RESEARCH)

Unranked 2007 U.S. NEWS MEDICAL SCHOOL RANKING (PRIMARY CARE)

ADMISSIONS

Admissions phone number: **(212) 263-5290**
Admissions email address: **admissions@med.nyu.edu**
Application website:
  http://www.med.nyu.edu/medicaldegree/admissions
Acceptance rate: **5.8%**
In-state acceptance rate: **9.4%**
Out-of-state acceptance rate: **5.0%**
Minority acceptance rate: **5.2%**
International acceptance rate: **4.4%**

Fall 2005 applications and acceptees

	Applied	Interviewed	Accepted	Enrolled
Total:	8,028	940	468	160
In-state:	1,467	235	138	67
Out-of-state:	6,561	705	330	93

Profile of admitted students

Average undergraduate grade point average: **3.73**
MCAT averages (scale: 1-15; writing test: J-T):
  Composite score: **11.0**
  Verbal reasoning score: **10.4**, Physical sciences score:
  11.1, Biological sciences score: **11.3**, Writing score: **Q**
Proportion with undergraduate majors in: Biological
  sciences: **42%**, Physical sciences: **24%**, Non-sciences:
  29%, Other health professions: **0%**, Mixed disciplines
  and other: **5%**
Percentage of students not coming directly from college
  after graduation: **28%**

Dates and details

The American Medical College Application Service
  (AMCAS) application is accepted.
School asks for a school-specific application as part of the
  admissions process.
Oldest MCAT considered for Fall 2007 entry: **2003**
Earliest application date for the 2007-2008 first-year class:
  June 1, 2006
Latest application date: **October 15, 2006**
Acceptance dates for regular application for the class
  entering in fall 2007:

Earliest: **January 15, 2007**
Latest: **N/A**
The school considers requests for deferred entrance.
Starting month for the class entering in 2007-2008:
  August
The school doesn't have an Early Decision Plan (EDP).
A personal interview is required for admission.

Undergraduate coursework required

Medical school requires undergraduate work in these subjects: biology, English, organic chemistry, inorganic (general) chemistry, physics.

ADMISSIONS POLICY
(TEXT PROVIDED BY SCHOOL):

The selection process involves judging the applicant on the
basis of several criteria. In the evaluation, the Admissions
Committee takes into account the candidate's undergraduate course work; his/her ability as judged by college instructors and/or pre-medical committees; results of the Medical
College Admissions Test, and results of a personal interview
at the New York University School of Medicine. The majority of entering first-year students range in age from 21 to
24. However, older candidates of exceptional merit are given
serious consideration for admission. In the 2005 entering
class, 28 percent took at least one year off before applying to
medical school. In recent years, women students have con-
stituted approximately 50 percent of the entering class.

It is not possible to interview all applicants. Only those
candidates who, on the basis of application data, appear to
merit serious consideration for admission are selected for an
interview. The strength of the applicant pool is such that last
year, interviews were granted to only 12 percent of applicants.

After acceptance, the student is given a two-week interval
before a response is required. Matriculation is accomplished by sending a letter of acceptance and a deposit of
$100 to the Admissions Office. The deposit is applied to the
first-year tuition and is refundable until May 15. Final registration becomes official only after the student has satisfactorily completed all admissions requirements and has passed
a physical examination given by the Student Health Service.

Students who have failed in another medical school are not eligible to apply for admission to the New York University School of Medicine.

COSTS AND FINANCIAL AID

Financial aid phone number: **(212) 263-5286**
Tuition, 2005-2006 academic year: **$38,175**
Room and board: **$12,000**
Percentage of students receiving financial aid in 2005-06: **77%**
Percentage of students receiving: Loans: **70%**, Grants/scholarships: **65%**, Work-study aid: **15%**
Average medical school debt for the Class of 2004: **$95,935**

STUDENT BODY

Fall 2005 full-time enrollment: **703**
Men: **50%**, Women: **50%**, In-state: **48%**, Minorities: **36%**, American Indian: **0.1%**, Asian-American: **25.2%**, African-American: **5.4%**, Hispanic-American: **5.0%**, White: **54.1%**, International: **1.0%**, Unknown: **9.2%**

ACADEMIC PROGRAMS

The school's curriculum frequently gives first-year students substantial contact with patients.
There are opportunities for first- or second-year students to work in community health clinics.
Program offerings: AIDS, drug/alcohol abuse, family medicine, geriatrics, internal medicine, pediatrics, rural medicine, women's health
Joint degrees awarded: M.D./Ph.D., M.D./MPH
Total National Institutes of Health (NIH) grants awarded to the medical school and affiliated hospitals: **$138.8 million**

CURRICULUM

(TEXT PROVIDED BY SCHOOL):
The central goal of the curriculum is to create physician-scholars who lead in every field of medical endeavor and who, throughout their professional careers, approach the practice of medicine with intellectual discipline, compassion, and professionalism. We do so in a learning environment that encourages students to apply the scientific method and critical thinking to advance both patient care and medical knowledge. Curriculum evaluation and reform are constant. In this process, students work closely with the faculty to improve the educational program. In the fall of 2001, the School of Medicine implemented a new curriculum. Under this unique and innovative program, the basic science courses were reorganized into thematic modules composed of interrelated units such as Macroscopic Structure and Development of the Human Body, From Molecules to Cells, Cells and Basic Tissues, Host Defense, Brain and Behavior, organ-system based Foundation for Medicine and Mechanisms of Disease, and the Skills and Science of Doctoring. Traditional lecture hours were

reduced, and the educational program now employs novel teaching methodologies, including cross-disciplinary, inter-active, multimedia, case-based computer modules that are specifically designed to nurture an increasingly independent and self-reliant student. The clinical sciences core curriculum consists of nine core clerkships in Medicine, Surgery, Pediatrics, Psychiatry, Obstetrics and Gynecology, Neurology, Ambulatory Care, Critical Care, and an acting internship in Advanced Medicine. Although the basic element of teaching in the clinical clerkship is bedside instruction, skills are developed through multiple media that reinforce interactive, interdisciplinary learning. Topics introduced in the preclinical years are revisited in renewed depth and with different perspectives through case-based exercises that vertically span the curriculum. The transition to clinical sciences is facilitated by a two-week, interdepartmental clerkship orientation, and entry into the final year of medical school begins with a thematic, in depth, seminar- and original literature-based selective in Advanced Science. Students select from a palette of topics drawn from the frontiers of translational medicine and biomedical technology, making choices based upon their own individualized interests and emerging differentiated career goals.

FACULTY PROFILE (FALL 2005)

Total teaching faculty: **1,531 (full-time)**, **3,420 (part-time)**
Of full-time faculty, those teaching in basic sciences: **20%**; in clinical programs: **80%**
Of part-time faculty, those teaching in basic sciences: **5%**; in clinical programs: **95%**
Full-time faculty/student ratio: **2.2**

SUPPORT SERVICES

The school offers students these services for dealing with stress: expanded-hour gym access, peer counseling, professional counseling, religious support, support groups.

RESIDENCY PROFILE

Most popular residency and specialty programs chosen by the 2004 and 2005 M.D. graduating classes: anesthesiology, dermatology, internal medicine, neurology, obstetrics and gynecology, ophthalmology, orthopaedic surgery, pediatrics, radiology–diagnostic, surgery–general.

WHERE GRADS GO

38.8%
Proportion of 2003-2005 graduates who entered primary care specialties

52.1%
Proportion of 2004-2005 graduates who accepted in-state residencies

Northeastern Ohio Universities

COLLEGE OF MEDICINE

- 4209 State Route 44, PO Box 95, Rootstown, OH 44272-0095
- **Public**
- **Year Founded:** 1973
- **Tuition, 2005-2006:** In-state: $24,599; Out-of-state: $47,906
- **Enrollment 2005-2006 academic year:** 461
- **Website:** http://www.neoucom.edu
- **Specialty ranking:** N/A

3.79 AVERAGE GPA, ENTERING CLASS FALL 2005

9.2 AVERAGE MCAT, ENTERING CLASS FALL 2005

14.9% ACCEPTANCE RATE, ENTERING CLASS FALL 2005

Unranked 2007 U.S. NEWS MEDICAL SCHOOL RANKING (RESEARCH)

Unranked 2007 U.S. NEWS MEDICAL SCHOOL RANKING (PRIMARY CARE)

ADMISSIONS

Admissions phone number: **(330) 325-6270**
Admissions email address: **admission@neoucom.edu**
Application website:
  http://www.neoucom.edu/students/ADMI
Acceptance rate: **14.9%**
In-state acceptance rate: **21.5%**
Out-of-state acceptance rate: **2.8%**
Minority acceptance rate: **18.5%**
International acceptance rate: **N/A**

Fall 2005 applications and acceptees

	Applied	Interviewed	Accepted	Enrolled
Total:	1,623	368	242	120
In-state:	1,049	333	226	115
Out-of-state:	574	35	16	5

Profile of admitted students

Average undergraduate grade point average: **3.79**
MCAT averages (scale: 1-15; writing test: J-T):
  Composite score: **9.2**
  Verbal reasoning score: **9.2**, Physical sciences score: **9.2**, Biological sciences score: **9.3**, Writing score: **O**
Proportion with undergraduate majors in: Biological sciences: **87%**, Physical sciences: **2%**, Non-sciences: **3%**, Other health professions: **1%**, Mixed disciplines and other: **7%**
Percentage of students not coming directly from college after graduation: **13%**

Dates and details

The American Medical College Application Service (AMCAS) application is accepted.
School asks for a school-specific application as part of the admissions process.
Oldest MCAT considered for Fall 2007 entry: **2004**
Earliest application date for the 2007-2008 first-year class: **June 1, 2006**
Latest application date: **November 1, 2006**
Acceptance dates for regular application for the class entering in fall 2007:

Earliest: **October 15, 2006**
Latest: **August 15, 2007**
The school doesn't consider requests for deferred entrance.
Starting month for the class entering in 2007–2008:
  August
The school has an Early Decision Plan (EDP).
A personal interview is required for admission.

Undergraduate coursework required

Medical school requires undergraduate work in these subjects: organic chemistry, physics.

ADMISSIONS POLICY

(TEXT PROVIDED BY SCHOOL):
A candidate for the M.D. degree must be able to demonstrate intellectual-conceptual, integrative, and quantitative abilities; skills in observation, communication, and motor functions; and mature behavioral and social attributes. For a more detailed explanation of the above, please contact the Office of Admissions at (800) 686-2511.

NEOUCOM is a publicly chartered and funded institution in the state of Ohio. Therefore, as a result of this public support, its charter mandates giving admission preference to residents of the state of Ohio, as defined by the Board of Regents.

Only U.S. citizens and permanent residents may be considered for admission to NEOUCOM; candidates must have such status upon application.

COSTS AND FINANCIAL AID

Financial aid phone number: **(330) 325-6481**
Tuition, 2005-2006 academic year: **In-state: $24,599; Out-of-state: $47,906**
Room and board: **$10,000**
Percentage of students receiving financial aid in 2005-06: **82%**
Percentage of students receiving: Loans: **81%**, Grants/scholarships: **26%**, Work-study aid: **0%**
Average medical school debt for the Class of 2004: **$98,494**

STUDENT BODY

Fall 2005 full-time enrollment: **461**

Men: 50%, Women: 50%, In-state: 94%, Minorities: 40%, American Indian: 0.7%, Asian-American: 34.1%, African-American: 3.9%, Hispanic-American: 1.1%, White: 59.7%, International: 0.0%, Unknown: 0.7%

ACADEMIC PROGRAMS

The school's curriculum occasionally gives first-year students substantial contact with patients.

There are opportunities for first- or second-year students to work in community health clinics.

Program offerings: AIDS, drug/alcohol abuse, family medicine, geriatrics, internal medicine, pediatrics, rural medicine, women's health

Joint degrees awarded: N/A

Total National Institutes of Health (NIH) grants awarded to the medical school and affiliated hospitals: **$2.4 million**

CURRICULUM

(TEXT PROVIDED BY SCHOOL):

Students of the Northeastern Ohio Universities College of Medicine (NEOUCOM) receive quality medical education that not only emphasizes the science of medicine, but also the art of healing. As a BS/M.D. program, students at NEOUCOM have generally completed two years of baccalaureate training at the University of Akron, Kent State University, or Youngstown State University.

NEOUCOM began implementation of its new Integrated Steps Curriculum in the 2005-2006 academic year, with full implementation in the 2006-2007 academic year. A spiral curriculum approach is taken in the new plan, which emphasizes principles of adult learning, teaches by building on the knowledge and skills gained in previous steps, decreases the hours that students spend in the instructional setting, and provides an integrated and comprehensive assessment structure. In the new curriculum, efforts will be directed toward the measurement of concrete outcomes and a better coordination of the assessment strategies across the four years.

Integrated courses in the first step of the five step curriculum include human development and structure, as well as molecules to cells. These are basic courses essential to the understanding of the science of medicine. The second step features three courses to provide a transition in understanding the science and practice of medicine: physiological basis of medicine; brain, mind and behavior; and infection and immunity. The third step of the curriculum features an integration of principles of medicine, radiology, pathology and pharmacology in a systems-based approach to medical practice. Step four provides theoretical and practical founda-

tions in the clinical disciplines. Working with clinical faculty and residents in eight major teaching hospitals, NEOUCOM students learn diagnostic and therapeutic skills, gain experience in patient management, and examine the ethical dilemmas of contemporary medicine. Students are required to complete experiences ranging from six to ten weeks in family medicine, internal medicine, obstetrics/gynecology, pediatrics, psychiatry, and surgery. Learners may opt to participate in a four-week elective in one of six areas: research, community service, community health, continuity of patient care, exploration of a medical specialty, or professionalism/inquiry.

Guided by advisors and working within requirements, seniors design their own curricula based on their educational and career priorities. Students take at least five clinical electives that reflect a balance in clinical experience. Students are required to participate in a month-long human values in medicine experience to help students gain awareness of their own and others' value systems and their role in the physician/patient relationship.

FACULTY PROFILE (FALL 2005)

Total teaching faculty: **260 (full-time)**, **1,670 (part-time)**

Of full-time faculty, those teaching in basic sciences: **18%**; in clinical programs: **82%**

Of part-time faculty, those teaching in basic sciences: **6%**; in clinical programs: **94%**

Full-time faculty/student ratio: **0.6**

SUPPORT SERVICES

The school offers students these services for dealing with stress: expanded-hour gym access, peer counseling, professional counseling, support groups.

RESIDENCY PROFILE

Most popular residency and specialty programs chosen by the 2004 and 2005 M.D. graduating classes: anesthesiology, emergency medicine, family practice, internal medicine, obstetrics and gynecology, ophthalmology, orthopaedic surgery, pediatrics, radiology–diagnostic.

WHERE GRADS GO

33%

Proportion of 2003-2005 graduates who entered primary care specialties

50%

Proportion of 2004-2005 graduates who accepted in-state residencies

Northwestern University

FEINBERG

- 303 E. Chicago Avenue, Morton Building 1-606, Chicago, IL 60611
- Private
- Year Founded: 1859
- Tuition, 2005-2006: $40,001
- Enrollment 2005-2006 academic year: 678
- Website: http://www.feinberg.northwestern.edu
- Specialty ranking: AIDS: 12, internal medicine: 20, pediatrics: 12, women's health: 15

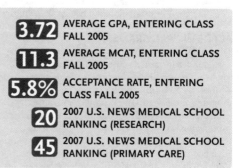

3.72 AVERAGE GPA, ENTERING CLASS FALL 2005

11.3 AVERAGE MCAT, ENTERING CLASS FALL 2005

5.8% ACCEPTANCE RATE, ENTERING CLASS FALL 2005

20 2007 U.S. NEWS MEDICAL SCHOOL RANKING (RESEARCH)

45 2007 U.S. NEWS MEDICAL SCHOOL RANKING (PRIMARY CARE)

ADMISSIONS

Admissions phone number: (312) 503-8206
Admissions email address: med-admissions@northwestern.edu
Application website:
http://www.medschool.northwestern.edu/admissions/md/
Acceptance rate: 5.8%
In-state acceptance rate: 5.5%
Out-of-state acceptance rate: 5.8%
Minority acceptance rate: 6.7%
International acceptance rate: 4.9%

Fall 2005 applications and acceptees

	Applied	Interviewed	Accepted	Enrolled
Total:	6,897	713	399	171
In-state:	884	113	49	47
Out-of-state:	6,013	600	350	124

Profile of admitted students

Average undergraduate grade point average: 3.72
MCAT averages (scale: 1-15; writing test: J-T):
  Composite score: 11.3
  Verbal reasoning score: 10.7, Physical sciences score: 11.6, Biological sciences score: 11.5, Writing score: Q
Proportion with undergraduate majors in: Biological sciences: 41%, Physical sciences: 28%, Non-sciences: 25%, Other health professions: 1%, Mixed disciplines and other: 5%
Percentage of students not coming directly from college after graduation: 25%

Dates and details

The American Medical College Application Service (AMCAS) application is accepted.
School asks for a school-specific application as part of the admissions process.
Oldest MCAT considered for Fall 2007 entry: 2004
Earliest application date for the 2007-2008 first-year class: June 1, 2006
Latest application date: October 16, 2006

Acceptance dates for regular application for the class entering in fall 2007:
  Earliest: November 30, 2006
  Latest: February 28, 2007
The school considers requests for deferred entrance.
Starting month for the class entering in 2007–2008: August
The school doesn't have an Early Decision Plan (EDP).
A personal interview is required for admission.

Undergraduate coursework required

Medical school requires undergraduate work in these subjects: biology, English, organic chemistry, inorganic (general) chemistry, physics.

ADMISSIONS POLICY

(TEXT PROVIDED BY SCHOOL):

The Committee on Admissions seeks applicants who have demonstrated academic excellence, leadership qualities, intellectual curiosity and personal maturity. Applicants should be liberally educated men and women who have studied subjects beyond the conventional required premedical courses. The Medical School has a particular interest in students with promise as physician scholars. Experience in research and evidence of a commitment to medicine as a service profession are positive factors for selection.

The Medical School maintains the richest possible educational environment through the enrollment of a diverse student body that represents applicants from underrepresented populations, applicants having prior work experience and applicants from the smallest to the largest of our nation's universities. The Feinberg School attracts students from all areas of the United States and the world. No preference is given to Illinois residents.

The equivalent of three years of college (or the equivalent) is the minimum required for entrance into the medical school. A bachelor's degree is not required, but it is preferred. The following coursework is recommended: Modern Biology, General Physics, Inorganic Chemistry, Organic Chemistry, English.

Applications from international students are welcome, provided that at least 3 years of course work have been completed at an accredited U.S. or Canadian university, including study at the undergraduate or graduate levels. This policy applies to all applicants, regardless of their citizenship status.

The MCAT is required of all applicants. Only scores from tests administered within the last three years will be accepted.

An AMCAS Application, submitted electronically, is required; it may be submitted as of June 1 and must be submitted to Feinberg no later than October 15 of the calendar year prior to matriculation. A Feinberg supplemental application, a processing fee, and letters of recommendation are required from selected applicants after preliminary review of AMCAS applications.

Interviews are held from September through mid-February at the Feinberg School of Medicine on the Chicago campus of Northwestern University. Admissions decisions are finalized solely upon the recommendation of the Feinberg Committee on Admissions. All decisions are mailed to applicants by the end of February of the matriculation year.

COSTS AND FINANCIAL AID
Financial aid phone number: (312) 503-8722
Tuition, 2005-2006 academic year: $40,001
Room and board: $14,625
Percentage of students receiving financial aid in 2005-06: 76%
Percentage of students receiving: Loans: 71%, Grants/scholarships: 58%, Work-study aid: 0%
Average medical school debt for the Class of 2004: $132,346

STUDENT BODY
Fall 2005 full-time enrollment: 678
Men: 51%, Women: 49%, In-state: 28%, Minorities: 51%, American Indian: 1.2%, Asian-American: 39.5%, African-American: 5.0%, Hispanic-American: 5.5%, White: 42.3%, International: 3.7%, Unknown: 2.8%

ACADEMIC PROGRAMS
The school's curriculum occasionally gives first-year students substantial contact with patients.
There are opportunities for first- or second-year students to work in community health clinics.
Program offerings: AIDS, drug/alcohol abuse, family medicine, geriatrics, internal medicine, pediatrics, rural medicine, women's health
Joint degrees awarded: M.D./Ph.D., M.D./MBA, M.D./MPH, M.D./M.A.
Total National Institutes of Health (NIH) grants awarded to the medical school and affiliated hospitals: $205.9 million

CURRICULUM
(TEXT PROVIDED BY SCHOOL):
The first- and second-year curriculum are composed of three courses. Each course is interdisciplinary and draws faculty from a number of departments. There are two courses in the basic medical sciences. Each involves approximately 10 hours of lecture per week for the entire academic year, complemented by problem-based-learning sessions, laboratories, and small-group discussions and tutorials. The first-year course begins with a review of cell and molecular

biology, genetics, and signal transduction, then addresses gross and microscopic anatomy, biochemistry, and physiology. The second year begins with an overview of immunology, microbiology, and infectious diseases and then details the pathology, pathophysiology, and pharmacology specific to each organ system.

Medical Decision Making occupies three short blocks of time in the first and second years. This course allows students to develop knowledge and skills in information management, epidemiology, biostatistics, and clinical problem solving.

Patient, Physician & Society is devoted to the development of clinical skills and professional perspectives, providing each student opportunity to develop mentoring relationships with faculty preceptors. The class is divided into four "colleges," each led by an experienced clinician. Colleges meet two afternoons per week throughout the first two years. One afternoon offers learning experiences centered around clinical skills development and the provision of an integrated biopsychosocial perspective on illness and patient care. The other afternoon's course sequence addresses medical ethics and humanities, public health, and health policy.

The third year requires 48 weeks of rotation through clerkships in the major clinical disciplines. In the fourth year, three specific clinical experiences are required: a six-week acting internship in either internal medicine or pediatrics, a four-week clerkship in emergency medicine and in intensive care, and a two-week clerkship in physical medicine and rehabilitation. The remainder of the fourth year consists of elective clerkships and research experiences.

FACULTY PROFILE (FALL 2005)
Total teaching faculty: 1,761 (full-time), 214 (part-time)
Of full-time faculty, those teaching in basic sciences: 8%; in clinical programs: 92%
Of part-time faculty, those teaching in basic sciences: 2%; in clinical programs: 98%
Full-time faculty/student ratio: 2.6

SUPPORT SERVICES
The school offers students these services for dealing with stress: professional counseling, religious support, support groups.

RESIDENCY PROFILE
Most popular residency and specialty programs chosen by the 2004 and 2005 M.D. graduating classes: anesthesiology, emergency medicine, internal medicine, orthopaedic surgery, pediatrics, physical medicine and rehabilitation, radiology–diagnostic, surgery–general, urology, transitional year.

WHERE GRADS GO
| 40.5% |
Proportion of 2003-2005 graduates who entered primary care specialties

| 34.7% |
Proportion of 2004-2005 graduates who accepted in-state residencies

Ohio State University

- 200 Meiling Hall, 370 W. Ninth Avenue, Columbus, OH 43210-1238
- Public
- Year Founded: 1834
- Tuition, 2005-2006: In-state: $23,872; Out-of-state: $28,717
- Enrollment 2005-2006 academic year: 839
- Website: http://medicine.osu.edu
- Specialty ranking: family medicine: 26, rural medicine: 30, women's health: 21

3.72 AVERAGE GPA, ENTERING CLASS FALL 2005

10.8 AVERAGE MCAT, ENTERING CLASS FALL 2005

9.6% ACCEPTANCE RATE, ENTERING CLASS FALL 2005

32 2007 U.S. NEWS MEDICAL SCHOOL RANKING (RESEARCH)

33 2007 U.S. NEWS MEDICAL SCHOOL RANKING (PRIMARY CARE)

ADMISSIONS

Admissions phone number: **(614) 292-7137**
Admissions email address: **medicine@osu.edu**
Application website:
   http://www.aamc.org/stuapps/start.htm
Acceptance rate: **9.6%**
In-state acceptance rate: **17.9%**
Out-of-state acceptance rate: **6.9%**
Minority acceptance rate: **7.7%**
International acceptance rate: **0.0%**

Fall 2005 applications and acceptees

	Applied	Interviewed	Accepted	Enrolled
Total:	4,180	665	400	210
In-state:	1,021	258	183	119
Out-of-state:	3,159	407	217	91

Profile of admitted students

Average undergraduate grade point average: **3.72**
MCAT averages (scale: 1-15; writing test: J-T):
   Composite score: **10.8**
   Verbal reasoning score: **10.3**, Physical sciences score: **10.9**, Biological sciences score: **11.2**, Writing score: **P**
Proportion with undergraduate majors in: Biological sciences: **57%**, Physical sciences: **12%**, Non-sciences: **6%**, Other health professions: **4%**, Mixed disciplines and other: **21%**
Percentage of students not coming directly from college after graduation: **10%**

Dates and details

The American Medical College Application Service (AMCAS) application is accepted.
School asks for a school-specific application as part of the admissions process.
Oldest MCAT considered for Fall 2007 entry: **2004**
Earliest application date for the 2007-2008 first-year class: **June 1, 2006**
Latest application date: **December 1, 2006**
Acceptance dates for regular application for the class entering in fall 2007:

Earliest: **October 15, 2006**
Latest: **August 13, 2007**
The school considers requests for deferred entrance.
Starting month for the class entering in 2007–2008: **August**
The school has an Early Decision Plan (EDP).
A personal interview is required for admission.

Undergraduate coursework required

Medical school requires undergraduate work in these subjects: biology, biology/zoology, organic chemistry, inorganic (general) chemistry, physics.

ADMISSIONS POLICY

(TEXT PROVIDED BY SCHOOL):
Application for admission is initiated through the American Medical College Application Service (AMCAS). Applicants designating The Ohio State University on the AMCAS application will receive an email from the College of Medicine directing them to the web-based secondary application. Applications are reviewed upon receipt of the AMCAS application, the secondary application, and MCAT scores. Applicants have access to the status of their application including: receipt of AMCAS application; receipt of secondary application; interview invitation with capability to confirm or reschedule via the web; admissions decision with a multimedia message for accepted students. On-site interviews are conducted from mid-September through March. Admission decisions are made on a rolling basis. Applicants interviewing in September are notified of their admission decision on October 15. Applicants interviewing in October through March are notified within two weeks of their interview.

The College of Medicine Admissions Committee will evaluate applicants by competitive admission standards. Along with strong academic performance, we look for applicants to be self-motivated, compassionate, with strong integrity and interpersonal skills to match the intellectual, physical, and emotional capacities needed to master the medical curriculum. Diverse interests and backgrounds are helpful in establishing the balanced view of society necessary for success in medical practice. We encourage applicants to include subjects such as philosophy, literature, writing, history, arts, and languages in the traditional undergraduate premedical curriculum. Applicants must embody high ethical standards, especially honesty and concern for others, and must be free from substance abuse, addictions, and violent behaviors. They must also possess the skills required to practice direct patient care. No specific undergraduate curriculum or college major is required. However the prerequisite requirements must be met prior to matriculation. In addition to the prerequisite requirements, coursework in biochemistry or cellular and molecular biology is strongly recommended.

COSTS AND FINANCIAL AID

Financial aid phone number: **(614) 292-8771**
Tuition, 2005-2006 academic year: **In-state: $23,872; Out-of-state: $28,717**
Room and board: **$7,080**
Percentage of students receiving financial aid in 2005-06: **87%**
Percentage of students receiving: Loans: **80%**, Grants/scholarships: **58%**, Work-study aid: **0%**
Average medical school debt for the Class of 2004: **$109,139**

STUDENT BODY

Fall 2005 full-time enrollment: **839**
Men: **63%**, Women: **37%**, In-state: **88%**, Minorities: **32%**, American Indian: **1.1%**, Asian-American: **21.7%**, African-American: **6.2%**, Hispanic-American: **2.5%**, White: **66.9%**, International: **1.0%**, Unknown: **0.7%**

ACADEMIC PROGRAMS

The school's curriculum frequently gives first-year students substantial contact with patients.
There are opportunities for first- or second-year students to work in community health clinics.
Program offerings: AIDS, drug/alcohol abuse, family medicine, geriatrics, internal medicine, pediatrics, rural medicine, women's health
Joint degrees awarded: M.D./Ph.D., M.D./MBA, M.D./MPH, M.D./JD, M.D./M.H.A.
Total National Institutes of Health (NIH) grants awarded to the medical school and affiliated hospitals: **$227.1 million**

CURRICULUM

(TEXT PROVIDED BY SCHOOL):
All preclinical students are enrolled in two courses throughout both preclinical years—Patient-Centered Medicine (PCM) and Physician Development (PD). PCM is taught in a small-group, case-based format and deals with topics including ethics, professionalism, self-care, diversity, and substance abuse, as well as a community project. PD includes the doctor-patient relationship, clinical interviewing, and physical examination, and a geriatric longitudinal

care experience. A newly constructed clinical skills laboratory is available to assist instruction through the use of standardized patients and simulations.

The preclinical curriculum also allows students to choose between two curricular pathways for the core scientific content—Integrated (IP) and Independent Study (ISP). IP is a two-year curriculum that integrates basic and clinical sciences in organ-specific modules. It was implemented in 2002. ISP presents the curriculum in an independent study format guided by written learning objectives related to readings. ISP has a 30-year history of success.

The third year consists of six- to 12-week blocks of the core clinical clerkships: internal medicine (eight weeks), pediatrics (eight weeks), psychiatry/neurology (eight weeks), surgery (six weeks), obstetrics/gynecology (six weeks), and ambulatory (12 weeks). All core clerkships must be taken at one of the affiliated teaching hospitals.

The fourth year consists of four-week blocks, of which four blocks must be selected from the Differentiation of Care (DOC) selectives and four are elective choices. Three blocks are available for preparation for USMLE Step 2, residency interviews, or vacation. All DOC selectives must be taken at an affiliated institution. Electives may be taken at any location, including a variety of international health experiences.

FACULTY PROFILE (FALL 2005)

Total teaching faculty: **1,907 (full-time)**, **1,122 (part-time)**
Of full-time faculty, those teaching in basic sciences: **18%**; in clinical programs: **82%**
Of part-time faculty, those teaching in basic sciences: **16%**; in clinical programs: **84%**
Full-time faculty/student ratio: **2.3**

SUPPORT SERVICES

The school offers students these services for dealing with stress: expanded-hour gym access, professional counseling, support groups.

RESIDENCY PROFILE

Most popular residency and specialty programs chosen by the 2004 and 2005 M.D. graduating classes: emergency medicine, family practice, internal medicine, obstetrics and gynecology, orthopaedic surgery, pathology–anatomic and clinical, pediatrics, psychiatry, surgery–general, internal medicine/pediatrics.

WHERE GRADS GO

43%
Proportion of 2003-2005 graduates who entered primary care specialties

48.5%
Proportion of 2004-2005 graduates who accepted in-state residencies

Oregon Health and Science University

- 3181 S.W. Sam Jackson Park Road, L102, Portland, OR 97239-3098
- Public
- **Year Founded:** 1887
- **Tuition, 2005-2006:** In-state: $28,760; Out-of-state: $38,760
- **Enrollment 2005-2006 academic year:** 489
- **Website:** http://www.ohsu.edu/som
- **Specialty ranking:** family medicine: 5, rural medicine: 4, women's health: 16

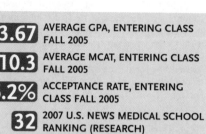

3.67	AVERAGE GPA, ENTERING CLASS FALL 2005
10.3	AVERAGE MCAT, ENTERING CLASS FALL 2005
6.2%	ACCEPTANCE RATE, ENTERING CLASS FALL 2005
32	2007 U.S. NEWS MEDICAL SCHOOL RANKING (RESEARCH)
3	2007 U.S. NEWS MEDICAL SCHOOL RANKING (PRIMARY CARE)

ADMISSIONS
Admissions phone number: **(503) 494-2998**
Admissions email address: **N/A**
Application website:
  http://www.ohsu.edu/som/dean/md/admissions
Acceptance rate: **6.2%**
In-state acceptance rate: **23.7%**
Out-of-state acceptance rate: **4.3%**
Minority acceptance rate: **4.4%**
International acceptance rate: **N/A**

Fall 2005 applications and acceptees
	Applied	Interviewed	Accepted	Enrolled
Total:	3,601	521	223	112
In-state:	359	168	85	68
Out-of-state:	3,242	353	138	44

Profile of admitted students
Average undergraduate grade point average: **3.67**
MCAT averages (scale: 1-15; writing test: J-T):
  Composite score: **10.3**
  Verbal reasoning score: **10.3**, Physical sciences score: **10.0**, Biological sciences score: **10.6**, Writing score: **P**
Proportion with undergraduate majors in: Biological sciences: **40%**, Physical sciences: **11%**, Non-sciences: **21%**, Other health professions: **4%**, Mixed disciplines and other: **24%**
Percentage of students not coming directly from college after graduation: **81%**

Dates and details
The American Medical College Application Service (AMCAS) application is accepted.
School asks for a school-specific application as part of the admissions process.
Oldest MCAT considered for Fall 2007 entry: **2003**
Earliest application date for the 2007-2008 first-year class: **July 1, 2006**
Latest application date: **October 15, 2006**
Acceptance dates for regular application for the class entering in fall 2007:

Earliest: **November 1, 2006**
Latest: **August 13, 2007**
The school doesn't consider requests for deferred entrance.
Starting month for the class entering in 2007–2008: **August**
The school doesn't have an Early Decision Plan (EDP).
A personal interview is required for admission.

Undergraduate coursework required
Medical school requires undergraduate work in these subjects: biology, English, organic chemistry, inorganic (general) chemistry, physics, biochemistry, humanities, mathematics, demonstration of writing skills, calculus, social sciences, general chemistry.

ADMISSIONS POLICY
(TEXT PROVIDED BY SCHOOL):
The Admissions Committee seeks students who have demonstrated academic excellence and readiness for the profession of medicine and who will contribute to the diversity necessary to enhance the medical education of all students. Applicants are selected on the basis of demonstrated motivation for medicine, humanistic attitudes, and a realistic understanding of the role of the physician in providing excellent health care to all communities in need of care. The ideal student will demonstrate evidence of strong communication skills; altruism, empathy, personal integrity; self-appraisal and emotional maturity; and an ability to make a positive contribution to society and the profession.

Attention is paid to achievements that demonstrate applicants' breadth of interests and experiences, commitment to others, and leadership among their peers and ability to contribute diverse and innovative perspectives to problem-solving in medicine and health care. Evaluation of applicants includes the academic record as demonstration of scholarship; the MCAT; recommendations from undergraduate or graduate school faculty, employers and health care and community service experiences; experiences in health care and other settings and other volunteer commitments; and the personal interview.

COSTS AND FINANCIAL AID

Financial aid phone number: **(503) 494-7800**
Tuition, 2005-2006 academic year: **In-state: $28,760; Out-of-state: $38,760**
Room and board: **$15,000**
Percentage of students receiving financial aid in 2005-06: **95%**
Percentage of students receiving: Loans: **90%**, Grants/scholarships: **80%**, Work-study aid: **2%**
Average medical school debt for the Class of 2004: **$124,486**

STUDENT BODY

Fall 2005 full-time enrollment: **489**
Men: **44%**, Women: **56%**, In-state: **52%**, Minorities: **12%**, American Indian: **1.6%**, Asian-American: **13.3%**, African-American: **1.4%**, Hispanic-American: **2.0%**, White: **81.6%**, International: **0.0%**, Unknown: **0.0%**

ACADEMIC PROGRAMS

The school's curriculum very frequently gives first-year students substantial contact with patients.
There are opportunities for first- or second-year students to work in community health clinics.
Program offerings: AIDS, drug/alcohol abuse, family medicine, geriatrics, internal medicine, pediatrics, rural medicine, women's health
Joint degrees awarded: M.D./Ph.D., M.D./MPH
Total National Institutes of Health (NIH) grants awarded to the medical school and affiliated hospitals: **$188.5 million**

CURRICULUM

(TEXT PROVIDED BY SCHOOL):
The goal of the School of Medicine's curriculum is to present a four-year continuum that balances emphasis on the scientific basis of medicine with early clinical experience; offers progressive patient-care responsibilities for students; and permits students to individualize their educational programs as well as enhance their independent-learning and problem-solving skills. The sciences basic to medicine are presented in an interdisciplinary format, focusing initially on the scientific principles of medicine and ultimately progressing to disease process.

Highlights include: centralized responsibility; integrated and multidisciplinary basic science courses with enhanced clinical relevance and logical sequencing; lecture and non-lecture learning balanced in half-day sessions; courses given in a series to avoid competing with other courses; instructional objective-based education; early and longitudinal clinical preceptorship; required clinical experience in a rural and/or underserved area; strong emphasis on ambulatory and primary care; and performance-based assessment of students utilizing standardized patients.

FACULTY PROFILE (FALL 2005)

Total teaching faculty: **1,466 (full-time)**, **292 (part-time)**
Of full-time faculty, those teaching in basic sciences: **12%**; in clinical programs: **88%**
Of part-time faculty, those teaching in basic sciences: **12%**; in clinical programs: **88%**
Full-time faculty/student ratio: **3.0**

SUPPORT SERVICES

The school offers students these services for dealing with stress: expanded-hour gym access, peer counseling, professional counseling, religious support, support groups.

RESIDENCY PROFILE

Most popular residency and specialty programs chosen by the 2004 and 2005 M.D. graduating classes: anesthesiology, emergency medicine, family practice, internal medicine, obstetrics and gynecology, pediatrics, psychiatry, radiology–diagnostic, surgery–general, internal medicine/pediatrics.

WHERE GRADS GO

41%
Proportion of 2003-2005 graduates who entered primary care specialties

31%
Proportion of 2004-2005 graduates who accepted in-state residencies

Rosalind Franklin

UNIVERSITY OF MEDICINE AND SCIENCE

- 3333 Green Bay Road, North Chicago, IL 60064
- Private
- Year Founded: 1912
- Tuition, 2005-2006: $36,900
- Enrollment 2005-2006 academic year: 756
- Website: http://www.rosalindfranklin.edu
- Specialty ranking: N/A

3.45 AVERAGE GPA, ENTERING CLASS FALL 2005

9.5 AVERAGE MCAT, ENTERING CLASS FALL 2005

7.5% ACCEPTANCE RATE, ENTERING CLASS FALL 2005

Unranked 2007 U.S. NEWS MEDICAL SCHOOL RANKING (RESEARCH)

Unranked 2007 U.S. NEWS MEDICAL SCHOOL RANKING (PRIMARY CARE)

ADMISSIONS

Admissions phone number: **(847) 578-3204**
Admissions email address:
  cms.admissions@rosalindfranklin.edu
Application website: **N/A**
Acceptance rate: **7.5%**
In-state acceptance rate: **8.2%**
Out-of-state acceptance rate: **7.4%**
Minority acceptance rate: **3.6%**
International acceptance rate: **4.5%**

Fall 2005 applications and acceptees

	Applied	Interviewed	Accepted	Enrolled
Total:	6,442	589	485	185
In-state:	1,240	104	102	37
Out-of-state:	5,202	485	383	148

Profile of admitted students

Average undergraduate grade point average: **3.45**
MCAT averages (scale: 1-15; writing test: J-T):
  Composite score: **9.5**
  Verbal reasoning score: **9.0**, Physical sciences score:
  10.0, Biological sciences score: **10.0**, Writing score: **O**
Proportion with undergraduate majors in: Biological
sciences: **71%**, Physical sciences: **12%**, Non-sciences: **9%**,
Other health professions: **1%**, Mixed disciplines and
other: **7%**
Percentage of students not coming directly from college
after graduation: **N/A**

Dates and details

The American Medical College Application Service
  (AMCAS) application is accepted.
School asks for a school-specific application as part of the
  admissions process.
Oldest MCAT considered for Fall 2007 entry: **2004**
Earliest application date for the 2007-2008 first-year class:
  June 1, 2006
Latest application date: **November 15, 2006**
Acceptance dates for regular application for the class
  entering in fall 2007:

Earliest: **December 1, 2006**
Latest: **July 1, 2007**
The school considers requests for deferred entrance.
Starting month for the class entering in 2007–2008:
  August
The school has an Early Decision Plan (EDP).
A personal interview is required for admission.

Undergraduate coursework required

Medical school requires undergraduate work in these subjects: biology/zoology, organic chemistry, inorganic (general) chemistry, physics.

ADMISSIONS POLICY
(TEXT PROVIDED BY SCHOOL):

The Chicago Medical School Student Admissions
Committee has the sole responsibility of selecting candidates for each entering class. The committee is comprised
of basic scientists, clinicians and senior medical students.
The process begins when the completed AMCAS application form is received. The applicant is then sent a supplemental information form from the Medical School
Admissions Office, additionally requesting that three letters
of evaluation be submitted. These evaluations may be submitted in the form of a single composite from the applicant's pre-professional advisory committee, or they may be
submitted from individual professors under whom the
applicant has studied. CMS requires a minimum of three
letters; two must be from professors the applicant has taken
classes from (does not have to be two science professors),
and the third letter should be from someone the student
feels relevant enough to make comments on their behalf.
CMS does not have a maximum number of letters to send
in to support their medical school application; therefore,
potential students should feel free to send additional letters.
Such letters of evaluation must come directly from the
authors or the school. Following the receipt of all required
information, each application is thoroughly screened to
determine which applicants will be invited for a personal
interview. Although the interview is somewhat structured,
applicants are encouraged to relate any information they

deem important in consideration of their application by the Student Admissions Committee. Invited applicants are interviewed by two or more committee members. Generally, around 5 percent of all applicants are invited for interview. Those candidates who have been interviewed are subsequently re-evaluated by committee members with respect to all data now at their disposal. The committee members meet approximately once a month, beginning in December, to make acceptances. If an applicant is not accepted the first round, they will go the following month, and so on. No one who has been interviewed will receive a rejection letter until after orientation week. Up until that time, anyone interviewed remains a viable candidate to CMS. All correspondences are generated by the Admissions Office. Invitation for interview or acceptances is not driven by in state residency; we are a private institution. Any applicant that receives a rejection letter are welcome to set up a counseling call with the Director of Admissions, Records, and Financial Aid.

COSTS AND FINANCIAL AID
Financial aid phone number: (847) 578-3216
Tuition, 2005-2006 academic year: $36,900
Room and board: $16,000
Percentage of students receiving financial aid in 2005-06: 81%
Percentage of students receiving: Loans: 81%, Grants/scholarships: 39%, Work-study aid: 5%
Average medical school debt for the Class of 2004: $174,932

STUDENT BODY
Fall 2005 full-time enrollment: 756
Men: 55%, Women: 45%, In-state: 23%, Minorities: 50%, American Indian: 0.3%, Asian-American: 43.8%, African-American: 4.8%, Hispanic-American: 1.5%, White: 47.1%, International: 2.2%, Unknown: 0.4%

ACADEMIC PROGRAMS
There are opportunities for first- or second-year students to work in community health clinics.
Program offerings: AIDS, drug/alcohol abuse, family medicine, geriatrics, internal medicine, pediatrics, women's health
Joint degrees awarded: M.D./Ph.D., M.D./MS
Total National Institutes of Health (NIH) grants awarded to the medical school and affiliated hospitals: $26.7 million

CURRICULUM
(TEXT PROVIDED BY SCHOOL):
The Chicago Medical School curriculum offers a strong grounding in the sciences basic to medicine along with

assuring competency in skills necessary for the practice of medicine. The CMS curriculum features a unique interprofessional approachs, with interaction among a broad range of health professional, students and practitioners. The curriculum is a mix of lectures, labs, small group discussions, team-based learning, and opportunities for peer to peer learning. Our educational information system, Desire to Learn, provides 24 hour a day access to learning materials.

Currently, the four year curriculum consists of 14 terms. Of the 6 terms of basic science, the first 3 are devoted primarily to the study of the structure and function of the human body. Topic integration across courses and a unique Interprofessional Teams course are the hallmark of the M1 curriculum. Students have early clinical experiences in our state of the art evaluation and education center as well as opportunities to connect with physician preceptors. The following 3 terms are devoted to the study of disease etiology, processes, therapy, and prevention. The required junior clinical clerkships include Medicine, Ambulatory Care, Surgery, Family Medicine, Obstetrics/Gynecology, Psychiatry, MedCore, Pediatrics, Neurology and Emergency Medicine. The senior requirements include four weeks in a Medicine or Pediatrics Subinternship, plus 32 weeks of approved electives (14 of which must be intramural). The elective period gives students an opportunity, through both intramural and extramural experiences, to explore and strengthen their personal career interests. Along with passing all courses and clerkships, students are required to pass Step 1 and Step 2 of the USMLE examinations as a requisite for graduation.

FACULTY PROFILE (FALL 2005)
Total teaching faculty: 683 (full-time), N/A (part-time)
Of full-time faculty, those teaching in basic sciences: 10%; in clinical programs: 90%
Of part-time faculty, those teaching in basic sciences: N/A; in clinical programs: N/A
Full-time faculty/student ratio: 0.9

SUPPORT SERVICES
The school offers students these services for dealing with stress: expanded-hour gym access, peer counseling, professional counseling, religious support, support groups.

RESIDENCY PROFILE
Most popular residency and specialty programs chosen by the 2004 and 2005 M.D. graduating classes: anesthesiology, emergency medicine, family practice, internal medicine, obstetrics and gynecology, orthopaedic surgery, pediatrics, radiology–diagnostic, surgery–general.

Rush University

- 600 S. Paulina Street, Chicago, IL 60612
- Private
- Year Founded: 1837
- Tuition, 2005-2006: $39,024
- Enrollment 2005-2006 academic year: 511
- Website: http://www.rushu.rush.edu/medcol/
- Specialty ranking: AIDS: 21

3.65 AVERAGE GPA, ENTERING CLASS FALL 2005

10.1 AVERAGE MCAT, ENTERING CLASS FALL 2005

6.2% ACCEPTANCE RATE, ENTERING CLASS FALL 2005

Unranked 2007 U.S. NEWS MEDICAL SCHOOL RANKING (RESEARCH)

Unranked 2007 U.S. NEWS MEDICAL SCHOOL RANKING (PRIMARY CARE)

ADMISSIONS

Admissions phone number: **(312) 942-6913**
Admissions email address: **RMC_Admissions@rush.edu**
Application website: **http://www.aamc.org**
Acceptance rate: **6.2%**
In-state acceptance rate: **14.7%**
Out-of-state acceptance rate: **2.4%**
Minority acceptance rate: **5.1%**
International acceptance rate: **N/A**

Fall 2005 applications and acceptees

	Applied	Interviewed	Accepted	Enrolled
Total:	4,247	458	263	128
In-state:	1,322	363	194	106
Out-of-state:	2,925	95	69	22

Profile of admitted students

Average undergraduate grade point average: **3.65**
MCAT averages (scale: 1-15; writing test: J-T):
   Composite score: **10.1**
   Verbal reasoning score: **9.8**, Physical sciences score:
   10.3, Biological sciences score: **10.3**, Writing score: **P**
Proportion with undergraduate majors in: Biological
   sciences: **48%**, Physical sciences: **13%**, Non-sciences:
   9%, Other health professions: **1%**, Mixed disciplines and
   other: **29%**
Percentage of students not coming directly from college
   after graduation: **48%**

Dates and details

The American Medical College Application Service
   (AMCAS) application is accepted.
School asks for a school-specific application as part of the
   admissions process.
Oldest MCAT considered for Fall 2007 entry: **2002**
Earliest application date for the 2007-2008 first-year class:
   June 1, 2006
Latest application date: **November 1, 2006**
Acceptance dates for regular application for the class
   entering in fall 2007:
   Earliest: **October 15, 2006**

Latest: **September 1, 2007**
The school considers requests for deferred entrance.
Starting month for the class entering in 2007-2008:
   September
The school doesn't have an Early Decision Plan (EDP).
A personal interview is required for admission.

Undergraduate coursework required

Medical school requires undergraduate work in these subjects: biology, organic chemistry, inorganic (general) chemistry, physics.

ADMISSIONS POLICY
(TEXT PROVIDED BY SCHOOL):

Rush Medical College is committed to the selection of individuals who will become vital members of the medical community as students, practitioners, educators and
researchers. Although admission depends on the satisfactory completion of a minimum of 90 semester hours of
undergraduate study prior to matriculation, 100 percent
obtained their baccalaureate degree. Rush requires entering
students to have at least eight semester hours of biology,
inorganic chemistry, organic chemistry and physics. Four
semester hours of biochemistry may be substituted in lieu
of the second semester of organic chemistry. Survey courses
in the sciences will not meet these requirements.

Rush Medical College is a member of the American
Medical College Application Service and all formal applications to Rush must be initiated through AMCAS. Upon
receipt of the AMCAS application, candidates are invited to
complete the Supplemental Application and submit supporting documentation. Only those applicants who have
U.S. citizenship or permanent residency status will be considered for admission to the college. In addition, all applicants must take the MCAT in order to be considered for
admission. Since full consideration by the Committee on
Admissions cannot be given to a candidate until MCAT
scores are received, applicants are encouraged to take the
examination in April of the year of application. The
Committee on Admissions will review only those candidates with complete applications. Preference is given to res-

idents of Illinois although it is expected that approximately 25 percent of the entering class will come from outside of Illinois.

Applicants invited to visit Rush Medical College will receive an overview of the medical college, will be interviewed by two faculty members, tour Rush University Medical Center and the Armour Academic Center, and have an opportunity to meet our current medical students. Applicants will be notified of a decision within 4 weeks from the date of their interview. Each year over 400 candidates will be interviewed and only those candidates invited for interview will be considered for acceptance.

COSTS AND FINANCIAL AID
Financial aid phone number: **(312) 942-6256**
Tuition, 2005-2006 academic year: **$39,024**
Room and board: **$8,560**
Percentage of students receiving financial aid in 2005-06: **87%**
Percentage of students receiving: Loans: **85%**, Grants/scholarships: **60%**, Work-study aid: **4%**
Average medical school debt for the Class of 2004: **$136,663**

STUDENT BODY
Fall 2005 full-time enrollment: **511**
Men: **45%**, Women: **55%**, In-state: **83%**, Minorities: **44%**, American Indian: **1.2%**, Asian-American: **35.8%**, African-American: **3.1%**, Hispanic-American: **1.6%**, White: **56.6%**, International: **0.0%**, Unknown: **1.8%**

ACADEMIC PROGRAMS
The school's curriculum occasionally gives first-year students substantial contact with patients.
There are opportunities for first- or second-year students to work in community health clinics.
Program offerings: AIDS, drug/alcohol abuse, family medicine, geriatrics, internal medicine, pediatrics, rural medicine, women's health
Joint degrees awarded: M.D./Ph.D., M.D./MS
Total National Institutes of Health (NIH) grants awarded to the medical school and affiliated hospitals: **$37.8 million**

CURRICULUM
(TEXT PROVIDED BY SCHOOL):
Rush Medical College provides educational opportunities in an environment that emphasizes competence and compassion in the provision of patient care and services.

The four-year curriculum provides an appropriate background for individuals with a diversity of professional career goals. Courses in the M1 year include anatomy, histology, biochemistry, physiology, neurobiology, ethics, health of the public, fundamentals of behavior, and behavior in the life cycle. Courses in the M2 year include pathology, pharmacology, pathophysiology, microbiology, immunology, interviewing and communication, introduction to psychopathology, epidemiology/biostatistics, and physical diagnosis. The Generalist Curriculum, which is taught across the first and second years, has three components that complement the basic science curriculum: the preceptorship experience and courses in physical diagnosis skills and communication skills. The preceptorship experience partners students with primary care physicians and their patients in outpatient settings throughout the Chicago metropolitan area.

The curriculum of the third and fourth years provides students with training in clinical skills, diagnosis and patient management in a variety of patient care settings. The third year includes required core clerkships in family medicine, internal medicine, neurology, obstetrics/gynecology, pediatrics, psychiatry, and surgery. In the fourth year, students enroll in one four-week sub-internship in their choice of family medicine, internal medicine, pediatrics or surgery, which provides students with the opportunity to function at an advanced level similar to an intern, with close supervision by the faculty.

A minimum of 18 weeks of elective study in areas of special interest to the student is also required.

Students at Rush Medical College receive their clinical training primarily at Rush University Medical Center, a voluntary, not-for-profit hospital with a professional staff of 1549 physicians and scientists, 625 house staff and fellows in graduate medical education, representing over 30 specialties. The John H. Stroger, Jr. Hospital of Cook County (formerly Cook County Hospital) is a major teaching affiliate of Rush and provides students with the opportunity to complete both core and elective clerkships in an environment that provides outstanding health care to the medically underserved.

FACULTY PROFILE (FALL 2005)
Total teaching faculty: **462 (full-time)**, **179 (part-time)**
Of full-time faculty, those teaching in basic sciences: **22%**; in clinical programs: **78%**
Of part-time faculty, those teaching in basic sciences: **7%**; in clinical programs: **93%**
Full-time faculty/student ratio: **0.9**

SUPPORT SERVICES
The school offers students these services for dealing with stress: expanded-hour gym access, professional counseling, support groups.

RESIDENCY PROFILE
Most popular residency and specialty programs chosen by the 2004 and 2005 M.D. graduating classes: anesthesiology, emergency medicine, family practice, internal medicine, neurology, obstetrics and gynecology, orthopaedic surgery, pediatrics, radiology–diagnostic, surgery–general.

WHERE GRADS GO
45%
Proportion of 2003-2005 graduates who entered primary care specialties

56%
Proportion of 2004-2005 graduates who accepted in-state residencies

Southern Illinois University—Springfield

- 801 N. Rutledge, PO Box 19620, Springfield, IL 62794-9620
- Public
- Year Founded: 1970
- Tuition, 2005-2006: In-state: $19,985; Out-of-state: $56,609
- Enrollment 2005-2006 academic year: 291
- Website: http://www.siumed.edu/
- Specialty ranking: family medicine: 26, rural medicine: 30

3.50	AVERAGE GPA, ENTERING CLASS FALL 2005
8.8	AVERAGE MCAT, ENTERING CLASS FALL 2005
19.0%	ACCEPTANCE RATE, ENTERING CLASS FALL 2005
Unranked	2007 U.S. NEWS MEDICAL SCHOOL RANKING (RESEARCH)
Unranked	2007 U.S. NEWS MEDICAL SCHOOL RANKING (PRIMARY CARE)

ADMISSIONS

Admissions phone number: **(217) 545-6013**
Admissions email address: **admissions@siumed.edu**
Application website: **N/A**
Acceptance rate: **19.0%**
In-state acceptance rate: **19.5%**
Out-of-state acceptance rate: **5.0%**
Minority acceptance rate: **N/A**
International acceptance rate: **N/A**

Fall 2005 applications and acceptees

	Applied	Interviewed	Accepted	Enrolled
Total:	1,013	284	192	72
In-state:	973	281	190	72
Out-of-state:	40	3	2	0

Profile of admitted students

Average undergraduate grade point average: **3.50**
MCAT averages (scale: 1-15; writing test: J-T):
  Composite score: **8.8**
  Verbal reasoning score: **8.9**, Physical sciences score: **8.5**,
  Biological sciences score: **9.0**, Writing score: **O**
Proportion with undergraduate majors in: Biological
  sciences: **68%**, Physical sciences: **8%**, Non-sciences:
  10%, Other health professions: **3%**, Mixed disciplines
  and other: **11%**
Percentage of students not coming directly from college
  after graduation: **30%**

Dates and details

The American Medical College Application Service
  (AMCAS) application is accepted.
School asks for a school-specific application as part of the
  admissions process.
Oldest MCAT considered for Fall 2007 entry: **2004**
Earliest application date for the 2007-2008 first-year class:
  June 1, 2006
Latest application date: **November 15, 2006**
Acceptance dates for regular application for the class
  entering in fall 2007:
  Earliest: **October 15, 2006**

Latest: **N/A**
The school considers requests for deferred entrance.
Starting month for the class entering in 2007–2008:
  August
The school doesn't have an Early Decision Plan (EDP).
A personal interview is required for admission.

ADMISSIONS POLICY
(TEXT PROVIDED BY SCHOOL):

SIU School of Medicine begins by looking for applications
with competitive GPA's and MCAT scores. Applicants are
expected to have a good foundation in the natural sciences,
social sciences and humanities, and be able to demonstrate
facility in writing and speaking the English language. The
Admissions Committee also looks for evidence of responsibility, maturity, integrity, social awareness, compassion,
service orientation, proper motivation, exploration of medicine as a career, and good interpersonal skills. We also look
for identification with the goals and nature of the School,
since our mission is to help the people of central and southern Illinois in meeting their health care needs through education, clinical care and research. A majority of our
graduates enter primary care specialties. Applications are
accepted from Illinois residents who are U.S. citizens or foreign citizens with a permanent resident visa. Preference is
given to established residents of downstate Illinois and
other underserved locations in the state of Illinois (including rural and inner-city areas). A limited number of out-of-
state residents are considered for the M.D./JD program
only. Applicants should display evidence of participation in
extracurricular and volunteer activities and employed positions.

COSTS AND FINANCIAL AID

Financial aid phone number: **(217) 545-2224**
Tuition, 2005-2006 academic year: **In-state: $19,985; Out-
  of-state: $56,609**
Room and board: **$6,956**
Percentage of students receiving financial aid in 2005-06:
  93%

Percentage of students receiving: Loans: **91%**,
  Grants/scholarships: **40%**, Work-study aid: **0%**
Average medical school debt for the Class of 2004:
  $109,255

STUDENT BODY

Fall 2005 full-time enrollment: **291**
Men: **48%**, Women: **52%**, In-state: **100%**, Minorities: **25%**,
  American Indian: **1.4%**, Asian-American: **10.3%**,
  African-American: **10.7%**, Hispanic-American: **3.1%**,
  White: **74.6%**, International: **0.0%**, Unknown: **0.0%**

ACADEMIC PROGRAMS

The school's curriculum very frequently gives first-year
  students substantial contact with patients.
There are opportunities for first- or second-year students to
  work in community health clinics.
Program offerings: AIDS, drug/alcohol abuse, family
  medicine, geriatrics, internal medicine, pediatrics, rural
  medicine, women's health
Joint degrees awarded: M.D./JD
Total National Institutes of Health (NIH) grants awarded to
  the medical school and affiliated hospitals: **N/A**

CURRICULUM

(TEXT PROVIDED BY SCHOOL):
SIU School of Medicine is a public medical school established in 1970 and focused on the healthcare needs of
downstate Illinois. We have always been a leader in medical
education and recognized for innovative teaching and testing techniques, including a competency-base curriculum,
the use of simulated patients, and courses in medical
humanities. (Most U.S. medical schools studied our curriculum before updating theirs in the 1980s.)

  The overall focus of our curriculum is on clinical, case-
based, self-directed learning in a small-group setting. Our
goal is to foster the integration of basic and clinical science
knowledge as students solve patient problems. Students
work toward competency, focusing on what they should
learn rather than on what teachers want to teach. Our community-based structure places students in physicians'
offices and local hospitals so they are educated as adult

learners in the real world of medicine. Clinical experiences
also include continuity clinic assignments and a doctoring
curriculum. These extensive clinical activities in all four
years help students become caring and competent physicians.

  We continue SIU's emphasis on treating patients as people rather than solely as medical conditions in various ways,
including emphasizing community healthcare and the psychosocial issues of medicine. Development of lifelong learning skills also is important in our program.

FACULTY PROFILE (FALL 2005)

Total teaching faculty: **301 (full-time)**, **930 (part-time)**
Of full-time faculty, those teaching in basic sciences: **41%**;
  in clinical programs: **59%**
Of part-time faculty, those teaching in basic sciences: **19%**;
  in clinical programs: **81%**
Full-time faculty/student ratio: **1.0**

SUPPORT SERVICES

The school offers students these services for dealing with
stress: peer counseling, professional counseling, support
groups.

RESIDENCY PROFILE

Most popular residency and specialty programs chosen by
the 2004 and 2005 M.D. graduating classes: anesthesiology,
emergency medicine, family practice, internal medicine,
obstetrics and gynecology, pediatrics, psychiatry, radiology–diagnostic, surgery–general, internal medicine/pedi-
atrics.

WHERE GRADS GO

42.5%
*Proportion of 2003-2005 graduates who entered primary
care specialties*

35%
*Proportion of 2004-2005 graduates who accepted in-state
residencies*

Stanford University

- 300 Pasteur Drive, Suite M121, Stanford, CA 94305
- Private
- Year Founded: 1858
- Tuition, 2005-2006: $38,431
- Enrollment 2005-2006 academic year: 476
- Website: http://med.stanford.edu
- Specialty ranking: AIDS: 17, drug/alcohol abuse: 18, internal medicine: 12, pediatrics: 11, women's health: 16

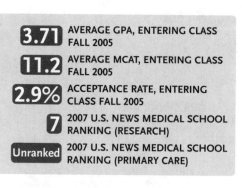

3.71 AVERAGE GPA, ENTERING CLASS FALL 2005

11.2 AVERAGE MCAT, ENTERING CLASS FALL 2005

2.9% ACCEPTANCE RATE, ENTERING CLASS FALL 2005

7 2007 U.S. NEWS MEDICAL SCHOOL RANKING (RESEARCH)

Unranked 2007 U.S. NEWS MEDICAL SCHOOL RANKING (PRIMARY CARE)

ADMISSIONS

Admissions phone number: **(650) 723-6861**
Admissions email address: **mdadmissions@stanford.edu**
Application website: **http://www.aamc.org**
Acceptance rate: **2.9%**
In-state acceptance rate: **2.4%**
Out-of-state acceptance rate: **3.1%**
Minority acceptance rate: **3.2%**
International acceptance rate: **3.8%**

Fall 2005 applications and acceptees

	Applied	Interviewed	Accepted	Enrolled
Total:	5,648	362	163	86
In-state:	2,055	135	50	32
Out-of-state:	3,593	227	113	54

Profile of admitted students

Average undergraduate grade point average: **3.71**
MCAT averages (scale: 1-15; writing test: J-T):
  Composite score: **11.2**
  Verbal reasoning score: **10.5**, Physical sciences score: **11.3**, Biological sciences score: **11.8**, Writing score: **Q**
Proportion with undergraduate majors in: Biological sciences: **25%**, Physical sciences: **43%**, Non-sciences: **8%**, Other health professions: **0%**, Mixed disciplines and other: **24%**
Percentage of students not coming directly from college after graduation: **64%**

Dates and details

The American Medical College Application Service (AMCAS) application is accepted.
School asks for a school-specific application as part of the admissions process.
Oldest MCAT considered for Fall 2007 entry: **2004**
Earliest application date for the 2007-2008 first-year class: **June 1, 2006**
Latest application date: **October 15, 2006**
Acceptance dates for regular application for the class entering in fall 2007:
  Earliest: **January 12, 2006**

Latest: **May 4, 2006**
The school considers requests for deferred entrance.
Starting month for the class entering in 2007–2008:
  August
The school has an Early Decision Plan (EDP).
A personal interview is required for admission.

Undergraduate coursework required

Medical school requires undergraduate work in these subjects: biology, organic chemistry, inorganic (general) chemistry, physics.

ADMISSIONS POLICY

(TEXT PROVIDED BY SCHOOL):

Stanford University School of Medicine is interested in candidates who have a strong humanitarian commitment and whose accomplishments show originality, creativity, and a capacity for independent, critical thinking. Enthusiasm for the basic sciences and humanities is prerequisite for admission to the school. An undergraduate major in any field is acceptable. The committee values applications from students who have tested their interest in working in the healthcare environment, in the laboratory, in activities involving the care of others, and in community services that include a working knowledge of the human condition beyond one's own socioeconomic and cultural group.

Grade-point average and Medical College Admission Test scores are important variables but do not entirely govern the process. Recently admitted applicants have had a mean GPA of about 3.7 and mean MCAT scores as follows: verbal reasoning, 10; physical sciences, 11; writing sample, O; biological sciences, 11. The MCAT should be taken in April, but in no case later than the late summer of the year in which the application is submitted. Applications are not processed until the Office of Admissions receives the MCAT scores.

Minimum course requirements for admission include: biological sciences (the equivalent of one full academic year), chemistry (the equivalent of two full academic years, including organic chemistry), and physics (the equivalent of one full academic year), including laboratory work in each of these subjects. Waivers may occasionally be given.

Knowledge of a modern foreign language, specifically Spanish or an Asian language, and coursework in behavioral sciences, calculus, physical chemistry, cellular biology, genetics, and, in particular, biochemistry are strongly recommended.

Foreign students must have studied for at least one year in an accredited college or university in the United States, Canada, or the United Kingdom before applying. In-state residency does not grant special consideration in the admissions process.

COSTS AND FINANCIAL AID
Financial aid phone number: **(650) 723-6958**
Tuition, 2005-2006 academic year: **$38,431**
Room and board: **$19,053**
Percentage of students receiving financial aid in 2005-06: **65%**
Percentage of students receiving: Loans: **57%**, Grants/scholarships: **52%**, Work-study aid: **8%**
Average medical school debt for the Class of 2004: **$61,566**

STUDENT BODY
Fall 2005 full-time enrollment: **476**
Men: **51%**, Women: **49%**, In-state: **43%**, Minorities: **53%**, American Indian: **1.5%**, Asian-American: **31.3%**, African-American: **5.0%**, Hispanic-American: **15.1%**, White: **42.9%**, International: **4.2%**, Unknown: **0.0%**

ACADEMIC PROGRAMS
The school's curriculum very frequently gives first-year students substantial contact with patients.
There are opportunities for first- or second-year students to work in community health clinics.
Program offerings: AIDS, drug/alcohol abuse, family medicine, geriatrics, internal medicine, pediatrics, rural medicine, women's health
Joint degrees awarded: M.D./Ph.D., M.D./MPH
Total National Institutes of Health (NIH) grants awarded to the medical school and affiliated hospitals: **N/A**

CURRICULUM
(TEXT PROVIDED BY SCHOOL):
The Stanford School of Medicine stepped into the education reform spotlight in the fall of 2003 with the launch of a new curriculum aimed at instilling a lifelong passion for learning, while equipping students with the tools to translate laboratory discoveries into life-enhancing therapies throughout their careers.

The new curriculum strengthens clinical training earlier in the education process, adds basic science "refreshers" during the clinical years, and requires students to participate in a scholarly concentration in which they can hone their research skills while developing early expertise in a topic that excites them.

Key elements of the curriculum include: in-depth study in a scholarly concentration area that will span the student's years at Stanford; better integration of the basic science and clinical portions of the curriculum; restructuring courses to focus on individual organ systems to avoid the redundancies that occur by teaching each discipline as a separate subject; and reducing weekly classroom instruction to give students more time for research and academic exploration.

A primary goal of the new curriculum is to prepare students to continue learning throughout their careers. In addition to the science coursework during the first two years of the curriculum, students will get refreshers on basic science topics during the latter two years of medical school. Students will also develop their clinical skills each week of the first two years and work with patients experiencing the disorders being studied in the classroom.

Students will be expected to devote at least 200 hours to a project in the scholarly concentration area they select. The 12 concentration areas are bioengineering; biomedical ethics and medical humanities; biomedical informatics; cardiovascular and pulmonary sciences; clinical research; community health and public service; health services and policy research; immunology; molecular basis of medicine; neuroscience, behavior and cognition; women's health, and independent design.

FACULTY PROFILE (FALL 2005)
Total teaching faculty: **736 (full-time)**, **21 (part-time)**
Of full-time faculty, those teaching in basic sciences: **13%**; in clinical programs: **87%**
Of part-time faculty, those teaching in basic sciences: **33%**; in clinical programs: **67%**
Full-time faculty/student ratio: **1.5**

SUPPORT SERVICES
The school offers students these services for dealing with stress: expanded-hour gym access, peer counseling, professional counseling, religious support, support groups.

RESIDENCY PROFILE
Most popular residency and specialty programs chosen by the 2004 and 2005 M.D. graduating classes: anesthesiology, dermatology, emergency medicine, family practice, internal medicine, orthopaedic surgery, pediatrics, psychiatry, radiology–diagnostic, surgery–general.

WHERE GRADS GO

32.1%
Proportion of 2003-2005 graduates who entered primary care specialties

61%
Proportion of 2004-2005 graduates who accepted in-state residencies

St. Louis University

- 1402 S. Grand Boulevard, St. Louis, MO 63104
- Private
- Year Founded: 1836
- Tuition, 2005-2006: $41,092
- Enrollment 2005-2006 academic year: 614
- Website: http://medschool.slu.edu
- Specialty ranking: geriatrics: 12

3.70 AVERAGE GPA, ENTERING CLASS FALL 2005

10.5 AVERAGE MCAT, ENTERING CLASS FALL 2005

8.7% ACCEPTANCE RATE, ENTERING CLASS FALL 2005

Unranked 2007 U.S. NEWS MEDICAL SCHOOL RANKING (RESEARCH)

Unranked 2007 U.S. NEWS MEDICAL SCHOOL RANKING (PRIMARY CARE)

ADMISSIONS

Admissions phone number: **(314) 977-9870**
Admissions email address: **slumd@slu.edu**
Application website:
  http://medschool.slu.edu/admissions/index.phtml?page =forms
Acceptance rate: **8.7%**
In-state acceptance rate: **24.0%**
Out-of-state acceptance rate: **7.4%**
Minority acceptance rate: **6.6%**
International acceptance rate: **5.7%**

Fall 2005 applications and acceptees

	Applied	Interviewed	Accepted	Enrolled
Total:	5,687	N/A	493	164
In-state:	433	N/A	104	60
Out-of-state:	5,254	N/A	389	104

Profile of admitted students

Average undergraduate grade point average: **3.70**
MCAT averages (scale: 1-15; writing test: J-T):
  Composite score: **10.5**
  Verbal reasoning score: **10.1**, Physical sciences score: **10.4**, Biological sciences score: **10.8**, Writing score: **P**
Proportion with undergraduate majors in: Biological sciences: **58%**, Physical sciences: **21%**, Non-sciences: **14%**, Other health professions: **2%**, Mixed disciplines and other: **5%**
Percentage of students not coming directly from college after graduation: **N/A**

Dates and details

The American Medical College Application Service (AMCAS) application is accepted.
School asks for a school-specific application as part of the admissions process.
Oldest MCAT considered for Fall 2007 entry: **2003**
Earliest application date for the 2007-2008 first-year class: **June 1, 2006**
Latest application date: **December 15, 2006**

Acceptance dates for regular application for the class entering in fall 2007:
  Earliest: **October 15, 2006**
  Latest: **N/A**
The school considers requests for deferred entrance. Starting month for the class entering in 2007–2008: **August**
The school has an Early Decision Plan (EDP).
A personal interview is required for admission.

Undergraduate coursework required

Medical school requires undergraduate work in these subjects: biology/zoology, English, organic chemistry, inorganic (general) chemistry, physics, humanities, behavioral science.

ADMISSIONS POLICY

(TEXT PROVIDED BY SCHOOL):
Saint Louis University School of Medicine is a private institution that considers applications from national and international students. The school encourages applications from students who have achieved a high level of academic performance and who manifest in their personal lives those human qualities compatible with a career of service to society. The university's mission statement affirms the value of a diverse educational environment to prepare students for life and work in a global society. To foster this mission, the School of Medicine strives to recruit, admit, retain, and graduate a diverse student body. Besides ethnicity, this diversity encompasses differences based on gender, culture, and economic circumstances.

Specific academic requirements include a minimum of 90 semester hours (135 quarter hours) in undergraduate arts and sciences courses. Virtually all accepted applicants complete a baccalaureate degree of at least 120 semester hours (180 quarter hours) from an accredited college or university. In all cases, the Committee on Admissions is more concerned with the quality of the applicant's education than with the number of hours or years of premedical training. Students who have received their education in a foreign school must complete at least one academic year of coursework in an accredited North American college or university prior to making application.

The course requirements for admission are: general biology or zoology (eight semester hours, with lab); inorganic chemistry (eight semester hours, with lab); organic chemistry (eight semester hours, with lab); physics (eight semester hours, with lab); English (six semester hours); and other humanities and behavioral sciences (12 semester hours).

The Medical College Admission Test is required.

COSTS AND FINANCIAL AID

Financial aid phone number: **(314) 977-9840**
Tuition, 2005-2006 academic year: **$41,092**
Room and board: **$15,518**

STUDENT BODY

Fall 2005 full-time enrollment: **614**
Men: **56%**, Women: **44%**, In-state: **43%**, Minorities: **26%**,
  American Indian: **0.2%**, Asian-American: **19.9%**,
  African-American: **3.7%**, Hispanic-American: **1.8%**,
  White: **60.1%**, International: **1.8%**, Unknown: **12.5%**

ACADEMIC PROGRAMS

The school's curriculum frequently gives first-year students substantial contact with patients.

There are opportunities for first- or second-year students to work in community health clinics.

Program offerings: AIDS, drug/alcohol abuse, family medicine, geriatrics, internal medicine, pediatrics, rural medicine, women's health

Joint degrees awarded: M.D./Ph.D., M.D./MBA, M.D./MPH.

Total National Institutes of Health (NIH) grants awarded to the medical school and affiliated hospitals: **$40.4 million**

CURRICULUM

(TEXT PROVIDED BY SCHOOL):
The M.D. degree program curriculum at Saint Louis University School of Medicine has undergone extensive changes in order to adapt to the needs of the evolving healthcare environment. The goal is to prepare students for the practice of medicine in the society they will face. The new curriculum is the result of several years of study by committees composed of faculty and students. However, the curriculum designed to attain the M.D. degree is only one phase of a continuum of learning in the practice of medicine. It is expected that students will pursue graduate study to further advance their skills before being able to practice without supervision.

The new curriculum offers better coordination and integration of subjects than the curriculum that was replaced. Additionally, it follows established principles of adult learning, and so contains fewer lectures, more small-group activities, earlier clinical activities, and more problem-solving exercises.

The first two years of the four-year curriculum (Phase 1 and Phase 2) are primarily devoted to the study of the fundamental sciences basic to medicine, while the last two years concentrate on the acquisition of clinical skills. Year 3 and Year 4 have been combined into one continuous period, Phase 3. This new structure enables students to pursue curricular offerings during the first half of Phase 3 that were previously unavailable, such as neurology, electives, and a family medicine requirement.

The total time of instruction in the four-year curriculum is 158 weeks.

FACULTY PROFILE (FALL 2005)

Total teaching faculty: **548 (full-time)**, **1,160 (part-time)**
Of full-time faculty, those teaching in basic sciences: **16%**;
  in clinical programs: **84%**
Of part-time faculty, those teaching in basic sciences: **0%**;
  in clinical programs: **100%**
Full-time faculty/student ratio: **0.9**

SUPPORT SERVICES

The school offers students these services for dealing with stress: expanded-hour gym access, peer counseling, professional counseling, religious support, support groups.

RESIDENCY PROFILE

Most popular residency and specialty programs chosen by the 2004 and 2005 M.D. graduating classes: anesthesiology, family practice, internal medicine, internal medicine–pediatrics, obstetrics and gynecology, pathology–anatomic and clinical, pediatrics, psychiatry, radiology–diagnostic, surgery–general.

WHERE GRADS GO

46.6%
Proportion of 2003-2005 graduates who entered primary care specialties

23.4%
Proportion of 2004-2005 graduates who accepted in-state residencies

Stony Brook University

- Office of Admissions, Health Science Center, L4, Stony Brook, NY 11794-8434
- Public
- **Year Founded:** 1971
- **Tuition, 2005-2006:** In-state: $19,736; Out-of-state: $34,436
- **Enrollment 2005-2006 academic year:** 447
- **Website:** http://www.hsc.sunysb.edu/som/
- **Specialty ranking:** N/A

3.60	AVERAGE GPA, ENTERING CLASS FALL 2005
10.7	AVERAGE MCAT, ENTERING CLASS FALL 2005
10.5%	ACCEPTANCE RATE, ENTERING CLASS FALL 2005
50	2007 U.S. NEWS MEDICAL SCHOOL RANKING (RESEARCH)
Unranked	2007 U.S. NEWS MEDICAL SCHOOL RANKING (PRIMARY CARE)

ADMISSIONS

Admissions phone number: **(631) 444-2113**
Admissions email address:
  somadmissions@stonybrook.edu
Application website: **http://www.hsc.sunysb.edu/som/**
Acceptance rate: **10.5%**
In-state acceptance rate: **13.6%**
Out-of-state acceptance rate: **3.1%**
Minority acceptance rate: **9.2%**
International acceptance rate: **1.5%**

Fall 2005 applications and acceptees

	Applied	Interviewed	Accepted	Enrolled
Total:	2,755	573	288	101
In-state:	1,939	520	263	94
Out-of-state:	816	53	25	7

Profile of admitted students

Average undergraduate grade point average: **3.60**
MCAT averages (scale: 1-15; writing test: J-T):
  Composite score: **10.7**
  Verbal reasoning score: **10.0**, Physical sciences score: **11.0**, Biological sciences score: **11.0**, Writing score: **P**
Proportion with undergraduate majors in: Biological sciences: **42%**, Physical sciences: **13%**, Non-sciences: **12%**, Other health professions: **0%**, Mixed disciplines and other: **33%**
Percentage of students not coming directly from college after graduation: **58%**

Dates and details

The American Medical College Application Service (AMCAS) application is accepted.
School asks for a school-specific application as part of the admissions process.
Oldest MCAT considered for Fall 2007 entry: **2002**
Earliest application date for the 2007-2008 first-year class:
  June 1, 2006
Latest application date: **December 15, 2006**
Acceptance dates for regular application for the class entering in fall 2007:

Earliest: **October 15, 2006**
Latest: **N/A**
The school considers requests for deferred entrance.
Starting month for the class entering in 2007–2008:
  August
The school has an Early Decision Plan (EDP).
A personal interview is required for admission.

Undergraduate coursework required

Medical school requires undergraduate work in these subjects: biology, English, organic chemistry, inorganic (general) chemistry, physics.

ADMISSIONS POLICY
(TEXT PROVIDED BY SCHOOL):

Grades, Medical College Admission Test scores, letters of evaluation, and extracurricular and work experiences are carefully examined. Motivational and personal characteristics as indicated in the application, letters of evaluation, and a personal interview are also a major part of the admissions assessment. There is no discrimination in the admissions review and selection process on the basis of sex, race, religion, national origin, age, marital status, or handicap.

Students learn from one another as well as from their teachers, textbooks, and parents; therefore, the school attempts to acquire a class representative of a variety of backgrounds and academic interests. Indeed, given the demands on physicians in the 21st century, breadth of individual background is particularly important. Stony Brook hopes to attract a significant representation of groups that have historically been underrepresented in medicine. Applicants from foreign schools must have completed at least one year in an American college or university. Residents of New York constitute the majority of the applicants and entrants; however, out-of-state applicants will be given due consideration, particularly those to special programs, such as the Medical Scientist Training Program (M.D./Ph.D.)

Required supporting documents include official transcripts of all college work and a letter of official evaluation from the applicant's premedical adviser (or, when no adviser exists at the applicant's college, from two instructors, one of whom must be from a science field). If other individuals are in a position to provide important information, the school would be happy to receive letters from them. Personal interviews will be arranged at the initiative of the school for candidates who appear to be serious contenders for admission.

COSTS AND FINANCIAL AID

Financial aid phone number: **(631) 444-2341**
Tuition, 2005-2006 academic year: **In-state: $19,736; Out-of-state: $34,436**
Room and board: **$21,350**
Percentage of students receiving financial aid in 2005-06: 87%
Percentage of students receiving: Loans: **84%**, Grants/scholarships: **35%**, Work-study aid: **9%**
Average medical school debt for the Class of 2004: **$120,300**

STUDENT BODY

Fall 2005 full-time enrollment: **447**
Men: **47%**, Women: **53%**, In-state: **98%**, Minorities: **51%**, American Indian: **0.9%**, Asian-American: **37.1%**, African-American: **9.2%**, Hispanic-American: **4.0%**, White: **48.3%**, International: **0.4%**, Unknown: **0.0%**

ACADEMIC PROGRAMS

The school's curriculum frequently gives first-year students substantial contact with patients.
There are opportunities for first- or second-year students to work in community health clinics.
Program offerings: AIDS, drug/alcohol abuse, family medicine, geriatrics, internal medicine, pediatrics, women's health
Joint degrees awarded: M.D./Ph.D., M.D./MPH
Total National Institutes of Health (NIH) grants awarded to the medical school and affiliated hospitals: **$75.3 million**

CURRICULUM

(TEXT PROVIDED BY SCHOOL):
The curriculum of the School of Medicine is designed to provide the opportunity for extensive training in the basic medical sciences and teaching in the clinical disciplines of medicine. The curriculum requires the acquisition and utilization of a variety of skills in basic and clinical sciences. The faculty has determined that a successful candidate for the M.D. degree must pass each unit of curriculum and that waiver of units of curriculum is offered only to those who because of prior experience are able to place out through examination.

The first year of the curriculum consists of integrated instruction in the basic sciences and introduction to clinical skills, human behavior, nutrition, and preventive medicine. The second-year curriculum includes microbiology, pharmacology, and an interdisciplinary course in pathophysiology of the different systems. In both the first and second years, students participate in the Introduction to Clinical Medicine and Medicine in Contemporary Society courses.

In the third year, students move to a series of clinical clerkships in medicine, surgery, pediatrics, obstetrics and gynecology, psychiatry, and family medicine, where opportunities for problem solving and patient responsibility are presented. Additional experiences are provided in radiology and emergency medicine. Clinical teaching in the Introduction to Clinical Medicine course, in the systems program, and in the clinical clerkships takes place at the University Hospital and various clinical facilities affiliated with the School of Medicine. The clerkship program is followed by selectives and electives in the fourth year. The curriculum emphasizes social issues in medicine and bioethics at each level of medical training.

FACULTY PROFILE (FALL 2005)

Total teaching faculty: **500 (full-time)**, **74 (part-time)**
Of full-time faculty, those teaching in basic sciences: **19%**; in clinical programs: **81%**
Of part-time faculty, those teaching in basic sciences: **0%**; in clinical programs: **100%**
Full-time faculty/student ratio: **1.1**

SUPPORT SERVICES

The school offers students these services for dealing with stress: expanded-hour gym access, peer counseling, professional counseling, religious support, support groups.

RESIDENCY PROFILE

Most popular residency and specialty programs chosen by the 2004 and 2005 M.D. graduating classes: anesthesiology, emergency medicine, internal medicine, obstetrics and gynecology, pediatrics, psychiatry, surgery–general.

WHERE GRADS GO

44.1%
Proportion of 2003-2005 graduates who entered primary care specialties

69.3%
Proportion of 2004-2005 graduates who accepted in-state residencies

SUNY–Syracuse

■ 766 Irving Avenue, Syracuse, NY 13210
■ Public
■ Year Founded: 1834
■ Tuition, 2005-2006: In-state: $19,840; Out-of-state: $34,540
■ Enrollment 2005-2006 academic year: 615
■ Website: http://www.upstate.edu
■ Specialty ranking: rural medicine: 30

3.54 AVERAGE GPA, ENTERING CLASS FALL 2005

9.8 AVERAGE MCAT, ENTERING CLASS FALL 2005

12.3% ACCEPTANCE RATE, ENTERING CLASS FALL 2005

Unranked 2007 U.S. NEWS MEDICAL SCHOOL RANKING (RESEARCH)

Unranked 2007 U.S. NEWS MEDICAL SCHOOL RANKING (PRIMARY CARE)

ADMISSIONS

Admissions phone number: **(315) 464-4570**
Admissions email address: **admiss@upstate.edu**
Application website:
  http://www.aamc.org/audienceamcas.htm
Acceptance rate: **12.3%**
In-state acceptance rate: **16.2%**
Out-of-state acceptance rate: **6.8%**
Minority acceptance rate: **11.0%**
International acceptance rate: **15.0%**

Fall 2005 applications and acceptees

	Applied	Interviewed	Accepted	Enrolled
Total:	3,227	908	396	153
In-state:	1,875	660	304	122
Out-of-state:	1,352	248	92	31

Profile of admitted students

Average undergraduate grade point average: **3.54**
MCAT averages (scale: 1-15; writing test: J-T):
  Composite score: **9.8**
  Verbal reasoning score: **9.6**, Physical sciences score: **9.9**,
  Biological sciences score: **10.1**, Writing score: **P**
Proportion with undergraduate majors in: Biological
  sciences: **48%**, Physical sciences: **28%**, Non-sciences:
  4%, Other health professions: **8%**, Mixed disciplines and
  other: **12%**
Percentage of students not coming directly from college
  after graduation: **52%**

Dates and details

The American Medical College Application Service
  (AMCAS) application is accepted.
School asks for a school-specific application as part of the
  admissions process.
Oldest MCAT considered for Fall 2007 entry: **2002**
Earliest application date for the 2007-2008 first-year class:
  June 1, 2006
Latest application date: **November 1, 2006**
Acceptance dates for regular application for the class
  entering in fall 2007:

Earliest: **October 15, 2006**
Latest: **N/A**
The school considers requests for deferred entrance.
Starting month for the class entering in 2007–2008:
  August
The school has an Early Decision Plan (EDP).
A personal interview is required for admission.

Undergraduate coursework required

Medical school requires undergraduate work in these subjects: biology, biology/zoology, English, organic chemistry,
inorganic (general) chemistry, physics.

ADMISSIONS POLICY
(TEXT PROVIDED BY SCHOOL):
The Admissions Committee considers the following factors
when selecting applicants: academic achievement in the sciences, academic achievement in the humanities and social
sciences, volunteer and clinical experience, communication
skills, meaningful experiences dealing with and relating to
people, character, and motivation for selecting a career in
medicine.

COSTS AND FINANCIAL AID
Financial aid phone number: **(315) 464-4329**
Tuition, 2005-2006 academic year: **In-state: $19,840; Out-
of-state: $34,540**
Room and board: **N/A**
Percentage of students receiving financial aid in 2005-06:
  89%
Percentage of students receiving: Loans: **83%**,
  Grants/scholarships: **44%**, Work-study aid: **7%**
Average medical school debt for the Class of 2004:
  $113,231

STUDENT BODY
Fall 2005 full-time enrollment: **615**
Men: **52%**, Women: **48%**, In-state: **95%**, Minorities: **29%**,
  American Indian: **0.7%**, Asian-American: **22.0%**,
  African-American: **5.5%**, Hispanic-American: **0.5%**,
  White: **68.1%**, International: **3.3%**, Unknown: **0.0%**

ACADEMIC PROGRAMS

The school's curriculum frequently gives first-year students substantial contact with patients.

There are opportunities for first- or second-year students to work in community health clinics.

Program offerings: AIDS, drug/alcohol abuse, family medicine, geriatrics, internal medicine, pediatrics, rural medicine, women's health

Joint degrees awarded: M.D./Ph.D.

Total National Institutes of Health (NIH) grants awarded to the medical school and affiliated hospitals: **$18.9 million**

CURRICULUM

(TEXT PROVIDED BY SCHOOL):

The organ-based curriculum integrates the basic and clinical sciences—with basic science courses teaching the clinical implications of the material—and provides clinical experience starting in the first semester. The organ systems approach enables an efficient, in-depth study of major concepts.

FACULTY PROFILE (FALL 2005)

Total teaching faculty: **366 (full-time)**, **182 (part-time)**

Of full-time faculty, those teaching in basic sciences: **N/A**; in clinical programs: **N/A**

Of part-time faculty, those teaching in basic sciences: **N/A**; in clinical programs: **N/A**

Full-time faculty/student ratio: **0.6**

SUPPORT SERVICES

The school offers students these services for dealing with stress: professional counseling, religious support, support groups.

RESIDENCY PROFILE

Most popular residency and specialty programs chosen by the 2004 and 2005 M.D. graduating classes: emergency medicine, family practice, internal medicine, surgery–general.

WHERE GRADS GO

50.2%

Proportion of 2003-2005 graduates who entered primary care specialties

52.6%

Proportion of 2004-2005 graduates who accepted in-state residencies

Temple University

- 3420 N. Broad Street, MRB 102, Philadelphia, PA 19140
- Public
- **Year Founded:** 1901
- **Tuition, 2005-2006:** In-state: $34,305; Out-of-state: $41,885
- **Enrollment 2005-2006 academic year:** 725
- **Website:** http://www.medschool.temple.edu
- **Specialty ranking:** N/A

3.59 AVERAGE GPA, ENTERING CLASS FALL 2005

10.0 AVERAGE MCAT, ENTERING CLASS FALL 2005

7.8% ACCEPTANCE RATE, ENTERING CLASS FALL 2005

Unranked 2007 U.S. NEWS MEDICAL SCHOOL RANKING (RESEARCH)

Unranked 2007 U.S. NEWS MEDICAL SCHOOL RANKING (PRIMARY CARE)

ADMISSIONS

Admissions phone number: **(215) 707-3656**
Admissions email address: **medadmissions@temple.edu**
Application website:
  http://www.medschool.temple.edu/main/prospective_st
  udents.html
Acceptance rate: **7.8%**
In-state acceptance rate: **23.5%**
Out-of-state acceptance rate: **5.6%**
Minority acceptance rate: **7.6%**
International acceptance rate: **0.0%**

Fall 2005 applications and acceptees

	Applied	Interviewed	Accepted	Enrolled
Total:	7,504	978	589	176
In-state:	948	253	223	93
Out-of-state:	6,556	725	366	83

Profile of admitted students

Average undergraduate grade point average: **3.59**
MCAT averages (scale: 1-15; writing test: J-T):
  Composite score: **10.0**
  Verbal reasoning score: **9.5**, Physical sciences score: **10.0**, Biological sciences score: **10.4**, Writing score: **P**
Proportion with undergraduate majors in: Biological sciences: **60%**, Physical sciences: **17%**, Non-sciences: **19%**, Other health professions: **2%**, Mixed disciplines and other: **2%**
Percentage of students not coming directly from college after graduation: **48%**

Dates and details

The American Medical College Application Service (AMCAS) application is accepted.
School asks for a school-specific application as part of the admissions process.
Oldest MCAT considered for Fall 2007 entry: **2004**
Earliest application date for the 2007-2008 first-year class: **June 1, 2006**
Latest application date: **December 15, 2006**

Acceptance dates for regular application for the class entering in fall 2007:
  Earliest: **October 15, 2006**
  Latest: **August 1, 2007**
The school considers requests for deferred entrance.
Starting month for the class entering in 2007–2008: **August**
The school has an Early Decision Plan (EDP).
A personal interview is required for admission.

Undergraduate coursework required

Medical school requires undergraduate work in these subjects: biology, organic chemistry, inorganic (general) chemistry, physics, humanities.

ADMISSIONS POLICY
(TEXT PROVIDED BY SCHOOL):

The Admissions Committee at Temple interviews about 20 percent of the applicants who complete their applications. That statistic says a lot about Temple's admissions philosophy: Yes, standards are high—many applicants will be screened out early because they don't meet the minimum academic requirements for admission. But standards are not rigid, and what's more, they're not purely quantitative. An applicant's performance during the interview may weigh just as heavily as test scores and grades, and grade progress in college (i.e., a real improvement) could tip the scales in an applicant's favor. In the end, many nontraditional students are admitted to Temple—older "second career" students, minorities, and, generally, people with a wide variety of social, ethnic, and scholastic backgrounds that have led to the school's notable reputation for pluralism.

As a state-related school, Temple shows preference to residents of Pennsylvania; however, a significant percentage of matriculants may be residents of other states. Nonresidents with a particular interest in Temple and strong credentials are encouraged to apply. Foreign nationals without permanent-resident status are ineligible for consideration.

Once invited for an interview, you will schedule a meeting with a single faculty member of the Admissions Committee.

What does the Temple interviewer look for in an applicant? The associate dean for admissions singles out these attributes (by no means an exhaustive list): strong interpersonal skills, poise, tact, appropriate sense of humor, ability to listen and take another's point of view; self-confident; articulate; compassionate; socially conscious. After the interviewer has briefed the committee on the applicant's qualifications and personal qualities, a full vote is called. Students are notified of the decision several weeks after the interview, but not before October 15 of the year before admission.

COSTS AND FINANCIAL AID

Financial aid phone number: **(215) 707-2667**
Tuition, 2005-2006 academic year: **In-state: $34,305; Out-of-state: $41,885**
Room and board: **$13,776**
Percentage of students receiving financial aid in 2005-06: **89%**
Percentage of students receiving: Loans: **88%**, Grants/scholarships: **45%**, Work-study aid: **6%**
Average medical school debt for the Class of 2004: **$140,266**

STUDENT BODY

Fall 2005 full-time enrollment: **725**
Men: **54%**, Women: **46%**, In-state: **62%**, Minorities: **38%**, American Indian: **0.1%**, Asian-American: **22.8%**, African-American: **8.8%**, Hispanic-American: **6.1%**, White: **61.7%**, International: **0.0%**, Unknown: **0.6%**

ACADEMIC PROGRAMS

The school's curriculum occasionally gives first-year students substantial contact with patients.
There are opportunities for first- or second-year students to work in community health clinics.
Program offerings: AIDS, drug/alcohol abuse, family medicine, geriatrics, internal medicine, pediatrics, rural medicine, women's health
Joint degrees awarded: M.D./Ph.D., M.D./MBA, M.D./MPH.
Total National Institutes of Health (NIH) grants awarded to the medical school and affiliated hospitals: **$26.0 million**

CURRICULUM

(TEXT PROVIDED BY SCHOOL):
The curriculum of the program leading to the M.D. degree provides a traditional general professional education that prepares students for all career options in medicine.

Instruction in the basic sciences takes place in the first two years. It is designed to provide students with an understanding of the scientific concepts underlying the practice of medicine and to instill habits of lifelong learning. First-year courses in anatomy, biochemistry, and physiology provide students with core knowledge of normal structure and function. The pathology, pathophysiology, and pharmacology courses in the second year have been integrated in a systems approach designed to cover basic mechanisms of disease and available treatment methods.

A hybrid of instructional methods is used in the first biennium, including didactic lectures, self-directed learning, and evidence-based principles. Relevance to the practice of medicine is emphasized through the use of clinical case-based conferences in all basic science courses. In addition, students learn the basics of patient interviewing, physical examination skills, and clinical problem solving. Topics in professionalism, humanism, medical ethics, cultural competence, and death and dying are incorporated throughout the courses. Standardized patients are used in the teaching and assessment of clinical skills throughout the curriculum.

The clinical education program of the third year includes required clerkships in family medicine, internal medicine, pediatrics, psychiatry, surgery (with a week of anesthesiology), and obstetrics and gynecology. In the fourth year, the program includes requirements in neurology, emergency medicine, and two sub-internships. Students are also required to take 20 weeks of selectives designed to allow students to pursue areas of individual interest.

Instruction and experience in patient care are provided in both ambulatory and hospital settings, with clinical sites in urban, suburban, and rural areas. The diverse settings of patient contact, including traditional hospital and intensive care units, emergency centers, and office-based medicine, ensure that students are well prepared for residency and all career options in medicine.

FACULTY PROFILE (FALL 2005)

Total teaching faculty: **458 (full-time), 69 (part-time)**
Of full-time faculty, those teaching in basic sciences: **28%**; in clinical programs: **72%**
Of part-time faculty, those teaching in basic sciences: **20%**; in clinical programs: **80%**
Full-time faculty/student ratio: **0.6**

SUPPORT SERVICES

The school offers students these services for dealing with stress: expanded-hour gym access, peer counseling, professional counseling, support groups.

RESIDENCY PROFILE

Most popular residency and specialty programs chosen by the 2004 and 2005 M.D. graduating classes: emergency medicine, family practice, internal medicine, obstetrics and gynecology, orthopaedic surgery, pediatrics, psychiatry, surgery–general.

WHERE GRADS GO

50%
Proportion of 2003-2005 graduates who entered primary care specialties

46%
Proportion of 2004-2005 graduates who accepted in-state residencies

Texas A&M University System

HEALTH SCIENCE CENTER

- 147 Joe H. Reynolds Medical Building, College Station, TX 77843-1114
- Public
- Year Founded: 1971
- Tuition, 2005-2006: In-state: $9,012; Out-of-state: $24,212
- Enrollment 2005-2006 academic year: 299
- Website: http://medicine.tamhsc.edu
- Specialty ranking: rural medicine: 30

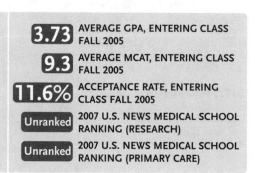

3.73	AVERAGE GPA, ENTERING CLASS FALL 2005
9.3	AVERAGE MCAT, ENTERING CLASS FALL 2005
11.6%	ACCEPTANCE RATE, ENTERING CLASS FALL 2005
Unranked	2007 U.S. NEWS MEDICAL SCHOOL RANKING (RESEARCH)
Unranked	2007 U.S. NEWS MEDICAL SCHOOL RANKING (PRIMARY CARE)

ADMISSIONS

Admissions phone number: **(979) 845-7743**
Admissions email address:
admissions@medicine.tamhsc.edu
Application website: **http://www.utsystem.edu/tmdsas/**
Acceptance rate: **11.6%**
In-state acceptance rate: **12.2%**
Out-of-state acceptance rate: **7.1%**
Minority acceptance rate: **10.8%**
International acceptance rate: **66.7%**

Fall 2005 applications and acceptees

	Applied	Interviewed	Accepted	Enrolled
Total:	2,108	694	245	81
In-state:	1,883	656	229	75
Out-of-state:	225	38	16	6

Profile of admitted students

Average undergraduate grade point average: **3.73**
MCAT averages (scale: 1-15; writing test: J-T):
Composite score: **9.3**
Verbal reasoning score: **8.8**, Physical sciences score: **9.3**,
Biological sciences score: **9.5**, Writing score: **Q**
Proportion with undergraduate majors in: Biological
sciences: **53%**, Physical sciences: **9%**, Non-sciences: **14%**,
Other health professions: **7%**, Mixed disciplines and
other: **17%**
Percentage of students not coming directly from college
after graduation: **46%**

Dates and details

The American Medical College Application Service
(AMCAS) application is not accepted.
School asks for a school-specific application as part of the
admissions process.
Oldest MCAT considered for Fall 2007 entry: **2002**
Earliest application date for the 2007-2008 first-year class:
May 1, 2006
Latest application date: **October 15, 2006**
Acceptance dates for regular application for the class
entering in fall 2007:

Earliest: **October 15, 2006**
Latest: **August 1, 2007**
The school considers requests for deferred entrance.
Starting month for the class entering in 2007–2008:
August
The school doesn't have an Early Decision Plan (EDP).
A personal interview is required for admission.

Undergraduate coursework required

Medical school requires undergraduate work in these subjects: biology, biology/zoology, English, organic chemistry,
inorganic (general) chemistry, physics, calculus.

ADMISSIONS POLICY
(TEXT PROVIDED BY SCHOOL):

The College of Medicine considers for enrollment individuals who have completed at least 90 credit hours of their
undergraduate course work at a fully accredited college or
university in the United States or its territories. By state
mandate, enrollment of individuals who are residents of
states other than Texas many not exceed 10%. In addition
to academic ability, successful applicants must demonstrate
the personal qualities necessary to interact with others in an
effective and compassionate manner. Most entering students have completed a baccalaureate degree before
enrolling. Exceptional applicants may be considered with
90 semester hours of college course work. Each year, 80
entering students are enrolled. The following courses are
required with at least a grade of "C" from a fully accredited
college or university in the U.S. or its territories and must
be completed before or by the time of matriculation: general
biology with labs, advanced biological sciences, general
chemistry with labs, organic chemistry with labs, college
physics with labs, calculus or math-based statistics, and
English. The process of screening applications for interview
is selective. Applicants are screened for interview on academic performance and intellectual capacity, dedication to
service and capacity for effective interactions, special life circumstances,and other compelling factors. Applicants are
invited for personal interviews based upon the competitive-
ness within the screening process described above.

Although intellectual ability and record of achievement are important elements contributing to the mastery of a challenging medical education experience, the admissions committee understands that other qualities are necessary to foster the development of a competent, compassionate and responsible physician.

COSTS AND FINANCIAL AID

Financial aid phone number: **(979) 845-8854**
Tuition, 2005-2006 academic year: **In-state: $9,012; Out-of-state: $24,212**
Room and board: **$10,884**
Percentage of students receiving financial aid in 2005-06: **86%**
Percentage of students receiving: Loans: **83%**, Grants/scholarships: **86%**, Work-study aid: **0%**
Average medical school debt for the Class of 2004: **$93,152**

STUDENT BODY

Fall 2005 full-time enrollment: **299**
Men: **49%**, Women: **51%**, In-state: **92%**, Minorities: **38%**, American Indian: **0.7%**, Asian-American: **21.7%**, African-American: **4.7%**, Hispanic-American: **10.7%**, White: **57.9%**, International: **1.7%**, Unknown: **2.7%**

ACADEMIC PROGRAMS

The school's curriculum occasionally gives first-year students substantial contact with patients.
There are opportunities for first- or second-year students to work in community health clinics.
Program offerings: AIDS, drug/alcohol abuse, family medicine, geriatrics, internal medicine, pediatrics, rural medicine
Joint degrees awarded: M.D./Ph.D., M.D./MBA, M.D./MPH.
Total National Institutes of Health (NIH) grants awarded to the medical school and affiliated hospitals: **$11.5 million**

CURRICULUM

(TEXT PROVIDED BY SCHOOL):
The Doctor of Medicine degree requires a minimum of four years of study. Students spend their first two years at the College Station campus studying basic medical sciences. The first year, organized in blocks over 36 weeks, is designed to lead the students through an introduction to fundamental concepts in cell and molecular biology to an in-depth, systems-based overview of the normal structure and function of the human body, and finally, to an introduction to the alterations in structure and function characteristic of the disease state. The Becoming a Clinician course runs concurrently with the basic science courses throughout the first year. The course serves as an introduction to patient care, and clinical instruction complements topics presented in the basic sciences courses.

The second year is a systems-oriented overview of pathogenesis organized in blocks over 36 weeks. Students also spend half a day each week learning fundamental clinical skills under the supervision of faculty members. The Becoming a Clinician II course ranges from biostatistics/epidemiology to human sexuality and clinical clerkship introductions. The ethical and social aspects of medical practice receive special emphasis.

During the third and fourth years in Temple, Texas, students receive clinical training in different patient care settings: the Central Texas Veterans' Health Care System, Scott and White Memorial Hospital and Clinic, Darnall Army Community Hospital at Fort Hood, and Driscoll Children's Hospital in Corpus Christi. Small classes permit individual attention and close working relationships between attending physician faculty and students. The third-year curriculum is structured over 51 weeks, immersing students in the traditional clerkships. The fourth-year curriculum is structured over 50 weeks and is distinguished by a four-week acting internship and its flexible schedule, which allows students 27 weeks of selective clerkships (20 weeks of which can be completed anywhere in the state or nation).

FACULTY PROFILE (FALL 2005)

Total teaching faculty: **719 (full-time)**, **81 (part-time)**
Of full-time faculty, those teaching in basic sciences: **7%**; in clinical programs: **93%**
Of part-time faculty, those teaching in basic sciences: **10%**; in clinical programs: **90%**
Full-time faculty/student ratio: **2.4**

SUPPORT SERVICES

The school offers students these services for dealing with stress: expanded-hour gym access, peer counseling, professional counseling, religious support, support groups.

RESIDENCY PROFILE

Most popular residency and specialty programs chosen by the 2004 and 2005 M.D. graduating classes: anesthesiology, emergency medicine, family practice, internal medicine, obstetrics and gynecology, pediatrics, psychiatry, radiology–diagnostic, surgery–general.

WHERE GRADS GO

42.1%
Proportion of 2003-2005 graduates who entered primary care specialties

54%
Proportion of 2004-2005 graduates who accepted in-state residencies

Texas Tech University

HEALTH SCIENCES CENTER

- 3601 Fourth Street, Lubbock, TX 79430
- Public
- Year Founded: 1969
- Tuition, 2005-2006: In-state: $10,807; Out-of-state: $23,907
- Enrollment 2005-2006 academic year: 538
- Website: http://www.ttuhsc.edu/SOM/
- Specialty ranking: rural medicine: 16

3.56 AVERAGE GPA, ENTERING CLASS FALL 2005

9.3 AVERAGE MCAT, ENTERING CLASS FALL 2005

6.5% ACCEPTANCE RATE, ENTERING CLASS FALL 2005

Unranked 2007 U.S. NEWS MEDICAL SCHOOL RANKING (RESEARCH)

Unranked 2007 U.S. NEWS MEDICAL SCHOOL RANKING (PRIMARY CARE)

ADMISSIONS

Admissions phone number: (806) 743-2297
Admissions email address: somadm@ttuhsc.edu
Application website: http://www.utsystem.edu/tmdsas/
Acceptance rate: 6.5%
In-state acceptance rate: 6.8%
Out-of-state acceptance rate: 4.4%
Minority acceptance rate: 7.0%
International acceptance rate: 0.0%

Fall 2005 applications and acceptees

	Applied	Interviewed	Accepted	Enrolled
Total:	2,656	776	173	140
In-state:	2,358	748	160	132
Out-of-state:	298	28	13	8

Profile of admitted students

Average undergraduate grade point average: 3.56
MCAT averages (scale: 1-15; writing test: J-T):
  Composite score: 9.3
  Verbal reasoning score: 9.0, Physical sciences score: 9.2, Biological sciences score: 9.9, Writing score: O
Proportion with undergraduate majors in: Biological sciences: 48%, Physical sciences: 21%, Non-sciences: 12%, Other health professions: 0%, Mixed disciplines and other: 19%
Percentage of students not coming directly from college after graduation: 10%

Dates and details

The American Medical College Application Service (AMCAS) application is not accepted.
School asks for a school-specific application as part of the admissions process.
Oldest MCAT considered for Fall 2007 entry: 2003
Earliest application date for the 2007-2008 first-year class: May 1, 2006
Latest application date: October 15, 2006
Acceptance dates for regular application for the class entering in fall 2007:
  Earliest: November 15, 2006

Latest: February 15, 2007
The school considers requests for deferred entrance.
Starting month for the class entering in 2007-2008:
  August
The school has an Early Decision Plan (EDP).
A personal interview is required for admission.

Undergraduate coursework required

Medical school requires undergraduate work in these subjects: biology, biology/zoology, English, organic chemistry, inorganic (general) chemistry, physics, mathematics, calculus.

ADMISSIONS POLICY
(TEXT PROVIDED BY SCHOOL):

At least three years of study (90 semester hours) in a U.S. or Canadian accredited college or university are required, and all prerequisite courses must be taken in a U.S. or Canadian school. A baccalaureate degree is highly desirable. Only students with superior credentials and definite evidence of maturity will be considered without a degree. Some preference is given to applicants from West Texas.

Specific course requirements have been kept at a minimum to permit maximum flexibility in the selection of well-rounded students. The prerequisite courses are: biology or zoology (12 hours), biology lab (two hours), inorganic chemistry with lab (eight hours), organic chemistry with lab (eight hours), physics with lab (eight hours), English (six hours), and calculus or math-based statistics (three hours). All graded prerequisite courses require a grade of C or better or Advanced Placement credit.

The Medical College Admission Test also is a requirement of admission. It is recommended that students take the MCAT in the spring of the year in which application will be made.

Applications are invited from qualified residents of Texas and neighboring counties of New Mexico and Oklahoma, which make up the service area of the school.

The Admissions Committee carefully reviews the applications of all individuals meeting the entrance requirements. Although evidence of high intellectual ability and a record of strong academic achievement are essential for success in the study of medicine, the committee recognizes that these are not the only qualities necessary for a physician's development. Compassion, motivation, the ability to communicate, maturity, and personal integrity also are deemed important. There is no discrimination on the basis of race, sex, creed, national origin, age, or disability.

COSTS AND FINANCIAL AID

Financial aid phone number: **(806) 743-3025**
Tuition, 2005-2006 academic year: **In-state: $10,807; Out-of-state: $23,907**
Room and board: **$10,210**
Percentage of students receiving financial aid in 2005-06: **78%**
Percentage of students receiving: Loans: **69%**, Grants/scholarships: **51%**, Work-study aid: **0%**
Average medical school debt for the Class of 2004: **$117,482**

STUDENT BODY

Fall 2005 full-time enrollment: **538**
Men: **57%**, Women: **43%**, In-state: **94%**, Minorities: **40%**, American Indian: **0.4%**, Asian-American: **25.1%**, African-American: **3.0%**, Hispanic-American: **11.2%**, White: **57.8%**, International: **0.4%**, Unknown: **2.2%**

ACADEMIC PROGRAMS

The school's curriculum very frequently gives first-year students substantial contact with patients.
There are opportunities for first- or second-year students to work in community health clinics.
Program offerings: AIDS, drug/alcohol abuse, family medicine, geriatrics, internal medicine, pediatrics, women's health
Joint degrees awarded: M.D./Ph.D., M.D./MBA.
Total National Institutes of Health (NIH) grants awarded to the medical school and affiliated hospitals: **$4.4 million**

CURRICULUM

(TEXT PROVIDED BY SCHOOL):
In the fall of 2005, the Texas Tech University Health Sciences Center School of Medicine launched a new 4-year curriculum focusing on integration of basic science and early clinical experience in Years 1 and 2. The redesign of Years 3 and 4 will be completed by 2006. Students spend their first two years on the Lubbock campus and receive subsequent clinical training on one of three SOM campuses—Lubbock, El Paso, or Amarillo.

The new curriculum increases integration of basic science and clinical medicine in all 4 years, ensures vertical and horizontal linkages of curricular experiences, and promotes student-directed lifelong learning. Through combined leadership of the Associate Dean for Curriculum, appointed in 2003, and the recently redefined Educational Policy Committee, which oversees educational programs, over 120 faculty from all campuses have now participated in the redesign process. Additional faculty teams are integrat-

ing seven major themes across all four years: cultural competence, geriatrics, genetics, medical informatics/evidence-based medicine, nutrition science, population health, and professionalism/communication.

The new Year 1 curriculum consists of 4 blocs: Foundations I (anatomy), Foundations II (biochemistry, histology and some pathology), Organs Systems (physiology, biochemistry, and related basic sciences, and Host Defense—microbiology, genetics, immunology). Early Clinical Experience allows Year 1 students to acquire specific clinical skills sets as they see patients in clinical settings with Master Teachers. Beginning in 2006-2007 Year 2 will combine organ systems blocs and small group clinical integration sessions; the Early Clinical Experience will move to community physician offices. Currently in Year 3 there are 6 required clerkships: Internal Medicine, Family Medicine, Pediatrics, Obstetrics-Gynecology, Psychiatry, and Surgery. Year 4 consists of 4 required one-month rotations (Ambulatory; Critical Care/Emergency Room; a sub-internship in Family Medicine, Internal Medicine, Pediatrics, or Surgery; and Neurology) and 4 months for electives. The redesign for Years 3 and 4 will feature about 50 percent ambulatory and chronic care continuity experiences, a geriatrics requirement, and new curricular elements to enhance student-centered learning and improve competencies in the six areas specified by the ACGME. The School has introduced OSCEs in Years 1 and 3; OSCEs will be added shortly to Years 2 and 4.

FACULTY PROFILE (FALL 2005)

Total teaching faculty: **482 (full-time), 82 (part-time)**
Of full-time faculty, those teaching in basic sciences: **13%**; in clinical programs: **87%**
Of part-time faculty, those teaching in basic sciences: **2%**; in clinical programs: **98%**
Full-time faculty/student ratio: **0.9**

SUPPORT SERVICES

The school offers students these services for dealing with stress: expanded-hour gym access, professional counseling.

RESIDENCY PROFILE

Most popular residency and specialty programs chosen by the 2004 and 2005 M.D. graduating classes: anesthesiology, emergency medicine, family practice, internal medicine, obstetrics and gynecology, orthopaedic surgery, pediatrics, psychiatry, radiology–diagnostic, surgery–general.

WHERE GRADS GO

36%
Proportion of 2003-2005 graduates who entered primary care specialties

52%
Proportion of 2004-2005 graduates who accepted in-state residencies

Tufts University

- 136 Harrison Avenue, Boston, MA 02111
- Private
- **Year Founded:** 1893
- **Tuition, 2005-2006:** $43,579
- **Enrollment 2005-2006 academic year:** 703
- **Website:** http://www.tufts.edu/med
- **Specialty ranking:** N/A

3.61	AVERAGE GPA, ENTERING CLASS FALL 2005
10.7	AVERAGE MCAT, ENTERING CLASS FALL 2005
7.0%	ACCEPTANCE RATE, ENTERING CLASS FALL 2005
42	2007 U.S. NEWS MEDICAL SCHOOL RANKING (RESEARCH)
57	2007 U.S. NEWS MEDICAL SCHOOL RANKING (PRIMARY CARE)

ADMISSIONS

Admissions phone number: **(617) 636-6571**
Admissions email address: **med-admissions@tufts.edu**
Application website:
   http://www.tufts.edu/med/admissions/fye_secondary_app.html
Acceptance rate: **7.0%**
In-state acceptance rate: **25.3%**
Out-of-state acceptance rate: **5.2%**
Minority acceptance rate: **5.4%**
International acceptance rate: **2.0%**

Fall 2005 applications and acceptees

	Applied	Interviewed	Accepted	Enrolled
Total:	6,794	893	473	168
In-state:	590	269	149	61
Out-of-state:	6,204	624	324	107

Profile of admitted students

Average undergraduate grade point average: **3.61**
MCAT averages (scale: 1-15; writing test: J-T):
   Composite score: **10.7**
   Verbal reasoning score: **10.2**, Physical sciences score:
   10.9, Biological sciences score: **11.1**, Writing score: **Q**
Proportion with undergraduate majors in: Biological
   sciences: **50%**, Physical sciences: **17%**, Non-sciences:
   27%, Other health professions: **1%**, Mixed disciplines
   and other: **5%**
Percentage of students not coming directly from college
   after graduation: **62%**

Dates and details

The American Medical College Application Service
   (AMCAS) application is accepted.
School asks for a school-specific application as part of the
   admissions process.
Oldest MCAT considered for Fall 2007 entry: **2004**
Earliest application date for the 2007-2008 first-year class:
   June 1, 2006
Latest application date: **November 1, 2006**

Acceptance dates for regular application for the class
   entering in fall 2007:
   Earliest: **October 15, 2006**
   Latest: **January 26, 2007**
The school considers requests for deferred entrance.
Starting month for the class entering in 2007–2008:
   August
The school has an Early Decision Plan (EDP).
A personal interview is required for admission.

Undergraduate coursework required

Medical school requires undergraduate work in these subjects: biology, organic chemistry, inorganic (general) chemistry, physics.

ADMISSIONS POLICY
(TEXT PROVIDED BY SCHOOL):

TUSM seeks a diverse and mature student body dedicated
to scholarly excellence and ongoing personal growth, with
strong interpersonal skills, compassion, and integrity, as
well as demonstrated commitment to medicine through
research or service experience. TUSM requires a number of
course prerequisites, the MCAT, the AMCAS online application, our secondary application, letters of recommendation,
and $95 fee (waived if AMCAS fee waived).

Applicants who complete a secondary application are
considered for a personal interview at the Boston campus.
Interviews are required for admission and occur from
September through April.

All complete applications remain under active consideration for an interview until the end of February. Applicants
receive either an invitation to interview or a letter of regret
by April 15.

The TUSM Admissions Committee meets periodically
during the interview season and admits selected applicants
on a rolling basis from November through May. Selected
applicants are admitted from the wait list during the summer.

The selection of applicants is based not only on performance in the required premedical courses but also on the
applicant's entire academic record and extracurricular expe-

riences. Letters of recommendation and information supplied by the applicant are reviewed for indications of promise and fitness for a medical career. Preference is given to U.S. citizens and permanent residents who will receive a bachelor's degree from an American college or university prior to matriculation.

See http://www.medicine.tufts.edu for specific application information.

COSTS AND FINANCIAL AID

Financial aid phone number: **(617) 636-6574**
Tuition, 2005-2006 academic year: **$43,579**
Room and board: **$7,820**
Percentage of students receiving financial aid in 2005-06: **77%**
Percentage of students receiving: Loans: **73%**, Grants/scholarships: **19%**, Work-study aid: **1%**
Average medical school debt for the Class of 2004: **$158,336**

STUDENT BODY

Fall 2005 full-time enrollment: **703**
Men: **54%**, Women: **46%**, In-state: **36%**, Minorities: **43%**, American Indian: **0.3%**, Asian-American: **31.7%**, African-American: **5.0%**, Hispanic-American: **5.8%**, White: **54.3%**, International: **0.7%**, Unknown: **2.1%**

ACADEMIC PROGRAMS

The school's curriculum very frequently gives first-year students substantial contact with patients.
There are opportunities for first- or second-year students to work in community health clinics.
Program offerings: AIDS, drug/alcohol abuse, family medicine, geriatrics, internal medicine, pediatrics, rural medicine
Joint degrees awarded: M.D./Ph.D., M.D./MBA, M.D./MPH.
Total National Institutes of Health (NIH) grants awarded to the medical school and affiliated hospitals: **$85.9 million**

CURRICULUM

(TEXT PROVIDED BY SCHOOL):
Tufts University School of Medicine (TUSM) in Boston, MA, a leader in curricular innovation, provides a vibrant, student-centered community for educating physicians to enter any field of medicine. The emphasis is on teamwork, not competition, where students learn from each other and their patients. TUSM balances sciences with the art of medicine, and imbues graduates with lifelong scientific, scholarly, and humanistic professional attitudes needed to competently face the rapid changes in healthcare, biomedicine, and technology in the 21st century.

To address the critical information and knowledge management needs of future physicians, TUSM features the Tufts University Sciences Knowledgebase (TUSK), an award-winning comprehensive multimedia knowledge management system. TUSK's online tools and resources support every phase of the curriculum, from interactive lectures to problem-based learning to virtual cases or labs to clerkship patient logs to independent research to student-generated resources.

Early clinical exposure, with real and standardized patients, is steadily reinforced and developed throughout the four years. Courses, presented in integrated "blocks" melding sciences with clinical application, emphasize clinical problem-solving and critical thinking. Clerkships, through an extensive and diverse network, provide experience in the full range of American health care from urban tertiary to rural primary care.

Students can elect to explore a wide range of clinical, enrichment, and research opportunities throughout years one and two, including summer research, with advanced research in year four. Active citizenship is highly valued; community service is required. TUSM offers five combined degree programs and several independent master's programs. Students actively participate in Tufts' outstanding continuous curriculum improvement system that promotes top-rated courses and clerkships in a nurturing and supportive environment with easy access to faculty and senior school leadership.

FACULTY PROFILE (FALL 2005)

Total teaching faculty: **1,346 (full-time)**, **2,556 (part-time)**
Of full-time faculty, those teaching in basic sciences: **9%**; in clinical programs: **91%**
Of part-time faculty, those teaching in basic sciences: **4%**; in clinical programs: **96%**
Full-time faculty/student ratio: **1.9**

SUPPORT SERVICES

The school offers students these services for dealing with stress: expanded-hour gym access, peer counseling, professional counseling, religious support, support groups.

RESIDENCY PROFILE

Most popular residency and specialty programs chosen by the 2004 and 2005 M.D. graduating classes: anesthesiology, emergency medicine, family practice, internal medicine, pediatrics, radiology–diagnostic, surgery–general.

WHERE GRADS GO

42%
Proportion of 2003-2005 graduates who entered primary care specialties

30%
Proportion of 2004-2005 graduates who accepted in-state residencies

UMDNJ

NEW JERSEY MEDICAL SCHOOL

- 185 S. Orange Avenue, PO Box 1709, Newark, NJ 07101-1709
- Public
- Year Founded: 1954
- Tuition, 2005-2006: In-state: $24,332; Out-of-state: $36,414
- Enrollment 2005-2006 academic year: 700
- Website: http://www.njms.umdnj.edu
- Specialty ranking: N/A

3.51	AVERAGE GPA, ENTERING CLASS FALL 2005
9.8	AVERAGE MCAT, ENTERING CLASS FALL 2005
10.2%	ACCEPTANCE RATE, ENTERING CLASS FALL 2005
Unranked	2007 U.S. NEWS MEDICAL SCHOOL RANKING (RESEARCH)
Unranked	2007 U.S. NEWS MEDICAL SCHOOL RANKING (PRIMARY CARE)

ADMISSIONS

Admissions phone number: **(973) 972-4631**
Admissions email address: **njmsadmiss@umdnj.edu**
Application website: **http://www.aamc.org**
Acceptance rate: **10.2%**
In-state acceptance rate: **31.4%**
Out-of-state acceptance rate: **3.3%**
Minority acceptance rate: **N/A**
International acceptance rate: **N/A**

Fall 2005 applications and acceptees

	Applied	Interviewed	Accepted	Enrolled
Total:	4,057	751	415	170
In-state:	1,003	N/A	315	141
Out-of-state:	3,054	N/A	100	29

Profile of admitted students

Average undergraduate grade point average: 3.51
MCAT averages (scale: 1-15; writing test: J-T):
   Composite score: 9.8
   Verbal reasoning score: 9.6, Physical sciences score: 9.8, Biological sciences score: 10.1, Writing score: O
Proportion with undergraduate majors in: Biological sciences: 50%, Physical sciences: 17%, Non-sciences: 21%, Other health professions: 5%, Mixed disciplines and other: 7%
Percentage of students not coming directly from college after graduation: N/A

Dates and details

The American Medical College Application Service (AMCAS) application is accepted.
School asks for a school-specific application as part of the admissions process.
Oldest MCAT considered for Fall 2007 entry: **N/A**
Earliest application date for the 2007-2008 first-year class: **June 1, 2006**
Latest application date: **December 1, 2006**
Acceptance dates for regular application for the class entering in fall 2007:
   Earliest: **October 15, 2006**

Latest: **August 20, 2007**
The school considers requests for deferred entrance.
Starting month for the class entering in 2007-2008: **August**
The school has an Early Decision Plan (EDP).
A personal interview is required for admission.

Undergraduate coursework required

Medical school requires undergraduate work in these subjects: biology, English, organic chemistry, inorganic (general) chemistry, physics.

ADMISSIONS POLICY

(TEXT PROVIDED BY SCHOOL):

Students are selected on the basis of scholastic achievement, aptitude for the study of medicine, and personal qualifications. Since success in medicine depends on a number of related factors in a student's development, of which scholastic accomplishments are only a part, the Admissions Committee also gives consideration to the use of language, special aptitudes, mechanical skill, stamina, perseverance, and motivation.

New Jersey Medical School applies no grade-point average or Medical College Admission Test cutoff levels in its selection process. It must be remembered, however, that competition is very keen, and applicants who are high in all determinable categories often receive the highest priority for acceptance. There are no restrictions as to race, creed, gender, national origin, age, or handicap. Applications from non-New Jersey residents are encouraged. New Jersey residents do get some preference in the selection process.

COSTS AND FINANCIAL AID

Financial aid phone number: **(973) 972-7030**
Tuition, 2005-2006 academic year: **In-state: $24,332; Out-of-state: $36,414**
Room and board: **$11,140**
Percentage of students receiving financial aid in 2005-06: **85%**
Percentage of students receiving: Loans: **82%**, Grants/scholarships: **35%**, Work-study aid: **6%**

Average medical school debt for the Class of 2004: $103,118

STUDENT BODY

Fall 2005 full-time enrollment: 700
Men: 51%, Women: 49%, In-state: 100%, Minorities: 58%,
   American Indian: 0.1%, Asian-American: 30.3%,
   African-American: 13.4%, Hispanic-American: 14.3%,
   White: 40.4%, International: 0.0%, Unknown: 1.4%

ACADEMIC PROGRAMS

The school's curriculum very frequently gives first-year
   students substantial contact with patients.
There are opportunities for first- or second-year students to
   work in community health clinics.
Program offerings: AIDS, drug/alcohol abuse, family
   medicine, geriatrics, internal medicine, pediatrics,
   women's health
Joint degrees awarded: M.D./Ph.D., M.D./MBA,
   M.D./MPH, M.D./JD.
Total National Institutes of Health (NIH) grants awarded to
   the medical school and affiliated hospitals: $54.6 million

CURRICULUM

(TEXT PROVIDED BY SCHOOL):
The curriculum of the New Jersey Medical School is undergoing a major revision beginning with academic year 2003-
2004. The changes that are being implemented are derived
from the following six goals, which form the overarching
principles of the medical school: 1) mastery of clinical
knowledge with integration of basic sciences, 2) excellence
in clinical skills, 3) excellence in professionalism and
humanism, 4) commitment to the health of the community
and appreciation of social/cultural diversity, 5) dedication to
lifelong learning, and 6) development of effective skills in
education and communication.

During the first two years of the curriculum, a doctoring
course will teach students how to perform a history and
physical examination. Early contact with patients will serve
as the opportunity to begin to address the moral, ethical,
and social issues that are critical to the practice of medicine.
The doctoring course will also train students in how to utilize evidence-based medicine to provide the most comprehensive and state-of-the-art clinical care.

Science courses will use a variety of teaching techniques,
including small-group learning, lectures, and laboratory
experiences. In the clinical years, students will rotate
through all of the major disciplines in medicine, including
surgery, obstetrics/gynecology, internal medicine, pediatrics,

family medicine, psychiatry, emergency medicine, rehabilitation medicine, and neurology. The medical school utilizes
numerous teaching hospitals, including an inner-city hospital, Veterans Affairs hospital, and community hospitals, to
ensure that students are exposed to multiple inpatient settings. Each rotation also has an outpatient component,
which provides students with the opportunity to interact
with patients in the ambulatory setting.

Throughout the four years of medical school, students
may become involved in a multitude of activities. There are
numerous student-run community organizations, including
a weekly student-directed healthcare clinic. Research opportunities are plentiful, and most students spend their summer between the first and second years of medical school
involved in research projects. During the final year of medical school, faculty members help guide students in making
career decisions for postgraduate training. It is also the perfect opportunity to utilize the school's elective program to
participate in electives throughout the world.

FACULTY PROFILE (FALL 2005)

Total teaching faculty: 737 (full-time), 93 (part-time)
Of full-time faculty, those teaching in basic sciences: 14%;
   in clinical programs: 86%
Of part-time faculty, those teaching in basic sciences: 10%;
   in clinical programs: 90%
Full-time faculty/student ratio: 1.1

SUPPORT SERVICES

The school offers students these services for dealing with
stress: peer counseling, professional counseling.

RESIDENCY PROFILE

Most popular residency and specialty programs chosen by
the 2004 and 2005 M.D. graduating classes: anesthesiology,
emergency medicine, family practice, internal medicine,
obstetrics and gynecology, orthopaedic surgery, pediatrics,
physical medicine and rehabilitation, radiology–diagnostic,
surgery–general.

WHERE GRADS GO

37%
*Proportion of 2003-2005 graduates who entered primary
care specialties*

31%
*Proportion of 2004-2005 graduates who accepted in-state
residencies*

UMDNJ

ROBERT WOOD JOHNSON MEDICAL SCHOOL

- 125 Paterson Street, New Brunswick, NJ 08903-0019
- Public
- **Year Founded:** 1961
- **Tuition, 2005-2006:** In-state: $24,392; Out-of-state: $36,474
- **Enrollment 2005-2006 academic year:** 642
- **Website:** http://rwjms.umdnj.edu
- **Specialty ranking:** N/A

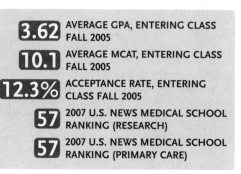

3.62 AVERAGE GPA, ENTERING CLASS FALL 2005

10.1 AVERAGE MCAT, ENTERING CLASS FALL 2005

12.3% ACCEPTANCE RATE, ENTERING CLASS FALL 2005

57 2007 U.S. NEWS MEDICAL SCHOOL RANKING (RESEARCH)

57 2007 U.S. NEWS MEDICAL SCHOOL RANKING (PRIMARY CARE)

ADMISSIONS
Admissions phone number: **(732) 235-4576**
Admissions email address: **rwjapadm@umdnj.edu**
Application website: **http://www.aamc.org**
Acceptance rate: **12.3%**
In-state acceptance rate: **29.4%**
Out-of-state acceptance rate: **2.5%**
Minority acceptance rate: **10.9%**
International acceptance rate: **0.0%**

Fall 2005 applications and acceptees

	Applied	Interviewed	Accepted	Enrolled
Total:	2,815	580	345	157
In-state:	1,020	474	300	155
Out-of-state:	1,795	106	45	2

Profile of admitted students
Average undergraduate grade point average: **3.62**
MCAT averages (scale: 1-15; writing test: J-T):
  Composite score: **10.1**
  Verbal reasoning score: **9.4**, Physical sciences score:
  10.2, Biological sciences score: **10.6**, Writing score: **P**
Proportion with undergraduate majors in: Biological
  sciences: **57%**, Physical sciences: **14%**, Non-sciences: **8%**,
  Other health professions: **N/A**, Mixed disciplines and
  other: **21%**
Percentage of students not coming directly from college
  after graduation: **34%**

Dates and details
The American Medical College Application Service
  (AMCAS) application is accepted.
School does not ask for a school-specific application as part
  of the admissions process.
Oldest MCAT considered for Fall 2007 entry: **2002**
Earliest application date for the 2007-2008 first-year class:
  June 1, 2006
Latest application date: **December 12, 2006**
Acceptance dates for regular application for the class
  entering in fall 2007:
  Earliest: **October 15, 2005**

Latest: **N/A**
The school considers requests for deferred entrance.
Starting month for the class entering in 2007–2008:
  August
The school has an Early Decision Plan (EDP).
A personal interview is required for admission.

Undergraduate coursework required
Medical school requires undergraduate work in these subjects: biology/zoology, English, organic chemistry, inorganic
(general) chemistry, physics, mathematics.

ADMISSIONS POLICY
(TEXT PROVIDED BY SCHOOL):
Robert Wood Johnson Medical School participates in the
American Medical College Application Service. All applications will be reviewed after the Admissions Committee
receives Medical College Admission Test scores and letters
of recommendation (a premedical advisory committee evaluation or three academic recommendations). Interviews will
be arranged at the invitation of the Admissions Committee.

Applicants must be U.S. citizens or permanent residents.
Preference for admission is given to New Jersey residents.
However, out-of-state applicants with outstanding creden-
tials are encouraged to apply.

Robert Wood Johnson Medical School places high value
on a balanced undergraduate education. It is expected that
applicants will have exposed themselves to coursework in
the humanities, the behavioral sciences, and the liberal arts
as well as the premedical sciences. Students with diverse
backgrounds and careers are encouraged to apply.

Students in post-baccalaureate programs are encouraged
to apply. The medical school has linkage agreements with
several such programs.

Admission requirements include the MCAT and a minimum of three years of college, consisting of 90 semester
hours of college work. The following undergraduate courses
are required: two semesters of biology or zoology (with laboratory); two semesters of inorganic chemistry (with laboratory); two semesters of organic chemistry (with laboratory);

two semesters of physics (with laboratory); one semester of college mathematics; and two semesters of English.

COSTS AND FINANCIAL AID
Financial aid phone number: **(732) 235-4689**
Tuition, 2005-2006 academic year: **In-state: $24,392; Out-of-state: $36,474**
Room and board: **$10,026**
Percentage of students receiving financial aid in 2005-06: **82%**
Percentage of students receiving: Loans: **79%**, Grants/scholarships: **43%**, Work-study aid: **6%**
Average medical school debt for the Class of 2004: **$103,897**

STUDENT BODY
Fall 2005 full-time enrollment: **642**
Men: **47%**, Women: **53%**, In-state: **100%**, Minorities: **54%**, American Indian: **0.2%**, Asian-American: **34.3%**, African-American: **12.9%**, Hispanic-American: **5.3%**, White: **46.4%**, International: **0.0%**, Unknown: **0.9%**

ACADEMIC PROGRAMS
The school's curriculum frequently gives first-year students substantial contact with patients.
There are opportunities for first- or second-year students to work in community health clinics.
Program offerings: AIDS, drug/alcohol abuse, family medicine, geriatrics, internal medicine, pediatrics, rural medicine, women's health
Joint degrees awarded: M.D./Ph.D., M.D./MBA, M.D./MPH, M.D./JD, M.D./MS.
Total National Institutes of Health (NIH) grants awarded to the medical school and affiliated hospitals: **$52.3 million**

CURRICULUM
(TEXT PROVIDED BY SCHOOL):
Our curriculum develops students who are competent to begin postgraduate training and become physicians who are humanitarian, compassionate, and focused on disease prevention, with the skills for self-directed/lifelong learning. Curricular goals and competencies have been defined, and courses, clerkships, and electives have learning objectives grouped as the ASK (attitudes, skills, and knowledge) curriculum.

Goal 1 is to develop enthusiastic, self-directed learners who possess essential knowledge in basic medical sciences and clinical medicine, and have the ability to assimilate new knowledge in these disciplines. Competencies include demonstrating knowledge in basic medical sciences and clinical medicine. Attitudes include enthusiasm for learning and commitment to problem solving, self-directed/lifelong learning, and data-based decision making.

Goal 2 is to produce humanitarian physicians with high moral and ethical standards. Competencies include ethical decision making and understanding ethical complexity. Attitudes include demonstrating personal integrity and honesty, providing service.

Goal 3 is to ensure students acquire the fundamental knowledge, skills, and attitudes necessary for a physician beginning residency training. Competencies include demonstrating attitudes, skills, and knowledge to provide quality care. Attitudes include a commitment to develop professional identity and responsibility, enthusiasm for collaboration and teamwork, and dedication to sound clinical decision making.

Goal 4 is to prepare physicians who appreciate the environmental, emotional, and social aspects of health and illness and who focus on disease prevention as well as on diagnosis and cure. Competencies include the ability to take into account the emotional, environmental, cultural, and societal aspects of health and illness and focus on disease prevention for individuals, families, and communities. Attitudes include valuing and respecting differences and appreciating complex individuals.

First year courses include anatomy, biochemistry, biostatistics, cellular and genetic mechanisms, epidemiology, physiology, histology, immunology, and neuroanatomy. Second year courses include behavioral science, clinical prevention, nutrition, pathology, pathophysiology, and pharmacology. Across the first two years, patient-centered medicine covers clinical diagnosis, cultural competency, interviewing, health care finance, human sexuality, legal medicine, medical ethics and professionalism. The third year has clerkships in family medicine, medicine, obstetrics and gynecology, pediatrics, psychiatry and surgery. Throughout the third and fourth year there are clinical electives, neurology, and an ambulatory primary care continuity experience. Fourth year rotations will include ambulatory subspecialties, critical care, emergency medicine, and subinternships.

FACULTY PROFILE (FALL 2005)
Total teaching faculty: **827 (full-time)**, **146 (part-time)**
Of full-time faculty, those teaching in basic sciences: **17%**; in clinical programs: **83%**
Of part-time faculty, those teaching in basic sciences: **16%**; in clinical programs: **84%**
Full-time faculty/student ratio: **1.3**

SUPPORT SERVICES
The school offers students these services for dealing with stress: peer counseling, professional counseling, religious support, support groups.

RESIDENCY PROFILE
Most popular residency and specialty programs chosen by the 2004 and 2005 M.D. graduating classes: anesthesiology, emergency medicine, family practice, internal medicine, obstetrics and gynecology, orthopaedic surgery, pediatrics, psychiatry, radiology–diagnostic, surgery–general.

WHERE GRADS GO
38.9%
Proportion of 2003-2005 graduates who entered primary care specialties

26.2%
Proportion of 2004-2005 graduates who accepted in-state residencies

Uniformed Services University

OF THE HEALTH SCIENCES (HEBERT)

- 4301 Jones Bridge Road, Bethesda, MD 20814
- Public
- Year Founded: 1972
- Tuition, 2005-2006: N/A
- Enrollment 2005-2006 academic year: 665
- Website: http://www.usuhs.mil
- Specialty ranking: N/A

3.52 AVERAGE GPA, ENTERING CLASS FALL 2005

9.7 AVERAGE MCAT, ENTERING CLASS FALL 2005

15.2% ACCEPTANCE RATE, ENTERING CLASS FALL 2005

Unranked 2007 U.S. NEWS MEDICAL SCHOOL RANKING (RESEARCH)

Unranked 2007 U.S. NEWS MEDICAL SCHOOL RANKING (PRIMARY CARE)

ADMISSIONS

Admissions phone number: **(800) 772-1743**
Admissions email address: **admissions@usuhs.mil**
Application website: **N/A**
Acceptance rate: **15.2%**
In-state acceptance rate: **N/A**
Out-of-state acceptance rate: **N/A**
Minority acceptance rate: **8.5%**
International acceptance rate: **N/A**

Fall 2005 applications and acceptees

	Applied	Interviewed	Accepted	Enrolled
Total:	1,725	498	263	169
In-state:	N/A	N/A	N/A	N/A
Out-of-state:	N/A	N/A	N/A	N/A

Profile of admitted students

Average undergraduate grade point average: **3.52**
MCAT averages (scale: 1-15; writing test: J-T):
Composite score: **9.7**
Verbal reasoning score: **9.4**, Physical sciences score: **9.8**,
Biological sciences score: **9.9**, Writing score: **O**
Proportion with undergraduate majors in: Biological
sciences: **41%**, Physical sciences: **17%**, Non-sciences: **8%**,
Other health professions: **3%**, Mixed disciplines and
other: **31%**
Percentage of students not coming directly from college
after graduation: **51%**

Dates and details

The American Medical College Application Service
(AMCAS) application is accepted.
School asks for a school-specific application as part of the
admissions process.
Oldest MCAT considered for Fall 2007 entry: **2004**
Earliest application date for the 2007-2008 first-year class:
June 1, 2006
Latest application date: **November 1, 2006**
Acceptance dates for regular application for the class
entering in fall 2007:
Earliest: **October 15, 2006**

Latest: **June 30, 2007**
The school considers requests for deferred entrance.
Starting month for the class entering in 2007–2008: **June**
The school doesn't have an Early Decision Plan (EDP).
A personal interview is required for admission.

Undergraduate coursework required

Medical school requires undergraduate work in these subjects: biology, English, organic chemistry, inorganic (general) chemistry, physics, calculus.

ADMISSIONS POLICY

(TEXT PROVIDED BY SCHOOL):
The School of Medicine subscribes fully to the policy of
equal educational opportunity. There are no quotas by race,
sex, religion, marital status, national origin, socioeconomic
background, or state of residence. There are no congres-
sional quotas or appointments.

All applicants are judged on personal merit in terms of
demonstrated aptitude, potential, and motivation for the
study and practice of military medicine. Only the best-quali-
fied, most promising candidates are selected.

Intellectual maturity, however, is an important consideration in admissions decisions. Applicants should be well-
informed, knowledgeable individuals who have
demonstrated competence in scholastic pursuits. They
should be adept in organizing, analyzing, and synthesizing
factual information. Mathematical ability and a background
in the sciences—natural, physical, and social—are expected.

Applicants are strongly encouraged by the Admissions
Committee to pursue some form of clinical work, e.g.,
emergency room, emergency medical technician, or shadowing a physician. Applicants are seldom accepted without
clinical experience.

The quality of an applicant's work at the preprofessional
level is of major interest to the school and is important in
admissions decisions. Although grades are not the only cri-
terion used in making decisions, college achievements are
scrutinized very carefully since academic performance
reflects achievement potential, interest, motivation, and self-
discipline.

While extracurricular activities, community service, employment, graduate study, military service, and personal accomplishments are considered in evaluating the applicant as a total individual, these factors cannot substitute entirely for a poor academic undergraduate record.

COSTS AND FINANCIAL AID

Financial aid phone number: **N/A**
Tuition, 2005-2006 academic year: **N/A**
Room and board: **$0**
Percentage of students receiving financial aid in 2005-06: **0%**
Percentage of students receiving: Loans: **0%**, Grants/scholarships: **0%**, Work-study aid: **0%**
Average medical school debt for the Class of 2004: **$0**

STUDENT BODY

Fall 2005 full-time enrollment: **665**
Men: **69%**, Women: **31%**, In-state: **6%**, Minorities: **20%**, American Indian: **1.1%**, Asian-American: **15.0%**, African-American: **3.0%**, Hispanic-American: **0.3%**, White: **74.7%**, International: **0.0%**, Unknown: **5.9%**

ACADEMIC PROGRAMS

The school's curriculum occasionally gives first-year students substantial contact with patients.
There are opportunities for first- or second-year students to work in community health clinics.
Program offerings: AIDS, drug/alcohol abuse, family medicine, geriatrics, internal medicine, pediatrics
Joint degrees awarded: M.D./Ph.D.
Total National Institutes of Health (NIH) grants awarded to the medical school and affiliated hospitals: **N/A**

CURRICULUM

(TEXT PROVIDED BY SCHOOL):
The school has a four-year program culminating in the doctor of medicine degree. Each of the first three academic years is 48 weeks, and the final year runs 40 weeks. Basic science instruction predominates in the initial two academic years, with the final two years being devoted to clinical education. Basic science instruction is correlated, as appropriate, both interdisciplinarily and clinically. The integration between the clinical and basic sciences is progressive and proceeds with involvement in patient-care activities

early in the curriculum, starting with the first semester of the freshman year.

While the overall program is designed to educate students to serve as providers of primary healthcare, there is sufficient flexibility to enable graduates to pursue postgraduate activities such as research. Elective courses are offered in clinical and research facilities in this country and in areas of the world where diseases rarely seen in the United States are responsible for 80 percent of the morbidity and mortality.

The curriculum also includes basic military orientation and concentration on unique aspects of military medicine. A conventional letter-grading system is employed to record student progress.

FACULTY PROFILE (FALL 2005)

Total teaching faculty: **269 (full-time)**, **1,837 (part-time)**
Of full-time faculty, those teaching in basic sciences: **41%**; in clinical programs: **59%**
Of part-time faculty, those teaching in basic sciences: **3%**; in clinical programs: **97%**
Full-time faculty/student ratio: **0.4**

SUPPORT SERVICES

The school offers students these services for dealing with stress: expanded-hour gym access, professional counseling, religious support, support groups.

RESIDENCY PROFILE

Most popular residency and specialty programs chosen by the 2004 and 2005 M.D. graduating classes: anesthesiology, emergency medicine, family practice, internal medicine, orthopaedic surgery, pediatrics, psychiatry, radiology–diagnostic, surgery–general, transitional year.

WHERE GRADS GO

35.0%
Proportion of 2003-2005 graduates who entered primary care specialties

N/A
Proportion of 2004-2005 graduates who accepted in-state residencies

University at Buffalo–SUNY

- 155 Biomedical Education Building, Buffalo, NY 14214
- Public
- **Year Founded:** 1846
- **Tuition, 2005-2006:** In-state: $20,099; Out-of-state: $34,799
- **Enrollment 2005-2006 academic year:** 561
- **Website:** http://www.smbs.buffalo.edu/ome
- **Specialty ranking:** rural medicine: 30

3.57 AVERAGE GPA, ENTERING CLASS FALL 2005

9.7 AVERAGE MCAT, ENTERING CLASS FALL 2005

12.9% ACCEPTANCE RATE, ENTERING CLASS FALL 2005

Unranked 2007 U.S. NEWS MEDICAL SCHOOL RANKING (RESEARCH)

Unranked 2007 U.S. NEWS MEDICAL SCHOOL RANKING (PRIMARY CARE)

ADMISSIONS

Admissions phone number: **(716) 829-3466**
Admissions email address: **jjrosso@buffalo.edu**
Application website: **http://www.aamc.org**
Acceptance rate: **12.9%**
In-state acceptance rate: **18.0%**
Out-of-state acceptance rate: **5.6%**
Minority acceptance rate: **N/A**
International acceptance rate: **N/A**

Fall 2005 applications and acceptees

	Applied	Interviewed	Accepted	Enrolled
Total:	2,772	548	358	136
In-state:	1,638	423	295	114
Out-of-state:	1,134	125	63	22

Profile of admitted students

Average undergraduate grade point average: **3.57**
MCAT averages (scale: 1-15; writing test: J-T):
  Composite score: **9.7**
  Verbal reasoning score: **9.3**, Physical sciences score: **9.9**,
  Biological sciences score: **10.1**, Writing score: **P**
Proportion with undergraduate majors in: Biological
  sciences: **49%**, Physical sciences: **23%**, Non-sciences:
  25%, Other health professions: **1%**, Mixed disciplines
  and other: **2%**
Percentage of students not coming directly from college
  after graduation: **N/A**

Dates and details

The American Medical College Application Service
  (AMCAS) application is accepted.
School asks for a school-specific application as part of the
  admissions process.
Oldest MCAT considered for Fall 2007 entry: **2003**
The school considers requests for deferred entrance.
Starting month for the class entering in 2007–2008:
  August
The school has an Early Decision Plan (EDP).
A personal interview is required for admission.

Undergraduate coursework required

Medical school requires undergraduate work in these subjects: biology, English, organic chemistry, inorganic (general) chemistry, physics.

ADMISSIONS POLICY
(TEXT PROVIDED BY SCHOOL):

The School of Medicine and Biomedical Sciences admits 135
students to its first-year class. Selection is based on scholastic achievement, aptitude, personal qualifications, and evidence of motivation toward medicine. These are judged
from the college record, the Medical College Admission
Test, letters of reference and evaluation, and a personal
interview. Students with a bachelor's degree from an accredited college or university are preferred. In exceptional cases,
those with shorter preparation will be considered for early
acceptance. In selecting a field of undergraduate concentration, the student should be strongly influenced by his or her
real inclinations. Medicine is a profession with many career
opportunities, and the exploration of almost any field in
depth is encouraged. Students presently matriculated in or
having graduated from another professional degree program are eligible to apply to the first-year class only.
Students presently enrolled in an American or Canadian or
other foreign medical or osteopathic school are ineligible to
apply to the first-year class but are eligible to apply to our
transfer program. All applicants must be U.S. citizens or
permanent residents and have had two full years or 60
credit hours of higher education in the United States or
Canada.

The school encourages minorities and disadvantaged students underrepresented in the medical profession to apply
and provides educational opportunities for them. A summer enrichment and support program is available to facilitate student retention in medical school. It is important that
students obtain a broad general education. In addition to
special scientific and academic prerequisites, students
should develop an educational background designed to
enjoy life and its varied experiences. It is not necessary to be
a science major to be admitted. In-state residency, while not
required, is looked upon favorably.

COSTS AND FINANCIAL AID

Financial aid phone number: **(716) 645-2450**
Tuition, 2005-2006 academic year: **In-state: $20,099; Out-of-state: $34,799**
Room and board: **$9,301**
Percentage of students receiving financial aid in 2005-06: **88%**
Percentage of students receiving: Loans: **84%**, Grants/scholarships: **70%**, Work-study aid: **0%**
Average medical school debt for the Class of 2004: **$134,121**

STUDENT BODY

Fall 2005 full-time enrollment: **561**
Men: **45%**, Women: **55%**, In-state: **100%**, Minorities: **50%**, American Indian: **0.4%**, Asian-American: **25.7%**, African-American: **5.9%**, Hispanic-American: **1.6%**, White: **66.5%**, International: **0.0%**, Unknown: **0.0%**

ACADEMIC PROGRAMS

The school's curriculum frequently gives first-year students substantial contact with patients.
There are opportunities for first- or second-year students to work in community health clinics.
Program offerings: AIDS, drug/alcohol abuse, family medicine, geriatrics, internal medicine, pediatrics, rural medicine
Joint degrees awarded: M.D./Ph.D., M.D./MBA, M.D./MPH.
Total National Institutes of Health (NIH) grants awarded to the medical school and affiliated hospitals: **$68.0 million**

CURRICULUM

(TEXT PROVIDED BY SCHOOL):
The four-year medical curriculum at the University at Buffalo begins with years 1 and 2 dominated by an organ-based, interdisciplinary core curriculum. The first-semester Foundations lecture module is designed to give all students a basic foundation of information in molecular and cell biology and epidemiology. Other modular lecture sections are dedicated to organs of interest. The modules incorporate the anatomy, histology, physiology, biochemistry, pathology, microbiology, pharmacology and toxicology associated with the organ and its diseases. Gross anatomy is provided as a course in the first semester of study. In addition to didactic lectures, students are expected to participate in small-group, problem-based learning sessions. The students also get practical experience in the Clinical Practice of Medicine course. In the third and fourth years, students rotate in the specialty clinical areas.

The University at Buffalo relies on a consortium of hospitals to provide training to our medical students. This association with hospitals such as Roswell Park Cancer Memorial Institute, Buffalo General Hospital, and Women's and Children's Hospital of Buffalo provides a rich source of experience for our students.

In addition to formal clinical training, students are in an atmosphere infused with exciting research. The school attracted approximately $45 million in research grants in 2004. The research faculty is involved in research relating to Parkinson disease, diabetes, obesity, multiple sclerosis, vaccine development, and cardiology, among others. The newly created Center of Excellence in Bioinformatics promises to be a world-class center for developing new drugs and therapeutic approaches involving genomics and unique protein identification. Medical students are encouraged to participate in a clinical or laboratory research experience, and there is a yearly celebration of research where the students present their findings and compete for prizes. The University at Buffalo allows medical students to explore their talents, benefit from a talented faculty, and prepare for a rewarding and creative career.

FACULTY PROFILE (FALL 2005)

Total teaching faculty: **440 (full-time), 26 (part-time)**
Of full-time faculty, those teaching in basic sciences: **25%**; in clinical programs: **75%**
Of part-time faculty, those teaching in basic sciences: **58%**; in clinical programs: **42%**
Full-time faculty/student ratio: **0.8**

SUPPORT SERVICES

The school offers students these services for dealing with stress: professional counseling, religious support.

RESIDENCY PROFILE

Most popular residency and specialty programs chosen by the 2004 and 2005 M.D. graduating classes: anesthesiology, emergency medicine, family practice, internal medicine, neurology, obstetrics and gynecology, pediatrics, psychiatry, radiology–diagnostic, surgery–general.

WHERE GRADS GO

43.1%
Proportion of 2003-2005 graduates who entered primary care specialties

67%
Proportion of 2004-2005 graduates who accepted in-state residencies

University of Alabama–Birmingham

■ Medical Student Services, VH Suite 100, Birmingham, AL
  35294-0019
■ Public
■ Year Founded: 1859
■ Tuition, 2005-2006: In-state: $15,478; Out-of-state: $38,210
■ Enrollment 2005-2006 academic year: 683
■ Website: http://www.uab.edu/uasom/admissions
■ Specialty ranking: AIDS: 5, geriatrics: 14, internal medicine:
  17, pediatrics: 20, rural medicine: 20, women's health: 8

3.72 AVERAGE GPA, ENTERING CLASS FALL 2005

10.1 AVERAGE MCAT, ENTERING CLASS FALL 2005

12.3% ACCEPTANCE RATE, ENTERING CLASS FALL 2005

22 2007 U.S. NEWS MEDICAL SCHOOL RANKING (RESEARCH)

28 2007 U.S. NEWS MEDICAL SCHOOL RANKING (PRIMARY CARE)

ADMISSIONS

Admissions phone number: **(205) 934-2330**
Admissions email address: **medschool@uab.edu**
Application website: **N/A**
Acceptance rate: **12.3%**
In-state acceptance rate: **41.3%**
Out-of-state acceptance rate: **2.5%**
Minority acceptance rate: **7.9%**
International acceptance rate: **N/A**

Fall 2005 applications and acceptees

	Applied	Interviewed	Accepted	Enrolled
Total:	1,734	346	213	160
In-state:	436	271	180	144
Out-of-state:	1,298	75	33	16

Profile of admitted students

Average undergraduate grade point average: **3.72**
MCAT averages (scale: 1-15; writing test: J-T):
  Composite score: **10.1**
  Verbal reasoning score: **9.8**, Physical sciences score:
  10.1, Biological sciences score: **10.4**, Writing score: **N/A**
Proportion with undergraduate majors in: Biological
  sciences: **48%**, Physical sciences: **21%**, Non-sciences:
  11%, Other health professions: **1%**, Mixed disciplines and
  other: **19%**
Percentage of students not coming directly from college
  after graduation: **N/A**

Dates and details

The American Medical College Application Service
  (AMCAS) application is accepted.
School asks for a school-specific application as part of the
  admissions process.
Oldest MCAT considered for Fall 2007 entry: **2004**
Earliest application date for the 2007-2008 first-year class:
  June 1, 2006
Latest application date: **November 1, 2006**
Acceptance dates for regular application for the class
  entering in fall 2007:
  Earliest: **August 1, 2006**

Latest: **N/A**
The school considers requests for deferred entrance.
Starting month for the class entering in 2007–2008:
  August
The school has an Early Decision Plan (EDP).
A personal interview is required for admission.

Undergraduate coursework required

Medical school requires undergraduate work in these subjects: biology, English, organic chemistry, inorganic (general) chemistry, physics, humanities, mathematics.

COSTS AND FINANCIAL AID

Financial aid phone number: **(205) 934-8223**
Tuition, 2005-2006 academic year: **In-state: $15,478; Out-
  of-state: $38,210**
Room and board: **$10,780**
Percentage of students receiving financial aid in 2005-06:
  85%
Percentage of students receiving: Loans: **81%**,
  Grants/scholarships: **22%**, Work-study aid: **N/A**
Average medical school debt for the Class of 2004:
  $96,786

STUDENT BODY

Fall 2005 full-time enrollment: **683**
Men: **59%**, Women: **41%**, In-state: **93%**, Minorities: **22%**,
  American Indian: **1.2%**, Asian-American: **12.9%**,
  African-American: **6.7%**, Hispanic-American: **0.9%**,
  White: **77.9%**, International: **N/A**, Unknown: **0.4%**

ACADEMIC PROGRAMS

Program offerings: AIDS, drug/alcohol abuse, family
  medicine, geriatrics, internal medicine, pediatrics, rural
  medicine, women's health
Joint degrees awarded: M.D./Ph.D., M.D./MPH
Total National Institutes of Health (NIH) grants awarded to
  the medical school and affiliated hospitals: **N/A**

FACULTY PROFILE (FALL 2005)

Total teaching faculty: **1,065 (full-time)**, **45 (part-time)**

Of full-time faculty, those teaching in basic sciences: **21%**; in clinical programs: **79%**
Of part-time faculty, those teaching in basic sciences: **13%**; in clinical programs: **87%**
Full-time faculty/student ratio: **1.6**

RESIDENCY PROFILE

Most popular residency and specialty programs chosen by the 2004 and 2005 M.D. graduating classes: anesthesiology, emergency medicine, family practice, internal medicine, neurology, obstetrics and gynecology, orthopaedic surgery, pediatrics, radiology–diagnostic, surgery–general.

WHERE GRADS GO

38%

Proportion of 2003-2005 graduates who entered primary care specialties

46%

Proportion of 2004-2005 graduates who accepted in-state residencies

University of Arizona

- 1501 N. Campbell Avenue, Tucson, AZ 85724
- Public
- Year Founded: 1967
- Tuition, 2005-2006: $14,462
- Enrollment 2005-2006 academic year: 461
- Website: http://www.medicine.arizona.edu
- Specialty ranking: family medicine: 22

3.67 AVERAGE GPA, ENTERING CLASS FALL 2005

9.9 AVERAGE MCAT, ENTERING CLASS FALL 2005

28.4% ACCEPTANCE RATE, ENTERING CLASS FALL 2005

57 2007 U.S. NEWS MEDICAL SCHOOL RANKING (RESEARCH)

Unranked 2007 U.S. NEWS MEDICAL SCHOOL RANKING (PRIMARY CARE)

ADMISSIONS

Admissions phone number: **(520) 626-6214**
Admissions email address:
   admissions@medicine.arizona.edu
Application website: **N/A**
Acceptance rate: **28.4%**
In-state acceptance rate: **28.4%**
Out-of-state acceptance rate: **30.8%**
Minority acceptance rate: **N/A**
International acceptance rate: **N/A**

Fall 2005 applications and acceptees

	Applied	Interviewed	Accepted	Enrolled
Total:	538	538	153	110
In-state:	525	525	149	109
Out-of-state:	13	13	4	1

Profile of admitted students

Average undergraduate grade point average: **3.67**
MCAT averages (scale: 1-15; writing test: J-T):
   Composite score: **9.9**
   Verbal reasoning score: **9.8**, Physical sciences score: **9.8**,
   Biological sciences score: **10.2**, Writing score: **P**
Proportion with undergraduate majors in: Biological
sciences: **56%**, Physical sciences: **17%**, Non-sciences:
12%, Other health professions: **7%**, Mixed disciplines
and other: **7%**
Percentage of students not coming directly from college
after graduation: **N/A**

Dates and details

The American Medical College Application Service
   (AMCAS) application is accepted.
School asks for a school-specific application as part of the
   admissions process.
Oldest MCAT considered for Fall 2007 entry: **2003**
Earliest application date for the 2007-2008 first-year class:
   June 1, 2006
Latest application date: **November 1, 2006**
Acceptance dates for regular application for the class
   entering in fall 2007:

Earliest: **January 1, 2007**
Latest: **August 1, 2007**
The school considers requests for deferred entrance.
Starting month for the class entering in 2007–2008:
   August
The school doesn't have an Early Decision Plan (EDP).
A personal interview is required for admission.

Undergraduate coursework required

Medical school requires undergraduate work in these subjects: biology/zoology, English, organic chemistry, inorganic
(general) chemistry, physics.

ADMISSIONS POLICY
(TEXT PROVIDED BY SCHOOL):

Acceptance to The University of Arizona College of
Medicine is based upon an assessment of the applicant's
intellectual and personal traits and fulfillment of certain
prerequisites outlined below. Applicants who wish to be
considered must be U.S. citizens (or have permanent resident visas) and residents of Arizona. Native Americans
whose reservation land lies partly in Arizona and partly in
an adjoining state and who are residents of such a reservation are also considered. In addition, consideration is given
to highly qualified applicants who are residents of Montana
and Wyoming, are certified, and will receive full and unin-
terrupted funding by the Western Interstate Commission
for Higher Education (WICHE). Applicants from states
other than these cannot be considered. No preference is
given to any particular type of undergraduate major.
Acceptance is based on the qualifications of the applicant
and not on the specific university attended. Many Arizona
residents and patients who receive care at the Arizona
Health Sciences Center and its affiliated clinics and hospitals speak Spanish as their primary language and it would
be helpful for University of Arizona medical students to be
conversant in Spanish. The Admissions Committee uses six
major criteria in the selection of students: academic record,
Medical College Admission Test (MCAT) scores, personal
statements, letters of recommendation, evaluations of the
personal interviews, and relevant experience. Consideration

of the academic record includes not only grades, but trends in the grade point average, course loads, work experience while going to school, breadth of the undergraduate education, extent of extracurricular interests and pursuits, and other factors which might directly or indirectly influence the individual's total academic performance. The MCAT scores provide a national comparison of each student with all those seeking admission to medical school. Personal statements in the AMCAS are used to determine applicants' interest in medicine, motivation, career goals and personal character. Interview summaries help the committee assess applicants' communication skills and character.

COSTS AND FINANCIAL AID
Financial aid phone number: **(520) 626-7145**
Tuition, 2005-2006 academic year: **$14,462**
Room and board: **$9,070**
Percentage of students receiving financial aid in 2005-06: **93%**
Percentage of students receiving: Loans: **88%**, Grants/scholarships: **88%**, Work-study aid: **4%**
Average medical school debt for the Class of 2004: **$85,706**

STUDENT BODY
Fall 2005 full-time enrollment: **461**
Men: **50%**, Women: **50%**, In-state: **99%**, Minorities: **29%**, American Indian: **2.8%**, Asian-American: **14.1%**, African-American: **1.5%**, Hispanic-American: **10.2%**, White: **71.4%**, International: **0.0%**, Unknown: **0.0%**

ACADEMIC PROGRAMS
The school's curriculum very frequently gives first-year students substantial contact with patients.
There are opportunities for first- or second-year students to work in community health clinics.
Program offerings: AIDS, drug/alcohol abuse, family medicine, geriatrics, internal medicine, pediatrics, rural medicine, women's health
Joint degrees awarded: M.D./Ph.D., M.D./MPH
Total National Institutes of Health (NIH) grants awarded to the medical school and affiliated hospitals: **N/A**

CURRICULUM
(TEXT PROVIDED BY SCHOOL):
The overall purpose of the educational program is to give students the desire for lifelong learning in medicine by creating study habits that call for the continuous pursuit of knowledge and the capacity to modify previously acquired information. The program also aims to give students the skills to conduct patient care activities as well as the professional attitudes consonant with the charge to provide patients with preventive and curative advice and treatment.

Biologic, cultural, psychosocial, economic and sociological concepts and data are provided in the core curriculum. Increasing emphasis is placed on problem-solving ability, beginning with initial instruction and carried through to graduation. Excellence in performance is encouraged and facilitated. Awareness of the milieu in which medicine is practiced is also encouraged.

The core curriculum comprises three years of required studies and one year of elective rotations. The learning environment encompasses lectures, small-group discussion and problem-solving sessions, independent study, clinical clerkships, practice in physical diagnosis, computer-based instruction, and a variety of other modes for the learner. Students learn in the classroom, conference room, laboratory, clinic and physician's office, bed units of hospitals, special sites for diagnostic and therapeutic maneuvers, University Medical Center, and a variety of inpatient and outpatient settings in Tucson, Phoenix, and throughout Arizona. All medical students will participate in an educational experience with an underserved population sometime during medical school. Upon graduation the physician is equipped to continue post-graduate education in general or specialty practice, teaching, or research.

FACULTY PROFILE (FALL 2005)
Total teaching faculty: **834 (full-time)**, **35 (part-time)**
Of full-time faculty, those teaching in basic sciences: **12%**; in clinical programs: **88%**
Of part-time faculty, those teaching in basic sciences: **17%**; in clinical programs: **83%**
Full-time faculty/student ratio: **1.8**

SUPPORT SERVICES
The school offers students these services for dealing with stress: expanded-hour gym access, peer counseling, professional counseling, religious support, support groups.

RESIDENCY PROFILE
Most popular residency and specialty programs chosen by the 2004 and 2005 M.D. graduating classes: anesthesiology, emergency medicine, family practice, internal medicine, obstetrics and gynecology, pediatrics, psychiatry, radiology–diagnostic, surgery–general.

WHERE GRADS GO

39%
Proportion of 2003-2005 graduates who entered primary care specialties

45%
Proportion of 2004-2005 graduates who accepted in-state residencies

University of Arkansas

FOR MEDICAL SCIENCES

- 4301 W. Markham Street, Slot 551, Little Rock, AR 72205
- Public
- Year Founded: 1879
- Tuition, 2005-2006: In-state: $14,861; Out-of-state: $28,949
- Enrollment 2005-2006 academic year: 581
- Website: http://www.uams.edu
- Specialty ranking: geriatrics: 10

3.62 AVERAGE GPA, ENTERING CLASS FALL 2005

9.2 AVERAGE MCAT, ENTERING CLASS FALL 2005

24.9% ACCEPTANCE RATE, ENTERING CLASS FALL 2005

Unranked 2007 U.S. NEWS MEDICAL SCHOOL RANKING (RESEARCH)

38 2007 U.S. NEWS MEDICAL SCHOOL RANKING (PRIMARY CARE)

ADMISSIONS

Admissions phone number: **(501) 686-5354**
Admissions email address: **southtomg@uams.edu**
Application website: **N/A**
Acceptance rate: **24.9%**
In-state acceptance rate: **59.2%**
Out-of-state acceptance rate: **4.2%**
Minority acceptance rate: **18.0%**
International acceptance rate: **N/A**

Fall 2005 applications and acceptees

	Applied	Interviewed	Accepted	Enrolled
Total:	694	315	173	150
In-state:	262	249	155	141
Out-of-state:	432	66	18	9

Profile of admitted students

Average undergraduate grade point average: **3.62**
MCAT averages (scale: 1-15; writing test: J-T):
   Composite score: **9.2**
   Verbal reasoning score: **9.4**, Physical sciences score: **8.8**, Biological sciences score: **9.4**, Writing score: **O**
Proportion with undergraduate majors in: Biological sciences: **57%**, Physical sciences: **23%**, Non-sciences: **19%**, Other health professions: **1%**, Mixed disciplines and other: **0%**
Percentage of students not coming directly from college after graduation: **27%**

Dates and details

The American Medical College Application Service (AMCAS) application is accepted.
School asks for a school-specific application as part of the admissions process.
Oldest MCAT considered for Fall 2007 entry: **2004**
Earliest application date for the 2007-2008 first-year class: **July 1, 2006**
Latest application date: **November 1, 2006**
Acceptance dates for regular application for the class entering in fall 2007:
   Earliest: **December 15, 2006**

Latest: **August 3, 2007**
The school considers requests for deferred entrance.
Starting month for the class entering in 2007–2008: **August**
The school doesn't have an Early Decision Plan (EDP).
A personal interview is required for admission.

Undergraduate coursework required

Medical school requires undergraduate work in these subjects: biology, biology/zoology, English, organic chemistry, inorganic (general) chemistry, physics, mathematics, demonstration of writing skills, calculus.

ADMISSIONS POLICY
(TEXT PROVIDED BY SCHOOL):

Preference is given to Arkansas residents, although non-Arkansas residents are encouraged to apply. Non-Arkansas residents should have strong ties to Arkansas and have excellent academic credentials. The applicant must perform well inside the classroom, i.e. GPA and MCAT, as well as outside the classroom, i.e., volunteerism, community service, exposure to patient care, research, clinical or hospital environment. Letters of recommendation, especially the composite evaluation provided by the applicant's Premedical Advisory Committee, are essential.

COSTS AND FINANCIAL AID

Financial aid phone number: **(501) 686-5813**
Tuition, 2005-2006 academic year: **In-state: $14,861; Out-of-state: $28,949**
Room and board: **$0**
Percentage of students receiving financial aid in 2005-06: **94%**
Percentage of students receiving: Loans: **89%**, Grants/scholarships: **44%**, Work-study aid: **0%**
Average medical school debt for the Class of 2004: **$98,582**

STUDENT BODY

Fall 2005 full-time enrollment: **581**

Men: 58%, Women: 42%, In-state: 98%, Minorities: 12%,
American Indian: 1.4%, Asian-American: 7.9%, African-
American: 5.9%, Hispanic-American: 0.2%, White:
84.7%, International: 0.0%, Unknown: 0.0%

ACADEMIC PROGRAMS
The school's curriculum occasionally gives first-year
students substantial contact with patients.
There are opportunities for first- or second-year students to
work in community health clinics.
Program offerings: AIDS, drug/alcohol abuse, family
medicine, geriatrics, internal medicine, pediatrics, rural
medicine, women's health
Joint degrees awarded: M.D./Ph.D., M.D./MBA,
M.D./MPH, M.D./JD.
Total National Institutes of Health (NIH) grants awarded to
the medical school and affiliated hospitals: **$52.7 million**

FACULTY PROFILE (FALL 2005)
Total teaching faculty: 962 (full-time), 0 (part-time)
Of full-time faculty, those teaching in basic sciences: 25%;
in clinical programs: 75%
Of part-time faculty, those teaching in basic sciences: N/A;
in clinical programs: N/A
Full-time faculty/student ratio: 1.7

SUPPORT SERVICES
The school offers students these services for dealing with
stress: expanded-hour gym access, peer counseling, professional counseling, support groups.

RESIDENCY PROFILE
Most popular residency and specialty programs chosen by
the 2004 and 2005 M.D. graduating classes: family practice, internal medicine, internal medicine–pediatrics, obstetrics and gynecology, pediatrics, psychiatry.

WHERE GRADS GO

52%

*Proportion of 2003-2005 graduates who entered primary
care specialties*

57%

*Proportion of 2004-2005 graduates who accepted in-state
residencies*

University of California–Davis

■ 1 Shields Avenue, Davis, CA 95616-8661
■ Public
■ Year Founded: 1966
■ Tuition, 2005-2006: In-state: $22,820; Out-of-state: $35,065
■ Enrollment 2005-2006 academic year: 404
■ Website: http://som.ucdavis.edu
■ Specialty ranking: family medicine: 12, rural medicine: 25

3.61 AVERAGE GPA, ENTERING CLASS FALL 2005

10.3 AVERAGE MCAT, ENTERING CLASS FALL 2005

4.9% ACCEPTANCE RATE, ENTERING CLASS FALL 2005

48 2007 U.S. NEWS MEDICAL SCHOOL RANKING (RESEARCH)

21 2007 U.S. NEWS MEDICAL SCHOOL RANKING (PRIMARY CARE)

ADMISSIONS

Admissions phone number: **(530) 752-2717**
Admissions email address: **medadmisinfo@ucdavis.edu**
Application website: **N/A**
Acceptance rate: **4.9%**
In-state acceptance rate: **5.7%**
Out-of-state acceptance rate: **1.4%**
Minority acceptance rate: **4.9%**
International acceptance rate: **N/A**

Fall 2005 applications and acceptees

	Applied	Interviewed	Accepted	Enrolled
Total:	4,109	392	202	91
In-state:	3,334	377	191	88
Out-of-state:	775	15	11	3

Profile of admitted students

Average undergraduate grade point average: **3.61**
MCAT averages (scale: 1-15; writing test: J-T):
  Composite score: **10.3**
  Verbal reasoning score: **10.0**, Physical sciences score: **10.0**, Biological sciences score: **11.0**, Writing score: **Q**
Proportion with undergraduate majors in: Biological sciences: **43%**, Physical sciences: **35%**, Non-sciences: **19%**, Other health professions: **1%**, Mixed disciplines and other: **2%**
Percentage of students not coming directly from college after graduation: **35%**

Dates and details

The American Medical College Application Service (AMCAS) application is accepted.
School asks for a school-specific application as part of the admissions process.
Oldest MCAT considered for Fall 2007 entry: **2003**
Earliest application date for the 2007-2008 first-year class: **June 1, 2006**
Latest application date: **November 1, 2006**
Acceptance dates for regular application for the class entering in fall 2007:
  Earliest: **October 15, 2006**

Latest: **August 1, 2007**
The school considers requests for deferred entrance.
Starting month for the class entering in 2007–2008:
  August
The school doesn't have an Early Decision Plan (EDP).
A personal interview is required for admission.

Undergraduate coursework required

Medical school requires undergraduate work in these subjects: biology, English, organic chemistry, inorganic (general) chemistry, physics, molecular and cell biology, biochemistry, mathematics, calculus.

ADMISSIONS POLICY

(TEXT PROVIDED BY SCHOOL):

The School of Medicine seeks to attract students who are curious, motivated, and intelligent with a view toward meeting the needs of society. The ideal student will have a demonstrated track record of achievement and leadership in an area of interest, demonstrable humanistic attitudes, and a realistic vision of the role they hope to play in health care delivery. In their pursuit of excellence, they will have demonstrated strong interpersonal skills, ethical judgment, and explored methods of inquiry. The School embraces diversity in its student body. This is reflected in the School's commitment to expand opportunities in medical education for individuals from groups underrepresented in medicine as a result of social discrimination and to increase the number of physicians practicing in underserved areas.
Therefore, the Admissions Committee, which is composed of individuals from a variety of cultural and professional backgrounds, evaluates each applicant in terms of total person, carefully considering all relevant factors. These include academic credentials, with due regard to how they have been affected by disadvantages experienced by the applicant; such personal traits as character and motivation; experience in the health sciences and/or the community; career objectives; and the ability of the individual to make a positive contribution to society, the profession, and the school.
  Factors considered for admission include the applicant's scholastic record, GPA, MCAT performance, community

service, leadership, reports of teachers and advisors regarding intellectual capacity, motivation, and emotional stability. Characteristics that make applicants particularly attractive to the Admissions Committee are outstanding non-academic achievements, capability for independent study, maturity, and other factors that suggest good academic and leadership potential. A personal interview will normally be required of each applicant who is accepted. Regional interviews are not normally available. We now expect that 10% of our entering class will come from outside the State of California. UC Davis School of Medicine participates in the WICHE Professional Student Exchange Program for applicants from certain western states that do not have a medical school.

COSTS AND FINANCIAL AID

Financial aid phone number: (530) 752-6618
Tuition, 2005-2006 academic year: **In-state: $22,820; Out-of-state: $35,065**
Room and board: **$11,229**
Percentage of students receiving financial aid in 2005-06: 95%
Percentage of students receiving: Loans: 90%, Grants/scholarships: 93%, Work-study aid: 0%
Average medical school debt for the Class of 2004: $69,345

STUDENT BODY

Fall 2005 full-time enrollment: 404
Men: 46%, Women: 54%, In-state: 100%, Minorities: 55%, American Indian: 1.7%, Asian-American: 40.1%, African-American: 3.5%, Hispanic-American: 9.7%, White: 44.8%, International: 0.2%, Unknown: 0.0%

ACADEMIC PROGRAMS

The school's curriculum frequently gives first-year students substantial contact with patients.
There are opportunities for first- or second-year students to work in community health clinics.
Program offerings: AIDS, drug/alcohol abuse, family medicine, geriatrics, internal medicine, pediatrics, rural medicine, women's health
Joint degrees awarded: M.D./Ph.D., M.D./MBA, M.D./MPH, M.D./MS, M.D./M.A.
Total National Institutes of Health (NIH) grants awarded to the medical school and affiliated hospitals: **$72.8 million**

CURRICULUM

(TEXT PROVIDED BY SCHOOL):
The UC Davis School of Medicine offers a four-year, comprehensive curriculum leading to a medical degree. Students are exposed to patient management at the start of their first year. The curriculum is designed to integrate basic and clinical sciences, promote active learning and critical thinking, and foster the highest standards of professionalism. The school has a strong tradition of community service by students through participation in several community clinics. The faculty also strongly encourages students to pursue research opportunities and advanced degrees. There are many new and exciting curriculum changes on the horizon for the UC Davis School of Medicine. For a detailed look at our current curriculum and updates on future changes, please visit our website.

FACULTY PROFILE (FALL 2005)

Total teaching faculty: **560 (full-time)**, **82 (part-time)**
Of full-time faculty, those teaching in basic sciences: 8%; in clinical programs: 92%
Of part-time faculty, those teaching in basic sciences: 15%; in clinical programs: 85%
Full-time faculty/student ratio: **1.4**

SUPPORT SERVICES

The school offers students these services for dealing with stress: peer counseling, professional counseling, support groups.

RESIDENCY PROFILE

Most popular residency and specialty programs chosen by the 2004 and 2005 M.D. graduating classes: emergency medicine, family practice, medical genetics, pediatrics, psychiatry, radiation oncology, transitional year.

WHERE GRADS GO

47.1%
Proportion of 2003-2005 graduates who entered primary care specialties

68.5%
Proportion of 2004-2005 graduates who accepted in-state residencies

University of California–Irvine

- 252 Irvine Hall, Irvine, CA 92697-3950
- **Public**
- **Year Founded:** 1967
- **Tuition, 2005-2006:** In-state: $22,820; Out-of-state: $35,065
- **Enrollment 2005-2006 academic year:** 388
- **Website:** http://www.ucihs.uci.edu
- **Specialty ranking:** N/A

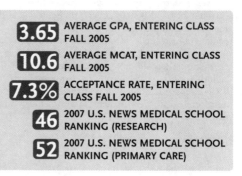

3.65 AVERAGE GPA, ENTERING CLASS FALL 2005

10.6 AVERAGE MCAT, ENTERING CLASS FALL 2005

7.3% ACCEPTANCE RATE, ENTERING CLASS FALL 2005

46 2007 U.S. NEWS MEDICAL SCHOOL RANKING (RESEARCH)

52 2007 U.S. NEWS MEDICAL SCHOOL RANKING (PRIMARY CARE)

ADMISSIONS

Admissions phone number: **(949) 824-5388**
Admissions email address: **medadmit@uci.edu**
Application website: **N/A**
Acceptance rate: **7.3%**
In-state acceptance rate: **8.2%**
Out-of-state acceptance rate: **0.6%**
Minority acceptance rate: **7.0%**
International acceptance rate: **0.0%**

Fall 2005 applications and acceptees

	Applied	Interviewed	Accepted	Enrolled
Total:	**3,798**	**455**	**277**	**103**
In-state:	**3,323**	**447**	**274**	**103**
Out-of-state:	**475**	**8**	**3**	**0**

Profile of admitted students

Average undergraduate grade point average: **3.65**
MCAT averages (scale: 1-15; writing test: J-T):
Composite score: **10.6**
Verbal reasoning score: **9.8**, Physical sciences score: **10.9**, Biological sciences score: **11.1**, Writing score: **Q**
Proportion with undergraduate majors in: Biological sciences: **68%**, Physical sciences: **14%**, Non-sciences: **15%**, Other health professions: **0%**, Mixed disciplines and other: **3%**
Percentage of students not coming directly from college after graduation: **N/A**

Dates and details

The American Medical College Application Service (AMCAS) application is accepted.
School asks for a school-specific application as part of the admissions process.
Oldest MCAT considered for Fall 2007 entry: **2004**
Earliest application date for the 2007-2008 first-year class: **June 1, 2006**
Latest application date: **November 1, 2006**
Acceptance dates for regular application for the class entering in fall 2007:
Earliest: **November 15, 2006**

Latest: **August 4, 2007**
The school considers requests for deferred entrance.
Starting month for the class entering in 2007–2008:
August
The school doesn't have an Early Decision Plan (EDP).
A personal interview is required for admission.

Undergraduate coursework required

Medical school requires undergraduate work in these subjects: biology, English, organic chemistry, inorganic (general) chemistry, physics, biochemistry, calculus.

ADMISSIONS POLICY

(TEXT PROVIDED BY SCHOOL):
The UCI School of Medicine seeks to admit students who are highly qualified to be trained in the practice of medicine and whose backgrounds, talents, and experiences contribute to a diverse student body. The Admissions Committee carefully reviews all applicants whose academic record and Medical College Admission Test scores indicate that they will be able to handle the rigorous medical school curriculum. Careful consideration is given to applicants from disadvantaged backgrounds (i.e., disadvantaged through social, cultural, and/or economic conditions). In addition to scholastic achievement, attributes deemed desirable in prospective students include leadership ability and participation in extracurricular activities, such as clinical and/or medically related research experience, as well as community service.

Information provided by the American Medical College Application Service application is used for preliminary screening. Based on decisions reached by the Admissions Committee, applicants may be sent a secondary application. Applicants receiving a secondary application are asked to submit additional materials, including a minimum of three letters of recommendation, supplemental information forms, and a nonrefundable application fee. Upon further review by the Admissions Committee, approximately 500 of those applicants receiving a secondary application will be invited to interview. Regional interviews are not available. Preference is given to California residents and applicants who are either U.S. citizens or permanent residents. The UCI School of Medicine does not accept transfer students.

COSTS AND FINANCIAL AID
Financial aid phone number: **(949) 824-6476**
Tuition, 2005-2006 academic year: **In-state: $22,820**; **Out-of-state: $35,065**
Room and board: **$10,520**
Percentage of students receiving financial aid in 2005-06: **87%**
Percentage of students receiving: Loans: **80%**, Grants/scholarships: **83%**, Work-study aid: **0%**
Average medical school debt for the Class of 2004: **$69,000**

STUDENT BODY
Fall 2005 full-time enrollment: **388**
Men: **52%**, Women: **48%**, In-state: **100%**, Minorities: **43%**, American Indian: **0.3%**, Asian-American: **31.7%**, African-American: **1.5%**, Hispanic-American: **9.5%**, White: **53.6%**, International: **0.0%**, Unknown: **3.4%**

ACADEMIC PROGRAMS
The school's curriculum frequently gives first-year students substantial contact with patients.
There are opportunities for first- or second-year students to work in community health clinics.
Program offerings: drug/alcohol abuse, family medicine, geriatrics, internal medicine, pediatrics, rural medicine, women's health
Joint degrees awarded: M.D./Ph.D., M.D./MBA.
Total National Institutes of Health (NIH) grants awarded to the medical school and affiliated hospitals: **$82.2 million**

CURRICULUM
(TEXT PROVIDED BY SCHOOL):
The first two years are devoted to basic science instruction and preclinical experiences. There is a vacation period between the first and second years; students may use this time for research in place of vacation. Between the second and third years there is a vacation period that students typically use to prepare for Step 1 of the United States Medical Licensing Examination (USMLE).

The third year is scheduled in six eight-week blocks, with one month off during the winter. The fourth year is scheduled in two- and four-week blocks. During the clinical third and fourth years, clerkships and elective rotations are taken. The sequence of these clinical rotations varys based on lottery assignments.

To become eligible for the M.D. degree, each student must demonstrate mastery of the material presented in the courses and programs of the curriculum. All of the following requirements must be completed in order for a student to be recommended for graduation: achievement of a passing grade in all courses in the M.D. curriculum; successful passage of the USMLE steps 1, 2CK and 2CS administered by the National Board of Medical Examiners (failure to pass any step precludes graduation, without exception); and passage of the Clinical Practice Examination near the end of the third year.

The Patient-Doctor Continuum is a four-year longitudinal, multidisciplinary, and multiple-course curriculum. The continuum begins with Patient, Doctor, and Society, a 55-hour interactive, didactic course that sets the tone and establishes the knowledge base.

The first-year course begins with supervised interviews that progressively increase in difficulty. Each student interviews a standardized patient while being observed from a monitoring room by his partner and the faculty preceptor. After four supervised practice interview sessions, students participate in six more complex, organ-based modules.

During the second year, students will spend one half-day a week participating in clinical service experiences, which are designed to provide them with real patient experience and exposure to the different fields of medicine. Students are assigned a "content theme" to explore during each four-week block and meet monthly with a faculty mentor for a problem-based learning session. Midway through their second year, students' clinical skills are tested through a practical examination.

FACULTY PROFILE (FALL 2005)
Total teaching faculty: **456 (full-time)**, **108 (part-time)**
Of full-time faculty, those teaching in basic sciences: **15%**; in clinical programs: **85%**
Of part-time faculty, those teaching in basic sciences: **1%**; in clinical programs: **99%**
Full-time faculty/student ratio: **1.2**

SUPPORT SERVICES
The school offers students these services for dealing with stress: expanded-hour gym access, peer counseling, professional counseling, religious support, support groups.

RESIDENCY PROFILE
Most popular residency and specialty programs chosen by the 2004 and 2005 M.D. graduating classes: anesthesiology, emergency medicine, family practice, internal medicine, obstetrics and gynecology, orthopaedic surgery, pediatrics, psychiatry, radiology–diagnostic, surgery–general.

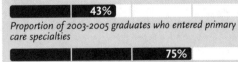

WHERE GRADS GO
43%
Proportion of 2003-2005 graduates who entered primary care specialties

75%
Proportion of 2004-2005 graduates who accepted in-state residencies

University of California–Los Angeles

GEFFEN

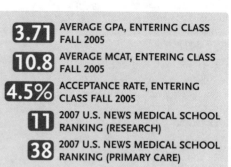

- 12-138 CHS, 10833 Le Conte Avenue, Los Angeles, CA 90095-1720
- Public
- Year Founded: 1951
- Tuition, 2005-2006: In-state: $21,506; Out-of-state: $33,751
- Enrollment 2005-2006 academic year: 690
- Website: http://www.medsch.ucla.edu
- Specialty ranking: AIDS: 8, drug/alcohol abuse: 4, geriatrics: 1, internal medicine: 15, pediatrics: 9, women's health: 12

3.71 AVERAGE GPA, ENTERING CLASS FALL 2005

10.8 AVERAGE MCAT, ENTERING CLASS FALL 2005

4.5% ACCEPTANCE RATE, ENTERING CLASS FALL 2005

11 2007 U.S. NEWS MEDICAL SCHOOL RANKING (RESEARCH)

38 2007 U.S. NEWS MEDICAL SCHOOL RANKING (PRIMARY CARE)

ADMISSIONS

Admissions phone number: **(310) 825-6081**
Admissions email address: **somadmiss@mednet.ucla.edu**
Application website:
http://www.medstudent.ucla.edu/admiss
Acceptance rate: **4.5%**
In-state acceptance rate: **5.4%**
Out-of-state acceptance rate: **3.1%**
Minority acceptance rate: **7.3%**
International acceptance rate: **1.0%**

Fall 2005 applications and acceptees

	Applied	Interviewed	Accepted	Enrolled
Total:	5,465	698	245	122
In-state:	3,350	486	180	99
Out-of-state:	2,115	212	65	23

Profile of admitted students

Average undergraduate grade point average: **3.71**
MCAT averages (scale: 1-15; writing test: J-T):
  Composite score: **10.8**
  Verbal reasoning score: **9.7**, Physical sciences score: **10.8**, Biological sciences score: **11.1**, Writing score: **Q**
Proportion with undergraduate majors in: Biological sciences: **55%**, Physical sciences: **20%**, Non-sciences: **20%**, Other health professions: **3%**, Mixed disciplines and other: **3%**
Percentage of students not coming directly from college after graduation: **5%**

Dates and details

The American Medical College Application Service (AMCAS) application is accepted.
School asks for a school-specific application as part of the admissions process.
Oldest MCAT considered for Fall 2007 entry: **2004**
Earliest application date for the 2007-2008 first-year class: **June 1, 2006**
Latest application date: **December 1, 2006**
Acceptance dates for regular application for the class entering in fall 2007:

Earliest: **January 1, 2007**
Latest: **August 6, 2007**
The school considers requests for deferred entrance.
Starting month for the class entering in 2007–2008:
  August
The school doesn't have an Early Decision Plan (EDP).
A personal interview is required for admission.

Undergraduate coursework required

Medical school requires undergraduate work in these subjects: biology, English, organic chemistry, inorganic (general) chemistry, physics, mathematics, calculus.

ADMISSIONS POLICY
(TEXT PROVIDED BY SCHOOL):

The David Geffen School of Medicine at UCLA seeks to admit students who embody the mission and goals of the school and will be future leaders in their communities, having distinguished careers in clinical practice, teaching, research, and public service.

The Admissions Committee gives preference to those applicants showing evidence of broad training and high achievement in their college education and possessing those traits of personality and character essential to succeeding in medicine and to providing quality, professional, and humane medical care. The committee looks for applicants who have demonstrated through coursework, school activities, community service, and research evidence of maturity, intellect, scholarship, and service to their communities and for those who are underprivileged and disadvantaged, culturally aware, and able to speak a second language, especially Spanish. We seek a student body with a broad diversity of backgrounds and interests. No preference is given to any particular undergraduate major. Final selections are made on the basis of individual qualifications and not on the basis of race, ethnicity, sex, age, sexual orientation, national origin, or disability.

Students submit their applications through the American Medical College Application Service. Applications are screened by the Admissions Committee. Students who pass this first screen are invited to submit a supplemental application, including letters of recommendation and transcripts. Successful applicants tend to have strong academic records, including firm and clear motivation for medicine. The committee looks for objective evidence that the applicant can handle the academic demands of the medical curriculum. Those judged to possess these necessary skills, knowledge, and attitudes are invited to interview.

Students interview with a faculty member and, if possible, a medical student, who are members of the Admissions Committee. Each student is given a thorough and personal review. Students are accepted each year beginning in January.

COSTS AND FINANCIAL AID

Financial aid phone number: (310) 825-4181
Tuition, 2005-2006 academic year: **In-state: $21,506; Out-of-state: $33,751**
Room and board: **$14,385**
Percentage of students receiving financial aid in 2005-06: **99%**
Percentage of students receiving: Loans: **93%**, Grants/scholarships: **99%**, Work-study aid: **0%**
Average medical school debt for the Class of 2004: **$86,122**

STUDENT BODY

Fall 2005 full-time enrollment: **690**
Men: **47%**, Women: **53%**, In-state: **98%**, Minorities: **64%**, American Indian: **0.4%**, Asian-American: **38.0%**, African-American: **8.8%**, Hispanic-American: **15.9%**, White: **32.8%**, International: **1.0%**, Unknown: **3.0%**

ACADEMIC PROGRAMS

The school's curriculum very frequently gives first-year students substantial contact with patients.
There are opportunities for first- or second-year students to work in community health clinics.
Program offerings: AIDS, drug/alcohol abuse, family medicine, geriatrics, internal medicine, pediatrics, women's health
Joint degrees awarded: M.D./Ph.D., M.D./MBA, M.D./MPH.
Total National Institutes of Health (NIH) grants awarded to the medical school and affiliated hospitals: **$426.8 million**

CURRICULUM

(TEXT PROVIDED BY SCHOOL):
The David Geffen School of Medicine at UCLA seeks to prepare its graduates for distinguished careers in clinical practice, teaching, research, and public service. Recognizing that medical school is but one phase in a physician's education, the curriculum is designed to create an environment in which students prepare for a future in which scientific knowledge, societal values, and human needs are ever changing.

Critical competencies developed throughout the curriculum include: an enthusiasm for lifelong learning; a commitment to humanistic, compassionate, and ethical care of individuals and families; skills in effective communication;

attainment of a broad and flexible base of knowledge and skills; an understanding of the scientific method and its application to clinical practice and research; a commitment to promote the community's health and well-being; ability to lead in settings of rapidly changing technology and societal needs; and a readiness to address complex societal and medical issues.

The UCLA curriculum consists of three phases. In Human Biology and Disease (Phase 1), students complete eight sequential, interdisciplinary block courses with an emphasis on the integration of basic, clinical, and social sciences. The grading system is pass/fail across all parts of the curriculum.

The Clinical Core (Phase 2) begins with a two-week foundation experience in which students prepare for working in ambulatory and hospital settings. This is followed by six core clerkships over a total of 48 weeks: inpatient medicine, ambulatory care (family medicine, internal medicine), obstetrics/gynecology, pediatrics, psychiatry/neurology, and surgery/ophthalmology. Students also participate in longitudinal courses: radiology, doctoring, and a preceptorship that allows them to work with community physicians.

Before beginning the College Phase (3), students join one of four colleges: Applied Anatomy, Acute Care, Primary Care, and Medical Sciences. Students enrolled in UCLA's joint degree programs for the MBA or MPH have a separate college on Healthcare Leadership.

FACULTY PROFILE (FALL 2005)

Total teaching faculty: 2,102 **(full-time)**, 217 **(part-time)**
Of full-time faculty, those teaching in basic sciences: **21%**; in clinical programs: **79%**
Of part-time faculty, those teaching in basic sciences: **33%**; in clinical programs: **67%**
Full-time faculty/student ratio: **3.0**

SUPPORT SERVICES

The school offers students these services for dealing with stress: expanded-hour gym access, professional counseling, religious support, support groups.

RESIDENCY PROFILE

Most popular residency and specialty programs chosen by the 2004 and 2005 M.D. graduating classes: anesthesiology, dermatology, emergency medicine, family practice, internal medicine, orthopaedic surgery, pediatrics, psychiatry, radiology–diagnostic, surgery–general.

WHERE GRADS GO

39.7%
Proportion of 2003-2005 graduates who entered primary care specialties

75%
Proportion of 2004-2005 graduates who accepted in-state residencies

University of California–San Diego

■ 9500 Gilman Drive, La Jolla, CA 92093-0602
■ Public
■ Year Founded: 1965
■ Tuition, 2005-2006: In-state: $22,008; Out-of-state: $34,253
■ Enrollment 2005-2006 academic year: 503
■ Website: http://meded.ucsd.edu/
■ Specialty ranking: AIDS: 6, drug/alcohol abuse: 8, family medicine: 17, internal medicine: 21, women's health: 21

3.73 AVERAGE GPA, ENTERING CLASS FALL 2005

11.0 AVERAGE MCAT, ENTERING CLASS FALL 2005

6.0% ACCEPTANCE RATE, ENTERING CLASS FALL 2005

14 2007 U.S. NEWS MEDICAL SCHOOL RANKING (RESEARCH)

33 2007 U.S. NEWS MEDICAL SCHOOL RANKING (PRIMARY CARE)

ADMISSIONS
Admissions phone number: **(858) 534-3880**
Admissions email address: **somadmissions@ucsd.edu**
Application website: **http://meded.ucsd.edu/admissions/**
Acceptance rate: **6.0%**
In-state acceptance rate: **8.0%**
Out-of-state acceptance rate: **2.3%**
Minority acceptance rate: **7.0%**
International acceptance rate: **0.0%**

Fall 2005 applications and acceptees

	Applied	Interviewed	Accepted	Enrolled
Total:	5,018	629	301	122
In-state:	3,249	522	261	113
Out-of-state:	1,769	107	40	9

Profile of admitted students
Average undergraduate grade point average: **3.73**
MCAT averages (scale: 1-15; writing test: J-T):
   Composite score: **11.0**
   Verbal reasoning score: **10.2**, Physical sciences score: **11.3**, Biological sciences score: **11.5**, Writing score: **Q**
Proportion with undergraduate majors in: Biological sciences: **52%**, Physical sciences: **25%**, Non-sciences: **10%**, Other health professions: **0%**, Mixed disciplines and other: **13%**
Percentage of students not coming directly from college after graduation: **66%**

Dates and details
The American Medical College Application Service (AMCAS) application is accepted.
School asks for a school-specific application as part of the admissions process.
Oldest MCAT considered for Fall 2007 entry: **2004**
Earliest application date for the 2007-2008 first-year class: **June 1, 2006**
Latest application date: **November 1, 2006**
Acceptance dates for regular application for the class entering in fall 2007:
   Earliest: **October 15, 2006**

   Latest: **September 1, 2007**
The school considers requests for deferred entrance.
Starting month for the class entering in 2007–2008:
   September
The school doesn't have an Early Decision Plan (EDP).
A personal interview is required for admission.

Undergraduate coursework required
Medical school requires undergraduate work in these subjects: biology, organic chemistry, inorganic (general) chemistry, physics, mathematics.

ADMISSIONS POLICY
(TEXT PROVIDED BY SCHOOL):
The University of California, San Diego School of Medicine's admission requirements include a minimum of three years of college or university education, at least one year of which has to have been undertaken in the United States. Consideration is given only to applicants who are U.S. citizens or permanent residents. Coursework requirements are: a year each of general/inorganic chemistry, organic chemistry, general physics, general biology, and mathematics (calculus or beyond, including statistics or computer science). Beyond the course requirements, applications are evaluated without regard to undergraduate major.
   Initially, the American Medical College Application Service application is evaluated by a member of the executive committee of the school's Recruitment and Admissions Committee (RAC). The application is examined to judge each applicant's academic preparation for medical school, knowledge and interest in a medical career, and motivation. Also considered are factors such as demonstrated ability to overcome social, economic, and educational disadvantage and/or willingness to practice medicine in an underserved region or community. Selected applicants are sent a secondary application. Additional material requested includes letters of reference, a personal autobiography, and further details about a candidate's leadership activities, community service, exposure to the clinical/medical workplace, and

research, as well as any extraordinary skills in sports, music, art, government, and so on.

Selected candidates are invited for a personal interview with two RAC members. Following the interview, each interviewer produces a summary of his or her impression of the candidate's suitability. The full RAC assigns each applicant a final rating. The school has a rolling admissions process. Offers of acceptance are made from October 15 on.

COSTS AND FINANCIAL AID

Financial aid phone number: (858) 534-4664
Tuition, 2005-2006 academic year: **In-state: $22,008; Out-of-state: $34,253**
Room and board: **$11,657**
Percentage of students receiving financial aid in 2005-06: **84%**
Percentage of students receiving: Loans: **82%**, Grants/scholarships: **63%**, Work-study aid: **2%**
Average medical school debt for the Class of 2004: **$66,642**

STUDENT BODY

Fall 2005 full-time enrollment: **503**
Men: **51%**, Women: **49%**, In-state: **97%**, Minorities: **49%**, American Indian: **1.0%**, Asian-American: **38.6%**, African-American: **2.0%**, Hispanic-American: **7.8%**, White: **37.4%**, International: **0.0%**, Unknown: **13.3%**

ACADEMIC PROGRAMS

The school's curriculum frequently gives first-year students substantial contact with patients.
There are opportunities for first- or second-year students to work in community health clinics.
Program offerings: AIDS, drug/alcohol abuse, family medicine, geriatrics, internal medicine, pediatrics, rural medicine, women's health
Joint degrees awarded: M.D./Ph.D., M.D./MPH, M.D./MS
Total National Institutes of Health (NIH) grants awarded to the medical school and affiliated hospitals: **$273.7 million**

CURRICULUM

(TEXT PROVIDED BY SCHOOL):
The UCSD School of Medicine seeks to train humanistic physicians and physician-scientists who are also highly skilled practitioners, innovators, and leaders. The goal of the curriculum is to prepare physicians who are scientifically expert, clinically astute, responsive to community problems, and compassionate in patient care.

The preclinical curriculum emphasizes not only basic sciences but also medical skills. In addition to courses like biochemistry and microbiology, curricular content includes doctor-patient communication, ethics, and alternative medicine. The school capitalizes on the superb basic science departments on UCSD's general campus. Scientists and clinicians work together in the school's clinical departments, and both are heavily involved in teaching the first two years

of medical school. During those two years, students complete 227 hours of preclinical electives, which may include everything from preceptorships to learning how to take a history in Spanish, Mandarin Chinese, or sign language.

During the third year, students complete 12-week rotations in medicine and surgery, six-week rotations in psychiatry and reproductive medicine, a four-week rotation in neurology, and an eight-week pediatric experience, in addition to a yearlong continuity clerkship in primary care. Fourth-year students may choose from several hundred electives. At least 12 weeks of direct patient care are required. Passing an examination that uses standardized patients is a graduation requirement. The fourth year also contains a 90-hour course entitled Principles to Practice, which integrates basic science principles into clinical medicine and prepares students better for residency. Students also must complete an independent study project before graduation. Students are required to pass both Step 1 and Step 2 of the U.S. Medical Licensing Examination to graduate.

Graduates are prepared to enter residencies in every surgical, medical, or hospital-based specialty offered today or to enter a career in primary-care medicine. Advanced training opportunities are available for medical students leading to master's and Ph.D degrees in multiple disciplines.

FACULTY PROFILE (FALL 2005)

Total teaching faculty: **797 (full-time)**, **34 (part-time)**
Of full-time faculty, those teaching in basic sciences: **26%**; in clinical programs: **74%**
Of part-time faculty, those teaching in basic sciences: **32%**; in clinical programs: **68%**
Full-time faculty/student ratio: **1.6**

SUPPORT SERVICES

The school offers students these services for dealing with stress: expanded-hour gym access, peer counseling, professional counseling, religious support, support groups.

RESIDENCY PROFILE

Most popular residency and specialty programs chosen by the 2004 and 2005 M.D. graduating classes: anesthesiology, pediatric anesthesiology, dermatology, emergency medicine, family practice, internal medicine, obstetrics and gynecology, pediatrics, psychiatry, radiology–diagnostic, surgery–general.

WHERE GRADS GO

41.4%
Proportion of 2003-2005 graduates who entered primary care specialties

70.3%
Proportion of 2004-2005 graduates who accepted in-state residencies

University of California–San Francisco

- 513 Parnassus Avenue, Room S224, San Francisco, CA 94143-0410
- Public
- **Year Founded:** 1864
- **Tuition, 2005-2006:** In-state: $22,328; Out-of-state: $34,573
- **Enrollment 2005-2006 academic year:** 600
- **Website:** http://medschool.ucsf.edu/
- **Specialty ranking:** AIDS: 1, drug/alcohol abuse: 5, family medicine: 10, geriatrics: 9, internal medicine: 2, pediatrics: 8, women's health: 2

3.79 AVERAGE GPA, ENTERING CLASS FALL 2005

11.3 AVERAGE MCAT, ENTERING CLASS FALL 2005

4.9% ACCEPTANCE RATE, ENTERING CLASS FALL 2005

4 2007 U.S. NEWS MEDICAL SCHOOL RANKING (RESEARCH)

10 2007 U.S. NEWS MEDICAL SCHOOL RANKING (PRIMARY CARE)

ADMISSIONS
Admissions phone number: **(415) 476-4044**
Admissions email address: **admissions@medsch.ucsf.edu**
Application website:
  http://medschool.ucsf.edu/admissions/
Acceptance rate: **4.9%**
In-state acceptance rate: **6.6%**
Out-of-state acceptance rate: **2.9%**
Minority acceptance rate: **6.1%**
International acceptance rate: **0.0%**

Fall 2005 applications and acceptees
	Applied	Interviewed	Accepted	Enrolled
Total:	5,298	538	257	141
In-state:	2,778	N/A	184	117
Out-of-state:	2,520	N/A	73	24

Profile of admitted students
Average undergraduate grade point average: **3.79**
MCAT averages (scale: 1-15; writing test: J-T):
  Composite score: **11.3**
  Verbal reasoning score: **10.6**, Physical sciences score: **11.5**, Biological sciences score: **11.7**, Writing score: **P**
Proportion with undergraduate majors in: Biological sciences: **N/A**, Physical sciences: **N/A**, Non-sciences: **N/A**, Other health professions: **N/A**, Mixed disciplines and other: **N/A**
Percentage of students not coming directly from college after graduation: **70%**

Dates and details
The American Medical College Application Service (AMCAS) application is accepted.
School asks for a school-specific application as part of the admissions process.
Oldest MCAT considered for Fall 2007 entry: **2004**
Earliest application date for the 2007-2008 first-year class: **June 1, 2006**
Latest application date: **November 1, 2006**
Acceptance dates for regular application for the class entering in fall 2007:

Earliest: **December 15, 2006**
Latest: **N/A**
The school considers requests for deferred entrance.
Starting month for the class entering in 2007–2008: **September**
The school doesn't have an Early Decision Plan (EDP).
A personal interview is required for admission.

Undergraduate coursework required
Medical school requires undergraduate work in these subjects: biology/zoology, organic chemistry, inorganic (general) chemistry, physics.

ADMISSIONS POLICY
(TEXT PROVIDED BY SCHOOL):
Please refer to the University of California, San Francisco School of Medicine admissions website for specific details regarding policies, preferences, criteria, selection factors, and procedures.

COSTS AND FINANCIAL AID
Financial aid phone number: **(415) 476-4181**
Tuition, 2005-2006 academic year: **In-state: $22,328; Out-of-state: $34,573**
Room and board: **$18,570**
Percentage of students receiving financial aid in 2005-06: **91%**
Percentage of students receiving: Loans: **85%**, Grants/scholarships: **88%**, Work-study aid: **1%**
Average medical school debt for the Class of 2004: **$76,573**

STUDENT BODY
Fall 2005 full-time enrollment: **600**
Men: **44%**, Women: **57%**, In-state: **95%**, Minorities: **49%**, American Indian: **1.3%**, Asian-American: **32.5%**, African-American: **4.3%**, Hispanic-American: **11.8%**, White: **48.8%**, International: **0.2%**, Unknown: **1.0%**

ACADEMIC PROGRAMS
The school's curriculum very frequently gives first-year students substantial contact with patients.

There are opportunities for first- or second-year students to work in community health clinics.

Program offerings: AIDS, drug/alcohol abuse, family medicine, geriatrics, internal medicine, pediatrics, rural medicine, women's health

Joint degrees awarded: M.D./Ph.D., M.D./MPH, M.D./MS

Total National Institutes of Health (NIH) grants awarded to the medical school and affiliated hospitals: **$422.9 million**

CURRICULUM

(TEXT PROVIDED BY SCHOOL):

UCSF's curriculum emphasizes interdisciplinary approaches and clinical context to prepare students for leadership and professional success in the science and service of health care for the future. The first two years, the Essential Core (EC) curriculum, is a series of integrated block courses weaving together basic, clinical, and social sciences. Extensive use of clinical cases motivates learners, increases retention, and enhances critical thinking. To promote self-directed and collaborative learning, formal class time is limited to 24 hours per week and small groups settings constitute half of all instructional hours. The electronic curriculum, iROCKET, fosters team learning through online forums and cooperative projects. Simulation labs support the development, integration and application of EC content and skill. Faculty-led advisory colleges serve as communities supporting professional development. EC courses include foundations of Patient Care: a longitudinal block that spans the entire EC and comprises clinical skills, professional development, and clinical reasoning.

The Clinical Core (CC), the third year, comprises required core clerkships in: Anesthesia; Family and Community Medicine; Internal Medicine; Neurology; Obstetrics and Gynecology; Pediatrics; Psychiatry; Surgery; and Surgical Specialties. Eight-week clerkship blocks are punctuated by three one-week Intersessions, when students discuss and reflect on clinical experiences, and focus on clinical decision-making, ethics, health policy and systems, and advances in medical science. Throughout the CC, every student participates in an ambulatory Longitudinal Clinical Experience, one half-day each week in a field of student choice. Clinical Skills Labs support the development, practice and assessment of clinical and communication skills.

Advanced Studies, the fourth year, prepares students for post-graduate study and offers ample elective options, including the Area of Concentration (AoC) program, where students work with faculty to identify a project, focus their inquiry, design a program of preparation, complete the project, and finally produce and present a tangible legacy. The AoCs include: Community Health and Social Advocacy; Global and Public Health; Humanities and Social Sciences in Medicine; Medical Education; The Health Care System and the Physician-Leader; The Science of Medicine and the Physician-Investigator.

For more information please see http://medschool.ucsf .edu/curriculum.

FACULTY PROFILE (FALL 2005)

Total teaching faculty: **1,604 (full-time), 59 (part-time)**
Of full-time faculty, those teaching in basic sciences: 9%; in clinical programs: 91%
Of part-time faculty, those teaching in basic sciences: 17%; in clinical programs: 83%
Full-time faculty/student ratio: 2.7

SUPPORT SERVICES

The school offers students these services for dealing with stress: expanded-hour gym access, professional counseling, support groups.

RESIDENCY PROFILE

Most popular residency and specialty programs chosen by the 2004 and 2005 M.D. graduating classes: anesthesiology, emergency medicine, family practice, internal medicine, obstetrics and gynecology, ophthalmology, pediatrics, psychiatry, radiology–diagnostic, surgery–general.

WHERE GRADS GO

34.5%
Proportion of 2003-2005 graduates who entered primary care specialties

63.7%
Proportion of 2004-2005 graduates who accepted in-state residencies

University of Chicago

PRITZKER

- 5841 S. Maryland Avenue, MC 1000, Chicago, IL 60637-5416
- Private
- **Year Founded:** 1927
- **Tuition, 2005-2006:** $34,701
- **Enrollment 2005-2006 academic year:** 416
- **Website:** http://pritzker.bsd.uchicago.edu
- **Specialty ranking:** drug/alcohol abuse: 19, internal medicine: 13

3.74 AVERAGE GPA, ENTERING CLASS FALL 2005

10.9 AVERAGE MCAT, ENTERING CLASS FALL 2005

7.2% ACCEPTANCE RATE, ENTERING CLASS FALL 2005

17 2007 U.S. NEWS MEDICAL SCHOOL RANKING (RESEARCH)

49 2007 U.S. NEWS MEDICAL SCHOOL RANKING (PRIMARY CARE)

ADMISSIONS

Admissions phone number: **(773) 702-1937**
Admissions email address:
  pritzkeradmissions@bsd.uchicago.edu
Application website: **N/A**
Acceptance rate: **7.2%**
In-state acceptance rate: **10.9%**
Out-of-state acceptance rate: **6.6%**
Minority acceptance rate: **9.0%**
International acceptance rate: **3.1%**

Fall 2005 applications and acceptees

	Applied	Interviewed	Accepted	Enrolled
Total:	3,830	599	277	104
In-state:	561	130	61	38
Out-of-state:	3,269	469	216	66

Profile of admitted students

Average undergraduate grade point average: **3.74**
MCAT averages (scale: 1-15; writing test: J-T):
  Composite score: **10.9**
  Verbal reasoning score: **10.5**, Physical sciences score:
  11.0, Biological sciences score: **11.3**, Writing score: **Q**
Proportion with undergraduate majors in: Biological
  sciences: **39%**, Physical sciences: **25%**, Non-sciences:
  14%, Other health professions: **0%**, Mixed disciplines
  and other: **22%**
Percentage of students not coming directly from college
  after graduation: **49%**

Dates and details

The American Medical College Application Service
  (AMCAS) application is accepted.
School asks for a school-specific application as part of the
  admissions process.
Oldest MCAT considered for Fall 2007 entry: **2004**
Earliest application date for the 2007-2008 first-year class:
  June 1, 2006
Latest application date: **December 1, 2006**
Acceptance dates for regular application for the class
  entering in fall 2007:

Earliest: **October 15, 2006**
Latest: **September 15, 2007**
The school considers requests for deferred entrance.
Starting month for the class entering in 2007–2008:
  September
The school has an Early Decision Plan (EDP).
A personal interview is required for admission.

Undergraduate coursework required

Medical school requires undergraduate work in these subjects: biology, organic chemistry, inorganic (general) chemistry, physics.

ADMISSIONS POLICY

(TEXT PROVIDED BY SCHOOL):

The goal of the University of Chicago Pritzker School of
Medicine is to graduate accomplished physicians who
aspire to excellence as outstanding physician-scientists,
medical educators and clinical scholars. Pritzker traditionally attracts and recruits culturally diverse student leaders
with strong academic backgrounds and personal accomplishments. By the time each class graduates, over 90 percent of students have explored scholarly pursuits outside
the required academic program. Pritzker graduates are
known to acquire superb skills in medical reasoning, problem-solving, team-building, and lifelong learning. These
skills ultimately help them assume leadership roles in their
residency training programs and clinical practices and as
faculty in academic medicine.

Once application materials are complete, the Committee
on Admissions reviews the candidate's entire application.
Applicants whose credentials are favorably reviewed are
invited to visit the campus for an interview day. The interviews provide the committee with an opportunity to get to
know the candidate, while the candidate has the opportunity
to ask questions and obtain insights into the school, curriculum, faculty, and student body. As part of the visit, candidates are given an orientation to Pritzker and the
University of Chicago, provided information on financial
aid, given a tour of the medical center, and given a lunch
hosted by medical students.

Offers of admission are made solely on the basis of ability, achievement, motivation, and humanistic qualities. Successful applicants have demonstrated a passion for lifelong learning, a commitment to others and to the goals of medicine, and leadership among their peers.

COSTS AND FINANCIAL AID
Financial aid phone number: **(773) 702-1938**
Tuition, 2005-2006 academic year: **$34,701**
Room and board: **$10,071**
Percentage of students receiving financial aid in 2005-06: **92%**
Percentage of students receiving: Loans: **79%**, Grants/scholarships: **85%**, Work-study aid: **2%**
Average medical school debt for the Class of 2004: **$144,900**

STUDENT BODY
Fall 2005 full-time enrollment: **416**
Men: **49%**, Women: **51%**, In-state: **35%**, Minorities: **34%**, American Indian: **0.2%**, Asian-American: **20.4%**, African-American: **8.2%**, Hispanic-American: **5.0%**, White: **62.5%**, International: **3.4%**, Unknown: **0.2%**

ACADEMIC PROGRAMS
The school's curriculum frequently gives first-year students substantial contact with patients.
There are opportunities for first- or second-year students to work in community health clinics.
Program offerings: AIDS, drug/alcohol abuse, family medicine, geriatrics, internal medicine, pediatrics, women's health
Joint degrees awarded: M.D./Ph.D., M.D./MBA, M.D./JD, M.D./M.S.W., M.D./MHA.
Total National Institutes of Health (NIH) grants awarded to the medical school and affiliated hospitals: **$197.8 million**

CURRICULUM
(TEXT PROVIDED BY SCHOOL):
At the University of Chicago, in an atmosphere of interdisciplinary scholarship and discovery, the Pritzker School of Medicine is dedicated to inspiring diverse students of exceptional promise to become leaders and innovators in science and medicine for the betterment of humanity. Pritzker operates on a pass/fail grading system to encourage students to develop teamwork skills, to discover and develop their unique talents and to promote cooperative learning through focused curricular and co-curricular activities.

These medical education programs include the following:
• Integration of basic science and clinical medicine across the four years of the curriculum;
• Clinical experiences with patients and standardized patients beginning the first quarter of medical school;
• Summer research training in which over 70 percent of students participate, as well as extensive opportunities to continue research throughout medical school;

• Required core clerkships combining ambulatory and inpatient experiences taught by full-time faculty to promote and model clinical proficiency;
• Web based programs and instruction in academic computing and medical informatics;
• Opportunities to participate in combined degree programs such as M.D./ Ph.D and M.D./JD, master degree programs (MBA, MPH, MPP) and other research experiences subscribed by a quarter of each class;
• Opportunities to develop teaching skills as assistants and in some medical courses;
• An extensive array of co-curricular activities that provide the arena for students to further develop their altruism, collegiality, leadership, and professionalism;
• Integration of humanism in medicine through programs such as the White Coat Ceremony, Student Symposia and Retreats, and the Clinical Reflections Ceremony.

The University of Chicago Pritzker School of Medicine provides more than training in medicine. It provides an immersion into the scholarship of a prestigious university, where the medical school, the hospitals, and the university share the same campus; where interdisciplinary research and teaching are the norm, not the exception; and where recognized experts from all disciplines contribute to the development of young physicians in training.

FACULTY PROFILE (FALL 2005)
Total teaching faculty: **781 (full-time)**, **247 (part-time)**
Of full-time faculty, those teaching in basic sciences: **15%**; in clinical programs: **85%**
Of part-time faculty, those teaching in basic sciences: **1%**; in clinical programs: **99%**
Full-time faculty/student ratio: **1.9**

SUPPORT SERVICES
The school offers students these services for dealing with stress: expanded-hour gym access, peer counseling, professional counseling, religious support, support groups.

RESIDENCY PROFILE
Most popular residency and specialty programs chosen by the 2004 and 2005 M.D. graduating classes: emergency medicine, internal medicine, orthopaedic surgery, pediatrics, plastic surgery, psychiatry, radiology–diagnostic, surgery–general, urology, transitional year.

WHERE GRADS GO
47%
Proportion of 2003-2005 graduates who entered primary care specialties

43%
Proportion of 2004-2005 graduates who accepted in-state residencies

University of Cincinnati

■ Office of Student Affairs and Admissions, Cincinnati, OH
45267-0552
■ Public
■ Year Founded: 1819
■ Tuition, 2005-2006: In-state: $23,580; Out-of-state: $41,004
■ Enrollment 2005-2006 academic year: 629
■ Website: http://www.med.uc.edu
■ Specialty ranking: pediatrics: 4

3.59 AVERAGE GPA, ENTERING CLASS FALL 2005

10.1 AVERAGE MCAT, ENTERING CLASS FALL 2005

11.5% ACCEPTANCE RATE, ENTERING CLASS FALL 2005

42 2007 U.S. NEWS MEDICAL SCHOOL RANKING (RESEARCH)

Unranked 2007 U.S. NEWS MEDICAL SCHOOL RANKING (PRIMARY CARE)

ADMISSIONS
Admissions phone number: **(513) 558-7314**
Admissions email address: **comadmis@ucmail.uc.edu**
Application website: **http://comdows.uc.edu/MedOneStop/**
Acceptance rate: **11.5%**
In-state acceptance rate: **24.5%**
Out-of-state acceptance rate: **5.4%**
Minority acceptance rate: **N/A**
International acceptance rate: **0.0%**

Fall 2005 applications and acceptees
	Applied	Interviewed	Accepted	Enrolled
Total:	2,971	627	343	160
In-state:	954	348	234	120
Out-of-state:	2,017	279	109	40

Profile of admitted students
Average undergraduate grade point average: **3.59**
MCAT averages (scale: 1-15; writing test: J-T):
Composite score: **10.1**
Verbal reasoning score: **9.7**, Physical sciences score: **10.1**,
Biological sciences score: **10.5**, Writing score: **O**
Proportion with undergraduate majors in: Biological
sciences: **51%**, Physical sciences: **20%**, Non-sciences:
18%, Other health professions: **2%**, Mixed disciplines
and other: **9%**
Percentage of students not coming directly from college
after graduation: **61%**

Dates and details
The American Medical College Application Service
(AMCAS) application is accepted.
School asks for a school-specific application as part of the
admissions process.
Oldest MCAT considered for Fall 2007 entry: **2004**
Earliest application date for the 2007-2008 first-year class:
June 1, 2006
Latest application date: **November 15, 2006**
Acceptance dates for regular application for the class
entering in fall 2007:
Earliest: **October 15, 2006**

Latest: **August 7, 2007**
The school considers requests for deferred entrance.
Starting month for the class entering in 2007–2008:
August
The school has an Early Decision Plan (EDP).
A personal interview is required for admission.

ADMISSIONS POLICY
(TEXT PROVIDED BY SCHOOL):
In addition to the American Medical College Application
Service application, the University of Cincinnati requires all
prospective students to complete an online supplementary
form. Applicants are directed to our website to complete
this secondary process. Once the secondary application and
letters of recommendation are received, the applicant will
be evaluated for an interview. In addition to the online
application, the website provides information about the
progress of each applicant in the admissions process.
The Interview Day Program is designed to present a brief
description of the college and student services. It will
include one interview, presentations on the admissions
process, the curriculum, student services, lunch, and a tour.
Notification of final decisions will be made typically
within three to five weeks. Prior to January, acceptances
may be sent on a weekly basis.
Offers of acceptance are based upon the overall evaluation of applicants' academic and personal qualities.
Postbaccalaureate and graduate coursework will be considered.

COSTS AND FINANCIAL AID
Financial aid phone number: **(513) 558-6797**
Tuition, 2005-2006 academic year: **In-state: $23,580; Out-
of-state: $41,004**
Room and board: **$15,191**
Percentage of students receiving financial aid in 2005-06:
87%
Percentage of students receiving: Loans: **85%**,
Grants/scholarships: **40%**, Work-study aid: **2%**
Average medical school debt for the Class of 2004:
$119,355

STUDENT BODY

Fall 2005 full-time enrollment: **629**

Men: **56%**, Women: **44%**, In-state: **94%**, Minorities: **28%**, American Indian: **0.0%**, Asian-American: **18.6%**, African-American: **8.4%**, Hispanic-American: **0.3%**, White: **72.7%**, International: **N/A**, Unknown: **N/A**

ACADEMIC PROGRAMS

The school's curriculum frequently gives first-year students substantial contact with patients.

There are opportunities for first- or second-year students to work in community health clinics.

Program offerings: AIDS, drug/alcohol abuse, family medicine, geriatrics, internal medicine, pediatrics, rural medicine, women's health

Joint degrees awarded: M.D./Ph.D., M.D./MBA.

Total National Institutes of Health (NIH) grants awarded to the medical school and affiliated hospitals: **$190.2 million**

CURRICULUM

(TEXT PROVIDED BY SCHOOL):

The College uses an integrated curricular approach and a variety of teaching modalities including lab, small group discussion, and team-based learning, along with traditional lectures. The major focus of the first year is the normal structure, function and development of the human body. The second year emphasizes the basis and mechanisms of human disease. The Clinical Foundations of Medical Practice Course in years 1 and 2 provides students with exposure to medical ethics, sexual health, nutrition, and end of life care. Clinical experiences in the medical interview and physical examination and diagnosis are fully integrated into the first two years, utilizing both standardized patients and visits to hospital, physicians' offices and clinics.

Year 3 includes required rotations through Family Medicine, Internal Medicine, OB/GYN, Pediatrics, Psychiatry, Surgery and Radiology. In year 4, students hone their clinical skills during the required Acting Internship and participate in a required Neuroscience rotation. The College offers more than 100 electives. Throughout, clinical training students are exposed to clinical procedures both in the Clinical Skills Lab and at the bedside. Realistic simulation programs, models and mannequins are utilized to prepare students for patient contact.

FACULTY PROFILE (FALL 2005)

Total teaching faculty: **1,365 (full-time)**, **115 (part-time)**

Of full-time faculty, those teaching in basic sciences: **8%**; in clinical programs: **92%**

Of part-time faculty, those teaching in basic sciences: **4%**; in clinical programs: **96%**

Full-time faculty/student ratio: **2.2**

SUPPORT SERVICES

The school offers students these services for dealing with stress: expanded-hour gym access, peer counseling, professional counseling, support groups.

RESIDENCY PROFILE

Most popular residency and specialty programs chosen by the 2004 and 2005 M.D. graduating classes: anesthesiology, emergency medicine, family practice, internal medicine, orthopaedic surgery, pathology–anatomic and clinical, pediatrics, psychiatry, radiology–diagnostic, surgery–general.

WHERE GRADS GO

36%

Proportion of 2003-2005 graduates who entered primary care specialties

48%

Proportion of 2004-2005 graduates who accepted in-state residencies

University of Colorado

HEALTH SCIENCES CENTER

- 4200 E. Ninth Avenue, Box C290, Denver, CO 80262
- Public
- Year Founded: 1883
- Tuition, 2005-2006: In-state: $21,218; Out-of-state: $72,791
- Enrollment 2005-2006 academic year: 561
- Website: http://www.uchsc.edu/sm/sm/mddgree.htm
- Specialty ranking: family medicine: 12, internal medicine: 26, pediatrics: 7

3.74 AVERAGE GPA, ENTERING CLASS FALL 2005

11.0 AVERAGE MCAT, ENTERING CLASS FALL 2005

9.7% ACCEPTANCE RATE, ENTERING CLASS FALL 2005

26 2007 U.S. NEWS MEDICAL SCHOOL RANKING (RESEARCH)

6 2007 U.S. NEWS MEDICAL SCHOOL RANKING (PRIMARY CARE)

ADMISSIONS

Admissions phone number: **(303) 315-7361**
Admissions email address: **somadmin@uchsc.edu**
Application website: **http://www.aamc.org**
Acceptance rate: **9.7%**
In-state acceptance rate: **24.2%**
Out-of-state acceptance rate: **5.4%**
Minority acceptance rate: **6.4%**
International acceptance rate: **4.5%**

Fall 2005 applications and acceptees

	Applied	Interviewed	Accepted	Enrolled
Total:	2,526	558	246	143
In-state:	583	330	141	108
Out-of-state:	1,943	228	105	35

Profile of admitted students

Average undergraduate grade point average: **3.74**
MCAT averages (scale: 1-15; writing test: J-T):
  Composite score: **11.0**
  Verbal reasoning score: **11.0**, Physical sciences score: **11.0**, Biological sciences score: **11.0**, Writing score: **Q**
Proportion with undergraduate majors in: Biological sciences: **32%**, Physical sciences: **25%**, Non-sciences: **20%**, Other health professions: **1%**, Mixed disciplines and other: **22%**
Percentage of students not coming directly from college after graduation: **80%**

Dates and details

The American Medical College Application Service (AMCAS) application is accepted.
School asks for a school-specific application as part of the admissions process.
Oldest MCAT considered for Fall 2007 entry: **2004**
Earliest application date for the 2007-2008 first-year class: **June 1, 2006**
Latest application date: **November 1, 2006**
Acceptance dates for regular application for the class entering in fall 2007:
  Earliest: **October 16, 2006**

Latest: **March 31, 2007**
The school considers requests for deferred entrance.
Starting month for the class entering in 2007-2008:
  August
The school doesn't have an Early Decision Plan (EDP).
A personal interview is required for admission.

Undergraduate coursework required

Medical school requires undergraduate work in these subjects: biology, English, organic chemistry, inorganic (general) chemistry, physics, mathematics.

ADMISSIONS POLICY

(TEXT PROVIDED BY SCHOOL):
Places are offered to the applicants who appear to the Admissions Committee to be the most highly qualified in terms of academic and intellectual achievement, character, motivation, maturity, service, and emotional stability. For this assessment, college grades, MCAT scores, letters of recommendation and personal interviews are used. Interviews are arranged for applicants who have a good chance of being accepted, and no applicant will be accepted without a personal interview.

Of the 144 places in each class, approximately 75 percent will be awarded to Colorado residents. Thereafter, preference will be given to applicants from certain western states participating in the WICHE program and to applicants from other states who have high GPAs and MCAT scores.

COSTS AND FINANCIAL AID

Financial aid phone number: **(303) 556-2866**
Tuition, 2005-2006 academic year: **In-state: $21,218; Out-of-state: $72,791**
Room and board: **$11,250**
Percentage of students receiving financial aid in 2005-06: **92%**
Percentage of students receiving: Loans: **89%**, Grants/scholarships: **56%**, Work-study aid: **4%**
Average medical school debt for the Class of 2004: **$105,755**

STUDENT BODY

Fall 2005 full-time enrollment: **561**
Men: **52%**, Women: **48%**, In-state: **92%**, Minorities: **19%**,
American Indian: **0.9%**, Asian-American: **8.2%**, African-
American: **2.9%**, Hispanic-American: **7.1%**, White:
80.9%, International: **0.0%**, Unknown: **0.0%**

ACADEMIC PROGRAMS

The school's curriculum frequently gives first-year students
substantial contact with patients.
There are opportunities for first- or second-year students to
work in community health clinics.
Program offerings: AIDS, drug/alcohol abuse, family
medicine, geriatrics, internal medicine, pediatrics, rural
medicine, women's health
Joint degrees awarded: M.D./Ph.D., M.D./MBA.
Total National Institutes of Health (NIH) grants awarded to
the medical school and affiliated hospitals: **$223.1 million**

CURRICULUM
(TEXT PROVIDED BY SCHOOL):

The University of Colorado School of Medicine is imple-
menting a new curriculum, beginning with the class entering in 2005, in which clinical and basic science material are
integrated throughout all 4 years. The Essentials Core curriculum comprises the first 18 months of medical education. It is separated into 2 phases, separated by a 10-week
break for individual activities. Each phase of the Essentials
Core consists of a series of interdisciplinary blocks that
present basic science material in a clinical context. Phase 1
includes 5 blocks: human body, molecules to medicine, disease & defense, blood & lymph, and cardiovascular, pulmonary, & renal. Phase 2 includes 4 blocks: nervous
system, metabolism, infectious disease, and life cycle. The
aim of the Essentials Core is to provide the scientific foundation for the student's further medical education and to
begin to equip each student for a lifetime of learning,
research and/or clinical care, and community service.

The Clinical Core (Phase 3) begins in April of the 2nd
year and fully immerses students in the culture of medicine
and direct patient care. It is comprised of six interdepartmental clerk shop blocks providing intensive clinical experiences in hospitals, ambulatory clinics, emergency and
operating rooms, and community, rural, and urban environments. In addition to a focus on clinical skills and clinical
reasoning, underlying basic science concepts will be reinforced and applied. Most of the clerkship blocks use AHEC
sites scattered throughout Colorado; each student is likely to
have at least one clerkship at a distant location.

The Foundations of Doctoring curriculum extends
through Phases 1-3, and is focused on physical exam and

communications skills, and includes a three-year ambulatory preceptor experience.

Phase 4 is advanced studies, which includes clinical electives, a sub-internship, residency preparation, and an
advanced basic science and clinical skills course.

Additional material on humanities, ethics, & professionalism; medicine & society; cultural competency & diversity,
and informatics & evidence-based medicine is threaded
through all 4 years, as is a program of mentored scholarly
activity.

A simulation center using standardized patients is utilized for both teaching and evaluation of students' knowledge, skills and attitudes. Gynecologic and urologic teaching
associates teach students the breast, pelvic, male genital,
rectal and prostate examination. Assessments are conducted
in the first three years. Students planning a career in academic medicine participate in the medical scientist training
program involving research and doctoral thesis work resulting in both the M.D. and Ph.D degrees.

FACULTY PROFILE (FALL 2005)

Total teaching faculty: **1,514 (full-time)**, **126 (part-time)**
Of full-time faculty, those teaching in basic sciences: **14%**;
in clinical programs: **86%**
Of part-time faculty, those teaching in basic sciences: **9%**;
in clinical programs: **91%**
Full-time faculty/student ratio: **2.7**

SUPPORT SERVICES

The school offers students these services for dealing with
stress: expanded-hour gym access, peer counseling, professional counseling, support groups.

RESIDENCY PROFILE

Most popular residency and specialty programs chosen by
the 2004 and 2005 M.D. graduating classes: anesthesiology,
emergency medicine, family practice, internal medicine,
neurology, obstetrics and gynecology, orthopaedic surgery,
pediatrics, psychiatry, radiology–diagnostic.

WHERE GRADS GO

42.7%
*Proportion of 2003-2005 graduates who entered primary
care specialties*

47.4%
*Proportion of 2004-2005 graduates who accepted in-state
residencies*

University of Connecticut

- 263 Farmington Avenue, Farmington, CT 06030-1905
- Public
- Year Founded: 1961
- Tuition, 2005-2006: In-state: $22,540; Out-of-state: $42,780
- Enrollment 2005-2006 academic year: 313
- Website: http://medicine.uchc.edu
- Specialty ranking: drug/alcohol abuse: 12

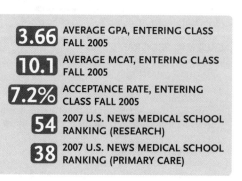

3.66 AVERAGE GPA, ENTERING CLASS FALL 2005

10.1 AVERAGE MCAT, ENTERING CLASS FALL 2005

7.2% ACCEPTANCE RATE, ENTERING CLASS FALL 2005

54 2007 U.S. NEWS MEDICAL SCHOOL RANKING (RESEARCH)

38 2007 U.S. NEWS MEDICAL SCHOOL RANKING (PRIMARY CARE)

ADMISSIONS

Admissions phone number: **(860) 679-3874**
Admissions email address: **sanford@ns01.uchc.edu**
Application website: **N/A**
Acceptance rate: **7.2%**
In-state acceptance rate: **27.3%**
Out-of-state acceptance rate: **3.7%**
Minority acceptance rate: **N/A**
International acceptance rate: **N/A**

Fall 2005 applications and acceptees

	Applied	Interviewed	Accepted	Enrolled
Total:	2,685	400	193	79
In-state:	396	230	108	60
Out-of-state:	2,289	170	85	19

Profile of admitted students

Average undergraduate grade point average: **3.66**
MCAT averages (scale: 1-15; writing test: J-T):
  Composite score: **10.1**
  Verbal reasoning score: **9.7**, Physical sciences score: **9.9**,
  Biological sciences score: **10.6**, Writing score: **Q**
Proportion with undergraduate majors in: Biological
  sciences: **54%**, Physical sciences: **20%**, Non-sciences:
  15%, Other health professions: **3%**, Mixed disciplines
  and other: **8%**
Percentage of students not coming directly from college
  after graduation: **66%**

Dates and details

The American Medical College Application Service
  (AMCAS) application is accepted.
School asks for a school-specific application as part of the
  admissions process.
Oldest MCAT considered for Fall 2007 entry: **2003**
Earliest application date for the 2007-2008 first-year class:
  June 1, 2006
Latest application date: **December 15, 2006**
Acceptance dates for regular application for the class
  entering in fall 2007:
  Earliest: **October 15, 2006**

Latest: **August 15, 2007**
The school considers requests for deferred entrance.
Starting month for the class entering in 2007–2008:
  August
The school has an Early Decision Plan (EDP).
A personal interview is required for admission.

Undergraduate coursework required

Medical school requires undergraduate work in these subjects: biology, biology/zoology, English, organic chemistry,
inorganic (general) chemistry, physics.

ADMISSIONS POLICY
(TEXT PROVIDED BY SCHOOL):

The aim of the University of Connecticut School of
Medicine is to admit a highly qualified and diverse student
body. As a state-supported school, approximatley 75 percent
of available positions are filled by resident students. Places
are offered only to those whose achievements and capabilities are consistent with the rigor and high standards of the
school's educational program. Early notification programs
are available. The factors considered by the Admissions
Committee are the applicant's achievements, ability, motivation, character and career and specialty interests. The applicant's grade point average and MCAT scores are considered
along with the difficulty of the academic program, evidence
of academic achievement beyond the regular coursework,
and evidence of intellectual growth and development.
Additional consideration is given for nonacademic activities
and involvements. Letters of recommendation are carefully
considered as well. Interviews are conducted at the request
of the Admissions Committee only.

University of Connecticut policy prohibits discrimination
in education, employment, and in the provision of services
on account of race, sex, age, marital status, national origin,
ancestry, sexual orientation, disabled veterans status, physical or mental disability, mental retardation, other specially
covered mental disabilities, and criminal records that are
not job related, in accordance with provisions of the Civil
Rights Act of 1964, Title IX Educational Amendments of
1972, the Rehabilitation Act of 1973, the Americans with

Disabilities Act, and other existing federal and state laws and executive orders pertaining to equal rights. The School of Medicine recruits disadvantaged applicants and applicants from groups underrepresented in medicine nationally and regionally. Applications are reviewed by the same general procedure used for all applicants. Candidates for admission receive a full and sensitive review and are selected on a competitive basis. The School of Medicine has developed high school and college summer enrichment programs for competitive candidates and for students from groups traditionally underrepresented in American medicine. The undergraduate campus and the medical center campus cooperate to offer a Combined Program in Medicine (4 year BA/BS followed by a four year medical program), as well as a Post Baccalaureate Program. A summer College Fellowship Program provides approximately 30 to 40 opportunities for interested college students.

COSTS AND FINANCIAL AID
Financial aid phone number: **(860) 679-3574**
Tuition, 2005-2006 academic year: **In-state: $22,540; Out-of-state: $42,780**
Room and board: **N/A**
Percentage of students receiving financial aid in 2005-06: **95%**
Percentage of students receiving: Loans: **90%**, Grants/scholarships: **45%**, Work-study aid: **0%**
Average medical school debt for the Class of 2004: **$79,000**

STUDENT BODY
Fall 2005 full-time enrollment: **313**
Men: **37%**, Women: **63%**, In-state: **58%**, Minorities: **34%**, American Indian: **0.6%**, Asian-American: **12.5%**, African-American: **14.1%**, Hispanic-American: **3.8%**, White: **65.2%**, International: **2.6%**, Unknown: **1.3%**

ACADEMIC PROGRAMS
The school's curriculum very frequently gives first-year students substantial contact with patients.
There are opportunities for first- or second-year students to work in community health clinics.
Program offerings: AIDS, drug/alcohol abuse, family medicine, geriatrics, internal medicine, pediatrics, women's health
Joint degrees awarded: M.D./Ph.D., M.D./MBA, M.D./MPH.
Total National Institutes of Health (NIH) grants awarded to the medical school and affiliated hospitals: **N/A**

CURRICULUM
(TEXT PROVIDED BY SCHOOL):
The curriculum plan for medical students is based on a multidepartmental approach. Basic medical sciences are taught from an organ-system approach. Normal structure/function is presented first, followed by pathophysiology and therapeutic approaches.

Patient contact begins in the first year as part of the clinical medicine course. Students learn medical history taking, physical diagnosis, and various other aspects of the physician-patient relationship. In addition, students participate in a longitudinal ambulatory clinical experience throughout all four years. In the third year, students rotate through ambulatory and inpatient activities in each of the major clinical disciplines. In the fourth year, students complete clinical rotations in emergent and urgent care and have five months of electives. To aid individual development, students are assigned significant amounts of free time during the first two years and a wide choice of elective subjects in the clinical years.

The National Board of Medical Examiners examinations are required of all students. The grading system is strictly pass/fail; there are no class rank scales or class standing. The third-year grading system is honors and pass/fail.

FACULTY PROFILE (FALL 2005)
Total teaching faculty: **430 (full-time)**, **117 (part-time)**
Of full-time faculty, those teaching in basic sciences: **44%**; in clinical programs: **56%**
Of part-time faculty, those teaching in basic sciences: **31%**; in clinical programs: **69%**
Full-time faculty/student ratio: **1.4**

SUPPORT SERVICES
The school offers students these services for dealing with stress: peer counseling, professional counseling, support groups.

RESIDENCY PROFILE
Most popular residency and specialty programs chosen by the 2004 and 2005 M.D. graduating classes: anesthesiology, emergency medicine, internal medicine, obstetrics and gynecology, pediatrics, psychiatry, surgery–general, internal medicine/pediatrics.

WHERE GRADS GO

50.3%
Proportion of 2003-2005 graduates who entered primary care specialties

30%
Proportion of 2004-2005 graduates who accepted in-state residencies

University of Florida

- Box 100215 UFHSC, Gainesville, FL 32610-0215
- Public
- Year Founded: 1956
- Tuition, 2005-2006: In-state: $20,036; Out-of-state: $47,073
- Enrollment 2005-2006 academic year: 491
- Website: http://www.med.ufl.edu
- Specialty ranking: N/A

3.65 AVERAGE GPA, ENTERING CLASS FALL 2005

10.5 AVERAGE MCAT, ENTERING CLASS FALL 2005

10.4% ACCEPTANCE RATE, ENTERING CLASS FALL 2005

50 2007 U.S. NEWS MEDICAL SCHOOL RANKING (RESEARCH)

52 2007 U.S. NEWS MEDICAL SCHOOL RANKING (PRIMARY CARE)

ADMISSIONS

Admissions phone number: (352) 392-4569
Admissions email address: robyn@dean.med.ufl.edu
Application website: http://www.aamc.org/amcas
Acceptance rate: 10.4%
In-state acceptance rate: 16.1%
Out-of-state acceptance rate: 1.4%
Minority acceptance rate: 3.7%
International acceptance rate: 0.0%

Fall 2005 applications and acceptees

	Applied	Interviewed	Accepted	Enrolled
Total:	2,048	362	212	131
In-state:	1,248	332	201	128
Out-of-state:	800	30	11	3

Profile of admitted students

Average undergraduate grade point average: 3.65
MCAT averages (scale: 1-15; writing test: J-T):
Composite score: 10.5
Verbal reasoning score: 10.1, Physical sciences score: 10.5, Biological sciences score: 10.9, Writing score: O
Proportion with undergraduate majors in: Biological sciences: 51%, Physical sciences: 13%, Non-sciences: 21%, Other health professions: 0%, Mixed disciplines and other: 15%
Percentage of students not coming directly from college after graduation: 12%

Dates and details

The American Medical College Application Service (AMCAS) application is accepted.
School asks for a school-specific application as part of the admissions process.
Oldest MCAT considered for Fall 2007 entry: 2004
Earliest application date for the 2007-2008 first-year class: June 5, 2006
Latest application date: December 1, 2006
Acceptance dates for regular application for the class entering in fall 2007:
Earliest: October 15, 2006

Latest: August 31, 2007
The school considers requests for deferred entrance.
Starting month for the class entering in 2007–2008:
August
The school doesn't have an Early Decision Plan (EDP).
A personal interview is required for admission.

Undergraduate coursework required

Medical school requires undergraduate work in these subjects: biology, organic chemistry, inorganic (general) chemistry, physics, biochemistry.

ADMISSIONS POLICY

(TEXT PROVIDED BY SCHOOL):

Admission to the University of Florida College of Medicine is highly competitive. We seek students who demonstrate personal and intellectual characteristics essential for physicians.

We appraise applicants on the basis of personal attributes, academic record, evaluation of past activities, the MCAT (taken within three years prior to anticipated matriculation), and letters of recommendation. The college does not discriminate on the basis of race, gender, age, disability, creed or national origin. We welcome applications from members of underserved minorities, as well as those who demonstrate a commitment to underserved populations.

Applicants must be U.S. citizens or permanent residents. They must receive a bachelor's degree or its equivalent from a Council on Higher Education-accredited institution prior to matriculation to the college. Preference is given to Florida residents.

It is not necessary for applicants to pursue an undergraduate major in the sciences but prior to matriculation applicants must complete eight semester hours each of general chemistry, general physics and biological sciences, as well as four hours each of organic chemistry and biochemistry. All courses must include a laboratory section.

Applicants submit an initial application to the American Medical College Application Service. The MCAT is required and must be taken within the three years prior to anticipated matriculation. Scores must be submitted before our

AMCAS application deadline. There is no minimum MCAT score or grade-point average required of applicants. The Medical Selection Committee invites competitive applicants to submit a second application directly to the college. Letters of recommendation accompany this application. Our deadline for receipt of all materials associated with the second application is January 15. After review of the entire application file, some applicants are invited for interviews. Interviews, required for admission to the college, occur from September through March. Following interviews, the MSC makes a recommendation regarding each applicant. With approval of the college dean, the committee chair makes the final determination of each applicant's status.

COSTS AND FINANCIAL AID
Financial aid phone number: **(352) 392-7800**
Tuition, 2005-2006 academic year: **In-state: $20,036; Out-of-state: $47,073**
Room and board: **$8,685**
Percentage of students receiving financial aid in 2005-06: **91%**
Percentage of students receiving: Loans: **86%**, Grants/scholarships: **77%**, Work-study aid: **0%**
Average medical school debt for the Class of 2004: **$75,975**

STUDENT BODY
Fall 2005 full-time enrollment: **491**
Men: **47%**, Women: **53%**, In-state: **97%**, Minorities: **34%**, American Indian: **0.6%**, Asian-American: **18.5%**, African-American: **6.3%**, Hispanic-American: **8.4%**, White: **65.0%**, International: **0.0%**, Unknown: **1.2%**

ACADEMIC PROGRAMS
The school's curriculum very frequently gives first-year students substantial contact with patients.
There are opportunities for first- or second-year students to work in community health clinics.
Program offerings: AIDS, drug/alcohol abuse, family medicine, geriatrics, internal medicine, pediatrics, rural medicine, women's health
Joint degrees awarded: M.D./Ph.D., M.D./MBA, M.D./MPH, M.D./JD, M.D./MS, M.D./M.A.
Total National Institutes of Health (NIH) grants awarded to the medical school and affiliated hospitals: **$82.7 million**

CURRICULUM
(TEXT PROVIDED BY SCHOOL):
Our curriculum is based on 12 educational principles and focuses on the development and assessment of competencies. We strive to provide a general and professional education.
Each course and clerkship develops learning objectives tied to specific competencies. Feedback is provided to students as they proceed. We emphasize the competency category of professionalism because it is crucial to our students' success.
Our first year includes traditional basic science courses. The Essentials of Patient Care course provides an early introduction to such clinical skills as the medical history

and physical examination. These are taught in the state-of-the-art Harrell Assessment and Development Center using our nationally recognized standardized patient program.
At the end of the first semester, each student is placed with a practicing physician for two weeks at sites throughout Florida. All first-year students also participate in a year-long interdisciplinary family health course, during which they visit volunteer families in their homes.
Second-year coursework includes pathology, immunology and medical microbiology, pharmacology, oncology, courses in medical ethics and evidence-based medicine, and continuance of Essentials of Patient Care. At four points during their training, students must pass a performance-based examination assessing clinical skills. All students must pass the National Board of Medical Examiners Step 1 test to proceed to their clinical years.
Our third year includes core clerkships in internal medicine, surgery, pediatrics, obstetrics and gynecology, psychiatry, family medicine and neurology. Additional required clerkships in the fourth year include geriatrics, emergency medicine and anesthesiology, and students must do a subinternship in internal medicine, family medicine or pediatrics. Much of the fourth year is elective time, to allow students to prepare for residency training.
We have two major clinical locations: Gainesville, including both Shands at the University of Florida and the Veterans Affairs Medical Center; and our urban campus location in Jacksonville at Shands Jacksonville.

FACULTY PROFILE (FALL 2005)
Total teaching faculty: **1,097 (full-time), 101 (part-time)**
Of full-time faculty, those teaching in basic sciences: **14%**; in clinical programs: **86%**
Of part-time faculty, those teaching in basic sciences: **4%**; in clinical programs: **96%**
Full-time faculty/student ratio: **2.2**

SUPPORT SERVICES
The school offers students these services for dealing with stress: expanded-hour gym access, peer counseling, professional counseling, religious support, support groups.

RESIDENCY PROFILE
Most popular residency and specialty programs chosen by the 2004 and 2005 M.D. graduating classes: anesthesiology, emergency medicine, family practice, internal medicine, neurological surgery, obstetrics and gynecology, pediatrics, psychiatry, surgery–general, transitional year.

WHERE GRADS GO
45%
Proportion of 2003-2005 graduates who entered primary care specialties

40.6%
Proportion of 2004-2005 graduates who accepted in-state residencies

University of Illinois—Chicago

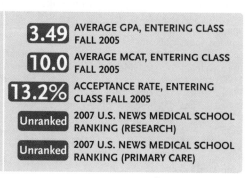

- 1853 W. Polk Street, M/C 784, Chicago, IL 60612
- Public
- Year Founded: 1881
- Tuition, 2005-2006: In-state: $26,230; Out-of-state: $54,284
- Enrollment 2005-2006 academic year: 1,403
- Website: http://www.uic.edu/depts/mcam
- Specialty ranking: N/A

3.49	AVERAGE GPA, ENTERING CLASS FALL 2005
10.0	AVERAGE MCAT, ENTERING CLASS FALL 2005
13.2%	ACCEPTANCE RATE, ENTERING CLASS FALL 2005
Unranked	2007 U.S. NEWS MEDICAL SCHOOL RANKING (RESEARCH)
Unranked	2007 U.S. NEWS MEDICAL SCHOOL RANKING (PRIMARY CARE)

ADMISSIONS

Admissions phone number: **(312) 996-5635**
Admissions email address: **medadmit@uic.edu**
Application website:
   http://www.aamc.org/students/amcas/start.htm
Acceptance rate: **13.2%**
In-state acceptance rate: **29.2%**
Out-of-state acceptance rate: **5.6%**
Minority acceptance rate: **12.2%**
International acceptance rate: **N/A**

Fall 2005 applications and acceptees

	Applied	Interviewed	Accepted	Enrolled
Total:	4,856	828	640	333
In-state:	1,560	572	455	248
Out-of-state:	3,296	256	185	85

Profile of admitted students

Average undergraduate grade point average: **3.49**
MCAT averages (scale: 1-15; writing test: J-T):
   Composite score: **10.0**
   Verbal reasoning score: **N/A**, Physical sciences score:
   N/A, Biological sciences score: **N/A**, Writing score: **N/A**
Proportion with undergraduate majors in: Biological
sciences: **48%**, Physical sciences: **17%**, Non-sciences:
11%, Other health professions: **0%**, Mixed disciplines
and other: **24%**
Percentage of students not coming directly from college
after graduation: **31%**

Dates and details

The American Medical College Application Service
   (AMCAS) application is accepted.
School asks for a school-specific application as part of the
   admissions process.
Oldest MCAT considered for Fall 2007 entry: **2004**
Earliest application date for the 2007-2008 first-year class:
   June 1, 2006
Latest application date: **December 1, 2006**
Acceptance dates for regular application for the class
   entering in fall 2007:

Earliest: **October 2, 2006**
Latest: **August 17, 2007**
The school considers requests for deferred entrance.
Starting month for the class entering in 2007–2008:
   August
The school has an Early Decision Plan (EDP).
A personal interview is required for admission.

Undergraduate coursework required

Medical school requires undergraduate work in these subjects: biology, organic chemistry, inorganic (general) chemistry, physics, behavioral science, social sciences.

ADMISSIONS POLICY
(TEXT PROVIDED BY SCHOOL):

The UIC College of Medicine selects applicants who, in the
judgment of the Committee on Admissions, demonstrate
the qualities that are necessary for the successful study and
practice of medicine and that best meet the needs of the citizenry of Illinois. These qualities include academic achievement, good communication skills, emotional stability,
maturity, integrity, diversity of interests, leadership, and
motivation. The committee considers the quality of all academic accomplishments of each applicant, including
achievement in advanced projects, as well as the work and
extracurricular experiences that demonstrate the applicant's
initiative and creativity.

COSTS AND FINANCIAL AID

Financial aid phone number: **(312) 413-0127**
Tuition, 2005-2006 academic year: **In-state: $26,230; Out-
of-state: $54,284**
Room and board: **$12,967**
Percentage of students receiving financial aid in 2005-06:
   N/A
Percentage of students receiving: Loans: **N/A**,
   Grants/scholarships: **N/A**, Work-study aid: **0%**
Average medical school debt for the Class of 2004:
   $97,556

STUDENT BODY

Fall 2005 full-time enrollment: 1,403
Men: 52%, Women: 48%, In-state: 78%, Minorities: 53%

ACADEMIC PROGRAMS

The school's curriculum frequently gives first-year students substantial contact with patients.

There are opportunities for first- or second-year students to work in community health clinics.

Program offerings: AIDS, drug/alcohol abuse, family medicine, geriatrics, internal medicine, pediatrics, rural medicine, women's health

Joint degrees awarded: M.D./Ph.D., M.D./MBA, M.D./MPH, M.D./M.H.I., M.D./JD, M.D./M.S.W., M.D./MS, M.D./M.A., M.D./M.H.A.

Total National Institutes of Health (NIH) grants awarded to the medical school and affiliated hospitals: **$84.4 million**

CURRICULUM

(TEXT PROVIDED BY SCHOOL):

The College of Medicine curriculum is designed to serve a variety of career choices. The educational program allows students to prepare for careers in medical practice, research, teaching, community medicine, medical administration, and other fields. The programs are diversified through relationships with many hospitals and other institutions, allowing for a wide range of learning opportunities in a variety of medical practice settings.

The curriculum is supported by a sound advising system and useful independent study aids. While all of these features are available in the curriculum, a student may seek even greater curricular independence through the College of Medicine at Chicago's Independent Study Program. The curriculum includes a wide variety of programs and courses. In addition to programs offered by the UIC College of Medicine at Chicago, there are opportunities available at other clinical sites.

The curriculum creates an environment for learning in which students will develop the willingness and competence to promote and contribute to improved healthcare and become responsible for their own continuing education

and, thereby, become able to cope with the ever-changing demands on physicians.

The learning environment is sufficiently flexible to allow for differences in student backgrounds, learning rates, and career goals. Proper emphasis is placed on the development of the attitudes necessary for effective interaction with individual patients, with health-professional colleagues, and with society at large. The curriculum stresses rational decision making and clinical problem solving based on an understanding of the basic biological, physical, and behavioral sciences; thus the integration of basic and clinical sciences is emphasized throughout the program.

FACULTY PROFILE (FALL 2005)

Total teaching faculty: **809 (full-time)**, **468 (part-time)**
Of full-time faculty, those teaching in basic sciences: **26%**; in clinical programs: **74%**
Of part-time faculty, those teaching in basic sciences: **4%**; in clinical programs: **96%**
Full-time faculty/student ratio: **0.6**

SUPPORT SERVICES

The school offers students these services for dealing with stress: expanded-hour gym access, peer counseling, professional counseling, religious support, support groups.

RESIDENCY PROFILE

Most popular residency and specialty programs chosen by the 2004 and 2005 M.D. graduating classes: anesthesiology, emergency medicine, family practice, internal medicine, neurology, orthopaedic surgery, pathology–anatomic and clinical, pediatrics, psychiatry, transitional year.

WHERE GRADS GO

47.3%
Proportion of 2003-2005 graduates who entered primary care specialties

47%
Proportion of 2004-2005 graduates who accepted in-state residencies

University of Iowa

ROY J. AND LUCILLE A. CARVER

- **200 CMAB, Iowa City, IA 52242-1101**
- **Public**
- **Year Founded:** 1847
- **Tuition, 2005-2006:** In-state: $21,076; Out-of-state: $40,282
- **Enrollment 2005-2006 academic year:** 562
- **Website:** http://www.medicine.uiowa.edu
- **Specialty ranking:** family medicine: 12, rural medicine: 4

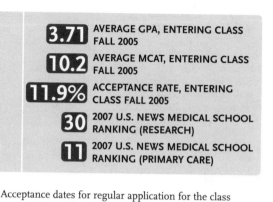

3.71	AVERAGE GPA, ENTERING CLASS FALL 2005
10.2	AVERAGE MCAT, ENTERING CLASS FALL 2005
11.9%	ACCEPTANCE RATE, ENTERING CLASS FALL 2005
30	2007 U.S. NEWS MEDICAL SCHOOL RANKING (RESEARCH)
11	2007 U.S. NEWS MEDICAL SCHOOL RANKING (PRIMARY CARE)

ADMISSIONS

Admissions phone number: **(319) 335-8052**
Admissions email address: **medical-admissions@uiowa.edu**
Application website:
http://www.medicine.uiowa.edu/osac/admissions
Acceptance rate: **11.9%**
In-state acceptance rate: **38.6%**
Out-of-state acceptance rate: **7.8%**
Minority acceptance rate: **9.2%**
International acceptance rate: **N/A**

Fall 2005 applications and acceptees

	Applied	Interviewed	Accepted	Enrolled
Total:	2,513	640	300	142
In-state:	337	263	130	97
Out-of-state:	2,176	377	170	45

Profile of admitted students
Average undergraduate grade point average: **3.71**
MCAT averages (scale: 1-15; writing test: J-T):
  Composite score: **10.2**
  Verbal reasoning score: **9.9**, Physical sciences score: **10.2**, Biological sciences score: **10.6**, Writing score: **P**
Proportion with undergraduate majors in: Biological sciences: **50%**, Physical sciences: **26%**, Non-sciences: **13%**, Other health professions: **1%**, Mixed disciplines and other: **10%**
Percentage of students not coming directly from college after graduation: **42%**

Dates and details
The American Medical College Application Service (AMCAS) application is accepted.
School asks for a school-specific application as part of the admissions process.
Oldest MCAT considered for Fall 2007 entry: **2001**
Earliest application date for the 2007-2008 first-year class: **June 1, 2006**
Latest application date: **November 1, 2006**

Acceptance dates for regular application for the class entering in fall 2007:
  Earliest: **October 15, 2006**
  Latest: **August 1, 2007**
The school considers requests for deferred entrance.
Starting month for the class entering in 2007–2008:
  August
The school has an Early Decision Plan (EDP).
A personal interview is required for admission.

Undergraduate coursework required
Medical school requires undergraduate work in these subjects: biology, organic chemistry, inorganic (general) chemistry, physics, mathematics.

COSTS AND FINANCIAL AID
Financial aid phone number: **(319) 335-8059**
Tuition, 2005-2006 academic year: **In-state: $21,076; Out-of-state: $40,282**
Room and board: **$9,000**
Percentage of students receiving financial aid in 2005-06: **96%**
Percentage of students receiving: Loans: **90%**, Grants/scholarships: **60%**, Work-study aid: **1%**
Average medical school debt for the Class of 2004: **$99,812**

STUDENT BODY
Fall 2005 full-time enrollment: **562**
Men: **53%**, Women: **47%**, In-state: **71%**, Minorities: **19%**, American Indian: **0.7%**, Asian-American: **6.8%**, African-American: **3.6%**, Hispanic-American: **7.8%**, White: **76.2%**, International: **0.0%**, Unknown: **5.0%**

ACADEMIC PROGRAMS
The school's curriculum occasionally gives first-year students substantial contact with patients.
There are opportunities for first- or second-year students to work in community health clinics.

Program offerings: AIDS, drug/alcohol abuse, family
  medicine, geriatrics, internal medicine, pediatrics, rural
  medicine
Joint degrees awarded: M.D./Ph.D., M.D./MBA,
  M.D./MPH., M.D./JD.
Total National Institutes of Health (NIH) grants awarded to
  the medical school and affiliated hospitals: **$145.9 million**

FACULTY PROFILE (FALL 2005)
Total teaching faculty: **870 (full-time), 467 (part-time)**
Of full-time faculty, those teaching in basic sciences: **11%**;
  in clinical programs: **89%**
Of part-time faculty, those teaching in basic sciences: **1%**;
  in clinical programs: **99%**
Full-time faculty/student ratio: **1.5**

SUPPORT SERVICES
The school offers students these services for dealing with
stress: peer counseling, professional counseling, support
groups.

RESIDENCY PROFILE
Most popular residency and specialty programs chosen by
the 2004 and 2005 M.D. graduating classes: anesthesiology,
emergency medicine, family practice, internal medicine,
obstetrics and gynecology, orthopaedic surgery,
pathology–anatomic and clinical, pediatrics, radiology–diagnostic, surgery–general.

WHERE GRADS GO

43.1%

*Proportion of 2003-2005 graduates who entered primary
care specialties*

30.1%

*Proportion of 2004-2005 graduates who accepted in-state
residencies*

University of Kansas Medical Center

- 3901 Rainbow Boulevard, Kansas City, KS 66160
- Public
- Year Founded: 1905
- Tuition, 2005-2006: In-state: $19,337; Out-of-state: $35,092
- Enrollment 2005-2006 academic year: 709
- Website: http://www.kumc.edu/som/som.html
- Specialty ranking: rural medicine: 25

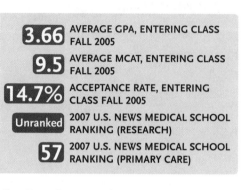

3.66	AVERAGE GPA, ENTERING CLASS FALL 2005
9.5	AVERAGE MCAT, ENTERING CLASS FALL 2005
14.7%	ACCEPTANCE RATE, ENTERING CLASS FALL 2005
Unranked	2007 U.S. NEWS MEDICAL SCHOOL RANKING (RESEARCH)
57	2007 U.S. NEWS MEDICAL SCHOOL RANKING (PRIMARY CARE)

ADMISSIONS

Admissions phone number: **(913) 588-5283**
Admissions email address: **smccurdy@kumc.edu**
Application website:
   http://www.kumc.edu/studentcenter/regacademic.html
Acceptance rate: **14.7%**
In-state acceptance rate: **41.6%**
Out-of-state acceptance rate: **5.2%**
Minority acceptance rate: **11.7%**
International acceptance rate: **0.0%**

Fall 2005 applications and acceptees

	Applied	Interviewed	Accepted	Enrolled
Total:	1,553	443	229	175
In-state:	406	307	169	142
Out-of-state:	1,147	136	60	33

Profile of admitted students

Average undergraduate grade point average: **3.66**
MCAT averages (scale: 1-15; writing test: J-T):
   Composite score: **9.5**
   Verbal reasoning score: **9.6**, Physical sciences score: **9.2**,
   Biological sciences score: **9.8**, Writing score: **P**
Proportion with undergraduate majors in: Biological
   sciences: **49%**, Physical sciences: **21%**, Non-sciences:
   14%, Other health professions: **1%**, Mixed disciplines
   and other: **15%**
Percentage of students not coming directly from college
   after graduation: **N/A**

Dates and details

The American Medical College Application Service
   (AMCAS) application is accepted.
School asks for a school-specific application as part of the
   admissions process.
Oldest MCAT considered for Fall 2007 entry: **2003**
Earliest application date for the 2007-2008 first-year class:
   July 1, 2006
Latest application date: **October 15, 2006**
Acceptance dates for regular application for the class
   entering in fall 2007:

Earliest: **November 15, 2006**
Latest: **N/A**
The school considers requests for deferred entrance.
Starting month for the class entering in 2007–2008:
   August
The school has an Early Decision Plan (EDP).
A personal interview is required for admission.

Undergraduate coursework required

Medical school requires undergraduate work in these subjects: biology, English, organic chemistry, inorganic (general) chemistry, physics, mathematics.

ADMISSIONS POLICY

(TEXT PROVIDED BY SCHOOL):
Applicants must have earned a bachelor's degree by the
time of enrollment into the University of Kansas School of
Medicine. While this degree may be in any discipline and
earned at any accredited institution, the courses listed on
this page are required of all applicants. Courses taken to
meet prerequisites should be one-year sequential courses
intended for students majoring in the sciences. Applicants
are expected to take course work that demonstrates the requisite intellectual discipline and analytical and problem solving skills necessary to succeed in medical school.

Applicants are encouraged to select courses, within their
major and outside, that they find stimulating and that fulfill
requirements for the baccalaureate degree. While not
required, statistics, biochemistry and upper level biology
courses are helpful in providing additional preparation for
the medical school curriculum. Students are strongly
advised to balance their work in the natural sciences with
the following disciplines: anthropology, communications,
computer science, economics, ethics, family life studies,
fine arts, human development, literature, philosophy, psychology, and sociology. A broad understanding of health
care and medicine is also expected. Work and/or volunteer
experiences (including physician shadowing) in settings
such as health care agencies, hospitals, and physician
offices are strongly recommended.

In order to earn assured admission to the University of Kansas School of Medicine, scholars must demonstrate academic achievements as well as a significant and informed interest in primary care.

COSTS AND FINANCIAL AID
Financial aid phone number: **(913) 588-5170**
Tuition, 2005-2006 academic year: **In-state: $19,337; Out-of-state: $35,092**
Room and board: **$22,464**
Percentage of students receiving financial aid in 2005-06: **95%**
Percentage of students receiving: Loans: **85%**, Grants/scholarships: **71%**, Work-study aid: **0%**
Average medical school debt for the Class of 2004: **$89,949**

STUDENT BODY
Fall 2005 full-time enrollment: **709**
Men: **55%**, Women: **45%**, In-state: **85%**, Minorities: **21%**, American Indian: **1.3%**, Asian-American: **10.6%**, African-American: **5.9%**, Hispanic-American: **2.8%**, White: **69.1%**, International: **0.0%**, Unknown: **10.3%**

ACADEMIC PROGRAMS
There are opportunities for first- or second-year students to work in community health clinics.
Program offerings: AIDS, drug/alcohol abuse, family medicine, geriatrics, internal medicine, pediatrics, rural medicine, women's health
Joint degrees awarded: M.D./Ph.D., M.D./MPH, M.D./MS, M.D./M.A., M.D./M.H.A.
Total National Institutes of Health (NIH) grants awarded to the medical school and affiliated hospitals: **N/A**

CURRICULUM
(TEXT PROVIDED BY SCHOOL):
The School of Medicine's curriculum ensures a sequential and interdisciplinary medical education with an emphasis on a generalist approach to the diagnosis, treatment and management of patient illnesses. This curriculum is designed to assist students in their acquisition of the knowledge, skills, and attitudes needed to become highly competent and caring physicians.

The first two years of the curriculum provide the basic biomedical and social sciences foundation essential to the practice of medicine. Didactic and self-directed learning are balanced between small group activities and lectures. In addition, first- and second-year medical students are paired with a mentoring physician in a longitudinal ambulatory care experience.

During years three and four, students participate in the delivery of health care in ambulatory and hospital settings, both in the community and at the KU Medical Center. The curriculum consists of required clerkships in the core clinical areas as well as a one-month preceptorship with a practicing Kansas physician. Students also choose from a large selection of basic science and clinical science electives to complete a well-rounded educational program. Seminars facilitate continuing student discussion of issues raised during their first two years of study, and a comprehensive advising system assists medical students with academic, personal, and professional development.

FACULTY PROFILE (FALL 2005)
Total teaching faculty: **515 (full-time)**, **127 (part-time)**
Of full-time faculty, those teaching in basic sciences: **26%**; in clinical programs: **74%**
Of part-time faculty, those teaching in basic sciences: **14%**; in clinical programs: **86%**
Full-time faculty/student ratio: **0.7**

SUPPORT SERVICES
The school offers students these services for dealing with stress: expanded-hour gym access, professional counseling, religious support, support groups.

RESIDENCY PROFILE
Most popular residency and specialty programs chosen by the 2004 and 2005 M.D. graduating classes: anesthesiology, emergency medicine, family practice, internal medicine, internal medicine–pediatrics, obstetrics and gynecology, pediatrics, psychiatry, radiology–diagnostic, surgery–general.

WHERE GRADS GO

45.2%
Proportion of 2003-2005 graduates who entered primary care specialties

42.7%
Proportion of 2004-2005 graduates who accepted in-state residencies

University of Kentucky

- Chandler Medical Center, 800 Rose Street, Lexington, KY 40536
- Public
- Year Founded: 1956
- Tuition, 2005-2006: In-state: $19,238; Out-of-state: $38,212
- Enrollment 2005-2006 academic year: 400
- Website: http://www.mc.uky.edu/medicine/
- Specialty ranking: rural medicine: 16

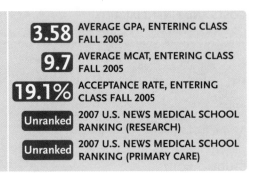

3.58 AVERAGE GPA, ENTERING CLASS FALL 2005

9.7 AVERAGE MCAT, ENTERING CLASS FALL 2005

19.1% ACCEPTANCE RATE, ENTERING CLASS FALL 2005

Unranked 2007 U.S. NEWS MEDICAL SCHOOL RANKING (RESEARCH)

Unranked 2007 U.S. NEWS MEDICAL SCHOOL RANKING (PRIMARY CARE)

ADMISSIONS

Admissions phone number: **(859) 323-6161**
Admissions email address: **kymedap@uky.edu**
Application website:
   http://www.aamc.org/students/amcas/start.htm
Acceptance rate: **19.1%**
In-state acceptance rate: **37.9%**
Out-of-state acceptance rate: **8.2%**
Minority acceptance rate: **N/A**
International acceptance rate: **N/A**

Fall 2005 applications and acceptees

	Applied	Interviewed	Accepted	Enrolled
Total:	1,002	322	191	103
In-state:	367	208	139	86
Out-of-state:	635	114	52	17

Profile of admitted students

Average undergraduate grade point average: **3.58**
MCAT averages (scale: 1-15; writing test: J-T):
   Composite score: **9.7**
   Verbal reasoning score: **9.8**, Physical sciences score: **9.7**,
   Biological sciences score: **9.9**, Writing score: **P**
Proportion with undergraduate majors in: Biological sciences: **54%**, Physical sciences: **18%**, Non-sciences: **11%**, Other health professions: **1%**, Mixed disciplines and other: **16%**
Percentage of students not coming directly from college after graduation: **25%**

Dates and details

The American Medical College Application Service (AMCAS) application is accepted.
School asks for a school-specific application as part of the admissions process.
Oldest MCAT considered for Fall 2007 entry: **2004**
Earliest application date for the 2007-2008 first-year class: **June 1, 2006**
Latest application date: **November 1, 2006**
Acceptance dates for regular application for the class entering in fall 2007:

Earliest: **October 15, 2006**
Latest: **N/A**
The school considers requests for deferred entrance.
Starting month for the class entering in 2007–2008:
   August
The school has an Early Decision Plan (EDP).
A personal interview is required for admission.

Undergraduate coursework required

Medical school requires undergraduate work in these subjects: biology, English, organic chemistry, inorganic (general) chemistry, physics.

ADMISSIONS POLICY
(TEXT PROVIDED BY SCHOOL):

Several factors are considered by the College of Medicine in the evaluation of candidates for admission: cumulative science grade-point average, cumulative non-science grade-point average, Medical College Admission Test performance, exposure to the medical profession, humanitarian or service activities, premedical references and evaluations, interpersonal or group accomplishments, and special characteristics, including residence in a physician-shortage area. Preference is also given to residents of the state of Kentucky.

COSTS AND FINANCIAL AID

Financial aid phone number: **(859) 323-6271**
Tuition, 2005-2006 academic year: **In-state: $19,238; Out-of-state: $38,212**
Room and board: **$10,175**
Percentage of students receiving financial aid in 2005-06: **95%**
Percentage of students receiving: Loans: **85%**, Grants/scholarships: **64%**, Work-study aid: **8%**
Average medical school debt for the Class of 2004: **$97,171**

STUDENT BODY

Fall 2005 full-time enrollment: **400**
Men: **57%**, Women: **43%**, In-state: **92%**, Minorities: **15%**, American Indian: **0.0%**, Asian-American: **8.3%**, African-

American: 4.8%, Hispanic-American: 0.5%, White: 83.3%, International: 2.3%, Unknown: 1.0%

ACADEMIC PROGRAMS

The school's curriculum occasionally gives first-year students substantial contact with patients.

There are opportunities for first- or second-year students to work in community health clinics.

Program offerings: AIDS, drug/alcohol abuse, family medicine, geriatrics, internal medicine, pediatrics, rural medicine, women's health

Joint degrees awarded: M.D./Ph.D., M.D./MBA, M.D./MPH.

Total National Institutes of Health (NIH) grants awarded to the medical school and affiliated hospitals: **N/A**

CURRICULUM

(TEXT PROVIDED BY SCHOOL):

The required course of study at the University of Kentucky College of Medicine provides an excellent foundation in medical science. The Kentucky medical curriculum relates scientific principles and concepts to the prevention of disease and to the delivery of cutting-edge, compassionate medical care. Because students with diverse backgrounds and interests embark upon a variety of medical careers, the curriculum provides the basic knowledge and skills essential for further professional development. We prepare our graduates for careers in all areas of medicine, including primary care, academic medicine, biomedical research, and the practice of medicine in specialized fields. In addition to the M.D. degree, M.D./Ph.D, M.D./MPH, and M.D./MBA degrees can be pursued. The curriculum is designed to be adapted to anticipated changes in medical practice and in the medical needs of our society.

The curriculum emphasizes early clinical experiences, integration of the basic and clinical sciences, teaching in ambulatory clinic settings, and primary care. It utilizes various learning methodologies, including standardized patients, clinical training models, computer-assisted instruction, problem-based learning, small-group tutorials, interactive lectures and laboratory exercises. The module block structure of the curriculum provides an intensive,

concentrated exposure to each content area. The first two years of study introduce students to the technical language, principles, and methods of investigation in the primary disciplines of biomedical science. The third-year curriculum provides the student with broad exposure to the principal medical disciplines in hospital and ambulatory care settings. At the end of third year, students complete a multi-station clinical performance examination. The fourth year of study is designed to allow students to further develop and demonstrate their clinical skills and includes 12 weeks of elective rotations at the University of Kentucky or other approved sites.

FACULTY PROFILE (FALL 2005)

Total teaching faculty: **658 (full-time)**, **145 (part-time)**

Of full-time faculty, those teaching in basic sciences: **26%**; in clinical programs: **74%**

Of part-time faculty, those teaching in basic sciences: **6%**; in clinical programs: **94%**

Full-time faculty/student ratio: **1.6**

SUPPORT SERVICES

The school offers students these services for dealing with stress: expanded-hour gym access, professional counseling, support groups.

RESIDENCY PROFILE

Most popular residency and specialty programs chosen by the 2004 and 2005 M.D. graduating classes: emergency medicine, family practice, internal medicine, internal medicine–pediatrics, obstetrics and gynecology, pediatrics, psychiatry, radiology–diagnostic, surgery–general.

WHERE GRADS GO

45%

Proportion of 2003-2005 graduates who entered primary care specialties

42%

Proportion of 2004-2005 graduates who accepted in-state residencies

University of Maryland

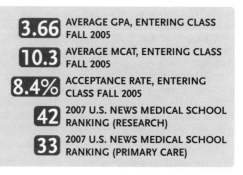

- 655 W. Baltimore Street, Room 14-029, Baltimore, MD 21201-1559
- Public
- Year Founded: 1807
- Tuition, 2005-2006: In-state: $20,262; Out-of-state: $36,129
- Enrollment 2005-2006 academic year: 604
- Website: http://medschool.umaryland.edu
- Specialty ranking: N/A

3.66 AVERAGE GPA, ENTERING CLASS FALL 2005

10.3 AVERAGE MCAT, ENTERING CLASS FALL 2005

8.4% ACCEPTANCE RATE, ENTERING CLASS FALL 2005

42 2007 U.S. NEWS MEDICAL SCHOOL RANKING (RESEARCH)

33 2007 U.S. NEWS MEDICAL SCHOOL RANKING (PRIMARY CARE)

ADMISSIONS

Admissions phone number: **(410) 706-7478**
Admissions email address: **mfoxwell@som.umaryland.edu**
Application website: **N/A**
Acceptance rate: **8.4%**
In-state acceptance rate: **25.5%**
Out-of-state acceptance rate: **4.0%**
Minority acceptance rate: **7.5%**
International acceptance rate: **0.0%**

Fall 2005 applications and acceptees

	Applied	Interviewed	Accepted	Enrolled
Total:	3,713	572	311	150
In-state:	748	325	191	123
Out-of-state:	2,965	247	120	27

Profile of admitted students

Average undergraduate grade point average: **3.66**
MCAT averages (scale: 1-15; writing test: J-T):
   Composite score: **10.3**
   Verbal reasoning score: **10.3**, Physical sciences score: **10.0**, Biological sciences score: **10.4**, Writing score: **P**
Proportion with undergraduate majors in: Biological sciences: **51%**, Physical sciences: **12%**, Non-sciences: **23%**, Other health professions: **3%**, Mixed disciplines and other: **11%**
Percentage of students not coming directly from college after graduation: **56%**

Dates and details

The American Medical College Application Service (AMCAS) application is accepted.
School asks for a school-specific application as part of the admissions process.
Oldest MCAT considered for Fall 2007 entry: **2003**
Earliest application date for the 2007-2008 first-year class: **June 1, 2006**
Latest application date: **November 1, 2006**
Acceptance dates for regular application for the class entering in fall 2007:
   Earliest: **October 15, 2006**

Latest: **N/A**
The school considers requests for deferred entrance.
Starting month for the class entering in 2007–2008: **August**
The school has an Early Decision Plan (EDP).
A personal interview is required for admission.

Undergraduate coursework required

Medical school requires undergraduate work in these subjects: biology/zoology, English, organic chemistry, inorganic (general) chemistry, physics.

ADMISSIONS POLICY
(TEXT PROVIDED BY SCHOOL):

The University of Maryland can consider for admission only those students who are citizens or permanent residents of the United States and Canada. Diversity is highly valued in the educational process and applications are encouraged from individuals from nontraditional and disadvantaged backgrounds.

The School of Medicine will admit only those who have documented that they possess the ability to successfully complete the academically rigorous curriculum. Academic excellence is expected. The Committee on Admissions seeks out evidence of maturity, character, integrity, good judgment, empathy, intellectual curiosity, motivation, leadership skills and commitment to excellence in the applicants' personal statement, extra curricular activities and life experiences, and in letters of recommendation.

Applications may be rejected without an interview. Applicants who possess competitive academic credentials and the personal characteristics noted above may be invited to interview. Interviews provide candidates with an opportunity to discuss their personal history and motivation. Interview evaluations are the last important factor considered by the admissions committee in their deliberations on an applicant's candidacy for admission.

COSTS AND FINANCIAL AID

Financial aid phone number: **(410) 706-7347**

Tuition, 2005-2006 academic year: **In-state: $20,262; Out-of-state: $36,129**

Room and board: **$18,315**

Percentage of students receiving financial aid in 2005-06: **88%**

Percentage of students receiving: Loans: **84%**, Grants/scholarships: **64%**, Work-study aid: **2%**

Average medical school debt for the Class of 2004: **$118,700**

STUDENT BODY

Fall 2005 full-time enrollment: **604**

Men: **40%**, Women: **60%**, In-state: **84%**, Minorities: **36%**, American Indian: **0.0%**, Asian-American: **21.2%**, African-American: **12.7%**, Hispanic-American: **1.7%**, White: **59.8%**, International: **1.2%**, Unknown: **3.5%**

ACADEMIC PROGRAMS

The school's curriculum frequently gives first-year students substantial contact with patients.

There are opportunities for first- or second-year students to work in community health clinics.

Program offerings: AIDS, drug/alcohol abuse, family medicine, geriatrics, internal medicine, pediatrics, rural medicine

Joint degrees awarded: M.D./Ph.D., M.D./MPH, M.D./M.H.I., M.D./MS

Total National Institutes of Health (NIH) grants awarded to the medical school and affiliated hospitals: **N/A**

CURRICULUM

(TEXT PROVIDED BY SCHOOL):

The University of Maryland's curriculum is designed to maximize independent learning and participation in campus and community activities while preparing the student for outstanding performance in the clinical setting. Year I and Year II consist of interdisciplinary blocks rather than parallel courses, allowing students to focus on one subject at a time. Lecture and small group teaching is limited to the morning. Introduction to Clinical Medicine is taught one afternoon per week and includes instruction in interviewing, physical examination, intimate human behavior, problem-based learning, and medical ethics. Standardized patients are used in all four years for clinical skills instruction and evaluation.

Year III consists of clerkships with clinical training in community and academic health centers. Year IV includes two months of required sub-internship and two months in a rural ambulatory health setting. Electives round out year IV, allowing students to pursue their interest locally or in approved national/international locations.

All medical students are required to purchase a laptop computer. Electronic laboratories and computer simulation are growing additions to the curriculum, with Web-based lecture recordings available to all students.

FACULTY PROFILE (FALL 2005)

Total teaching faculty: **1,156 (full-time)**, **207 (part-time)**

Of full-time faculty, those teaching in basic sciences: **14%**; in clinical programs: **86%**

Of part-time faculty, those teaching in basic sciences: **1%**; in clinical programs: **99%**

Full-time faculty/student ratio: **1.9**

SUPPORT SERVICES

The school offers students these services for dealing with stress: expanded-hour gym access, peer counseling, professional counseling, support groups.

RESIDENCY PROFILE

Most popular residency and specialty programs chosen by the 2004 and 2005 M.D. graduating classes: emergency medicine, family practice, internal medicine, neurology, pediatrics, surgery–general.

WHERE GRADS GO

47%

Proportion of 2003-2005 graduates who entered primary care specialties

29%

Proportion of 2004-2005 graduates who accepted in-state residencies

University of Massachusetts—Worcester

■ 55 Lake Avenue N, Worcester, MA 01655
■ Public
■ Year Founded: 1970
■ Tuition, 2005-2006: $14,037
■ Enrollment 2005-2006 academic year: 412
■ Website: http://www.umassmed.edu
■ Specialty ranking: N/A

3.64 AVERAGE GPA, ENTERING CLASS FALL 2005

10.6 AVERAGE MCAT, ENTERING CLASS FALL 2005

22.8% ACCEPTANCE RATE, ENTERING CLASS FALL 2005

48 2007 U.S. NEWS MEDICAL SCHOOL RANKING (RESEARCH)

4 2007 U.S. NEWS MEDICAL SCHOOL RANKING (PRIMARY CARE)

ADMISSIONS

Admissions phone number: **(508) 856-2323**
Admissions email address: **admissions@umassmed.edu**
Application website:
 http://www.aamc.org/students/amcas/start.htm
Acceptance rate: **22.8%**
In-state acceptance rate: **26.2%**
Out-of-state acceptance rate: **4.1%**
Minority acceptance rate: **N/A**
International acceptance rate: **N/A**

Fall 2005 applications and acceptees

	Applied	Interviewed	Accepted	Enrolled
Total:	795	440	181	102
In-state:	673	424	176	100
Out-of-state:	122	16	5	2

Profile of admitted students

Average undergraduate grade point average: **3.64**
MCAT averages (scale: 1-15; writing test: J-T):
 Composite score: **10.6**
 Verbal reasoning score: **10.3**, Physical sciences score:
 10.7, Biological sciences score: **10.7**, Writing score: **Q**
Proportion with undergraduate majors in: Biological
 sciences: **35%**, Physical sciences: **20%**, Non-sciences:
 17%, Other health professions: **1%**, Mixed disciplines
 and other: **27%**
Percentage of students not coming directly from college
 after graduation: **64%**

Dates and details

The American Medical College Application Service
 (AMCAS) application is accepted.
School asks for a school-specific application as part of the
 admissions process.
Oldest MCAT considered for Fall 2007 entry: **2003**
Earliest application date for the 2007-2008 first-year class:
 June 15, 2006
Latest application date: **November 1, 2006**
Acceptance dates for regular application for the class
 entering in fall 2007:

 Earliest: **October 1, 2006**
 Latest: **August 15, 2007**
The school considers requests for deferred entrance.
Starting month for the class entering in 2007–2008:
 August
The school has an Early Decision Plan (EDP).
A personal interview is required for admission.

Undergraduate coursework required

Medical school requires undergraduate work in these subjects: biology, biology/zoology, English, organic chemistry,
inorganic (general) chemistry, physics.

ADMISSIONS POLICY
(TEXT PROVIDED BY SCHOOL):

The admissions process promotes the UMMS mission by
selecting those qualified residents of Massachusetts who
will best serve the commonwealth's healthcare needs
through medical practice, public service, education, and
research, as stated in our educational goals and objectives:
"the training of physicians in the full range of medical disciplines with emphasis on practice in the primary-care specialties, in the public sector, and in underserved areas of
Massachusetts."

An Admissions Committee determines selection. Factors
considered include: residency in Massachusetts (application
to the Ph.D./M.D. program is not restricted to Massachusetts
residents); a baccalaureate degree and prior academic performance (grade-point average); performance on the Medical
College Admission Test; service activities that indicate an ability to work with people in a helping role; diversity of experience; extracurricular accomplishments; oral communication
and interpersonal skills; written communication skills;
achievement in scientific research and/or medically related
service; evidence of motivation and preparedness for medicine; and essential attributes and values for physicians,
including honesty, altruism, compassion, flexibility, maturity,
intellectual curiosity, self-awareness, and ability for self-
directed learning and working as team member.

The following coursework is required within the past
four years: one year of biology or zoology, with lab; one year

of both inorganic and organic chemistry, each with lab; one year of general physics, with lab; and English.

The committee reviews applications only when complete, as follows: the American Medical College Application Service and UMMS supplemental applications, including additional written materials; official transcript; letters of recommendation; MCAT within three years prior to application; notarized Proof of Massachusetts Residency Form; and nonrefundable application fee. Selected applicants receive two one-on-one interviews.

The final admissions decision is by vote of the entire committee. Applicants with disadvantaged status who do not otherwise meet the criteria for admission, but who show significant academic promise, may enter the UMMS postbaccalaureate program. If academically successful, they are encouraged to reapply to the medical school.

COSTS AND FINANCIAL AID
Financial aid phone number: **(508) 856-2265**
Tuition, 2005-2006 academic year: **$14,037**
Room and board: **$12,563**
Percentage of students receiving financial aid in 2005-06: **89%**
Percentage of students receiving: Loans: **89%**, Grants/scholarships: **26%**, Work-study aid: **0%**
Average medical school debt for the Class of 2004: **$92,069**

STUDENT BODY
Fall 2005 full-time enrollment: **412**
Men: **45%**, Women: **55%**, In-state: **99%**, Minorities: **20%**, American Indian: **1.0%**, Asian-American: **14.6%**, African-American: **3.2%**, Hispanic-American: **1.7%**, White: **79.4%**, International: **0.0%**, Unknown: **0.2%**

ACADEMIC PROGRAMS
The school's curriculum very frequently gives first-year students substantial contact with patients.
There are opportunities for first- or second-year students to work in community health clinics.
Program offerings: AIDS, drug/alcohol abuse, family medicine, geriatrics, internal medicine, pediatrics, rural medicine, women's health
Joint degrees awarded: M.D./Ph.D.
Total National Institutes of Health (NIH) grants awarded to the medical school and affiliated hospitals: **N/A**

CURRICULUM
(TEXT PROVIDED BY SCHOOL):
Our curriculum teaches core knowledge, skills, attitudes, and values, as the foundation for training the "undifferentiated" physician. Given this emphasis on preparing students for the generalist specialties, UMMS successfully meets its goal of 50 percent of graduates entering primary care fields. However, our students leave UMMS with an outstanding preparation for all medical specialties.

Our curriculum emphasizes early patient-care exposure from day one: strong clinical skills development; student activism in community service and advocacy; and lifelong learning skills. Our educational philosophy values partnership with students in teaching and learning, respect and dignity in the doctor-patient and student-learner relationship, and a milieu of collegiality, collaboration, and diversity.

The first two years' curriculum provides a strong foundation in the medical sciences; a focus on health and wellness as well as disease states; and early exposure to patient care and development of clinical skills through a longitudinal preceptorship program that spans both years. The basic science courses emphasize problem solving, cross-disciplinary teaching, interactive small-group learning, and technology-based teaching. Introductory clinical skills, medical ethics, communications, physical diagnosis, and the doctor-patient relationship are taught across both years in the Physician, Patient, and Society course.

The third year begins with a comprehensive orientation that serves as a transition to the six required clerkships: medicine, surgery, pediatrics, obstetrics/gynecology, psychiatry, and family medicine. A total of 13 weeks are devoted to primary care with placements in office-based practices across the state. Each clerkship features a robust core curriculum and the extensive use of standardized patients to teach and assess clinical skills. At the end of year 3, all students must complete a comprehensive exam of core clinical skills.

Year 4 includes required rotations in neurology and a subinternship, with 24 weeks of elective opportunity.

FACULTY PROFILE (FALL 2005)
Total teaching faculty: **939 (full-time)**, **65 (part-time)**
Of full-time faculty, those teaching in basic sciences: **24%**; in clinical programs: **76%**
Of part-time faculty, those teaching in basic sciences: **20%**; in clinical programs: **80%**
Full-time faculty/student ratio: **2.3**

SUPPORT SERVICES
The school offers students these services for dealing with stress: expanded-hour gym access, peer counseling, professional counseling, religious support, support groups.

RESIDENCY PROFILE
Most popular residency and specialty programs chosen by the 2004 and 2005 M.D. graduating classes: anesthesiology, emergency medicine, family practice, internal medicine, internal medicine–pediatrics, obstetrics and gynecology, orthopaedic surgery, pediatrics, psychiatry, radiology–diagnostic.

WHERE GRADS GO

57%
Proportion of 2003-2005 graduates who entered primary care specialties

51%
Proportion of 2004-2005 graduates who accepted in-state residencies

University of Miami

MILLER SCHOOL OF MEDICINE

- 1600 N.W. 10th Avenue, Miami, FL 33136
- Private
- Year Founded: 1952
- Tuition, 2005-2006: $29,848
- Enrollment 2005-2006 academic year: 641
- Website: http://www.miami.edu/medical-admissions
- Specialty ranking: AIDS: 11, geriatrics: 17

3.71 AVERAGE GPA, ENTERING CLASS FALL 2005

9.8 AVERAGE MCAT, ENTERING CLASS FALL 2005

8.6% ACCEPTANCE RATE, ENTERING CLASS FALL 2005

56 2007 U.S. NEWS MEDICAL SCHOOL RANKING (RESEARCH)

Unranked 2007 U.S. NEWS MEDICAL SCHOOL RANKING (PRIMARY CARE)

ADMISSIONS

Admissions phone number: **(305) 243-6791**
Admissions email address: **med.admissions@miami.edu**
Application website: **N/A**
Acceptance rate: **8.6%**
In-state acceptance rate: **19.0%**
Out-of-state acceptance rate: **3.5%**
Minority acceptance rate: **9.2%**
International acceptance rate: **4.5%**

Fall 2005 applications and acceptees

	Applied	Interviewed	Accepted	Enrolled
Total:	3,739	473	323	182
In-state:	1,247	312	237	150
Out-of-state:	2,492	161	86	32

Profile of admitted students

Average undergraduate grade point average: **3.71**
MCAT averages (scale: 1-15; writing test: J-T):
   Composite score: **9.8**
   Verbal reasoning score: **9.6**, Physical sciences score: **9.7**,
   Biological sciences score: **10.0**, Writing score: **P**
Proportion with undergraduate majors in: Biological
   sciences: **48%**, Physical sciences: **31%**, Non-sciences:
   18%, Other health professions: **2%**, Mixed disciplines
   and other: **1%**
Percentage of students not coming directly from college
   after graduation: **14%**

Dates and details

The American Medical College Application Service
   (AMCAS) application is accepted.
School asks for a school-specific application as part of the
   admissions process.
Oldest MCAT considered for Fall 2007 entry: **2004**
Earliest application date for the 2007-2008 first-year class:
   June 1, 2006
Latest application date: **December 1, 2006**
Acceptance dates for regular application for the class
   entering in fall 2007:
   Earliest: **October 15, 2006**

Latest: **August 1, 2007**
The school considers requests for deferred entrance.
Starting month for the class entering in 2007–2008:
   August
The school doesn't have an Early Decision Plan (EDP).
A personal interview is required for admission.

Undergraduate coursework required

Medical school requires undergraduate work in these subjects: biology/zoology, English, organic chemistry, inorganic
(general) chemistry, physics.

ADMISSIONS POLICY
(TEXT PROVIDED BY SCHOOL):

The UMMSM participates in the American Medical College
Application Service and accepts applications only from U.S.
citizens and permanent residents. To receive a secondary
application, Florida residents must have a 3.2 or higher
undergraduate cumulative grade-point average or a postbaccalaureate or graduate GPA of at least 3.5 (minimum of
15 credits). Non-Floridians must have a cumulative undergraduate GPA of at least 3.6 to receive a secondary application.

Applicants are evaluated in the following dimensions:
quality of undergraduate education and preparedness to
study medicine, MCAT scores, diversity of life experiences,
meaningfulness of direct patient contact experiences, writing ability, and quality of letters of recommendation.

Applicants with the highest ratings are invited for an
interview. Interviews are arranged only at the initiative of
the Office of Admissions and are held on the medical campus. Some of the factors evaluated at the time of interview
are: maturity, knowledge about the profession of medicine,
interpersonal skills, depth and source of motivation to study
medicine, and desire to serve others. Applicants' files are
reviewed without regard to race, creed, sex, national origin,
or age.

COSTS AND FINANCIAL AID

Financial aid phone number: **(305) 243-6211**
Tuition, 2005-2006 academic year: **$29,848**

Room and board: **$22,917**
Percentage of students receiving financial aid in 2005-06:
   88%
Percentage of students receiving: Loans: **88%**,
   Grants/scholarships: **27%**, Work-study aid: **0%**
Average medical school debt for the Class of 2004:
   $139,100

STUDENT BODY

Fall 2005 full-time enrollment: **641**
Men: **51%**, Women: **49%**, In-state: **80%**, Minorities: **43%**,
   American Indian: **0.6%**, Asian-American: **22.0%**,
   African-American: **6.2%**, Hispanic-American: **14.0%**,
   White: **56.5%**, International: **0.3%**, Unknown: **0.3%**

ACADEMIC PROGRAMS

The school's curriculum very frequently gives first-year
   students substantial contact with patients.
There are opportunities for first- or second-year students to
   work in community health clinics.
Program offerings: AIDS, drug/alcohol abuse, family
   medicine, geriatrics, internal medicine, pediatrics, rural
   medicine, women's health
Joint degrees awarded: M.D./Ph.D., M.D./MPH.
Total National Institutes of Health (NIH) grants awarded to
   the medical school and affiliated hospitals: **$82.5 million**

CURRICULUM

(TEXT PROVIDED BY SCHOOL):
The University of Miami Miller School of Medicine
(UMMSM) medical curriculum integrates the teaching of
the basic and clinical sciences by beginning the first year of
study with one semester of Fundamentals of the Biomedical
Sciences followed by three semesters of integrated organ system modules. Basic science concepts relevant to organ systems are introduced and assimilated in the context of
common disease processes and clinical relevance. The third
and fourth clinical years have been combined so that students can explore areas of clinical medicine and research
that interest them before completion of their core clinical
clerkships. Clinical experiences at the sub-internship level in
medical and surgical specialties are required for graduation.

The curriculum also includes nontraditional areas of
study to prepare physicians to practice in today's healthcare
system (e.g. cultural diversity, public-health issues, healthcare delivery systems, quality management, professionalism, population medicine). Various learning methodologies
are used including self-directed problem-based learning. In
addition to knowledge acquisition, professional qualities,
attitudes, and behaviors are evaluated in all phases of the
curriculum.

FACULTY PROFILE (FALL 2005)

Total teaching faculty: **1,146 (full-time)**, **9 (part-time)**
Of full-time faculty, those teaching in basic sciences: **37%**;
   in clinical programs: **63%**
Of part-time faculty, those teaching in basic sciences: **56%**;
   in clinical programs: **44%**
Full-time faculty/student ratio: **1.8**

SUPPORT SERVICES

The school offers students these services for dealing with
stress: expanded-hour gym access, professional counseling.

RESIDENCY PROFILE

Most popular residency and specialty programs chosen by the
2004 and 2005 M.D. graduating classes: anesthesiology,
emergency medicine, family practice, internal medicine,
neurology, obstetrics and gynecology, pathology–anatomic
and clinical, pediatrics, radiology–diagnostic, surgery–general.

WHERE GRADS GO

39%
*Proportion of 2003-2005 graduates who entered primary
care specialties*

43%
*Proportion of 2004-2005 graduates who accepted in-state
residencies*

University of Michigan–Ann Arbor

- 1301 Catherine Road, Ann Arbor, MI 48109-0624
- Public
- **Year Founded:** 1848
- **Tuition, 2005-2006:** In-state: $22,435; Out-of-state: $34,787
- **Enrollment 2005-2006 academic year:** 688
- **Website:** http://www.med.umich.edu/medschool/
- **Specialty ranking:** drug/alcohol abuse: 19, family medicine: 6, geriatrics: 4, internal medicine: 8, pediatrics: 15, women's health: 7

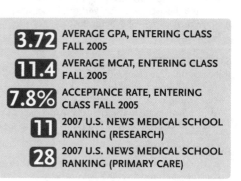

3.72 AVERAGE GPA, ENTERING CLASS FALL 2005

11.4 AVERAGE MCAT, ENTERING CLASS FALL 2005

7.8% ACCEPTANCE RATE, ENTERING CLASS FALL 2005

11 2007 U.S. NEWS MEDICAL SCHOOL RANKING (RESEARCH)

28 2007 U.S. NEWS MEDICAL SCHOOL RANKING (PRIMARY CARE)

ADMISSIONS
Admissions phone number: **(734) 764-6317**
Admissions email address: **umichmedadmiss@umich.edu**
Application website: **N/A**
Acceptance rate: **7.8%**
In-state acceptance rate: **10.1%**
Out-of-state acceptance rate: **7.3%**
Minority acceptance rate: **N/A**
International acceptance rate: **N/A**

Fall 2005 applications and acceptees

	Applied	Interviewed	Accepted	Enrolled
Total:	4,938	807	387	177
In-state:	890	240	90	79
Out-of-state:	4,048	567	297	98

Profile of admitted students
Average undergraduate grade point average: **3.72**
MCAT averages (scale: 1-15; writing test: J-T):
- Composite score: **11.4**
- Verbal reasoning score: **10.8**, Physical sciences score: **11.7**, Biological sciences score: **11.8**, Writing score: **Q**

Proportion with undergraduate majors in: Biological sciences: **50%**, Physical sciences: **14%**, Non-sciences: **20%**, Other health professions: **6%**, Mixed disciplines and other: **10%**
Percentage of students not coming directly from college after graduation: **54%**

Dates and details
The American Medical College Application Service (AMCAS) application is accepted.
School asks for a school-specific application as part of the admissions process.
Oldest MCAT considered for Fall 2007 entry: **2003**
Earliest application date for the 2007-2008 first-year class: **June 1, 2006**
Latest application date: **November 15, 2006**
Acceptance dates for regular application for the class entering in fall 2007:
- Earliest: **October 15, 2006**
- Latest: **August 1, 2007**

The school considers requests for deferred entrance.
Starting month for the class entering in 2007–2008:
- **August**

The school doesn't have an Early Decision Plan (EDP).
A personal interview is required for admission.

Undergraduate coursework required
Medical school requires undergraduate work in these subjects: biology, English, organic chemistry, inorganic (general) chemistry, physics, biochemistry, humanities.

ADMISSIONS POLICY
(TEXT PROVIDED BY SCHOOL):
Applicants to the Medical School are screened for academic and personal characteristics that predict success in the curriculum and as a future physician. Of the approximately 4900 applicants in 2004, 800 received interviews. The class size is 170.

The Admissions Committee, composed of student and faculty volunteers, is charged with conducting interviews and evaluating candidates. Each applicant has three one-on-one interviews with a committee member. Selection criteria currently in use by this committee include quality of education, knowledge of medicine, research activities, service to others, life experiences and extracurricular activities, leadership roles, letters of reference, communication skills, and overall attributes.

An Admissions Executive Committee, appointed by the dean from the pool of experienced interviewers, meets regularly to give final ranking scores to all applicants after the interviews. The assistant dean of admissions chairs this committee and directs the admissions program. In recent years, about half of the entering class has consisted of residents of the state of Michigan.

COSTS AND FINANCIAL AID
Financial aid phone number: **(734) 763-4147**
Tuition, 2005-2006 academic year: **In-state: $22,435; Out-of-state: $34,787**
Room and board: **$20,880**

Percentage of students receiving financial aid in 2005-06: 83%

Percentage of students receiving: Loans: 76%, Grants/scholarships: 56%, Work-study aid: 0%

Average medical school debt for the Class of 2004: $110,738

STUDENT BODY

Fall 2005 full-time enrollment: 688

Men: 55%, Women: 45%, In-state: 46%, Minorities: 47%, American Indian: 1.2%, Asian-American: 29.9%, African-American: 10.3%, Hispanic-American: 5.4%, White: 51.5%, International: 0.0%, Unknown: 1.7%

ACADEMIC PROGRAMS

The school's curriculum frequently gives first-year students substantial contact with patients.

There are opportunities for first- or second-year students to work in community health clinics.

Program offerings: AIDS, drug/alcohol abuse, family medicine, geriatrics, internal medicine, pediatrics, rural medicine, women's health

Joint degrees awarded: M.D./Ph.D., M.D./MBA, M.D./MPH, M.D./JD, M.D./M.S.W., M.D./MS.

Total National Institutes of Health (NIH) grants awarded to the medical school and affiliated hospitals: $315.2 million

CURRICULUM

(TEXT PROVIDED BY SCHOOL):

The University of Michigan Medical School's curriculum provides students with the opportunity to develop the knowledge, skills, attitudes, and behaviors for entry into all fields of graduate medical education and to assume leadership roles in the areas of clinical medicine, research, and teaching.

The first-year curriculum is interdisciplinary, with basic sciences presented in an organ-system format, covering the normal cell and organ systems, immunology, and infectious diseases. As appropriate, material is presented in a clinical context and supported by patient cases. An introductory Patients & Populations course provides students with a foundation in genetics and disease, and equips them with the knowledge and skills to construct clinical questions, conduct literature searches, and evaluate evidence. The second-year curriculum continues to be interdisciplinary and organ-system based, covering the abnormal organ systems.

Within most of the organ-systems sequences, a longitudinal patient case is introduced and discussed in small groups with clinical faculty facilitators. Each case includes personal, cultural, and medical information and is accompanied by specific questions and problems to augment learning and help students understand how patients and families experience illness.

Students begin the two-year Family-Centered Experience early in the first year. Pairs of students are assigned to families that have been recruited to help them understand how health changes, chronic conditions, and serious illnesses

affect patients and those close to them. Students explore connections between healthcare and culture, health beliefs, age, gender, and support systems. They also learn about rapport between patients and their physicians.

Clinical Foundations in Medicine modules are scheduled during breaks between the sequences in years 1 and 2 to allow students to focus on the development of clinical and communication skills.

Third- and fourth-year clinical clerkships are discipline based and include both inpatient and ambulatory experiences. Throughout the third year, students assume increasing responsibility for patient care under faculty supervision. Required clerkships include internal medicine, surgery, obstetrics/gynecology/women's health, pediatrics, family medicine, neurology, and psychiatry. Weekly Seminars in Medicine provide learning in more complex clinical contexts. Emergency medicine, sub-internship, advanced medical therapeutics, and intensive care unit rotations are required fourth-year experiences, complemented by up to seven months of elective clerkships.

Standardized patient instructors are an integral learning and assessment tool across the four-year curriculum. Comprehensive clinical assessments at the end of the second year and after completion of the required clinical clerkships assure that all students graduate with the necessary communication and clinical skills to succeed as first-year residents.

FACULTY PROFILE (FALL 2005)

Total teaching faculty: 1,905 (full-time), 468 (part-time)

Of full-time faculty, those teaching in basic sciences: 10%; in clinical programs: 90%

Of part-time faculty, those teaching in basic sciences: 5%; in clinical programs: 95%

Full-time faculty/student ratio: 2.8

SUPPORT SERVICES

The school offers students these services for dealing with stress: expanded-hour gym access, peer counseling, professional counseling, support groups.

RESIDENCY PROFILE

Most popular residency and specialty programs chosen by the 2004 and 2005 M.D. graduating classes: anesthesiology, emergency medicine, family practice, internal medicine, obstetrics and gynecology, ophthalmology, pediatrics, psychiatry, radiology–diagnostic, surgery–general.

WHERE GRADS GO

29.9%

Proportion of 2003-2005 graduates who entered primary care specialties

33%

Proportion of 2004-2005 graduates who accepted in-state residencies

University of Minnesota

- 420 Delaware Street SE, MMC 293, Minneapolis, MN 55455
- Public
- **Year Founded:** 1851
- **Tuition, 2005-2006:** In-state: $30,875; Out-of-state: $37,769
- **Enrollment 2005-2006 academic year:** 937
- **Website:** http://www.med.umn.edu
- **Specialty ranking:** family medicine: 15, pediatrics: 22, rural medicine: 7

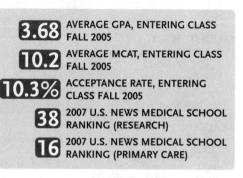

3.68 AVERAGE GPA, ENTERING CLASS FALL 2005

10.2 AVERAGE MCAT, ENTERING CLASS FALL 2005

10.3% ACCEPTANCE RATE, ENTERING CLASS FALL 2005

38 2007 U.S. NEWS MEDICAL SCHOOL RANKING (RESEARCH)

16 2007 U.S. NEWS MEDICAL SCHOOL RANKING (PRIMARY CARE)

ADMISSIONS

Admissions phone number: **(612) 625-7977**
Admissions email address: **meded@umn.edu**
Application website: **N/A**
Acceptance rate: **10.3%**
In-state acceptance rate: **22.1%**
Out-of-state acceptance rate: **4.6%**
Minority acceptance rate: **8.1%**
International acceptance rate: **12.4%**

Fall 2005 applications and acceptees

	Applied	Interviewed	Accepted	Enrolled
Total:	3,239	664	334	220
In-state:	1,052	431	233	170
Out-of-state:	2,187	233	101	50

Profile of admitted students

Average undergraduate grade point average: **3.68**
MCAT averages (scale: 1-15; writing test: J-T):
  Composite score: **10.2**
  Verbal reasoning score: **9.9**, Physical sciences score: **10.2**, Biological sciences score: **10.5**, Writing score: **Q**
Proportion with undergraduate majors in: Biological sciences: **28%**, Physical sciences: **22%**, Non-sciences: **10%**, Other health professions: **2%**, Mixed disciplines and other: **38%**
Percentage of students not coming directly from college after graduation: **54%**

Dates and details

The American Medical College Application Service (AMCAS) application is accepted.
School asks for a school-specific application as part of the admissions process.
Oldest MCAT considered for Fall 2007 entry: **2003**
Earliest application date for the 2007-2008 first-year class: **June 1, 2006**
Latest application date: **November 15, 2006**
Acceptance dates for regular application for the class entering in fall 2007:
  Earliest: **October 1, 2006**

Latest: **May 15, 2007**
The school considers requests for deferred entrance.
Starting month for the class entering in 2007–2008:
  August
The school has an Early Decision Plan (EDP).
A personal interview is required for admission.

Undergraduate coursework required

Medical school requires undergraduate work in these subjects: biology, English, organic chemistry, inorganic (general) chemistry, physics, biochemistry, humanities, mathematics, behavioral science, calculus, social sciences.

ADMISSIONS POLICY
(TEXT PROVIDED BY SCHOOL):

The two campuses have independent but similar application processes for early decision (decision by October 1) and for regular applications. Applications submitted under the regular application process are the majority and are submitted to the American Medical College Application Service between June 1 and November 15 each year.

The application is screened by admissions committee members. Qualified candidates receive a supplemental application (SA) packet, which includes instructions on completing the online portion of the SA, including a form that must accompany all recommendation letters. Applicants also must submit a $75 application fee and a current photograph. Applicants who have been granted a fee waiver by AMCAS are eligible to have the application fee waived. Applicants are given 30 days to complete the SA.

Admissions committee members evaluate candidates holistically, with the goal of educating physicians who excel both in science and in compassion. After review, qualified candidates are asked to come to each campus for interviews. Applicants are informed of the final decision no later than May 15.

COSTS AND FINANCIAL AID

Financial aid phone number: **(612) 625-4998**

Tuition, 2005-2006 academic year: **In-state: $30,875; Out-of-state: $37,769**

Room and board: **$11,220**

Percentage of students receiving financial aid in 2005-06: **93%**

Percentage of students receiving: Loans: **81%**, Grants/scholarships: **73%**, Work-study aid: **1%**

Average medical school debt for the Class of 2004: **$119,868**

STUDENT BODY

Fall 2005 full-time enrollment: **937**

Men: **50%**, Women: **50%**, In-state: **77%**, Minorities: **20%**, American Indian: **2.8%**, Asian-American: **11.8%**, African-American: **1.9%**, Hispanic-American: **2.2%**, White: **79.3%**, International: **1.9%**, Unknown: **N/A**

ACADEMIC PROGRAMS

The school's curriculum very frequently gives first-year students substantial contact with patients.

There are opportunities for first- or second-year students to work in community health clinics.

Program offerings: AIDS, drug/alcohol abuse, family medicine, geriatrics, internal medicine, pediatrics, rural medicine, women's health

Joint degrees awarded: M.D./Ph.D., M.D./MBA, M.D./MPH, M.D./M.H.I., M.D./JD.

Total National Institutes of Health (NIH) grants awarded to the medical school and affiliated hospitals: **$148.4 million**

CURRICULUM

(TEXT PROVIDED BY SCHOOL):

The University of Minnesota Medical School educates skilled, compassionate, and socially responsible physicians. The school has campuses in the Twin Cities and Duluth serving diverse populations in urban and rural Minnesota. The Duluth campus focuses on training primary care physicians for rural communities, including American Indian communities. The curriculum includes learning science fundamental to medicine, contact with patients (real and virtual) in the first year, professional skills, and a focus on interprofessionalism: Medical students learn with fellow U

of M students in pharmacy, nursing, and other disciplines. In addition, the Rural Physician Associate Program places some 35 third-year students annually with preceptors in small towns throughout Minnesota for nine months.

To graduate, students must master 13 educational objectives and the course of study for the M.D. that requires 152 weeks of academic work. A recent innovation is the Flexible M.D., in which medical students may take from 3.5 to 6 years to complete the M.D. program, at no additional cost. The school offers dual-degree programs: M.D./Ph.D., M.D./MPH, M.D./JD, M.D./MBA, M.D./MS in biomedical engineering, and M.D./M.H.I. (health informatics).

FACULTY PROFILE (FALL 2005)

Total teaching faculty: **1,585 (full-time)**, **107 (part-time)**

Of full-time faculty, those teaching in basic sciences: **15%**; in clinical programs: **85%**

Of part-time faculty, those teaching in basic sciences: **12%**; in clinical programs: **88%**

Full-time faculty/student ratio: **1.7**

SUPPORT SERVICES

The school offers students these services for dealing with stress: peer counseling, professional counseling, support groups.

RESIDENCY PROFILE

Most popular residency and specialty programs chosen by the 2004 and 2005 M.D. graduating classes: anesthesiology, emergency medicine, family practice, internal medicine, obstetrics and gynecology, orthopaedic surgery, pediatrics, psychiatry, radiology–diagnostic, surgery–general.

WHERE GRADS GO

47.4%

Proportion of 2003-2005 graduates who entered primary care specialties

52.1%

Proportion of 2004-2005 graduates who accepted in-state residencies

University of Missouri–Columbia

- ■ 1 Hospital Drive, Columbia, MO 65212
- ■ Public
- ■ **Year Founded:** 1872
- ■ **Tuition, 2005-2006:** In-state: $21,895; Out-of-state: $42,620
- ■ **Enrollment 2005-2006 academic year:** 368
- ■ **Website:** http://www.muhealth.org/~medicine/
- ■ **Specialty ranking:** family medicine: 3, rural medicine: 12

3.75 AVERAGE GPA, ENTERING CLASS FALL 2005

9.9 AVERAGE MCAT, ENTERING CLASS FALL 2005

16.2% ACCEPTANCE RATE, ENTERING CLASS FALL 2005

Unranked 2007 U.S. NEWS MEDICAL SCHOOL RANKING (RESEARCH)

16 2007 U.S. NEWS MEDICAL SCHOOL RANKING (PRIMARY CARE)

ADMISSIONS

Admissions phone number: **(573) 882-9219**
Admissions email address: **nolkej@health.missouri.edu**
Application website: **N/A**
Acceptance rate: **16.2%**
In-state acceptance rate: **31.1%**
Out-of-state acceptance rate: **5.4%**
Minority acceptance rate: **10.7%**
International acceptance rate: **N/A**

Fall 2005 applications and acceptees

	Applied	Interviewed	Accepted	Enrolled
Total:	959	301	155	96
In-state:	402	225	125	86
Out-of-state:	557	76	30	10

Profile of admitted students

Average undergraduate grade point average: **3.75**
MCAT averages (scale: 1-15; writing test: J-T):
  Composite score: **9.9**
  Verbal reasoning score: **10.0**, Physical sciences score: **9.6**, Biological sciences score: **10.2**, Writing score: **P**
Proportion with undergraduate majors in: Biological sciences: **57%**, Physical sciences: **20%**, Non-sciences: **15%**, Other health professions: **0%**, Mixed disciplines and other: **8%**
Percentage of students not coming directly from college after graduation: **N/A**

Dates and details

The American Medical College Application Service (AMCAS) application is accepted.
School asks for a school-specific application as part of the admissions process.
Oldest MCAT considered for Fall 2007 entry: **2000**
Earliest application date for the 2007-2008 first-year class: **June 1, 2006**
Latest application date: **November 1, 2006**
Acceptance dates for regular application for the class entering in fall 2007:
  Earliest: **November 15, 2006**

Latest: **August 1, 2007**
The school considers requests for deferred entrance.
Starting month for the class entering in 2007–2008:
  August
The school has an Early Decision Plan (EDP).
A personal interview is required for admission.

Undergraduate coursework required

Medical school requires undergraduate work in these subjects: biology, English, organic chemistry, inorganic (general) chemistry, physics, mathematics, demonstration of writing skills.

ADMISSIONS POLICY
(TEXT PROVIDED BY SCHOOL):

Applicants must have completed at least 90 semester hours (not including physical education and military science) at a recognized college or university. Required coursework includes: English composition or writing intensive (two semesters); college-level mathematics (one semester); general biology with lab (eight hours); general chemistry with lab (eight hours); organic chemistry with lab (eight hours); and general physics with lab (eight hours).

One or two courses in biochemistry are strongly recommended, and one or two additional biology or chemistry courses are recommended. Only those courses required for science majors are acceptable; introductory survey science courses are not.

The Medical College Admission Test is required.

COSTS AND FINANCIAL AID

Financial aid phone number: **(573) 882-2923**
Tuition, 2005-2006 academic year: **In-state: $21,895; Out-of-state: $42,620**
Room and board: **$8,433**
Percentage of students receiving financial aid in 2005-06: **95%**
Percentage of students receiving: Loans: **95%**, Grants/scholarships: **44%**, Work-study aid: **0%**
Average medical school debt for the Class of 2004: **$108,805**

STUDENT BODY

Fall 2005 full-time enrollment: **368**
Men: **52%**, Women: **48%**, In-state: **98%**, Minorities: **16%**,
American Indian: **0.0%**, Asian-American: **7.3%**, African-
American: **5.7%**, Hispanic-American: **1.4%**, White:
85.6%, International: **0.0%**, Unknown: **0.0%**

ACADEMIC PROGRAMS

The school's curriculum frequently gives first-year students
substantial contact with patients.
There are opportunities for first- or second-year students to
work in community health clinics.
Program offerings: AIDS, drug/alcohol abuse, family
medicine, geriatrics, internal medicine, pediatrics, rural
medicine, women's health
Joint degrees awarded: M.D./Ph.D., M.D./MS
Total National Institutes of Health (NIH) grants awarded to
the medical school and affiliated hospitals: **$15.3 million**

CURRICULUM

(TEXT PROVIDED BY SCHOOL):
Each year, 96 first-year slots are available. The School of
Medicine is a pioneer in the style of medical education that
emphasizes problem solving, self-directed learning, and
early clinical experience. In addition, the Bryant Scholars
Program and the Rural Track Program offered through the
school give students an opportunity to gain education and
experience practicing medicine in a rural area.

A faculty of 91 basic scientists and 451 clinicians joins
350 residents to supervise patient care, student teaching and
research. The school provides postgraduate medical training
in virtually all specialties and subspecialties.

As part of the Health Sciences Center, the school continues to revolutionize medicine by exploring innovative ways
to deliver healthcare to the residents of Missouri. Its faculty
and administrators are leading a major initiative that allows
rural physicians and their patients to consult with Health
Sciences Center specialists via telemedicine technology.

FACULTY PROFILE (FALL 2005)

Total teaching faculty: **451 (full-time), 91 (part-time)**
Of full-time faculty, those teaching in basic sciences: **20%**;
in clinical programs: **80%**
Of part-time faculty, those teaching in basic sciences: **18%**;
in clinical programs: **82%**
Full-time faculty/student ratio: **1.2**

SUPPORT SERVICES

The school offers students these services for dealing with
stress: peer counseling, professional counseling, support
groups.

RESIDENCY PROFILE

Most popular residency and specialty programs chosen by the
2004 and 2005 M.D. graduating classes: anesthesiology,
emergency medicine, family practice, internal medicine, pediatrics, radiology–diagnostic, internal medicine/pediatrics.

WHERE GRADS GO

52%
*Proportion of 2003-2005 graduates who entered primary
care specialties*

44%
*Proportion of 2004-2005 graduates who accepted in-state
residencies*

University of Nebraska

COLLEGE OF MEDICINE

- 986585 Nebraska Medical Center, Omaha, NE 68198-6585
- Public
- Year Founded: N/A
- Tuition, 2005-2006: In-state: $21,475; Out-of-state: $49,105
- Enrollment 2005-2006 academic year: 476
- Website: http://www.unmc.edu/UNCOM/
- Specialty ranking: rural medicine: 9

3.75 AVERAGE GPA, ENTERING CLASS FALL 2005

9.7 AVERAGE MCAT, ENTERING CLASS FALL 2005

15.3% ACCEPTANCE RATE, ENTERING CLASS FALL 2005

Unranked 2007 U.S. NEWS MEDICAL SCHOOL RANKING (RESEARCH)

11 2007 U.S. NEWS MEDICAL SCHOOL RANKING (PRIMARY CARE)

ADMISSIONS

Admissions phone number: **(402) 559-2259**
Admissions email address: **grrogers@unmc.edu**
Application website: **N/A**
Acceptance rate: **15.3%**
In-state acceptance rate: **45.6%**
Out-of-state acceptance rate: **4.3%**
Minority acceptance rate: **8.2%**
International acceptance rate: **0.0%**

Fall 2005 applications and acceptees

	Applied	Interviewed	Accepted	Enrolled
Total:	1,101	382	169	122
In-state:	294	270	134	105
Out-of-state:	807	112	35	17

Profile of admitted students

Average undergraduate grade point average: **3.75**
MCAT averages (scale: 1-15; writing test: J-T):
  Composite score: **9.7**
  Verbal reasoning score: **9.6**, Physical sciences score: **9.5**,
  Biological sciences score: **10.0**, Writing score: **N/A**
Proportion with undergraduate majors in: Biological
  sciences: **46%**, Physical sciences: **22%**, Non-sciences:
  31%, Other health professions: **0%**, Mixed disciplines
  and other: **1%**
Percentage of students not coming directly from college
  after graduation: **N/A**

Dates and details

The American Medical College Application Service
  (AMCAS) application is accepted.
School asks for a school-specific application as part of the
  admissions process.
Oldest MCAT considered for Fall 2007 entry: **2004**
Earliest application date for the 2007-2008 first-year class:
  June 1, 2006
Latest application date: **November 1, 2006**
Acceptance dates for regular application for the class
  entering in fall 2007:
  Earliest: **December 1, 2006**

Latest: **August 15, 2007**
The school doesn't consider requests for deferred entrance.
Starting month for the class entering in 2007–2008:
  August
The school has an Early Decision Plan (EDP).
A personal interview is required for admission.

Undergraduate coursework required

Medical school requires undergraduate work in these subjects: biology, English, organic chemistry, inorganic (general) chemistry, physics, biochemistry, humanities, calculus.

ADMISSIONS POLICY

(TEXT PROVIDED BY SCHOOL):

Students are selected on the basis of a total assessment of
each candidate's motivation, interest, character, demonstrated intellectual ability, previous academic record including its trends, personal interviews, scores on the MCAT and
general fitness and promise for a career in medicine.
Academic credentials are evaluated on the basis of course
level and load, involvement in co-curricular activities or
employment as well as other influential factors. The personal comments section of the AMCAS application is considered extremely important by the Admissions Committee
and should be utilized. Cut-off levels for GPAs or for scores
on the MCAT are not used; however, applicants are
reminded of the competition for entrance and are advised to
be realistic. Personal attributes are assessed through letters
of reference and in the interview. The College makes every
effort in each stage of the review process to consider each
applicant as an individual; therefore, the interview is an
important element of the selection process. Although preference is given to residents of Nebraska, students from
other states are considered for admission. Approximately
one-forth of Nebraska applicants receive acceptances.
Students from rural areas, small towns or disadvantaged
backgrounds are encouraged to apply. The potential for
service to underserved communities is taken into consideration during the admissions evaluation.

COSTS AND FINANCIAL AID

Financial aid phone number: **(402) 559-4199**

Tuition, 2005-2006 academic year: **In-state: $21,475; Out-of-state: $49,105**

Room and board: **$13,500**

Percentage of students receiving financial aid in 2005-06: **100%**

Percentage of students receiving: Loans: **93%**, Grants/scholarships: **64%**, Work-study aid: **0%**

Average medical school debt for the Class of 2004: **$100,875**

STUDENT BODY

Fall 2005 full-time enrollment: **476**

Men: **59%**, Women: **41%**, In-state: **87%**, Minorities: **8%**, American Indian: **0.6%**, Asian-American: **3.8%**, African-American: **2.1%**, Hispanic-American: **1.1%**, White: **91.8%**, International: **0.0%**, Unknown: **0.6%**

ACADEMIC PROGRAMS

The school's curriculum very frequently gives first-year students substantial contact with patients.

There are opportunities for first- or second-year students to work in community health clinics.

Program offerings: AIDS, drug/alcohol abuse, family medicine, geriatrics, internal medicine, pediatrics, rural medicine, women's health

Joint degrees awarded: M.D./Ph.D.

Total National Institutes of Health (NIH) grants awarded to the medical school and affiliated hospitals: **$33.0 million**

CURRICULUM

(TEXT PROVIDED BY SCHOOL):

The College of Medicine enjoys a distinguished record of excellence in medical education. Our innovative medical curriculum provides early exposure to patient care. The spectrum of these clinical experiences are carefully integrated into and correlated with basic medical sciences subject matter in the first two years. Traditionally, in the past, these two years of the curriculum have been dedicated almost exclusively to basic science courses. Unique components of the integrated clinical experiences include clinical problem-based learning in small groups, the use of "standardized" patients as case examples, a longitudinal clinical experience assigned to a primary care physician and a block clinical rotation in rural Nebraska. The integration of subject matter continues in the last two years, but this time, basic sciences are woven into the clinical clerkships to reinforce their importance to the understanding of pathophysiology and therapeutics. A few selected students might choose a combined M.D./Ph.D program that has a reputation of producing academic physicians and, thus, provides opportunities for research education.

FACULTY PROFILE (FALL 2005)

Total teaching faculty: **579 (full-time)**, **114 (part-time)**

Of full-time faculty, those teaching in basic sciences: **15%**; in clinical programs: **85%**

Of part-time faculty, those teaching in basic sciences: **5%**; in clinical programs: **95%**

Full-time faculty/student ratio: **1.2**

SUPPORT SERVICES

The school offers students these services for dealing with stress: expanded-hour gym access, professional counseling, religious support, support groups.

RESIDENCY PROFILE

Most popular residency and specialty programs chosen by the 2004 and 2005 M.D. graduating classes: emergency medicine, family practice, internal medicine, pediatrics, psychiatry, surgery–general, internal medicine/pediatrics.

WHERE GRADS GO

61%

Proportion of 2003-2005 graduates who entered primary care specialties

39%

Proportion of 2004-2005 graduates who accepted in-state residencies

University of New Mexico

■ Basic Medical Sciences Building, Room 107, Albuquerque, NM 87131
■ Public
■ Year Founded: 1964
■ Tuition, 2005-2006: In-state: $14,642; Out-of-state: $38,781
■ Enrollment 2005-2006 academic year: 325
■ Website: http://hsc.unm.edu/som/
■ Specialty ranking: family medicine: 7, rural medicine: 2

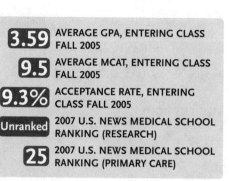

3.59 AVERAGE GPA, ENTERING CLASS FALL 2005

9.5 AVERAGE MCAT, ENTERING CLASS FALL 2005

9.3% ACCEPTANCE RATE, ENTERING CLASS FALL 2005

Unranked 2007 U.S. NEWS MEDICAL SCHOOL RANKING (RESEARCH)

25 2007 U.S. NEWS MEDICAL SCHOOL RANKING (PRIMARY CARE)

ADMISSIONS

Admissions phone number: **(505) 272-4766**
Admissions email address:
  somadmissions@salud.unm.edu
Application website: **http://hsc.unm.edu/som/admiss**
Acceptance rate: **9.3%**
In-state acceptance rate: **37.6%**
Out-of-state acceptance rate: **0.5%**
Minority acceptance rate: **9.0%**
International acceptance rate: **N/A**

Fall 2005 applications and acceptees

	Applied	Interviewed	Accepted	Enrolled
Total:	994	197	92	75
In-state:	234	190	88	71
Out-of-state:	760	7	4	4

Profile of admitted students

Average undergraduate grade point average: **3.59**
MCAT averages (scale: 1-15; writing test: J-T):
  Composite score: **9.5**
  Verbal reasoning score: **9.5**, Physical sciences score: **9.1**, Biological sciences score: **9.8**, Writing score: **N/A**
Proportion with undergraduate majors in: Biological sciences: **42%**, Physical sciences: **26%**, Non-sciences: **7%**, Other health professions: **1%**, Mixed disciplines and other: **24%**
Percentage of students not coming directly from college after graduation: **N/A**

Dates and details

The American Medical College Application Service (AMCAS) application is accepted.
School asks for a school-specific application as part of the admissions process.
Oldest MCAT considered for Fall 2007 entry: **2002**
Earliest application date for the 2007-2008 first-year class: **June 1, 2006**
Latest application date: **November 15, 2006**
Acceptance dates for regular application for the class entering in fall 2007:

Earliest: **March 15, 2006**
Latest: **March 15, 2006**
The school considers requests for deferred entrance.
Starting month for the class entering in 2007–2008: **August**
The school has an Early Decision Plan (EDP).
A personal interview is required for admission.

Undergraduate coursework required

Medical school requires undergraduate work in these subjects: biology, organic chemistry, inorganic (general) chemistry, physics, biochemistry.

ADMISSIONS POLICY
(TEXT PROVIDED BY SCHOOL):

Information that is essential in the decision making process is gleaned from the application form, letters of recommendation and interviews with members of the Committee on Admissions. At this time, all applicants to the University of New Mexico School of Medicine are given two interviews. Members of the Committee on Admissions interview applicants and make the final acceptance decisions. The medical school feels that it has an obligation to help meet the physician manpower needs of the state by selection of students who are likely to train in specialty areas of current need and have a strong motivation to remain in or return to the areas in New Mexico that are medically underserved areas of the state. An important factor in considering students for admission is the residency status of the student. As a state-supported institution in a state where health care needs are great, the medical school feels strongly that most of the accepted applicants should be residents of New Mexico. The school acknowledges a secondary obligation to students from Montana, Idaho and Wyoming, states without medical schools, through participation in the Western Interstate Commission on Higher Education (WICHE) program and will continue to accept one or two of these students each year. All non-resident applicants, including those from Montana, Idaho and Wyoming, must apply during the Early Decision Program to be given consideration. During the last several years more than 95 percent of the accepted students have been residents of this state. The UNM School of Medicine has a compelling interest in assuring a regional representation of diversity among our faculty, staff and student body to comprehensively achieve our educational mission and effectively meet our obligation to the state in addressing statewide health care access problems. It is imperative that the UNM School of Medicine endeavors to obtain a critical mass of both Hispanic and Native American students, as well as faculty role models, and that we assure a learning environment that enhances cultural sensitivity and competence. To this end, the UNM School of Medicine will attempt to recruit and accept qualified Hispanic and Native American applicants from New Mexico into the MD degree program.

COSTS AND FINANCIAL AID

Financial aid phone number: **(505) 272-8008**
Tuition, 2005-2006 academic year: **In-state: $14,642**; **Out-of-state: $38,781**
Room and board: **$8,312**
Percentage of students receiving financial aid in 2005-06: **89%**
Percentage of students receiving: Loans: **86%**, Grants/scholarships: **81%**, Work-study aid: **0%**
Average medical school debt for the Class of 2004: **$92,687**

STUDENT BODY

Fall 2005 full-time enrollment: **325**
Men: **43%**, Women: **57%**, In-state: **98%**, Minorities: **40%**, American Indian: **4.0%**, Asian-American: **7.4%**, African-American: **0.6%**, Hispanic-American: **28.0%**, White: **59.7%**, International: **0.0%**, Unknown: **0.3%**

ACADEMIC PROGRAMS

The school's curriculum very frequently gives first-year students substantial contact with patients.
There are opportunities for first- or second-year students to work in community health clinics.
Program offerings: AIDS, drug/alcohol abuse, family medicine, geriatrics, internal medicine, pediatrics, rural medicine, women's health
Joint degrees awarded: M.D./Ph.D., M.D./MPH
Total National Institutes of Health (NIH) grants awarded to the medical school and affiliated hospitals: **$40.1 million**

CURRICULUM

(TEXT PROVIDED BY SCHOOL):
The primary goal of the School of Medicine is to produce competent, humanistic physicians capable of pursuing a complete spectrum of medical careers. The educational program strives to imbue the medical student with a deep concern for continuing intellectual growth that will lead to a lifelong commitment to self-education. UNM seeks to recruit and retain educationally disadvantaged New Mexicans in healthcare professions.

Unique aspects of the UNM School of Medicine include problem-based and student-centered learning; early clinical skills learning coupled with sustained, community-based learning; the incorporation of a population and behavioral

perspective into the clinical years; peer teaching; computer-assisted instruction; and biweekly seminars on professional responsibility. The curriculum also addresses the historically unmet as well as changing healthcare needs of New Mexico's population.

Integration of learning throughout the four years includes consideration of normal and abnormal; biology, behavior, and population; primary and tertiary care; and urban and rural community experiences. The curriculum consists of three phases:

Phase 1 (18 months) is organized around organ systems, each incorporating three perspectives: biologic, behavioral, and population. Hands-on medical skills are gained through weekly clinical skills and laboratory sessions. Students have the opportunity to apply these skills in a weekly continuity clinic. At the end of the first academic year, students participate in an in-depth Practical Immersion Experience in a professional setting in either a rural or urban community.

In Phase 2 (12 months), students spend half of their time in an ambulatory setting and half on inpatient services. This phase features continued reinforcement of basic and clinical science integration and development of basic science learning resources for use on clinical services.

Phase 3 (15 months) features more hospital-based clinical experiences in which the student has progressive responsibility for patient care under the supervision of house staff and faculty. One month is spent working with a practicing physician.

FACULTY PROFILE (FALL 2005)

Total teaching faculty: **636 (full-time)**, **137 (part-time)**
Of full-time faculty, those teaching in basic sciences: **10%**; in clinical programs: **90%**
Of part-time faculty, those teaching in basic sciences: **7%**; in clinical programs: **93%**
Full-time faculty/student ratio: **2.0**

SUPPORT SERVICES

The school offers students these services for dealing with stress: expanded-hour gym access, peer counseling, professional counseling, support groups.

RESIDENCY PROFILE

Most popular residency and specialty programs chosen by the 2004 and 2005 M.D. graduating classes: anesthesiology, emergency medicine, family practice, internal medicine, obstetrics and gynecology, orthopaedic surgery, pediatrics, psychiatry, radiology–diagnostic, surgery–general.

WHERE GRADS GO

43%
Proportion of 2003-2005 graduates who entered primary care specialties

36%
Proportion of 2004-2005 graduates who accepted in-state residencies

University of North Carolina–Chapel Hill

■ CB #7000, 125 MacNider Building, Chapel Hill, NC 27599-7000
■ **Public**
■ **Year Founded:** 1879
■ **Tuition, 2005-2006:** In-state: $10,740; Out-of-state: $34,406
■ **Enrollment 2005-2006 academic year:** 732
■ **Website:** http://www.med.unc.edu/admit/
■ **Specialty ranking:** AIDS: 9, drug/alcohol abuse: 13, family medicine: 2, internal medicine: 16, pediatrics: 21, rural medicine: 4, women's health: 9

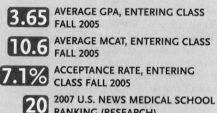

3.65 AVERAGE GPA, ENTERING CLASS FALL 2005

10.6 AVERAGE MCAT, ENTERING CLASS FALL 2005

7.1% ACCEPTANCE RATE, ENTERING CLASS FALL 2005

20 2007 U.S. NEWS MEDICAL SCHOOL RANKING (RESEARCH)

2 2007 U.S. NEWS MEDICAL SCHOOL RANKING (PRIMARY CARE)

ADMISSIONS
Admissions phone number: **(919) 962-8331**
Admissions email address: **admissions@med.unc.edu**
Application website: **N/A**
Acceptance rate: **7.1%**
In-state acceptance rate: **22.4%**
Out-of-state acceptance rate: **1.6%**
Minority acceptance rate: **5.8%**
International acceptance rate: **8.1%**

Fall 2005 applications and acceptees

	Applied	Interviewed	Accepted	Enrolled
Total:	3,154	565	224	160
In-state:	832	480	186	142
Out-of-state:	2,322	85	38	18

Profile of admitted students
Average undergraduate grade point average: **3.65**
MCAT averages (scale: 1-15; writing test: J-T):
  Composite score: **10.6**
  Verbal reasoning score: **10.3**, Physical sciences score: **10.5**, Biological sciences score: **10.9**, Writing score: **N**
Proportion with undergraduate majors in: Biological sciences: **48%**, Physical sciences: **13%**, Non-sciences: **10%**, Other health professions: **3%**, Mixed disciplines and other: **27%**
Percentage of students not coming directly from college after graduation: **55%**

Dates and details
The American Medical College Application Service (AMCAS) application is accepted.
School asks for a school-specific application as part of the admissions process.
Oldest MCAT considered for Fall 2007 entry: **2003**
Earliest application date for the 2007-2008 first-year class: **June 1, 2006**
Latest application date: **November 15, 2006**
Acceptance dates for regular application for the class entering in fall 2007:
  Earliest: **October 15, 2006**

Latest: **August 15, 2007**
The school considers requests for deferred entrance.
Starting month for the class entering in 2007–2008:
  August
The school has an Early Decision Plan (EDP).
A personal interview is required for admission.

Undergraduate coursework required
Medical school requires undergraduate work in these subjects: biology, English, organic chemistry, inorganic (general) chemistry, physics.

ADMISSIONS POLICY
(TEXT PROVIDED BY SCHOOL):
The Committee on Admissions evaluates the qualifications of all applicants to select those with the greatest potential for accomplishment in one of the many careers open to medical graduates. Preference is given to North Carolina residents. The University of North Carolina does not discriminate on the basis of race, national origin, religion, sex, age, or handicap. The American Medical College Application Service application is used for initial screening. In making its final selections from the group of qualified applicants, the committee considers evidence of each candidate's motivation, maturity, leadership, integrity, and a variety of other personal qualifications and accomplishments in addition to the scholastic record. No special admission tracks or quotas are applied among applicants. The undergraduate major is not an important consideration, but excellence in the chosen field is expected.

COSTS AND FINANCIAL AID
Financial aid phone number: **(919) 962-6117**
Tuition, 2005-2006 academic year: **In-state: $10,740; Out-of-state: $34,406**
Room and board: **$24,384**
Percentage of students receiving financial aid in 2005-06: **84%**
Percentage of students receiving: Loans: **80%**, Grants/scholarships: **80%**, Work-study aid: **0%**

Average medical school debt for the Class of 2004:
$74,605

STUDENT BODY
Fall 2005 full-time enrollment: **732**
Men: **48%**, Women: **52%**, In-state: **84%**, Minorities: **29%**

ACADEMIC PROGRAMS
The school's curriculum frequently gives first-year students
substantial contact with patients.
There are opportunities for first- or second-year students to
work in community health clinics.
Program offerings: AIDS, drug/alcohol abuse, family
medicine, geriatrics, internal medicine, pediatrics, rural
medicine, women's health
Joint degrees awarded: M.D./Ph.D.
Total National Institutes of Health (NIH) grants awarded to
the medical school and affiliated hospitals: **$212.3
million**

CURRICULUM
(TEXT PROVIDED BY SCHOOL):
The curriculum encompasses 144 weeks of instruction,
preparing students for career options through a comprehensive set of learning experiences. Students are taught fundamental principles of medicine and their underlying
scientific foundations with an emphasis on developing critical thinking and medical problem-solving skills. The new
first and second year interdisciplinary block curricula,
organized by organ systems, are primarily devoted to the
study of basic sciences, pathophysiology and disease
processes. Several integrated clinical cases provide opportunities to study specific issues as a means of operationalizing
the clinical relevance of the basic sciences. First and second
year students acquire basic clinical skills through the two-
year Introduction to Clinical Medicine course.
   A new clinical curriculum will be implemented starting
in July 2006. The third year will include core clerkships in
medicine, ob/gyn, psychiatry and neurology, family medicine, surgery, and pediatrics. The fourth-year curriculum
will include selective offerings in critical care, ambulatory

care, fundamentals of acute care, a week-long capstone case
in complex issues of practice, and more time for students to
explore early career options through the electives program
of over 300 offerings. The clinical curriculum will offer core
clinical training within a framework of flexibility that supports both students who are prepared to specialize early and
those who seek a greater range of experience.

FACULTY PROFILE (FALL 2005)
Total teaching faculty: **1,238 (full-time)**, **127 (part-time)**
Of full-time faculty, those teaching in basic sciences: **18%**;
in clinical programs: **82%**
Of part-time faculty, those teaching in basic sciences: **6%**;
in clinical programs: **94%**
Full-time faculty/student ratio: **1.7**

SUPPORT SERVICES
The school offers students these services for dealing with
stress: peer counseling, professional counseling, support
groups.

RESIDENCY PROFILE
Most popular residency and specialty programs chosen by
the 2004 and 2005 M.D. graduating classes: anesthesiology,
emergency medicine, family practice, internal medicine,
pediatrics, psychiatry, surgery–general.

WHERE GRADS GO

48%
*Proportion of 2003-2005 graduates who entered primary
care specialties*

31%
*Proportion of 2004-2005 graduates who accepted in-state
residencies*

University of North Dakota

- 501 N. Columbia Road, PO Box 9037, Grand Forks, ND 58202-9037
- Public
- **Year Founded:** 1905
- **Tuition, 2005-2006:** In-state: $20,125; Out-of-state: $51,699
- **Enrollment 2005-2006 academic year:** 236
- **Website:** http://www.med.und.nodak.edu
- **Specialty ranking:** rural medicine: 12

3.70	AVERAGE GPA, ENTERING CLASS FALL 2005
9.1	AVERAGE MCAT, ENTERING CLASS FALL 2005
33.6%	ACCEPTANCE RATE, ENTERING CLASS FALL 2005
Unranked	2007 U.S. NEWS MEDICAL SCHOOL RANKING (RESEARCH)
Unranked	2007 U.S. NEWS MEDICAL SCHOOL RANKING (PRIMARY CARE)

ADMISSIONS

Admissions phone number: **(701) 777-4221**
Admissions email address: **jdheit@medicine.nodak.edu**
Application website:
http://www.med.und.nodak.edu/admissions.html
Acceptance rate: **33.6%**
In-state acceptance rate: **43.8%**
Out-of-state acceptance rate: **23.0%**
Minority acceptance rate: **N/A**
International acceptance rate: **N/A**

Fall 2005 applications and acceptees

	Applied	Interviewed	Accepted	Enrolled
Total:	250	153	84	61
In-state:	128	94	56	44
Out-of-state:	122	59	28	17

Profile of admitted students

Average undergraduate grade point average: **3.70**
MCAT averages (scale: 1-15; writing test: J-T):
Composite score: **9.1**
Verbal reasoning score: **8.9**, Physical sciences score: **8.9**,
Biological sciences score: **9.7**, Writing score: **O**
Proportion with undergraduate majors in: Biological sciences: **61%**, Physical sciences: **16%**, Non-sciences: **11%**, Other health professions: **3%**, Mixed disciplines and other: **8%**
Percentage of students not coming directly from college after graduation: **27%**

Dates and details

The American Medical College Application Service (AMCAS) application is not accepted.
School does not ask for a school-specific application as part of the admissions process.
Oldest MCAT considered for Fall 2007 entry: **2003**
Earliest application date for the 2007-2008 first-year class: **July 1, 2006**
Latest application date: **November 1, 2006**
Acceptance dates for regular application for the class entering in fall 2007:

Earliest: **January 15, 2007**
Latest: **August 1, 2007**
The school considers requests for deferred entrance.
Starting month for the class entering in 2007–2008: **August**
The school doesn't have an Early Decision Plan (EDP).
A personal interview is required for admission.

Undergraduate coursework required

Medical school requires undergraduate work in these subjects: biology/zoology, English, organic chemistry, inorganic (general) chemistry, physics, mathematics, behavioral science.

ADMISSIONS POLICY
(TEXT PROVIDED BY SCHOOL):

It is the university's policy that there shall be no discrimination in admissions based on race, religion, age, creed, color, sex, disability, sexual orientation, national origin, marital status, veteran status, or political belief or affiliation. Preference in admission is given to residents of North Dakota. A resident is any applicant who has lived in North Dakota for 12 months prior to November 1 of the year of application and who is a U.S. citizen or legal permanent resident. Applicants certified by the Western Interstate Commission on Higher Education receive equal preference for up to six positions in each entering class. Residents of Minnesota also are considered for admission on a limited basis. Enrolled members of federally recognized tribes, regardless of state of residency, may apply through the school's INMED Program.

Application forms may be submitted either electronically or in paper format, no later than November 1. The school does not use the American Medical College Application Service. The completed application folder consists of the application form, a personal statement, four letters of recommendation, Medical College Admission Test scores, official academic transcripts, and a $50 nonrefundable application fee. Prior to admission, a minimum of 90 semester hours of credit from an approved college or university must be completed. Preference is given to applicants who will have completed an undergraduate degree and who are broadly educated in the sciences and humanities. A minimum cumulative and science grade-point average of 3.0 is expected. Applicants favorably considered for admission are invited for personal interviews with the Committee on Admissions. In addition to high academic achievement, selection is based on a number of factors, including qualities such as motivation and commitment to a medical career, empathy and compassion in interpersonal relationships, maturity and flexibility in dealing with problems, and the ability to work with others

COSTS AND FINANCIAL AID

Financial aid phone number: **(701) 777-2849**
Tuition, 2005-2006 academic year: **In-state: $20,125; Out-of-state: $51,699**
Room and board: **$8,704**
Percentage of students receiving financial aid in 2005-06: **98%**
Percentage of students receiving: Loans: **95%**, Grants/scholarships: **55%**, Work-study aid: **0%**
Average medical school debt for the Class of 2004: **$108,710**

STUDENT BODY

Fall 2005 full-time enrollment: **236**
Men: **48%**, Women: **52%**, In-state: **85%**, Minorities: **11%**, American Indian: **8.9%**, Asian-American: **1.7%**, African-American: **N/A**, Hispanic-American: **0.8%**, White: **88.6%**, International: **N/A**, Unknown: **N/A**

ACADEMIC PROGRAMS

The school's curriculum frequently gives first-year students substantial contact with patients.
There aren't opportunities for first- or second-year students to work in community health clinics.
Program offerings: AIDS, drug/alcohol abuse, family medicine, geriatrics, internal medicine, pediatrics, rural medicine, women's health
Joint degrees awarded: M.D./Ph.D., M.D./MPH, M.D./MS
Total National Institutes of Health (NIH) grants awarded to the medical school and affiliated hospitals: **N/A**

CURRICULUM

(TEXT PROVIDED BY SCHOOL):
The University of North Dakota School of Medicine and Health Sciences is a university-based, community-integrated medical education program. Students spend the initial two years attending classes at the main campus in Grand Forks. The third year is taken at one of three regional campuses in Bismarck, Fargo, or Grand Forks. Minot is added as one of four area campuses for completion of the senior year.

The curriculum for years 1 and 2 is organized in eight 10-week blocks. Using an interdisciplinary approach, Block 1 presents the basic foundation for understanding the functional biology of cells and tissue. An organ-system approach is utilized for the remainder of the first year (blocks 2-4).

Blocks 5-8, the second-year curriculum, stress pathobiology. The teaching of foundational clinical sciences also occurs on a continuing basis. The curriculum is presented through lectures and small-group sessions. Within a patient-centered learning format, the small-group sessions are designed to facilitate the integration of basic sciences with clinically relevant cases. To be successful, students must synthesize large amounts of information, effectively apply science concepts to clinical problems, and integrate concepts across disciplines.

The third year consists of six core clerkships of eight weeks' duration and a two-hour, didactic community medicine and epidemiology course. The clerkships include internal medicine, surgery, obstetrics and gynecology, pediatrics, psychiatry, and family medicine. A limited number of students also may complete 28 weeks of the third year in a rural community through the Rural Opportunities in Medical Education program. The fourth year consists of two acting internships of four weeks each, one in medicine and the other in surgery; six electives of four weeks each; and a final one-week transitional classroom activity.

The school utilizes a grading system of satisfactory/unsatisfactory only for the first year; the system changes to honors/satisfactory/unsatisfactory for the final three years.

FACULTY PROFILE (FALL 2005)

Total teaching faculty: **160 (full-time), 1,218 (part-time)**
Of full-time faculty, those teaching in basic sciences: **46%**; in clinical programs: **54%**
Of part-time faculty, those teaching in basic sciences: **3%**; in clinical programs: **97%**
Full-time faculty/student ratio: **0.7**

SUPPORT SERVICES

The school offers students these services for dealing with stress: expanded-hour gym access, professional counseling, religious support, support groups.

RESIDENCY PROFILE

Most popular residency and specialty programs chosen by the 2004 and 2005 M.D. graduating classes: emergency medicine, family practice, internal medicine, neurology, obstetrics and gynecology, orthopaedic surgery, pathology–anatomic and clinical, pediatrics, radiology–diagnostic, surgery–general.

WHERE GRADS GO

28%
Proportion of 2003-2005 graduates who entered primary care specialties

19.2%
Proportion of 2004-2005 graduates who accepted in-state residencies

University of Oklahoma

- PO Box 26901, BMSB 357, Oklahoma City, OK 73190
- Public
- Year Founded: 1900
- Tuition, 2005-2006: In-state: $17,021; Out-of-state: $39,109
- Enrollment 2005-2006 academic year: 582
- Website: http://www.medicine.ouhsc.edu
- Specialty ranking: N/A

3.68	AVERAGE GPA, ENTERING CLASS FALL 2005
9.6	AVERAGE MCAT, ENTERING CLASS FALL 2005
19.6%	ACCEPTANCE RATE, ENTERING CLASS FALL 2005
Unranked	2007 U.S. NEWS MEDICAL SCHOOL RANKING (RESEARCH)
Unranked	2007 U.S. NEWS MEDICAL SCHOOL RANKING (PRIMARY CARE)

ADMISSIONS

Admissions phone number: **(405) 271-2331**
Admissions email address: **adminmed@ouhsc.edu**
Application website: **http://www.aamc.org**
Acceptance rate: **19.6%**
In-state acceptance rate: **44.1%**
Out-of-state acceptance rate: **4.9%**
Minority acceptance rate: **16.3%**
International acceptance rate: **N/A**

Fall 2005 applications and acceptees

	Applied	Interviewed	Accepted	Enrolled
Total:	1,012	241	198	152
In-state:	379	203	167	137
Out-of-state:	633	38	31	15

Profile of admitted students

Average undergraduate grade point average: **3.68**
MCAT averages (scale: 1-15; writing test: J-T):
  Composite score: **9.6**
  Verbal reasoning score: **9.7**, Physical sciences score: **9.5**,
  Biological sciences score: **9.7**, Writing score: **O**
Proportion with undergraduate majors in: Biological
  sciences: **40%**, Physical sciences: **24%**, Non-sciences:
  13%, Other health professions: **2%**, Mixed disciplines
  and other: **21%**
Percentage of students not coming directly from college
  after graduation: **18%**

Dates and details

The American Medical College Application Service
  (AMCAS) application is accepted.
School does not ask for a school-specific application as part
  of the admissions process.
Oldest MCAT considered for Fall 2007 entry: **2001**
Earliest application date for the 2007-2008 first-year class:
  June 1, 2006
Latest application date: **October 15, 2006**
Acceptance dates for regular application for the class
  entering in fall 2007:
  Earliest: **November 15, 2006**

Latest: **March 15, 2007**
The school doesn't consider requests for deferred entrance.
Starting month for the class entering in 2007–2008:
  August
The school doesn't have an Early Decision Plan (EDP).
A personal interview is required for admission.

Undergraduate coursework required

Medical school requires undergraduate work in these subjects: biology/zoology, English, organic chemistry, inorganic
(general) chemistry, physics, molecular and cell biology,
humanities, social sciences.

ADMISSIONS POLICY
(TEXT PROVIDED BY SCHOOL):

The University of Oklahoma College of Medicine participates in the American Medical College Application Service.
Applicants to the M.D. program begin the online application process during the spring or summer, a year in
advance of when they wish to be admitted.

As a general rule, the College of Medicine will consider
applicants with 90 or more hours of college work. No particular major is given preference, but the applicant must
understand and be able to utilize scientific information. A
broad education is encouraged. A letter grade of C or better
is required in all prerequisite courses. Pass/fail grading,
Advanced Placement, and College Level Examination
Program courses are accepted if a subsequent higher course
is taken for a grade.

Preference in admission is given to Oklahoma residents.
Only nonresidents with superior academic records and ties
to the state should apply.

All applicants are required to take the Medical College
Admission Test. Eligible applicants to the College of
Medicine are those students with a grade-point average of
3.0 or better and a MCAT average score of 7.0 or better.
Applicants must be U.S. citizens or hold a permanent visa.

All applicants selected for final consideration will be
interviewed between December and February. The College
of Medicine endeavors to have a class selected by March 1.

Approximately 150 students are admitted to the first-year class, at least 85 percent from within Oklahoma.

Admissions decisions are based on an applicant's indications and probabilities of successfully completing medical school, intellectual ability, academic achievement, character, motivation, and maturity. The assessment utilizes college grades, MCAT scores, letters of recommendation, personal statements, and interview results.

Intellectual ability and academic achievement alone are not sufficient to assure the professional development and commitment required of a physician. Traits of personality, maturity, and character also are necessary.

COSTS AND FINANCIAL AID
Financial aid phone number: **(405) 271-2118**
Tuition, 2005-2006 academic year: **In-state: $17,021; Out-of-state: $39,109**
Room and board: **N/A**
Percentage of students receiving financial aid in 2005-06: **90%**
Percentage of students receiving: Loans: **86%**, Grants/scholarships: **42%**, Work-study aid: **0%**
Average medical school debt for the Class of 2004: **$118,000**

STUDENT BODY
Fall 2005 full-time enrollment: **582**
Men: **61%**, Women: **39%**, In-state: **96%**, Minorities: **24%**, American Indian: **7.2%**, Asian-American: **14.6%**, African-American: **1.4%**, Hispanic-American: **0.7%**, White: **73.9%**, International: **0.0%**, Unknown: **2.2%**

ACADEMIC PROGRAMS
The school's curriculum very frequently gives first-year students substantial contact with patients.
There are opportunities for first- or second-year students to work in community health clinics.
Program offerings: AIDS, drug/alcohol abuse, family medicine, geriatrics, internal medicine, pediatrics, rural medicine, women's health
Joint degrees awarded: M.D./Ph.D., M.D./MPH, M.D./MS, M.D./M.H.A.
Total National Institutes of Health (NIH) grants awarded to the medical school and affiliated hospitals: **$37.0 million**

CURRICULUM
(TEXT PROVIDED BY SCHOOL):
The curriculum is designed to provide an integrated overview of human biology and behavior. Classroom and laboratory studies are complemented with clinical demonstrations and case studies, problem- and team-based learning, and an extensive online curriculum called Hippocrates. Patient contact is a major component of each of the four years of medical school, beginning with simulated patients and extending to hospital and ambulatory settings.

Students are required to pass Step 1 of the U.S. Medical Licensing Examination prior to beginning third-year clinical rotations. Students must take the USMLE Step 2 examination during the fourth year and report scores. All basic science courses are conducted on the campus of the Health Sciences Center in Oklahoma City. Up to 25 percent of the class choose to undertake clinical training at the College of Medicine-Tulsa.

First-year courses focus on knowledge of structure and function of human biology, critical thinking skills, and the management of medical information. Second-year courses address the pathophysiology of diseases and form a bridge into the clinical portion of the curriculum. A significant feature of this curriculum is early exposure to patients in the two Principles of Clinical Medicine courses. Students learn interviewing skills on actual and simulated patients, and work with local physicians and clinical faculty throughout the entire first and second years. Faculty members recognize the importance of self-directed learning, small-group discussion sessions, independent learning modules, computer-assisted instruction, and integrated medical problem solving.

In the third year, all students are required to take core clerkships in family medicine, geriatrics, internal medicine, neuroscience, obstetrics/gynecology, pediatrics, psychiatry, and surgery. Fourth-year students have a required ambulatory care experience, a rural preceptorship under the guidance of an Oklahoma physician, and six months of clinical electives. Over the past 10 years, 49 percent of our students selected primary-care disciplines, and 50 percent remained in Oklahoma for residency.

FACULTY PROFILE (FALL 2005)
Total teaching faculty: **734 (full-time)**, **162 (part-time)**
Of full-time faculty, those teaching in basic sciences: **11%**; in clinical programs: **89%**
Of part-time faculty, those teaching in basic sciences: **1%**; in clinical programs: **99%**
Full-time faculty/student ratio: **1.3**

SUPPORT SERVICES
The school offers students these services for dealing with stress: professional counseling, support groups.

RESIDENCY PROFILE
Most popular residency and specialty programs chosen by the 2004 and 2005 M.D. graduating classes: anesthesiology, emergency medicine, family practice, internal medicine, internal medicine–pediatrics, pediatrics, psychiatry, radiology–diagnostic, surgery–general, internal medicine/pediatrics.

WHERE GRADS GO

46.8%
Proportion of 2003-2005 graduates who entered primary care specialties

37.4%
Proportion of 2004-2005 graduates who accepted in-state residencies

University of Pennsylvania

- 237 John Morgan Building, 3620 Hamilton Walk, Philadelphia, PA 19104-6055
- Private
- Year Founded: 1765
- Tuition, 2005-2006: $39,467
- Enrollment 2005-2006 academic year: 617
- Website: http://www.med.upenn.edu
- Specialty ranking: AIDS: 14, drug/alcohol abuse: 6, geriatrics: 12, internal medicine: 5, pediatrics: 2, women's health: 4

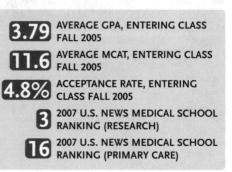

3.79 AVERAGE GPA, ENTERING CLASS FALL 2005

11.6 AVERAGE MCAT, ENTERING CLASS FALL 2005

4.8% ACCEPTANCE RATE, ENTERING CLASS FALL 2005

3 2007 U.S. NEWS MEDICAL SCHOOL RANKING (RESEARCH)

16 2007 U.S. NEWS MEDICAL SCHOOL RANKING (PRIMARY CARE)

ADMISSIONS

Admissions phone number: **(215) 898-8001**
Admissions email address: **admiss@mail.med.upenn.edu**
Application website:
   http://www.med.upenn.edu/admiss/applications.html
Acceptance rate: **4.8%**
In-state acceptance rate: **8.8%**
Out-of-state acceptance rate: **4.3%**
Minority acceptance rate: **4.8%**
International acceptance rate: **4.9%**

Fall 2005 applications and acceptees

	Applied	Interviewed	Accepted	Enrolled
Total:	4,671	833	223	147
In-state:	533	148	47	37
Out-of-state:	4,138	685	176	110

Profile of admitted students

Average undergraduate grade point average: **3.79**
MCAT averages (scale: 1-15; writing test: J-T):
   Composite score: **11.6**
   Verbal reasoning score: **11.0**, Physical sciences score: **11.8**, Biological sciences score: **11.8**, Writing score: **Q**
Proportion with undergraduate majors in: Biological sciences: **56%**, Physical sciences: **16%**, Non-sciences: **24%**, Other health professions: **0%**, Mixed disciplines and other: **4%**
Percentage of students not coming directly from college after graduation: **51%**

Dates and details

The American Medical College Application Service (AMCAS) application is accepted.
School asks for a school-specific application as part of the admissions process.
Oldest MCAT considered for Fall 2007 entry: **2002**
Earliest application date for the 2007-2008 first-year class: **June 1, 2006**
Latest application date: **October 15, 2006**
Acceptance dates for regular application for the class entering in fall 2007:

Earliest: **March 15, 2007**
Latest: **August 1, 2007**
The school considers requests for deferred entrance.
Starting month for the class entering in 2007–2008: **August**
The school has an Early Decision Plan (EDP).
A personal interview is required for admission.

Undergraduate coursework required

Medical school requires undergraduate work in these subjects: biology, English, organic chemistry, physics, mathematics, general chemistry.

ADMISSIONS POLICY
(TEXT PROVIDED BY SCHOOL):

The University of Pennsylvania School of Medicine selects students based on academic and personal excellence. In accordance with the mission of the school, diversity is valued in the selection process, recognizing that differences enhance learning and enrich the school community.

Academic excellence is measured by the academic performance of the student, the rigorousness of the courses taken, the school attended, intellectual curiosity, and national testing measures, such as the MCAT. In addition, the Committee on Admissions takes into account the student's record of activity in extracurricular college and community affairs, special talents or abilities, employment, and other life experiences. Sustained contributions to organizations, communities, research, and activities over time indicate a commitment and in-depth involvement. Leadership is strongly considered and encouraged.

Personal excellence is evidenced by behavior associated with extracurricular activities and accomplishments, life experiences, personal insight, and maturity. These characteristics are corroborated by letters of recommendation from faculty, premedical advisers, and others. Selection characteristics prized by the school are integrity, respect for and concern about others, inner strength, personal effectiveness and communication, compassion, and desire to make a contribution in healthcare.

COSTS AND FINANCIAL AID

Financial aid phone number: **(215) 573-3423**
Tuition, 2005-2006 academic year: **$39,467**
Room and board: **$16,050**
Percentage of students receiving financial aid in 2005-06:
  84%
Percentage of students receiving: Loans: **73%**,
  Grants/scholarships: **61%**, Work-study aid: **1%**
Average medical school debt for the Class of 2004:
  $101,318

STUDENT BODY

Fall 2005 full-time enrollment: **617**
Men: **50%**, Women: **50%**, In-state: **41%**, Minorities: **36%**,
  American Indian: **0.6%**, Asian-American: **18.8%**,
  African-American: **9.1%**, Hispanic-American: **7.3%**,
  White: **63.7%**, International: **0.5%**, Unknown: **N/A**

ACADEMIC PROGRAMS

The school's curriculum frequently gives first-year students
  substantial contact with patients.
There are opportunities for first- or second-year students to
  work in community health clinics.
Program offerings: AIDS, drug/alcohol abuse, family
  medicine, geriatrics, internal medicine, pediatrics, rural
  medicine, women's health
Joint degrees awarded: M.D./Ph.D., M.D./MBA,
  M.D./MPH, M.D./JD, M.D./MS
Total National Institutes of Health (NIH) grants awarded to
  the medical school and affiliated hospitals: **$500.8
  million**

CURRICULUM

*(TEXT PROVIDED BY SCHOOL):*The four-year curriculum is
built on three themes: science of medicine; technology and
practice of medicine; and professionalism and humanism.
It is designed with flexibility So that students can participate
in other graduate programs offered at the University of
Pennsylvania and School of Medicine.

Module 1 is a four-month module divided into four
blocks: Developmental and Molecular Biology; Cell
Physiology and Metabolism; Human Body, Structure and
Function; and Host Defenses. Module 1 gives students the
foundation of basic sciences necessary to enter a series of
organ-system blocks, where basic sciences are integrated
across each organ system. This module is pass/fail, and all
students must successfully complete each component.

Module 2, Integrative Systems and Diseases, which
begins in January of Year 1, is composed of organ systems
and disease blocks. Topics are organized by organ systems
in the following structure: Normal Development; Normal
Processes; Abnormal Processes; Therapeutics and Disease
Management; Epidemiology/Evidence-Based Medicine; and
Prevention and Nutrition.

Module 3, Technology and Practice of Medicine, spans
modules 1 and 2, and concludes upon the start of Module 4,
Core Clerkships. This program is designed to achieve a level

of competency across epidemiology and biostatistics, decision making, economics of healthcare, population-based
medicine, and the basics of clinical medicine.

Module 6, Professionalism and Humanism, runs concurrently throughout the curriculum and covers topics on
bioethics, multiculturalism, spirituality, research ethics, and
confidentiality.

Upon successful completion of modules 1, 2, 3, and part
of 6, all students enter the required clerkships known as
Module 4. Module 4 begins in January of the second year
and is composed of 48 weeks of required clinical clerkships,
ending in December of the third year. All students must
complete all of the core clerkships before moving on to
Module 5. The clerkships are divided into four cross-disciplinary experiences of three months each: internal medi-
cine/family medicine; obstetrics/gynecology/pediatrics;
surgery/anesthesia/emergency medicine; and
psychiatry/neurology and clinical specialties, orthopedics,
otorhinolaryngology, and ophthalmology.

Module 5 begins in January of the third year and is the
final 16 months of medical school. All students completing
a four-year M.D. degree are required to complete six additional electives; a subinternship in either general medicine
or general pediatrics; 12 weeks of a scholarly pursuit with a
mentor, and four weeks of the Frontiers in Medical Science
courses.

FACULTY PROFILE (FALL 2005)

Total teaching faculty: **2,047 (full-time)**, **936 (part-time)**
Of full-time faculty, those teaching in basic sciences: **10%**;
  in clinical programs: **90%**
Of part-time faculty, those teaching in basic sciences: **11%**;
  in clinical programs: **89%**
Full-time faculty/student ratio: **3.3**

SUPPORT SERVICES

The school offers students these services for dealing with
stress: peer counseling, professional counseling, support
groups.

RESIDENCY PROFILE

Most popular residency and specialty programs chosen by
the 2004 and 2005 M.D. graduating classes: emergency
medicine, internal medicine, ophthalmology, orthopaedic
surgery, pediatrics, psychiatry, radiology–diagnostic, surgery–general.

WHERE GRADS GO

37%

*Proportion of 2003-2005 graduates who entered primary
care specialties*

31%

*Proportion of 2004-2005 graduates who accepted in-state
residencies*

University of Pittsburgh

- 401 Scaife Hall, Pittsburgh, PA 15261
- Public
- Year Founded: 1886
- Tuition, 2005-2006: In-state: $32,868; Out-of-state: $37,608
- Enrollment 2005-2006 academic year: 584
- Website: http://www.medschool.pitt.edu
- Specialty ranking: AIDS: 17, drug/alcohol abuse: 13, geriatrics: 11, internal medicine: 23, pediatrics: 17, women's health: 5

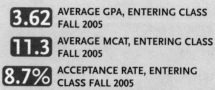

3.62 AVERAGE GPA, ENTERING CLASS FALL 2005

11.3 AVERAGE MCAT, ENTERING CLASS FALL 2005

8.7% ACCEPTANCE RATE, ENTERING CLASS FALL 2005

16 2007 U.S. NEWS MEDICAL SCHOOL RANKING (RESEARCH)

33 2007 U.S. NEWS MEDICAL SCHOOL RANKING (PRIMARY CARE)

ADMISSIONS

Admissions phone number: (412) 648-9891
Admissions email address:
admissions@medschool.pitt.edu
Application website: **https://admissions.medschool.pitt.edu**
Acceptance rate: **8.7%**
In-state acceptance rate: **8.2%**
Out-of-state acceptance rate: **8.8%**
Minority acceptance rate: **6.7%**
International acceptance rate: **0.0%**

Fall 2005 applications and acceptees

	Applied	Interviewed	Accepted	Enrolled
Total:	5,300	1,188	462	148
In-state:	794	164	65	23
Out-of-state:	4,506	1,024	397	125

Profile of admitted students

Average undergraduate grade point average: **3.62**
MCAT averages (scale: 1-15; writing test: J-T):
Composite score: **11.3**
Verbal reasoning score: **10.6**, Physical sciences score: **11.6**, Biological sciences score: **11.6**, Writing score: **P**
Proportion with undergraduate majors in: Biological sciences: **41%**, Physical sciences: **28%**, Non-sciences: **24%**, Other health professions: **0%**, Mixed disciplines and other: **7%**
Percentage of students not coming directly from college after graduation: **58%**

Dates and details

The American Medical College Application Service (AMCAS) application is accepted.
School asks for a school-specific application as part of the admissions process.
Oldest MCAT considered for Fall 2007 entry: **2004**
Earliest application date for the 2007-2008 first-year class: **June 1, 2006**
Latest application date: **December 1, 2006**
Acceptance dates for regular application for the class entering in fall 2007:

Earliest: **October 15, 2006**
Latest: **August 13, 2007**
The school considers requests for deferred entrance.
Starting month for the class entering in 2007–2008: **August**
The school doesn't have an Early Decision Plan (EDP).
A personal interview is required for admission.

Undergraduate coursework required

Medical school requires undergraduate work in these subjects: biology, English, organic chemistry, inorganic (general) chemistry, physics.

ADMISSIONS POLICY

(TEXT PROVIDED BY SCHOOL):

We are an American Medical College Application Service school. AMCAS forwards to us applicants' academic credentials. Our supplemental application, sent to competitive applicants, asks for three academic letters of recommendation or a committee letter; the student must also answer questions in essay form. (Applicants who request a supplemental application, after having received our letter denying it, are allowed to apply.)

Each applicant is interviewed by a faculty member and a first- or second-year medical student. No applicant is admitted without an interview. Both interview reports and the remainder of the applicant's credentials are brought before the Admissions Committee. Each committee member ranks the applicant on a scale of 1 (low) to 10 (high) in whole numbers. State of residence does not play a part in consideration. Applicants are accepted, rejected, or placed on a wait list on a rolling basis after October 15.

The Admissions Committee seeks to admit a diverse, intellectually competent student body. Intellectual competence is judged not only by numerical academic criteria but also on the basis of recommendation letters. Applicants should have some medical exposure to test their decision to enter medicine. Extracurricular activities are weighted heavily. We seek to admit students who have evidenced longtime dedication to some praiseworthy activity. This may be sports, research, a community activity, or an artistic endeavor. During the interview, the applicant must communicate his or her motivation to enter medicine and establish a relationship with the interviewer. We seek to admit well-rounded applicants, and this facet of an individual's persona should be evident during the interview. In addition, a broad education is a major plus in consideration of the applicant's credentials.

COSTS AND FINANCIAL AID
Financial aid phone number: **(412) 648-9891**
Tuition, 2005-2006 academic year: **In-state: $32,868; Out-of-state: $37,608**
Room and board: **$15,000**
Percentage of students receiving financial aid in 2005-06: **86%**
Percentage of students receiving: Loans: **75%**, Grants/scholarships: **59%**, Work-study aid: **0%**
Average medical school debt for the Class of 2004: **$123,256**

STUDENT BODY
Fall 2005 full-time enrollment: **584**
Men: **53%**, Women: **47%**, In-state: **29%**, Minorities: **39%**, American Indian: **0.0%**, Asian-American: **26.7%**, African-American: **9.6%**, Hispanic-American: **2.6%**, White: **61.1%**, International: **0.0%**, Unknown: **0.0%**

ACADEMIC PROGRAMS
The school's curriculum frequently gives first-year students substantial contact with patients.
There are opportunities for first- or second-year students to work in community health clinics.
Program offerings: AIDS, drug/alcohol abuse, family medicine, geriatrics, internal medicine, pediatrics, rural medicine, women's health
Joint degrees awarded: M.D./Ph.D., M.D./MPH, M.D./M.A.
Total National Institutes of Health (NIH) grants awarded to the medical school and affiliated hospitals: **$330.0 million**

CURRICULUM
(TEXT PROVIDED BY SCHOOL):
The Patient of Today and the Medicine of Tomorrow describes the curriculum at the University of Pittsburgh School of Medicine. The patient focus begins on Day 1, in the Introduction to Being a Physician course. Students interview patients and visit community settings to develop an early understanding of their role as medical professionals.

Patient interviewing and physical diagnosis courses follow, along with exercises examining physician life in society, in ethical settings, and at the patient bedside. Throughout the first two years, students apply their new skills in local practices and hospitals, one afternoon per week.

Foundations for mastery of the Medicine of Tomorrow begin with the basic science block that runs through three fourths of the first year. This block provides the language

and concepts that underlie the scientific basis of medical practice.

Organ system courses integrate physiology, pathophysiology, pharmacology, and introduction to medicine for the major organ systems. Students continually focus on the patient with concurrent courses in the patient care and patient-doctor relationship blocks.

The unique Biomedical Scientist Training Program and the Clinical Scientist Training Program prepare students for a career in academic medicine. Others opt to participate in area of concentration (AOC) programs. AOCs are offered in disabilities medicine, medical humanities, service learning (underserved populations), geriatrics, women's health, informatics, global health, and biomedical research. Since 1983, our Medical Scientist Training Program has offered the M.D./Ph.D.

During the first two years, mentored student groups engage in problem-based learning (PBL) exercises based on clinical cases. The PBL learning experience culminates in the Integrated Case Studies course at the end of Year 2, which serves as a bridge to patient care responsibilities during Year 3.

All third-year students take clerkships in adult inpatient medicine, clinical neurosciences, ambulatory care, surgical subspecialties, obstetrics and gynecology, pediatrics, surgery and perioperative care, and family medicine. In Year 4, students enjoy a wide range of elective options.

FACULTY PROFILE (FALL 2005)
Total teaching faculty: **1,777 (full-time)**, **51 (part-time)**
Of full-time faculty, those teaching in basic sciences: **9%**; in clinical programs: **91%**
Of part-time faculty, those teaching in basic sciences: **0%**; in clinical programs: **100%**
Full-time faculty/student ratio: **3.0**

SUPPORT SERVICES
The school offers students these services for dealing with stress: expanded-hour gym access, peer counseling, professional counseling, support groups.

RESIDENCY PROFILE
Most popular residency and specialty programs chosen by the 2004 and 2005 M.D. graduating classes: anesthesiology, emergency medicine, family practice, internal medicine, obstetrics and gynecology, orthopaedic surgery, pediatrics, psychiatry, radiology–diagnostic, surgery–general.

WHERE GRADS GO

34.9%
Proportion of 2003-2005 graduates who entered primary care specialties

32.5%
Proportion of 2004-2005 graduates who accepted in-state residencies

University of Rochester

- 601 Elmwood Avenue, Box 706, Rochester, NY 14642
- Private
- Year Founded: 1925
- Tuition, 2005-2006: $37,379
- Enrollment 2005-2006 academic year: 408
- Website: http://www.urmc.rochester.edu/smd/
- Specialty ranking: family medicine: 26, geriatrics: 15, internal medicine: 26, pediatrics: 22

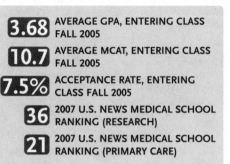

3.68 AVERAGE GPA, ENTERING CLASS FALL 2005

10.7 AVERAGE MCAT, ENTERING CLASS FALL 2005

7.5% ACCEPTANCE RATE, ENTERING CLASS FALL 2005

36 2007 U.S. NEWS MEDICAL SCHOOL RANKING (RESEARCH)

21 2007 U.S. NEWS MEDICAL SCHOOL RANKING (PRIMARY CARE)

ADMISSIONS
Admissions phone number: **(585) 275-4542**
Admissions email address:
mdadmish@urmc.rochester.edu
Application website:
https://admissions.urmc.rochester.edu/studentlogin.cfm
Acceptance rate: **7.5%**
In-state acceptance rate: **9.7%**
Out-of-state acceptance rate: **6.8%**
Minority acceptance rate: **6.3%**
International acceptance rate: **N/A**

Fall 2005 applications and acceptees
	Applied	Interviewed	Accepted	Enrolled
Total:	3,449	636	260	100
In-state:	932	216	90	37
Out-of-state:	2,517	420	170	63

Profile of admitted students
Average undergraduate grade point average: **3.68**
MCAT averages (scale: 1-15; writing test: J-T):
    Composite score: **10.7**
    Verbal reasoning score: **10.5**, Physical sciences score: **10.8**, Biological sciences score: **11.0**, Writing score: **P**
Proportion with undergraduate majors in: Biological sciences: **53%**, Physical sciences: **15%**, Non-sciences: **25%**, Other health professions: **1%**, Mixed disciplines and other: **6%**
Percentage of students not coming directly from college after graduation: **64%**

Dates and details
The American Medical College Application Service (AMCAS) application is accepted.
School asks for a school-specific application as part of the admissions process.
Oldest MCAT considered for Fall 2007 entry: **2003**
Earliest application date for the 2007-2008 first-year class: **June 1, 2006**
Latest application date: **October 15, 2006**

Acceptance dates for regular application for the class entering in fall 2007:
    Earliest: **October 15, 2006**
    Latest: **August 13, 2007**
The school considers requests for deferred entrance.
Starting month for the class entering in 2007–2008: **August**
The school doesn't have an Early Decision Plan (EDP).
A personal interview is required for admission.

Undergraduate coursework required
Medical school requires undergraduate work in these subjects: biology, biology/zoology, English, organic chemistry, inorganic (general) chemistry, physics, humanities, demonstration of writing skills, social sciences.

ADMISSIONS POLICY
(TEXT PROVIDED BY SCHOOL):
A strong academic record and good scores on the MCAT are necessary but not sufficient criteria for admission. The Admissions Committee looks for evidence of scholarship and research, service to the community, clinical volunteer experiences, leadership abilities, integrity, maturity, and excellent interpersonal skills. Rochester seeks students who value human diversity, exhibit a love of learning, have an appreciation of the science and art of medicine, and are called to serve others.

Applications are reviewed by the committee beginning in July. Selected applicants are granted interviews at the medical center from September to the middle of March. Acceptances are mailed out in late October and continue on a rolling basis until the class is filled.

COSTS AND FINANCIAL AID
Financial aid phone number: **(585) 275-4523**
Tuition, 2005-2006 academic year: **$37,379**
Room and board: **$15,000**
Percentage of students receiving financial aid in 2005-06: **92%**
Percentage of students receiving: Loans: **84%**, Grants/scholarships: **46%**, Work-study aid: **22%**

Average medical school debt for the Class of 2004:
$129,342

STUDENT BODY

Fall 2005 full-time enrollment: **408**

Men: **45%**, Women: **55%**, In-state: **41%**, Minorities: **31%**, American Indian: **0.0%**, Asian-American: **20.6%**, African-American: **7.6%**, Hispanic-American: **2.9%**, White: **66.7%**, International: **0.0%**, Unknown: **2.2%**

ACADEMIC PROGRAMS

The school's curriculum very frequently gives first-year students substantial contact with patients.

There are opportunities for first- or second-year students to work in community health clinics.

Program offerings: AIDS, drug/alcohol abuse, family medicine, geriatrics, internal medicine, pediatrics, rural medicine, women's health

Joint degrees awarded: M.D./Ph.D., M.D./MBA, M.D./MPH, M.D./MS

Total National Institutes of Health (NIH) grants awarded to the medical school and affiliated hospitals: **$140.6 million**

CURRICULUM

(TEXT PROVIDED BY SCHOOL):

The Rochester Double Helix Curriculum weaves basic science and clinical medicine throughout the four years. Each element of the curriculum strengthens Rochester's biopsychosocial tradition by fostering knowledge, skills, attitudes, and behaviors of the physician/scientist/humanist, by combining cutting-edge, evidence-based medical science with the relationship-centered art that is medicine's distinctive trademark.

The Rochester curriculum is designed to train lifelong learners of medicine with emphasis on knowledge acquisition skills and use and the incorporation of cutting edge research discoveries. Sensitivity to the world of the patient is encompassed in the biopsychosocial integration of the curriculum and the learning experience. By ensuring adequate and early electives for students to enhance their special interests, the Double Helix Curriculum generates a knowledge base characterized by depth, breadth, rigor, and flexibility.

Courses are interdisciplinary; basic sciences are integrated with one another, and basic and clinical sciences are woven together as the strands of the Double Helix Curriculum throughout the four years. Emphasis is on active student learning through the schoolwide use of multidisciplinary, problem-based learning (PBL) cases in all courses. Interdepartmental, multidisciplinary faculty teams direct major curricular blocks, which usually include three two-hour PBL tutorials per week, lectures, labs, and conferences. Adequate time for self-study is provided by keeping two afternoons per week free of curricular activities. We expect students to treat the educational enterprise with the same seriousness of purpose with which we all treat patient care and research, and participation in course/clerkship assessment for continuous improvement of the curriculum is expected.

Clinical exposure begins during the first week of medical school. Students complete their introduction to clinical medicine in the fall of the first year and then participate in the ambulatory care clerkship beginning their first spring semester. This experience includes the ambulatory components of family medicine, pediatrics, internal medicine, women's health, and ambulatory surgery, and is completed by the end of the second year. The clinical skills training 1 leads not to shadowing experiences in clinics but to the start of real clinical work as part of the healthcare team while still in the first year.

Third-year inpatient clerkships focus on acute-care experiences in adult medicine, women's and children's health, and mind/brain/behavior. Blocks of time in the third year are dedicated to more in-depth basic science principles and applications.

Fourth-year students can choose from a wide variety of clinical electives. They also participate in the Community Health Improvement Clerkship, a sub-internship, Emergency Medicine, Process of Discovery, and Successful Interning.

There are many opportunities for meaningful research including our Academic Research Track that leads to a Master's degree. In addition, the medical school offers international health experiences and community volunteer experiences through our Students of Rochester outreach program.

FACULTY PROFILE (FALL 2005)

Total teaching faculty: **1,320 (full-time)**, **1,242 (part-time)**

Of full-time faculty, those teaching in basic sciences: **16%**; in clinical programs: **84%**

Of part-time faculty, those teaching in basic sciences: **2%**; in clinical programs: **98%**

Full-time faculty/student ratio: **3.2**

SUPPORT SERVICES

The school offers students these services for dealing with stress: expanded-hour gym access, peer counseling, professional counseling, religious support, support groups.

RESIDENCY PROFILE

Most popular residency and specialty programs chosen by the 2004 and 2005 M.D. graduating classes: emergency medicine, family practice, internal medicine, neurology, neurology–child neurology, obstetrics and gynecology, pathology–anatomic and clinical, pediatrics, psychiatry, surgery–general.

WHERE GRADS GO

32.1%

Proportion of 2003-2005 graduates who entered primary care specialties

33.4%

Proportion of 2004-2005 graduates who accepted in-state residencies

University of South Carolina

- School of Medicine, Columbia, SC 29208
- Public
- Year Founded: 1974
- Tuition, 2005-2006: In-state: $19,570; Out-of-state: $56,496
- Enrollment 2005-2006 academic year: 319
- Website: http://www.med.sc.edu
- Specialty ranking: N/A

3.55 AVERAGE GPA, ENTERING CLASS FALL 2005

9.2 AVERAGE MCAT, ENTERING CLASS FALL 2005

10.0% ACCEPTANCE RATE, ENTERING CLASS FALL 2005

Unranked 2007 U.S. NEWS MEDICAL SCHOOL RANKING (RESEARCH)

Unranked 2007 U.S. NEWS MEDICAL SCHOOL RANKING (PRIMARY CARE)

ADMISSIONS

Admissions phone number: **(803) 733-3325**
Admissions email address: **jeanette@gw.sc.edu**
Application website: **N/A**
Acceptance rate: **10.0%**
In-state acceptance rate: **31.3%**
Out-of-state acceptance rate: **2.3%**
Minority acceptance rate: **5.5%**
International acceptance rate: **N/A**

Fall 2005 applications and acceptees

	Applied	Interviewed	Accepted	Enrolled
Total:	1,383	265	138	80
In-state:	368	205	115	70
Out-of-state:	1,015	60	23	10

Profile of admitted students
Average undergraduate grade point average: **3.55**
MCAT averages (scale: 1-15; writing test: J-T):
   Composite score: **9.2**
   Verbal reasoning score: **9.6**, Physical sciences score: **8.5**,
   Biological sciences score: **9.4**, Writing score: **O**
Proportion with undergraduate majors in: Biological
   sciences: **50%**, Physical sciences: **17%**, Non-sciences: **5%**,
   Other health professions: **14%**, Mixed disciplines and
   other: **14%**
Percentage of students not coming directly from college
   after graduation: **23%**

Dates and details
The American Medical College Application Service
   (AMCAS) application is accepted.
School asks for a school-specific application as part of the
   admissions process.
Oldest MCAT considered for Fall 2007 entry: **2002**
Earliest application date for the 2007-2008 first-year class:
   June 1, 2006
Latest application date: **December 1, 2006**
Acceptance dates for regular application for the class
   entering in fall 2007:
   Earliest: **October 15, 2006**

Latest: **August 1, 2007**
The school considers requests for deferred entrance.
Starting month for the class entering in 2007–2008:
   August
The school has an Early Decision Plan (EDP).
A personal interview is required for admission.

Undergraduate coursework required
Medical school requires undergraduate work in these subjects: biology/zoology, English, organic chemistry, inorganic
(general) chemistry, physics.

ADMISSIONS POLICY
(TEXT PROVIDED BY SCHOOL):
Applicants admitted to the University of South Carolina
School of Medicine are selected by an Admissions
Committee composed of members of the basic science and
clinical science faculties of the School of Medicine, university faculty, medical students, and area clinicians. In making selections from each year's group of applicants,
members of the Admissions Committee recognize that they
are selecting future physicians. The admissions procedure
is therefore an effort to select applicants who possess the
individual characteristics required for both the study and
the practice of medicine.

The Admissions Committee considers all aspects of a
prospective student's application in the decision-making
process. The selection criteria for admission are weighted as
one third for the Medical College Admission Test score and
grade-point average, one third for letters of recommendation and work/volunteer experiences, and one third for
interviews and personal attributes.

COSTS AND FINANCIAL AID
Financial aid phone number: **(803) 733-3135**
Tuition, 2005-2006 academic year: **In-state: $19,570; Out-
of-state: $56,496**
Room and board: **$10,930**
Percentage of students receiving financial aid in 2005-06:
   91%

Percentage of students receiving: Loans: 86%,
   Grants/scholarships: 39%, Work-study aid: 0%
Average medical school debt for the Class of 2004: $86,311

STUDENT BODY
Fall 2005 full-time enrollment: 319
Men: 52%, Women: 48%, In-state: 94%, Minorities: 17%,
   American Indian: 0.3%, Asian-American: 10.7%,
   African-American: 6.0%, Hispanic-American: 0.0%,
   White: 82.8%, International: 0.0%, Unknown: 0.3%

ACADEMIC PROGRAMS
The school's curriculum occasionally gives first-year
   students substantial contact with patients.
There are opportunities for first- or second-year students to
   work in community health clinics.
Program offerings: family medicine, geriatrics, internal
   medicine, pediatrics, rural medicine
Joint degrees awarded: M.D./Ph.D., M.D./MPH
Total National Institutes of Health (NIH) grants awarded to
   the medical school and affiliated hospitals: $7.6 million

CURRICULUM
(TEXT PROVIDED BY SCHOOL):
Basic sciences: During the first two years of medical education, students study a core curriculum of basic sciences and
clinical disciplines necessary for an understanding of the
structure and function of human systems. During Year 1,
students gain a basic understanding of normal structure,
function, and development. During Year 2, emphasis is
placed on pathology and general therapeutic principles.
Throughout the first two years, clinical correlations to basic
science material are integral components of the curriculum,
as is the four-semester Introduction to Clinical Medicine
course continuum. Interdisciplinary material on nutrition,
substance abuse, human values, genetics, and geriatrics is
also presented in vertical curricula over four years. The
Introduction to Clinical Medicine course and correlations
provides students with the background and skills to prepare
them for clinical clerkships in the third and fourth years.
Introduction to Clinical Medicine courses also emphasize
active, independent, and cooperative learning in a small-
group format and include components devoted to problem-
based learning.
   Clinical clerkships: Clerkship experiences in the third
year include rotations of eight weeks each in medicine, surgery, obstetrics and gynecology, psychiatry, family medicine,
and pediatrics. Year 4 includes required rotations of four
weeks each in neurology, surgery, medicine, and an acting
internship. Also required is "capstone month," a multidisciplinary four-week rotation that concludes the process of
undergraduate medical education and prepares students for
the transition to residency training and clinical practice. The
remainder of the fourth year is devoted to a selective/elec-
tive program, which allows for flexibility and the pursuit of
individual interests. Students actively participate in the clinical setting, where emphasis is placed on the correlation of
basic science and clinical material. This correlation is further nurtured by small tutorial seminars, lectures, and
group discussions.

FACULTY PROFILE (FALL 2005)
Total teaching faculty: 223 (full-time), 13 (part-time)
Of full-time faculty, those teaching in basic sciences: 25%;
   in clinical programs: 75%
Of part-time faculty, those teaching in basic sciences: 8%;
   in clinical programs: 92%
Full-time faculty/student ratio: 0.7

SUPPORT SERVICES
The school offers students these services for dealing with
stress: expanded-hour gym access, peer counseling, professional counseling.

RESIDENCY PROFILE
Most popular residency and specialty programs chosen by the
2004 and 2005 M.D. graduating classes: anesthesiology,
emergency medicine, family practice, internal medicine,
obstetrics and gynecology, ophthalmology, pathology–
anatomic and clinical, pediatrics, psychiatry, surgery–general.

WHERE GRADS GO

45.9%

*Proportion of 2003-2005 graduates who entered primary
care specialties*

43.9%

*Proportion of 2004-2005 graduates who accepted in-state
residencies*

University of South Dakota

- 1400 W. 22nd Street, Sioux Falls, SD 57105
- Public
- Year Founded: 1907
- Tuition, 2005-2006: In-state: $16,731; Out-of-state: $35,197
- Enrollment 2005-2006 academic year: 206
- Website: http://www.usd.edu/med/md
- Specialty ranking: rural medicine: 10

3.66 AVERAGE GPA, ENTERING CLASS FALL 2005

9.3 AVERAGE MCAT, ENTERING CLASS FALL 2005

9.2% ACCEPTANCE RATE, ENTERING CLASS FALL 2005

Unranked 2007 U.S. NEWS MEDICAL SCHOOL RANKING (RESEARCH)

Unranked 2007 U.S. NEWS MEDICAL SCHOOL RANKING (PRIMARY CARE)

ADMISSIONS

Admissions phone number: **(605) 677-6886**
Admissions email address: **usdsmsa@usd.edu**
Application website: **N/A**
Acceptance rate: **9.2%**
In-state acceptance rate: **43.1%**
Out-of-state acceptance rate: **0.7%**
Minority acceptance rate: **1.6%**
International acceptance rate: **0.0%**

Fall 2005 applications and acceptees

	Applied	Interviewed	Accepted	Enrolled
Total:	717	158	66	50
In-state:	144	132	62	48
Out-of-state:	573	26	4	2

Profile of admitted students

Average undergraduate grade point average: **3.66**
MCAT averages (scale: 1-15; writing test: J-T):
  Composite score: **9.3**
  Verbal reasoning score: **9.4**, Physical sciences score: **8.9**,
  Biological sciences score: **9.7**, Writing score: **O**
Proportion with undergraduate majors in: Biological
  sciences: **54%**, Physical sciences: **18%**, Non-sciences:
  18%, Other health professions: **0%**, Mixed disciplines
  and other: **10%**
Percentage of students not coming directly from college
  after graduation: **34%**

Dates and details

The American Medical College Application Service
  (AMCAS) application is accepted.
School asks for a school-specific application as part of the
  admissions process.
Oldest MCAT considered for Fall 2007 entry: **2004**
Earliest application date for the 2007-2008 first-year class:
  June 1, 2006
Latest application date: **November 15, 2006**
Acceptance dates for regular application for the class
  entering in fall 2007:
  Earliest: **November 20, 2006**

Latest: **March 15, 2007**
The school considers requests for deferred entrance.
Starting month for the class entering in 2007–2008:
  August
The school doesn't have an Early Decision Plan (EDP).
A personal interview is required for admission.

Undergraduate coursework required

Medical school requires undergraduate work in these subjects: biology, organic chemistry, inorganic (general) chemistry, physics, mathematics.

ADMISSIONS POLICY

(TEXT PROVIDED BY SCHOOL):

Only applicants who have earned at least 64 semester credits of college coursework will be considered for admission.
Prior to acceptance, applicants must have taken the Medical
College Admission Test (MCAT). Prior to matriculation,
applicants must have submitted transcripts of all college
credits earned, indicating at least 90 semester credit hours
or, preferably, a baccalaureate degree from an accredited
institution.

In preparation for medical school, students are strongly
encouraged to obtain a broad background in the natural and
social sciences and the humanities; in addition, good oral
and written communication skills are considered essential.
However, selection of majors and other coursework at the
baccalaureate level should be on the basis of the student's
own interest. No single field is given preference in the
selection process. The School of Medicine expects courses
in English (especially literature and composition), the social
and behavioral sciences, and the humanities to be included
in the requirement for completion of the baccalaureate
degree.

In addition, the faculty of the School of Medicine
requires that students preparing for admission to the school
obtain appropriate background (usually one year each),
including laboratory experience, in the following areas: biology, general (inorganic) chemistry, organic chemistry, mathematics, and physics. If Advanced Placement or College
Level Examination Program credits are on the college tran-

script, these may be accepted as a fulfillment of a prerequisite providing that there is evidence of proficiency in the subject. Examples of proficiency may be successful completion of a more advanced course in that field or a strong MCAT score. Required courses should be the same as those required of majors in each area. Correspondence courses are not considered acceptable substitutes.

All residents of South Dakota are offered an interview, and a select few applicants with strong ties to the state are also invited to interview. Transfers may be considered from students who are currently in good standing at a Liaison Committee on Medical Education-accredited medical school.

COSTS AND FINANCIAL AID
Financial aid phone number: **(605) 677-5112**
Tuition, 2005-2006 academic year: **In-state: $16,731**; **Out-of-state: $35,197**
Room and board: **$19,375**
Percentage of students receiving financial aid in 2005-06: **96%**
Percentage of students receiving: Loans: **93%**, Grants/scholarships: **74%**, Work-study aid: **2%**
Average medical school debt for the Class of 2004: **$104,497**

STUDENT BODY
Fall 2005 full-time enrollment: **206**
Men: **52%**, Women: **48%**, In-state: **96%**, Minorities: **5%**, American Indian: **3.4%**, Asian-American: **1.9%**, African-American: **0.0%**, Hispanic-American: **0.0%**, White: **94.7%**, International: **0.0%**, Unknown: **0.0%**

ACADEMIC PROGRAMS
The school's curriculum occasionally gives first-year students substantial contact with patients.
There are opportunities for first- or second-year students to work in community health clinics.
Program offerings: drug/alcohol abuse, family medicine, geriatrics, internal medicine, pediatrics, rural medicine
Joint degrees awarded: M.D./Ph.D.
Total National Institutes of Health (NIH) grants awarded to the medical school and affiliated hospitals: **$11.8 million**

CURRICULUM
(TEXT PROVIDED BY SCHOOL):
A thorough knowledge of the basic biomedical sciences is emphasized during the first two years. These include anatomy, biochemistry, histology, neuroscience, physiology,

microbiology, pharmacology, and pathology. In addition, the students receive clinical instruction in courses called Introduction to Clinical Medicine that are taught throughout both years. The second year is capped with a one-month family medicine preceptorship.

The junior year in Sioux Falls or Rapid City consists of six major clerkships taught in pairs during three blocks of 16 weeks: family medicine and internal medicine, surgery and psychiatry, obstetrics/gynecology and pediatrics. The junior year in Yankton is ambulatory-based, emphasizing continuity of care, and students rotate through all clerkships for the entire year.

Clerkships in emergency medicine, family medicine, and several surgery subspecialties are required in the senior year, with a variety of other clerkships available on an elective basis. Primary-care medicine is emphasized in all four years of the curriculum. Longitudinal, ambulatory care clinical experience is part of the curriculum at all three clinical training sites.

FACULTY PROFILE (FALL 2005)
Total teaching faculty: **246 (full-time)**, **696 (part-time)**
Of full-time faculty, those teaching in basic sciences: **15%**; in clinical programs: **85%**
Of part-time faculty, those teaching in basic sciences: **0%**; in clinical programs: **100%**
Full-time faculty/student ratio: **1.2**

SUPPORT SERVICES
The school offers students professional counseling for dealing with stress.

RESIDENCY PROFILE
Most popular residency and specialty programs chosen by the 2004 and 2005 M.D. graduating classes: anesthesiology, dermatology, emergency medicine, family practice, internal medicine, obstetrics and gynecology, orthopaedic surgery, pediatrics, surgery–general, transitional year.

WHERE GRADS GO

32.3%
Proportion of 2003-2005 graduates who entered primary care specialties

24.3%
Proportion of 2004-2005 graduates who accepted in-state residencies

University of Southern California

KECK SCHOOL OF MEDICINE

- 1975 Zonal Avenue, KAM 500, Los Angeles, CA 90033
- Private
- Year Founded: 1895
- Tuition, 2005-2006: $40,454
- Enrollment 2005-2006 academic year: 665
- Website: http://www.usc.edu/keck
- Specialty ranking: N/A

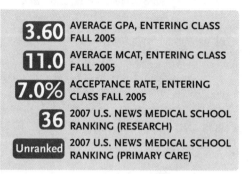

3.60 AVERAGE GPA, ENTERING CLASS FALL 2005

11.0 AVERAGE MCAT, ENTERING CLASS FALL 2005

7.0% ACCEPTANCE RATE, ENTERING CLASS FALL 2005

36 2007 U.S. NEWS MEDICAL SCHOOL RANKING (RESEARCH)

Unranked 2007 U.S. NEWS MEDICAL SCHOOL RANKING (PRIMARY CARE)

ADMISSIONS

Admissions phone number: **(323) 442-2552**
Admissions email address: **medadmit@usc.edu**
Application website: **http://www.usc.edu/keck**
Acceptance rate: **7.0%**
In-state acceptance rate: **8.3%**
Out-of-state acceptance rate: **5.2%**
Minority acceptance rate: **6.0%**
International acceptance rate: **3.8%**

Fall 2005 applications and acceptees

	Applied	Interviewed	Accepted	Enrolled
Total:	5,461	625	384	171
In-state:	3,212	416	266	125
Out-of-state:	2,249	209	118	46

Profile of admitted students

Average undergraduate grade point average: **3.60**
MCAT averages (scale: 1-15; writing test: J-T):
  Composite score: **11.0**
  Verbal reasoning score: **10.5**, Physical sciences score:
  11.2, Biological sciences score: **11.4**, Writing score: **Q**
Proportion with undergraduate majors in: Biological
  sciences: **52%**, Physical sciences: **19%**, Non-sciences:
  18%, Other health professions: **1%**, Mixed disciplines
  and other: **10%**
Percentage of students not coming directly from college
  after graduation: **39%**

Dates and details

The American Medical College Application Service
  (AMCAS) application is accepted.
School asks for a school-specific application as part of the
  admissions process.
Oldest MCAT considered for Fall 2007 entry: **2004**
Earliest application date for the 2007-2008 first-year class:
  June 1, 2006
Latest application date: **November 1, 2006**
Acceptance dates for regular application for the class
  entering in fall 2007:
  Earliest: **October 15, 2006**

Latest: **August 6, 2007**
The school considers requests for deferred entrance.
Starting month for the class entering in 2007–2008:
  August
The school has an Early Decision Plan (EDP).
A personal interview is required for admission.

Undergraduate coursework required

Medical school requires undergraduate work in these subjects: biology, organic chemistry, inorganic (general) chemistry, physics, molecular and cell biology, biochemistry,
humanities, social sciences.

ADMISSIONS POLICY
(TEXT PROVIDED BY SCHOOL):

The Keck School of Medicine of the University of Southern
California's Admissions Committee is committed to
recruiting a diverse group of accomplished and promising
students to its M.D. programs through its unique admissions process.

Each year there are many more qualified candidates than
there are positions available. The B.A./M.D. and early-deci-
sion programs provide additional options for those interested in earning medical degrees.

Undergraduate students must meet course requirements
and take the MCAT well before the application process
begins. In general, applications must be received between
June 1 and November 1 for admission in August of the following year.

All applicants to the M.D. program must have completed
a minimum of four full years or 120 semester hours of academic work at an accredited college or university at the time
of matriculation. Applicants are strongly encouraged to have
their basic science requirements completed at the time of
application.

The Admissions Committee views the personal attributes
of each medical school applicant holistically. The following
factors influence admission decisions: college GPA; MCAT
scores; personal characteristics, such as communication
skills, compassion, and empathy; history of leadership, civic
service, and commitment to social justice; and interest in

teaching, research, or providing patient care to underserved populations.

The Keck School encourages applications from all qualified students. USC does not discriminate against students or applicants for admission on the basis of race, color, ancestry, religion, sexual orientation, national origin, age, marital status, or status as a disabled veteran. An otherwise qualified individual shall not be excluded solely by reason of his or her physical handicap or medical condition.

COSTS AND FINANCIAL AID

Financial aid phone number: (323) 442-1016
Tuition, 2005-2006 academic year: $40,454
Room and board: $12,950
Percentage of students receiving financial aid in 2005-06: 90%
Percentage of students receiving: Loans: 90%, Grants/scholarships: 35%, Work-study aid: 0%
Average medical school debt for the Class of 2004: $146,300

STUDENT BODY

Fall 2005 full-time enrollment: 665
Men: 51%, Women: 49%, In-state: 79%, Minorities: 45%, American Indian: 0.2%, Asian-American: 32.6%, African-American: 3.5%, Hispanic-American: 9.2%, White: 49.3%, International: 1.5%, Unknown: 3.8%

ACADEMIC PROGRAMS

The school's curriculum very frequently gives first-year students substantial contact with patients.
There are opportunities for first- or second-year students to work in community health clinics.
Program offerings: AIDS, drug/alcohol abuse, family medicine, geriatrics, internal medicine, pediatrics, rural medicine, women's health
Joint degrees awarded: M.D./Ph.D., M.D./MBA, M.D./MPH, M.D./M.S.W., M.D./MS, M.D./M.H.A.
Total National Institutes of Health (NIH) grants awarded to the medical school and affiliated hospitals: $159.0 million

CURRICULUM

(TEXT PROVIDED BY SCHOOL):
The Keck School of Medicine revised its four-year curriculum in 2001. The new curriculum enhances students' understanding of the basic sciences and their relevance to clinical medicine. New educational methodology improves students' problem-solving and independent study skills.

In the first two years of the curriculum, the teaching and learning of basic and clinical sciences are fully integrated. The curriculum begins with 19 weeks of Core Principles of Health and Disease, followed by 49 weeks of organ system study, and ending with a seven-week integrated case study section. Cadaver dissection remains a teaching tool.

In Professionalism and the Practice of Medicine, students meet weekly with faculty mentors in small groups. The second year concludes with the integrated cases section, where students in small groups study more complex cases.

The Introduction to Clinical Medicine program expresses the curriculum's patient-centered orientation. Throughout

the first two years, students interact with patients at the Los Angeles County/USC Medical Center and other hospitals. Major content areas include communication in illness settings, the unified concept of health and disease (or biopsychosocial model), basic clinical skills, and correlating basic science with clinical medicine. Small groups of students spend four to eight hours each week with an instructor from the clinical faculty, who remains with the group for one to two years.

In the third year, the curriculum is organized into a track system where all five six-week required clerkships and one 12-week surgery clerkship follow a specific sequence.

In year 4, students complete two four-week clerkships, Medicine II and Neurology, along with electives and selectives. As they acquire knowledge and skills during these clerkships, students assume more clinical responsibility. In the Year IV Medicine II clerkship, students are assigned responsibilities equivalent to those of first-year graduate residents.

Humanities, Economics, Art and the Law is a four-year curriculum that begins in the first year with collaborative discourse where students learn to identify, analyze and resolve clinical ethical problems. The program continues with ethical discernment and action in simulated settings and the human dimensions of medicine in the second year. The third year is devoted to ethics education by clinical role models and encompasses instruction in the core clerkship by ethical standard bearers, followed by home hospice experience and pain management, and the fourth year concludes with a series of student retreats on contemporary health care and the physician's role in society.

FACULTY PROFILE (FALL 2005)

Total teaching faculty: 1,222 (full-time), 31 (part-time)
Of full-time faculty, those teaching in basic sciences: 12%; in clinical programs: 88%
Of part-time faculty, those teaching in basic sciences: 10%; in clinical programs: 90%
Full-time faculty/student ratio: 1.8

SUPPORT SERVICES

The school offers students these services for dealing with stress: expanded-hour gym access, peer counseling, professional counseling, religious support, support groups.

RESIDENCY PROFILE

Most popular residency and specialty programs chosen by the 2004 and 2005 M.D. graduating classes: anesthesiology, family practice, internal medicine, obstetrics and gynecology, pediatrics, psychiatry, radiology–diagnostic, surgery–general, transitional year.

WHERE GRADS GO

43%
Proportion of 2003-2005 graduates who entered primary care specialties

79%
Proportion of 2004-2005 graduates who accepted in-state residencies

University of South Florida

- 12901 Bruce B. Downs Boulevard, Box 3, Tampa, FL 33612
- Public
- Year Founded: 1965
- Tuition, 2005-2006: In-state: $18,431; Out-of-state: $50,515
- Enrollment 2005-2006 academic year: 458
- Website: http://www.hsc.usf.edu/medicine/mdadmissions
- Specialty ranking: N/A

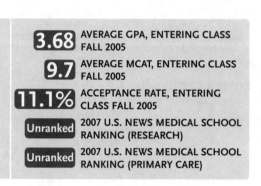

3.68 AVERAGE GPA, ENTERING CLASS FALL 2005

9.7 AVERAGE MCAT, ENTERING CLASS FALL 2005

11.1% ACCEPTANCE RATE, ENTERING CLASS FALL 2005

Unranked 2007 U.S. NEWS MEDICAL SCHOOL RANKING (RESEARCH)

Unranked 2007 U.S. NEWS MEDICAL SCHOOL RANKING (PRIMARY CARE)

ADMISSIONS

Admissions phone number: **(813) 974-2229**
Admissions email address: **md-admissions@lyris.hsc.usf.edu**
Application website: **N/A**
Acceptance rate: **11.1%**
In-state acceptance rate: **15.0%**
Out-of-state acceptance rate: **1.5%**
Minority acceptance rate: **11.0%**
International acceptance rate: **N/A**

Fall 2005 applications and acceptees

	Applied	Interviewed	Accepted	Enrolled
Total:	1,822	336	202	120
In-state:	1,291	324	194	115
Out-of-state:	531	12	8	5

Profile of admitted students

Average undergraduate grade point average: **3.68**
MCAT averages (scale: 1-15; writing test: J-T):
   Composite score: **9.7**
   Verbal reasoning score: **9.4**, Physical sciences score: **9.7**, Biological sciences score: **9.9**, Writing score: **N/A**
Proportion with undergraduate majors in: Biological sciences: **50%**, Physical sciences: **13%**, Non-sciences: **8%**, Other health professions: **4%**, Mixed disciplines and other: **25%**
Percentage of students not coming directly from college after graduation: **50%**

Dates and details

The American Medical College Application Service (AMCAS) application is accepted.
School asks for a school-specific application as part of the admissions process.
Oldest MCAT considered for Fall 2007 entry: **2004**
Earliest application date for the 2007-2008 first-year class: **N/A**
Latest application date: **December 1, 2006**
Acceptance dates for regular application for the class entering in fall 2007:

Earliest: **October 15, 2005**
Latest: **N/A**
The school considers requests for deferred entrance.
Starting month for the class entering in 2007-2008: **August**
The school has an Early Decision Plan (EDP).
A personal interview is required for admission.

Undergraduate coursework required

Medical school requires undergraduate work in these subjects: biology, English, organic chemistry, inorganic (general) chemistry, physics, mathematics.

ADMISSIONS POLICY

(TEXT PROVIDED BY SCHOOL):
The school traditionally accepts Florida students only, but we are now able to take a limited number of superior, out-of-state applicants.

COSTS AND FINANCIAL AID

Financial aid phone number: **(813) 974-2068**
Tuition, 2005-2006 academic year: **In-state: $18,431; Out-of-state: $50,515**
Room and board: **$9,420**
Percentage of students receiving financial aid in 2005-06: **83%**
Percentage of students receiving: Loans: **79%**, Grants/scholarships: **42%**, Work-study aid: **0%**
Average medical school debt for the Class of 2004: **$100,823**

STUDENT BODY

Fall 2005 full-time enrollment: **458**
Men: **47%**, Women: **53%**, In-state: **99%**, Minorities: **37%**, American Indian: **2.0%**, Asian-American: **18.1%**, African-American: **7.0%**, Hispanic-American: **9.6%**, White: **63.1%**, International: **0.0%**, Unknown: **0.2%**

ACADEMIC PROGRAMS

The school's curriculum frequently gives first-year students substantial contact with patients.

There are opportunities for first- or second-year students to work in community health clinics.

Program offerings: AIDS, drug/alcohol abuse, family medicine, geriatrics, internal medicine, pediatrics, rural medicine, women's health

Joint degrees awarded: M.D./Ph.D., M.D./MBA, M.D./MPH

Total National Institutes of Health (NIH) grants awarded to the medical school and affiliated hospitals: **$63.8 million**

CURRICULUM
(TEXT PROVIDED BY SCHOOL):
The curriculum is highly integrated with clinical care, skills testing, and medical professionalism.

FACULTY PROFILE (FALL 2005)
Total teaching faculty: **504 (full-time), 93 (part-time)**
Of full-time faculty, those teaching in basic sciences: 23%; in clinical programs: 77%
Of part-time faculty, those teaching in basic sciences: 47%; in clinical programs: 53%
Full-time faculty/student ratio: **1.1**

SUPPORT SERVICES
The school offers students these services for dealing with stress: expanded-hour gym access, professional counseling, support groups.

RESIDENCY PROFILE
Most popular residency and specialty programs chosen by the 2004 and 2005 M.D. graduating classes: anesthesiology, dermatology, emergency medicine, family practice, internal medicine, obstetrics and gynecology, pediatrics, psychiatry, radiology–diagnostic, surgery–general.

WHERE GRADS GO

41.1%
Proportion of 2003-2005 graduates who entered primary care specialties

46.3%
Proportion of 2004-2005 graduates who accepted in-state residencies

University of Tennessee

HEALTH SCIENCE CENTER

- 62 S. Dunlap, Suite 400 , Memphis, TN 38163
- Public
- Year Founded: 1911
- Tuition, 2005-2006: In-state: $18,065; Out-of-state: $34,949
- Enrollment 2005-2006 academic year: 600
- Website: http://www.utmem.edu/Medicine/
- Specialty ranking: N/A

3.58	AVERAGE GPA, ENTERING CLASS FALL 2005
9.3	AVERAGE MCAT, ENTERING CLASS FALL 2005
23.6%	ACCEPTANCE RATE, ENTERING CLASS FALL 2005
Unranked	2007 U.S. NEWS MEDICAL SCHOOL RANKING (RESEARCH)
Unranked	2007 U.S. NEWS MEDICAL SCHOOL RANKING (PRIMARY CARE)

ADMISSIONS

Admissions phone number: **(901) 448-5559**
Admissions email address: **diharris@utmem.edu**
Application website:
  http://www.utmem.edu/Medicine/Admissions/
Acceptance rate: **23.6%**
In-state acceptance rate: **39.1%**
Out-of-state acceptance rate: **5.6%**
Minority acceptance rate: **21.3%**
International acceptance rate: **0.0%**

Fall 2005 applications and acceptees

	Applied	Interviewed	Accepted	Enrolled
Total:	1,051	375	248	150
In-state:	565	324	221	141
Out-of-state:	486	51	27	9

Profile of admitted students

Average undergraduate grade point average: **3.58**
MCAT averages (scale: 1-15; writing test: J-T):
  Composite score: **9.3**
  Verbal reasoning score: **9.0**, Physical sciences score: **9.0**,
  Biological sciences score: **10.0**, Writing score: **O**
Proportion with undergraduate majors in: Biological
  sciences: **51%**, Physical sciences: **22%**, Non-sciences:
  11%, Other health professions: **1%**, Mixed disciplines and
  other: **15%**
Percentage of students not coming directly from college
  after graduation: **45%**

Dates and details

The American Medical College Application Service
  (AMCAS) application is accepted.
School asks for a school-specific application as part of the
  admissions process.
Oldest MCAT considered for Fall 2007 entry: **2001**
Earliest application date for the 2007-2008 first-year class:
  June 1, 2006
Latest application date: **November 15, 2006**
Acceptance dates for regular application for the class
  entering in fall 2007:

Earliest: **October 15, 2006**
Latest: **August 6, 2007**
The school considers requests for deferred entrance.
Starting month for the class entering in 2007–2008:
  August
The school doesn't have an Early Decision Plan (EDP).
A personal interview is required for admission.

Undergraduate coursework required

Medical school requires undergraduate work in these subjects: biology, English, organic chemistry, inorganic (general) chemistry, physics.

ADMISSIONS POLICY

(TEXT PROVIDED BY SCHOOL):
Selection Factors: The criteria the Committee on
Admissions use in the selection process are the academic
record, MCAT scores, preprofessional evaluations, and personal interviews. Applicants must be citizens or permanent
residents of the U.S. at the time of application. Applications
are considered from Tennessee and its contiguous states
(Mississippi, Arkansas, Missouri, Kentucky, Virginia, North
Carolina, Georgia, and Alabama). Children of UT alumni
may also be considered, regardless of their state of residence. Since priority is given to qualified Tennesseans, non-
residents must possess superior qualifications to be
considered by the committee. Only 10% of the entering
class may be non-residents. Upon initial review of the
AMCAS application, a supplemental application will be sent
to applicants considered competitive for further review.

COSTS AND FINANCIAL AID

Financial aid phone number: **(901) 448-5568**
Tuition, 2005-2006 academic year: **In-state: $18,065; Out-
of-state: $34,949**
Room and board: **$13,251**
Percentage of students receiving financial aid in 2005-06:
  89%
Percentage of students receiving: Loans: **84%**,
  Grants/scholarships: **42%**, Work-study aid: **1%**

Average medical school debt for the Class of 2004:
$103,193

STUDENT BODY
Fall 2005 full-time enrollment: **600**
Men: **62%**, Women: **38%**, In-state: **97%**, Minorities: **23%**,
 American Indian: **0.5%**, Asian-American: **12.0%**,
 African-American: **9.3%**, Hispanic-American: **1.3%**,
 White: **75.0%**, International: **0.0%**, Unknown: **1.8%**

ACADEMIC PROGRAMS
The school's curriculum occasionally gives first-year
 students substantial contact with patients.
There are opportunities for first- or second-year students to
 work in community health clinics.
Program offerings: family medicine, geriatrics, internal
 medicine, pediatrics, women's health
Joint degrees awarded: M.D./Ph.D.
Total National Institutes of Health (NIH) grants awarded to
 the medical school and affiliated hospitals: **N/A**

CURRICULUM
(TEXT PROVIDED BY SCHOOL):
The biomedical sciences are approximately 72 weeks. The
first year begins in August and includes Gross Anatomy;
Prevention, Community and Culture (PCC); Doctoring:
Recognizing Signs and Symptoms (DRS); Molecular Basis
of Disease; and Physiology and ends in March. In April and
May of year 1, basic concepts from the Pathophysiology,
Microbiology, Pathology, and Pharmacology courses are pre-
sented. Year 2 begins in August with Pharmacology,
Microbiology, Pathology, Pathophysiology, Neurosciences,
PCC and DRS. Students are introduced to clinical medicine
in their first semester through PCC and DRS. These
courses expose students to the practice of medicine by placing them in a community physician's office and emphasiz-

ing professionalism. In the third-year clerkships, students
focus on patient problem-solving and experience an increasing level of responsibility. The fourth year consists of six 4-
week clerkships, one week of PCC, and four 4-week
electives.

FACULTY PROFILE (FALL 2005)
Total teaching faculty: **721 (full-time)**, **141 (part-time)**
Of full-time faculty, those teaching in basic sciences: **18%**;
 in clinical programs: **82%**
Of part-time faculty, those teaching in basic sciences: **4%**;
 in clinical programs: **96%**
Full-time faculty/student ratio: **1.2**

SUPPORT SERVICES
The school offers students these services for dealing with
stress: expanded-hour gym access, peer counseling, professional counseling, religious support, support groups.

RESIDENCY PROFILE
Most popular residency and specialty programs chosen by the
2004 and 2005 M.D. graduating classes: anesthesiology,
emergency medicine, family practice, internal medicine,
internal medicine–pediatrics, obstetrics and gynecology,
pediatrics, psychiatry, radiology–diagnostic, surgery–general.

WHERE GRADS GO

30%
*Proportion of 2003-2005 graduates who entered primary
care specialties*

38%
*Proportion of 2004-2005 graduates who accepted in-state
residencies*

University of Texas

HEALTH SCIENCE CENTER—HOUSTON

- 6431 Fannin, MSB G.420, Houston, TX 77030
- Public
- Year Founded: 1969
- Tuition, 2005-2006: In-state: $11,505; Out-of-state: $24,605
- Enrollment 2005-2006 academic year: 848
- Website: http://www.med.uth.tmc.edu
- Specialty ranking: N/A

3.66	AVERAGE GPA, ENTERING CLASS FALL 2005
9.5	AVERAGE MCAT, ENTERING CLASS FALL 2005
7.9%	ACCEPTANCE RATE, ENTERING CLASS FALL 2005
57	2007 U.S. NEWS MEDICAL SCHOOL RANKING (RESEARCH)
Unranked	2007 U.S. NEWS MEDICAL SCHOOL RANKING (PRIMARY CARE)

ADMISSIONS

Admissions phone number: **(713) 500-5116**
Admissions email address: **msadmissions@uth.tmc.edu**
Application website: **http://www.utsystem.edu/tmdsas**
Acceptance rate: **7.9%**
In-state acceptance rate: **8.9%**
Out-of-state acceptance rate: **2.0%**
Minority acceptance rate: **4.9%**
International acceptance rate: **0.0%**

Fall 2005 applications and acceptees

	Applied	Interviewed	Accepted	Enrolled
Total:	3,245	1,212	256	210
In-state:	2,749	1,186	246	202
Out-of-state:	496	26	10	8

Profile of admitted students

Average undergraduate grade point average: **3.66**
MCAT averages (scale: 1-15; writing test: J-T):
  Composite score: **9.5**
  Verbal reasoning score: **9.3**, Physical sciences score: **9.3**,
  Biological sciences score: **10.0**, Writing score: **P**
Proportion with undergraduate majors in: Biological
  sciences: **58%**, Physical sciences: **14%**, Non-sciences:
  11%, Other health professions: **1%**, Mixed disciplines and
  other: **16%**
Percentage of students not coming directly from college
  after graduation: **N/A**

Dates and details

The American Medical College Application Service
  (AMCAS) application is not accepted.
School does not ask for a school-specific application as part
  of the admissions process.
Oldest MCAT considered for Fall 2007 entry: **2002**
Earliest application date for the 2007-2008 first-year class:
  May 1, 2006
Latest application date: **October 15, 2006**
The school doesn't consider requests for deferred entrance.
The school doesn't have an Early Decision Plan (EDP).
A personal interview is required for admission.

Undergraduate coursework required

Medical school requires undergraduate work in these subjects: biology, English, organic chemistry, inorganic (general) chemistry, physics, calculus.

ADMISSIONS POLICY
(TEXT PROVIDED BY SCHOOL):

The UTHSC-H Medical School, in conformity with the purpose assigned it by the Texas Legislature and its mission statement, selects the best qualified students for its entering class who demonstrate a potential to become competent and caring physicians and who will serve the identified needs of the State of Texas. To that end, the Admissions Committee considers the totality of each application and gives importance to the following factors: 1.Intellectual capacity.; 2.Interpersonal and communication skills; 3.Breadth and depth of pre-medical educational experience; 4.Potential for service to the State of Texas; 5.Motivation; and 6.Integrity. It is important that evidence of scholarly interest and achievement in some branch of academic endeavor be demonstrated. A liberal arts education is an excellent basis for a medical career. Accordingly, applicants may have majored is such areas as classics, languages, history, English literature, belles letters, music, or philosophy, provided the specific scientific requirements listed below are fulfilled. Because the study of medicine is based upon science, majors in the scientific disciplines are satisfactory. Technological, vocational (e.g., pharmacy), engineering, or business courses of study are not viewed as favorably as those providing a broad educational background. Students must complete at least 90 undergraduate credit hours, including the specific pre-medical credits listed below, at a United States or Canadian university. English–one year. Biology–two years, as required for science majors and must include formal laboratory work. Mathematics—one-half year of college calculus given by the mathematics department. Physics—one year, as required for science majors, and must include laboratory experience. Chemistry—two years, one year of general chemistry and one year of organic chemistry as required for science majors and must include the corresponding laboratory experience.

The Medical and Dental schools of The University of Texas System are authorized to accept only a limited number of non-Texas residents in an entering class. Non-resident students who do not have outstanding qualifications and students who have been dismissed or who have withdrawn from a medical school are not encourage to apply.

All individuals, without exception, who apply for admission to UTHSC-H Medical School must be able to perform specific essential functions. An applicant who cannot perform the Medical School's essential functions—either with or without reasonable accommodations—will not be considered for admission. Application for admission to The UTHSC-H Medial School is made through the Texas Medical and Dental Schools Application Service (TMDSAS).

COSTS AND FINANCIAL AID
Financial aid phone number: **(713) 500-3860**
Tuition, 2005-2006 academic year: **In-state: $11,505; Out-of-state: $24,605**
Room and board: **$12,410**
Percentage of students receiving financial aid in 2005-06: **98%**
Percentage of students receiving: Loans: **98%**, Grants/scholarships: **49%**, Work-study aid: **0%**
Average medical school debt for the Class of 2004: **$98,345**

STUDENT BODY
Fall 2005 full-time enrollment: **848**
Men: **52%**, Women: **48%**, In-state: **97%**, Minorities: **27%**, American Indian: **0.2%**, Asian-American: **11.6%**, African-American: **2.9%**, Hispanic-American: **12.7%**, White: **69.9%**, International: **0.2%**, Unknown: **2.4%**

ACADEMIC PROGRAMS
There are opportunities for first- or second-year students to work in community health clinics.
Program offerings: AIDS, family medicine, geriatrics, internal medicine, pediatrics, rural medicine, women's health
Joint degrees awarded: M.D./Ph.D., M.D./MPH
Total National Institutes of Health (NIH) grants awarded to the medical school and affiliated hospitals: **$52.4 million**

CURRICULUM
(TEXT PROVIDED BY SCHOOL):
The basic four-year program outlined below is required for the M.D. degree. Variations and adjustments may be made as the Curriculum Committee deems necessary.

Basic sciences: The first academic year includes 18 weeks of required courses in the fall semester, including biochemistry, developmental anatomy, gross anatomy, histology, and introduction to clinical medicine (which is continued in the spring semester). The 19-week spring term also includes immunology, microbiology, neuroscience, and physiology.

Year 2 also is divided into an 18-week fall semester and a 19-week spring semester. Required courses include behavioral sciences, genetics, fundamentals of clinical medicine (with problem-based learning), pathology, physical diagnosis, reproductive biology, radiology (one week), and technical skills.

Clinical sciences: The third academic year begins the first week of July and lasts 48 weeks. It is divided into two 24-week rotation periods with four weeks of vacation. Required clerkships include medicine (12 weeks), obstetrics/gynecology (eight weeks), pediatrics (eight weeks), psychiatry (eight weeks), surgery (eight weeks), and family practice (four weeks). Year 4 begins in July and lasts 11 months. It includes required clerkships in family practice, medicine, neurology, and surgery; a minimum of five one-month electives; and two months for vacation or additional electives.

The Medical School's elective and preceptorship programs in the fourth year permit students to seek clinical opportunities away from Houston, ranging from family practice in rural communities to experiences in the most sophisticated settings requiring advanced technology. International clinical and research electives also are available. The school is fortunate regarding the wealth of clinical opportunities available to its students.

FACULTY PROFILE (FALL 2005)
Total teaching faculty: **795 (full-time), 105 (part-time)**
Of full-time faculty, those teaching in basic sciences: **14%**; in clinical programs: **86%**
Of part-time faculty, those teaching in basic sciences: **2%**; in clinical programs: **98%**
Full-time faculty/student ratio: **0.9**

SUPPORT SERVICES
The school offers students these services for dealing with stress: expanded-hour gym access, peer counseling, professional counseling, religious support, support groups.

RESIDENCY PROFILE
Most popular residency and specialty programs chosen by the 2004 and 2005 M.D. graduating classes: anesthesiology, emergency medicine, family practice, internal medicine, obstetrics and gynecology, pathology–anatomic and clinical, pediatrics, psychiatry, surgery–general.

WHERE GRADS GO
35.3%
Proportion of 2003-2005 graduates who entered primary care specialties

57.9%
Proportion of 2004-2005 graduates who accepted in-state residencies

University of Texas Medical Branch–Galveston

- 301 University Boulevard, Galveston, TX 77555-0133
- Public
- Year Founded: N/A
- Tuition, 2005-2006: In-state: $9,378; Out-of-state: $22,478
- Enrollment 2005-2006 academic year: 830
- Website: http://www.utmb.edu/
- Specialty ranking: N/A

3.72 AVERAGE GPA, ENTERING CLASS FALL 2005

9.3 AVERAGE MCAT, ENTERING CLASS FALL 2005

8.4% ACCEPTANCE RATE, ENTERING CLASS FALL 2005

57 2007 U.S. NEWS MEDICAL SCHOOL RANKING (RESEARCH)

Unranked 2007 U.S. NEWS MEDICAL SCHOOL RANKING (PRIMARY CARE)

ADMISSIONS

Admissions phone number: **(409) 772-3517**
Admissions email address: **lauthoma@utmb.edu**
Application website:
   https://www2.utmb.edu/utmbapp/app_options.htm
Acceptance rate: **8.4%**
In-state acceptance rate: **8.8%**
Out-of-state acceptance rate: **5.7%**
Minority acceptance rate: **9.4%**
International acceptance rate: **0.0%**

Fall 2005 applications and acceptees

	Applied	Interviewed	Accepted	Enrolled
Total:	3,154	974	265	210
In-state:	2,719	890	240	198
Out-of-state:	435	84	25	12

Profile of admitted students

Average undergraduate grade point average: **3.72**
MCAT averages (scale: 1-15; writing test: J-T):
   Composite score: **9.3**
   Verbal reasoning score: **9.0**, Physical sciences score: **9.0**,
   Biological sciences score: **10.0**, Writing score: **P**
Proportion with undergraduate majors in: Biological
   sciences: **47%**, Physical sciences: **22%**, Non-sciences:
   9%, Other health professions: **10%**, Mixed disciplines
   and other: **12%**
Percentage of students not coming directly from college
   after graduation: **10%**

Dates and details

The American Medical College Application Service
   (AMCAS) application is not accepted.
School does not ask for a school-specific application as part
   of the admissions process.
Oldest MCAT considered for Fall 2007 entry: **2001**
Earliest application date for the 2007-2008 first-year class:
   June 1, 2006
Latest application date: **October 15, 2006**
Acceptance dates for regular application for the class
   entering in fall 2007:

Earliest: **November 1, 2006**
Latest: **N/A**
The school considers requests for deferred entrance.
Starting month for the class entering in 2007–2008:
   August
The school doesn't have an Early Decision Plan (EDP).
A personal interview is required for admission.

Undergraduate coursework required

Medical school requires undergraduate work in these subjects: biology, English, organic chemistry, inorganic (general) chemistry, physics, calculus.

COSTS AND FINANCIAL AID

Financial aid phone number: **(409) 772-4955**
Tuition, 2005-2006 academic year: In-state: **$9,378**; Out-
   of-state: **$22,478**
Room and board: **N/A**
Percentage of students receiving financial aid in 2005-06:
   84%
Percentage of students receiving: Loans: **80%**,
   Grants/scholarships: **60%**, Work-study aid: **8%**
Average medical school debt for the Class of 2004: **$98,517**

STUDENT BODY

Fall 2005 full-time enrollment: **830**
Men: **50%**, Women: **50%**, In-state: **94%**, Minorities: **43%**,
   American Indian: **0.5%**, Asian-American: **17.5%**,
   African-American: **9.5%**, Hispanic-American: **15.4%**,
   White: **51.3%**, International: **0.7%**, Unknown: **5.1%**

ACADEMIC PROGRAMS

The school's curriculum very frequently gives first-year
   students substantial contact with patients.
There are opportunities for first- or second-year students to
   work in community health clinics.
Program offerings: family medicine, geriatrics, internal
   medicine, pediatrics, rural medicine, women's health
Joint degrees awarded: M.D./Ph.D.
Total National Institutes of Health (NIH) grants awarded to
   the medical school and affiliated hospitals: **$100.8 million**

CURRICULUM

(TEXT PROVIDED BY SCHOOL):

UTMB's Integrated Medical Curriculum (IMC) is a four-year program emphasizing continuous integration of bio-medical sciences with clinical medicine, early clinical skills and clinical experiences, and professionalism. In this student-centered curriculum, which utilizes small-group problem-based learning, computer-assisted instruction, lectures, and labs, the biomedical sciences are learned in clinical contexts. Beyond knowledge acquisition, the IMC emphasizes problem solving, clinical data gathering and decision making, independent study, and lifelong learning throughout all four years. Its organ-system approach and clinical science contexts promote basic science integration across disciplines. Performance of UTMB students on the USMLE Step 1 exam confirms their mastery of basic science, consistently exceeding national averages.

Through all four years of the IMC, there is a heavy emphasis on the acquisition and refinement of clinical skills. Students work with standardized patients (SPs) beginning the first week of medical school to learn interview and examination techniques, and they begin seeing patients in physicians' offices in the fall of year 1. Progressively more advanced clinical experiences continue during the first two years. Learning and assessment exercises with SPs continue through all four years, with far more SP exercises than most medical schools, giving students ample preparation for the USMLE Clinical Skills Examination. The increasing use of medical simulation provides UTMB students with a truly state-of-the-art medical education.

Years 3 and 4 of the IMC, revised in 2003, emphasize ambulatory and inpatient experiences in standard clerkships, emergency medicine, and neurology. UTMB's role as a referral hospital for many counties throughout the state provides unparalleled depth and breadth of clinical experiences for students. A unique feature of the third-year curriculum is an elective month, allowing students to explore potential career interests before beginning residency application early in year four. A growing collaboration with

Brackenridge Hospital in Austin provides many third- and fourth-year students the option to take some or all of their required rotations in Austin. The fourth year includes an acting internship, community-based ambulatory medicine, and a scholarly project in which a basic science or medical humanities topic is explored in depth. An extensive network of international relationships affords a wide variety of experiences for interested students.

FACULTY PROFILE (FALL 2005)

Total teaching faculty: **1,074 (full-time)**, **N/A (part-time)**
Of full-time faculty, those teaching in basic sciences: **N/A**; in clinical programs: **N/A**
Of part-time faculty, those teaching in basic sciences: **N/A**; in clinical programs: **N/A**
Full-time faculty/student ratio: **1.3**

SUPPORT SERVICES

The school offers students these services for dealing with stress: expanded-hour gym access, professional counseling, religious support, support groups.

RESIDENCY PROFILE

Most popular residency and specialty programs chosen by the 2004 and 2005 M.D. graduating classes: anesthesiology, emergency medicine, family practice, internal medicine, obstetrics and gynecology, orthopaedic surgery, pediatrics, psychiatry, radiology–diagnostic, surgery–general.

WHERE GRADS GO

44.3%
Proportion of 2003-2005 graduates who entered primary care specialties

62.5%
Proportion of 2004-2005 graduates who accepted in-state residencies

University of Texas

SOUTHWESTERN MEDICAL CENTER–DALLAS

- 5323 Harry Hines Boulevard, Dallas, TX 75390
- Public
- Year Founded: 1943
- Tuition, 2005-2006: In-state: $10,632; Out-of-state: $23,732
- Enrollment 2005-2006 academic year: 904
- Website: http://www.utsouthwestern.edu/
- Specialty ranking: internal medicine: 9, women's health: 16

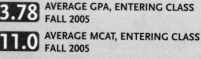

3.78 AVERAGE GPA, ENTERING CLASS FALL 2005

11.0 AVERAGE MCAT, ENTERING CLASS FALL 2005

13.3% ACCEPTANCE RATE, ENTERING CLASS FALL 2005

19 2007 U.S. NEWS MEDICAL SCHOOL RANKING (RESEARCH)

20 2007 U.S. NEWS MEDICAL SCHOOL RANKING (PRIMARY CARE)

ADMISSIONS

Admissions phone number: **(214) 648-5617**
Admissions email address:
 admissions@utsouthwestern.edu
Application website:
 http://www.utsouthwestern.edu/medapp
Acceptance rate: **13.3%**
In-state acceptance rate: **14.4%**
Out-of-state acceptance rate: **9.0%**
Minority acceptance rate: **13.7%**
International acceptance rate: **5.6%**

Fall 2005 applications and acceptees

	Applied	Interviewed	Accepted	Enrolled
Total:	3,268	723	434	229
In-state:	2,590	622	373	193
Out-of-state:	678	101	61	36

Profile of admitted students

Average undergraduate grade point average: **3.78**
MCAT averages (scale: 1-15; writing test: J-T):
 Composite score: **11.0**
 Verbal reasoning score: **10.3**, Physical sciences score:
 11.3, Biological sciences score: **11.4**, Writing score: **P**
Proportion with undergraduate majors in: Biological
 sciences: **45%**, Physical sciences: **27%**, Non-sciences:
 18%, Other health professions: **0%**, Mixed disciplines
 and other: **10%**
Percentage of students not coming directly from college
 after graduation: **27%**

Dates and details

The American Medical College Application Service
 (AMCAS) application is not accepted.
School asks for a school-specific application as part of the
 admissions process.
Oldest MCAT considered for Fall 2007 entry: **2002**
Earliest application date for the 2007-2008 first-year class:
 May 1, 2006
Latest application date: **October 15, 2006**

Acceptance dates for regular application for the class
 entering in fall 2007:
 Earliest: **October 15, 2006**
 Latest: **N/A**
The school considers requests for deferred entrance.
Starting month for the class entering in 2007–2008:
 August
The school doesn't have an Early Decision Plan (EDP).
A personal interview is required for admission.

Undergraduate coursework required

Medical school requires undergraduate work in these subjects: biology/zoology, English, organic chemistry, inorganic
(general) chemistry, physics, calculus.

ADMISSIONS POLICY
(TEXT PROVIDED BY SCHOOL):
Application is made through the Texas Medical and Dental
Schools Application Service (TMDSAS) between May 1 and
October 15 each year for enrollment into the following
year's entering class. Application to the combined
M.D./Ph.D program is made through the American
Medical Colleges Application Service (AMCAS). The
Admissions Committee considers all of the following in
evaluating each applicant's acceptability: academic performance in college as reflected in the undergraduate GPA; the
rigor of the undergraduate curriculum; scores from the
Medical College Admissions Test (MCAT); recommendation
letters from the college premedical committee or faculty;
research experience; extracurricular activities; socioeconomic background; race/ethnicity; any time spent in outside employment; personal integrity and compassion for
others; the ability to communicate in English; other personal qualities and individual factors, such as leadership,
self-appraisal, determination, social/family support, and
maturity/coping capabilities; the applicant's motivation for
a career in medicine. In addition, applicants are evaluated
with regard to the mission of Southwestern Medical School,
which emphasizes the importance of training primary-care
physicians, educating doctors who will practice in medically
underserved areas of Texas, and preparing physician-scien-

tists who seek careers in academic medicine or research. A personal interview is required and is initiated by invitation from the Admissions Committee. Interviews are conducted between September and mid-January each year. Applicants are notified of admission decisions beginning on October 15. Texas law requires that no more than 10 percent of each class be non-Texas residents.

COSTS AND FINANCIAL AID

Financial aid phone number: **(214) 648-3611**
Tuition, 2005-2006 academic year: **In-state: $10,632; Out-of-state: $23,732**
Room and board: **$15,277**
Percentage of students receiving financial aid in 2005-06: **92%**
Percentage of students receiving: Loans: **84%**, Grants/scholarships: **66%**, Work-study aid: **6%**
Average medical school debt for the Class of 2004: **$75,400**

STUDENT BODY

Fall 2005 full-time enrollment: **904**
Men: **56%**, Women: **44%**, In-state: **86%**, Minorities: **43%**, American Indian: **0.3%**, Asian-American: **26.3%**, African-American: **5.9%**, Hispanic-American: **10.6%**, White: **51.5%**, International: **0.8%**, Unknown: **4.5%**

ACADEMIC PROGRAMS

The school's curriculum occasionally gives first-year students substantial contact with patients.
There are opportunities for first- or second-year students to work in community health clinics.
Program offerings: AIDS, drug/alcohol abuse, family medicine, geriatrics, internal medicine, pediatrics, rural medicine, women's health
Joint degrees awarded: M.D./Ph.D., M.D./MBA, M.D./MPH, M.D./MS
Total National Institutes of Health (NIH) grants awarded to the medical school and affiliated hospitals: **$187.9 million**

CURRICULUM

(TEXT PROVIDED BY SCHOOL):
The mission of Southwestern Medical School is to produce physicians and scientists who will be inspired to maintain lifelong medical scholarship and who will apply the knowledge gained from the formal and informal curriculum in a responsible and humanistic manner to the care of patients. The basic medical degree curriculum provides a general professional education that exposes and prepares students for all medical career options. A general overview of the curriculum scheduling can be seen at http://medschool .swmed.edu. The first-year begins with a study of the normal human body and its processes. An introduction to clinical ethics in medicine is provided at this time as well. A program of pre-clinical electives in humanities and related topics complements the required courses. Available summer programs include research opportunities and precep-

torships in the community. Some students continue with research experience full-time, obtaining a Ph.D as a member of the Medical Scientist Training Program (M.D., Ph.D). Other combined degree programs include M.D., MPH and M.D., MBA. The second year offers the student an opportunity to study disease processes and therapeutics. Contact with patients begins early in the second year with history taking, physical examination, and hospital experiences. The third and fourth years offer intense clinical experiences and direct patient care. The third year occupies 12 months. It offers rotations of eight weeks each in surgery and pediatrics, six weeks each in psychiatry and obstetrics, four weeks in family practice and neurology, with 12 weeks in internal medicine. During these rotations, a rich and varied patient population is encountered at county, Veteran's Affairs and university hospitals. The fourth year consists of seven individual four-week clinical rotations. Three rotations are mandatory, a medicine sub-internship, ambulatory medicine and acute care, with each one providing a choice of the specific clinical experiences. Four electives, each of four weeks duration, are chosen from an extensive list of options to fulfill the remaining course requirements. The curriculum is dynamic and responds to the changing requirements for medical education. Faculty and students review the curriculum regularly, and changes are introduced almost every year.

FACULTY PROFILE (FALL 2005)

Total teaching faculty: **1,458 (full-time)**, **209 (part-time)**
Of full-time faculty, those teaching in basic sciences: **17%**; in clinical programs: **83%**
Of part-time faculty, those teaching in basic sciences: **6%**; in clinical programs: **94%**
Full-time faculty/student ratio: **1.6**

SUPPORT SERVICES

The school offers students these services for dealing with stress: expanded-hour gym access, professional counseling, support groups.

RESIDENCY PROFILE

Most popular residency and specialty programs chosen by the 2004 and 2005 M.D. graduating classes: anesthesiology, emergency medicine, family practice, internal medicine, obstetrics and gynecology, pediatrics, radiology–diagnostic, surgery–general.

WHERE GRADS GO

44%
Proportion of 2003-2005 graduates who entered primary care specialties

50%
Proportion of 2004-2005 graduates who accepted in-state residencies

University of Utah

- 30 N. 1900 E, Salt Lake City, UT 84132-2101
- Public
- Year Founded: 1941
- Tuition, 2005-2006: In-state: $17,646; Out-of-state: $32,805
- Enrollment 2005-2006 academic year: 398
- Website: http://uuhsc.utah.edu/som
- Specialty ranking: women's health: 21

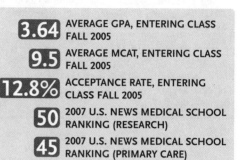

3.64 AVERAGE GPA, ENTERING CLASS FALL 2005

9.5 AVERAGE MCAT, ENTERING CLASS FALL 2005

12.8% ACCEPTANCE RATE, ENTERING CLASS FALL 2005

50 2007 U.S. NEWS MEDICAL SCHOOL RANKING (RESEARCH)

45 2007 U.S. NEWS MEDICAL SCHOOL RANKING (PRIMARY CARE)

ADMISSIONS

Admissions phone number: **(801) 581-7498**
Admissions email address:
  deans.admissions@hsc.utah.edu
Application website:
  http://www.uuhsc.utah.edu/som/admissions/
Acceptance rate: **12.8%**
In-state acceptance rate: **21.9%**
Out-of-state acceptance rate: **6.9%**
Minority acceptance rate: **5.7%**
International acceptance rate: **11.4%**

Fall 2005 applications and acceptees

	Applied	Interviewed	Accepted	Enrolled
Total:	1,074	442	138	102
In-state:	424	281	93	75
Out-of-state:	650	161	45	27

Profile of admitted students

Average undergraduate grade point average: **3.64**
MCAT averages (scale: 1-15; writing test: J-T):
  Composite score: **9.5**
  Verbal reasoning score: **9.3**, Physical sciences score: **9.2**,
  Biological sciences score: **10.1**, Writing score: **O**
Proportion with undergraduate majors in: Biological sciences: **21%**, Physical sciences: **21%**, Non-sciences: **13%**, Other health professions: **16%**, Mixed disciplines and other: **29%**
Percentage of students not coming directly from college after graduation: **18%**

Dates and details

The American Medical College Application Service (AMCAS) application is accepted.
School asks for a school-specific application as part of the admissions process.
Oldest MCAT considered for Fall 2007 entry: **2004**
Earliest application date for the 2007-2008 first-year class:
  June 1, 2006
Latest application date: **November 1, 2006**

Acceptance dates for regular application for the class entering in fall 2007:
  Earliest: **October 15, 2006**
  Latest: **August 1, 2007**
The school considers requests for deferred entrance.
Starting month for the class entering in 2007–2008:
  August
The school doesn't have an Early Decision Plan (EDP).
A personal interview is required for admission.

Undergraduate coursework required

Medical school requires undergraduate work in these subjects: biology, organic chemistry, inorganic (general) chemistry, physics, molecular and cell biology, biochemistry, humanities, demonstration of writing skills, social sciences.

ADMISSIONS POLICY
(TEXT PROVIDED BY SCHOOL):

Admissions requirements: AMCAS application with a recent MCAT (within two years of matriculation) and at least 3 years of college in an accredited U.S. or Canadian school. Classes must include 8 credit hours of biology/zoology, inorganic chemistry, organic chemistry, and general physics (with labs); and 6 hours each of English and behavioral or social sciences. Biochemistry and cellular/molecular biology are highly recommended as well as strong communication skills, previous community service, and physician shadowing or medical experiences. On-site interviews are required. West Virginia residents receive priority consideration, and those with strong ties to West Virginia or strong interest in rural medicine will also be considered.

The 2005 entering class profile: 60 percent West Virginia residents; 44 percent women; 88 percent in science related majors; 44 percent attended West Virginia schools; 3.65 overall mean GPA; mean MCAT scores of 9.0 verbal reasoning, 9.2 physical sciences, 9.6 biological sciences, and O writing sample.

COSTS AND FINANCIAL AID

Financial aid phone number: **(801) 581-6474**

Tuition, 2005-2006 academic year: **In-state: $17,646; Out-of-state: $32,805**
Room and board: **$8,604**
Percentage of students receiving financial aid in 2005-06: **91%**
Percentage of students receiving: Loans: **89%**, Grants/scholarships: **50%**, Work-study aid: **0%**
Average medical school debt for the Class of 2004: **$65,386**

STUDENT BODY
Fall 2005 full-time enrollment: **398**
Men: **62%**, Women: **38%**, In-state: **76%**, Minorities: **15%**, American Indian: **0.5%**, Asian-American: **6.5%**, African-American: **1.8%**, Hispanic-American: **1.8%**, White: **84.2%**, International: **4.0%**, Unknown: **1.3%**

ACADEMIC PROGRAMS
The school's curriculum occasionally gives first-year students substantial contact with patients.
There are opportunities for first- or second-year students to work in community health clinics.
Program offerings: family medicine, geriatrics, internal medicine, pediatrics
Joint degrees awarded: M.D./Ph.D., M.D./MPH
Total National Institutes of Health (NIH) grants awarded to the medical school and affiliated hospitals: **$101.7 million**

CURRICULUM
(TEXT PROVIDED BY SCHOOL):
The four years of medical education constitute but a brief introduction to a broad, deep, and rapidly changing discipline. The mastery of medical knowledge and technical skills requires lifelong self-education.

The curriculum is designed to provide students with the knowledge, skills, and attitudes necessary to practice medicine. Students spend the first two years in the sciences basic to medicine, including anatomy, biochemistry, physiology, microbiology, genetics, pharmacology, pathology, and behavioral science. Concepts and skills necessary to manage clinical illness, to understand the social issues in medicine, and to be well grounded in the ethics of medical practice are introduced early and explored in depth as the curriculum progresses. Emphasis is placed on prevention, diagnosis, and management of disease states and in the systematic application of these concepts to organ-specific diseases.

The first year includes courses in gross anatomy, embryology, histology, biochemistry, human genetics, medical immunology, medical microbiology, pathology, pharmacology, physical diagnosis, physiology, psychiatry, the science of medicine, social medicine, and the doctor-patient relationship.

During the second year, the aim is to integrate basic scientific facts with specific diseases and clinical problems. A multidisciplinary course, organized by specific organ systems, emphasizes pathophysiologic processes, clinical manifestations, and treatment. Courses include geriatrics, neuroanatomy, organ systems, pathology, pediatrics, pharmacology, physical diagnosis, physiology, psychiatry, the science of medicine, and the doctor-patient relationship.

In the third year, emphasis is on the integration of basic science knowledge with clinical, ethical, diagnostic, and problem-solving skills. Clinical clerkships, during which students learn patient management as members of the health-care team, include family practice, internal medicine, obstetrics and gynecology, pediatrics, psychiatry, and surgery. The Topics of Medicine course reviews a series of simulated patients with common medical problems seen in ambulatory medicine. Students are also required to complete a four-week clinical neurology clerkship before graduation.

Seniors must complete a minimum of 36 weeks of credit, including a medical ethics course, a hospital-based subinternship, a public-health project, and clinical electives.

FACULTY PROFILE (FALL 2005)
Total teaching faculty: **951 (full-time)**, **265 (part-time)**
Of full-time faculty, those teaching in basic sciences: **18%**; in clinical programs: **82%**
Of part-time faculty, those teaching in basic sciences: **8%**; in clinical programs: **92%**
Full-time faculty/student ratio: **2.4**

SUPPORT SERVICES
The school offers students these services for dealing with stress: peer counseling, professional counseling, support groups.

RESIDENCY PROFILE
Most popular residency and specialty programs chosen by the 2004 and 2005 M.D. graduating classes: anesthesiology, emergency medicine, internal medicine, pediatrics, surgery–general.

WHERE GRADS GO

36.3%
Proportion of 2003-2005 graduates who entered primary care specialties

25.7%
Proportion of 2004-2005 graduates who accepted in-state residencies

University of Vermont

- E-126 Given Building, 89 Beaumont Avenue, Burlington, VT 05405
- Public
- **Year Founded:** 1822
- **Tuition, 2005-2006:** In-state: $25,477; Out-of-state: $43,487
- **Enrollment 2005-2006 academic year:** 410
- **Website:** https://www.med.uvm.edu
- **Specialty ranking:** rural medicine: 25

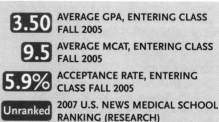

3.50	AVERAGE GPA, ENTERING CLASS FALL 2005
9.5	AVERAGE MCAT, ENTERING CLASS FALL 2005
5.9%	ACCEPTANCE RATE, ENTERING CLASS FALL 2005
Unranked	2007 U.S. NEWS MEDICAL SCHOOL RANKING (RESEARCH)
14	2007 U.S. NEWS MEDICAL SCHOOL RANKING (PRIMARY CARE)

ADMISSIONS

Admissions phone number: **(802) 656-2154**
Admissions email address: **medadmissions@uvm.edu**
Application website:
  http://www.aamc.org/students/amcas/application.htm
Acceptance rate: **5.9%**
In-state acceptance rate: **55.4%**
Out-of-state acceptance rate: **4.5%**
Minority acceptance rate: **3.6%**
International acceptance rate: **1.8%**

Fall 2005 applications and acceptees

	Applied	Interviewed	Accepted	Enrolled
Total:	3,482	497	205	102
In-state:	92	66	51	43
Out-of-state:	3,390	431	154	59

Profile of admitted students

Average undergraduate grade point average: **3.50**
MCAT averages (scale: 1-15; writing test: J-T):
  Composite score: **9.5**
  Verbal reasoning score: **9.8**, Physical sciences score: **9.1**,
  Biological sciences score: **9.6**, Writing score: **Q**
Proportion with undergraduate majors in: Biological sciences: **56%**, Physical sciences: **5%**, Non-sciences: **36%**, Other health professions: **1%**, Mixed disciplines and other: **2%**
Percentage of students not coming directly from college after graduation: **50%**

Dates and details

The American Medical College Application Service (AMCAS) application is accepted.
School asks for a school-specific application as part of the admissions process.
Oldest MCAT considered for Fall 2007 entry: **2003**
Earliest application date for the 2007-2008 first-year class: **June 1, 2006**
Latest application date: **November 1, 2006**
Acceptance dates for regular application for the class entering in fall 2007:

Earliest: **November 15, 2006**
Latest: **August 6, 2007**
The school considers requests for deferred entrance.
Starting month for the class entering in 2007–2008:
  August
The school has an Early Decision Plan (EDP).
A personal interview is required for admission.

Undergraduate coursework required

Medical school requires undergraduate work in these subjects: biology, organic chemistry, inorganic (general) chemistry, physics.

ADMISSIONS POLICY
(TEXT PROVIDED BY SCHOOL):

Applicants must have completed at least three years of undergraduate study at a U.S. or Canadian institution accredited by the National Committee of Regional Accrediting Agencies. The baccalaureate degree is strongly encouraged. An applicant's undergraduate studies must include one year or eight credits each of biology, physics, general chemistry, and organic chemistry. One year of laboratory must be included with each of these prerequisites. In addition, we recommend one course in biochemistry or molecular genetics be taken. The required courses should be completed at the time of application. If they are not, detailed plans for completion by the end of the spring semester for the entering year must be listed on the transcript portion of the American Medical College Application Service (AMCAS) application. High school advanced placement courses will be accepted only if credit appears on the college transcript and subsequently appears on the AMCAS transcript portion of the application.

We encourage students who have a broad and balanced educational background during their undergraduate years. In addition to prerequisite courses in the sciences, recommended areas of study include literature, mathematics, behavioral sciences, history, philosophy, and the arts. College work must demonstrate intellectual drive, independent thinking, curiosity, and self-discipline.

A career in medicine calls for excellent oral and written communication skills. Applicants should seek out opportunities to develop such skills during their college years. Successful applicants often have a history of service to community.

COSTS AND FINANCIAL AID

Financial aid phone number: **(802) 656-8293**
Tuition, 2005-2006 academic year: **In-state: $25,477**; **Out-of-state: $43,487**
Room and board: **$9,767**
Percentage of students receiving financial aid in 2005-06: **90%**
Percentage of students receiving: Loans: **88%**, Grants/scholarships: **64%**, Work-study aid: **0%**
Average medical school debt for the Class of 2004: **$131,945**

STUDENT BODY

Fall 2005 full-time enrollment: **410**
Men: **38%**, Women: **62%**, In-state: **32%**, Minorities: **17%**, American Indian: **0.2%**, Asian-American: **15.1%**, African-American: **0.5%**, Hispanic-American: **0.7%**, White: **78.5%**, International: **0.7%**, Unknown: **4.1%**

ACADEMIC PROGRAMS

The school's curriculum frequently gives first-year students substantial contact with patients.
There are opportunities for first- or second-year students to work in community health clinics.
Program offerings: AIDS, drug/alcohol abuse, family medicine, geriatrics, internal medicine, pediatrics, rural medicine, women's health
Joint degrees awarded: M.D./Ph.D.
Total National Institutes of Health (NIH) grants awarded to the medical school and affiliated hospitals: **N/A**

CURRICULUM

(TEXT PROVIDED BY SCHOOL):
For the past seven years, our school has been in the process of self-examination and curriculum reform as we worked to design a new curriculum that will provide the knowledge, skills, and attributes needed for a physician in the 21st century. The Vermont Integrated Curriculum (VIC) was fully implemented in the fall of 2003. VIC will integrate sciences and clinical medicine from the beginning of medical school, provide continuous assessment of student competency, and foster the skills needed to engage in "education" throughout a lifetime. Instruction in the art and science of medicine is woven throughout the VIC with a focus on patients, families, and communities.

The VIC progresses through three phases—from the study of the basic foundations of medicine, both clinical and basic science, to applications in clinical clerkships to senior scholarship and supervised patient management in an "advanced integration" fourth-year experience.

Integrated comprehensive examinations are administered at the end of the first year, the end of the foundations phase, the closing of clinical clerkships, and after completion of two acting internships.

Foundations studies are organized into three phases: fundamentals, systems integration, and convergence. These present a progression from basic vocabulary, concepts, and methods to relationships of organ systems in health and disease to complex presentations of pathophysiology. Principles of professionalism are integrated throughout this phase through weekly Medical Student Leadership Groups.

The clinical clerkship year is composed of three 15-week segments of departmentally based clinical experience and didactic programs, three one-week blocks of bridge clerkship, and a final performance examination before students are allowed to move into advanced integration.

Each student must complete two months of acting internships at a teaching hospital, including one in internal medicine. In addition, students must complete a four-week elective in emergency medicine. In a two-week teaching practicum, fourth-year students help to teach first-year students under faculty supervision.

The goal of our new curriculum is to integrate the ever expanding universe of knowledge with a desire for continued lifelong learning. Students will be measured both in and between courses to ensure their competency in mastering well-defined learning objectives through an extensive program of assessment involving the use of standardized patients in addition to standard examination formats.

FACULTY PROFILE (FALL 2005)

Total teaching faculty: **512 (full-time)**, **1,285 (part-time)**
Of full-time faculty, those teaching in basic sciences: **15%**; in clinical programs: **85%**
Of part-time faculty, those teaching in basic sciences: **2%**; in clinical programs: **98%**
Full-time faculty/student ratio: **1.2**

SUPPORT SERVICES

The school offers students these services for dealing with stress: expanded-hour gym access, peer counseling, professional counseling, religious support, support groups.

RESIDENCY PROFILE

Most popular residency and specialty programs chosen by the 2004 and 2005 M.D. graduating classes: anesthesiology, emergency medicine, family practice, internal medicine, obstetrics and gynecology, pediatrics, psychiatry, radiology–diagnostic, surgery–general.

WHERE GRADS GO

55%
Proportion of 2003-2005 graduates who entered primary care specialties

22.9%
Proportion of 2004-2005 graduates who accepted in-state residencies

University of Virginia

- PO Box 800793, McKim Hall, Charlottesville, VA 22908-0793
- **Public**
- **Year Founded:** 1819
- **Tuition, 2005-2006:** In-state: $28,700; Out-of-state: $38,524
- **Enrollment 2005-2006 academic year:** 563
- **Website:** http://www.med.virginia.edu
- **Specialty ranking:** internal medicine: 28, rural medicine: 30

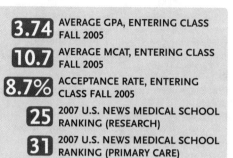

3.74 AVERAGE GPA, ENTERING CLASS FALL 2005

10.7 AVERAGE MCAT, ENTERING CLASS FALL 2005

8.7% ACCEPTANCE RATE, ENTERING CLASS FALL 2005

25 2007 U.S. NEWS MEDICAL SCHOOL RANKING (RESEARCH)

31 2007 U.S. NEWS MEDICAL SCHOOL RANKING (PRIMARY CARE)

ADMISSIONS

Admissions phone number: **(434) 924-5571**
Admissions email address: **medsch-adm@virginia.edu**
Application website: **N/A**
Acceptance rate: **8.7%**
In-state acceptance rate: **18.5%**
Out-of-state acceptance rate: **6.3%**
Minority acceptance rate: **8.8%**
International acceptance rate: **6.1%**

Fall 2005 applications and acceptees

	Applied	Interviewed	Accepted	Enrolled
Total:	3,604	505	314	141
In-state:	712	181	132	93
Out-of-state:	2,892	324	182	48

Profile of admitted students

Average undergraduate grade point average: **3.74**
MCAT averages (scale: 1-15; writing test: J-T):
   Composite score: **10.7**
   Verbal reasoning score: **10.4**, Physical sciences score: **10.9**, Biological sciences score: **11.0**, Writing score: **P**
Proportion with undergraduate majors in: Biological sciences: **51%**, Physical sciences: **18%**, Non-sciences: **21%**, Other health professions: **3%**, Mixed disciplines and other: **7%**
Percentage of students not coming directly from college after graduation: **47%**

Dates and details

The American Medical College Application Service (AMCAS) application is accepted.
School asks for a school-specific application as part of the admissions process.
Oldest MCAT considered for Fall 2007 entry: **2004**
Earliest application date for the 2007-2008 first-year class: **June 1, 2006**
Latest application date: **November 1, 2006**
Acceptance dates for regular application for the class entering in fall 2007:
   Earliest: **October 15, 2006**

Latest: **March 10, 2007**
The school considers requests for deferred entrance.
Starting month for the class entering in 2007–2008:
   August
The school doesn't have an Early Decision Plan (EDP).
A personal interview is required for admission.

Undergraduate coursework required

Medical school requires undergraduate work in these subjects: biology, organic chemistry, inorganic (general) chemistry, physics.

ADMISSIONS POLICY
(TEXT PROVIDED BY SCHOOL):

The Admissions Committee of the University of Virginia School of Medicine, in selecting medical school matriculants, places high value on academic excellence; diversity of culture, ethnicity, and experience; human compassion; and strong interpersonal skills. Preference is given to Virginia residents, with approximately 65 percent of the class having Virginia residence.

The school participates in the American Medical College Application Service. The deadline for receiving AMCAS applications is November 1 of the year prior to enrollment. However, because the University of Virginia utilizes a rolling admission process, it is in the best interest of the applicant to apply as early as possible. After submitting the AMCAS application, applicants will be directed to the University of Virginia School of Medicine's Web-based supplemental application. A $75 nonrefundable processing fee must accompany the supplemental application. Applicants who have been granted an AMCAS fee waiver will also be granted a supplemental application fee waiver.

A select group of applicants will be invited to the School of Medicine for interviews with members of the Admissions Committee. Students are selected and notified of their acceptance on a rolling admissions basis after October 15 until the class is filled. Applicants generally receive notice of their admission status the week following their interview.

All applicants must have completed a minimum of 90 semester hours of coursework in an accredited U.S. or Canadian college or university. The following college science courses must be completed prior to matriculation: one year each of biology, general chemistry, organic chemistry, and physics, all with lab. Biochemistry may be substituted for the second semester of organic chemistry. These courses should not be taken pass/fail, credit/no credit, or through a long-distance learning program. The Medical College Admission Test is required of all applicants.

COSTS AND FINANCIAL AID
Financial aid phone number: **(434) 924-0033**
Tuition, 2005-2006 academic year: **In-state: $28,700; Out-of-state: $38,524**
Room and board: **$16,549**
Percentage of students receiving financial aid in 2005-06: **87%**
Percentage of students receiving: Loans: **84%**, Grants/scholarships: **65%**, Work-study aid: **0%**
Average medical school debt for the Class of 2004: **$78,790**

STUDENT BODY
Fall 2005 full-time enrollment: **563**
Men: **49%**, Women: **51%**, In-state: **70%**, Minorities: **28%**

ACADEMIC PROGRAMS
The school's curriculum frequently gives first-year students substantial contact with patients.
There are opportunities for first- or second-year students to work in community health clinics.
Program offerings: AIDS, drug/alcohol abuse, family medicine, geriatrics, internal medicine, pediatrics, rural medicine, women's health
Joint degrees awarded: M.D./Ph.D., M.D./MPH, M.D./MS, M.D./M.A.
Total National Institutes of Health (NIH) grants awarded to the medical school and affiliated hospitals: **N/A**

CURRICULUM
(TEXT PROVIDED BY SCHOOL):
The M.D. program is designed to prepare leaders in the field of medicine. The curriculum equips graduates to enter careers in clinical practice, research, medical education, or medical administration. The four-year course of instruction consists of lectures, laboratories, small group discussions, and a variety of clinical experiences on inpatient wards and in outpatient clinics and physicians' offices. Humanism and community service are part of the integrated professional experience. Students associate with practicing physicians throughout the four years of medical school. Formal course work during the first two years includes gross and developmental anatomy, biochemistry, cell and tissue

structure/physiology, medical and molecular genetics, medical neuroscience, introduction to human behavior, pharmacology, pathology, introduction to psychiatric medicine, epidemiology, and microbiology. A nearly two-year practice of medicine course, taught primarily in small group tutorials and with frequent patient encounters, provides a forum for learning the fundamental attitudes, skills, knowledge and reasoning required of a physician for clinical problem solving.

Clinical studies include required clerkships in family medicine, internal medicine, neurology, obstetrics and gynecology, pediatrics, psychiatric medicine, and surgery. These are followed by career-focused basic science and health care systems courses. The remainder of the post clerkship period is an elective/selective experience of the student's choosing, which is planned in association with a faculty advisor.

The curriculum is supervised by the associate dean for curriculum and the Curriculum Committee. Two major subcommittees, the Principles of Medicine and Clinical Medicine Committees, consist of course directors and student representatives.

FACULTY PROFILE (FALL 2005)
Total teaching faculty: **882 (full-time), 104 (part-time)**
Of full-time faculty, those teaching in basic sciences: **20%**; in clinical programs: **80%**
Of part-time faculty, those teaching in basic sciences: **8%**; in clinical programs: **92%**
Full-time faculty/student ratio: **1.6**

SUPPORT SERVICES
The school offers students these services for dealing with stress: expanded-hour gym access, peer counseling, professional counseling, religious support, support groups.

RESIDENCY PROFILE
Most popular residency and specialty programs chosen by the 2004 and 2005 M.D. graduating classes: anesthesiology, emergency medicine, family practice, internal medicine, obstetrics and gynecology, orthopaedic surgery, pediatrics, radiology–diagnostic, surgery–general.

WHERE GRADS GO

37%
Proportion of 2003-2005 graduates who entered primary care specialties

26%
Proportion of 2004-2005 graduates who accepted in-state residencies

University of Washington

- Box 356340, Seattle, WA 98195
- Public
- **Year Founded:** 1946
- **Tuition, 2005-2006:** In-state: $14,859; Out-of-state: $34,697
- **Enrollment 2005-2006 academic year:** 810
- **Website:** http://www.uwmedicine.org
- **Specialty ranking:** AIDS: 4, drug/alcohol abuse: 13, family medicine: 1, geriatrics: 7, internal medicine: 6, pediatrics: 10, rural medicine: 1, women's health: 6

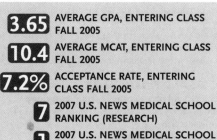

3.65 AVERAGE GPA, ENTERING CLASS FALL 2005

10.4 AVERAGE MCAT, ENTERING CLASS FALL 2005

7.2% ACCEPTANCE RATE, ENTERING CLASS FALL 2005

7 2007 U.S. NEWS MEDICAL SCHOOL RANKING (RESEARCH)

1 2007 U.S. NEWS MEDICAL SCHOOL RANKING (PRIMARY CARE)

ADMISSIONS

Admissions phone number: **(206) 543-7212**
Admissions email address: **askuwsom@u.washington.edu**
Application website: **N/A**
Acceptance rate: **7.2%**
In-state acceptance rate: **20.1%**
Out-of-state acceptance rate: **1.5%**
Minority acceptance rate: **5.2%**
International acceptance rate: **N/A**

Fall 2005 applications and acceptees

	Applied	Interviewed	Accepted	Enrolled
Total:	3,224	803	232	180
In-state:	990	703	199	164
Out-of-state:	2,234	100	33	16

Profile of admitted students

Average undergraduate grade point average: **3.65**
MCAT averages (scale: 1-15; writing test: J-T):
  Composite score: **10.4**
  Verbal reasoning score: **10.2**, Physical sciences score: **10.1**, Biological sciences score: **10.7**, Writing score: **Q**
Proportion with undergraduate majors in: Biological sciences: **33%**, Physical sciences: **13%**, Non-sciences: **17%**, Other health professions: **1%**, Mixed disciplines and other: **36%**
Percentage of students not coming directly from college after graduation: **46%**

Dates and details

The American Medical College Application Service (AMCAS) application is accepted.
School asks for a school-specific application as part of the admissions process.
Oldest MCAT considered for Fall 2007 entry: **2004**
Earliest application date for the 2007-2008 first-year class: **June 1, 2006**
Latest application date: **June 1, 2006**
Acceptance dates for regular application for the class entering in fall 2007:
  Earliest: **November 1, 2006**

Latest: **March 31, 2007**
The school considers requests for deferred entrance.
Starting month for the class entering in 2007–2008:
  August
The school doesn't have an Early Decision Plan (EDP).
A personal interview is required for admission.

Undergraduate coursework required

Medical school requires undergraduate work in these subjects: biology, inorganic (general) chemistry, physics.

ADMISSIONS POLICY

(TEXT PROVIDED BY SCHOOL):
Residents from the states of Washington, Wyoming, Alaska, Montana, and Idaho are eligible to apply. Proof of residency is required. Residents from outside the region who come from disadvantaged backgrounds and/or who have demonstrated a commitment to serving underserved populations will be considered. Individuals with a demonstrated interest in research may apply for the M.D./Ph.D. program regardless of residency.

Candidates for admission are considered on the basis of academic performance, motivation, maturity, personal integrity, and demonstrated humanitarian qualities. Knowledge of the needs of individuals and society and an awareness of healthcare delivery systems are expected, and direct exposure is desired. Extenuating circumstances in an applicant's background are evaluated as they relate to selection factors.

Applicants must submit scores for the 2003, 2004, or 2005 Medical College Admission Test. This exam must be taken no later than the autumn of the year before possible matriculation.

The premedical course requirements should be completed by the time of application and must be completed by matriculation. These requirements include a total of 32 semester hours or 48 quarter hours in undergraduate science courses divided as follows: biology, eight semester hours or 12 quarter hours; chemistry, 12 semester/18 quarter hours, which can be satisfied by taking any combination of inorganic, organic, biochemistry, or molecular biology courses; physics, four semester/six quarter hours; and open science subjects, eight semester/12 quarter hours in the previously mentioned study areas. Biochemistry is strongly suggested for entering students.

All candidates must demonstrate substantial ability in their field; be proficient in English; be able to use basic mathematics; and have an understanding of personal computing and information technologies. Recent accepted applicants had a mean grade-point average of 3.67 with MCAT scores of 10.2 on verbal reasoning, 10.4 in physical sciences, 10.9 in biological sciences, and a Q in the writing sample.

COSTS AND FINANCIAL AID
Financial aid phone number: (206) 685-9229
Tuition, 2005-2006 academic year: **In-state: $14,859; Out-of-state: $34,697**
Room and board: **$12,603**
Percentage of students receiving financial aid in 2005-06: 92%
Percentage of students receiving: Loans: 85%, Grants/scholarships: 60%, Work-study aid: 0%
Average medical school debt for the Class of 2004: **$85,953**

STUDENT BODY
Fall 2005 full-time enrollment: **810**
Men: **48%**, Women: **52%**, In-state: **88%**, Minorities: **24%**, American Indian: **1.6%**, Asian-American: **15.2%**, African-American: **2.2%**, Hispanic-American: **5.1%**, White: **73.6%**, International: **0.0%**, Unknown: **2.3%**

ACADEMIC PROGRAMS
The school's curriculum very frequently gives first-year students substantial contact with patients.
There are opportunities for first- or second-year students to work in community health clinics.
Program offerings: AIDS, drug/alcohol abuse, family medicine, geriatrics, internal medicine, pediatrics, rural medicine, women's health
Joint degrees awarded: M.D./Ph.D., M.D./MPH
Total National Institutes of Health (NIH) grants awarded to the medical school and affiliated hospitals: **$538.8 million**

CURRICULUM
(TEXT PROVIDED BY SCHOOL):
All students are assigned to one of five colleges and to a faculty mentor within their college with whom they interact throughout their medical education.

In the first year, students receive instruction in courses taught from specific departments or disciplines including biochemistry, physiology, pathology, immunology, behavioral sciences, microbiology, and anatomy and embryology. Critical reading, informatics, and evidence-based medicine are also introduced. Students begin instruction in interviewing skills, history-taking and recording techniques, and the physical examination.

The second year involves the organ systems teaching method with 12 courses such as cardiovascular system, res-

piratory system and hematology and adds two discipline-based courses in pharmacology. Students have a weekly opportunity to learn clinical skills at the bedside, working in small groups with their college mentors.

The third and fourth years consist of required and elective clinical clerkships. Required clerkships are in family medicine, internal medicine, obstetrics and gynecology, pediatrics, psychiatry, and surgery. Rehabilitation medicine, emergency medicine, neurology, and an additional four-week selective in surgery or a surgical subspecialty are also required.

Because the UW School of Medicine serves as a regional school for the states of Washington, Wyoming, Alaska, Montana, and Idaho and because of the value of seeing healthcare delivered in different settings, all students take at least one or two clerkships outside of the Seattle area. Most clinical electives are taken in the fourth year. Typically, fourth-year schedules permit advanced coursework in preparation for assuming patient-care responsibilities in residency training.

Students must also complete a continuity curriculum and required preceptorship; four nonclinical selective credits; 32 elective credits (16 weeks); a "capstone course" held in the fourth year, focusing on refresher topics and preresidency skills; and an independet research study in medical sciences. Each student participates in the Objective Structured Clinical Examination at the end of the second year and beginning of the fourth.

FACULTY PROFILE (FALL 2005)
Total teaching faculty: **1,977 (full-time)**, **278 (part-time)**
Of full-time faculty, those teaching in basic sciences: **17%**; in clinical programs: **83%**
Of part-time faculty, those teaching in basic sciences: **17%**; in clinical programs: **83%**
Full-time faculty/student ratio: **2.4**

SUPPORT SERVICES
The school offers students these services for dealing with stress: expanded-hour gym access, peer counseling, professional counseling, support groups.

RESIDENCY PROFILE
Most popular residency and specialty programs chosen by the 2004 and 2005 M.D. graduating classes: anesthesiology, emergency medicine, family practice, internal medicine, obstetrics and gynecology, orthopaedic surgery, pediatrics, psychiatry, radiology–diagnostic, surgery–general.

WHERE GRADS GO

46%
Proportion of 2003-2005 graduates who entered primary care specialties

41%
Proportion of 2004-2005 graduates who accepted in-state residencies

University of Wisconsin–Madison

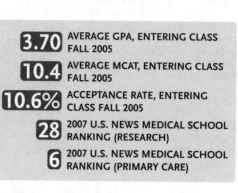

- 750 Highland Avenue, Madison, WI 53705-2221
- Public
- Year Founded: 1848
- Tuition, 2005-2006: In-state: $21,818; Out-of-state: $32,942
- Enrollment 2005-2006 academic year: 619
- Website: http://www.med.wisc.edu/Education
- Specialty ranking: family medicine: 3, geriatrics: 15, internal medicine: 28, rural medicine: 30, women's health: 21

3.70 AVERAGE GPA, ENTERING CLASS FALL 2005

10.4 AVERAGE MCAT, ENTERING CLASS FALL 2005

10.6% ACCEPTANCE RATE, ENTERING CLASS FALL 2005

28 2007 U.S. NEWS MEDICAL SCHOOL RANKING (RESEARCH)

6 2007 U.S. NEWS MEDICAL SCHOOL RANKING (PRIMARY CARE)

ADMISSIONS

Admissions phone number: **(608) 265-6344**
Admissions email address: **eamenzer@wisc.edu**
Application website:
  http://www.med.wisc.edu/Education/md/admissions
Acceptance rate: **10.6%**
In-state acceptance rate: **30.9%**
Out-of-state acceptance rate: **4.1%**
Minority acceptance rate: **6.0%**
International acceptance rate: **N/A**

Fall 2005 applications and acceptees

	Applied	Interviewed	Accepted	Enrolled
Total:	2,602	630	277	163
In-state:	637	502	197	139
Out-of-state:	1,965	128	80	24

Profile of admitted students

Average undergraduate grade point average: **3.70**
MCAT averages (scale: 1-15; writing test: J-T):
  Composite score: **10.4**
  Verbal reasoning score: **10.1**, Physical sciences score: **10.4**, Biological sciences score: **10.7**, Writing score: **P**
Proportion with undergraduate majors in: Biological sciences: **62%**, Physical sciences: **14%**, Non-sciences: **19%**, Other health professions: **3%**, Mixed disciplines and other: **3%**
Percentage of students not coming directly from college after graduation: **39%**

Dates and details

The American Medical College Application Service (AMCAS) application is accepted.
School asks for a school-specific application as part of the admissions process.
Oldest MCAT considered for Fall 2007 entry: **2002**
Earliest application date for the 2007-2008 first-year class: **June 1, 2006**
Latest application date: **November 1, 2006**
Acceptance dates for regular application for the class entering in fall 2007:

Earliest: **October 15, 2006**
Latest: **August 15, 2007**
The school considers requests for deferred entrance.
Starting month for the class entering in 2007–2008: **August**
The school has an Early Decision Plan (EDP).
A personal interview is required for admission.

Undergraduate coursework required

Medical school requires undergraduate work in these subjects: biology, biology/zoology, English, organic chemistry, inorganic (general) chemistry, physics, biochemistry, mathematics, demonstration of writing skills.

ADMISSIONS POLICY
(TEXT PROVIDED BY SCHOOL):

The Admissions Committee attempts to select a class in which all members have a level of past academic performance that predicts the student's academic success in medical school; personal characteristics that will enable the student to provide sympathetic and intelligent patient care; and an interest in others as might be demonstrated by community service, extracurricular activities, and/or leadership.

In the selection of candidates for admission, the committee considers undergraduate and graduate academic performance and Medical College Admission Test scores; extracurricular activities; the applicant's employment record; the personal, educational, and socioeconomic background of the applicant and the response of the applicant to any challenges; the applicant's character with reference to honesty and integrity, empathy, maturity, leadership, self-discipline, and emotional stability; the ability of the applicant to communicate and relate well with others; motivation to pursue a career in medicine; and the interest and suitability of the applicant for special programs and/or future specific careers.

Furthermore, in the interests of both enriching the educational environment for all students and better meeting the future medical, educational, and scientific needs of society, the committee makes a special effort to select a class whose members represent a broad range of diverse life experiences, backgrounds, and interests. This diversity may include ethnic or racial background; socioeconomic background; educational background; regional and geographic background; interests and/or aptitudes for different medical careers; and other cultural experiences.

It is the responsibility of the faculty and students who serve on the Admissions Committee to select the entering class. Our admissions policy does not allow the dean or anyone else to grant special consideration for applicants to the University of Wisconsin School of Medicine and Public Health. It is the goal of the Admissions Committee to seek students capable of benefiting from the educational opportunities available at the University of Wisconsin-Madison and who give evidence that they will contribute to meeting the healthcare needs of the people of the state of Wisconsin and the nation.

Preference is given to residents of Wisconsin.

COSTS AND FINANCIAL AID

Financial aid phone number: **(608) 262-3060**
Tuition, 2005-2006 academic year: **In-state: $21,818; Out-of-state: $32,942**
Room and board: **$13,860**
Percentage of students receiving financial aid in 2005-06: **85%**
Percentage of students receiving: Loans: **85%**, Grants/scholarships: **25%**, Work-study aid: **0%**
Average medical school debt for the Class of 2004: **$130,000**

STUDENT BODY

Fall 2005 full-time enrollment: **619**
Men: **47%**, Women: **53%**, In-state: **88%**, Minorities: **20%**, American Indian: **0.5%**, Asian-American: **7.9%**, African-American: **4.0%**, Hispanic-American: **4.2%**, White: **82.6%**, International: **0.0%**, Unknown: **0.8%**

ACADEMIC PROGRAMS

The school's curriculum frequently gives first-year students substantial contact with patients.
There are opportunities for first- or second-year students to work in community health clinics.
Program offerings: AIDS, drug/alcohol abuse, family medicine, geriatrics, internal medicine, pediatrics, rural medicine, women's health
Joint degrees awarded: M.D./Ph.D.
Total National Institutes of Health (NIH) grants awarded to the medical school and affiliated hospitals: **$182.8 million**

CURRICULUM

(TEXT PROVIDED BY SCHOOL):
The University of Wisconsin medical curriculum emphasizes the acquisition of core doctoring skills in a humane and nurturing environment. Students spend time in doctors' offices from the first month of medical school and continue to build their doctoring skills throughout the four years through a core curriculum component, which is interdisciplinary and longitudinal.

In the first year, the core curriculum is a cohesive series of courses designed to build a firm base in the sciences fundamental to clinical medicine; the focus is on the functional, morphological, molecular, metabolic, pathologic, and developmental principles of the human body. In the second year, the courses emphasize organ systems, mechanisms of disease and abnormalities, and therapeutic intervention. Throughout the first two years, a mixture of didactic, small-group, standardized-patient, and clinical experiences help to provide a lively and varied medical education.

Beginning in the third year, clerkships expose students to a wide variety of clinical settings, including outpatient, inpatient, community-based, rural, and inner city. Our "statewide campus" includes clinical training sites in nine communities throughout Wisconsin, with principal locations in Madison, La Crosse, Marshfield, and Milwaukee as well as at 34 preceptor sites and the Area Health Education Centers.

Students emerging from their clinical years at the UW Medical School do very well in competing for residencies, and residency supervisors rate our graduates very highly. Our graduates also look back on their medical education and rate it favorably in preparing them for residency.

FACULTY PROFILE (FALL 2005)

Total teaching faculty: **1,031 (full-time)**, **190 (part-time)**
Of full-time faculty, those teaching in basic sciences: **14%**; in clinical programs: **86%**
Of part-time faculty, those teaching in basic sciences: **2%**; in clinical programs: **98%**
Full-time faculty/student ratio: **1.7**

SUPPORT SERVICES

The school offers students these services for dealing with stress: expanded-hour gym access, professional counseling, support groups.

RESIDENCY PROFILE

Most popular residency and specialty programs chosen by the 2004 and 2005 M.D. graduating classes: anesthesiology, emergency medicine, family practice, internal medicine, pediatrics, radiology–diagnostic, surgery–general.

WHERE GRADS GO

46.6%
Proportion of 2003-2005 graduates who entered primary care specialties

32.3%
Proportion of 2004-2005 graduates who accepted in-state residencies

Vanderbilt University

- 21st Avenue S and Garland Avenue, Nashville, TN 37232-2104
- Private
- Year Founded: 1875
- Tuition, 2005-2006: $36,001
- Enrollment 2005-2006 academic year: 436
- Website: http://www.mc.vanderbilt.edu/medschool/
- Specialty ranking: internal medicine: 18, pediatrics: 19

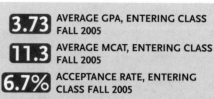

3.73 AVERAGE GPA, ENTERING CLASS FALL 2005

11.3 AVERAGE MCAT, ENTERING CLASS FALL 2005

6.7% ACCEPTANCE RATE, ENTERING CLASS FALL 2005

17 2007 U.S. NEWS MEDICAL SCHOOL RANKING (RESEARCH)

57 2007 U.S. NEWS MEDICAL SCHOOL RANKING (PRIMARY CARE)

ADMISSIONS

Admissions phone number: **(615) 322-2145**
Admissions email address: **N/A**
Application website:
  http://www.mc.vanderbilt.edu/medschool/admissions/online_app.php
Acceptance rate: **6.7%**
In-state acceptance rate: **6.6%**
Out-of-state acceptance rate: **6.7%**
Minority acceptance rate: **7.2%**
International acceptance rate: **10.6%**

Fall 2005 applications and acceptees

	Applied	Interviewed	Accepted	Enrolled
Total:	4,369	993	291	105
In-state:	317	45	21	17
Out-of-state:	4,052	948	270	88

Profile of admitted students

Average undergraduate grade point average: **3.73**
MCAT averages (scale: 1-15; writing test: J-T):
  Composite score: **11.3**
  Verbal reasoning score: **10.6**, Physical sciences score: **11.5**, Biological sciences score: **11.7**, Writing score: **Q**
Proportion with undergraduate majors in: Biological sciences: **50%**, Physical sciences: **21%**, Non-sciences: **15%**, Other health professions: **N/A**, Mixed disciplines and other: **13%**
Percentage of students not coming directly from college after graduation: **44%**

Dates and details

The American Medical College Application Service (AMCAS) application is accepted.
School asks for a school-specific application as part of the admissions process.
Oldest MCAT considered for Fall 2007 entry: **2003**
Earliest application date for the 2007-2008 first-year class: **June 1, 2006**
Latest application date: **November 15, 2006**

Acceptance dates for regular application for the class entering in fall 2007:
  Earliest: **October 15, 2006**
  Latest: **N/A**
The school considers requests for deferred entrance.
Starting month for the class entering in 2007–2008:
  August
The school has an Early Decision Plan (EDP).
A personal interview is required for admission.

Undergraduate coursework required

Medical school requires undergraduate work in these subjects: biology, English, organic chemistry, inorganic (general) chemistry, physics.

ADMISSIONS POLICY
(TEXT PROVIDED BY SCHOOL):

The initial stage involves review of material provided to the AMCAS. There is a holistic review of the academic performance and non-academic factors such as patient care experiences, research, extracurricular involvement, leadership, athletic activities, applicants from underserved populations, and applicants who would enhance the diversity of the class and enhance the educational experience. Selected candidates will be offered an opportunity to file a secondary application, which consists of three additional essays along with a $50 application fee. This second stage also includes a one-on-one personal interview conducted on the Vanderbilt campus by a faculty member who is not necessarily a member of the Admissions Committee. The interviewer reviews the AMCAS primary application, essay, and biographical data, but the secondary and recommendations are not available to him/her. When all relevant admission materials are completed, which includes a primary AMCAS application, the Vanderbilt secondary application, the written report of the interviewer, and letters of recommendation, each candidate will be assigned for detailed review to three members of the Admissions Committee which is composed of active faculty and three student representatives. The three reviewers will present the credentials of the applicant along with a suggested action to the entire committee. Admission Committee meetings are held weekly from Fall to the beginning of April, and actions are taken in a rolling admissions process. Approximately 250 immediate admissions are offered for the 104 places. A Second Visit Weekend is held in early Spring for students holding admissions. After the May 15 decision date for students, the School determines how many waiting list places are required to be filled, and applicants accepted from the waiting list are notified. Approximately 10 positions in the medical school are reserved for the MSTP (M.D./Ph.D.) program, which has a separate Admissions Committee and screening process. Places are also available for early decision applicants using the same criteria as the standard applicant pool, at two early time points, upon matriculation as undergraduates and at the completion of the second year at the university. The goal for each of these programs is to identify the best of the Vanderbilt undergraduate applicants who upon admission to the medical school have been relieved of the time and effort of the standard medical school application process, allowing them to pursue independent study.

COSTS AND FINANCIAL AID
Financial aid phone number: **(615) 343-6310**
Tuition, 2005-2006 academic year: **$36,001**
Room and board: **$8,640**
Percentage of students receiving financial aid in 2005-06: **86%**
Percentage of students receiving: Loans: **71%**, Grants/scholarships: **58%**, Work-study aid: **N/A**
Average medical school debt for the Class of 2004: **$103,200**

STUDENT BODY
Fall 2005 full-time enrollment: **436**
Men: **53%**, Women: **47%**, In-state: **30%**, Minorities: **30%**, American Indian: **0.2%**, Asian-American: **17.9%**, African-American: **7.6%**, Hispanic-American: **1.6%**, White: **67.4%**, International: **4.1%**, Unknown: **1.1%**

ACADEMIC PROGRAMS
The school's curriculum occasionally gives first-year students substantial contact with patients.
There are opportunities for first- or second-year students to work in community health clinics.
Program offerings: AIDS, drug/alcohol abuse, family medicine, geriatrics, internal medicine, pediatrics, rural medicine, women's health
Joint degrees awarded: M.D./Ph.D., M.D./MBA, M.D./MPH, M.D./JD, M.D./MS
Total National Institutes of Health (NIH) grants awarded to the medical school and affiliated hospitals: **$249.3 million**

CURRICULUM
(TEXT PROVIDED BY SCHOOL):
Throughout the four years at Vanderbilt, students learn from both clinical and didactic experiences, with classroom based learning more dominant in the first two years, and clinical experience in the last two.

During the first year, students study anatomy, biochemistry, microbiology and immunology, physiology and histology. In addition, they learn about social and economic factors in medicine and the psychological aspects of health

and disease. All students participate in a clinical preceptorship during the first semester. Vanderbilt recently launched a new required course that provides students with the critical thinking and research skills to become leaders and scholars in medicine.

Each student performs a two year project in one of the following nine areas: medical humanities, law and medicine, health services research, community health initiatives, laboratory based research, patient centered research, medical education, medical informatics, and global health. Each project is supervised, and students record their progress in an electronic learning portfolio. Students devote eight weeks to their emphasis projects during the summer after their first year, and complete their projects during the second year. At the end of the second year, they present their findings at an all-school seminar.

In the second year, students study pathology, neuroscience, psychiatry, radiology, genetics, clinical nutrition, preventive medicine, and laboratory diagnosis. They are required to choose one elective each semester from a list that allows laboratory and clinical experiences. Students may also use elective time for additional clinical experience.

In the third year, students participate in six required clinical clerkships: medicine, surgery, neurology, psychiatry, obstetrics and gynecology, and pediatrics.

In the fourth year, students are required to complete a medicine and a surgery sub-internship, emergency medicine, and ambulatory care. In addition, they are required to choose four other electives.

FACULTY PROFILE (FALL 2005)
Total teaching faculty: **1,630 (full-time)**, **996 (part-time)**
Of full-time faculty, those teaching in basic sciences: **24%**; in clinical programs: **76%**
Of part-time faculty, those teaching in basic sciences: **6%**; in clinical programs: **94%**
Full-time faculty/student ratio: **3.7**

SUPPORT SERVICES
The school offers students these services for dealing with stress: expanded-hour gym access, peer counseling, professional counseling, religious support, support groups.

RESIDENCY PROFILE
Most popular residency and specialty programs chosen by the 2004 and 2005 M.D. graduating classes: dermatology, emergency medicine, internal medicine, orthopaedic surgery, pathology–anatomic and clinical, pediatrics, psychiatry, radiology–diagnostic, surgery–general, internal medicine/pediatrics.

WHERE GRADS GO

31%		

Proportion of 2003-2005 graduates who entered primary care specialties

25%		

Proportion of 2004-2005 graduates who accepted in-state residencies

Virginia Commonwealth University

■ PO Box 980565, Richmond, VA 23298-0565
■ Public
■ Year Founded: 1838
■ Tuition, 2005-2006: In-state: $24,137; Out-of-state: $38,166
■ Enrollment 2005-2006 academic year: 737
■ Website: http://www.medschool.vcu.edu
■ Specialty ranking: N/A

3.50	AVERAGE GPA, ENTERING CLASS FALL 2005
9.4	AVERAGE MCAT, ENTERING CLASS FALL 2005
7.5%	ACCEPTANCE RATE, ENTERING CLASS FALL 2005
Unranked	2007 U.S. NEWS MEDICAL SCHOOL RANKING (RESEARCH)
Unranked	2007 U.S. NEWS MEDICAL SCHOOL RANKING (PRIMARY CARE)

ADMISSIONS

Admissions phone number: **(804) 828-9629**
Admissions email address: **somume@hsc.vcu.edu**
Application website: **http://www.admissions.som.vcu.edu**
Acceptance rate: **7.5%**
In-state acceptance rate: **23.2%**
Out-of-state acceptance rate: **4.4%**
Minority acceptance rate: **10.0%**
International acceptance rate: **N/A**

Fall 2005 applications and acceptees

	Applied	Interviewed	Accepted	Enrolled
Total:	4,877	685	368	184
In-state:	809	317	188	104
Out-of-state:	4,068	368	180	80

Profile of admitted students

Average undergraduate grade point average: **3.50**
MCAT averages (scale: 1-15; writing test: J-T):
   Composite score: **9.4**
   Verbal reasoning score: **9.0**, Physical sciences score: **9.4**,
   Biological sciences score: **9.8**, Writing score: **O**
Proportion with undergraduate majors in: Biological
   sciences: **48%**, Physical sciences: **23%**, Non-sciences:
   26%, Other health professions: **3%**, Mixed disciplines
   and other: **0%**
Percentage of students not coming directly from college
   after graduation: **47%**

Dates and details

The American Medical College Application Service
   (AMCAS) application is accepted.
School asks for a school-specific application as part of the
   admissions process.
Oldest MCAT considered for Fall 2007 entry: **2003**
Earliest application date for the 2007-2008 first-year class:
   June 1, 2006
Latest application date: **October 15, 2006**
Acceptance dates for regular application for the class
   entering in fall 2007:
   Earliest: **October 15, 2006**

Latest: **August 6, 2007**
The school considers requests for deferred entrance.
Starting month for the class entering in 2007–2008:
   August
The school has an Early Decision Plan (EDP).
A personal interview is required for admission.

Undergraduate coursework required

Medical school requires undergraduate work in these subjects: biology, biology/zoology, English, organic chemistry,
physics, mathematics, demonstration of writing skills, general chemistry.

ADMISSIONS POLICY

(TEXT PROVIDED BY SCHOOL):
Applicants are selected on the basis of their potential as
prospective physicians as well as students of medicine.
Attributes of character, personality factors, academic skills,
and exposure to medicine are considered along with academic performance, grade-point average, Medical College
Admission Test scores, letters of recommendation, and personal interviews at the School of Medicine.

The school gives preference to bona fide residents of the
Commonwealth of Virginia and does not discriminate on
the basis of age, race, sex, creed, national origin, or handicap. Foreign nationals must be permanent residents at the
time of application.

COSTS AND FINANCIAL AID

Financial aid phone number: **(804) 828-4006**
Tuition, 2005-2006 academic year: **In-state: $24,137; Out-
of-state: $38,166**
Room and board: **$9,372**
Percentage of students receiving financial aid in 2005-06:
   93%
Percentage of students receiving: Loans: **86%**,
   Grants/scholarships: **38%**, Work-study aid: **0%**
Average medical school debt for the Class of 2004:
   $115,314

STUDENT BODY

Fall 2005 full-time enrollment: 737
Men: 52%, Women: 48%, In-state: 59%, Minorities: 28%,
American Indian: 0.3%, Asian-American: 28.0%,
African-American: 6.6%, Hispanic-American: 0.1%,
White: 58.2%, International: 0.0%, Unknown: 6.8%

ACADEMIC PROGRAMS

The school's curriculum very frequently gives first-year
students substantial contact with patients.
There are opportunities for first- or second-year students to
work in community health clinics.
Program offerings: AIDS, drug/alcohol abuse, family
medicine, geriatrics, internal medicine, pediatrics, rural
medicine, women's health
Joint degrees awarded: M.D./Ph.D., M.D./MPH,
M.D./M.H.A.
Total National Institutes of Health (NIH) grants awarded to
the medical school and affiliated hospitals: N/A

CURRICULUM

(TEXT PROVIDED BY SCHOOL):
The first year is spent studying normal structure and function in a traditional discipline format. The second year
emphasizes pathogenesis of disease manifestations, and
principles of management are discussed in each of the
major body systems. There is a longitudinal experience in
clinical medicine for first- and second-year students.
Students spend two afternoons per month in a small group
learning the fundamentals of clinical medicine. This is supplemented by a clinical experience in the office of a primary-care physician two afternoons per month. This unique
clinical experience is integrated with the basic science curriculum in a way that enhances and enriches the student's
learning. There is a computer lab with over 40 workstations
and a full array of commercial and in-house, faculty-devel-
oped educational software.
  In the third year, the clinical rotations are at the university and Veterans Affairs hospitals, with ambulatory care
rotations at nonuniversity primary-care sites. Computer

educational workstations, distributed throughout the hospitals and clinics, give students access to the university library
databases, expert decision support systems, and educational
software programs.
  During the fourth year, the student may choose from a
wide variety of electives both at the university and throughout the United States. In addition, there are elective programs serving the first and second years.

FACULTY PROFILE (FALL 2005)

Total teaching faculty: 749 (full-time), 40 (part-time)
Of full-time faculty, those teaching in basic sciences: 22%;
in clinical programs: 78%
Of part-time faculty, those teaching in basic sciences: 33%;
in clinical programs: 68%
Full-time faculty/student ratio: 1.0

SUPPORT SERVICES

The school offers students these services for dealing with
stress: expanded-hour gym access, peer counseling, professional counseling, religious support, support groups.

RESIDENCY PROFILE

Most popular residency and specialty programs chosen by
the 2004 and 2005 M.D. graduating classes: emergency
medicine, family practice, internal medicine, obstetrics and
gynecology, pathology–anatomic and clinical, pediatrics,
psychiatry, radiology–diagnostic, surgery–general, transitional year.

WHERE GRADS GO

42%
*Proportion of 2003-2005 graduates who entered primary
care specialties*

41%
*Proportion of 2004-2005 graduates who accepted in-state
residencies*

Wake Forest University

- Medical Center Boulevard, Winston-Salem, NC 27157
- Private
- Year Founded: 1941
- Tuition, 2005-2006: $34,006
- Enrollment 2005-2006 academic year: 431
- Website: http://www.wfubmc.edu
- Specialty ranking: family medicine: 18, geriatrics: 20

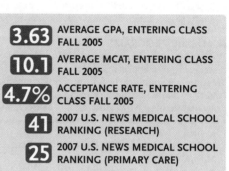

3.63 AVERAGE GPA, ENTERING CLASS FALL 2005

10.1 AVERAGE MCAT, ENTERING CLASS FALL 2005

4.7% ACCEPTANCE RATE, ENTERING CLASS FALL 2005

41 2007 U.S. NEWS MEDICAL SCHOOL RANKING (RESEARCH)

25 2007 U.S. NEWS MEDICAL SCHOOL RANKING (PRIMARY CARE)

ADMISSIONS

Admissions phone number: **(336) 716-4264**
Admissions email address: **medadmit@wfubmc.edu**
Application website: **http://www.aamc.org/stuapps**
Acceptance rate: **4.7%**
In-state acceptance rate: **12.4%**
Out-of-state acceptance rate: **3.8%**
Minority acceptance rate: **N/A**
International acceptance rate: **N/A**

Fall 2005 applications and acceptees

	Applied	Interviewed	Accepted	Enrolled
Total:	5,983	518	280	108
In-state:	627	140	78	41
Out-of-state:	5,356	378	202	67

Profile of admitted students

Average undergraduate grade point average: **3.63**
MCAT averages (scale: 1-15; writing test: J-T):
 Composite score: **10.1**
 Verbal reasoning score: **10.1**, Physical sciences score: **10.1**, Biological sciences score: **10.1**, Writing score: **P**
Proportion with undergraduate majors in: Biological sciences: **40%**, Physical sciences: **23%**, Non-sciences: **26%**, Other health professions: **0%**, Mixed disciplines and other: **11%**
Percentage of students not coming directly from college after graduation: **51%**

Dates and details

The American Medical College Application Service (AMCAS) application is accepted.
School asks for a school-specific application as part of the admissions process.
Oldest MCAT considered for Fall 2007 entry: **2003**
Earliest application date for the 2007-2008 first-year class: **June 1, 2006**
Latest application date: **November 1, 2006**
Acceptance dates for regular application for the class entering in fall 2007:
 Earliest: **October 15, 2006**

Latest: **July 30, 2007**
The school considers requests for deferred entrance.
Starting month for the class entering in 2007–2008: **July**
The school has an Early Decision Plan (EDP).
A personal interview is required for admission.

Undergraduate coursework required

Medical school requires undergraduate work in these subjects: biology, biology/zoology, organic chemistry, inorganic (general) chemistry, physics.

ADMISSIONS POLICY

(TEXT PROVIDED BY SCHOOL):
Medical College Admission Test scores and grade-point average are considered, and personal qualities are assessed in the interviews.
 A national pool of applicants is considered, so state of residence is inconsequential.

COSTS AND FINANCIAL AID

Financial aid phone number: **(336) 716-2889**
Tuition, 2005-2006 academic year: **$34,006**
Room and board: **$15,040**
Percentage of students receiving financial aid in 2005-06: **86%**
Percentage of students receiving: Loans: **82%**, Grants/scholarships: **76%**, Work-study aid: **0%**
Average medical school debt for the Class of 2004: **$126,634**

STUDENT BODY

Fall 2005 full-time enrollment: **431**
Men: **56%**, Women: **44%**, In-state: **36%**, Minorities: **30%**, American Indian: **1.2%**, Asian-American: **14.2%**, African-American: **11.4%**, Hispanic-American: **3.7%**, White: **64.5%**, International: **5.1%**, Unknown: **0.0%**

ACADEMIC PROGRAMS

The school's curriculum frequently gives first-year students substantial contact with patients.

There are opportunities for first- or second-year students to work in community health clinics.

Program offerings: AIDS, drug/alcohol abuse, family medicine, geriatrics, internal medicine, pediatrics, rural medicine, women's health

Joint degrees awarded: M.D./Ph.D., M.D./MBA, M.D./MS

Total National Institutes of Health (NIH) grants awarded to the medical school and affiliated hospitals: **N/A**

CURRICULUM
(TEXT PROVIDED BY SCHOOL):

The curriculum, Prescription for Excellence: A Physician's Pathway to Lifelong Learning, is organized to meet the goals of the undergraduate medical education program: the development of proficiency in self-directed learning and life-long learning skills, and the acquisition of appropriate core biomedical science knowledge, clinical skills, problem-solving/clinical reasoning skills, interviewing and communication skills, information management skills, and professional attitudes and behavior.

Students study the basic and clinical sciences in an integrated fashion across the five phases of the four-year curriculum, utilizing a variety of educational methods including small-group, problem-based learning. Community-based clinical experiences in the first year, as well as a focus on general population health, are hallmarks of the curriculum. Humanistic and professionalism issues are addressed longitudinally across the curriculum in formats designed to provide students with a clear understanding of the role and responsibilities of physicians within society. Information technology has been integrated into the curriculum, and all incoming students are provided with a laptop computer.

Phase 1 serves as the foundation for the remainder of the curriculum and consists of seven courses: Human Structure and Development, Cellular and Subcellular Processes, Basic and Clinical Science Problems I, Foundations of Clinical Medicine I (FCM), Medicine as a Profession I (MAAP), Population Health and Epidemiology/Evidence Based Medicine, and Community Practice Experience(CPE).

Phase 2 is composed of five courses. Systems Pathophysiology begins in Phase 2, with the remaining four courses (Basic and Clinical Science Problems, FCM, MAAP, and CPE) being continuations of courses begun in Phase 1. The Systems Pathophysiology course is intended to be an introduction to clinical medicine—integrating basic science with clinical material built around nine organ-based topics: infectious disease/microbiology, hematology/lymph, endocrinology/reproduction, cardiovascular, pulmonary, renal, nervous system, digestive diseases/nutrition, and integument and musculoskeletal.

Phase 3 is composed of three 16-week blocks; approximately one third of the class is assigned to each block at any given time. Core clinical clerkships include: inpatient inter-

nal medicine, ambulatory internal medicine, surgery, obstetrics/gynecology/women's health, pediatrics, psychiatry, neurology/rehabilitation, and family medicine. There are also one-week clerkships in anesthesiology and radiology.

Phase 4 consists of 10 four-week blocks (four required, six elective) and four weeks of vacation. Numerous elective opportunities are available intramurally and externally at approved institutions. Students have the opportunity to participate in electives in foreign countries; the medical school maintains formal affiliation agreements with a number of medical schools. The four required clerkship months are advanced inpatient management (AIM), clerkships (students complete two monthlong AIM clerkships selected from two separate disciplines: surgery, psychiatry, family medicine, obstetrics and gynecology, internal medicine, and pediatrics), emergency medicine, and intensive care. The primary goal of these clerkship experiences is the development of students' abilities in complete patient management. Students are actively involved in all aspects of patient care.

Phase 5 is a five-week capstone experience for students and includes small-group problem-based learning, journal clubs, medical Spanish, and a series of basic and clinical science lectures, aimed at enhancing the abilities and preparing the soon-to-graduate student for the challenges of residency and beyond.

FACULTY PROFILE (FALL 2005)
Total teaching faculty: **869 (full-time)**, **491 (part-time)**
Of full-time faculty, those teaching in basic sciences: **28%**; in clinical programs: **72%**
Of part-time faculty, those teaching in basic sciences: **11%**; in clinical programs: **89%**
Full-time faculty/student ratio: **2.0**

SUPPORT SERVICES
The school offers students these services for dealing with stress: professional counseling, religious support.

RESIDENCY PROFILE
Most popular residency and specialty programs chosen by the 2004 and 2005 M.D. graduating classes: anesthesiology, emergency medicine, internal medicine, pediatrics, surgery–general.

WHERE GRADS GO

49%

Proportion of 2003-2005 graduates who entered primary care specialties

26%

Proportion of 2004-2005 graduates who accepted in-state residencies

Washington University in St. Louis

- 660 S. Euclid Avenue, St. Louis, MO 63110
- Private
- Year Founded: 1891
- Tuition, 2005-2006: $39,720
- Enrollment 2005-2006 academic year: 593
- Website: http://medschool.wustl.edu
- Specialty ranking: AIDS: 21, drug/alcohol abuse: 10, internal medicine: 7, pediatrics: 6, women's health: 10

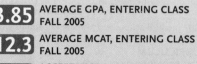

3.85 AVERAGE GPA, ENTERING CLASS FALL 2005

12.3 AVERAGE MCAT, ENTERING CLASS FALL 2005

9.9% ACCEPTANCE RATE, ENTERING CLASS FALL 2005

4 2007 U.S. NEWS MEDICAL SCHOOL RANKING (RESEARCH)

52 2007 U.S. NEWS MEDICAL SCHOOL RANKING (PRIMARY CARE)

ADMISSIONS

Admissions phone number: **(314) 362-6858**
Admissions email address: **wumscoa@wustl.edu**
Application website:
   http://medschool.wustl.edu/admissions/
Acceptance rate: **9.9%**
In-state acceptance rate: **7.0%**
Out-of-state acceptance rate: **10.0%**
Minority acceptance rate: **10.7%**
International acceptance rate: **11.7%**

Fall 2005 applications and acceptees

	Applied	Interviewed	Accepted	Enrolled
Total:	3,298	1,195	326	123
In-state:	157	53	11	6
Out-of-state:	3,141	1,142	315	117

Profile of admitted students

Average undergraduate grade point average: **3.85**
MCAT averages (scale: 1-15; writing test: J-T):
   Composite score: **12.3**
   Verbal reasoning score: **11.6**, Physical sciences score:
   12.7, Biological sciences score: **12.8**, Writing score: **Q**
Proportion with undergraduate majors in: Biological
   sciences: **41%**, Physical sciences: **44%**, Non-sciences:
   13%, Other health professions: **0%**, Mixed disciplines
   and other: **2%**
Percentage of students not coming directly from college
   after graduation: **37%**

Dates and details

The American Medical College Application Service
   (AMCAS) application is accepted.
School asks for a school-specific application as part of the
   admissions process.
Oldest MCAT considered for Fall 2007 entry: **2003**
Earliest application date for the 2007-2008 first-year class:
   July 1, 2006
Latest application date: **December 1, 2006**
Acceptance dates for regular application for the class
   entering in fall 2007:

Earliest: **November 1, 2006**
Latest: **August 1, 2007**
The school considers requests for deferred entrance.
Starting month for the class entering in 2007–2008:
   August
The school doesn't have an Early Decision Plan (EDP).
A personal interview is required for admission.

Undergraduate coursework required

Medical school requires undergraduate work in these subjects: biology, organic chemistry, inorganic (general) chemistry, physics, mathematics, calculus.

ADMISSIONS POLICY

(TEXT PROVIDED BY SCHOOL):
Washington University School of Medicine enrolls bright, energetic, compassionate students who want to learn to practice medicine at the edge of what is known. The recruitment and selection process identifies people who are personally and academically accomplished and who are energized by interacting with and improving the well being of others. Applications are especially encouraged from women and members of underrepresented minority groups as well as those from diverse life experiences and backgrounds.

Each year the Medical Scientist Training Program (MSTP) and the Committee on Admissions accept up to 25 incoming students who enroll in the combined MD-PhD degree program and receive full-tuition scholarships plus stipends for living expenses. MSTP selection emphasizes scientific experience, accomplishments, commitment to a combined career of scientific investigation with clinical practice, and potential for success in this research training environment.

Coursework required for admission includes one year of biology, general (inorganic) chemistry, organic chemistry, physics, and mathematics through differential calculus. One semester of statistics can be substituted for one semester of calculus and one semester of biochemistry can replace one semester of organic chemistry. Biochemistry, though not required, is encouraged.

The application is then evaluated to determine whether the candidate will be invited for an interview. This evaluation considers the applicant's entire undergraduate and, where applicable, graduate records. Items scrutinized include rigor of the curriculum, grades, MCAT scores, recommendation letters, extracurricular activities, life experiences, and AMCAS essay.

Once accepted, applicants may request deferred entry into the class for activities such as research, teaching, public service or travel.

COSTS AND FINANCIAL AID
Financial aid phone number: (314) 362-6845
Tuition, 2005-2006 academic year: $39,720
Room and board: $8,824
Percentage of students receiving financial aid in 2005-06: 92%
Percentage of students receiving: Loans: 52%, Grants/scholarships: 76%, Work-study aid: 0%
Average medical school debt for the Class of 2004: $92,501

STUDENT BODY
Fall 2005 full-time enrollment: 593
Men: 53%, Women: 47%, In-state: 7%, Minorities: 34%, American Indian: 0.7%, Asian-American: 26.1%, African-American: 4.7%, Hispanic-American: 2.2%, White: 58.7%, International: 4.4%, Unknown: 3.2%

ACADEMIC PROGRAMS
The school's curriculum frequently gives first-year students substantial contact with patients.
There are opportunities for first- or second-year students to work in community health clinics.
Program offerings: AIDS, drug/alcohol abuse, family medicine, geriatrics, internal medicine, pediatrics, rural medicine
Joint degrees awarded: M.D./Ph.D., M.D./M.A.
Total National Institutes of Health (NIH) grants awarded to the medical school and affiliated hospitals: $358.9 million

CURRICULUM
(TEXT PROVIDED BY SCHOOL):
The first-year curriculum focuses on the acquisition of a core knowledge of human biology, as well as on an introduction to the essentials of good patient care. Courses are graded pass/fail, and a variety of didactic means are made available, including lectures, small groups, extensive course syllabi, clinical correlations, and a Lotus Notes computerized curriculum database. The Practice of Medicine I uses regular patient interactions and integrative cases to teach students to skillfully interview and examine patients, as well as the fundamentals of bioethics, health promotion/disease prevention, biostatistics, and epidemiology.

The second-year curriculum is focused on human pathophysiology and pathology. Students acquire broad, detailed knowledge of mechanisms of disease pathogenesis, clinopathological relationships, and fundamental principles of therapy. The Practice of Medicine II continues students' introduction to the fundamentals of patient care, and emphasizes organizing and interpreting clinical information.

The overall goal of the third year is implementation of fundamental interactive clinical skills necessary for the practice of medicine at the highest possible level of excellence. Students achieve this goal by participating in intensive, closely supervised training experiences in the core clinical clerkships involving inpatient and ambulatory settings and interactions with patients who present a spectrum of clinical problems. Through these experiences, students exhibit growth and maturation in their abilities to take medical histories, perform complete physical examinations, synthesize findings into a diagnosis, formulate treatment plans, and document and present information in a concise, logical, and organized fashion.

The overall goals of the fourth year are to consolidate, enhance, and refine the basic clinical skills developed during the clinical clerkships and to explore specialty areas within the field of medicine.

FACULTY PROFILE (FALL 2005)
Total teaching faculty: 1,501 (full-time), 79 (part-time)
Of full-time faculty, those teaching in basic sciences: 10%; in clinical programs: 90%
Of part-time faculty, those teaching in basic sciences: 5%; in clinical programs: 95%
Full-time faculty/student ratio: 2.5

SUPPORT SERVICES
The school offers students these services for dealing with stress: expanded-hour gym access, peer counseling, professional counseling, religious support, support groups.

RESIDENCY PROFILE
Most popular residency and specialty programs chosen by the 2004 and 2005 M.D. graduating classes: anesthesiology, dermatology, emergency medicine, internal medicine, ophthalmology, orthopaedic surgery, pediatrics, radiology–diagnostic, surgery–general.

WHERE GRADS GO
30%
Proportion of 2003-2005 graduates who entered primary care specialties

35.5%
Proportion of 2004-2005 graduates who accepted in-state residencies

Wayne State University

- 540 E. Canfield, Detroit, MI 48201
- Public
- **Year Founded:** 1868
- **Tuition, 2005-2006:** In-state: $23,314; Out-of-state: $46,766
- **Enrollment 2005-2006 academic year:** 1,063
- **Website:** http://www.med.wayne.edu/Admissions
- **Specialty ranking:** N/A

N/A	AVERAGE GPA, ENTERING CLASS FALL 2005
N/A	AVERAGE MCAT, ENTERING CLASS FALL 2005
N/A	ACCEPTANCE RATE, ENTERING CLASS FALL 2005
Unranked	2007 U.S. NEWS MEDICAL SCHOOL RANKING (RESEARCH)
Unranked	2007 U.S. NEWS MEDICAL SCHOOL RANKING (PRIMARY CARE)

ADMISSIONS
Admissions phone number: **(313) 577-1466**
Admissions email address: **admissions@med.wayne.edu**

Dates and details
The American Medical College Application Service (AMCAS) application is accepted.
School asks for a school-specific application as part of the admissions process.
The school has an Early Decision Plan (EDP).
A personal interview is required for admission.

Undergraduate coursework required
Medical school requires undergraduate work in these subjects: biology, English, organic chemistry, inorganic (general) chemistry, physics.

ADMISSIONS POLICY
(TEXT PROVIDED BY SCHOOL):
The Committee on Admissions will select those applicants who, in its judgment, will make the best students and physicians. Consideration is given to the entire record, grade-point average, Medical College Admission Test scores, recommendations, and interview results as these reflect the applicant's personality, maturity, character, and suitability for medicine. Additionally, the committee regards as desirable certain healthcare experiences, such as volunteering or working in hospitals, hospices, nursing homes, or doctor's offices. The committee also values experience in biomedical laboratory research.

Following an initial screening process, students with competitive applications are selected to complete a secondary application. Special encouragement is given to candidates from medically underserved areas in Michigan.

COSTS AND FINANCIAL AID
Financial aid phone number: **(313) 577-1039**
Tuition, 2005-2006 academic year: **In-state: $23,314; Out-of-state: $46,766**
Room and board: **$18,733**

Percentage of students receiving financial aid in 2005-06: **87%**
Percentage of students receiving: Loans: **86%**, Grants/scholarships: **41%**, Work-study aid: **3%**
Average medical school debt for the Class of 2004: **$113,000**

STUDENT BODY
Fall 2005 full-time enrollment: **1,063**
Men: **52%**, Women: **48%**, In-state: **92%**, Minorities: **30%**, American Indian: **0.2%**, Asian-American: **16.1%**, African-American: **12.9%**, Hispanic-American: **0.8%**, White: **65.9%**, International: **2.1%**, Unknown: **2.1%**

ACADEMIC PROGRAMS
There are opportunities for first- or second-year students to work in community health clinics.
Program offerings: AIDS, drug/alcohol abuse, family medicine, geriatrics, internal medicine, pediatrics, women's health
Joint degrees awarded: M.D./Ph.D.
Total National Institutes of Health (NIH) grants awarded to the medical school and affiliated hospitals: **N/A**

CURRICULUM
(TEXT PROVIDED BY SCHOOL):
The Medical School curriculum is a four-academic-year course of study, beginning in August of one year and ending in May 45 months later.

Traditionally, the first two years are designated as the basic science curriculum. The curriculum in Year 1 deals with normal structure and function of the human body. It includes courses in human gross anatomy, histology, embryology, biochemistry, physiology, neuroscience, genetics, nutrition, and clinical medicine. Neuroscience is the only integrated course in the first year, combining portions of neuroanatomy, physiology, psychiatry, and biochemistry. All courses include problem-solving sessions as part of their curriculum. The clinical medicine program is largely a problem-based course that is integrated over all four years.

The Year 2 curriculum focuses on the abnormal structure and function of the human body. The first term is composed of courses in immunology/microbiology/infectious disease, psychiatry, pharmacology, pathobiology, and clinical medicine. The second term is made up of eight pathophysiology units that integrate pathology, medicine, and pharmacology for gastrointestinal, hematology, connective tissues/dermatology, neurology, respiratory, cardiovascular, and endocrine systems. Running concurrently with this program is Clinical Medicine, which involves twice-weekly sessions in area hospitals where students work in small groups with teams of physicians to learn physical diagnostic skills.

Upon completion of the basic science curriculum, students must pass the United States Medical Licensing Examination Step 1 before promotion to the third year of medical school.

The clinical science curriculum includes eight required clerkships during 11 months in the third year and three required courses during the eight months of study making up the fourth year.

The third-year required clerkships are pediatrics (two months), internal medicine (two months), family medicine (one month), and continuity of care (six months, concurrent with other clerkships), general surgery (two months), obstetrics and gynecology (two months), neurology (one month), and psychiatry (one month). One month is reserved for an elective.

The fourth-year required clerkships are Emergency Medicine (one month); Inpatient Medicine (adult or pediatric, one month); and Outpatient Medicine (adult or pediatric, one month).

During the clinical science curriculum, students must take a minimum of six electives, typically taken as one elective in the third year and five in the fourth year. It is required that students plan a balanced program of study.

Midway through the third year, students typically begin to choose an adviser and focus on postgraduate (residency) training. The residency application process begins in the summer of the fourth year, with interviews for most specialties in the fall and early winter. Match lists for the National Residency Matching Program are due in February of the senior year, with results announced in mid-March. Senior students are required to take the USMLE Step 2 before graduation, and, beginning with Class of 2005, passage of this examination will be a requirement for graduation.

FACULTY PROFILE (FALL 2005)
Total teaching faculty: **N/A (full-time), N/A (part-time)**
Of full-time faculty, those teaching in basic sciences: **N/A**;
   in clinical programs: **N/A**
Of part-time faculty, those teaching in basic sciences: **N/A**;
   in clinical programs: **N/A**
Full-time faculty/student ratio: **N/A**

SUPPORT SERVICES
The school offers students these services for dealing with stress: expanded-hour gym access, peer counseling, professional counseling, support groups.

West Virginia University

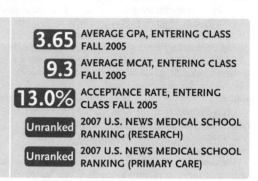

- 1146 Health Sciences N, Morgantown, WV 26506-9111
- Public
- **Year Founded:** 1902
- **Tuition, 2005-2006:** In-state: $16,454; Out-of-state: $37,452
- **Enrollment 2005-2006 academic year:** 424
- **Website:** http://www.hsc.wvu.edu/som/students
- **Specialty ranking:** rural medicine: 12

3.65 AVERAGE GPA, ENTERING CLASS FALL 2005

9.3 AVERAGE MCAT, ENTERING CLASS FALL 2005

13.0% ACCEPTANCE RATE, ENTERING CLASS FALL 2005

Unranked 2007 U.S. NEWS MEDICAL SCHOOL RANKING (RESEARCH)

Unranked 2007 U.S. NEWS MEDICAL SCHOOL RANKING (PRIMARY CARE)

ADMISSIONS

Admissions phone number: **(304) 293-2408**
Admissions email address: **medadmissions@hsc.wvu.edu**
Application website: **http://www.aamc.org**
Acceptance rate: **13.0%**
In-state acceptance rate: **45.7%**
Out-of-state acceptance rate: **7.6%**
Minority acceptance rate: **27.8%**
International acceptance rate: **N/A**

Fall 2005 applications and acceptees

	Applied	Interviewed	Accepted	Enrolled
Total:	1,307	258	170	98
In-state:	186	118	85	55
Out-of-state:	1,121	140	85	43

Profile of admitted students

Average undergraduate grade point average: **3.65**
MCAT averages (scale: 1-15; writing test: J-T):
　Composite score: **9.3**
　Verbal reasoning score: **9.0**, Physical sciences score: **9.2**,
　Biological sciences score: **9.6**, Writing score: **O**
Proportion with undergraduate majors in: Biological sciences: **54%**, Physical sciences: **30%**, Non-sciences: **12%**, Other health professions: **4%**, Mixed disciplines and other: **0%**
Percentage of students not coming directly from college after graduation: **8%**

Dates and details

The American Medical College Application Service (AMCAS) application is accepted.
School asks for a school-specific application as part of the admissions process.
Oldest MCAT considered for Fall 2007 entry: **2005**
Earliest application date for the 2007-2008 first-year class: **June 1, 2006**
Latest application date: **November 15, 2006**
Acceptance dates for regular application for the class entering in fall 2007:
　Earliest: **October 15, 2006**

Latest: **August 15, 2007**
The school considers requests for deferred entrance.
Starting month for the class entering in 2007–2008:
　August
The school has an Early Decision Plan (EDP).
A personal interview is required for admission.

Undergraduate coursework required

Medical school requires undergraduate work in these subjects: biology/zoology, English, organic chemistry, inorganic (general) chemistry, physics, behavioral science, social sciences.

COSTS AND FINANCIAL AID

Financial aid phone number: **(304) 293-3706**
Tuition, 2005-2006 academic year: **In-state: $16,454; Out-of-state: $37,452**
Room and board: **$8,226**
Percentage of students receiving financial aid in 2005-06: **88%**
Percentage of students receiving: Loans: **82%**, Grants/scholarships: **41%**, Work-study aid: **0%**
Average medical school debt for the Class of 2004: **$95,308**

STUDENT BODY

Fall 2005 full-time enrollment: **424**
Men: **61%**, Women: **39%**, In-state: **75%**, Minorities: **11%**, American Indian: **0.0%**, Asian-American: **9.7%**, African-American: **0.7%**, Hispanic-American: **1.9%**, White: **87.7%**, International: **0.0%**, Unknown: **0.0%**

ACADEMIC PROGRAMS

The school's curriculum frequently gives first-year students substantial contact with patients.
There are opportunities for first- or second-year students to work in community health clinics.
Program offerings: AIDS, drug/alcohol abuse, family medicine, geriatrics, internal medicine, pediatrics, rural medicine, women's health
Joint degrees awarded: M.D./Ph.D., M.D./MPH

Total National Institutes of Health (NIH) grants awarded to the medical school and affiliated hospitals: **$15.5 million**

FACULTY PROFILE (FALL 2005)
Total teaching faculty: **584 (full-time)**, **113 (part-time)**
Of full-time faculty, those teaching in basic sciences: **12%**; in clinical programs: **88%**
Of part-time faculty, those teaching in basic sciences: **0%**; in clinical programs: **100%**
Full-time faculty/student ratio: **1.4**

SUPPORT SERVICES
The school offers students these services for dealing with stress: expanded-hour gym access, professional counseling, support groups.

RESIDENCY PROFILE
Most popular residency and specialty programs chosen by the 2004 and 2005 M.D. graduating classes: emergency medicine, family practice, internal medicine, obstetrics and gynecology, pediatrics, surgery–general, transitional year, internal medicine/pediatrics.

WHERE GRADS GO

41%
Proportion of 2003-2005 graduates who entered primary care specialties

45%
Proportion of 2004-2005 graduates who accepted in-state residencies

Wright State University

- PO Box 1751, Dayton, OH 45401-1751
- Public
- Year Founded: 1974
- Tuition, 2005-2006: In-state: $24,082; Out-of-state: $32,806
- Enrollment 2005-2006 academic year: 386
- Website: http://www.med.wright.edu
- Specialty ranking: N/A

3.58 AVERAGE GPA, ENTERING CLASS FALL 2005

9.0 AVERAGE MCAT, ENTERING CLASS FALL 2005

8.3% ACCEPTANCE RATE, ENTERING CLASS FALL 2005

Unranked 2007 U.S. NEWS MEDICAL SCHOOL RANKING (RESEARCH)

Unranked 2007 U.S. NEWS MEDICAL SCHOOL RANKING (PRIMARY CARE)

ADMISSIONS

Admissions phone number: **(937) 775-2934**
Admissions email address: **som_saa@wright.edu**
Application website:
  https://somms2.med.wright.edu/saa/oasys/login.asp
Acceptance rate: **8.3%**
In-state acceptance rate: **19.6%**
Out-of-state acceptance rate: **2.2%**
Minority acceptance rate: **N/A**
International acceptance rate: **N/A**

Fall 2005 applications and acceptees

	Applied	Interviewed	Accepted	Enrolled
Total:	2,710	451	225	100
In-state:	950	368	186	86
Out-of-state:	1,760	83	39	14

Profile of admitted students

Average undergraduate grade point average: **3.58**
MCAT averages (scale: 1-15; writing test: J-T):
  Composite score: **9.0**
  Verbal reasoning score: **9.1**, Physical sciences score: **8.6**,
  Biological sciences score: **9.3**, Writing score: **O**
Proportion with undergraduate majors in: Biological sciences: **50%**, Physical sciences: **15%**, Non-sciences: **15%**, Other health professions: **5%**, Mixed disciplines and other: **15%**
Percentage of students not coming directly from college after graduation: **15%**

Dates and details

The American Medical College Application Service (AMCAS) application is accepted.
School asks for a school-specific application as part of the admissions process.
Oldest MCAT considered for Fall 2007 entry: **2003**
Earliest application date for the 2007-2008 first-year class: **June 1, 2006**
Latest application date: **November 15, 2006**
Acceptance dates for regular application for the class entering in fall 2007:

Earliest: **November 1, 2006**
Latest: **August 1, 2007**
The school considers requests for deferred entrance.
Starting month for the class entering in 2007–2008: **August**
The school has an Early Decision Plan (EDP).
A personal interview is required for admission.

Undergraduate coursework required

Medical school requires undergraduate work in these subjects: biology, English, organic chemistry, inorganic (general) chemistry, physics, mathematics.

ADMISSIONS POLICY
(TEXT PROVIDED BY SCHOOL):

It is the policy of the School of Medicine to seek a student body of diverse social, ethnic, and educational backgrounds. Women, minority students, and applicants from rural Ohio backgrounds are particularly encouraged to apply. However, applicants are admitted solely on the basis of individual qualifications without regard to race, religion, gender, sexual orientation, disability, veteran status, national origin, age, or ancestry.

Dedication to human concerns, compassion, intellectual capacity, and personal maturity in the applicant are of greater importance than specific areas of preprofessional preparation. The Admissions Committee, which is broadly based, also seeks positive evidence of motivation, altruism, selflessness, and human empathy in the prospective student.

Upon receipt of the application from the American Medical College Application Service, all applicants are invited to submit secondary applications and letters of recommendation. After review of all submitted material, applicants are selected for interviews. The committee carefully reviews the application, the academic record, Medical College Admission Test performance, letters of recommendation, and the results of personal interviews (by invitation only) in making its final selections. Ohio residents are given preference, but nonresidents are encouraged to apply.

COSTS AND FINANCIAL AID

Financial aid phone number: **(937) 775-2934**
Tuition, 2005-2006 academic year: **In-state: $24,082; Out-of-state: $32,806**
Room and board: **$10,560**

STUDENT BODY

Fall 2005 full-time enrollment: **386**
Men: **45%**, Women: **55%**, In-state: **96%**, Minorities: **22%**, American Indian: **0.5%**, Asian-American: **13.2%**, African-American: **8.8%**, Hispanic-American: **2.6%**, White: **74.4%**, International: **0.0%**, Unknown: **0.5%**

ACADEMIC PROGRAMS

The school's curriculum very frequently gives first-year students substantial contact with patients.
There are opportunities for first- or second-year students to work in community health clinics.
Program offerings: AIDS, drug/alcohol abuse, family medicine, geriatrics, internal medicine, pediatrics, rural medicine, women's health
Joint degrees awarded: M.D./Ph.D., M.D./MBA, M.D./MPH
Total National Institutes of Health (NIH) grants awarded to the medical school and affiliated hospitals: **N/A**

CURRICULUM

(TEXT PROVIDED BY SCHOOL):
The primary goal of the educational program is to educate students to provide comprehensive care to patients and their families.

During the first two years, students are taught in an interdisciplinary fashion using large-group lectures, small-group discussions, computer-based instruction, case-based learning, and team learning. The curriculum introduces students to normal structure and functioning in an integrated fashion. Instruction progresses through various organizational levels from molecular to organ.

Throughout the first two years, the curriculum integrates the behavioral sciences, humanities, wellness, and disease prevention. Regular didactic instruction by clinical faculty is provided. Students are taught medical history-taking, physi-cal examination skills, and evaluation of patients' concerns, and they are provided an understanding of catastrophic illnesses. Students meet regularly with preceptors to develop clinical skills. To provide additional opportunities for clinical exposure and enrichment, clinically based electives are offered in the first two years.

In the third year, students are exposed to the basic disciplines of medicine through six clerkship rotations. Primary-care clerkships are offered as part of block rotations to coordinate instruction among multiple disciplines.

The fourth year includes rotations, time for board study, and junior internships. Students may choose from over 140 monthly electives.

FACULTY PROFILE (FALL 2005)

Total teaching faculty: **333 (full-time)**, **1,251 (part-time)**
Of full-time faculty, those teaching in basic sciences: **14%**; in clinical programs: **86%**
Of part-time faculty, those teaching in basic sciences: **2%**; in clinical programs: **98%**
Full-time faculty/student ratio: **0.9**

SUPPORT SERVICES

The school offers students these services for dealing with stress: professional counseling, support groups.

RESIDENCY PROFILE

Most popular residency and specialty programs chosen by the 2004 and 2005 M.D. graduating classes: emergency medicine, family practice, internal medicine, obstetrics and gynecology, pediatrics, psychiatry, surgery–general.

WHERE GRADS GO

45%
Proportion of 2003-2005 graduates who entered primary care specialties

40%
Proportion of 2004-2005 graduates who accepted in-state residencies

Yale University

- 333 Cedar Street, PO Box 208055, New Haven, CT 06520-8055
- Private
- Year Founded: 1810
- Tuition, 2005-2006: $37,655
- Enrollment 2005-2006 academic year: 441
- Website: http://info.med.yale.edu/ysm
- Specialty ranking: drug/alcohol abuse: 1, geriatrics: 8, internal medicine: 9, pediatrics: 18, women's health: 12

3.75 AVERAGE GPA, ENTERING CLASS FALL 2005

11.6 AVERAGE MCAT, ENTERING CLASS FALL 2005

5.9% ACCEPTANCE RATE, ENTERING CLASS FALL 2005

9 2007 U.S. NEWS MEDICAL SCHOOL RANKING (RESEARCH)

Unranked 2007 U.S. NEWS MEDICAL SCHOOL RANKING (PRIMARY CARE)

ADMISSIONS

Admissions phone number: **(203) 785-2643**
Admissions email address: **medical.admissions@yale.edu**
Application website:
   http://info.med.yale.edu/education/admissions
Acceptance rate: **5.9%**
In-state acceptance rate: **12.7%**
Out-of-state acceptance rate: **5.5%**
Minority acceptance rate: **5.6%**
International acceptance rate: **7.4%**

Fall 2005 applications and acceptees

	Applied	Interviewed	Accepted	Enrolled
Total:	3,708	767	220	100
In-state:	205	75	26	20
Out-of-state:	3,503	692	194	80

Profile of admitted students

Average undergraduate grade point average: **3.75**
MCAT averages (scale: 1-15; writing test: J-T):
   Composite score: **11.6**
   Verbal reasoning score: **11.1**, Physical sciences score: **11.9**, Biological sciences score: **11.9**, Writing score: **R**
Proportion with undergraduate majors in: Biological sciences: **51%**, Physical sciences: **25%**, Non-sciences: **22%**, Other health professions: **0%**, Mixed disciplines and other: **2%**
Percentage of students not coming directly from college after graduation: **52%**

Dates and details

The American Medical College Application Service (AMCAS) application is accepted.
School asks for a school-specific application as part of the admissions process.
Oldest MCAT considered for Fall 2007 entry: **2003**
Earliest application date for the 2007-2008 first-year class: **June 1, 2006**
Latest application date: **October 15, 2006**
Acceptance dates for regular application for the class entering in fall 2007:

Earliest: **March 31, 2007**
Latest: **August 31, 2007**
The school considers requests for deferred entrance. Starting month for the class entering in 2007–2008: **August**
The school has an Early Decision Plan (EDP).
A personal interview is required for admission.

Undergraduate coursework required

Medical school requires undergraduate work in these subjects: biology/zoology, organic chemistry, inorganic (general) chemistry, physics.

ADMISSIONS POLICY

(TEXT PROVIDED BY SCHOOL):

The Yale School of Medicine seeks to enroll a diverse class of accomplished, mature, motivated students who aspire to careers of leadership in medicine and the biomedical sciences. In making admissions decisions, the entire application is considered. There are no "cut-offs" for GPA or MCAT scores. The applicant's state of residence is not a factor; nor is the applicant's country of citizenship or residence. Students from all backgrounds are encouraged to apply.

AMCAS applications must be submitted by October 15 and Yale Supplemental Applications by November 15. To be eligible for acceptance, applicants must have attended a four-year college of arts and sciences or institute of technology, with at least one year of study in the United States or Canada. Before matriculation, accepted students must have completed, in the United States or Canada, full-year college or university courses (with laboratory) in general biology or zoology, general chemistry, organic chemistry, and general physics.

The application review process begins in September. Personal interviews are required for admission and are conducted from September to March. All final decisions are made on or before March 31. Offers of admission to applicants on the waiting list are made as needed through the spring and summer.

Students are expected to matriculate in the fall of the year in which they are accepted, but deferred matriculation is allowed if a student has a valid reason to delay medical school. Requests for deferred matriculation must be made by June 30.

In addition to its MD and MD/PhD programs, the Yale School of Medicine administers a combined degree program in Public Health (MD/MPH). Yale also offers combined degree programs in collaboration with the Yale Law School (MD/JD), the Yale School of Management (MD/MBA), and the Yale Divinity School (MD/MDiv). Detailed information regarding application requirements may be obtained from the Admissions Office.

COSTS AND FINANCIAL AID
Financial aid phone number: **(203) 785-2645**
Tuition, 2005-2006 academic year: **$37,655**
Room and board: **$10,150**
Percentage of students receiving financial aid in 2005-06: **82%**
Percentage of students receiving: Loans: **69%**, Grants/scholarships: **55%**, Work-study aid: **0%**
Average medical school debt for the Class of 2004: **$94,568**

STUDENT BODY
Fall 2005 full-time enrollment: **441**
Men: **45%**, Women: **55%**, In-state: **12%**, Minorities: **36%**, American Indian: **0.9%**, Asian-American: **21.1%**, African-American: **7.3%**, Hispanic-American: **6.3%**, White: **54.9%**, International: **6.8%**, Unknown: **2.7%**

ACADEMIC PROGRAMS
The school's curriculum very frequently gives first-year students substantial contact with patients.
There are opportunities for first- or second-year students to work in community health clinics.
Program offerings: AIDS, drug/alcohol abuse, family medicine, geriatrics, internal medicine, pediatrics, rural medicine, women's health
Joint degrees awarded: M.D./Ph.D., M.D./MBA, M.D./MPH, M.D./JD
Total National Institutes of Health (NIH) grants awarded to the medical school and affiliated hospitals: **$300.7 million**

CURRICULUM
(TEXT PROVIDED BY SCHOOL):
The educational mission of the Yale School of Medicine is to educate and inspire scholars and future leaders who will advance the practice of medicine and the biomedical sciences. Guiding this mission is the Yale System, an educational philosophy which encourages students to become independent and scientific thinkers. At the core of the Yale System is the supposition that medical students are already strongly motivated to learn, requiring guidance and stimulation rather than pressure of competition. Examinations are given anonymously and class ranks are not calculated, thus freeing students from the anxieties provoked by competition and encouraging their participation in electives and

research. Yale students are required to complete an original research project, closely mentored and culminating in a thesis. In the preclinical years, time is set aside for students to enroll in graduate-level electives to spark their interests in various disciplines. In the clinical years, students are able to schedule their required clerkships so that there is opportunity to complete their research projects.

The core medical curriculum is divided into the preclinical years (1 and 2) and clinical years (3 and 4). In the preclinical years the scientific basis of health and disease is presented in a core curriculum that includes courses in Human Anatomy and Development, Biochemistry, Cell Biology, Histology, Physiology, Neurobiology, Biological Basis of Behavior, Pathology, Genetics, Immunobiology, Microbiology, Pharmacology, Child and Adolescent Development, Epidemiology and Public Health, and the organ and system-based modules. Complementing the core curriculum are opportunities to explore the leading edge of scientific discovery and to master scientific reasoning. Students participate in weekly small group skill-building sessions and meetings with a clinical tutor. Students also study ethical and informed medical decision-making in Professional Responsibility, Epidemiology and Biostatistics, and the History of Medicine.

In the clinical years students rotate through clerkships. Medical decision-making and clinical skills are taught, developed, and assessed with ward teams, in private offices, and in a Preceptorship Program, which matches students with senior clinical faculty.

FACULTY PROFILE (FALL 2005)
Total teaching faculty: **999 (full-time)**, **39 (part-time)**
Of full-time faculty, those teaching in basic sciences: **17%**; in clinical programs: **83%**
Of part-time faculty, those teaching in basic sciences: **3%**; in clinical programs: **97%**
Full-time faculty/student ratio: **2.3**

SUPPORT SERVICES
The school offers students these services for dealing with stress: expanded-hour gym access, peer counseling, professional counseling, religious support, support groups.

RESIDENCY PROFILE
Most popular residency and specialty programs chosen by the 2004 and 2005 M.D. graduating classes: dermatology, emergency medicine, internal medicine, obstetrics and gynecology, ophthalmology, pediatrics, radiology–diagnostic, surgery–general, transitional year.

WHERE GRADS GO
30.2%
Proportion of 2003-2005 graduates who entered primary care specialties

25%
Proportion of 2004-2005 graduates who accepted in-state residencies

Yeshiva University

ALBERT EINSTEIN

- 1300 Morris Park Avenue, Bronx, NY 10461
- Private
- Year Founded: 1955
- Tuition, 2005-2006: $39,800
- Enrollment 2005-2006 academic year: 732
- Website: http://www.aecom.yu.edu
- Specialty ranking: N/A

3.65 AVERAGE GPA, ENTERING CLASS FALL 2005

10.5 AVERAGE MCAT, ENTERING CLASS FALL 2005

8.8% ACCEPTANCE RATE, ENTERING CLASS FALL 2005

38 2007 U.S. NEWS MEDICAL SCHOOL RANKING (RESEARCH)

31 2007 U.S. NEWS MEDICAL SCHOOL RANKING (PRIMARY CARE)

ADMISSIONS

Admissions phone number: **(718) 430-2106**
Admissions email address: **admissions@aecom.yu.edu**
Application website:
http://www.aecom.yu.edu/home/admissions/Default.htm
Acceptance rate: **8.8%**
In-state acceptance rate: **12.9%**
Out-of-state acceptance rate: **7.5%**
Minority acceptance rate: **7.5%**
International acceptance rate: **8.4%**

Fall 2005 applications and acceptees

	Applied	Interviewed	Accepted	Enrolled
Total:	6,307	1,368	552	180
In-state:	1,442	428	186	80
Out-of-state:	4,865	940	366	100

Profile of admitted students

Average undergraduate grade point average: **3.65**
MCAT averages (scale: 1-15; writing test: J-T):
Composite score: **10.5**
Verbal reasoning score: **9.9**, Physical sciences score:
10.7, Biological sciences score: **11.0**, Writing score: **Q**
Proportion with undergraduate majors in: Biological
sciences: **61%**, Physical sciences: **15%**, Non-sciences:
16%, Other health professions: **0%**, Mixed disciplines
and other: **8%**
Percentage of students not coming directly from college
after graduation: **20%**

Dates and details

The American Medical College Application Service
(AMCAS) application is accepted.
School asks for a school-specific application as part of the
admissions process.
Oldest MCAT considered for Fall 2007 entry: **N/A**
Earliest application date for the 2007-2008 first-year class:
June 1, 2006
Latest application date: **November 1, 2006**

Acceptance dates for regular application for the class
entering in fall 2007:
Earliest: **January 15, 2005**
Latest: **N/A**
The school considers requests for deferred entrance.
Starting month for the class entering in 2007–2008:
August
The school has an Early Decision Plan (EDP).
A personal interview is required for admission.

Undergraduate coursework required

Medical school requires undergraduate work in these subjects: biology, English, organic chemistry, inorganic (general) chemistry, physics, mathematics.

ADMISSIONS POLICY
(TEXT PROVIDED BY SCHOOL):

The M.D. Committee on Admissions considers several
thousand applicants each year and recommends to the
Dean the acceptance of 180 students. Approximately 15 of
them enter the Medical Scientist Training Program leading
to the M.D. and Ph.D. degrees. The committee selects for
admission a diverse and well-prepared group of students
who show great promise of becoming respected members
of the medical community. Serious consideration is given to
participation in extracurricular activities, community service, research and other scholarly work, practical experience
in clinical settings, and sincere and realistic motivation for
pursuing a career in medicine.

The undergraduate experience should not be considered
primarily as preparation for entrance to medical school.
Students are encouraged to take advantage of the diverse
educational opportunities provided at their college or university and plan a course of study that meets their particular
interests.

In addition to completing minimal requirements in the
biological and physical sciences, it is recommended that
students take at least another year of instruction in a discipline such as biochemistry, genetics or neurobiology.
Acquisition of a knowledge base in these subjects is not
only beneficial to the effective learning of biomedical sci-

ence during medical school; it also provides a basis for appreciating and understanding numerous remarkable advances in clinical medicine.

If it all possible, preparation in mathematics should include a working knowledge of biostatistics and understanding of probabilistic science concepts.

The continuing rapid growth in the volume and complexity of medical information is beyond the range of human cognitive abilities. It is becoming increasingly necessary, therefore, for students of medicine and practicing physicians to be acquainted with computer-based information systems and be able to use computers to manage and access information.

The education of students seeking careers in medicine should also include courses in the social and behavioral sciences because physicians need to focus no less attention on preventing illness and promoting health than on diagnosis and treatment. Successful practice of clinical prevention and health promotion requires knowledge of the sociocultural and behavioral factors that increase the risk of illness and influence the course of disease.

The quality of a physician's communication and interpersonal skills determines to a large extent whether he/she is able to conduct a proper history, change a patient's maladaptive behavior or obtain a patient's compliance with therapeutic advice. Students interested in medicine should therefore participate in extracurricular and workplace activities that enable them to hone these skills prior to starting medical school.

COSTS AND FINANCIAL AID
Financial aid phone number: **(718) 430-2336**
Tuition, 2005-2006 academic year: **$39,800**
Room and board: **$14,300**
Percentage of students receiving financial aid in 2005-06: **80%**
Percentage of students receiving: Loans: **80%**, Grants/scholarships: **45%**, Work-study aid: **0%**
Average medical school debt for the Class of 2004: **$95,000**

STUDENT BODY
Fall 2005 full-time enrollment: **732**
Men: **47%**, Women: **53%**, In-state: **45%**, Minorities: **29%**, American Indian: **0.3%**, Asian-American: **24.2%**, African-American: **7.4%**, Hispanic-American: **3.7%**, White: **56.4%**, International: **1.6%**, Unknown: **6.4%**

ACADEMIC PROGRAMS
The school's curriculum frequently gives first-year students substantial contact with patients.
There are opportunities for first- or second-year students to work in community health clinics.
Program offerings: AIDS, drug/alcohol abuse, family medicine, geriatrics, internal medicine, pediatrics, rural medicine, women's health

Joint degrees awarded: M.D./Ph.D., M.D./MS
Total National Institutes of Health (NIH) grants awarded to the medical school and affiliated hospitals: **$203.8 million**

CURRICULUM
(TEXT PROVIDED BY SCHOOL):
The 19-month long pre-clerkship curriculum is devoted primarily to interdisciplinary courses in biomedical sciences taking place in lecture halls, conference rooms and laboratories. There are also courses in which students interact with patients, learn the basics of patient-doctor communication, acquire physical examination skills, study medical ethics and learn how psychosocial and cultural factors affect patient behavior. During the last two years of the curriculum, students learn the rational application of biomedical science knowledge and communication skills to problems of human disease and illness in clinical settings located in three different boroughs of New York City. Twenty small-group case based conference sessions during the clerkship year deal with issues of prevention, ethics and professionalism. In addition to required courses/clerkships, there are abundant, mostly funded opportunities throughout all four years for students to participate in research and community and global health projects.

FACULTY PROFILE (FALL 2005)
Total teaching faculty: **2,530 (full-time)**, **317 (part-time)**
Of full-time faculty, those teaching in basic sciences: **14%**; in clinical programs: **86%**
Of part-time faculty, those teaching in basic sciences: **9%**; in clinical programs: **91%**
Full-time faculty/student ratio: **3.5**

SUPPORT SERVICES
The school offers students these services for dealing with stress: peer counseling, professional counseling, religious support, support groups.

RESIDENCY PROFILE
Most popular residency and specialty programs chosen by the 2004 and 2005 M.D. graduating classes: anesthesiology–pediatric anesthesiology, emergency medicine–pediatric emergency medicine, internal medicine, neurology, ophthalmology, pediatrics, psychiatry, radiology–diagnostic, surgery–general.

WHERE GRADS GO

55%
Proportion of 2003-2005 graduates who entered primary care specialties

60%
Proportion of 2004-2005 graduates who accepted in-state residencies

A.T. Still University

KIRKSVILLE COLLEGE OF OSTEOPATHIC MEDICINE

- 800 W. Jefferson Street, Kirksville, MO 63501
- Private
- Year Founded: 1892
- Tuition, 2005-2006: $33,945
- Enrollment 2005-2006 academic year: 671
- Website: http://www.atsu.edu
- Specialty ranking: rural medicine: 16

3.47	AVERAGE GPA, ENTERING CLASS FALL 2005
8.4	AVERAGE MCAT, ENTERING CLASS FALL 2005
14.7%	ACCEPTANCE RATE, ENTERING CLASS FALL 2005
Unranked	2007 U.S. NEWS MEDICAL SCHOOL RANKING (RESEARCH)
Unranked	2007 U.S. NEWS MEDICAL SCHOOL RANKING (PRIMARY CARE)

ADMISSIONS

Admissions phone number: **(866) 626-2878**
Admissions email address: **admissions@atsu.edu**
Application website: **http://www.aacom.org**
Acceptance rate: **14.7%**
In-state acceptance rate: **41.0%**
Out-of-state acceptance rate: **13.5%**
Minority acceptance rate: **10.1%**
International acceptance rate: **15.8%**

Fall 2005 applications and acceptees

	Applied	Interviewed	Accepted	Enrolled
Total:	2,634	538	388	172
In-state:	117	50	48	28
Out-of-state:	2,517	488	340	144

Profile of admitted students

Average undergraduate grade point average: **3.47**
MCAT averages (scale: 1-15; writing test: J-T):
Composite score: **8.4**
Verbal reasoning score: **8.3**, Physical sciences score: **8.2**,
Biological sciences score: **8.8**, Writing score: **O**
Proportion with undergraduate majors in: Biological
sciences: **54%**, Physical sciences: **12%**, Non-sciences:
9%, Other health professions: **4%**, Mixed disciplines and
other: **21%**
Percentage of students not coming directly from college
after graduation: **40%**

Dates and details

The American Medical College Application Service
(AMCAS) application is not accepted.
School asks for a school-specific application as part of the
admissions process.
Oldest MCAT considered for Fall 2007 entry: **2003**
Earliest application date for the 2007-2008 first-year class:
May 15, 2006
Latest application date: **February 15, 2006**
Acceptance dates for regular application for the class
entering in fall 2007:
Earliest: **October 15, 2006**

Latest: **N/A**
The school considers requests for deferred entrance.
Starting month for the class entering in 2007–2008:
August
The school has an Early Decision Plan (EDP).
A personal interview is required for admission.

Undergraduate coursework required

Medical school requires undergraduate work in these subjects: biology, English, organic chemistry, inorganic (general) chemistry, physics.

ADMISSIONS POLICY
(TEXT PROVIDED BY SCHOOL):

The Admissions Committee seeks those individuals capable
of meeting the college's academic rigor.

Applicants are screened for academic achievement, clinical involvement, interpersonal relations, leadership and
service, maturity, motivation, and osteopathic awareness.
Applicants who reach the final phase of the selection
process will be invited to visit the college for an interview.
All applicants selected for admission are interviewed prior
to acceptance. As a private institution and the national college of osteopathic medicine, the Kirksville College of
Osteopathic Medicine seeks students from all parts of the
United States who are interested in a career in osteopathic
medicine; no preference is given to in-state applicants. The
college seeks students who are underrepresented in today's
current physician population.

The Admissions Committee reserves the right to accept,
reject, or defer an application. Applicants are notified as
soon as the Admissions Committee decides on their status.
Successful applicants are granted a specified time period to
notify the Office of Admissions of their intention to enroll.
This letter of intent must be accompanied by payment of a
nonrefundable acceptance fee. Complete official transcripts
from each school attended must be on file with the Office of
the Registrar prior to matriculation. Admission, after
acceptance, is subject to the satisfactory completion of all
academic requirements.

COSTS AND FINANCIAL AID

Financial aid phone number: (660) 626-2529
Tuition, 2005-2006 academic year: $33,945
Room and board: $10,010
Percentage of students receiving financial aid in 2005-06: 94%
Percentage of students receiving: Loans: 94%, Grants/scholarships: 18%, Work-study aid: 18%
Average medical school debt for the Class of 2004: $144,801

STUDENT BODY

Fall 2005 full-time enrollment: 671
Men: 60%, Women: 40%, In-state: 16%, Minorities: 14%, American Indian: 0.6%, Asian-American: 12.7%, African-American: 0.6%, Hispanic-American: 1.8%, White: 79.9%, International: 1.6%, Unknown: 2.8%

ACADEMIC PROGRAMS

The school's curriculum occasionally gives first-year students substantial contact with patients.
There are opportunities for first- or second-year students to work in community health clinics.
Program offerings: AIDS, drug/alcohol abuse, family medicine, geriatrics, internal medicine, pediatrics, rural medicine, women's health
Joint degrees awarded: M.D./MPH, M.D./MS, M.D./M.H.A.
Total National Institutes of Health (NIH) grants awarded to the medical school and affiliated hospitals: $.2 million

CURRICULUM

(TEXT PROVIDED BY SCHOOL):
A.T. Still University/Kirksville College of Osteopathic Medicine offers a four-year program leading to the degree Doctor of Osteopathic medicine (D.O.). The curriculum is primarily discipline-based and begins with a year of medical basic science courses. High fidelity human patient simulators are utilized throughout the curriculum, beginning with orientation. The Complete Doctor is a longitudinal doctoring course beginning in the first year of medical school. It engages students in topics such as medical interviewing, physical exam skills, discussing difficult topics with patients, death and dying, caring for geriatric patients, medical ethics, issues surrounding human sexuality and topics in epidemiology and community medicine. During the summer of the first year, students participate in a two-week rotation with a primary care physician in Missouri.

The second year includes clinically-related basic science courses, infectious diseases, medical pharmacology and neuroscience, as well as introductions to the medical specialties, such as pathology, internal medicine and surgery. These classes provide a framework for each specialty prior to clinical rotations. A unique feature of the second year is a manikin-based clinical skills lab in which students learn suturing techniques, airway management, operating room protocols, bedside procedures, and other basic clinical skills.

In addition to the "traditional" medical school curriculum, additional enriched curricular experiences are delivered via societies. These are groups consisting of approximately 10-12 students per class and led by faculty mentors. These small socities explore topics including professionalism, peer review, humanities in medicine, health policy, and medical ethics. Student portfolios are developed via the societies that allow for the presentation of outcomes of student learning. Development of these portfolios provides an opportunity for the student to engage in reflective writing following various experiences. Not only does the portfolio project provide documentation of student learning, it also provides an opportunity for students to create presentation portfolios as they make application to residency programs.

Students are assigned to clinical regions for the third and fourth years. Each area has a dean and other clinical faculty. Required third-year rotations include family medicine, internal medicine, obstetrics/gynecology, pediatrics, surgery, psychiatry, radiology and anesthesiology. The fourth year requires additional time in family medicine, internal medicine (critical care), emergency medicine, orthopedics, neurology and pediatrics.

FACULTY PROFILE (FALL 2005)

Total teaching faculty: 70 (full-time), 15 (part-time)
Of full-time faculty, those teaching in basic sciences: 37%; in clinical programs: 63%
Of part-time faculty, those teaching in basic sciences: 0%; in clinical programs: 100%
Full-time faculty/student ratio: 0.1

SUPPORT SERVICES

The school offers students these services for dealing with stress: expanded-hour gym access, peer counseling, professional counseling, religious support, support groups.

RESIDENCY PROFILE

Most popular residency and specialty programs chosen by the 2004 and 2005 M.D. graduating classes: anesthesiology, emergency medicine, family practice, internal medicine, pediatrics, surgery–general, transitional year.

WHERE GRADS GO

| 45.7% |

Proportion of 2003-2005 graduates who entered primary care specialties

| 15% |

Proportion of 2004-2005 graduates who accepted in-state residencies

Chicago College of Osteopathic Medicine

- 555 31st Street, Downers Grove, IL 60515
- Private
- **Year Founded:** 1900
- **Tuition, 2005-2006:** $32,250
- **Enrollment 2005-2006 academic year:** 690
- **Website:** http://www.midwestern.edu
- **Specialty ranking:** N/A

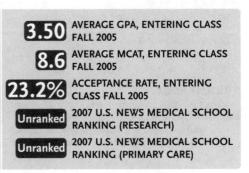

3.50 AVERAGE GPA, ENTERING CLASS FALL 2005

8.6 AVERAGE MCAT, ENTERING CLASS FALL 2005

23.2% ACCEPTANCE RATE, ENTERING CLASS FALL 2005

Unranked 2007 U.S. NEWS MEDICAL SCHOOL RANKING (RESEARCH)

Unranked 2007 U.S. NEWS MEDICAL SCHOOL RANKING (PRIMARY CARE)

ADMISSIONS

Admissions phone number: **(630) 515-7200**
Admissions email address: **admissil@midwestern.edu**
Application website: **N/A**
Acceptance rate: **23.2%**
In-state acceptance rate: **48.1%**
Out-of-state acceptance rate: **19.0%**
Minority acceptance rate: **18.5%**
International acceptance rate: **N/A**

Fall 2005 applications and acceptees

	Applied	Interviewed	Accepted	Enrolled
Total:	1,645	519	382	174
In-state:	239	154	115	71
Out-of-state:	1,406	365	267	103

Profile of admitted students

Average undergraduate grade point average: **3.50**
MCAT averages (scale: 1-15; writing test: J-T):
  Composite score: **8.6**
  Verbal reasoning score: **8.5**, Physical sciences score: **8.3**,
  Biological sciences score: **9.0**, Writing score: **N/A**
Percentage of students not coming directly from college
  after graduation: **N/A**

Dates and details

The American Medical College Application Service
  (AMCAS) application is not accepted.
School asks for a school-specific application as part of the
  admissions process.
Starting month for the class entering in 2007–2008:
  September
The school doesn't have an Early Decision Plan (EDP).
A personal interview is required for admission.

Undergraduate coursework required

Medical school requires undergraduate work in these subjects: biology, English, organic chemistry, inorganic (general) chemistry, physics, demonstration of writing skills.

COSTS AND FINANCIAL AID

Financial aid phone number: **(630) 515-6035**
Tuition, 2005-2006 academic year: **$32,250**
Room and board: **$9,735**

STUDENT BODY

Fall 2005 full-time enrollment: **690**
Men: **47%**, Women: **53%**, In-state: **46%**, Minorities: **24%**

College of Osteopathic Med. of the Pacific

WESTERN UNIVERSITY

- 309 E. Second Street, Pomona, CA 91766-1854
- Private
- Year Founded: 1977
- Tuition, 2005-2006: $35,260
- Enrollment 2005-2006 academic year: 724
- Website: http://www.westernu.edu/comp/home.xml
- Specialty ranking: N/A

3.45 AVERAGE GPA, ENTERING CLASS FALL 2005

8.9 AVERAGE MCAT, ENTERING CLASS FALL 2005

23.1% ACCEPTANCE RATE, ENTERING CLASS FALL 2005

Unranked 2007 U.S. NEWS MEDICAL SCHOOL RANKING (RESEARCH)

Unranked 2007 U.S. NEWS MEDICAL SCHOOL RANKING (PRIMARY CARE)

ADMISSIONS

Admissions phone number: **(909) 469-5335**
Admissions email address: **admissions@westernu.edu**
Application website: **http://www.aacom.org**
Acceptance rate: **23.1%**
In-state acceptance rate: **35.5%**
Out-of-state acceptance rate: **17.5%**
Minority acceptance rate: **21.3%**
International acceptance rate: **24.0%**

Fall 2005 applications and acceptees

	Applied	Interviewed	Accepted	Enrolled
Total:	2,342	601	542	212
In-state:	736	289	261	132
Out-of-state:	1,606	312	281	80

Profile of admitted students

Average undergraduate grade point average: **3.45**
MCAT averages (scale: 1-15; writing test: J-T):
  Composite score: **8.9**
  Verbal reasoning score: **8.5**, Physical sciences score: **8.9**,
  Biological sciences score: **9.6**, Writing score: **O**
Proportion with undergraduate majors in: Biological
  sciences: **47%**, Physical sciences: **16%**, Non-sciences:
  8%, Other health professions: **20%**, Mixed disciplines
  and other: **8%**
Percentage of students not coming directly from college
  after graduation: **3%**

Dates and details

The American Medical College Application Service
  (AMCAS) application is not accepted.
School asks for a school-specific application as part of the
  admissions process.
Oldest MCAT considered for Fall 2007 entry: **2004**
Earliest application date for the 2007-2008 first-year class:
  May 18, 2006
Latest application date: **April 15, 2006**
Acceptance dates for regular application for the class
  entering in fall 2007:
  Earliest: **September 15, 2006**

Latest: **August 15, 2007**
The school considers requests for deferred entrance.
Starting month for the class entering in 2007–2008:
  August
The school doesn't have an Early Decision Plan (EDP).
A personal interview is required for admission.

Undergraduate coursework required

Medical school requires undergraduate work in these subjects: biology/zoology, English, organic chemistry, inorganic
(general) chemistry, physics, behavioral science.

ADMISSIONS POLICY
(TEXT PROVIDED BY SCHOOL):

COMP accepts applications from all qualified candidates.
More applications are received from qualified candidates
than can be admitted. While grades and Medical College
Admission Test scores are important in selecting candidates
for admission and may suggest future academic success,
the Admissions Committee recognizes that these statistics,
by themselves, do not guarantee later success as a physician. Therefore, nonacademic criteria are also important in
making the selection.

COMP seeks a diverse and balanced student population
and considers factors such as well-rounded background,
work experiences, letters of recommendation, interest in
and knowledge of osteopathic medicine, and professional
promise. To ascertain these factors, an on-campus interview
is required prior to action on an application. The college
may exercise its discretion to rely upon additional consider-
ations. COMP is committed to admitting competitive, qualified individuals with disabilities.

COSTS AND FINANCIAL AID

Financial aid phone number: **(909) 469-5350**
Tuition, 2005-2006 academic year: **$35,260**
Room and board: **$10,430**
Percentage of students receiving financial aid in 2005-06:
  89%
Percentage of students receiving: Loans: **87%**,
  Grants/scholarships: **12%**, Work-study aid: **0%**

Average medical school debt for the Class of 2004:
$154,572

STUDENT BODY
Fall 2005 full-time enrollment: **724**
Men: **50%**, Women: **50%**, In-state: **69%**, Minorities: **46%**,
American Indian: **0.6%**, Asian-American: **39.8%**,
African-American: **1.2%**, Hispanic-American: **4.6%**,
White: **46.4%**, International: **1.5%**, Unknown: **5.9%**

ACADEMIC PROGRAMS
The school's curriculum frequently gives first-year students
substantial contact with patients.
There are opportunities for first- or second-year students to
work in community health clinics.
Program offerings: AIDS, drug/alcohol abuse, family
medicine, geriatrics, internal medicine, pediatrics, rural
medicine
Joint degrees awarded: M.D./MS
Total National Institutes of Health (NIH) grants awarded to
the medical school and affiliated hospitals: **$.1 million**

CURRICULUM
(TEXT PROVIDED BY SCHOOL):
The D.O. curriculum is divided into three phases: introduction to the basic sciences; correlated system teaching, incorporating basic and clinical sciences in the study of 10 organ
systems of the body; and clinical experiences.

The four-year curriculum has been developed to appro-
priately prepare the graduate for the postdoctoral training
years of their choice, with an emphasis on primary care.

In addition to the regular curriculum, COMP offers elective courses. These focus on the art of medicine and seek to
sensitize the future physician to the important aspects of
life and to instill a greater sense of ethics and human values. Various extracurricular activities also contribute to the
personal and professional growth of students, among them
a student drama troupe called SANUS.

Phase 1: The first semester of the first year is designed to
introduce the students to the basic concepts of anatomy
(gross, embryology, and histology), biochemistry, microbiology, pathology, pharmacology, and physiology. Interwoven
throughout the curriculum are osteopathic principles and
practice.

Phase 2: This phase begins in the second semester of the
first year and continues throughout the second year. The
basic and clinical sciences concerned with one particular
organ system of the body are integrated in classroom
instruction. This approach emphasizes the relevance of
basic sciences to clinical practice. The osteopathic approach
is continually emphasized by lecture and laboratory demonstration including manipulative techniques. Other courses

not directly related to a system are also included in Phase 2
as family medicine core courses.

Phase 3 (clinical training): Clinical training via rotation
through each of the major medical disciplines (family practice, internal medicine, surgery, pediatrics, obstetrics/gyne-
cology, pathology, psychiatry, emergency medicine, and
radiology) is accomplished in the third and forth years of
training. Twenty-two rotations of four weeks each provide
an opportunity for clinical skills development in primary-
care medicine. Several elective options are also offered during this two-year period.

The goal of COMP's clinical curriculum is to prepare
each and every student with the knowledge, attitudes, and
skills to excel in his or her chosen postdoctoral training program. Specifically, the student will be able, among other
skills, to: identify the wide range of normal human functioning; recognize, diagnose, and treat the most commonly
encountered health conditions in a primary-care practice;
recognize, diagnose, and treat the acute, life-threatening
conditions encountered by the primary-care physician; dif-
ferentiate health and common health problems from less
common diseases; recognize conditions or situations that
are best handled by consultation and/or referral; provide
continuity of healthcare beginning with initial patient contact; assess and treat chronic health conditions; develop
appropriate, professionally intimate relationships with
patients; understand a patient's individual concerns and
incorporate them into routine care; integrate osteopathic
philosophy and practices into routine patient care; and
understand and work with the family unit to improve the
health and welfare of the individual patient and his or her
family.

FACULTY PROFILE (FALL 2005)
Total teaching faculty: **36 (full-time)**, **4 (part-time)**
Of full-time faculty, those teaching in basic sciences: **50%**;
in clinical programs: **50%**
Of part-time faculty, those teaching in basic sciences: **50%**;
in clinical programs: **50%**
Full-time faculty/student ratio: **N/A**

SUPPORT SERVICES
The school offers students these services for dealing with
stress: expanded-hour gym access, peer counseling, professional counseling, religious support, support groups.

RESIDENCY PROFILE
Most popular residency and specialty programs chosen by
the 2004 and 2005 M.D. graduating classes: emergency
medicine, family practice, internal medicine, obstetrics and
gynecology, pediatrics, physical medicine and rehabilitation,
psychiatry, transitional year.

Des Moines University

OSTEOPATHIC MEDICAL CENTER

■ 3200 Grand Avenue, Des Moines, IA 50312
■ Private
■ Year Founded: 1898
■ Tuition, 2005-2006: $30,210
■ Enrollment 2005-2006 academic year: 819
■ Website: http://www.dmu.edu
■ Specialty ranking: family medicine: 26, rural medicine: 20

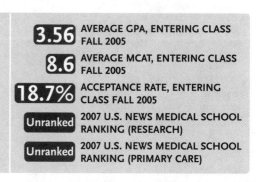

3.56 AVERAGE GPA, ENTERING CLASS FALL 2005

8.6 AVERAGE MCAT, ENTERING CLASS FALL 2005

18.7% ACCEPTANCE RATE, ENTERING CLASS FALL 2005

Unranked 2007 U.S. NEWS MEDICAL SCHOOL RANKING (RESEARCH)

Unranked 2007 U.S. NEWS MEDICAL SCHOOL RANKING (PRIMARY CARE)

ADMISSIONS

Admissions phone number: **(515) 271-1450**
Admissions email address: **doadmit@dmu.edu**
Application website: **N/A**
Acceptance rate: **18.7%**
In-state acceptance rate: **58.1%**
Out-of-state acceptance rate: **15.9%**
Minority acceptance rate: **10.6%**
International acceptance rate: **46.9%**

Fall 2005 applications and acceptees

	Applied	Interviewed	Accepted	Enrolled
Total:	2,387	579	446	215
In-state:	160	111	93	59
Out-of-state:	2,227	468	353	156

Profile of admitted students

Average undergraduate grade point average: **3.56**
MCAT averages (scale: 1-15; writing test: J-T):
  Composite score: **8.6**
  Verbal reasoning score: **8.5**, Physical sciences score: **8.3**,
  Biological sciences score: **9.0**, Writing score: **O**
Proportion with undergraduate majors in: Biological
  sciences: **59%**, Physical sciences: **15%**, Non-sciences:
  11%, Other health professions: **6%**, Mixed disciplines
  and other: **9%**
Percentage of students not coming directly from college
  after graduation: **64%**

Dates and details

The American Medical College Application Service
  (AMCAS) application is not accepted.
School asks for a school-specific application as part of the
  admissions process.
Oldest MCAT considered for Fall 2007 entry: **2003**
Earliest application date for the 2007-2008 first-year class:
  June 1, 2006
Latest application date: **February 1, 2006**
Acceptance dates for regular application for the class
  entering in fall 2007:
  Earliest: **October 2, 2006**

Latest: **August 1, 2007**
The school considers requests for deferred entrance.
Starting month for the class entering in 2007–2008:
  August
The school has an Early Decision Plan (EDP).
A personal interview is required for admission.

Undergraduate coursework required

Medical school requires undergraduate work in these subjects: biology/zoology, English, organic chemistry, inorganic
(general) chemistry, physics.

ADMISSIONS POLICY

(TEXT PROVIDED BY SCHOOL):
The admissions policies of the College of Osteopathic
Medicine ensure selection of students with appropriate
preparation. The policies define acceptable premedical education and designate admission procedures. All admission
requirements must be completed prior to matriculation.
Prospective students should carefully note specified deadlines.

The practice of osteopathic medicine requires good communication skills, an understanding of individuals within
their social environment, logical and quantitative thinking,
and a solid background in the sciences. To meet these
requirements, students are encouraged to complete a diversified undergraduate program.

The application process culminates with a personal interview at the college. Because of limited openings, the
Admissions Committee invites only those candidates considered to have the greatest professional promise. The committee bases decisions on academic achievement, activities,
personality, character, motivation, and promise shown by
candidates.

The college's curriculum integrates basic and clinical sciences. COM does not advise prospective students to enroll
in courses during their undergraduate years that must be
taken during their osteopathic medical curriculum.
Advanced standing based on prior coursework is not given.

COSTS AND FINANCIAL AID

Financial aid phone number: **(515) 271-1470**
Tuition, 2005-2006 academic year: **$30,210**
Room and board: **$14,690**
Percentage of students receiving financial aid in 2005-06:
  95%
Percentage of students receiving: Loans: **91%**,
  Grants/scholarships: **23%**, Work-study aid: **N/A**
Average medical school debt for the Class of 2004:
  $146,689

STUDENT BODY

Fall 2005 full-time enrollment: **819**
Men: **52%**, Women: **48%**, In-state: **24%**, Minorities: **11%**,
  American Indian: **0.5%**, Asian-American: **6.8%**, African-
  American: **1.1%**, Hispanic-American: **2.1%**, White:
  84.9%, International: **1.3%**, Unknown: **3.3%**

ACADEMIC PROGRAMS

The school's curriculum occasionally gives first-year
  students substantial contact with patients.
There are opportunities for first- or second-year students to
  work in community health clinics.
Program offerings: AIDS, drug/alcohol abuse, family
  medicine, geriatrics, internal medicine, pediatrics
Joint degrees awarded: M.D./MPH, M.D./M.H.A.
Total National Institutes of Health (NIH) grants awarded to
  the medical school and affiliated hospitals: **N/A**

CURRICULUM
(TEXT PROVIDED BY SCHOOL):

The College of Osteopathic Medicine has developed a highly
integrated systems approach that reflects the interrelationship and interdependence of body systems. The curriculum
combines case-based discussion, lecture, and laboratory
studies with clinical experience in teaching hospitals, college and private clinics, and community service agencies.

  The four years of osteopathic medical school preceding
graduate medical education are divided into a preclinical
and a clinical phase. The preclinical phase occupies the first
two years, and the clinical phase occupies the third and
fourth years. Basic science departments are largely responsible for the preclinical curriculum in the first year. During
the second year, basic and clinical sciences are integrated
into a case-based, organ-systems approach. The principal
method of instruction in the first two years is lecture, along

with small-group discussion, self-instruction, case-based
learning, and laboratory experiences. Concentration of basic
and clinical sciences in this integrated systems approach
ensures a strong base of knowledge that enables students to
function at the highest level in the clinical years.

  As an extension of the college's primary-care emphasis,
the curriculum includes a focus on preventive medicine as
a component of the second year. A series of preventive-med-
icine sources are presented as a corollary to the integrated
systems sequence. Prior to clinical rotations, a short course
designed to prepare students for the practical requirements
of clerkships is also presented.

  The clinical phase of the curriculum begins in
September of the third year and continues until graduation.
The periods of instruction are called clerkships.

FACULTY PROFILE (FALL 2005)

Total teaching faculty: **40 (full-time), 40 (part-time)**
Of full-time faculty, those teaching in basic sciences: **65%**;
  in clinical programs: **35%**
Of part-time faculty, those teaching in basic sciences: **3%**;
  in clinical programs: **98%**
Full-time faculty/student ratio: **N/A**

SUPPORT SERVICES

The school offers students these services for dealing with
stress: expanded-hour gym access, professional counseling.

RESIDENCY PROFILE

Most popular residency and specialty programs chosen by
the 2004 and 2005 M.D. graduating classes: anesthesiology,
emergency medicine, family practice, internal medicine,
obstetrics and gynecology, orthopaedic surgery, pediatrics,
psychiatry, surgery–general, transitional year.

WHERE GRADS GO

46.5%
*Proportion of 2003-2005 graduates who entered primary
care specialties*

17.9%
*Proportion of 2004-2005 graduates who accepted in-state
residencies*

Edward Via Virginia

COLLEGE OF OSTEOPATHIC MEDICINE

- 2265 Kraft Drive, Blacksburg, VA 24060
- Public
- **Year Founded:** 2003
- **Tuition, 2005-2006:** In-state: $29,500; Out-of-state: $29,500
- **Enrollment 2005-2006 academic year:** 470
- **Website:** http://www.vcom.vt.edu
- **Specialty ranking:** N/A

3.45 AVERAGE GPA, ENTERING CLASS FALL 2005

7.5 AVERAGE MCAT, ENTERING CLASS FALL 2005

15.3% ACCEPTANCE RATE, ENTERING CLASS FALL 2005

Unranked 2007 U.S. NEWS MEDICAL SCHOOL RANKING (RESEARCH)

Unranked 2007 U.S. NEWS MEDICAL SCHOOL RANKING (PRIMARY CARE)

ADMISSIONS

Admissions phone number: **(540) 231-6138**
Admissions email address: **mprice@vcom.vt.edu**
Application website: **http://www.aacom.org**
Acceptance rate: **15.3%**
In-state acceptance rate: **50.0%**
Out-of-state acceptance rate: **11.3%**
Minority acceptance rate: **12.2%**
International acceptance rate: **N/A**

Fall 2005 applications and acceptees

	Applied	Interviewed	Accepted	Enrolled
Total:	1,677	334	257	160
In-state:	174	102	87	70
Out-of-state:	1,503	232	170	90

Profile of admitted students

Average undergraduate grade point average: **3.45**
MCAT averages (scale: 1-15; writing test: J-T):
  Composite score: **7.5**
  Verbal reasoning score: **7.8**, Physical sciences score: **7.1**,
  Biological sciences score: **7.7**, Writing score: **P**
Proportion with undergraduate majors in: Biological
sciences: **58%**, Physical sciences: **12%**, Non-sciences:
18%, Other health professions: **9%**, Mixed disciplines
and other: **3%**
Percentage of students not coming directly from college
after graduation: **N/A**

Dates and details

The American Medical College Application Service
  (AMCAS) application is not accepted.
School asks for a school-specific application as part of the
  admissions process.
Oldest MCAT considered for Fall 2007 entry: **2003**
Earliest application date for the 2007-2008 first-year class:
  May 1, 2006
Latest application date: **February 15, 2006**
Acceptance dates for regular application for the class
  entering in fall 2007:
  Earliest: **October 1, 2006**

Latest: **May 1, 2007**
The school considers requests for deferred entrance.
Starting month for the class entering in 2007–2008:
  August
The school has an Early Decision Plan (EDP).
A personal interview is required for admission.

Undergraduate coursework required

Medical school requires undergraduate work in these subjects: biology, English, organic chemistry, inorganic (general) chemistry, physics.

ADMISSIONS POLICY

(TEXT PROVIDED BY SCHOOL):

The Edward Via Virginia College of Osteopathic Medicine
(VCOM) considers applicants who possess the academic,
professional, and individual promise to become exemplary
osteopathic physicians. VCOM seeks to admit a portion of
the class from qualified applicants based in Virginia, North
Carolina, West Virginia, and the Appalachian Region. Please
refer to the recruitment section of the catalog to learn more
about VCOM student recruitment. Although VCOM seeks
students from rural and Appalachian regions, all qualified
applicants are considered and students are accepted from
areas throughout the United States.

Once VCOM receives the primary application, we will
screen this document for three factors: requirements, academic factors, and non-academic factors.

Requirements: obtain an undergraduate degree before
matriculation; complete all required coursework before
matriculation; and a recent MCAT score no earlier than
April 2003.

Academic Factors: science GPA—minimum of 2.75
(average 3.4); and overall GPA—minimum of 2.75 (average
3.5). Non-Academic Factors: volunteer and work experience
in the healthcare field; extra-curricular activities; community service and outreach; and a personal statement.

Within its competitive admissions framework, VCOM
uses multiple criteria to select the most qualified candidates
from an applicant pool that will always exceed the number
of seats available. Candidates who present a competitive pri-

mary application will be invited, in writing, to submit a secondary application. VCOM requires two letters of recommendation as part of the secondary application—one from your pre-medical/pre-health committee (or science faculty member) and one from an osteopathic physician.

COSTS AND FINANCIAL AID

Financial aid phone number: **(540) 231-6021**
Tuition, 2005-2006 academic year: **In-state: $29,500; Out-of-state: $29,500**
Room and board: **$23,000**
Percentage of students receiving financial aid in 2005-06: **N/A**
Percentage of students receiving: Loans: **93%**, Grants/scholarships: **8%**, Work-study aid: **0%**
Average medical school debt for the Class of 2004: **N/A**

STUDENT BODY

Fall 2005 full-time enrollment: **470**
Men: **51%**, Women: **49%**, In-state: **36%**, Minorities: **20%**, American Indian: **0.4%**, Asian-American: **10.4%**, African-American: **7.0%**, Hispanic-American: **3.5%**, White: **74.8%**, International: **0.4%**, Unknown: **3.5%**

ACADEMIC PROGRAMS

The school's curriculum frequently gives first-year students substantial contact with patients.
There are opportunities for first- or second-year students to work in community health clinics.
Program offerings: AIDS, drug/alcohol abuse, family medicine, geriatrics, internal medicine, pediatrics, rural medicine, women's health
Joint degrees awarded: M.D./Ph.D., M.D./MBA, M.D./MPH, M.D./MS
Total National Institutes of Health (NIH) grants awarded to the medical school and affiliated hospitals: **$.9 million**

CURRICULUM

(TEXT PROVIDED BY SCHOOL):
The Curriculum at VCOM is innovative and modern. The faculty of VCOM recognize that students learn in a number of ways. Students generally assimilate a knowledge base through instruction, reading, and experience. Students who are in rigid problem-based, case-based, or discipline-based curriculums often complain of repetition and lack of variety. VCOM has developed a hybrid curriculum consisting of lectures, computerized case tutorials, laboratory experiences, clinical skills laboratories and clinical experiences throughout the four years.

All courses at VCOM are available to students on the computer through Blackboard. The computer based materials are placed on Blackboard in order to augment student learning where minimal note taking is required in class. This leaves valuable classroom time for faculty/student interaction. Computer-based instructional cases are the backbone of the clinical curriculum and demand preparation and performance prior to classroom instruction. Classroom instruction becomes concise case overviews rather than a detailed re-read of the text. The clinical cases are examples whereby students learn to apply their knowledge base to problem solving in clinical medicine. VCOM recognizes students also learn by pattern recognition. The symptom-based, case-based presentations advance students through the clinical curriculum and prepare them for the third-year clinical rotations.

Clinical experiences occur throughout the first and second years and include Geriatric centers, free clinics, doctor of pharmacy rounds, hospital rounds, and primary care experiences. Osteopathic manipulative medicine is taught throughout the curriculum by faculty physicians who practice primary care and osteopathic and sports medicine. The OMM curriculum is reinforced in the clinical years by providing clinical experiences with this same faculty, demonstrating the incorporation of the manipulative medicine skills into clinical practice. Osteopathic manipulative medicine skills labs continue through the third year.

The curriculum is directed toward the development of a primary care physician. VCOM faculty believe that the students who choose medical specialties will benefit from a broad-based primary care curriculum and a whole-patient approach to care. There are fellowship and curriculum tracts within the VCOM clinical curriculum for students who qualify and wish to enter research or missionary medicine training.

FACULTY PROFILE (FALL 2005)

Total teaching faculty: **43 (full-time)**, **24 (part-time)**
Of full-time faculty, those teaching in basic sciences: **40%**; in clinical programs: **60%**
Of part-time faculty, those teaching in basic sciences: **17%**; in clinical programs: **83%**
Full-time faculty/student ratio: **0.1**

SUPPORT SERVICES

The school offers students these services for dealing with stress: expanded-hour gym access, peer counseling, professional counseling, religious support.

Lake Erie College of Osteopathic Med.

- 1858 W. Grandview Boulevard, Erie, PA 16509
- Private
- Year Founded: 1992
- Tuition, 2005-2006: $25,220
- Enrollment 2005-2006 academic year: 1,206
- Website: http://www.lecom.edu
- Specialty ranking: N/A

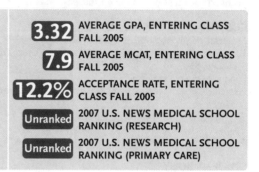

3.32 AVERAGE GPA, ENTERING CLASS FALL 2005

7.9 AVERAGE MCAT, ENTERING CLASS FALL 2005

12.2% ACCEPTANCE RATE, ENTERING CLASS FALL 2005

Unranked 2007 U.S. NEWS MEDICAL SCHOOL RANKING (RESEARCH)

Unranked 2007 U.S. NEWS MEDICAL SCHOOL RANKING (PRIMARY CARE)

ADMISSIONS

Admissions phone number: **(814) 866-6641**
Admissions email address: **admissions@lecom.edu**
Application website: **http://www.aacom.org**
Acceptance rate: **12.2%**
In-state acceptance rate: **37.1%**
Out-of-state acceptance rate: **9.1%**
Minority acceptance rate: **8.1%**
International acceptance rate: **100.0%**

Fall 2005 applications and acceptees

	Applied	Interviewed	Accepted	Enrolled
Total:	4,251	1,185	519	389
In-state:	469	297	174	123
Out-of-state:	3,782	888	345	266

Profile of admitted students

Average undergraduate grade point average: **3.32**
MCAT averages (scale: 1-15; writing test: J-T):
Composite score: **7.9**
Verbal reasoning score: **7.9**, Physical sciences score: **7.6**,
Biological sciences score: **8.2**, Writing score: **O**
Proportion with undergraduate majors in: Biological
sciences: **65%**, Physical sciences: **6%**, Non-sciences: **8%**,
Other health professions: **11%**, Mixed disciplines and
other: **10%**
Percentage of students not coming directly from college
after graduation: **20%**

Dates and details

The American Medical College Application Service
(AMCAS) application is not accepted.
School asks for a school-specific application as part of the
admissions process.
Oldest MCAT considered for Fall 2007 entry: **2003**
Earliest application date for the 2007-2008 first-year class:
June 1, 2006
Latest application date: **March 1, 2006**
Acceptance dates for regular application for the class
entering in fall 2007:
Earliest: **October 1, 2006**

Latest: **July 30, 2007**
The school considers requests for deferred entrance.
Starting month for the class entering in 2007–2008:
August
The school doesn't have an Early Decision Plan (EDP).
A personal interview is required for admission.

Undergraduate coursework required

Medical school requires undergraduate work in these subjects: biology, English, organic chemistry, inorganic (general) chemistry, physics, molecular and cell biology,
humanities, mathematics, behavioral science, social sciences.

ADMISSIONS POLICY

(TEXT PROVIDED BY SCHOOL):

Applicants must complete a baccalaureate degree from a
college or university by the time of enrollment. Applicants
participating in special affiliated programs with LECOM
and other exceptions to this policy will be considered on an
individual basis. LECOM recommends that the applicant
have an overall minimum grade point average of 3.0.
Successful candidates typically have both science and overall
grade point averages of 3.3 or above. Each candidate must
submit his or her most recent MCAT scores. MCAT scores
taken within the past three years are acceptable. The most
recent MCAT must be taken by the fall prior to the entering
year. Successful candidates typically have a mean MCAT
score of 24. Individuals interested in applying to LECOM
must complete an American Association of Colleges of
Osteopathic Medicine (AACOMAS) Application and a
LECOM Supplemental Application. LECOM requires a preprofessional committee letter or a letter from two science
professors along with a letter of recommendation from an
Osteopathic Physician. LECOM encourages applicants to
learn more about the profession by getting to know an
osteopathic physician. Receiving exposure to the osteopathic
profession will enhance awareness of osteopathic medical
philosophy. Working with a physician will prepare the applicant for the interview. The College looks for candidates who
exemplify the LECOM mission to prepare students to

become osteopathic physicians through programs of excellence in education, research, clinical care, and community service to enhance the quality of life through improved health for all humanity. The primary goal of LECOM is to educate students to become physicians practicing within the osteopathic concept. A secondary goal of the College is to educate and develop primary care physicians who will practice in the osteopathic tradition. The College imparts to its students a firm academic background enabling them to pursue advanced training in other fields of osteopathic medicine as well as primary care. The College encourages its students to participate in research to further advance their chosen profession.

COSTS AND FINANCIAL AID
Financial aid phone number: (814) 866-6641
Tuition, 2005-2006 academic year: $25,220
Room and board: $10,500
Percentage of students receiving financial aid in 2005-06: 92%
Percentage of students receiving: Loans: 92%, Grants/scholarships: 25%, Work-study aid: 0%
Average medical school debt for the Class of 2004: $140,000

STUDENT BODY
Fall 2005 full-time enrollment: 1,206
Men: 54%, Women: 46%, In-state: 34%, Minorities: 22%, American Indian: 0.3%, Asian-American: 15.8%, African-American: 2.3%, Hispanic-American: 3.9%, White: 77.5%, International: 0.1%, Unknown: 0.0%

ACADEMIC PROGRAMS
The school's curriculum very frequently gives first-year students substantial contact with patients.
There are opportunities for first- or second-year students to work in community health clinics.
Program offerings: AIDS, drug/alcohol abuse, family medicine, geriatrics, internal medicine, pediatrics, rural medicine, women's health
Joint degrees awarded: M.D./MS
Total National Institutes of Health (NIH) grants awarded to the medical school and affiliated hospitals: $.0 million

CURRICULUM
(TEXT PROVIDED BY SCHOOL):
Lake Erie College of Osteopathic Medicine has designed student-centered curriculums recognizing different learning styles: traditional Lecture-Discussion Pathway (LDP); small-group, Problem-Based Learning Pathway (PBL); or the self-learning Independent Study Pathway (ISP). LECOM offers the Doctor of Osteopathic Medicine Degree at two campuses. The Erie, Pennsylvania campus offers three learning pathways, while Bradenton, Florida students enroll in PBL. LECOM requires 12 weeks of Human Gross Anatomy lectures and labs with two years of Osteopathic Manipulative Medicine training.
LDP core curriculum starts with basic sciences and introductions to clinical education: microbiology, immunology, physiology, pharmacology, biochemistry, pathology, health

care management, spirituality, medicine and ethics. Beginning the first year, second semester, the LECOM systems curriculum integrates basic and clinical science of human organ systems. Lectures provide a physician's "real life" view of contemporary healthcare. Students begin clinical experience during the first year working with physician preceptors to learn how to conduct physical examinations.

PBL emphasizes student-centered, self-directed learning. Each group of eight students meets with a faculty facilitator three times per week. Students work independently and in small groups developing learning issues and discussing new information relevant to actual patient cases. Groups will request additional history and physical results and an EKG or an MRI as needed as students begin forming differential diagnoses. PBL students progress through basic science and onto clinical science as they become better at solving patient cases.

ISP provides significant flexibility for students during the first two years of medical school. For admission to ISP, the student must show excellent organizational and time management skills in order to proceed through the curriculum and meet strict examination deadlines. Though the program stresses independence, it is a closely directed course of study. ISP students use lists of highly structured learning objectives compiled into module booklets. Modules are divided into Core and Systems similar to the LDP curriculum. Core modules deal with fundamentals of basic science while systems modules integrate basic science and clinical disciplines in an organ systems approach to learning.

FACULTY PROFILE (FALL 2005)
Total teaching faculty: 85 (full-time), 1,162 (part-time)
Of full-time faculty, those teaching in basic sciences: 49%; in clinical programs: 51%
Of part-time faculty, those teaching in basic sciences: 2%; in clinical programs: 98%
Full-time faculty/student ratio: 0.1

SUPPORT SERVICES
The school offers students these services for dealing with stress: expanded-hour gym access, peer counseling, professional counseling, religious support, support groups.

RESIDENCY PROFILE
Most popular residency and specialty programs chosen by the 2004 and 2005 M.D. graduating classes: emergency medicine, family practice, internal medicine, obstetrics and gynecology, pediatrics, radiology–diagnostic, surgery–general, transitional year.

WHERE GRADS GO

61%
Proportion of 2003-2005 graduates who entered primary care specialties

31%
Proportion of 2004-2005 graduates who accepted in-state residencies

Michigan State University

COLLEGE OF OSTEOPATHIC MEDICINE

- A308 E. Fee Hall, East Lansing, MI 48824
- Public
- Year Founded: 1969
- Tuition, 2005-2006: In-state: $23,700; Out-of-state: $51,600
- Enrollment 2005-2006 academic year: 616
- Website: http://www.com.msu.edu
- Specialty ranking: family medicine: 18, rural medicine: 30

3.49 AVERAGE GPA, ENTERING CLASS FALL 2005

8.5 AVERAGE MCAT, ENTERING CLASS FALL 2005

17.2% ACCEPTANCE RATE, ENTERING CLASS FALL 2005

Unranked 2007 U.S. NEWS MEDICAL SCHOOL RANKING (RESEARCH)

4 2007 U.S. NEWS MEDICAL SCHOOL RANKING (PRIMARY CARE)

ADMISSIONS

Admissions phone number: **(517) 353-7740**
Admissions email address: **comadm@com.msu.edu**
Application website: **http://www.aacom.org**
Acceptance rate: **17.2%**
In-state acceptance rate: **46.6%**
Out-of-state acceptance rate: **5.7%**
Minority acceptance rate: **10.5%**
International acceptance rate: **N/A**

Fall 2005 applications and acceptees

	Applied	Interviewed	Accepted	Enrolled
Total:	1,943	375	335	205
In-state:	549	288	256	185
Out-of-state:	1,394	87	79	20

Profile of admitted students

Average undergraduate grade point average: **3.49**
MCAT averages (scale: 1-15; writing test: J-T):
Composite score: **8.5**
Verbal reasoning score: **8.5**, Physical sciences score: **8.2**,
Biological sciences score: **8.8**, Writing score: **O**
Proportion with undergraduate majors in: Biological
sciences: **57%**, Physical sciences: **12%**, Non-sciences:
21%, Other health professions: **9%**, Mixed disciplines
and other: **1%**
Percentage of students not coming directly from college
after graduation: **68%**

Dates and details

The American Medical College Application Service
(AMCAS) application is not accepted.
School asks for a school-specific application as part of the
admissions process.
Oldest MCAT considered for Fall 2007 entry: **2003**
Earliest application date for the 2007-2008 first-year class:
November 22, 2006
Latest application date: **May 24, 2006**
Acceptance dates for regular application for the class
entering in fall 2007:
Earliest: **March 29, 2007**

Latest: **November 28, 2007**
The school considers requests for deferred entrance.
Starting month for the class entering in 2007-2008: **July**
The school doesn't have an Early Decision Plan (EDP).
A personal interview is required for admission.

Undergraduate coursework required

Medical school requires undergraduate work in these subjects: biology, English, organic chemistry, inorganic (general) chemistry, physics, biochemistry, behavioral science.

ADMISSIONS POLICY

(TEXT PROVIDED BY SCHOOL):

MSUCOM looks for students who are academically accomplished, committed to service and well versed in the philosophy of osteopathic medicine. In each area of evaluation, we
examine applicants' accomplishments within the context of
their life experience. Much like the way D.O.s approach
their patients, we invite applicants to tell us their stories by
completing a comprehensive supplemental application.

Academic minimum standards for receiving a supplemental application are 2.70 science and overall grade-point
average, and total Medical College Admission Test score of
18, with subject-area minimums of 4 in verbal reasoning, 5
in physical sciences, and 6 in biological sciences.

The Admissions Committee meets weekly, beginning in
late August. Our weighted ranking, used to determine the
order in which applications are reviewed, is 60 percent academic and 40 percent nonacademic. Applicants should plan
to submit their AACOMAS applications no later than
August 1 to ensure inclusion in the selection process.

Review criteria may include: grade-point average; level
and types of coursework; academic honors; MCAT scores;
commitment to service; demonstrated skills in communication, leadership, collaboration, problem solving, and critical
thinking; fluency in multiple languages; military service;
participation in varsity sports; research experience; and
appreciation for diversity and cultural competence in healthcare.

Many applications are sufficiently thorough to allow the
committee to make an immediate decision to offer admis-

sion, a position on the waiting list or to deny the application. Some applicants are invited to have a single, one-hour interview. All committee decisions may be subject to review by the dean of the college.

Applicants offered admission or waiting list positions are invited to visit the college for an interview day. Those applicants who are invited for an interview have their interview in the morning, then join the rest of the group. The day consists of presentations on financial aid, curriculum, student organizations and outreach, the college community, international opportunities and local housing; a tour and lunch hosted by first and second year medical students, and open Q&A sessions with the Associate Dean, Student Services and the Director of Admissions

COSTS AND FINANCIAL AID

Financial aid phone number: **(517) 353-5188**
Tuition, 2005-2006 academic year: **In-state: $23,700;** Out-of-state: **$51,600**
Room and board: **$12,024**
Percentage of students receiving financial aid in 2005-06: **94%**
Percentage of students receiving: Loans: **92%,** Grants/scholarships: **88%,** Work-study aid: **0%**
Average medical school debt for the Class of 2004: **$141,850**

STUDENT BODY

Fall 2005 full-time enrollment: **616**
Men: **48%,** Women: **52%,** In-state: **91%,** Minorities: **16%,** American Indian: **0.6%,** Asian-American: **12.3%,** African-American: **2.1%,** Hispanic-American: **1.1%,** White: **83.8%,** International: **0.0%,** Unknown: **0.0%**

ACADEMIC PROGRAMS

The school's curriculum very frequently gives first-year students substantial contact with patients.
There are opportunities for first- or second-year students to work in community health clinics.
Program offerings: AIDS, drug/alcohol abuse, family medicine, geriatrics, internal medicine, pediatrics, rural medicine, women's health
Joint degrees awarded: M.D./Ph.D., M.D./MPH, M.D./MS
Total National Institutes of Health (NIH) grants awarded to the medical school and affiliated hospitals: **$7.5 million**

CURRICULUM

(TEXT PROVIDED BY SCHOOL):
The college is dedicated to helping to meet the ever-growing public demand for physicians who can provide comprehensive and continuing healthcare to all members of the family.
While the educational program of MSUCOM is geared to the training of primary-care physicians, the curriculum is also designed to meet the continuing need for medical specialists and teacher-investigators.

Traditionally, osteopathic education seeks to prepare physicians who are especially concerned with maintaining continuing personal relationships with patients, their families, and their optimum interaction with the community environmental patterns. This emphasis is reflected in the nature of the curriculum and particularly reinforced during clinical clerkship rotations through a variety of clinical disciplines in both hospital and nonhospital settings.

Early clinical involvement in patient care enables students to study the biological and behavioral sciences that are relevant to what they are seeing and doing in the clinical area. With the help of the faculties in the biological and behavioral sciences, students learn to apply current concepts and principles to clinical problems related to patient care. The entire teaching program emphasizes an important cooperative relationship between basic sciences and clinical practice.

During their medical undergraduate and graduate education, students must develop the foundation and motivation for a lifetime of learning, and the ability to apply new knowledge and skills as they evolve.

FACULTY PROFILE (FALL 2005)

Total teaching faculty: **180 (full-time),** 25 **(part-time)**
Of full-time faculty, those teaching in basic sciences: **27%;** in clinical programs: **73%**
Of part-time faculty, those teaching in basic sciences: **12%;** in clinical programs: **88%**
Full-time faculty/student ratio: **0.3**

SUPPORT SERVICES

The school offers students these services for dealing with stress: expanded-hour gym access, peer counseling, professional counseling, religious support, support groups.

RESIDENCY PROFILE

Most popular residency and specialty programs chosen by the 2004 and 2005 M.D. graduating classes: emergency medicine, family practice, internal medicine, obstetrics and gynecology, pediatrics, internal medicine/emergency medicine, internal medicine/pediatrics.

WHERE GRADS GO

 85.8%
Proportion of 2003-2005 graduates who entered primary care specialties

90%
Proportion of 2004-2005 graduates who accepted in-state residencies

New York College of Osteopathic Med.

- Old Westbury, Northern Boulevard, Long Island, NY 11568
- Private
- Year Founded: 1977
- Tuition, 2005-2006: $34,984
- Enrollment 2005-2006 academic year: 1,176
- Website: http://www.nyit.edu
- Specialty ranking: N/A

3.50 AVERAGE GPA, ENTERING CLASS FALL 2005

8.6 AVERAGE MCAT, ENTERING CLASS FALL 2005

16.4% ACCEPTANCE RATE, ENTERING CLASS FALL 2005

Unranked 2007 U.S. NEWS MEDICAL SCHOOL RANKING (RESEARCH)

Unranked 2007 U.S. NEWS MEDICAL SCHOOL RANKING (PRIMARY CARE)

ADMISSIONS

Admissions phone number: **(516) 686-3747**
Admissions email address: **rzaika@nyit.edu**
Application website: **http://www.aacom.org**
Acceptance rate: **16.4%**
In-state acceptance rate: **43.3%**
Out-of-state acceptance rate: **9.6%**
Minority acceptance rate: **16.4%**
International acceptance rate: **N/A**

Fall 2005 applications and acceptees

	Applied	Interviewed	Accepted	Enrolled
Total:	3,297	720	540	310
In-state:	660	367	286	198
Out-of-state:	2,637	353	254	112

Profile of admitted students

Average undergraduate grade point average: **3.50**
MCAT averages (scale: 1-15; writing test: J-T):
  Composite score: **8.6**
  Verbal reasoning score: **8.2**, Physical sciences score: **8.5**,
  Biological sciences score: **9.0**, Writing score: **O**
Proportion with undergraduate majors in: Biological
  sciences: **38%**, Physical sciences: **12%**, Non-sciences:
  15%, Other health professions **13%**, Mixed disciplines
  and other: **22%**
Percentage of students not coming directly from college
  after graduation: **27%**

Dates and details

The American Medical College Application Service
  (AMCAS) application is not accepted.
School asks for a school-specific application as part of the
  admissions process.
Oldest MCAT considered for Fall 2007 entry: **2002**
Earliest application date for the 2007-2008 first-year class:
  June 1, 2006
Latest application date: **February 1, 2006**
Acceptance dates for regular application for the class
  entering in fall 2007:
  Earliest: **December 22, 2005**

Latest: **August 1, 2006**
The school considers requests for deferred entrance.
Starting month for the class entering in 2007–2008:
  August
The school doesn't have an Early Decision Plan (EDP).
A personal interview is required for admission.

Undergraduate coursework required

Medical school requires undergraduate work in these subjects: biology, biology/zoology, English, organic chemistry,
inorganic (general) chemistry, physics.

ADMISSIONS POLICY

(TEXT PROVIDED BY SCHOOL):
Applicants for first-year-class admission to the college must
meet the following requirements prior to matriculation: 1)
hold a baccalaureate degree from an accredited college or
university; 2) must have completed an acceptable academic
year sequence, with a grade of "C" or better, in the following
pre-requisite courses: English (6hrs), biology (8hrs), general
chemistry (8hrs), organic chemistry (8hrs), physics (8hrs);
3) submit Medical College Admission Test scores; and 4)
complete a personal interview process. These are the minimum requirements for admission.

COSTS AND FINANCIAL AID

Financial aid phone number: **(516) 686-7960**
Tuition, 2005-2006 academic year: **$34,984**
Room and board: **$20,275**
Percentage of students receiving financial aid in 2005-06:
  94%
Percentage of students receiving: Loans: **87%**,
  Grants/scholarships: **27%**, Work-study aid: **0%**
Average medical school debt for the Class of 2004:
  $158,000

STUDENT BODY

Fall 2005 full-time enrollment: **1,176**
Men: **46%**, Women: **54%**, In-state: **64%**, Minorities: **45%**,
  American Indian: **0.2%**, Asian-American: **26.4%**,

African-American: **9.2%**, Hispanic-American: **7.1%**,
White: **55.6%**, International: **0.1%**, Unknown: **1.4%**

ACADEMIC PROGRAMS

The school's curriculum occasionally gives first-year
students substantial contact with patients.

There are opportunities for first- or second-year students to
work in community health clinics.

Program offerings: family medicine, geriatrics, internal
medicine, pediatrics, rural medicine, women's health

Joint degrees awarded: M.D./MBA, M.D./MS

Total National Institutes of Health (NIH) grants awarded to
the medical school and affiliated hospitals: **N/A**

CURRICULUM

(TEXT PROVIDED BY SCHOOL):

New York College of Osteopathic Medicine is committed to
training osteopathic physicians for a lifetime of medical
practice and learning based on established science and critical thinking, integrating osteopathic philosophy, principles,
and practice.

FACULTY PROFILE (FALL 2005)

Total teaching faculty: **38 (full-time), 1,528 (part-time)**

Of full-time faculty, those teaching in basic sciences: **55%**;
in clinical programs: **45%**

Of part-time faculty, those teaching in basic sciences: **0%**;
in clinical programs: **100%**

Full-time faculty/student ratio: **N/A**

SUPPORT SERVICES

The school offers students these services for dealing with
stress: expanded-hour gym access, peer counseling, professional counseling.

RESIDENCY PROFILE

Most popular residency and specialty programs chosen by
the 2004 and 2005 M.D. graduating classes: family practice, internal medicine, obstetrics and gynecology, pediatrics, psychiatry.

WHERE GRADS GO

45%

*Proportion of 2003-2005 graduates who entered primary
care specialties*

67%

*Proportion of 2004-2005 graduates who accepted in-state
residencies*

Nova Southeastern University

COLLEGE OF OSTEOPATHIC MEDICINE

- 3200 S. University Drive, Fort Lauderdale, FL 33328
- Private
- Year Founded: 1981
- Tuition, 2005-2006: $24,740
- Enrollment 2005-2006 academic year: 819
- Website: http://medicine.nova.edu
- Specialty ranking: N/A

3.41 AVERAGE GPA, ENTERING CLASS FALL 2005

8.3 AVERAGE MCAT, ENTERING CLASS FALL 2005

14.4% ACCEPTANCE RATE, ENTERING CLASS FALL 2005

Unranked 2007 U.S. NEWS MEDICAL SCHOOL RANKING (RESEARCH)

Unranked 2007 U.S. NEWS MEDICAL SCHOOL RANKING (PRIMARY CARE)

ADMISSIONS

Admissions phone number: **(954) 262-1101**
Admissions email address: **deliac@nsu.nova.edu**
Application website: **http://hpd.nova.edu/**
Acceptance rate: **14.4%**
In-state acceptance rate: **49.9%**
Out-of-state acceptance rate: **6.3%**
Minority acceptance rate: **N/A**
International acceptance rate: **N/A**

Fall 2005 applications and acceptees

	Applied	Interviewed	Accepted	Enrolled
Total:	2,541	423	366	236
In-state:	471	258	235	124
Out-of-state:	2,070	165	131	112

Profile of admitted students

Average undergraduate grade point average: **3.41**
MCAT averages (scale: 1-15; writing test: J-T):
  Composite score: **8.3**
  Verbal reasoning score: **8.4**, Physical sciences score: **8.0**,
  Biological sciences score: **8.6**, Writing score: **M**
Proportion with undergraduate majors in: Biological
  sciences: **25%**, Physical sciences: **9%**, Non-sciences:
  10%, Other health professions: **16%**, Mixed disciplines
  and other: **40%**
Percentage of students not coming directly from college
  after graduation: **16%**

Dates and details

The American Medical College Application Service
  (AMCAS) application is not accepted.
School asks for a school-specific application as part of the
  admissions process.
Oldest MCAT considered for Fall 2007 entry: **2004**
Acceptance dates for regular application for the class
  entering in fall 2007:
  Earliest: **January 6, 2006**
  Latest: **March 1, 2007**
The school considers requests for deferred entrance.

Starting month for the class entering in 2007–2008:
  August
The school doesn't have an Early Decision Plan (EDP).
A personal interview is required for admission.

Undergraduate coursework required

Medical school requires undergraduate work in these subjects: biology, English, organic chemistry, inorganic (general) chemistry, physics.

ADMISSIONS POLICY

(TEXT PROVIDED BY SCHOOL):

A personal interview is required; however, not all applicants
will be granted an interview nor does an interview guarantee acceptance. A letter of evaluation is required from the
preprofessional committee. If one does not exist, letters
from two science professors and one from a liberal arts professor must be submitted instead. A letter of evaluation
must also be submitted from an osteopathic physician.
Admission is highly competitive; the college receives
approximately 3,500 applicants per year, of whom only 230
are admitted. Florida residents are eligible to receive
reduced in-state tuition.

COSTS AND FINANCIAL AID

Financial aid phone number: **(954) 262-3380**
Tuition, 2005-2006 academic year: **$24,740**
Room and board: **$10,431**
Percentage of students receiving financial aid in 2005-06:
  95%
Percentage of students receiving: Loans: **95%**,
  Grants/scholarships: **20%**, Work-study aid: **3%**
Average medical school debt for the Class of 2004:
  $165,110

STUDENT BODY

Fall 2005 full-time enrollment: **819**
Men: **50%**, Women: **50%**, In-state: **52%**, Minorities: **32%**,
  American Indian: **0.7%**, Asian-American: **13.8%**,
  African-American: **3.8%**, Hispanic-American: **13.3%**,
  White: **62.0%**, International: **N/A**, Unknown: **6.3%**

ACADEMIC PROGRAMS

The school's curriculum frequently gives first-year students substantial contact with patients.

There are opportunities for first- or second-year students to work in community health clinics.

Program offerings: AIDS, drug/alcohol abuse, family medicine, geriatrics, internal medicine, pediatrics, rural medicine, women's health

Joint degrees awarded: M.D./MBA, M.D./MPH

Total National Institutes of Health (NIH) grants awarded to the medical school and affiliated hospitals: **$1.7 million**

CURRICULUM

(TEXT PROVIDED BY SCHOOL):

The NSU-COM curriculum is designed to fulfill its mission of training primary-care physicians. It emphasizes interdisciplinary collaboration, guiding students to develop a holistic and osteopathic approach to medicine.

Basic scientific information is correlated with fundamental clinical application. Students are exposed to clinical settings in their first semester, giving them an opportunity to prepare for the "real world" of medicine. The clinical exposure continues into the second year, when students have an increased opportunity to interact with standardized patients and with real patients under the supervision of physicians in office and hospital settings. A notable aspect of the clinical program is a required three-month rotation in a rural practice and/or inner city setting, providing care to patients who are medically underserved. Students learn to treat various patients whose lifestyles, practices, and attitudes toward health differ from those seen in more traditional training sites.

NSU promotes interdisciplinary cooperation whenever possible. Students share faculty members and facilities with NSU's pharmacy, dental, optometry, physician assistant, physical therapy, occupational therapy, public health, nursing, and medical science students.

FACULTY PROFILE (FALL 2005)

Total teaching faculty: **94 (full-time)**, **838 (part-time)**

Of full-time faculty, those teaching in basic sciences: **33%**; in clinical programs: **67%**

Of part-time faculty, those teaching in basic sciences: **0%**; in clinical programs: **100%**

Full-time faculty/student ratio: **0.1**

SUPPORT SERVICES

The school offers students professional counseling for dealing with stress.

RESIDENCY PROFILE

Most popular residency and specialty programs chosen by the 2004 and 2005 M.D. graduating classes: anesthesiology, dermatology, emergency medicine, internal medicine, obstetrics and gynecology, orthopaedic surgery, pediatrics, psychiatry, radiology–diagnostic, surgery–general.

WHERE GRADS GO

77%

Proportion of 2003-2005 graduates who entered primary care specialties

37%

Proportion of 2004-2005 graduates who accepted in-state residencies

Ohio University

- ■ Grosvenor and Irvine Halls, Athens, OH 45701
- ■ Public
- ■ Year Founded: 1975
- ■ Tuition, 2005-2006: In-state: $22,845; Out-of-state: $32,277
- ■ Enrollment 2005-2006 academic year: 430
- ■ Website: http://www.oucom.ohiou.edu
- ■ Specialty ranking: N/A

3.54	AVERAGE GPA, ENTERING CLASS FALL 2005
8.0	AVERAGE MCAT, ENTERING CLASS FALL 2005
6.7%	ACCEPTANCE RATE, ENTERING CLASS FALL 2005
Unranked	2007 U.S. NEWS MEDICAL SCHOOL RANKING (RESEARCH)
Unranked	2007 U.S. NEWS MEDICAL SCHOOL RANKING (PRIMARY CARE)

ADMISSIONS

Admissions phone number: **(740) 593-4313**
Admissions email address:
 admissions@exchange.oucom.ohiou.edu
Application website: **http://www.aacom.org**
Acceptance rate: **6.7%**
In-state acceptance rate: **35.7%**
Out-of-state acceptance rate: **1.3%**
Minority acceptance rate: **5.5%**
International acceptance rate: **0.0%**

Fall 2005 applications and acceptees

	Applied	Interviewed	Accepted	Enrolled
Total:	2,338	210	157	108
In-state:	367	169	131	94
Out-of-state:	1,971	41	26	14

Profile of admitted students

Average undergraduate grade point average: **3.54**
MCAT averages (scale: 1-15; writing test: J-T):
 Composite score: **8.0**
 Verbal reasoning score: **8.0**, Physical sciences score: **7.6**,
 Biological sciences score: **8.3**, Writing score: **O**
Proportion with undergraduate majors in: Biological
 sciences: **64%**, Physical sciences: **12%**, Non-sciences:
 9%, Other health professions: **6%**, Mixed disciplines
 and other: **9%**
Percentage of students not coming directly from college
 after graduation: **23%**

Dates and details

The American Medical College Application Service
 (AMCAS) application is not accepted.
School asks for a school-specific application as part of the
 admissions process.
Oldest MCAT considered for Fall 2007 entry: **2004**
Earliest application date for the 2007-2008 first-year class:
 May 1, 2006
Latest application date: **February 1, 2006**
Acceptance dates for regular application for the class
 entering in fall 2007:

Earliest: **July 31, 2006**
Latest: **April 15, 2007**
The school considers requests for deferred entrance.
Starting month for the class entering in 2007–2008:
 August
The school doesn't have an Early Decision Plan (EDP).
A personal interview is required for admission.

Undergraduate coursework required

Medical school requires undergraduate work in these subjects: biology, biology/zoology, English, organic chemistry,
inorganic (general) chemistry, physics, behavioral science,
social sciences.

ADMISSIONS POLICY
(TEXT PROVIDED BY SCHOOL):

Consideration for admission depends on strong academic
performance, a dedication to the humane delivery of medical care, motivation for osteopathic medicine, and strong
communication skills. It is preferred that students have
completed a 4-year baccalaureate degree from a regionally
accredited college or university. However, applicants with
90 semester hours or three years of exceptional work at a
college or university may be considered. Transfer applicants
will be evaluated only if they are osteopathic medical students in good academic standing. A state-assisted program,
OU-COM accepts non-residents, but gives preference to
Ohio residents. All applicants must be U.S. citizens or hold
a permanent visa, present letters of recommendation from
at least two natural science faculty they have had for instruction or a letter from a premedical committee, and have
completed a full academic year of: English, behavioral sciences, biology/zoology, general chemistry, physics and
organic chemistry, with appropriate labs. The MCAT must
be taken by August of the year preceding matriculation, and
may not be more than three years old. OU-COM utilizes a
rolling admissions process. Candidates learn the decision of
the admissions committee within a week of the interview.
All candidates seeking to gain admittance must meet health
and technical standards that include, but are not limited to,
a criminal background check and proof of immunization

titers. Computers are required for all entering students, laptops are preferred.

COSTS AND FINANCIAL AID
Financial aid phone number: **(740) 593-2152**
Tuition, 2005-2006 academic year: **In-state: $22,845; Out-of-state: $32,277**
Room and board: **$10,071**
Percentage of students receiving financial aid in 2005-06: **92%**
Percentage of students receiving: Loans: **90%**, Grants/scholarships: **31%**, Work-study aid: **2%**
Average medical school debt for the Class of 2004: **$124,795**

STUDENT BODY
Fall 2005 full-time enrollment: **430**
Men: **45%**, Women: **55%**, In-state: **97%**, Minorities: **24%**, American Indian: **0.7%**, Asian-American: **8.6%**, African-American: **10.7%**, Hispanic-American: **4.4%**, White: **75.6%**, International: **0.0%**, Unknown: **0.0%**

ACADEMIC PROGRAMS
The school's curriculum very frequently gives first-year students substantial contact with patients.
There are opportunities for first- or second-year students to work in community health clinics.
Program offerings: AIDS, drug/alcohol abuse, family medicine, geriatrics, internal medicine, pediatrics, rural medicine, women's health
Joint degrees awarded: M.D./Ph.D., M.D./MBA, M.D./M.S.W., M.D./MS, M.D./M.A., M.D./M.H.A.
Total National Institutes of Health (NIH) grants awarded to the medical school and affiliated hospitals: **$.0 million**

CURRICULUM
(TEXT PROVIDED BY SCHOOL):
The learning environment at the Ohio University College of Osteopathic Medicine (OU-COM) is constructed based on the principles of adult learning. Students enrolled in OU-COM study in one of two tracks, the Patient-Centered Continuum curriculum or the Clinical Presentation Continuum curriculum. Both view medical education as an organized building process that extends from the beginning of medical school through residency training and beyond. Students in both curricula begin interacting with real patients in the first weeks of their medical education and continue that interaction in physicians' offices and patient labs on a regular basis through the first two years.

The PCC curriculum provides opportunities for the integration of clinical, biomedical and social medicine fundamentals in the small group setting. Students work together to identify learning issues based on patient-centered cases designed by clinical and basic science faculty. Students in the PCC participate in small group, case-based learning activities 6 hours per week, problem sets with faculty 2-4 hours per week, clinical and science laboratories 6-13 hours per week, and clinical and community experience 4 hours per week.

The CPC curriculum is organized around important or common symptoms that bring patients to see a physician. Faculty-directed, structured learning activities are provided to help students learn the clinical, biomedical and social fundamentals of medicine. Students in the CPC are offered 8-14 hours per week of lecture, panel discussions, and problem sets related to the clinical presentation of the week. They participate in 4 hours of small group, case-based learning a week, and 6-10 hours of clinical and science labs. They also have 4 hours of clinical and community experience every other week.

During their third and fourth years, OU-COM students are assigned to a hospital in our Centers for Osteopathic Research and Education system throughout the state of Ohio to complete training.

The third- and fourth-year curriculum consists of 59 weeks of assigned services and 20 weeks of clinical electives. All students begin their clinical rotations with a six-week family medicine clerkship designed to ease the transition. The other assigned rotations include primary care, specialty medicine, and an innovative two-week rotation focusing on health care management. The 20 weeks of electives allow students to explore all areas of medicine, including research and international rotations. In addition, various types of didactic components are considered requirements throughout these years.

FACULTY PROFILE (FALL 2005)
Total teaching faculty: **80 (full-time), 506 (part-time)**
Of full-time faculty, those teaching in basic sciences: **49%**; in clinical programs: **51%**
Of part-time faculty, those teaching in basic sciences: **1%**; in clinical programs: **99%**
Full-time faculty/student ratio: **0.2**

SUPPORT SERVICES
The school offers students these services for dealing with stress: expanded-hour gym access, peer counseling, professional counseling, religious support, support groups.

RESIDENCY PROFILE
Most popular residency and specialty programs chosen by the 2004 and 2005 M.D. graduating classes: anesthesiology, emergency medicine, family practice, internal medicine, obstetrics and gynecology, orthopaedic surgery, pediatrics, physical medicine and rehabilitation, psychiatry, surgery–general.

WHERE GRADS GO

58%
Proportion of 2003-2005 graduates who entered primary care specialties

77%
Proportion of 2004-2005 graduates who accepted in-state residencies

Oklahoma State University

CENTER FOR HEALTH SCIENCES

- 1111 W. 17th Street, Tulsa, OK 74107-1898
- Public
- Year Founded: 1972
- Tuition, 2005-2006: In-state: $16,938; Out-of-state: $32,158
- Enrollment 2005-2006 academic year: 352
- Website: http://healthsciences.okstate.edu
- Specialty ranking: family medicine: 26, rural medicine: 20

3.59 AVERAGE GPA, ENTERING CLASS FALL 2005

8.5 AVERAGE MCAT, ENTERING CLASS FALL 2005

27.5% ACCEPTANCE RATE, ENTERING CLASS FALL 2005

Unranked 2007 U.S. NEWS MEDICAL SCHOOL RANKING (RESEARCH)

45 2007 U.S. NEWS MEDICAL SCHOOL RANKING (PRIMARY CARE)

ADMISSIONS

Admissions phone number: **(918) 561-8421**
Admissions email address: **ldhaines@chs.okstate.edu**
Application website: **http://www.aacom.org**
Acceptance rate: **27.5%**
In-state acceptance rate: **47.0%**
Out-of-state acceptance rate: **10.3%**
Minority acceptance rate: **22.3%**
International acceptance rate: **N/A**

Fall 2005 applications and acceptees

	Applied	Interviewed	Accepted	Enrolled
Total:	422	216	116	88
In-state:	198	175	93	76
Out-of-state:	224	41	23	12

Profile of admitted students

Average undergraduate grade point average: **3.59**
MCAT averages (scale: 1-15; writing test: J-T):
   Composite score: **8.5**
   Verbal reasoning score: **9.0**, Physical sciences score: **8.0**,
   Biological sciences score: **9.0**, Writing score: **O**
Proportion with undergraduate majors in: Biological
   sciences: **50%**, Physical sciences: **18%**, Non-sciences:
   8%, Other health professions: **10%**, Mixed disciplines
   and other: **14%**
Percentage of students not coming directly from college
   after graduation: **61%**

Dates and details

The American Medical College Application Service
   (AMCAS) application is not accepted.
School asks for a school-specific application as part of the
   admissions process.
Oldest MCAT considered for Fall 2007 entry: **3**
Earliest application date for the 2007-2008 first-year class:
   June 1, 2006
Latest application date: **February 1, 2006**
Acceptance dates for regular application for the class
   entering in fall 2007:
   Earliest: **October 15, 2006**

Latest: **August 15, 2007**
The school considers requests for deferred entrance.
Starting month for the class entering in 2007–2008:
   August
The school doesn't have an Early Decision Plan (EDP).
A personal interview is required for admission.

Undergraduate coursework required

Medical school requires undergraduate work in these subjects: biology, biology/zoology, English, organic chemistry,
inorganic (general) chemistry, physics, molecular and cell
biology, biochemistry.

ADMISSIONS POLICY
(TEXT PROVIDED BY SCHOOL):

Preference is given to applicants from Oklahoma. Non-U.S.
citizens who do not have a permanent resident visa (green
card) at the time of application cannot be considered for
admission. The Admissions Committee recommends applicants for admission. Final selection of candidates to be
offered admission is made by the dean.

The college considers all qualified candidates without
regard to age, gender, religion, race, or national origin. The
college actively recruits qualified minority students.

At the time of application, the applicant must have an
overall grade-point average of 3.0 (on 4.0 scale), a minimum of 7.0 on the Medical College Admission Test, and a
preprofessional science GPA of at least 2.75 (on 4.0 scale).
Under special circumstances, the College of Osteopathic
Medicine may use discretion to admit students who do not
meet these minimum requirements. The average MCAT
and GPA of recently admitted students are 9.0 and 3.5,
respectively.

At the time of entry, the applicant must have completed
at least three years (90 semester hours) and not less than 75
percent of the courses required for the baccalaureate degree
at a regionally accredited college or university. The applicant
must have completed the following courses, including laboratory, with no grade below C: English (six to eight semester
hours); biology (eight to 10 hours); physics (eight to 10
hours); general chemistry (eight to 10 hours); organic chem-

istry (eight to 10 hours), and at least one of the following undergraduate courses (three to five are strongly recommended): biochemistry, microbiology or molecular biology, histology, embryology, and comparative anatomy or cellular biology.

MCAT scores must be on file before an interview will be granted. An on-campus interview (by invitation only) is required. Interviews are conducted by clinical and basic science faculty members.

COSTS AND FINANCIAL AID
Financial aid phone number: **(918) 561-1228**
Tuition, 2005-2006 academic year: **In-state: $16,938; Out-of-state: $32,158**
Room and board: **$7,300**
Percentage of students receiving financial aid in 2005-06: **98%**
Percentage of students receiving: Loans: **94%**, Grants/scholarships: **44%**, Work-study aid: **25%**
Average medical school debt for the Class of 2004: **$136,000**

STUDENT BODY
Fall 2005 full-time enrollment: **352**
Men: **53%**, Women: **47%**, In-state: **89%**, Minorities: **22%**, American Indian: **11.6%**, Asian-American: **4.8%**, African-American: **4.3%**, Hispanic-American: **1.4%**, White: **76.4%**, International: **0.0%**, Unknown: **1.4%**

ACADEMIC PROGRAMS
The school's curriculum occasionally gives first-year students substantial contact with patients.
There are opportunities for first- or second-year students to work in community health clinics.
Program offerings: AIDS, drug/alcohol abuse, family medicine, geriatrics, internal medicine, pediatrics, rural medicine, women's health
Joint degrees awarded: M.D./Ph.D., M.D./MBA.
Total National Institutes of Health (NIH) grants awarded to the medical school and affiliated hospitals: **$.5 million**

CURRICULUM
(TEXT PROVIDED BY SCHOOL):
The curriculum includes hands-on clinical experiences, student-centered and problem-based methods of instruction, and frequent consultation with faculty members and community-based physicians. Development of problem-solving and information-retrieval skills are emphasized to produce osteopathic physicians with the capacity to be lifelong learners. In a spiral curriculum, study matter is continuously reintroduced to the student in greater depth and complexity, reinforcing prior learning and promoting meaningful retention. The curriculum emphasizes integration of basic sciences with clinical and behavioral sciences to permit full comprehension of the clinician's work and promote a holistic approach to the care of patients and their families.

The curriculum is designed to implement a 22-month clerkship program within the four-year program of professional education.

The first year is designed to bring all students to desired levels of competence in the biomedical sciences and preliminary clinical knowledge and skills. Here, students learn the terminology of medicine and acquire the knowledge for problem solving. During the first year, students are introduced to core concepts in anatomy, physiology, biochemistry, and microbiology. Students begin to develop competence in osteopathic clinical skills including physical examination, diagnosis and patient interviewing, and recognition of normal and abnormal patterns of physical conditions and diseases.

The second year emphasizes case-based learning, clinical problem-solving strategies, and recognition and understanding of common diseases and conditions. Small-group learning and independent study are keys to students' development of the critical thinking required for the clinical context. Students' clinical skills are honed through interactive lab sessions and simulated clinical experiences.

The final 22 months are clinically oriented and community based, consisting of clerkship experiences in hospitals and clinics, where students observe patients on a daily basis under physician-faculty supervision. The student rotates through primary-care services including surgery, obstetrics/gynecology, pediatrics, psychiatry, internal medicine, family medicine, and emergency medicine. The balance of the clerkship program consists of supervised patient contact in rural areas throughout Oklahoma as well as elective rotations chosen by the student.

FACULTY PROFILE (FALL 2005)
Total teaching faculty: **71 (full-time)**, **408 (part-time)**
Of full-time faculty, those teaching in basic sciences: **37%**; in clinical programs: **63%**
Of part-time faculty, those teaching in basic sciences: **7%**; in clinical programs: **93%**
Full-time faculty/student ratio: **0.2**

SUPPORT SERVICES
The school offers students these services for dealing with stress: peer counseling, professional counseling, religious support, support groups.

RESIDENCY PROFILE
Most popular residency and specialty programs chosen by the 2004 and 2005 M.D. graduating classes: anesthesiology, emergency medicine, family practice, internal medicine, obstetrics and gynecology, pediatrics, psychiatry, surgery–general, internal medicine/pediatrics.

WHERE GRADS GO

67%
Proportion of 2003-2005 graduates who entered primary care specialties

57.5%
Proportion of 2004-2005 graduates who accepted in-state residencies

Philadelphia College of Osteopathic Med.

■ 4170 City Avenue, Philadelphia, PA 19131
■ Private
■ Year Founded: 1899
■ Tuition, 2005-2006: $34,272
■ Enrollment 2005-2006 academic year: 1,041
■ Website: http://www.pcom.edu
■ Specialty ranking: N/A

3.23 AVERAGE GPA, ENTERING CLASS FALL 2005

8.3 AVERAGE MCAT, ENTERING CLASS FALL 2005

10.8% ACCEPTANCE RATE, ENTERING CLASS FALL 2005

Unranked 2007 U.S. NEWS MEDICAL SCHOOL RANKING (RESEARCH)

Unranked 2007 U.S. NEWS MEDICAL SCHOOL RANKING (PRIMARY CARE)

ADMISSIONS

Admissions phone number: **(800) 999-6998**
Admissions email address: **admissions@pcom.edu**
Application website: **http://www.aacom.org**
Acceptance rate: **10.8%**
In-state acceptance rate: **42.9%**
Out-of-state acceptance rate: **5.4%**
Minority acceptance rate: **2.2%**
International acceptance rate: **7.1%**

Fall 2005 applications and acceptees

	Applied	Interviewed	Accepted	Enrolled
Total:	3,825	568	414	266
In-state:	553	309	237	161
Out-of-state:	3,272	259	177	105

Profile of admitted students

Average undergraduate grade point average: **3.23**
MCAT averages (scale: 1-15; writing test: J-T):
  Composite score: **8.3**
  Verbal reasoning score: **8.4**, Physical sciences score: **8.1**,
  Biological sciences score: **8.6**, Writing score: **O**
Proportion with undergraduate majors in: Biological
  sciences: **58%**, Physical sciences: **9%**, Non-sciences: **3%**,
  Other health professions: **21%**, Mixed disciplines and
  other: **9%**
Percentage of students not coming directly from college
  after graduation: **9%**

Dates and details

The American Medical College Application Service
  (AMCAS) application is not accepted.
School asks for a school-specific application as part of the
  admissions process.
Oldest MCAT considered for Fall 2007 entry: **2004**
Earliest application date for the 2007-2008 first-year class:
  May 1, 2006
Latest application date: **February 1, 2006**
Acceptance dates for regular application for the class
  entering in fall 2007:
  Earliest: **October 1, 2006**

Latest: **August 1, 2007**
The school doesn't consider requests for deferred entrance.
Starting month for the class entering in 2007–2008:
  August
The school doesn't have an Early Decision Plan (EDP).
A personal interview is required for admission.

Undergraduate coursework required

Medical school requires undergraduate work in these subjects: biology, English, organic chemistry, inorganic (general) chemistry, physics.

ADMISSIONS POLICY

(TEXT PROVIDED BY SCHOOL):
Admission to PCOM is competitive and selective. We seek
well-rounded, achievement-oriented persons whose character, maturity, and sense of dedication point to a successful
and productive life as an osteopathic physician. We are an
institution that has historically sought diversity in our student population. We actively recruit underrepresented
minority students and nontraditional students, who often
offer exceptional potential for becoming outstanding physicians.

Grades and Medical College Admission Test scores are
important to us, as they are some of the best predictors of
success in medical school; however, we also look very carefully at extracurricular activities, community involvement,
motivation to study medicine, and letters of evaluation.

COSTS AND FINANCIAL AID

Financial aid phone number: **(215) 871-6170**
Tuition, 2005-2006 academic year: **$34,272**
Room and board: **N/A**
Percentage of students receiving financial aid in 2005-06:
  93%
Percentage of students receiving: Loans: **90%**,
  Grants/scholarships: **45%**, Work-study aid: **15%**
Average medical school debt for the Class of 2004:
  $172,491

STUDENT BODY

Fall 2005 full-time enrollment: 1,041
Men: 47%, Women: 53%, In-state: 57%, Minorities: 20%,
   American Indian: 0.2%, Asian-American: 11.0%,
   African-American: 5.9%, Hispanic-American: 3.0%,
   White: 76.4%, International: 0.8%, Unknown: 2.8%

ACADEMIC PROGRAMS

The school's curriculum occasionally gives first-year
   students substantial contact with patients.
There are opportunities for first- or second-year students to
   work in community health clinics.
Program offerings: AIDS, drug/alcohol abuse, family
   medicine, geriatrics, internal medicine, pediatrics, rural
   medicine, women's health
Joint degrees awarded: M.D./Ph.D., M.D./MBA,
   M.D./MPH, M.D./MS
Total National Institutes of Health (NIH) grants awarded to
   the medical school and affiliated hospitals: $.4 million

CURRICULUM

(TEXT PROVIDED BY SCHOOL):
A fundamental educational goal of Philadelphia College of
Osteopathic Medicine (PCOM) is to prepare students for
excellence in the practice of osteopathic medicine. The
course of medical study is a practitioner's program, with a
strong emphasis on primary care, prevention, and osteopathic concepts.

Each PCOM student progresses through a uniform and
comprehensive curriculum. Elective clinical clerkships
expose students to specialty or subspecialty fields, and later
they may specialize. At PCOM, students are trained first as
family practitioners and thus build solid foundations for
their careers. Throughout the curriculum, osteopathic concepts and methods are stressed.

Efficiency is also an educational goal. Innovations such
as computerized tutorials, classroom videos, and simulated
patient encounters will sharpen skills as a physician. Our
curriculum revision bridges departmental divisions and
joins related disciplines so that students relate different perspectives to a variety of conditions taught in a common
time frame.

The first two years lay the foundation with intense concentration on the basic sciences, anatomy, biochemistry,
molecular biology, neuroscience, physiology, microbiology,
pathology, and pharmacology. Coursework in ethics, patient
communication, human sexuality, medical law, public
health, and medical economics rounds out the curriculum.

The basic sciences are complemented by instruction in
clinical subjects. All students attend small-group sessions
during the first and second years to develop communication
and diagnostic skills. In addition, an active standardized
patient program introduces first- and second-year students
to patient care through examinations of patient-actors in a
simulated practice setting.

The last two years emphasize clinical training experiences. The program is designed to afford progressive student responsibility for all phases of patient care under the
direction of experienced physicians. Students rotate through
services in medicine, family practice, manipulative medicine, surgery, cardiology, obstetrics/gynecology, pediatrics,
psychiatry, otorhinolaryngology, and office-based preceptorships. All students receive additional training in osteopathic
manipulative medicine in the third year.

Each senior student serves 12 weeks in a healthcare center clerkship. Eight weeks are in our urban clinics, and four
weeks are in one of several rural centers. An alternative
rural selective is offered to a limited number of students in
an area of alternative healthcare delivery or a rural area of
intense medical need, such as India, Israel, Africa,
Appalachia, and Indian Health Service sites.

FACULTY PROFILE (FALL 2005)

Total teaching faculty: 55 (full-time), 39 (part-time)
Of full-time faculty, those teaching in basic sciences: 47%;
   in clinical programs: 53%
Of part-time faculty, those teaching in basic sciences: 3%;
   in clinical programs: 97%
Full-time faculty/student ratio: 0.1

SUPPORT SERVICES

The school offers students these services for dealing with
stress: expanded-hour gym access, peer counseling, professional counseling, support groups.

RESIDENCY PROFILE

Most popular residency and specialty programs chosen by
the 2004 and 2005 M.D. graduating classes: anesthesiology,
emergency medicine, family practice, internal medicine,
obstetrics and gynecology, orthopaedic surgery, pediatrics,
physical medicine and rehabilitation, radiology–diagnostic,
surgery–general.

WHERE GRADS GO

37%
*Proportion of 2003-2005 graduates who entered primary
care specialties*

52%
*Proportion of 2004-2005 graduates who accepted in-state
residencies*

Pikeville Coll. School of Osteopathic Med.

- 147 Sycamore Street, Pikeville, KY 41501
- Private
- Year Founded: 1997
- Tuition, 2005-2006: $28,000
- Enrollment 2005-2006 academic year: 284
- Website: http://www.pc.edu
- Specialty ranking: rural medicine: 30

3.30 AVERAGE GPA, ENTERING CLASS FALL 2005

7.3 AVERAGE MCAT, ENTERING CLASS FALL 2005

26.9% ACCEPTANCE RATE, ENTERING CLASS FALL 2005

Unranked 2007 U.S. NEWS MEDICAL SCHOOL RANKING (RESEARCH)

Unranked 2007 U.S. NEWS MEDICAL SCHOOL RANKING (PRIMARY CARE)

ADMISSIONS

Admissions phone number: **(606) 218-5400**
Admissions email address: **ahamilto@pc.edu**
Application website: **http://www.aacom.org**
Acceptance rate: **26.9%**
In-state acceptance rate: **87.7%**
Out-of-state acceptance rate: **19.4%**
Minority acceptance rate: **19.6%**
International acceptance rate: **0.0%**

Fall 2005 applications and acceptees

	Applied	Interviewed	Accepted	Enrolled
Total:	521	167	140	80
In-state:	57	54	50	36
Out-of-state:	464	113	90	44

Profile of admitted students

Average undergraduate grade point average: **3.30**
MCAT averages (scale: 1-15; writing test: J-T):
  Composite score: **7.3**
  Verbal reasoning score: **7.3**, Physical sciences score: **6.9**,
  Biological sciences score: **7.5**, Writing score: **N/A**
Proportion with undergraduate majors in: Biological
  sciences: **67%**, Physical sciences: **7%**, Non-sciences: **4%**,
  Other health professions: **11%**, Mixed disciplines and
  other: **11%**
Percentage of students not coming directly from college
  after graduation: **28%**

Dates and details

The American Medical College Application Service
  (AMCAS) application is not accepted.
School asks for a school-specific application as part of the
  admissions process.
Oldest MCAT considered for Fall 2007 entry: **2003**
Earliest application date for the 2007-2008 first-year class:
  June 1, 2006
Latest application date: **February 1, 2006**
Acceptance dates for regular application for the class
  entering in fall 2007:
  Earliest: **September 15, 2006**

Latest: **May 12, 2007**
The school considers requests for deferred entrance.
Starting month for the class entering in 2007–2008:
  August
The school doesn't have an Early Decision Plan (EDP).
A personal interview is required for admission.

Undergraduate coursework required

Medical school requires undergraduate work in these subjects: biology, English, organic chemistry, inorganic (general) chemistry, physics.

ADMISSIONS POLICY
(TEXT PROVIDED BY SCHOOL):

The school considers all applicants for admission and financial aid without respect to age, gender, sexual orientation,
race, color, creed, religion, handicap, or national origin.
Applicants are considered on their intellectual ability,
scholastic achievement, commitment, and suitability to succeed in the study of osteopathic medicine.

The PCSOM Admissions Committee will consider applications from all qualified individuals, but preference is
given to students who will provide medical healthcare for
Kentucky, other Appalachian regions, and rural, medically
underserved areas.

The minimum academic requirements for admission to
the first-year class are:

1. A baccalaureate degree, or completion of at least three
fourths (90 semester hours or 135 term credit hours) of the
required credits for a baccalaureate degree, from a regionally accredited college or university. The baccalaureate
degree is preferred.

COSTS AND FINANCIAL AID

Financial aid phone number: **(606) 218-5407**
Tuition, 2005-2006 academic year: **$28,000**
Room and board: **$0**
Percentage of students receiving financial aid in 2005-06:
  98%
Percentage of students receiving: Loans: **98%**,
  Grants/scholarships: **66%**, Work-study aid: **N/A**

Average medical school debt for the Class of 2004: **$128,000**

STUDENT BODY
Fall 2005 full-time enrollment: **284**
Men: **57%**, Women: **43%**, In-state: **45%**, Minorities: **10%**, American Indian: **0.4%**, Asian-American: **5.6%**, African-American: **2.1%**, Hispanic-American: **2.5%**, White: **85.9%**, International: **0.0%**, Unknown: **3.5%**

ACADEMIC PROGRAMS
The school's curriculum occasionally gives first-year students substantial contact with patients.
There are opportunities for first- or second-year students to work in community health clinics.
Program offerings: AIDS, drug/alcohol abuse, family medicine, geriatrics, internal medicine, pediatrics, rural medicine, women's health
Joint degrees awarded: M.D./MPH
Total National Institutes of Health (NIH) grants awarded to the medical school and affiliated hospitals: **$.0 million**

CURRICULUM
(TEXT PROVIDED BY SCHOOL):
The curriculum is structured around nine competencies that maximize the student's opportunity to train for a career in osteopathic primary care.

1. Osteopathic advocate: The PCSOM graduate is knowledgeable about, and an advocate for, the unique nature of the osteopathic medical profession. This includes integrating the four key principles of osteopathic philosophy into clinical practice. Those principles are: (A) the body is a unit—the person is a unit of body, mind, and spirit; (B) the body is capable of self-regulation, self-healing, and health maintenance; (C) structure and function are reciprocally interrelated; and (D) rational treatment is based upon an understanding of the basic principles of body unit, self-regulation, and the interrelationship of structure and function.

2. Effective communication: The PCSOM graduate will listen attentively and communicate clearly with patients, families, and other healthcare team members.

3. Basic clinical skills: The PCSOM graduate will obtain an appropriate history and perform skillful, comprehensive examinations. The graduate will correctly select, proficiently perform, and accurately interpret clinical procedures and laboratory findings.

4. Use of basic science to guide therapy: The PCSOM graduate will recognize, explain, and treat health problems based upon current scientific knowledge or understanding.

5. Diagnosis, management, and prevention: The PCSOM graduate will diagnose, manage, and educate in the prevention of common health problems of individuals, families, and communities in collaboration with them.

6. Lifelong learning: The PCSOM graduate actively sets clear learning goals, pursues them, and applies the knowledge gained to his or her practice of osteopathic medicine.

7. Self-awareness and self-care: The PCSOM graduate approaches the practice of osteopathic medicine with awareness of his or her limits, strengths, weaknesses, and personal vulnerabilities.

8. Social and community contexts of care: The PCSOM graduate provides guidance to patients by responding to the many factors that influence health besides those of a biological nature.

9. Moral reasoning and ethical judgment: The PCSOM graduate combines a willingness to recognize the nature of the value systems of patients and others with commitment to his or her own system and the ethical choices necessary to maintain his or her own ethical integrity.

FACULTY PROFILE (FALL 2005)
Total teaching faculty: **26 (full-time)**, **749 (part-time)**
Of full-time faculty, those teaching in basic sciences: **46%**; in clinical programs: **54%**
Of part-time faculty, those teaching in basic sciences: **N/A**; in clinical programs: **100%**
Full-time faculty/student ratio: **0.1**

SUPPORT SERVICES
The school offers students these services for dealing with stress: peer counseling, professional counseling, religious support, support groups.

RESIDENCY PROFILE
Most popular residency and specialty programs chosen by the 2004 and 2005 M.D. graduating classes: anesthesiology, emergency medicine, family practice, internal medicine, neurology, ophthalmology, pediatrics, psychiatry, surgery–general, transitional year.

WHERE GRADS GO
78%
Proportion of 2003-2005 graduates who entered primary care specialties

23%
Proportion of 2004-2005 graduates who accepted in-state residencies

Touro University

COLLEGE OF OSTEOPATHIC MEDICINE

- 1310 Johnson Lane, Vallejo, CA 94592
- Private
- Year Founded: 1997
- Tuition, 2005-2006: $33,200
- Enrollment 2005-2006 academic year: 526
- Website: http://www.tu.edu
- Specialty ranking: N/A

3.45 AVERAGE GPA, ENTERING CLASS FALL 2005

8.8 AVERAGE MCAT, ENTERING CLASS FALL 2005

13.3% ACCEPTANCE RATE, ENTERING CLASS FALL 2005

Unranked 2007 U.S. NEWS MEDICAL SCHOOL RANKING (RESEARCH)

Unranked 2007 U.S. NEWS MEDICAL SCHOOL RANKING (PRIMARY CARE)

ADMISSIONS

Admissions phone number: **(707) 638-5270**
Admissions email address: **haight@touro.edu**
Application website: **N/A**
Acceptance rate: **13.3%**
In-state acceptance rate: **N/A**
Out-of-state acceptance rate: **N/A**
Minority acceptance rate: **N/A**
International acceptance rate: **N/A**

Fall 2005 applications and acceptees

	Applied	Interviewed	Accepted	Enrolled
Total:	2,084	425	278	135
In-state:	N/A	N/A	N/A	N/A
Out-of-state:	N/A	N/A	N/A	N/A

Profile of admitted students

Average undergraduate grade point average: **3.45**
MCAT averages (scale: 1-15; writing test: J-T):
  Composite score: **8.8**
  Verbal reasoning score: **8.6**, Physical sciences score: **8.9**, Biological sciences score: **9.0**, Writing score: **O**

Dates and details

The American Medical College Application Service (AMCAS) application is not accepted.
School asks for a school-specific application as part of the admissions process.
Oldest MCAT considered for Fall 2007 entry: **2003**
Earliest application date for the 2007-2008 first-year class: **May 15, 2006**
Latest application date: **April 15, 2006**
Acceptance dates for regular application for the class entering in fall 2007:
  Earliest: **October 1, 2006**
  Latest: **June 30, 2007**
The school considers requests for deferred entrance.
Starting month for the class entering in 2007–2008: **August**
The school has an Early Decision Plan (EDP).
A personal interview is required for admission.

Undergraduate coursework required

Medical school requires undergraduate work in these subjects: biology, English, organic chemistry, inorganic (general) chemistry, physics, humanities.

ADMISSIONS POLICY
(TEXT PROVIDED BY SCHOOL):

1. TUCOM has no mandate to enroll any percentage of in-state residents.

2. Complete the primary online application with the American Association of Colleges of Osteopathic Medicine Application Service. TUCOM's code number is 618.

3. Qualified applicants will be instructed to complete TUCOM's supplemental application.

4. If eligible for a supplemental application, submit an evaluation from a preprofessional advisory committee or letters of recommendation from two science faculty members familiar with your work.

5. Submit a letter of recommendation from a physician (D.O. or M.D.).

6. If invited to do so, schedule a formal interview with the Admissions and Standards Committee.

COSTS AND FINANCIAL AID

Financial aid phone number: **(707) 638-5280**
Tuition, 2005-2006 academic year: **$33,200**
Room and board: **$14,798**
Percentage of students receiving financial aid in 2005-06: **94%**
Percentage of students receiving: Loans: **93%**, Grants/scholarships: **11%**, Work-study aid: **10%**
Average medical school debt for the Class of 2004: **$182,000**

STUDENT BODY

Fall 2005 full-time enrollment: **526**
Men: **N/A**, Women: **N/A**, In-state: **N/A**, Minorities: **N/A**, American Indian: **N/A**, Asian-American: **N/A**, African-American: **N/A**, Hispanic-American: **N/A**, White: **N/A**, International: **N/A**, Unknown: **N/A**

ACADEMIC PROGRAMS

There are opportunities for first- or second-year students to work in community health clinics.

Program offerings: AIDS, drug/alcohol abuse, family medicine, geriatrics, internal medicine, pediatrics, rural medicine

Joint degrees awarded: N/A

Total National Institutes of Health (NIH) grants awarded to the medical school and affiliated hospitals: **N/A**

CURRICULUM

(TEXT PROVIDED BY SCHOOL):

TUCOM students take courses in all of the subject areas one would expect any physician to master, including anatomy, pathology, microbiology, histology, osteopathic principles and practices, pharmacology, immunology, clinical skills, and doctor-patient communication, as well as systems courses that focus on each major system of the body, such as cardiovascular, respiratory, gastrointestinal, and so on.

Our goal is to prepare students for the realities of medicine as it presently exists, as well as how it is likely to be in the future. Practice in problem solving is part of the daily classroom clinic experience as we strive to deliver a curriculum consistent with emerging directions of healthcare.

FACULTY PROFILE (FALL 2005)

Total teaching faculty: **48 (full-time)**, **0 (part-time)**

Of full-time faculty, those teaching in basic sciences: **54%**; in clinical programs: **46%**

Of part-time faculty, those teaching in basic sciences: **N/A**; in clinical programs: **N/A**

Full-time faculty/student ratio: **0.1**

SUPPORT SERVICES

The school offers students these services for dealing with stress: expanded-hour gym access, peer counseling, professional counseling, religious support, support groups.

WHERE GRADS GO

52%

Proportion of 2003-2005 graduates who entered primary care specialties

40%

Proportion of 2004-2005 graduates who accepted in-state residencies

UMDNJ

SCHOOL OF OSTEOPATHIC MEDICINE

- 1 Medical Center Drive, Stratford, NJ 08084-1501
- Public
- Year Founded: 1977
- Tuition, 2005-2006: In-state: $23,977; Out-of-state: $36,059
- Enrollment 2005-2006 academic year: 382
- Website: http://som.umdnj.edu
- Specialty ranking: geriatrics: 20

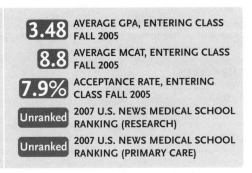

3.48 AVERAGE GPA, ENTERING CLASS FALL 2005

8.8 AVERAGE MCAT, ENTERING CLASS FALL 2005

7.9% ACCEPTANCE RATE, ENTERING CLASS FALL 2005

Unranked 2007 U.S. NEWS MEDICAL SCHOOL RANKING (RESEARCH)

Unranked 2007 U.S. NEWS MEDICAL SCHOOL RANKING (PRIMARY CARE)

ADMISSIONS

Admissions phone number: **(856) 566-7050**
Admissions email address: **somadm@umdnj.edu**
Application website: **N/A**
Acceptance rate: **7.9%**
In-state acceptance rate: **20.9%**
Out-of-state acceptance rate: **5.5%**
Minority acceptance rate: **3.9%**
International acceptance rate: **N/A**

Fall 2005 applications and acceptees

	Applied	Interviewed	Accepted	Enrolled
Total:	2,401	285	190	100
In-state:	373	115	78	100
Out-of-state:	2,028	170	112	0

Profile of admitted students

Average undergraduate grade point average: **3.48**
MCAT averages (scale: 1-15; writing test: J-T):
  Composite score: **8.8**
  Verbal reasoning score: **8.5**, Physical sciences score: **8.7**,
  Biological sciences score: **9.2**, Writing score: **Q**
Proportion with undergraduate majors in: Biological
  sciences: **50%**, Physical sciences: **20%**, Non-sciences:
  7%, Other health professions: **10%**, Mixed disciplines
  and other: **13%**
Percentage of students not coming directly from college
  after graduation: **69%**

Dates and details

The American Medical College Application Service
  (AMCAS) application is not accepted.
School asks for a school-specific application as part of the
  admissions process.
Oldest MCAT considered for Fall 2007 entry: **2001**
Acceptance dates for regular application for the class
  entering in fall 2007:
  Earliest: **September 20, 2006**
  Latest: **August 1, 2007**
The school considers requests for deferred entrance.

Starting month for the class entering in 2007–2008:
  August
The school doesn't have an Early Decision Plan (EDP).
A personal interview is required for admission.

Undergraduate coursework required

Medical school requires undergraduate work in these subjects: biology, English, organic chemistry, inorganic (general) chemistry, physics, mathematics, behavioral science.

COSTS AND FINANCIAL AID

Financial aid phone number: **(856) 566-6008**
Tuition, 2005-2006 academic year: **In-state: $23,977; Out-
  of-state: $36,059**
Room and board: **$10,000**
Percentage of students receiving financial aid in 2005-06:
  89%
Percentage of students receiving: Loans: **87%**,
  Grants/scholarships: **45%**, Work-study aid: **7%**
Average medical school debt for the Class of 2004:
  $104,005

STUDENT BODY

Fall 2005 full-time enrollment: 382
Men: **43%**, Women: **57%**, In-state: **99%**, Minorities: **53%**,
  American Indian: **0.3%**, Asian-American: **23.8%**,
  African-American: **21.7%**, Hispanic-American: **6.5%**,
  White: **47.4%**, International: **0.3%**, Unknown: **0.0%**

ACADEMIC PROGRAMS

The school's curriculum frequently gives first-year students
  substantial contact with patients.
There are opportunities for first- or second-year students to
  work in community health clinics.
Program offerings: AIDS, drug/alcohol abuse, family
  medicine, geriatrics, internal medicine, pediatrics, rural
  medicine, women's health
Joint degrees awarded: M.D./Ph.D., M.D./MPH, M.D./JD,
  M.D./MS
Total National Institutes of Health (NIH) grants awarded to
  the medical school and affiliated hospitals: **$4.6 million**

FACULTY PROFILE (FALL 2005)

Total teaching faculty: **165 (full-time)**, **34 (part-time)**

Of full-time faculty, those teaching in basic sciences: **19%**;
in clinical programs: **81%**

Of part-time faculty, those teaching in basic sciences: **9%**;
in clinical programs: **91%**

Full-time faculty/student ratio: **0.4**

SUPPORT SERVICES

The school offers students these services for dealing with stress: expanded-hour gym access, professional counseling.

RESIDENCY PROFILE

Most popular residency and specialty programs chosen by the 2004 and 2005 M.D. graduating classes: emergency medicine, family practice, family practice–geriatric medicine, internal medicine, internal medicine–critical care medicine, internal medicine–pulmonary disease and critical care medicine, obstetrics and gynecology, orthopaedic surgery, psychiatry, internal medicine–emergency medicine.

University of New England

COLLEGE OF OSTEOPATHIC MEDICINE

- 11 Hills Beach Road, Biddeford, ME 04005
- Private
- Year Founded: 1978
- Tuition, 2005-2006: $35,270
- Enrollment 2005-2006 academic year: 500
- Website: http://www.une.edu/com/
- Specialty ranking: family medicine: 26, rural medicine: 25

3.37 AVERAGE GPA, ENTERING CLASS FALL 2005

8.4 AVERAGE MCAT, ENTERING CLASS FALL 2005

9.0% ACCEPTANCE RATE, ENTERING CLASS FALL 2005

Unranked 2007 U.S. NEWS MEDICAL SCHOOL RANKING (RESEARCH)

Unranked 2007 U.S. NEWS MEDICAL SCHOOL RANKING (PRIMARY CARE)

ADMISSIONS

Admissions phone number: **(800) 477-4863**
Admissions email address: **unecomadmissions@une.edu**
Application website: **https://aacomas.aacom.org**
Acceptance rate: **9.0%**
In-state acceptance rate: **63.5%**
Out-of-state acceptance rate: **7.8%**
Minority acceptance rate: **2.2%**
International acceptance rate: **N/A**

Fall 2005 applications and acceptees

	Applied	Interviewed	Accepted	Enrolled
Total:	2,448	306	221	121
In-state:	52	37	33	28
Out-of-state:	2,396	269	188	93

Profile of admitted students

Average undergraduate grade point average: **3.37**
MCAT averages (scale: 1-15; writing test: J-T):
Composite score: **8.4**
Verbal reasoning score: **8.5**, Physical sciences score: **7.8**,
Biological sciences score: **8.6**, Writing score: **R**
Proportion with undergraduate majors in: Biological
sciences: **52%**, Physical sciences: **18%**, Non-sciences:
15%, Other health professions: **10%**, Mixed disciplines
and other: **5%**
Percentage of students not coming directly from college
after graduation: **78%**

Dates and details

The American Medical College Application Service
(AMCAS) application is not accepted.
School asks for a school-specific application as part of the
admissions process.
Oldest MCAT considered for Fall 2007 entry: **2004**
Earliest application date for the 2007-2008 first-year class:
May 14, 2006
Latest application date: **February 2, 2006**
Acceptance dates for regular application for the class
entering in fall 2007:
Earliest: **September 15, 2006**

Latest: **July 30, 2007**
The school doesn't consider requests for deferred entrance.
Starting month for the class entering in 2007–2008:
August
The school doesn't have an Early Decision Plan (EDP).
A personal interview is required for admission.

Undergraduate coursework required

Medical school requires undergraduate work in these subjects: biology, English, organic chemistry, inorganic (general) chemistry, physics, molecular and cellular biology, biochemistry.

ADMISSIONS POLICY
(TEXT PROVIDED BY SCHOOL):

All Maine residents meeting the college's stated minimum
entrance requirements are guaranteed an interview.
Preference is given to residents of the New England region.
Factors taken into consideration when determining appropriateness for interview include academic ability, level of
healthcare experience, extracurricular activities, applicants'
level of knowledge, and commitment to the profession and
to primary-care medicine.

COSTS AND FINANCIAL AID

Financial aid phone number: **(207) 283-0171**
Tuition, 2005-2006 academic year: **$35,270**
Room and board: **$11,000**
Percentage of students receiving financial aid in 2005-06:
93%
Percentage of students receiving: Loans: **92%**,
Grants/scholarships: **29%**, Work-study aid: **0%**
Average medical school debt for the Class of 2004:
$164,516

STUDENT BODY

Fall 2005 full-time enrollment: **500**
Men: **48%**, Women: **52%**, In-state: **19%**, Minorities: **10%**,
American Indian: **0.2%**, Asian-American: **7.8%**, African-American: **1.0%**, Hispanic-American: **1.0%**, White:
89.2%, International: **0.8%**, Unknown: **0.0%**

ACADEMIC PROGRAMS

The school's curriculum frequently gives first-year students substantial contact with patients.

There are opportunities for first- or second-year students to work in community health clinics.

Program offerings: AIDS, drug/alcohol abuse, family medicine, geriatrics, internal medicine, pediatrics, rural medicine, women's health

Joint degrees awarded: M.D./MPH

Total National Institutes of Health (NIH) grants awarded to the medical school and affiliated hospitals: **N/A**

CURRICULUM

(TEXT PROVIDED BY SCHOOL):

The four-year curriculum leading to the degree Doctor of Osteopathic Medicine is as follows:

Year 1: Basic sciences—gross anatomy, histology, embryology, biochemistry, immunology, nutrition, virology, bacteriology, parasitology, physiology, pharmacology, and pathology; Osteopathic Principles and Practices I; Medical Jurisprudence; Population Health; and Basic Life Support. Foundations of Doctoring is a yearlong course focusing on traditional physical diagnosis and medical humanities. Students in this course also gain early clinical exposure through the preceptor program. The Dermatology System course occurs at the end of the first year.

Year 2: A neuroanatomy course is followed by systems courses—nervous, psychiatry, musculoskeletal, respiratory, hematology, cardiovascular, renal, gastrointestinal, endocrine, and reproductive. Yearlong courses include Pharmacology and Therapeutics (I and II), Osteopathic Principles and Practices II, and Experiences in Doctoring, (a skills-based course). Emergency Medicine, Advanced Cardiac Life Support, and Clinical Decision Making (a capstone course) complete the year.

Year 3: Core rotation requirements include 12 weeks of internal medicine and six weeks each of surgery, obstetrics/gynecology, pediatrics, family practice, and psychiatry.

Year 4: Additional clinical requirements include four weeks each of internal medicine, surgery, osteopathic manipulative medicine, and rural and emergency medicine. The balance of the student's schedule is elective.

FACULTY PROFILE (FALL 2005)

Total teaching faculty: **101 (full-time), 431 (part-time)**

Of full-time faculty, those teaching in basic sciences: **18%**; in clinical programs: **82%**

Of part-time faculty, those teaching in basic sciences: **2%**; in clinical programs: **98%**

Full-time faculty/student ratio: **0.2**

SUPPORT SERVICES

The school offers students these services for dealing with stress: expanded-hour gym access, professional counseling.

RESIDENCY PROFILE

Most popular residency and specialty programs chosen by the 2004 and 2005 M.D. graduating classes: emergency medicine, family practice, internal medicine, obstetrics and gynecology, pediatrics, physical medicine and rehabilitation, radiology–diagnostic, surgery–general, transitional year.

WHERE GRADS GO

67.2%

Proportion of 2003-2005 graduates who entered primary care specialties

17.5%

Proportion of 2004-2005 graduates who accepted in-state residencies

U. of North Texas Health Sci. Center

(TEXAS COL. OF OSTEOPATHIC MEDICINE)

- 3500 Camp Bowie Boulevard, Fort Worth, TX 76107-2699
- Public
- Year Founded: 1966
- Tuition, 2005-2006: In-state: $10,974; Out-of-state: $26,724
- Enrollment 2005-2006 academic year: 520
- Website: http://www.hsc.unt.edu
- Specialty ranking: N/A

3.52 AVERAGE GPA, ENTERING CLASS FALL 2005

9.2 AVERAGE MCAT, ENTERING CLASS FALL 2005

10.4% ACCEPTANCE RATE, ENTERING CLASS FALL 2005

Unranked 2007 U.S. NEWS MEDICAL SCHOOL RANKING (RESEARCH)

28 2007 U.S. NEWS MEDICAL SCHOOL RANKING (PRIMARY CARE)

ADMISSIONS

Admissions phone number: **(800) 535-8266**
Admissions email address:
   TCOMAdmissions@hsc.unt.edu
Application website:
   **http://www.hsc.unt.edu/education/tcom/
   Admissions.cfm**
Acceptance rate: **10.4%**
In-state acceptance rate: **9.8%**
Out-of-state acceptance rate: **14.7%**
Minority acceptance rate: **8.1%**
International acceptance rate: **22.2%**

Fall 2005 applications and acceptees

	Applied	Interviewed	Accepted	Enrolled
Total:	1,701	569	177	135
In-state:	1,504	522	148	122
Out-of-state:	197	47	29	13

Profile of admitted students

Average undergraduate grade point average: **3.52**
MCAT averages (scale: 1-15; writing test: J-T):
   Composite score: **9.2**
   Verbal reasoning score: **9.0**, Physical sciences score: **8.9**,
   Biological sciences score: **9.6**, Writing score: **P**
Proportion with undergraduate majors in: Biological
   sciences: **55%**, Physical sciences: **14%**, Non-sciences:
   11%, Other health professions: **9%**, Mixed disciplines
   and other: **11%**
Percentage of students not coming directly from college
   after graduation: **44%**

Dates and details

The American Medical College Application Service
   (AMCAS) application is not accepted.
School asks for a school-specific application as part of the
   admissions process.
Oldest MCAT considered for Fall 2007 entry: **2002**
Earliest application date for the 2007-2008 first-year class:
   May 1, 2006
Latest application date: **October 15, 2006**

Acceptance dates for regular application for the class
   entering in fall 2007:
   Earliest: **October 15, 2006**
   Latest: **July 20, 2007**
The school considers requests for deferred entrance.
Starting month for the class entering in 2007–2008: **July**
The school has an Early Decision Plan (EDP).
A personal interview is required for admission.

Undergraduate coursework required

Medical school requires undergraduate work in these subjects: biology, biology/zoology, English, organic chemistry,
inorganic (general) chemistry, physics, mathematics,
demonstration of writing skills, calculus, general chemistry.

ADMISSIONS POLICY
(TEXT PROVIDED BY SCHOOL):

A minimum of 90 semester credit hours (or an equivalent
number of quarter hours) towards a bachelor's degree from
a regionally accredited college or university in the United
States is required at the time of application. The following
prerequisite courses in the sciences and humanities must
be satisfactorily completed in order for us to properly evaluate your application: general or inorganic chemistry; organic
chemistry; general biology; general physics; English or creative writing; calculus or statistics.

   Strong preference will be given to those who have completed all of their requirements for the bachelor's degree
before entering medical school. Applicants are also encouraged to complete their prerequisite course work with letter
grades rather than using a pass/fail option. Science
courses must include laboratory experience and must be at
the level taken by majors in those disciplines. Biology
courses should cover the cellular and molecular aspects
and the structure and function of living organisms. We
also urge you to broaden your education by taking courses
in the behavioral sciences and the humanities. Prospective
students should strive to become proficient in scientific
problem solving, critical thinking and writing. An applicant's academic record is important to us, but we do examine other factors when selecting our incoming class. We

look for students who demonstrate the greatest promise of becoming skilled osteopathic physicians. These qualities and attributes will be evaluated by several means. As a state-supported medical school, we are required to admit 90 percent Texas residents for each entering class of 125 students. Up to 10 percent of each entering class may be filled with non-residents with outstanding credentials. An alien living in the United States under a visa permitting permanent residence or who has filed a declaration of intention to become a citizen with the proper federal immigration authorities has the same privilege of qualifying for Texas residency as do citizens of the United States. TCOM admits applicants through the Texas Medical and Dental Schools Application Service (TMDSAS).

COSTS AND FINANCIAL AID

Financial aid phone number: **(800) 346-8266**
Tuition, 2005-2006 academic year: **In-state: $10,974; Out-of-state: $26,724**
Room and board: **$10,857**
Percentage of students receiving financial aid in 2005-06: **90%**
Percentage of students receiving: Loans: **90%**, Grants/scholarships: **41%**, Work-study aid: **1%**
Average medical school debt for the Class of 2004: **$93,207**

STUDENT BODY

Fall 2005 full-time enrollment: **520**
Men: **47%**, Women: **53%**, In-state: **95%**, Minorities: **37%**, American Indian: **0.8%**, Asian-American: **26.3%**, African-American: **1.9%**, Hispanic-American: **7.7%**, White: **62.5%**, International: **0.6%**, Unknown: **0.2%**

ACADEMIC PROGRAMS

The school's curriculum frequently gives first-year students substantial contact with patients.
There are opportunities for first- or second-year students to work in community health clinics.
Program offerings: AIDS, drug/alcohol abuse, family medicine, geriatrics, internal medicine, pediatrics, rural medicine, women's health
Joint degrees awarded: M.D./Ph.D., M.D./MPH, M.D./MS
Total National Institutes of Health (NIH) grants awarded to the medical school and affiliated hospitals: **$12.9 million**

CURRICULUM

(TEXT PROVIDED BY SCHOOL):
In the first two years of the D.O. program, students are taught basic sciences and clinical medicine through an integrated systems approach. A medical simulation laboratory is utilized in the first two years.

Years three and four resemble clinical education programs that are available in medical schools throughout the United States. In both phases, emphasis is placed on identification and treatment of illnesses, the promotion of health and wellness in patients, and on the necessity of treating each patient in the context of a wide variety of factors that influence health.

The first portion of the curriculum is designed to help students integrate basic and clinical sciences, further develop the ability to diagnose illness, and increase their understanding of the context within which medicine is practiced. The integrated systems approach is built on the same strong foundation of scientific and clinical knowledge that has long characterized TCOM's outstanding academic program.

The clinical years of the curriculum provide students a comprehensive understanding of the clinical practices of modern medicine. Students complete over 3,800 hours of medical training in hospitals and clinics; they are are required to complete both a set of core clinical rotations and elective rotations.

Beginning with the first semester, students are placed in a variety of clinics and agencies to help them become familiar with the many facets of community health care and the health problems that will play a role in their lives as health care providers. This provides a gradual transition from classroom to clinical settings.

Emphasis is placed on learning activities that help each student interact effectively with peers and promote cooperative relationships with others in the health professions. Central to all activities in the curriculum are the goals of teaching critical thinking and helping each student develop the skills to make decisions in the clinical setting.

FACULTY PROFILE (FALL 2005)

Total teaching faculty: **293 (full-time), 19 (part-time)**
Of full-time faculty, those teaching in basic sciences: **27%**; in clinical programs: **73%**
Of part-time faculty, those teaching in basic sciences: **26%**; in clinical programs: **74%**
Full-time faculty/student ratio: **0.6**

SUPPORT SERVICES

The school offers students these services for dealing with stress: expanded-hour gym access, peer counseling, professional counseling, religious support, support groups.

RESIDENCY PROFILE

Most popular residency and specialty programs chosen by the 2004 and 2005 M.D. graduating classes: anesthesiology, emergency medicine, family practice, internal medicine, obstetrics and gynecology, orthopaedic surgery, pediatrics, physical medicine and rehabilitation, psychiatry, surgery–general.

WHERE GRADS GO

77.7%
Proportion of 2003-2005 graduates who entered primary care specialties

57.6%
Proportion of 2004-2005 graduates who accepted in-state residencies

West Virginia School of Osteopathic Med.

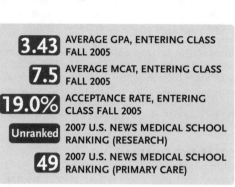

- 400 N. Lee Street, Lewisburg, WV 24901
- Public
- **Year Founded:** 1972
- **Tuition, 2005-2006:** In-state: $17,850; Out-of-state: $45,878
- **Enrollment 2005-2006 academic year:** 397
- **Website:** http://www.wvsom.edu
- **Specialty ranking:** rural medicine: 15

3.43 AVERAGE GPA, ENTERING CLASS FALL 2005

7.5 AVERAGE MCAT, ENTERING CLASS FALL 2005

19.0% ACCEPTANCE RATE, ENTERING CLASS FALL 2005

Unranked 2007 U.S. NEWS MEDICAL SCHOOL RANKING (RESEARCH)

49 2007 U.S. NEWS MEDICAL SCHOOL RANKING (PRIMARY CARE)

ADMISSIONS

Admissions phone number: **(800) 356-7836**
Admissions email address: **admissions@wvsom.edu**
Application website: **http://www.aacom.org**
Acceptance rate: **19.0%**
In-state acceptance rate: **48.8%**
Out-of-state acceptance rate: **16.5%**
Minority acceptance rate: **8.6%**
International acceptance rate: **N/A**

Fall 2005 applications and acceptees

	Applied	Interviewed	Accepted	Enrolled
Total:	1,635	420	310	104
In-state:	123	77	60	43
Out-of-state:	1,512	343	250	61

Profile of admitted students

Average undergraduate grade point average: **3.43**
MCAT averages (scale: 1-15; writing test: J-T):
 Composite score: **7.5**
 Verbal reasoning score: **7.8**, Physical sciences score: **7.1**,
 Biological sciences score: **7.4**, Writing score: **M**
Proportion with undergraduate majors in: Biological
 sciences: **56%**, Physical sciences: **18%**, Non-sciences: **3%**,
 Other health professions: **13%**, Mixed disciplines and
 other: **10%**
Percentage of students not coming directly from college
 after graduation: **47%**

Dates and details

The American Medical College Application Service
 (AMCAS) application is not accepted.
School asks for a school-specific application as part of the
 admissions process.
Oldest MCAT considered for Fall 2007 entry: **2004**
Earliest application date for the 2007-2008 first-year class:
 June 1, 2006
Latest application date: **February 15, 2006**
Acceptance dates for regular application for the class
 entering in fall 2007:
 Earliest: **September 1, 2006**

Latest: **April 30, 2007**
The school doesn't consider requests for deferred entrance.
Starting month for the class entering in 2007–2008:
 August
The school has an Early Decision Plan (EDP).
A personal interview isn't required for admission.

Undergraduate coursework required

Medical school requires undergraduate work in these subjects: biology/zoology, English, organic chemistry, inorganic
(general) chemistry, physics.

ADMISSIONS POLICY

(TEXT PROVIDED BY SCHOOL):
Students are the key to the West Virginia School of
Osteopathic Medicine's commitment to improving healthcare. The Admissions Committee strives to fill the class
each year with men and women who are motivated toward
small-community or rural primary care.

Students come to Lewisburg with diverse academic and
professional backgrounds, ranging from those possessing
the minimum admission requirements to those holding
advanced degrees in various fields. First preference is given
to West Virginia residents.

The admission process is initiated by completing the
American Association of Colleges of Osteopathic Medicine
Application Service online application. Supplemental applications are provided only to those applicants who are
granted an interview. The interview process begins in the
latter part of August of the year preceding entry and continues through mid-April.

The basic requirements for admission to the first-year
class include:
 1. Ninety semester hours or three fourths of the credits
required for a baccalaureate degree from an accredited college or university.
 2. Medical College Admission Test scores.
 3. Six semester hours (or its equivalent) of English; eight
semester hours each in general biology or zoology, physics
(algebra and trigonometry based), inorganic or general
chemistry, and organic chemistry (including aliphatic and

aromatic compounds), all with laboratories; and 52 semester hours of electives.

4. Cardiopulmonary resuscitation (CPR) certification prior to matriculation.

5. Letters of evaluation from the student's premedical adviser, premedical advising committee, or approved science faculty member and an osteopathic physician.

It is strongly recommended that a prospective applicant consider the following courses: biochemistry, cell biology, cell physiology, microbiology, modern genetics, comparative anatomy, embryology, histology, human anatomy, and mammalian physiology.

The Admissions Committee has the responsibility of accepting applicants on the basis of aptitude, maturity, ability to relate to people, motivation for osteopathic medicine, personal conduct, and scholarship. A personal interview may be required.

COSTS AND FINANCIAL AID

Financial aid phone number: (800) 356-7836
Tuition, 2005-2006 academic year: **In-state: $17,850; Out-of-state: $45,878**
Room and board: N/A
Percentage of students receiving financial aid in 2005-06: **97%**
Percentage of students receiving: Loans: **94%**, Grants/scholarships: **12%**, Work-study aid: **11%**
Average medical school debt for the Class of 2004: **$148,147**

STUDENT BODY

Fall 2005 full-time enrollment: **397**
Men: **53%**, Women: **47%**, In-state: **55%**, Minorities: **11%**, American Indian: **0.5%**, Asian-American: **8.3%**, African-American: **0.5%**, Hispanic-American: **1.3%**, White: **88.7%**, International: **0.0%**, Unknown: **0.8%**

ACADEMIC PROGRAMS

The school's curriculum frequently gives first-year students substantial contact with patients.
There are opportunities for first- or second-year students to work in community health clinics.
Program offerings: AIDS, drug/alcohol abuse, family medicine, geriatrics, internal medicine, pediatrics, rural medicine, women's health
Joint degrees awarded: N/A
Total National Institutes of Health (NIH) grants awarded to the medical school and affiliated hospitals: **$.0 million**

CURRICULUM

(TEXT PROVIDED BY SCHOOL):
The West Virginia School of Osteopathic Medicine provides two curricular tracts for students, Systems and Problem-Based Learning. In the Systems track, students spend the first year taking basic science courses, including both lab and lecture formats with a full-body dissection lab in anatomy. Second-year students take an integrated systems approach to medicine, plus courses such as pharmacology, physical diagnosis, and physician skills. An Osteopathic Principles and Practice course is given in both years. First-

and second-year students participate in a unique community clinic experience, where local community patients are diagnosed and treated osteopathically free of charge by the students, under faculty supervision.

In the Problem-Based Learning track, students are taught through the small-group learning process. Each group of seven or eight students is presented patient cases, which are revealed through progressive disclosure. Each group has two faculty facilitators, one basic scientist and one clinician. Students research issues, discuss their findings, and the case continues until all issues have been covered. Students also work on specific problem sets that help direct their learning. They have a full anatomy dissection course and participate with Systems students in the Osteopathic Principles and Practices course. These students begin physical diagnosis in the first year, and this expands into a physician skills course the second year. PBL students also participate in the free community clinic.

Promotion to the clinical curriculum requires passage of Part I of the National Osteopathic Board Examination. The clinical years are identical for both programs. Students are scheduled with clinician preceptors for their clerkships. Students are required to do three months of rural rotations and five months of family medicine throughout their third and fourth years. Other required rotations include obstetrics/gynecology, surgery, emergency medicine, pediatrics, internal medicine, psychiatry, and geriatrics. Graduation requires successful passage of Part II of the National Osteopathic Board Examination

FACULTY PROFILE (FALL 2005)

Total teaching faculty: **39 (full-time)**, **98 (part-time)**
Of full-time faculty, those teaching in basic sciences: **51%**; in clinical programs: **49%**
Of part-time faculty, those teaching in basic sciences: **0%**; in clinical programs: **100%**
Full-time faculty/student ratio: **0.1**

SUPPORT SERVICES

The school offers students these services for dealing with stress: expanded-hour gym access, peer counseling, professional counseling, religious support, support groups.

RESIDENCY PROFILE

Most popular residency and specialty programs chosen by the 2004 and 2005 M.D. graduating classes: anesthesiology, emergency medicine, family practice, internal medicine, obstetrics and gynecology, pathology–anatomic and clinical, pediatrics, psychiatry, surgery–general, transitional year.

WHERE GRADS GO

87.3%
Proportion of 2003-2005 graduates who entered primary care specialties

34%
Proportion of 2004-2005 graduates who accepted in-state residencies

Additional Schools

Basic contact information for those schools that did not respond to the U.S. News survey is provided below.

LOMA LINDA UNIVERSITY
- Loma Linda, CA 92350
- Private
- Website: http://www.llu.edu

LSU SCHOOL OF MEDICINE–NEW ORLEANS
- Admissions Office, 1901 Perdido Street, New Orleans, LA 70112-1393
- Public
- Year Founded: 1941
- Website: http://www.medschool.lsumc.edu

LSU SCHOOL OF MEDICINE–SHREVEPORT
- P.O. Box 33932, Shreveport, LA 71130-3932
- Public
- Year Founded: 1969
- Website: http://www.sh.lsumc.edu

MARSHALL UNIVERSITY (EDWARDS)
- 1600 Medical Center Drive, Huntington, WV 25701-3655
- Public
- Year Founded: 1977
- Website: http://musom.marshall.edu

MEHARRY MEDICAL COLLEGE
- 1005 D.B. Todd Jr. Boulevard, Nashville, TN
- Private
- Year Founded: 1876
- Website: http://www.mmc.edu

PENNSYLVANIA STATE UNIVERSITY COLLEGE OF MEDICINE
- 500 University Drive, Hershey, PA 17033
- Public
- Year Founded: 1967
- Website: http://www.hmc.psu.edu

SUNY–DOWNSTATE MEDICAL CENTER
- 450 Clarkson Avenue, Box 60, Brooklyn, NY 11203
- Public
- Year Founded: 1860
- Website: http://www.hscbklyn.edu

TULANE UNIVERSITY
- 1430 Tulane Avenue, SL67, New Orleans, LA 70112-2699
- Private
- Year Founded: 1834
- Website: http://www.mcl.tulane.edu

UNIVERSITY OF HAWAII–MANOA (BURNS)
- 1960 East-West Road, Honolulu, HI 96822
- Public
- Year Founded: 1967
- Website: http://hawaiimed.hawaii.edu

UNIVERSITY OF LOUISVILLE
- Abell Administration Center, H.S.C., Louisville, KY 40202
- Public
- Year Founded: 1876
- Website: http://www.louisville.edu

UNIVERSITY OF MISSISSIPPI
- 2500 N. Slate Street, Jackson, MS 39216-4505
- Public
- Year Founded: 1903
- Website: http://www.umc.edu

UNIVERSITY OF MISSOURI–KANSAS CITY
- 2411 Holmes, Kansas City, MO 64108
- Public
- Year Founded: 1971
- Website: http://www.med.umkc.edu

UNIVERSITY OF NEVADA–RENO
- Pennington Building, Mailstop 357, Reno, NV 89557-0029
- Public
- Year Founded: 1969
- Website: http://www.unr.edu/med

UNIVERSITY OF SOUTH ALABAMA
- 307 University Boulevard, 170 CSAB, Mobile, AL 36688
- Public
- Website: http://southmed.usouthal.edu

UNIVERSITY OF TEXAS HEALTH SCIENCE CENTER–SAN ANTONIO
- 7703 Floyd Curl Drive, San Antonio, TX 78229-3900
- Public
- Website: http://www.uthscsa.edu

ARIZONA COLLEGE OF OSTEOPATHIC MEDICINE (MIDWESTERN UNIVERSITY)
- 19555 N. 59th Avenue, Glendale, AZ 85308
- Private
- Year Founded: 1995
- Website: http://www.midwestern.edu

UNIVERSITY OF HEALTH SCIENCES COLLEGE OF OSTEOPATHIC MEDICINE
- 1750 Independence Avenue, Kansas City, MO 64106-1453
- Private
- Year Founded: 1916
- Website: http://www.uhs.edu

Resources for Late Starters

Postbaccalaureate programs for nonscientists

What if you come late to your decision to apply to med school and have little or no science background? Here are several highly regarded postbaccalaureate programs designed to help career-changers make their dreams come true. They offer all the science courses you'll need as well as advice and support when it comes time to apply to medical school; students who successfully complete the coursework are "sponsored" by the program, meaning the program vouches for their readiness to go on. (For a complete list of postbac premed programs, go to www.aamc.org.) Once you complete a program, it usually takes another year to apply to medical school, unless the program has "linkage" with one or more medical schools—an arrangement that allows qualified students to go directly to those med schools when they complete the postbac program.

BRYN MAWR COLLEGE

Canwyll House
101 North Merion Avenue
Bryn Mawr, PA 19010-2899
(610) 526-7350
Website: www.brynmawr.edu/postbac
Year started: 1972
Description: One-year program. Full-time, days only. Three courses per semester. Each usually has a laboratory. Classes are predominantly postbac classes although some are open to undergrads.
Enrollment: 75
Admissions requirements: Minimum undergraduate GPA of 3.0; standardized testing required. Interview required for competitive applicants.
Acceptance rate: 60%
Average MCAT score of those who apply to medical school: 31.5
Acceptance rate into medical school in 2003: 100% (over past 5 years: 99%)
Tuition: $17,280; $1,550 per summer session
Financial aid: (610) 526-5267
Linkage with: Brown University School of Medicine, Dartmouth Medical College, Drexel University College of Medicine, George Washington University School of Medicine, Jefferson Medical College, SUNY at Downstate College of Medicine, SUNY Stony Brook School of Medicine, Health Sciences Center, Temple University School of Medicine, University of Rochester School of Medicine

COLUMBIA UNIVERSITY

Lewisohn Hall, Room 408
Mail Code 4101
2970 Broadway
New York, NY 10027
(212) 854-2772
Website: www.columbia.edu/cu/gs/postbacc
Year started: 1955
Description: Two-year program. Full-time or part-time, days or evenings. General chemistry prerequisite for both bio and organic chemistry. Minimum 120 hours of clinical volunteer work; 18–20 hours research volunteer work required. Postbac students are mixed with undergrad premed students.
Enrollment: 427

Admissions requirements: Minimum undergraduate GPA of 3.0; standardized testing, if taken, must be submitted. Interview not required.

Acceptance rate into program: 50–60%

Average MCAT score of those sponsored: 31

Acceptance rate into medical school of those sponsored in 2001 (last year available): 92%

Tuition: $10,000 per year ($976 per credit; need 20 credits to get certificate). Full program is 38 credits: $37,088.

Financial aid: (212) 854-5410

Linkage with: Ben Gurion University of the Negev; Brown University School of Medicine; Jefferson Medical College of Thomas Jefferson University; Drexel University College of Medicine; National University of Ireland, University College, Cork; New York Medical College; SUNY Brooklyn School of Medicine; SUNY Stony Brook School of Medicine; Temple University School of Medicine; Trinity College–Dublin; UMDNJ–New Jersey Medical School; UMDNJ–Robert Wood Johnson Medical School

GOUCHER COLLEGE

Postbaccalaureate Premedical Program
1021 Dulaney Valley Road
Baltimore, MD 21204-2794
(800) 414-3437
Website: www.goucher.edu/postbac
Year started: 1980
Description: One-year program. Full-time, days only. Classes separate from undergrads. Three courses per semester; intensive general chemistry over the summer. Volunteer work required.
Enrollment: 25–30
Admissions requirements: Standardized testing required. Interview required.
Acceptance rate into program: 20–30%

Average MCAT score of those sponsored: 32

Acceptance rate into medical school for those sponsored in 2003: 100%

Tuition: $2,590 per course. The typical curriculum consists of eight courses, bringing total tuition to $20,720.

Financial aid: (410) 337-6430

Linkage with: Brown Medical School, George Washington University School of Medicine, Drexel University School of Medicine, SUNY Stony Brook School of Medicine, Temple University School of Medicine, Tulane University School of Medicine, University of Pittsburgh School of Medicine

HARVARD UNIVERSITY

Health Careers Program
Harvard University Extension School
51 Brattle Street
Cambridge, MA 02138
(617) 495-2926
Website: www.extension.harvard.edu
Year started: 1980
Description: Two-year program, part-time evenings only. Postbac students are separated from undergrad premed students. Standard load is two courses per term. Students expected to find patient-contact work, either paid or volunteer.
Enrollment: 200 plus
Admissions requirements: Minimum undergraduate GPA of 2.7, no standardized test required. No interview required.
Acceptance rate into program: 90%
Average MCAT score of those sponsored: 32
Acceptance rate into medical school for those sponsored in 2003: 89%
Tuition: $800 per course
Financial aid: (617) 495-4293

JOHNS HOPKINS UNIVERSITY

3400 North Charles Street

Wyman Park Building, Suite G1

Baltimore, MD 21218

(410) 516-7748

Website: www.jhu.edu/postbac

Description: One-year program. Full-time, days only. Four or five courses with no more than two lab science courses each semester. Students participate in a "journal club" and "mini-medical school" to learn about and discuss contemporary medical/health care issues. Students engage in a wide choice of clinical activities, including medical tutorials with medical school faculty, structured hospital internships and volunteer programs, and volunteer work in the community. Postbac students are mixed in with undergrad premed students.

Enrollment: 25–30

Admissions requirements: Minimum undergraduate GPA of 3.0 plus; standardized testing (SAT, ACT, or GRE) required. Interview required.

Acceptance rate into program: 19%

Average MCAT Score of medical school applicants: approximately 31

Acceptance rate into medical school of applicants in 2003: 100%

Tuition: $22,600

Financial aid: (410) 516-4688

Linkage with: George Washington University School of Medicine, UMDNJ–Robert Wood Johnson Medical School, and University of Rochester

MILLS COLLEGE

5000 MacArthur Boulevard

Oakland, CA 94613

(510) 430-2317

Website: www.mills.edu

Year started: 1979

Description: One- or two-year program. Full-time or part-time, days only. Students take two or three courses per semester. Volunteer work not required, but encouraged. Postbac students are separated from undergrad premed students.

Enrollment: 60

Admissions requirements: Minimum undergraduate GPA of 3.0; standardized testing required. No interview required.

Acceptance rate into program: Varies considerably from year to year; approximately 75%

Average MCAT score of those sponsored: 31

Acceptance rate into medical school for those sponsored in 2003: 87.5%

Tuition: $15,000–$25,000 per year, depending on number of courses

Financial aid: Need to respond on application; Mills College will not discuss aid over the phone.

Linkage with: Tulane University Medical School

SCRIPPS COLLEGE W.M. KECK SCIENCE CENTER

925 N. Mills Avenue

Claremont, CA 91711

(909) 621-8764

Website: www.jsd.claremont.edu/postbac

Year started: 1994

Description: One- or two-year program. Full-time or part-time, days only. Postbac students are mixed with undergrad premed students. Students in the one-year program take three or four courses per semester and two summer courses each summer. Students in the two-year program take two courses per semester and are required to work at least 20 hours a week. Internships and volunteer work required.

Enrollment: 60

Admissions requirements: Minimum undergraduate GPA of 3.0; standardized testing required. Interview required.

Acceptance rate into program: 27%

Average MCAT score of those sponsored: 31.2

Acceptance rate into medical school for those sponsored in 2003: 100%

Tuition: $20,000–$26,000 per year, depending on number of courses

Financial aid: (909) 621-8275

Linkage with: University of Pittsburgh School of Medicine, Drexel University School of Medicine, George Washington School of Medicine, Temple University School of Medicine, Western University School of Medicine, College of Osteopathic Medicine of the Pacific

TUFTS UNIVERSITY

419 Boston Ave. Dowling Hall
Medford, MA 02155
(617) 627-2321

Website: http://studentservices.tufts.edu/postbac

Year started: 1988

Description: 11 to 20 months depending on student. Full-time, days only. Two laboratory science courses per semester and other electives available. Volunteer or paid part-time work recommended. Postbac students are mixed in with undergrad premed students.

Enrollment: 40

Admissions requirements: Minimum undergraduate GPA of 3.0; standardized testing required. No interview required.

Acceptance rate into program: 30–40%

Average MCAT score of those sponsored: 30–31

Acceptance rate into medical school of those sponsored in 2003: 90%

Tuition: $10,001–15,000 per year, depending on number of courses

Financial aid: Once admitted, students can discuss it with counselors.

Linkage with: Tufts University School of Medicine and University of New England College of Osteopathic Medicine

UNIVERSITY OF PENNSYLVANIA

3440 Market Street, Suite 100
College of General Studies
Philadelphia, PA 19104-3335
(215) 898-3110

Website: www.sas.upenn.edu/CGS/postbac/premed

Year started: 1977

Description: One- or two-year program. Full-time or part-time, days, or evenings. Postbac students are separated from undergrad premed students.

Enrollment: 50–70

Admissions requirements: Minimum undergraduate GPA of 3.0; standardized testing required. Interview required.

Acceptance rate into program: N/A

Average MCAT score of those sponsored: N/A

Acceptance rate into medical school of those sponsored in 2003: 100%

Tuition: $12,000 per academic year

Financial aid: www.sfs.upenn.edu/home

Linkage with: George Washington University School of Medicine, Jefferson Medical College, Drexel University College of Medicine, Temple University School of Medicine, UMDNJ–Robert Wood Johnson School of Medicine, University of Pittsburgh School of Medicine

Overseas Options
Foreign medical schools that welcome Americans

If you don't get into an American medical school, one possible alternate route is a foreign or "off-shore" school that accepts a significant number of U.S. applicants (see Chapter 6, page 55). Before you make a choice, be sure you know what you're getting into: Visit the school, find out what kind of program it offers and how many Americans attend, how students do on the United States Medical Licensing Examination (USMLE), and how many end up with residencies in the States. Below is a sampling of programs that accept Americans.

AMERICAN UNIVERSITY OF THE CARIBBEAN SCHOOL OF MEDICINE

Jordan Road
Cupecoy
St. Maarten, N.A.
Admissions: Medical Education Information Office
901 Ponce de Leon Boulevard, Suite 201
Coral Gables, Florida 33134
(866) 372-2282
Website: www.aucmed.edu
Year founded: 1978. AUC offers basic medical sciences in St. Maarten and clinical rotations at affiliated hospitals in the U.S., U.K., and Ireland. Graduates include more than 3,500 licensed physicians practicing in the U.S. Semesters begin in January, May, and September.
Enrollment: 380 in basic sciences; 235 in clinical sciences (May 2004)
Percentage of U.S. citizens (or permanent residents): 88.4

Admissions information: Entering class 2003: average GPA: 3.1; average MCAT: 22
Acceptance rate: 51%
Language: Courses taught in English
Pass rate on USMLE Step 1: N/A
Percentage of first-year residency placements in U.S.: 81.5% (110 of 135 graduates)
Tuition: $9,500 per semester (semesters 1–5); $10,000 per semester thereafter
Financial aid: (305) 446-0600, ext. 22 or 23

BEN-GURION UNIVERSITY OF THE NEGEV

Beer Sheva, Israel
M.D. Program in International Health and Medicine in collaboration with Columbia University Medical Center
Admissions: 630 W. 168th Street, PH15E-1512
New York, New York 10032
(212) 305-9587
Website: http://cpmcnet.columbia.edu/dept/bgcu-md
Year founded: 1996
Enrollment: Average entering class size is 30; currently 123 students in the four-year program.
Percentage of U.S. citizens: 66%
Admissions information: Average undergraduate GPA of 3.4 ; average MCAT score: 27. Interview is required.
Acceptance rate: 46%
Language: courses taught in English
Pass rate on USMLE Step 1: more than 95% for U.S. students

Percentage of first-year residency placements in U.S.: 100% in 2004

Tuition: $25,850 (2003–2004)

Financial aid: American students may use Stafford and alternative loans; and after the first semester, all students may apply for limited scholarships based on financial need.

Average attrition rate: From 1998–2004, about 4%. The rate this year for the 2003 entering class is 3.4%.

ROSS UNIVERSITY SCHOOL OF MEDICINE

Dominica, West Indies

Admissions: 499 Thornall St, 10th Floor Edison, NJ 08837

(732) 978-5300

Website: www.rossmed.edu

Year founded: 1978

Enrollment: 2,500'plus

Percentage of U.S. citizens: 93%

Admissions information: Mean undergraduate GPA of 3.25; MCAT score: N/A (though now required). Interview is required.

Acceptance rate: Approximately 55%

Language: Courses taught in English

Pass rate on USMLE Step 1: 88% for 2002 first-time test takers; 94% for first- and second-time test takers.

Percentage of first-year residency placements in U.S.: 64.2% through the match; 16.3% prematch; 19.5% outside the match. Typically, 96% of eligible graduates achieve a residency position in the States.

Tuition: $20,200

Financial aid: (732) 978-5300

Average attrition: 17%

ST. GEORGE'S UNIVERSITY MEDICAL SCHOOL

Grenada, West Indies

Admissions: The North American Correspondent c/o University Services, Ltd.

1 East Main Street Bay Shore, NY 11706

(800) 899-6337, ext. 280 or (631) 665-8500

Website: www.sgu.edu

Year founded: 1976

Enrollment: 2,349

Percentage of U.S. citizens: 75%

Admissions information: average undergraduate GPA for the 2003 entering class of 3.3; MCAT Score: 24. Interview required

Language: Courses taught in English

Pass rate on USMLE Step 1: 90%

Percentage of first-year residency placements in U.S.: 99% of those eligible U.S. graduates who applied obtained residency positions in 650 hospitals throughout 50 states.

Tuition: $30,000

Financial aid: 1-631-665-8500, ext. 232

TECHNION-ISRAEL INSTITUTE OF TECHNOLOGY

The Technion American Medical Students (TEAMS) Program

12th Efron St., P.O. Box 9649

Haifa, 31096, Israel

011-972-829-5248

Website: http://teams.technion.ac.il

Year founded: 1983

Enrollment: 60 Americans

Percentage of U.S. citizens: 100% in the TEAMS program (U.S. citizens make up 10–15% of Technion student body).

Admissions information: Average GPA of above 3.4 and average MCAT score of 24 are required Interview is required.

Acceptance rate into program: 70%

Language: Courses taught in English

Pass rate on USMLE Step 1: 98%

Percentage of first-year residency placements in U.S.: 100%

Tuition: $19,120

Financial aid: Federal and private

Attrition rate: Less than 1 percent

TEL AVIV UNIVERSITY SACKLER SCHOOL OF MEDICINE

New York State/American Program

Ramat Aviv Israel

Admissions: 17 E. 62nd Street

New York, NY 10021

(212) 688-8811

Website: www.tau.ac.il/medicine

Year founded: 1976

Enrollment: 300

Percentage of U.S. citizens: 100%

Admissions information: Minimum undergraduate GPA of 3.0. MCAT score: minimum of 8 on each section. Interview required.

Acceptance rate: 50%

Language: Courses are taught in English.

Pass rate on USMLE Step 1: 98%

Percentage of first-year residency placements in U.S.: 100%

Tuition: $22,000

Financial aid: Federal Stafford loan and several private loans

UNIVERSIDAD AUTÓNOMA DE GUADALAJARA

Av. Patria # 1201, Lomas del Valle, 3a. Sección

Guadalajara, Jalisco, México C.P. 44100

Admissions: 4715 Fredericksburg Road, Suite 300,

San Antonio, TX 78229

(800) 531-5494

20 Corporate Woods Boulevard, Suite 205,

Albany, NY 12211- 2370

(866) 434-7392

Website: www.uag.mx

Year founded: 1935

Enrollment: 4,000 plus

Percentage of U.S. citizens: 20%

Admissions information: Average GPA of 2.9; MCAT: 24. Interview required.

Acceptance rate: 33%

Language: Lectures and some labs taught in English for only the first two years, then Spanish.

Pass rate on USMLE Step 1: 82%

Percentage of first-year residency placements in U.S.: 92%

Tuition: $17,580

Financial aid: Yes

Alphabetical Index of Schools

A.T. Still University of Health Sciences (Kirksville), 320
Albany Medical College, 107
Arizona College of Osteopathic Medicine (Midwestern University), 356

Baylor College of Medicine, 108
Boston University, 110
Brown University, 112

Case Western Reserve University, 114
Chicago College of Osteopathic Medicine, 322
College of Osteopathic Medicine of the Pacific (Western University), 324
Columbia University College of Physicians and Surgeons, 116
Cornell University (Weill), 118
Creighton University, 120

Dartmouth Medical School, 122
Des Moines University Osteopathic Medical Center, 326
Drexel University, 124
Duke University, 126

East Carolina University (Brody), 128
East Tennessee State University (Quillen), 132
Eastern Virginia Medical School, 130
Edward Via Virginia College of Osteopathic Medicine, 328
Emory University, 134

Florida State University, 136

George Washington University, 140
Georgetown University, 138

Harvard University, 142
Howard University, 144

Indiana University–Indianapolis, 146

Jefferson Medical College, 148
Johns Hopkins University, 150

Lake Erie College of Osteopathic Medicine, 330
Loma Linda University, 356
Loyola University Chicago (Stritch), 152
LSU School of Medicine–New Orleans, 356
LSU School of Medicine–Shreveport, 356

Marshall University (Edwards), 356
Mayo Medical School, 154
Medical College of Georgia, 156
Medical College of Wisconsin, 158
Medical University of Ohio, 160
Medical University of South Carolina, 162
Meharry Medical College, 356
Mercer University, 164
Michigan State University, 166
Michigan State University College of Osteopathic Medicine, 332
Morehouse School of Medicine, 168
Mount Sinai School of Medicine, 170

New York College of Osteopathic Medicine, 334
New York Medical College, 172
New York University, 174
Northeastern Ohio Universities College of Medicine, 176
Northwestern University (Feinberg), 178
Nova Southeastern University College of Osteopathic Medicine, 336

Ohio State University, 180

Ohio University, 338
Oklahoma State University Center for Health Sciences, 340
Oregon Health and Science University, 182

Pennsylvania State University College of Medicine, 356
Philadelphia College of Osteopathic Medicine, 342
Pikeville College School of Osteopathic Medicine, 344

Rosalind Franklin University of Medicine and Science, 184
Rush University, 186

Southern Illinois University–Springfield, 188
St. Louis University, 192
Stanford University, 190
Stony Brook University, 194
SUNY–Downstate Medical Center, 356
SUNY–Syracuse, 196

Temple University, 198
Texas A&M University System Health Science Center, 200
Texas Tech University Health Sciences Center, 202
Touro University College of Osteopathic Medicine, 346
Tufts University, 204
Tulane University, 356

U. of North Texas Health Sci. Center (Texas Col. of Osteopathic Medicine), 352
UMDNJ-New Jersey Medical School, 206
UMDNJ-Robert Wood Johnson Medical School, 208
UMDNJ–School of Osteopathic Medicine, 348
Uniformed Services University of the Health Sciences (Hebert), 210

University at Buffalo–SUNY, 212
University of
  Alabama–Birmingham, 214
University of Arizona, 216
University of Arkansas for
  Medical Sciences, 218
University of California–Davis,
  220
University of California–Irvine,
  222
University of California–Los
  Angeles (Geffen), 224
University of California–San
  Diego, 226
University of California–San
  Francisco, 228
University of Chicago (Pritzker),
  230
University of Cincinnati, 232
University of Colorado–Denver
  and Health Sciences Center, 234
University of Connecticut, 236
University of Florida, 238
University of Hawaii–Manoa
  (Burns), 356
University of Health Sciences
  College of Osteopathic
  Medicine, 356
University of Illinois–Chicago,
  240
University of Iowa (Carver), 242
University of Kansas Medical
  Center, 244
University of Kentucky, 246

University of Louisville, 356
University of Maryland, 248
University of
  Massachusetts–Worcester, 250
University of Miami (Miller), 252
University of Michigan–Ann
  Arbor, 254
University of Minnesota Medical
  School, 256
University of Mississippi, 356
University of Missouri–Columbia,
  258
University of Missouri–Kansas
  City, 356
University of Nebraska College of
  Medicine, 260
University of Nevada–Reno, 356
University of New England
  College of Osteopathic
  Medicine, 350
University of New Mexico, 262
University of North
  Carolina–Chapel Hill, 264
University of North Dakota, 266
University of Oklahoma, 268
University of Pennsylvania, 270
University of Pittsburgh, 272
University of Rochester, 274
University of South Alabama, 356
University of South Carolina, 276
University of South Dakota, 278
University of South Florida, 282
University of Southern California
  (Keck), 280

University of Tennessee Health
  Science Center, 284
University of Texas Health Science
  Center–Houston, 286
University of Texas Health Science
  Center–San Antonio, 356
University of Texas Medical
  Branch–Galveston, 288
University of Texas Southwestern
  Medical Center–Dallas, 290
University of Utah, 292
University of Vermont, 294
University of Virginia, 296
University of Washington, 298
University of Wisconsin–Madison,
  300

Vanderbilt University, 302
Virginia Commonwealth
  University, 304

Wake Forest University, 306
Washington University in St.
  Louis, 308
Wayne State University, 310
West Virginia School of
  Osteopathic Medicine, 354
West Virginia University, 312
Wright State University, 314

Yale University, 316
Yeshiva University (Einstein), 318

Index of Schools by State

Alabama
University of
  Alabama–Birmingham, 214
University of South Alabama, 356

Arizona
Arizona College of Osteopathic
  Medicine (Midwestern
  University), 356
University of Arizona, 216

Arkansas
University of Arkansas for
  Medical Sciences, 218

California
College of Osteopathic Medicine
  of the Pacific (Western
  University), 324
Loma Linda University, 356
Stanford University, 190

Touro University College of
  Osteopathic Medicine, 346
University of California–Davis, 220
University of California–Irvine, 222
University of California–Los
  Angeles (Geffen), 224
University of California–San Diego,
  226
University of California–San
  Francisco, 228

University of Southern California (Keck), 280

Colorado
University of Colorado–Denver and Health Sciences Center, 234

Connecticut
University of Connecticut, 236
Yale University, 316

District of Columbia
George Washington University, 140
Georgetown University, 138
Howard University, 144

Florida
Florida State University, 136
Nova Southeastern University College of Osteopathic Medicine, 336
University of Florida, 238
University of Miami (Miller), 252
University of South Florida, 282

Georgia
Emory University, 134
Medical College of Georgia, 156
Mercer University, 164
Morehouse School of Medicine, 168

Hawaii
University of Hawaii—Manoa (Burns), 356

Illinois
Chicago College of Osteopathic Medicine, 322
Loyola University Chicago (Stritch), 152
Northwestern University (Feinberg), 178
Rosalind Franklin University of Medicine and Science, 184
Rush University, 186
Southern Illinois University—Springfield, 188
University of Chicago (Pritzker), 230
University of Illinois—Chicago, 240

Indiana
Indiana University–Indianapolis, 146

Iowa
Des Moines University Osteopathic Medical Center, 326
University of Iowa (Carver), 242

Kansas
University of Kansas Medical Center, 244

Kentucky
Pikeville College School of Osteopathic Medicine, 344
University of Kentucky, 246
University of Louisville, 356

Louisiana
LSU School of Medicine–New Orleans, 356
LSU School of Medicine–Shreveport, 356
Tulane University, 356

Maine
University of New England College of Osteopathic Medicine, 350

Maryland
Johns Hopkins University, 150
Uniformed Services University of the Health Sciences (Hebert), 210
University of Maryland, 248

Massachusetts
Boston University, 110
Harvard University, 142
Tufts University, 204
University of Massachusetts–Worcester, 250

Michigan
Michigan State University, 166
Michigan State University College of Osteopathic Medicine, 332

University of Michigan–Ann Arbor, 254
Wayne State University, 310

Minnesota
Mayo Medical School, 154
University of Minnesota Medical School, 256

Mississippi
University of Mississippi, 356

Missouri
A.T. Still University of Health Sciences (Kirksville), 320
St. Louis University, 192
University of Health Sciences College of Osteopathic Medicine, 356
University of Missouri–Columbia, 258
University of Missouri–Kansas City, 356
Washington University in St. Louis, 308

Nebraska
Creighton University, 120
University of Nebraska College of Medicine, 260

Nevada
University of Nevada–Reno, 356

New Hampshire
Dartmouth Medical School, 122

New Jersey
UMDNJ-New Jersey Medical School, 206
UMDNJ-Robert Wood Johnson Medical School, 208
UMDNJ–School of Osteopathic Medicine, 248

New Mexico
University of New Mexico, 262

New York
Albany Medical College, 107
Columbia University College of
  Physicians and Surgeons, 116
Cornell University (Weill), 118
Mount Sinai School of Medicine,
  170
New York College of Osteopathic
  Medicine, 334
New York Medical College, 172
New York University, 174
Stony Brook University, 194
SUNY–Downstate Medical Center,
  356
SUNY–Syracuse, 196
University at Buffalo–SUNY, 212
University of Rochester, 274
Yeshiva University (Einstein), 318

North Carolina
Duke University, 126
East Carolina University (Brody),
  128
University of North
  Carolina–Chapel Hill, 264
Wake Forest University, 306

North Dakota
University of North Dakota, 266

Ohio
Case Western Reserve University,
  114
Medical University of Ohio, 160
Northeastern Ohio Universities
  College of Medicine, 176
Ohio State University, 180
Ohio University, 338
University of Cincinnati, 232
Wright State University, 314

Oklahoma
Oklahoma State University Center
  for Health Sciences, 340

University of Oklahoma, 268

Oregon
Oregon Health and Science
  University, 182

Pennsylvania
Drexel University, 124
Jefferson Medical College, 148
Lake Erie College of Osteopathic
  Medicine, 330
Pennsylvania State University
  College of Medicine, 356
Philadelphia College of
  Osteopathic Medicine, 342
Temple University, 198
University of Pennsylvania, 270
University of Pittsburgh, 272

Rhode Island
Brown University, 112

South Carolina
Medical University of South
  Carolina, 162
University of South Carolina, 276

South Dakota
University of South Dakota, 278

Tennessee
East Tennessee State University
  (Quillen), 132
Meharry Medical College, 356
University of Tennessee Health
  Science Center, 284
Vanderbilt University, 302

Texas
Baylor College of Medicine, 108
Texas A&M University System
  Health Science Center, 200
Texas Tech University Health
  Sciences Center, 202

U. of North Texas Health Sci.
  Center (Texas Col. of
  Osteopathic Medicine), 352
University of Texas Health Science
  Center–Houston, 284
University of Texas Health Science
  Center–San Antonio, 356
University of Texas Medical
  Branch–Galveston, 288
University of Texas Southwestern
  Medical Center–Dallas, 290

Utah
University of Utah, 292

Vermont
University of Vermont, 294

Virginia
Eastern Virginia Medical School,
  130
Edward Via Virginia College of
  Osteopathic Medicine, 328
University of Virginia, 296
Virginia Commonwealth
  University, 304

Washington
University of Washington, 298

West Virginia
Marshall University (Edwards), 356
West Virginia School of
  Osteopathic Medicine, 354
West Virginia University, 312

Wisconsin
Medical College of Wisconsin, 158
University of Wisconsin–Madison,
  300

About the Authors & Editors

Founded in 1933, Washington, D.C.–based *U.S.News & World Report* delivers a unique brand of weekly magazine journalism to its 12.2 million readers. In 1983, *U.S. News* began its exclusive annual rankings of American colleges and universities. The *U.S. News* education franchise is second to none, with its annual college and graduate school rankings among the most eagerly anticipated magazine issues in the country.

Josh Fischman, the book's lead writer and editor, covers health and science for *U.S. News & World Report*. Previously, he was editor-in-chief at *Earth*, deputy news editor at *Science*, and a senior editor at *Discover*. He has also cowritten the children's book *101 Things Every Kid Should Know about Dinosaurs*. He has won the Blakeslee Award for excellence in medical reporting from the American Heart Association.

Anne McGrath, editor, is a deputy editor at *U.S.News & World Report*, where she covers health. Previously, she was managing editor of "America's Best Colleges" and "America's Best Graduate Schools," the two *U.S. News* annual publications featuring rankings of the country's colleges and universities.

Robert Morse is the director of data research at *U.S.News & World Report*. He is in charge of the research, data collection, methodologies, and survey design for the annual "America's Best Colleges" rankings and the "America's Best Graduate Schools" rankings.

Brian Kelly is the executive editor of *U.S.News & World Report*. As the magazine's No. 2 editor, he oversees the weekly magazine, the website, and a series of newsstand books. He is a former editor at the *Washington Post* and the author of three books.

Other writers who contributed chapters or passages to the book are **Ulrich Boser, Kristin Davis, Justin Ewers, Helen Fields, Dan Gilgoff, Vicky Hallett, Cory Hatch, Bernadine Healy, Caroline Hsu, Katy Kelly, Carolyn Kleiner Butler, Samantha Levine, Marianne Szegedy-Maszak, Stacy Schultz, Nancy Shute, Rachel K. Sobel**, and **Amanda Spake**. The work involved in producing the directory and *U.S. News* Insider's Index was handled by **Sam Flanigan**. Thanks to **David Griffin** for his work in designing the book and to **Sara Sklaroff** for project editing. Thanks as well to **James Bock** for his copyediting assistance and to members of the *U.S. News* **factchecking team** for making sure we got it right.